Technology Development and Platform Enhancements for Successful Global E–Government Design

Kelvin Joseph Bwalya
University of Botswana, Botswana & Senior Research Fellow, University of Johannesburg, South Africa

A volume in the Advances in Electronic Government, Digital Divide, and Regional Development (AEGDDRD) Book Series

Information Science REFERENCE
An Imprint of IGI Global

Managing Director:	Lindsay Johnston
Production Manager:	Jennifer Yoder
Development Editor:	Austin DeMarco
Acquisitions Editor:	Kayla Wolfe
Typesetter:	John Crodian
Cover Design:	Jason Mull

Published in the United States of America by
Information Science Reference (an imprint of IGI Global)
701 E. Chocolate Avenue
Hershey PA 17033
Tel: 717-533-8845
Fax: 717-533-8661
E-mail: cust@igi-global.com
Web site: http://www.igi-global.com

Library of Congress Cataloging-in-Publication Data

CIP Data Pending

ISBN: 978-1-4666-4900-2 (hardcover)
ISBN: 978-1-4666-4901-9 (ebook)
ISBN: 978-1-4666-4902-6 (print & perpetucal access)

This book is published in the IGI Global book series Advances in Electronic Government, Digital Divide, and Regional Development (AEGDDRD) (ISSN: 2326-9103; eISSN: 2326-9111)

British Cataloguing in Publication Data
A Cataloguing in Publication record for this book is available from the British Library.

For electronic access to this publication, please contact: eresources@igi-global.com.

Advances in Electronic Government, Digital Divide, and Regional Development (AEGDDRD) Book Series

ISSN: 2326-9103
EISSN: 2326-9111

Mission

The successful use of digital technologies (including social media and mobile technologies) to provide public services and foster economic development has become an objective for governments around the world. The development towards electronic government (or e-government) not only affects the efficiency and effectiveness of public services, but also has the potential to transform the nature of government interactions with its citizens. Current research and practice on the adoption of electronic/digital government and the implementation in organizations around the world aims to emphasize the extensiveness of this growing field.

The Advances in Electronic Government, Digital Divide & Regional Development (AEGDDRD) book series aims to publish authored, edited and case books encompassing the current and innovative research and practice discussing all aspects of electronic government development, implementation and adoption as well the effective use of the emerging technologies (including social media and mobile technologies) for a more effective electronic governance (or e-governance).

Coverage

- Digital Democracy
- E-Citizenship
- Electronic & Digital Government
- ICT Adoption in Developing Countries
- ICT within Government & Public Sectors
- Knowledge Divide
- Public Information Management
- Regional Planning
- Urban & Rural Development
- Web 2.0 in Government

IGI Global is currently accepting manuscripts for publication within this series. To submit a proposal for a volume in this series, please contact our Acquisition Editors at Acquisitions@igi-global.com or visit: http://www.igi-global.com/publish/.

Titles in this Series

For a list of additional titles in this series, please visit: www.igi-global.com

Technology Development and Platform Enhancements for Successful Global E-Government Design
Kelvin Joseph Bwalya (University of Botswana, Botswana & University of Johannesburg, South Africa)
Information Science Reference • copyright 2014 • 340pp • H/C (ISBN: 9781466649002) • US $180.00 (our price)

IT in the Public Sphere Applications in Administration, Government, Politics, and Planning
Zaigham Mahmood (University of Derby, UK & North West University, South Africa)
Information Science Reference • copyright 2014 • 300pp • H/C (ISBN: 9781466647190) • US $180.00 (our price)

Globalization and Governance in the International Political Economy
Ümit Hacioğlu (Beykent University, Turkey) and Hasan Dinçer (Beykent University, Turkey)
Information Science Reference • copyright 2014 • 435pp • H/C (ISBN: 9781466646391) • US $175.00 (our price)

Developing E-Government Projects Frameworks and Methodologies
Zaigham Mahmood (University of Derby, UK & North West University, South Africa)
Information Science Reference • copyright 2013 • 461pp • H/C (ISBN: 9781466642454) • US $180.00 (our price)

Citizen E-Participation in Urban Governance Crowdsourcing and Collaborative Creativity
Carlos Nunes Silva (University of Lisbon, Portugal)
Information Science Reference • copyright 2013 • 392pp • H/C (ISBN: 9781466641693) • US $180.00 (our price)

E-Government Success around the World Cases, Empirical Studies, and Practical Recommendations
J. Ramon Gil-Garcia (Centro de Investigación y Docencia Económicas (CIDE), Mexico)
Information Science Reference • copyright 2013 • 467pp • H/C (ISBN: 9781466641730) • US $180.00 (our price)

E-Government Success Factors and Measures Theories, Concepts, and Methodologies
J. Ramon Gil-Garcia (Centro de Investigación y Docencia Económicas (CIDE), Mexico)
Information Science Reference • copyright 2013 • 424pp • H/C (ISBN: 9781466640580) • US $180.00 (our price)

E-Government Implementation and Practice in Developing Countries
Zaigham Mahmood (University of Derby, UK & North West University, South Africa)
Information Science Reference • copyright 2013 • 348pp • H/C (ISBN: 9781466640900) • US $180.00 (our price)

Global Sustainable Development and Renewable Energy Systems
Phillip Olla (Madonna University, USA)
Information Science Reference • copyright 2012 • 354pp • H/C (ISBN: 9781466616257) • US $180.00 (our price)

www.igi-global.com

701 E. Chocolate Ave., Hershey, PA 17033
Order online at www.igi-global.com or call 717-533-8845 x100
To place a standing order for titles released in this series, contact: cust@igi-global.com
Mon-Fri 8:00 am - 5:00 pm (est) or fax 24 hours a day 717-533-8661

Table of Contents

Section 1
Fundamentals for E-Government Technology and Application Design

Detailed Table of Contents

Section 1
Fundamentals for E-Government Technology and Application Design

Chapter 1
Kelvin Joseph Bwalya, University of Botswana, Botswana & Senior Research Fellow,
University of Johannesburg, South Africa

Although a lot has been achieved with regards to technology development for e-Government applications, there are still no global technological conceptual frameworks and models that define e-Government platform design and implementation the world over. This has partly been attributed to the differing local contexts and organisational cultures in the public services departments (even within the same government). Because of this scenario, there is need to review the different technology design endeavours geared towards achieving process automation and application integration in the different government departments to achieve meaningful and robust e-Government development. This lead chapter intends to review the different approaches that have been done on the technology front of e-Government (especially design of interoperability frameworks and ontology platforms) in different parts of the world and outlines the future works that e-Government researchers and practitioners need to concentrate on. This chapter sets the tone for the remaining chapters of this book, which discuss various aspects of e-Government implementation from the technological front (deployment, design, and customization of e-Government solutions). The chapter posits that with the current pace of technological advancements and efforts by the OASIS forum and other interested parties, it is not difficult to notice that global technological models of e-Government are to be realized in the foreseeable future.

Chapter 2

Jean Vincent Fonou-Dombeu, Vaal University of Technology, South Africa

Magda Huisman, North-West University, South Africa

The ultimate goal of e-Governance is to reach the stage of seamless service delivery in one-stop e-Government. This raises the engineering issues of integration, reusability, maintenance, and interoperability of autonomous e-Government systems of government departments and agencies. Therefore, appropriate methodologies that consistently address the aforementioned engineering issues throughout clearly defined e-Government development phases are needed. This chapter provides the design and specification, of a framework that amalgamates features from maturity models, software engineering and Semantic Web domains for semantic-enabled development of e-Government systems. Firstly, the methods and techniques used for the planning, design, and implementation of e-Government systems worldwide are investigated; a critical analysis is carried out to identify their advantages and disadvantages, as well as their contribution towards addressing the aforementioned engineering issues. Secondly, the proposed framework is drawn and specified. Finally, support tools including a business process model, an alignment matrix of stages and phases of development, and a weighting matrix of the intensity of semantic activities at various phases of development is drawn and described.

Chapter 3

Lefkothea Spiliotopoulou, University of the Aegean, Greece

Yannis Charalabidis, University of the Aegean, Greece

There has been significant research in the private sector towards systematic exploitation of the emerging Web 2.0/Web 3.0 and social media paradigms. However, not much has been achieved with regards to the embodiment of similar technologies. Currently, governments and organizations are making considerable efforts, trying to enhance citizens' participation in decision-making and policy-formulation processes. This chapter presents a novel policy analysis framework, proposing a Web-based platform that enables publishing content and micro-applications to multiple Web 2.0 social media and collecting citizens' interactions (e.g. comments, ratings) with efficient use of Application Programming Interfaces (APIs) of these media. Citizens' opinions and interactions can then be processed through different techniques or methods (Web analytics, opinion mining, simulation modeling) in order to use the extracted conclusions as support to government decision and policy makers.

Chapter 4

Bongani Ngwenya, Solusi University, Zimbabwe

The literature suggests that the elaboration of ontology contributes to the standardization and classification of concepts and terminologies, and it has been happening in some sectors, such as software engineering, e-Government services implementation, and project management. In the area of e-Government, knowledge plays a critical role in the development of e-Government transformation project management ontology, which aims at adopting and customizing the existing project management approaches according to the specific challenges encountered in the e-Government environment. It is in this context that this chapter presents an ontological representation of the concepts of e-Government project management in one of the developing countries in southern Africa. The chapter further intends to collaborate in the excellence and productivity of the management of the e-Government project process. This will also enable the interoperability and knowledge reuse between all factors and stakeholders related with the implementation of such types of projects as a lesson for developing countries. The data was collected by use of an interview protocol or schedule, and the researcher interviewed relevant employees of the two ministries, the Ministry of Information Technology and the Ministry of Information and Communication. The data was then analyzed qualitatively to draw a model that the Zimbabwean government is adopting.

Chapter 5

This chapter addresses the design challenge of providing Information and Communication Technology(ies) ICT(s) systems for public e-Service provision. Public sector services differ qualitatively from private sector services in that they aim to provide not just value for money but also public value. Generally speaking, public value is created when public organizations successfully meet the needs of citizens. Therefore, public sector ICTs have unique requirements that are not all thoroughly supported by traditional ICTs and their respective design theories. This chapter presents a design theory to guide developers of public sector ICTs on how to produce systems that provide public e-Services through secure and inclusive information systems. These systems will, in turn, create public value by tackling digital inequality and easing citizens' online privacy concerns. The design theory was created while designing and deploying a digital postal system. By abstracting from the experience of building the system, a design theory for ICTs providing public e-Services was formulated. This new design theory is an important theoretical contribution because it provides guidance to developers and sets an agenda for IS research into public sector information systems design. It achieves this by articulating theory-based principles outlining how public value can be created through the development of appropriate ICTs. The design principles outlined by the theory are also subject to empirical, as well as practical, validation.

Chapter 6

This chapter intends to present information systems philosophies on design of affluent e-Government platform design. The chapter looks at e-Government platform design in two ways. First, it looks at it as a prevailing concept and philosophy that emanate through the combination of literature in the academic disciplines of government and governance, ICT and information society, and e-Business. Hence, the chapter argues that these fields of study provided the theoretical basis influencing e-Government platform design. Second, the chapter proposes that if the philosophies embedded in the literature dealing with systems thinking and performance measurement are included as part of the theories for e-Government conceptualization, this may culminate into developing a new philosophy. This philosophy may be based on asking relevant and appropriate socio-cultural questions that may facilitate the design of better e-Government platforms. The chapter proposes a model for incorporating the said philosophical standpoints into actual e-Government design. The anticipation is that such a platform may culminate into e-Government platforms that may meet social requirements necessary for requisite e-Government platforms.

Ontologies are used to represent human knowledge in a machine-understandable format. Knowledge exists in all domains and the proper capture and utilization of the knowledge is very important. Many ontology engineering methodologies are available for the development of ontologies. However, they suffer from their heavy weight nature and make the development process tedious. In addition, the resulting ontologies are monolithic ontologies and are not easy to reuse. Therefore, an agile and modular method is proposed to develop ontologies. The ease of use of the method is tested by a group of 68 inexperienced ontology engineers who compare it with Ontology 101 by developing ontologies in the e-Government domain using both methods.

E-Government open source system is now becoming commonplace. The e-Government open system requires at each review stage the relevant official input, the date, and the time when each application is processed. Free access to the status of an application makes applicants realize that there is no need to contact officials or to provide a bribe to complete the process. No doubt, e-Government open system is a very useful system currently being used by a majority of governments in developing world countries. However, extant review of literature has shown that some developing countries governments are now also making frantic effort to implement the open system although the practice seems to have gone farther in developed nations. In light of this, this chapter discusses e-Government open source system in developing countries and compares this to what is happening in the developed countries, examines the role OSS/SF has played in developing e-Government solutions or applications in the developing world, identifies the benefits and challenges of OSS/SF in the developing countries' context, and discusses possible ways forward. The chapter posits that open source plays a significant role in designing e-Government applications.

Section 2
Design and Use of E-Government Applications

Fast development of geospatial technologies has made it possible to integrate existing user operational information and value-added services in a single harmonized infrastructure. This has made it possible to utilize geospatial technologies in the e-Government context. The emerging technologies have made it possible for natural disaster monitoring and mitigation for early warning in order for effective actions under emergency situation, such as natural disaster and chemical accident, to be taken. Natural disasters may include fires, explosions, leakages, or releases of toxic or hazardous materials that can cause people illness, injury, disability, or death. With emerging geospatial technology capabilities and applications such as Google Earth, GIS, and GPS, computer modeling and simulation can provide the inverse identification of emission profile and location. The modeling result can further present the forward prediction of the likely impact of any disaster event. Therefore, the community can acquire the situation in time to form spontaneous emergency response planning, which will also help the other stakeholders such as government and responsible community team. This modeling tool can form a virtual e-Government solution requisite for effective monitoring and mitigation. This chapter highlights the current research trends and future prospects with regards to integrating technologies for managing spatio-temporal information with e-Government conceptualization.

Chapter 10
Anti-Corruption Capabilities of Public E-Procurement Technologies: Principal-Agent Theory 185
Arjun Neupane, University of Southern Queensland, Australia
Jeffrey Soar, University of Southern Queensland, Australia
Kishor Vaidya, University of Southern Queensland, Australia & University of Canberra, Australia

Public procurement is an important area warranting further attention in government reform, as electronic systems for procurement have enormous potential to help reduce corruption. Public e-Procurement is the use of an Internet or Web-based system by government institutions for the acquisition of goods and services, which can improve transparency and accountability. This chapter discusses different types of e-Procurement technologies with case examples from different countries that demonstrate how the e-Procurement technologies have great potential as the anti-corruption technologies. The chapter reviews the Principal-Agent Theory and discusses other relevant theories including Transaction Cost Theory, Fraud Triangle Theory, Diffusion of Innovation Theory, and the Technology Acceptance Model. Following a discussion of the potential of e-Procurement systems in mitigating corruption, a theoretical research model is proposed for identifying public e-Procurement anti-corruption capabilities.

Chapter 11
Smartphone-Based Digital Government Model: The Case of the Beyaz Masa (White Table) App in Turkey 204
Ronan de Kervenoael, Sabanci University, Turkey & Aston Business School, UK
Egemen Sekeralp, Pordiva Bilisim Teknolojileri A.S., Turkey

M-Government services are now at the forefront of both user expectations and technology capabilities. Within the current setting, there is growing evidence that interoperability is becoming a key issue towards service sustainability. Thus, the objective of this chapter is to highlight the case of "Beyas Masa" – a Turkish application for infrastructure repair services. This application requires different stakeholders from different cultural background and geographically dispersed regions to work together. The major aim of this chapter to showcase experiences in as far as implementation and adoption of m-Government is concerned in the case of Turkey. The study utilizes the co-creation literature to investigate the factors influencing successful implementation of the Beyas Masa. This study reveals that initiatives are fragmented due to differences in the characteristics of the targeted audience, the marketing strategy, technology supply, distribution, and media utilized to promote its awareness. The chapter posits that in order to have affluent m-Government implementation in Turkey, it is important that many of the standalone applications are integrated to encourage interoperability and that socio-cultural behaviours should be re-shaped to encourage active engagement and interactive government service provisions that unlock the power of ICT.

Chapter 12

Hakikur Rahman, University of Minho, Portugal
Isabel Ramos, University of Minho, Portugal

E-Government and e-Governance are the two terms within the governance system that need to be attended through clarity, distinctness, and justification. No matter how the stages of the governance system evolve, where they have been applied, and in which stages they are at a present moment, these two prominently distinct elements of the governance systems are yet to be watched closely and minutely. After synthesizing existing e-Government maturity models and exploring relevant literature, this chapter proposes a new model that may guide e-Government implementation in a developing world context. It is expected that the proposed model would assist researchers, academics, and policy makers in establishing sustained e-Government model in emerging and developing economies.

Chapter 13

Hilda Moraa, iHub Research, Kenya
Anne Salim, iHub Research, Kenya
Albert Otieno, iHub Research, Kenya

iHub Research conducted a study on 896 citizens to establish whether citizens raise alarm when faced with problems related to water. The study aimed to ascertain the communication channels they use to forward complaints to relevant authorities and the level of satisfaction obtained by the citizens after their complaints have been received. The study found that 68% of the respondents had faced challenges while trying to access their main source of water and were not able to complain to anyone about the problems affecting them due to inexistence of appropriate communication channels. A lack of understanding with regards to whom or where to complain was cited as one of the major reasons as to why most respondents do not complain about the water service levels. Majority of the citizens interviewed use face-to-face communication to raise their water grievances. Levels of satisfaction were found to vary when it comes to rating the action taken on water complaints raised. This study opines that with the emergence of Information and Communication Technologies (ICTs) this scenario is poised to change. The study participants revealed that they are motivated to utilise ICTs to air their complaints with regards to their levels of service satisfaction. Emerging ICT applications, especially those accessible on mobile devices, provide a lot of promise for enhancing water service delivery in Kenya because feedback on water/service quality can be received ubiquitously.

Chapter 14

Malgorzata Pankowska, University of Economics in Katowice, Poland

E-Government and e-Democracy system development is enabled by Internet technology. The implementation of Information and Communication Technologies (ICTs) accelerates the transformation of government institutions and their methods of operations. The use of ICTs at municipality institutions not only opens up possibilities for improving services to citizens and businesses, but also increases their involvement in local community governance. The general objective of this chapter is to reveal, at the municipality level, the opportunity for local community development and stronger citizen involvement in governing processes (e-Democracy). The chapter aims to present the new sources of knowledge, particularly through the involvement of individuals in local government development. The chapter aims to understand challenges in developing open information infrastructures that support municipality innovation and development. The chapter utilizes extensive literature reviews and the analysis of the content of selected e-Government portals to inform its positions.

Chapter 15

Camilius Aloyce Sanga, Sokoine University of Agriculture, Tanzania

Siza D. Tumbo, Sokoine University of Agriculture, Tanzania

Malongo R. S. Mlozi, Sokoine University of Agriculture, Tanzania

The major purpose of this chapter is to explore the options of Information and Communication Technologies (ICTs) to complement conventional agricultural extension services in Tanzania. Group discussions and meetings were conducted to investigate the role of ICTs in extension services delivery using CAT-WOE framework of Soft Systems Methodology. The findings of the study reveal that the use of SSM helped the researchers to understand easily the problematic areas of the current situation of agricultural extension services. In addition, it was easy to plan feasible actions to be taken to improve the situation. The framework for the conceptual model towards improving the agricultural extension services in Kilosa District of Tanzania was developed. These results have been used in the development of an ICT-based system (Web- and Mobile-Based Farmers' Advisory Information Systems) to supplement the conventional agricultural extension system. The roadmap developed as the implementation plan for this research can be used in any e-Government project. The need to improve the way agricultural extension is done in Tanzania through integration of relevant and affordable ICTs is well researched. This book chapter presents how this can be done using SSM approach in an action and participatory research. This is the first presentation of SSM intervention in agricultural informatics in Tanzania. The approach used in this study can be adopted by researchers doing any e-Government research.

Chapter 16

Rafiat A. Oyekunle, University of Ilorin, Nigeria

H. B. Akanbi-Ademolake, University of Ilorin, Nigeria

This chapter presents an overview of e-Government technological divide in developing countries. Technological divide here does not consist simply of telecommunications and computer equipment (i.e. ICTs), but it is also e-Readiness (i.e. the available capacity as indicated by workforce capacity to build, deploy, and maintain ICT infrastructure), ICT literacy (using digital technology, communication tools, and/or networks appropriately to access, manage, integrate, evaluate, and create information), e-Inclusion and/or e-Exclusion (i.e. no one is left behind in enjoying the benefits of ICT), etc., which are factors also necessary in order for people to be able to use and benefit from e-Government applications. Most of the currently published works on e-Government strategies are based on successful experiences from developed countries, which may not be directly applicable to developing countries. Based on a literature review, this chapter reveals the status of e-Government technological divide in developing countries and also underscores the challenges associated with e-Government in developing countries, thus bringing to the limelight the factors that influence the growth of the technological divide and different approaches that have been put in place to overcome the divide. In conclusion, this chapter advocates education and training, local content development, enhancing network infrastructure, and capacity building, among others, as ways of bridging the divide.

Chapter 17

Tatjana Bilevičienė, Mykolas Romeris University, Lithuania

Eglė Bilevičiūtė, Mykolas Romeris University, Lithuania

Social technologies are slowly occupying the central place of available and emerging solution for a variety of socio-economic problems. Although not a panacea, it cannot be overemphasized that social technologies have an influence on the social effects of humans, social groups, hierarchical social structures (such as public administrations, local authorities, non-governmental organizations, etc.), and behaviour. Of late, there has been an escalation in the use of social technologies in the legal fraternity. The Lithuanian government has started putting in place interventions that promote the utilization of social technologies into legal administrative processes. This came after the realization that Lithuanian citizens have the right to full and truthful information about administrative law and administrative processes. Using extensive literature reviews, this chapter probes the key success factors that need to be considered in the successful utilization of social technologies in legal administrative processes. The chapter posits that within the e-Government realm, the opportunities to be amassed from the use of Information and Communication Technologies are immense.

Chapter 18

This chapter introduces and analyzes the best practices and development methods for Information Communication Technologies (ICTs) in South Korea in the realm of e-Government. To the present, national informatization in South Korea has focused on e-Government. This is because e-Government can lead to transformation in national information infrastructure and the public services sector, leading to increased efficiencies. Thus, firstly, this chapter focuses on defining the key concepts of e-Government. Secondly, it analyzes public document systems for the best practices of e-Government in South Korea in the following categories: Government for Citizens (G4C), Government e-Procurement Systems (GePS), the governance system, the On-Nara Business Process System, and the Home Tax Service (HTS). E-Government has reduced the number of documents and therefore reduced costs. In particular, the e-Procurement system has proven effective. This chapter explains the theoretical concepts of e-Government in South Korea via a literature review. Finally, this chapter analyzes instances of success and suggests avenues for future e-Government growth.

There are many different benefits that a government can obtain from encouraging the use of Information and Communication Technologies (ICTs) in its public sector delivery frameworks. Utilization of ICTs as a socio-economic stimulant has long been recognized by governments the world over. Electronic government utilizes ICTs to provide all the access to a wide range of public services. Today, different government departments and/or units at all levels of the governance hierarchy respond to millions of citizen demands electronically. The rising interest of many stakeholders in e-Government calls for a conceptual model that will guide implementation regardless of context. This chapter argues that several key success factors are appropriate and need to be considered for successful e-Government implementation. About one hundred e-Government Websites were examined upon those key success factors. Sixty-one university students took part in this investigation. Using t-test, the chapter investigates the appropriateness of the proposed model.

Chapter 20

This chapter utilizes extensive literature reviews to assess the different perspectives of e-Government development in developing world contexts. In order to do that, the chapter presents a case study from Jordan assessing the design and reality gaps of e-Government interventions using the ITPOSMO model. The chapter posits that e-Government for development is likely to grow only if there is deliberate cognisance of culture, real work practices, and of the broader technical and socio-political environment with which the e-Government projects are introduced and applied in the developing world.

Shauneen Furlong, University of Liverpool, UK

Throughout the millennia, project management methodologies were developed, and as projects were completed, both theoreticians and practitioners contributed to the development of project management science and codification. Throughout this time, project management science grappled with the problem of delineating project activities from on-going operational activities. Projects require project management while operations require business process management or operations management (PMI, 2008). In the project methodology world, a project is defined as unique, temporary, a definite start and finish (PMI, 2008). Without this definition, the science of project management cannot be applied. It is this definition that provides the credence for the creation and application of project management processes, tools, and techniques. However, the science of project management exists irrespective of a project. In fact, it is the application of project management to any endeavor that creates a project. Effective project management that will drive the design and implementation of transformational e-Government must be enhanced. This chapter proposes project management enhancements to the design, direction, management, and implementation of e-Government projects that focus on project problems rather than methodological processes. The enhanced project management solution provides the tools and educates the user to take into account the impact of the holistic, synergistic challenges and barriers that surround and influence e-Government projects – heretofore, in an unmanageable way that has inhibited change instead of promoting it. The enhanced project management solution is "exogenous" of the e-Government solution; it is its external driver.

Preface

Many texts on e-Government have attempted to investigate what factors influence e-Government adoption and usage and report the experiences in e-Government implementation. There are very few texts that have attempted to share their experiences in as far as technology design of e-Government implementation is concerned. While it cannot be denied that there are myriad technology solutions that can be employed to design affluent technology applications and solutions, developing e-Government is a different undertaking altogether because context is very much at play in influencing its success or failure. This book, therefore, intends to outline the technology principles and fundamentals that should be cornerstones of e-Government applications design.

Successful e-Government implementation demands that there is equilibrium between the supply (interventions towards the promotion of e-Government) and demand (citizens' and businesses' willingness to engage in e-Government) sides of e-Government. In general, there is a dearth of information on the supply side of e-Government especially with regards to implementation and design of e-Government from the technology front. For example, only the recent works (on going) of the OASIS e-Government Technical Committee have put up concerted efforts in developing interoperability platforms that can bring about integration of e-Government applications.

This book therefore intends to unearth the different technological nuances that need to be incorporated into successful e-Government designs. It provides a platform for e-Government designers and practitioners to share their experiences with emphasis on technological design and how to map technology to the unique characteristics of systems where e-Government is to be implemented. The book, therefore, brings out cases that complement the work of international committees such OASIS towards achieving a common interoperable technology solution for e-Government design regardless of whether it is implemented in a developed or resource-constrained economy.

The impact of this book is imaginable owing to the fact that there is no reference book devoted solely to discussing issues of technology design of e-Government applications in its entirety, especially from both a developing and developed world context. The thesis of the book is that inappropriate technology design may be one of the major causes of failure of many e-Government projects worldwide; therefore, this publication calls for experiences of best-practice to be shared. The overall objective of this book is to provide a platform for researchers, designers, and practitioners to share experiences in technology design of e-Government platforms. The book showcases the heterogeneous technology solutions implemented in different parts of the world in the realm of e-Government, helps e-Government designers understand what technology platforms are likely to work given their context, and provides a reference source for both researchers and academics concerning current and emerging research trends in technology designs of e-Government applications.

Because of the many benefits that come about with the implementation of e-Government, many governments have started implementing it. However, many e-Government designs are adopted without tailoring the technology (arguably the main enabler) to the local context and its heterogeneity. The result of this is that many of these projects fail to deliver on their promises. The chapters presented in this book will enable e-Government planners/designers to tailor their projects to the characteristics of the local context and therefore reduce the chance for e-Government projects to fail.

As aforementioned, although technology solutions are readily available to be potentially utilized in the design of e-Government applications, context plays a major role in determining the success rate of e-Government design interventions. Therefore, this book intends to present the nitty-gritty of e-Government technology design. Essentially, the book has two sections: The first section looks discusses fundamentals that guide the designs of e-Government technology and application platforms. The second section presents real-world cases of technology design and applications of e-Government solutions. In short, whilst the first section highlights the design principles, section two presents the application of the said principles in real world environments, providing a near hands-on feeling of e-Government to the readers of this book. The detailed snapshots of the chapters included in this book are outlined below.

The 1st chapter is an editorial comment that aims to highlight the overview of the best practices and foresights in technology design of e-Government applications development. The chapter posits that although a lot has been achieved in technology development for e-Government applications, there are still no global technological conceptual frameworks and models that define e-Government implementation the world over. Further, the current pace of technological advancements supporting requisite e-Government applications and efforts put in by the OASIS forum and other interested parties, it is not difficult to notice that global technological models of e-Government are to be realized in the foreseeable future.

The 2nd chapter by Fonou Vincent-Dombeu and Magda Huisman proposes a semantic-enabled framework for e-Government systems development. The chapter provides the design and specification of a framework which amalgamates features from maturity models, software engineering, and Semantic Web domains for semantic-enabled development of e-Government systems. Firstly, the chapter investigates the techniques utilized in the planning, design and implementation of e-Government systems worldwide, proposes the semantic-enabled framework, and then presents the support tools such as the business process model and the alignment matrix to articulate intensity of semantic activities at various stages of the phases for e-Government development.

Chapter 3 explores the prospects of socio media (Web 2.0) in e-Government environments. The chapter proposes a novel policy analysis framework, proposing a Web-based platform that enables publishing content and micro-applications to multiple Web 2.0 social media and collecting citizens' interactions (e.g. comments, ratings) with efficient use of Application Programming Interfaces (APIs) of these media.

Chapter 4 discusses an ontology development process in e-Government Project Management environments with a specific focus on Zimbabwe. The chapter underscores the role of Project Management in the e-Government technology developing process cycle.

In chapter 5, Liam Church and Maria Moloney outline the design principles for e-Government applications design. The chapter presents a design theory to guide developers of public sector ICTs on how to produce systems that provide public e-services through secure and inclusive information systems. The design principles outlined by the theory are also subject to empirical, as well as practical, validation therefore opening future research directions for e-Government researchers.

Chapter 6 utilizes systems thinking and performance management frameworks to aid e-Government applications design. The chapter presents concepts, which should be utilized by e-Government platform designers if they must reach their goals of designing and implementing an e-Government platform that will meet social requirements necessary for designing good e-Government platforms.

In chapter 7, Gobin presents an agile and modular approach for developing ontologies, which may inform effervescent e-Government designs. The chapter posits that many ontology engineering methodologies available suffer from their heavy weight nature and make the development process tedious.

The 8th chapter by Adeyinka and Adetayo explores the literature to investigate the promise of Open Source system or software for developing requisite e-Government solutions for the developing world. The chapter posits that open source plays a significant role in e-Government application and its benefits are overwhelming as it results to less corruption, increased transparency, greater convenience, revenue growth, and/or cost reductions. However, it adoption is not without challenges.

Section 2, which present chapters focusing on the design and use of e-Government application in real world scenarios, starts with Tianxing Cai's chapter, which looks at the geospatial technologies implemented on an e-Government conceptualization safeguarding the environment as a public good.

Chapter 10 by Neupane, Solar, and Vaidya discusses e-Procurement technologies with a goal of mitigating corruption levels in the public sector and utilizes the Principal-Agent theory to investigate the role of technologies in creating social sanity. The chapter reviews the principal-agent theory and discusses other relevant theories including transaction cost theory, fraud triangle theory, diffusion of innovation theory, and technology acceptance model. Following a discussion of the anti-corruption potential of e-procurement systems, a theoretical research model is proposed for identifying public e-procurement anti-corruption capabilities.

Chapter 11 discusses the Smartphone Base Digital Government Model in Turkey. The chapter posits that the different m-Government initiatives in Turkey are fragmented due to differences in audience, marketing strategy, technology supply, and distribution and media leading to reduced interoperability, and that apart from technologies, socio-cultural behaviours should be re-shaped to encourage active engagement and interactive government service provision that unlock the power of ICT.

Chapter 12 by Rahman and Ramos discusses the different stages of e-Government maturity models and provides some projectile of how contemporary e-Government initiatives can be designed and measured. The chapter proposes a grassroots e-Government model that emphasizes that affluent e-Government initiatives or technology focuses should be geared towards understanding the inherent attributes of the community setups.

The 13th chapter discusses the prospects brought about by technology utilization in the water sector using mobile technologies (m-Government). The chapter outlines the emerging ICT applications, especially those accessible on mobile devices, provide a lot of promise for enhancing water service delivery in Kenya because feedback on water/service quality can be received ubiquitously.

Chapter 14, by Malgorzata Pankowska, discusses the concept of Government 2.0 and outlines the different platforms promoting innovation for e-Democracy by particularly surveying open information infrastructures that support municipality innovation and development. The chapter utilizes extensive literature reviews and the analysis of the content of selected e-Government portals to inform its positions.

Chapter 15 discusses the different ICT applications utilized for linking small-scale farmers and agricultural extension service delivery. Using Soft Systems Methodology, the chapter proposes a framework for a conceptual model towards improving the agricultural extension services in Kilosa District of Tanzania was developed. The results were utilized in the development of an ICT-based system (Web-

and Mobile-Based Farmers' Advisory Information Systems) to supplement conventional agricultural extension system. The roadmap developed as the implementation plan for this research can be used in any e-Government projects.

Oyekunle and Akanbi-Ademolake discuss e-Government technology divide in developing world contexts in chapter 16. The chapter highlights the different factors that may influence e-Government especially in resource-constrained countries.

In chapter 17, Tatjana Bilevičienė and Eglė Bilevičiūtė explore the possibilities of the use of ICTs in the judicial delivery platforms (e-Justice) in the context of e-Government. This is an eye-opener for e-Government domain researchers to explore and design applications to be utilized in law-enforcement agencies.

In chapter 18, Young Jun Shin extends the discussion of e-Procurement in e-Government environments started in chapter 10. The chapter presents Korea the following best practices of e-Government: Government for Citizens (G4C), Government e-Procurement Systems (GePS), the governance system, the On-Nara Business Process System, and the Home Tax Service (HTS).

Chapter 19 by Sagheb-Tehrani discusses the key factors influencing e-Government implementation. The chapter aims to discuss different contexts that may shape the success or failure of e-Government implementation.

Chapter 20 by Afolayan discusses the critical perspectives of e-Government in developing world contexts. This chapter utilizes extensive literature reviews to assess the different perspectives of e-Government development in developing world contexts. The chapter presents a Case Study from Jordan assessing the design and reality gaps of e-Government interventions using the ITPOSMO model.

In the final chapter in this book, Furlong discusses the role of Project Management in e-Government environments. The chapter outlines the need for effervescent Project Management approaches given the transformational e-Government models taking shape in most of the developing world contexts. The enhanced project management solution is "exogenous" of the e-Government solution.

As aforementioned, this book will go a long way in articulating the technology design fundamentals in the design of e-Government applications. I believe the carefully chosen chapters presented in this book will go a long way in acting as a major reference source for e-Government research and practice both in the developing and developed world.

Kelvin Joseph Bwalya
University of Botswana, Botswana & Senior Research Fellow, University of Johannesburg, South Africa

Acknowledgment

I would like to express my thanks to the authors who invested a considerable amount of their time in contributing to this book project. Without the authors' contributions, this project would not have materialized. My conscience would not let me off the hook if I ignored the valuable contributions to this book by the reviewers of the submitted chapters. This book is the way it is because of the sleepless nights endured by the authors and reviewers. Any credit that this book may garner should, therefore, go to them.

I am also particularly indebted to the IGI Global team for the technical and managerial assistance rendered to us during all stages of the publishing cycle of this book. Particularly, I would like to recognize the valuable contribution by the following people: Julia Mosemann – Director of Book Publications, (Ms) Jan Travers – Director of Intellectual Property and Contracts, Erika Carter – Acquisitions Editor, Myla Harty – Editorial Assistant at the Development Division, and Austin M. DeMarco – Editorial Assistant, Editorial Content Division – Book Development. Austin's support during the different development stages of this book was exceptional.

I would also like to thank colleagues at the Department of Library and Information Studies (DLIS) for any support rendered towards this project. Many thanks to the University of Botswana for providing a conducive academic and research environment, without which this publication would not have been possible. Further, special thanks are attributed to the Center for Information and Knowledge Management, University of Johannesburg, for the technical support.

Last but not least, thanks to my family for the support.

Kelvin Joseph Bwalya
University of Botswana, Botswana & Senior Research Fellow, University of Johannesburg, South Africa

Section 1
Fundamentals for E–Government Technology and Application Design

Chapter 1

Foresights and Practice in Technology Development for E-Government Applications:
A Global Compendium of Approaches

Kelvin Joseph Bwalya
University of Botswana, Botswana & Senior Research Fellow,
University of Johannesburg, South Africa

ABSTRACT

Although a lot has been achieved with regards to technology development for e-government applications, there are still no global technological conceptual frameworks and models that define e-government platform design and implementation the world over. This has partly been attributed to the differing local contexts and organisational cultures in the public services departments (even within the same government). Because of this scenario, there is need to review the different technology design endeavours geared towards achieving process automation and application integration in the different government departments to achieve meaningful and robust e-Government development. This lead chapter intends to review the different approaches that have been done on the technology front of e-Government (especially design of interoperability frameworks and ontology platforms) in different parts of the world and outlines the future works that e-Government researchers and practitioners need to concentrate on. This chapter sets the tone for the remaining chapters of this book, which discuss various aspects of e-Government implementation from the technological front (deployment, design, and customization of e-Government solutions). The chapter posits that with the current pace of technological advancements and efforts by the OASIS forum and other interested parties, it is not difficult to notice that global technological models of e-Government are to be realized in the foreseeable future.

DOI: 10.4018/978-1-4666-4900-2.ch001

E-GOVERNMENT CONCEPTUALIZATION

It cannot be overemphasized that many private organizations have long recognized information as a key resource for enriching business competitiveness and sustainability. Information is an enzyme that guides appropriate requisite evidence-based decision making which ensures that there is reduced wastage of business resources employed towards achieving a set business objective. In order for the full value of information to be amassed, it is important that it is, as much as possible, integrated into the different organisational business processes at all levels of the organisation hierarchy. This integration of information in different organisational business value chains can be achieved with requisite use of Information and Communication Technologies (ICTs). Although private organizations have lead the crusade towards mainstreaming information in their business activities, many public organizations and government departments are now following suit and slowly charging up. Through e-Government, government departments are now emphasizing on requisite usage of ICTs in their back-end and front-end business processes to achieve effectiveness and efficiencies and therefore amass the many benefits that come with e-Government implementation. Contemporary e-Government services aim towards satisfying the needs of citizens and businesses by providing seamless flow of information across government organizations (Borras, 2004). The seamless flow of information cannot be achieved with carefully-thought technology solutions. Against this background, this book intends to bring out the different e-Government technology design approaches and strategies from both renowned and emerging e-Government practioners and researchers.

Designing global e-Government technology platforms and applications is not a simple undertaking because of the multi-dimensionality nature of e-Government and because a robust e-Government technology model should consider the different political, cultural, and socio-economic contexts (Carbo & Williams, 2004). It cannot be denied that the task of designing requisite e-Government solutions is further hardened by technology designs' over-dependence on semantics and software syntax which defines how technology interacts and how different technology systems can interchange data. Given this difficulty in realizing the full potential of technology for designing dynamic e-Government solutions, several interventions for e-Government technology platforms have adopted open international standards together with XML and XSL as core standards for data integration (Borras, 2004). In this regard, Borras (2004) has outlined the ongoing work at an international level by the OASIS e-Government Technical Committee that aims to develop technology standards for interoperability with a goal of supporting the establishment of e-Government solutions worldwide.

This chapter intends to provide an overview of what technology principles and design guidelines currently exist and discuss how different e-Government solutions have been designed especially in the developing world economies. By doing that, it is anticipated that core technology focuses will be discussed in a bid to bring about a compendium of best practices in as far as e-Government design and implementation is concerned.

BACKGROUND

The wider recognition of information as a strategic resource to organizations has led to what are called 'Knowledge-Based-Economies (KBEs)'. KBEs are basically economical setups which have bought-into the idea that the different knowledge types (tacit and explicit) need to be amassed appropriately and integrated into the different organisational business processes. The emergence of knowledge economies entails that knowledge is the major sources of competitive advantage distinct to the old economic models which recognized land, labour and capital as vital factors of production and therefore competitiveness (Drucker, 1995; 1999; Stiglitz, 2003; Butler et al., 2004). Recognition of the role information plays in business contexts and the need for it flow across organisation silos entails that process integration and dynamic technology applications are needed. For the case of e-Government, technology is one of the main enablers. Therefore, there is need to check what advancements have been achieved by both e-Government practitioners and researchers on the technology front. In order to appreciate the role of technology in the e-Government landscape, Figure 1 below shows a six-stage e-Government development roadmap.

This roadmap shows that e-Government development starts from back-office process automation where the organisation has procured one

Figure 1. A six stage e-government roadmap (Adapted from: Forrester Research, Inc.)

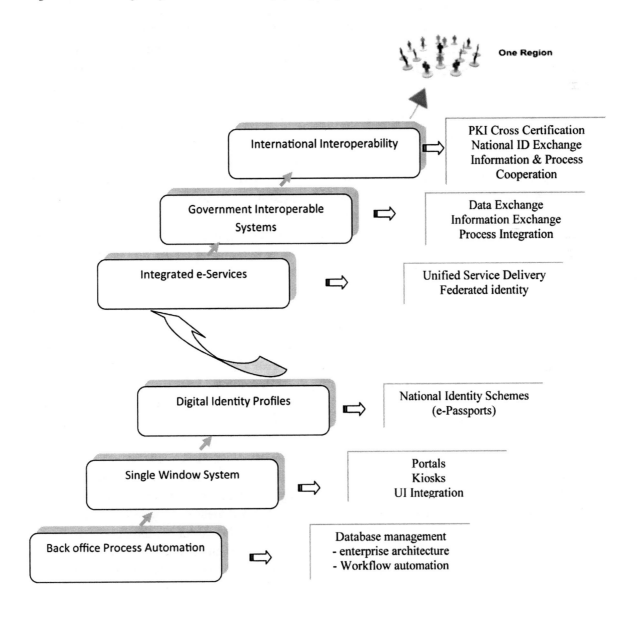

or two types of databases, the enterprise architecture has been established and the workflow automation has been put in place. The advanced stage comprises the existence of interoperable government systems which lead to ubiquitous governance systems. The future development stage of e-Government will vie towards international interoperability where government systems from across borders of different countries will be integrated. At each of these stages, it is important to note that technology is extensively utilised. Therefore, as much as other non-technology strategies are cardinal to the success of e-Government, ignoring requisite technology design frameworks for e-Government applications is a huge opportunity cost as most e-Government interventions done with a lame focus on the design of requisite technology platforms fail.

In order to design requisite e-Government applications commensurate for the different stages of the e-Government roadmap as shown in Figure 1, there is need to completely understand the major trends and tenets of e-Government in a given context. The major technology tenets and challenges in e-Government include:

1. How to design the back-office and front-office technology consoles so that they are adequately and appropriately integrated?
2. What technology platforms to use to design graphical user interfaces commensurate to the types of users in any given environment (ease-to-use e-Government portals and databases according to user profiles)?
3. How to integrate e-Government solutions across departmental and organisational silos?
4. How to design open, scalable and highly interoperable e-Government systems (technology that evolve with evolving technology)? and
5. How to build durable and secure e-Government systems?

Amongst all the various technology tenets mentioned above, it is vital to mention that most e-Government interventions have devoted their efforts to designing highly interoperable and integrated e-Government systems, advanced e-Government portals and database components. These technology focuses are basically the technology success factors for e-Government implementation. Choudrie, Ghinea & Weerakkody (2004) evaluated a cross-section of e-Government portals using a common set of performance metrics and Web diagnostic engines (such as *WebXact, Netmechanic*- http://www.netmechanic.com*), W3C's HTML validator (*http://validator.w3.org*). Their study posited that significant amount of work needs to be done before portals can be examples of 'best practice' e-Government services. This entails that there is still a lot of work to be done in this area and active researchers and practitioners should therefore tap in to this void in the knowledge gaps. Another important component of successful e-Government is the database. E-Government applications should have a very responsive database component which appropriately responds to the database queries timely. Such a database can be build based on the Resource Description Framework (RDF) and the Simple Protocol and RDF Query Language - SPARQL (Harris et al., 2008). Researchers and practitioners are therefore implored to come up with strategies that would inform the design of context-aware e-Government database applications.

As mentioned above, one of the core success factors for e-Government includes designing requisite context-aware e-Government systems which are able to provide seamless flow of information amongst departments. In order to achieve this, technical policies and specifications guiding interoperability and technology coherence (Government organizations need to agree upon data schemas for use throughout the public sector) across government departments needs to be achieved. That said, let us now look at the different technology nuances which act as a pivot to e-Government platform and applications design.

TECHNOLOGY NUANCES

As outlined above, one of the core tenets of technology in e-Government design is the need to design seamless data flow amongst different standalone systems. For this to be achieved, it is necessary to have highly integrated and interoperable systems that can seamlessly exchange data. Of late, research in designing interoperability frameworks has taken centre-stage in e-Government design and practice. Despite being predominantly looked at from the technical side, interoperability can also be an organisational issue (ownership, people and business processes). In any competitive e-Government design, the importance of requisite interoperability frameworks cannot be overemphasized. Therefore, the design of interoperability strategy is a cornerstone for designing any e-Government information system (Jarrari, Deik, & Farraj, 2009).

There are different definitions of interoperability: the Institute of Electrical and Electronics Engineers (IEEE) defines interoperability as the inherent capacity and ability of two independent information systems entities or components to exchange information. The ISO/IEC 2382-01 defines it as the mere ability for two or more systems to communicate and execute programs and thereby transfer data among various functional units where the user is expected to have little or no knowledge of what is happening behind the systems (Tschumperlin, 2009). The main obstacles for integration of e-Government applications stem from technical (great variety of legacy systems already installed and running in government departments), semantic (difference in data/information standards) and human (adoption of interoperable solutions by government officers) issues (Saekow & Boonmee, 2009).

Many of the e-Government technology platforms have been based on XML architecture. The XML family consists of the XML documents and the schemas themselves. There are basically two types of XML documents: XML Instance Documents which contain the actual data, and XML Schemas which define allowable XML constraints. The schemas are further sub-divided into XML Document Schemas and XML Library Schemas (Tschumperlin, 2009). The successful design of e-Government applications should be based as much as possible on XML-based technologies because most technological solutions and applications are based on XML for easy interoperability.

According to Al-Khouri (2013), some of the common technological platforms for developing e-Government applications are:

- Cybersecurity & access control (such as WS-Security, SAML, XACML, KMIP, DSS & XSPA);
- Office documents and smart semantic documents (such as OpenDocument, DITA, DocBook & CMIS); and
- Electronic commerce (including SOA and web services, such as BPEL, ebXML, WS-Reliable Messaging & the WS-Transaction standards)

Other technology standards with a view of complementing on efforts by OASIS have been produced such as the following (Al-Khouri, 2013):

- UBL and Business Document Exchange (for e-procurement)
- CAP and EDML (for emergency first-responder notifications); and
- LegalXML (for electronic court filing data).

Utilization of open-source software in the design of e-Government is now getting prominence (Butler et al., 2004; Sourouni et al., 2008; Jarrari, Deik, & Farraj, 2009; Al-Khouri, 2013). One of the widely-used open-source software has been the *Portable Knowledge Asset Development System* (*p*KADS) which is a desktop-based knowledge management system which aims to facilitate the sharing of knowledge in government and non-governmental organizations.

Sourouni et al., (2008) described the design of a Web portal with focus on thorough description of the application ontology and repositories for e-Government. The Web portal was developed using ASP.NET and the DBMS component was based on SQL Server 2005 and utilized HTTP compression filter to make optimal usage of the available bandwidth. Reviewing different e-Government ontologies, Sourouni et al., (2008) proposed an e-Government Knowledge Interoperability Ontology (eGKI) which is a two-layer ontology enveloping the knowledge management conceptualization into public services business processes. The eGKI was formalized using OWL.

Meneklis et al., (2005) designed a Web Services based platform for e-Government, the eMayor platform, which was based on the ISO/RM-ODP standard which supports the integration of distribution, interworking, interoperability and portability of e-Government applications. It can be observed from above paragraphs that the design of requisite e-Government is influenced by a variety of factors such as ontologies (which may take care of the context) and Web portals and Web Services being designed using different technologies to ensure that context is taken into consideration. Also coming up is the role of Open-Source systems and software and the issues that they bring on board to e-Government platform design. The next paragraph discusses the issues of interoperability and looks at ways on which such technologies allow integration of different e-Government systems from different government departments.

The heterogeneity of data in the public sector entails that there needs to be developed adaptive systems that are able to handle all types of data. Technology platforms and standards such as RosettaNet (B2B data exchange standard), EDIFACT (Electronic Data Interchange for Administration, Commerce, and Transport), XML and Electronic Data Interchange (EDI) have enabled different government departments to exchange data through common interoperable systems (Muthaiyah & Kerschberg, 2008). Despite the existence of these technology solutions, including the Service Oriented Architecture (SOA) and Web Services, the problem of data handling given its heterogeneity, has not been resolved by e-Government. Therefore, there is need to ensure for researchers and practitioners to engage and find ways on how this can be resolved (Muthaiyah & Kerschberg, 2008).

E-Government interoperability enables seamless exchange of information across government sectors. The main technology frameworks guiding this have been the Government Interoperability Frameworks (GIFs) and of Enterprise Architectures (EAs). One of the most pronounced GIFs has been the European Union Interoperability Framework (EUIF) which is further discussed in the next section. The EUIF acts as a guideline for e-Government interventions at the member state level. Some of the e-Government design programs at country level includes the following:

1. The Italian e-Government Architecture (SPCoop Enterprise Architecture) which follows a Service Oriented Architecture (SOA). It also uses the *Zinna*r ontology build from ORM notation;

2. The Estonian Semantic Interoperability Architecture (X-Road) also based on the *Zinnar* ontology; and

3. The UK e-Government Interoperability Framework (e-GIF) which has the following basic components: the e-Government Metadata Standard (e-GMS) – which defines the elements, refinements and encoding schemes for creating e-Government metadata;; the Integrated Public Sector Vocabulary (IPSV/GCL) – vocabulary and encoding scheme for e-GMS; the Government Data

Standards Catalogue (GDSC) – outlines the agreed set of core government data standards; XML Schemas – describing all the data in the e-Government environment (Jarrar, Deik, & Farraj, 2011).

Saekow and Boonmee (2009) designed an approach called 'interoperability Practical Implementation Support (IPIS)' which utilizes UN/CEFACTs Modeling Methodology (UMM) for modeling or specifying organisational business processes, UN/CEFACT CCTS as the semantic tool for data standardization or harmonization, and the XML Naming and Design Rules, and Recommend 34.

Lee, Yee and Cheung (2009) has suggested that interoperability framework comprise two parts: 1) definitions of recommended technical specifications; and 2) frameworks data exchanges based on XML standards (Schema design and design guide and its applications). Requisite technology applications interoperability has been based on the XML Schema Design and Management Guide which posits that there are basically three dimensions of interoperability (Lee, Yee, & Cheung2009).

1. **Technical interoperability**: Outlines what communication protocols and message formats needs to be utilised when one entity sends information to another in an e-Government environment. An example could be two applications processes agreeing using a three handshake system that packets will be encoded in XML, defined using a specific XML Schema, XML Encryption (or Secure Socket Layer - SSL channel) and XML Signature, and packet sent via HTTP;

2. **Data interoperability**: Two communication entities agree on what data should be sent across their networking media and in what format it should be. Another important roadblock to affective highly interoperable e-Government systems has been the issue of

data interoperability. Data interoperability is concerned with how different systems exchange data and how to represent data for common understanding. There are different standards that guide the achievement of data interoperability and these should be consulted if it were to be achieved. For example, they may agree to utilize ISO 8601 standard; and

3. **Process interoperability**: Provides details on agreements on how business activities effect each other and how they should be integrated (functional integration). This can be achieved, for example, using SOAP V.1.1., WSDL v. 1.1., and UDDI v.2

Ellis (2004) and Jarrari, Deik and Farraj (2009) distinguish four types of interoperability within the European Union *viz* political interoperability (political support for improved public services), legal interoperability (provision of European legal frameworks for data exchange among member states), organisational interoperability (definition of business goals and processes), semantic interoperability (applications' ability to precisely understand the exchanged information and re-engineering of business processes), and technical interoperability (covering technical issues such as need for open interfaces, middleware, accessibility and security services). Tschumperlin (2007) has submitted that apart from the four types of interoperability discussed above, there are also higher levels of interoperability such as syntactic interoperability (common protocols for sharing information such as XML syntax) and others such as Pragmatic, Dynamic, Conceptual, Legal, International interoperability.

It is important to recognize that apart from the design, technology deployment and process re-engineering are some of the key success factors for successful e-Government. To this regard, the Salford Process Re-engineering method Involving New Technologies (SPRINT) was designed to introduce programs to counter the risk and complexity of e-Government projects (Eddowes, 2004).

Based on Systems Oriented Architecture (SOA), Widodo et al (2013) attempted to create an Enterprise Architecture Framework (EAF) as a basis for data integration and system interoperability for e-Government applications in Indonesia. The architecture described the anticipated government applications platform using the Web Services Description Language (WSDL) and in order to make applications and business process integration easier, suggested technical specifications for the Government Service Bus (GSB) which was realized using the Business Process Execution Language (BPEL). The design of this EAF was to come up with a scalable interoperable e-Government systems environment which could easily support Web Services. The SOA was intended to make applications distribution and therefore present integration and interoperability as a not far-fetched dream. Distributed technology such as CORBA, COM/DCOM, EJB, JAVA RMI was used to implement interoperability between applications.

During the design of e-Government systems, it is important to note the importance of including modeling of data interaction as one of the core attributes. Business Process Modeling Methodology is clearly defined by the XML Schema Design and extends the *ebXML Core Components Technical Specification* (CCTS) (UN/CEFACT 2003). This allows business analysts monitoring e-Government business processes to specify data elements and documents for a variety of models such as *Aggregate Business Information Entity* (ABIE), *Association Business Information Entity* (ASBIE) and *Core Component Type* (CCT) used for modeling singular or complex property in an object class (Lee, Hon, & Cheung, 2009).

One of the approaches towards solving semantic interoperability is the design of semantically enriched Web Services. Muthaiyah and Kerschberg (2008) proposed an hierarchical repository which was based on two-part semantic mediation

approach using Semantic Relatedness Scores (SRS) and Semantic Web Rule Language (SWRL) which are necessary for schema heterogeneity. This repository employed the a rule-based engine that reads and executes SWRL rules (i.e. RacerPro) and utilised several tools such as Protégé (i.e. ontology editor) and JESS (Java Expert Shell System (Muthaiyah & Kerschberg, 2008). The semantic Web technologies are being supplemented with a metadata registry based upon ISO/IEC 11179 standard. The ISO/IEC 11179 allows the maintaining of semantics and metadata independently.

Fonou Dombeu, Huisman and Szpak (2011) provide a framework that may be used to generate semantic model ontologies in OWL syntax that may be used to construct e-Government applications. In achieving this, they used an ontology editor – Protégé. On the ontology aspects, the Simple Knowledge Organisation System (SKOS), an RDF vocabulary designed to represent terminologies, thesauri and classification schemes has been used extensively in applications development (Harris, Gibbons, Davies, & Crichton, 2008).

The need for a drive by e-Government researchers and practitioners towards global technology approaches for designing e-Government applications is a very urgent matter. Efforts to design context-aware interoperability frameworks cannot be overemphasized as there is currently no global semantic model that would aid such efforts. Even at the technology level, some standards do not 'talk to each other'. An example includes the XML standards developed by OASIS UBL which are incompatible with the OASIS xNAL (Tschumperlin, 2009).

ADVANCES IN TECHNOLOGY DESIGNS

The different technology specifications aimed towards open interoperable defined by common ontologies, schemas and meta-languages towards harmonizing heterogeneous e-Government applications as specified in e-Government Interoperability Frameworks (e-GIFs). The Organization for the Advancement of Structured Information Standards (OASIS) is an international forum that is mandated to spearhead development of e-Government technology specifications towards global technology models. OASIS is one of the largest and oldest global open data standards consortia, founded in 1993 as SGML Open. OASIS has over 5000 active participants representing about 600 member organizations and individual members in over 80 countries. OASIS has the e-Government Technical Committee is specifically mandated to rehearse with governments throughout the world on their needs for XML-based technologies (e.g. ebXML, Web Services, SOAP, Web Services) for e-Government applications design (Borras, 2004). OASIS concentrates on providing technology interventions and evolving e-Government technology design paradigms so that e-Government solutions are relevant at any one given time.

In order to achieve this, the following program domains are currently pursued by OASIS (Borras, 2004):

1. Search Service Interoperability;
2. **EbXML messaging for use within e-Government:** Produced a requirements document detailing compliance with government issues and how to integrate this with ebXML;
3. **Common data definitions:** Common definitions facilitating data exchange within processes as a basis for application integration (Borras, 2004);
4. **Use by governments of ebXML registries:** Efforts towards coming up with common standards for governments' data dictionaries, XML schema repositories and other registries storing information of the technology components used in e-Government platforms;

5. **Use by government of the eprXML standard:** developed by the Norwegian Government, the eprXML Standards covers electronic processes and is used is used to describe how data support can be organized in a unified and standardized manner (Borras, 2004);
6. **Semantic interoperability and business implementation guidelines:** Project ongoing to extend the XML syntactic interoperability capability into semantic interoperability (where systems are able to talk and understand each other);
7. **Workflow standards:** To enable systems to underpin e-Services especially in cases where a government business process needs input from several departments (such as the vehicle fitness license issuing office needs to check with the police traffic department whether a particular customer was implicated in road mal practices such s over-speeding at any time); and
8. **Naming and design rules for XML schemas:** Project is ongoing which aims to define the Naming and Design rules for use in XML Schemas towards future data sharing across governments using networked distributed e-Government systems (Borras, 2004).

The European Union has come up with the European Interoperability Framework (EIF) which aims to guide the interoperability of government services at both the country level and across countries and organisational silos (Ellis, 2004). The European e-GIF was necessary so as to clear barriers that are caused by accessibility, multilingualism among European nations and promote secure applications using Open-Source standards and providing multilateral solutions.

The Minimum Information Interoperability Standards (MIOS) sets out the South African Government's policies and standards for achieving interoperability and seamless information flow across government as well as the wider public sector (Segole, 2010).

The MIOS provides a framework that outlines the principles needed for successful implementation of e-Government across government departments: these principles are as follows (Segole, 2010):

1. Management process, how to successfully integrate information systems across government departments;
2. Lobbying for a government-wide Enterprise Architecture (GWEA) framework which details the composition of the governance layer comprising best practices, policies and interoperability standards
3. Stakeholder engagement as a fundamental objective towards success
4. Outlining of minimum set of standards such as:
   a. Drivers of interoperability – technical policies and standards necessary to achieve interoperability and seamless information flows across government departments; universal adoption of standards across government departments, adoption of XML as primary data interoperability standard and use of XML Schema to support Web Services through Web Services Description Language (WSDL) based interfaces, etc.
   b. Outlining of principles relating to networks (migration from IPv4 to IPv6), security (based on provisions of ISO 17799), e-mail (SMTP/MIME)
5. Principle statement relating to data interoperability (use of RDF, OWL and RSS for metadata framework; UML and XMI for exchange of information and system design modeling, use of Extensible Stylesheet Language (XSL) for data transformation).

Despite the positive promises of e-GIFs, it cannot be ignored that because of the multiplicity and diversity in the public sector, it is very difficult to realize complete e-Government applications integration (Charalabidis & Askounis, 2008). Successful e-Government design does not only focus on design requisite e-Government applications but also aims to look at non-technical aspects. An example of a non-technology solution in e-Government projects has been the New Institutional Economics (NIE) which is aimed at delivering transformational change towards successfully accepting e-Government as a delivery platform (Elis, 2004). The NIE combines two theoretical approaches to economic organization i.e. Transactional Cost Economic (TCE) and Agency Theory (AT). Technology design or deployment cannot succeed without requisite Project Management strategy. In order to emphasize the role of Project Management in e-Governments, Sarantis, Charalabidis and Askounis (2011) outlined a goal-driven and knowledge-based framework to manage critical e-Government projects thereby emphasizing that technology is not all it takes to achieve competitive and sustainable e-Government design.

FUTURE PROSPECTS

With the emergence of smart or ubiquitous e-Government systems, there is need to come up with novel, robust, scalable and easy-to-adapt e-Government platforms. This can be achieved by utilizing the emerging technology platforms which have shown much promise. The emergency of open-source e-Government platforms, tools and software ensures that the different e-Government interventions throughout the world should be designed with unison platforms. This entails that researchers and practititoners should consider digging deeper the future role of Open-

Source software/systems in designing requisite e-Government solutions.

Another open area is to check the likely impact of regional e-Government interventions. For example, the European Union has done a lot in as far as enacting laws to support e-Government growth in its member countries. Not all these interventions may be appropriate to successfully supporting e-Government growth. For example, Baldoni et al., (2009) reported that a legal framework supporting e-Government in most European countries presents a major stumbling block for e-Government proliferation. Future research should delve deeper in understanding how such regional interventions should be designed.

CONCLUSION

This lead chapter has provided a synopsis of what is going on at the world stage in as far as e-Government technological platform design is concerned. Despite quantifiable accomplishments on the technology front of e-Government, it is still evident that there is a lot of work that needs to be done if all the anticipated organization and individual benefits of e-Government were to be realized. Researchers and practitioners are implored to take advantage of the gaps outlined in this chapter.

REFERENCES

Al-Khouri, A. M. (2013). e-Government in Arab countries: A 6-staged roadmap to develop the public sector. *Journal of Management and Strategy*, *4*(1), 80–107. doi:10.5430/jms.v4n1p80

Baldoni, B., Fuligni, S., Mecella, M., & Tortorelli, F. (2009). The Italian *e*-government service oriented architecture: Strategic vision and technical solutions. *Electronic. Journal of E-Government*, *7*(4), 318–390.

Borras, J. (2004). International technical standards for e-government. *Electronic. Journal of E-Government*, *2*(2), 75–80.

Butler, T., Feller, J., Pope, P., Barry, P., & Murphy, C. (2004). Promoting knowledge sharing in government and non-government organizations using open source software: The pKADS story. *Electronic. Journal of E-Government*, *2*(2), 81–94.

Carbo, T., & Williams, J. G. (2004). Models and metrics for evaluating local electronic government systems and services. *Electronic. Journal of E-Government*, *2*(2), 95–104.

Charalabidis, Y., & Askounis, D. (2008). Interoperability registries in e-government: Developing a semantically rich repository for electronic services and documents of the new public administration. In *Proceedings of the 41st Hawaii International Conference on System Sciences*. IEEE.

Choudrie, J., Ghinea, G., & Weerakkody, V. (2004). Evaluating global e-government sites: A view using web diagnostic tools. *Electronic. Journal of E-Government*, *2*(2), 105–114.

Drucker, P. F. (1999). *Management challenges for the 21st century*. Oxford, UK: Butterworth-Heinemann.

Eddowes, L. A. (2004). The application of methodologies in e-government. *Electronic. Journal of E-Government*, *2*(2), 115–126.

Ellis, A. (2004). Using the new institutional economics in e-government to deliver transformational change. *Electronic. Journal of E-Government*, *2*(2), 126–138.

Fonou Dombeu, V. F., Huisman, M., & Szpak, Z. (2011). A framework for semantic model ontologies generation for e-government applications. In *Proceedings of ICDS 2011: The Fifth International Conference on Digital Society*. ICDS.

Harris, S., Gibbons, J., Davies, J., & Crichton, C. (2008). *Semantic technologies in electronic government: Tutorial and workshop.* Retrieved May 2, 2013, from http://www.cs.ox.ac.uk/people/jeremy.gibbons/publications/semantech-egov.pdf

Jarrar, M., Deik, A., & Farraj, B. (2011). *Ontology-based data and process governance framework-The case of e-government interoperability in Palestine.* Retrieved March 18, 2013 from http://www.jarrar.info/publications/JDF11.pdf

Lee, T., Hon, C. T., & Cheung, D. (2009). XML schema design and management for e-government data interoperability. *Electronic. Journal of E-Government, 7*(4), 381–390.

Lee, T. Y., Yee, P. K., & Cheung, D. W. (2009). E-government data interoperability framework in Hong Kong. In *Proceedings - 2009 International Conference On Interoperability For Enterprise Software and Applications* (IESA 2009). IESA. http://dx.doi.org/10.1109/I-ESA.2009.12

Meneklis, B., Kaliontzoglou, A., Douligeris, C., & Polemi, D. (2005). Engineering and technology aspects of an e-government architecture based on web services. In *Proceedings of the ECOWS '05 Proceedings of the Third European Conference on Web Services.* ECOWS.

Muthaiyah, S., & Kerschberg, L. (2008). Achieving interoperability in e-government services with two modes of semantic bridging: SRS and SWRL. *Journal of Theoretical and Applied Electronic Commerce Research, 3*(3), 52–63. doi:10.4067/S0718-18762008000200005

Saekow, A., & Boonmee, C. (2009). A pragmatic approach to interoperability practical implementation support (IPIS) for e-government interoperability. *Electronic. Journal of E-Government, 7*(4), 403–414.

Sarantis, D., Charalabidis, Y., & Askounis, D. (2011). A goal-driven management framework for electronic government transformation projects implementation. *Government Information Quarterly, 28,* 117–128. doi:10.1016/j.giq.2009.10.006

Segole, J. (2010). South *African government interoperability framework using enterprise architecture to achieve interoperability.* Retrieved March 18, 2013 from http://www.gif4dev.net/wp-content/uploads/2010/05/South-Africa-Julius-Segole.pdf

Sourouni, A.-M., Lampathaki, F., Mouzakitis, S., Charalabidis, F., & Askounis, D. (2008). *Paving the way to eGovernment transformation: Interoperability registry infrastructure development.* Paper presented at the DEXA eGOV 2008 Conference. Torino, Italy.

Stiglitz, J. (2003). Democratising the international monetary fund and the world bank: Governance and accountability. *Governance: An International Journal of Policy, Administration and Institutions, 16*(1), L11–L139. doi:10.1111/1468-0491.00207

Tschumperlin, J. (2009). Model-driven semantic interoperability using open standards: A case study, New Zealand education sector architecture framework (ESAF). In *Proceedings of the 10th Annual International Conference on Digital Government Research: Social Networks: Making Connections between Citizens, Data and Government,* (pp. 63-72). Academic Press.

Widodo, A. P., Istiyanto, J. E., Wardoyo, R., & Santoso, P. (2013). E-government interoperability framework based on a real time architecture. *International Journal of Computer Science Issues, 10*(1), 469–477.

ADDITIONAL READING

Baldoni, R., Fuligni, S., Mecella, M., & Tortorelli, F. (2008). The Italian e-Government Enterprise Architecture: A Comprehensive Introduction with Focus on the SLA Issue. 5th International Service Availability Symposium, ISAS 2008, Tokyo, Japan, May 19-21. LNC 5017. Springer, pp. 1–12.

Bussler, C. (2001). B2B Protocol Standards and their Role in Semantic B2B Integration Engines. *A Quarterly Bulletin of the Computer Society of the IEEE Technical Committee on Data Engineering, 24*(1), 3–11.

Jarrar, M. (2005). Towards methodological principles for ontology engineering. PhD Thesis. Vrije Universiteit Brussel. Unpublished. Retrieved July 17, 2013 from http://www.jarrar.info/publications/.

Juric, M. B., Mathew, B., & Sarang, P. (2004). Business Process Execution Language for Web Services: BPEL and BPEL4WS: Packt Publishing. Khoshafian, S.

Kassoff, M., Kato, D., & Mohsin, W. (2003). Creating GUIs for Web Services. *IEEE Internet Computing, 7*(5), 66–73. doi:10.1109/MIC.2003.1232520

Kubicek, H., & Cimander, R. (2009). The dimensions of organizational interoperability: Insights from recent studies for improving interoperability frame-works. In *European Journal of ePractice*, www.epracticejournal.eu NO 6. ISSN: 1988-625X. Foley, P., Alfonso, X., & Ghani, S. (2002). The digital divide in a world city (Greater London Authority, London).

Ouksel, A., & Sheth, A. (1999). Semantic Interoperability in Global Information Systems: A brief introduction to the research area and the special section. *SIGMOD Record Special Interest Group on Management of Data, 28*(1), 5–12. doi:10.1145/309844.309849

Shaffer, D., & Dayton, B. (2004). Orchestrating Web Services: The case for a BPEL server, oracle white paper, June 2004. Retrieved February 16, 2012 from http://www.oracle.com/solutions/integration/BPEL_whitepaper.pdf.

Vetere, G. (2007). SPCoop: Semantic Integration of Italian e-Government Services. INFINT Workshop – Bertinoro, Rome, Italia, September 30 - October 4, 2007. Retrieved July 17, 2013 from http://www.dis.uniroma1.it/~lenzerin/INFINT2007/material/Vetere.pdf.

KEY TERMS AND DEFINITIONS

E-GIF: This is an acronym that stands for E-Government Interoperability Framework, provides best practice or minimum technological and managerial characteristics that should inform e-government design and implementation in a given context.

E-Government: The use of Information and Communication Technologies in public service delivery networks.

Interoperability: Is a characteristic of technology (applications and processes) that makes it possible for two independent processes to communicate and exchange data.

OASIS: Which stands for Organization for the Advancement of Structured Information Standards is an international forum that is mandated to spearhead development of e-Government technology specifications towards global technology models.

Ontology: The philosophical description of nature of 'being', 'becoming', 'existence' or 'reality' and description of their relations.

RDF: Which stands for 'Resource Description Framework' is is a family of World Wide Web Consortium (W3C) specifications originally designed as a metadata data model.

SOA: Which stands for 'Service Oriented Architecture' details the software desiign and provides architectural specification based on structured collections of discrete software modules, known as services, outlining complete functionality of a large software application.

XML: Which stands for 'Extensible Markup Language' is a meta-language which forms the basis of technology interoperability of e-Government applications.

Chapter 2
A Semantic–Enabled Framework for E–Government Systems Development

Jean Vincent Fonou-Dombeu
Vaal University of Technology, South Africa

Magda Huisman
North-West University, South Africa

ABSTRACT

The ultimate goal of e-Governance is to reach the stage of seamless service delivery in one-stop e-Government. This raises the engineering issues of integration, reusability, maintenance, and interoperability of autonomous e-Government systems of government departments and agencies. Therefore, appropriate methodologies that consistently address the aforementioned engineering issues throughout clearly defined e-Government development phases are needed. This chapter provides the design and specification, of a framework that amalgamates features from maturity models, software engineering and Semantic Web domains for semantic-enabled development of e-Government systems. Firstly, the methods and techniques used for the planning, design, and implementation of e-Government systems worldwide are investigated; a critical analysis is carried out to identify their advantages and disadvantages, as well as their contribution towards addressing the aforementioned engineering issues. Secondly, the proposed framework is drawn and specified. Finally, support tools including a business process model, an alignment matrix of stages and phases of development, and a weighting matrix of the intensity of semantic activities at various phases of development is drawn and described.

DOI: 10.4018/978-1-4666-4900-2.ch002

INTRODUCTION

In recent years, many countries worldwide have adopted e-Governance, resulting in several Web-based applications being developed in various government departments and agencies for online services delivery to citizens. The increasing number of these autonomous e-Government applications has raised several software engineering issues such as reusability, maintenance, integration and interoperability of these applications (Choudrie & Weerrakody 2007; Saekow & Boonmee 2009). These applications have been raised in the context of one-stop e-Government which requires e-Government applications to be accessed at a single point and function as a whole for better efficiency and seamless services delivery (Wimmer 2002; Lee et al. 2009).

On the other hand, e-Government is a broad research field with several research works being undertaken in various domains (Lofstedt 2005). These research endeavours aim to address simultaneously political, institutional, legal, technological, cultural and societal issues for effective electronic services (e-Services) delivery to citizens. However, the development and deployment of e-Services in one-stop portal/shop remain a key and challenging priority in e-Government development. In fact, (1), e-Government strategies of various countries include e-Services development as a vehicle for effective online delivery to citizens and stakeholders.

In order to understand what it takes to implement e-Government, it is important to reference examples of successful e-Government implementation from countries such as Singapore (Devadoss et al. 2003), Australia (Teicher and Dow 2002), Taiwan (Sang et al. 2005) and UK (Beynon-Davies 2005); and (2), research studies reporting on successful e-Government implementation show that few countries have reached the stage of one-stop portal where citizens can seamlessly access all government's services (Chen *et al.,* 2006). Therefore, it is important to look at appropriate methodologies for developing e-Government applications which provides structured guidelines for the design, implementation and deployment of various government services on the Web to citizens, while consistently addressing the aforementioned engineering issues in an incremental and iterative manner, towards one-stop e-Government portals. A review of current literature in e-Government implementation has allowed identifying three main methods and techniques that deal with the planning, design, implementation and deployment of e-Services for effective online delivery to citizens. These include maturity models (MM), software engineering (SE) and Semantic Web (SW) techniques.

Considerable research has been conducted by public administrators for e-Government planning and implementation. These different researchers propose different stages for e-Government development in maturity models or "stage of growth" models (Layne and Lee 2001; Howard 2001; Deloitte and Touche 2001; Moon 2002; United Nation 2003; West 2004; Zarei et al. 2008; Bri 2009). A maturity model or 'stage of growth' model is designed as a sequence of stages of e-Government growth and constitutes a guiding and benchmarking tool for e-Government planning and development. Each maturity model stage prescribes a list of Web features that are needed online or mechanisms required to create changes at that particular stage of e-Government development. An example of e-Government initiative that has used the Layne and Lee (2001) model is the Integrated Acquisition Environment (IAE) e-Government project in the United States (Sang et al. 2005). The shortcoming of maturity models or 'stage of growth' models is that they lack design guidelines throughout their various stages. Furthermore, maturity models emphasize e-Government services integration at advanced stages of e-Government growth but they do not mention how this can be done. Despite their shortcomings mentioned above, maturity models provide useful methodological features for e-Government planning and development, especially at a higher level of abstraction (Estevez et al. 2007). However, the aforementioned shortcomings could be addressed with software engineering and Semantic Web techniques as described below.

In the software engineering field, it is believed that an e-Government application is a software system; existing software development methodologies (SDM) are used in e-Government projects and existing standards are employed for services integration and interoperability (Vassilakis et al. 2002; Heeks 2006; Janowski et al. 2007; Salhofer and Ferbas 2007; Sanati and Lu 2007; Arif 2008; Lee et al. 2009). Here and after, existing SDM or traditional software engineering techniques refers to structured and object-oriented analysis and design methods, and agile methods. The advantages of software engineering techniques is that they provide a large range of tools and mechanisms for analyzing and describing the requirements of the complex public administration systems (Arif 2008; Janowski et al. 2007; Lee et al. 2009), and provides platforms for implementing and deploying Web-based e-Government applications. However, traditional software development methodologies are inappropriate for the planning and benchmarking of e-Services development as public administrators do with maturity models. Furthermore, the traditional software engineering techniques use existing Web services standards for e-Services integration and interoperability as described in Arif (2008) and Lee et al. (2009). However, Muthaiyah and Kerschberg (2008) have demonstrated that existing Web services standards provide only syntactical interoperability and that the trend is towards semantic interoperability which is more reliable. This is in line with the work of Sanati and Lu (2007) who argued that traditional software engineering methodologies provide only limited solutions to the problem of services integration in e-Government. They recommended that more research work be carried out to develop new methodological approaches that

provide appropriate solutions to the integration problem in e-Government. To this end, semantic technologies have emerged as promising solutions (Muthaiyah and Kerschberg 2008; Sabucedo et al. 2010).

The Semantic Web techniques use ontology to model e-Government systems (Apostolou et al. 2005a, 2005b; Xiao et al. 2007; Muthaiyah and Kerschberg 2008; Sanati and Lu 2009; Sabucedo et al. 2010), facilitating their semantic integration and interoperability. The advantage of Semantic Web techniques is that they provide efficient and reliable solutions to the engineering issues of integration, reusability, maintenance and interoperability in e-Government (Sanati and Lu 2007; Muthaiyah and Kerschberg 2008). Further, the Semantic Web techniques share some tools and platforms with traditional software engineering techniques (Sanati and Lu 2007) for the analysis and design of e-Services, and the development of Web-based e-Government applications. However, the semantic ontology models being developed in the e-Government domain are mainly ad hoc solutions and are not aligned to any e-Government development phases or stages as proposed by maturity models, which might make it extremely difficult to plan and benchmark a semantic-driven e-Government project. Furthermore, various ontologies are being used in different research projects for the modelling and specification of e-Services, but it is unclear which kinds of ontologies were used (Muthaiyah and Kerschberg 2008; Saekow and Boonmee 2009) and when and in which circumstances of e-Services development the proposed ontologies are required (Apostolou 2005b; Xiao et al. 2007; Sanati and Lu 2009), nor how to represent them from the complex public administration system (Apostolou 2005b; Xiao et al. 2007; Sanati and Lu 2009; Sabucedo et al. 2010). Finally, none of current semantic based e-Government solutions provides a stepwise methodology for a semantic-driven planning and implementation of e-Government systems.

The following sections present a framework which amalgamates features from maturity models, software engineering and Semantic Web domains for semantic-enabled development of future e-Government systems.

PRESENTATION AND SPECIFICATION OF PROPOSED FRAMEWORK

The proposed framework architecture is depicted in Figure 1. It displays an overlay of features from maturity models (top layer), software engineering (middle layer) and Semantic Web (bottom layer) domains. These layers are presented in three phases of e-Government systems development namely: scope definition, identification and categorization of services and Web service development. The next sub-sections specify the layers, phases and semantic content of the framework.

Specification of the Framework base on its Layers

First of all, from a software engineering perspective, e-Government systems implementation entails gathering the requirements of the government services to be delivered online to citizens, analyze, design, implement and deploy the e-Service on the Web for online interaction with citizens. These processes could be carried out iteratively and incrementally with state-of-the-art software engineering techniques. In view of the complexity of the public administration system, e-Government implementation as described above requires, (1) mechanisms for the planning and implementation of e-Services at various stages or phases of e-Government development, (2) state-of-the-art software engineering techniques and platforms for the design and implementation of e-Services, as well as (3) emerging technologies as the Semantic Web technologies which have potential to facilitate

Figure 1. Proposed three phase framework for semantic-enabled development of e-Government systems

Framework Layers	Phase 1	Phase 2	Phase 3
Maturity Model Stages		Web Presence / Enhanced Presence	Interactive Presence / Transactional Presence / Seamless Service
Services Development	Scope Definition	Identification and categorization of Sevices	Wed Services Development
Ontology	domain ontologies	Ontology Modelling task and domain ontologies	representation or meta ontologies

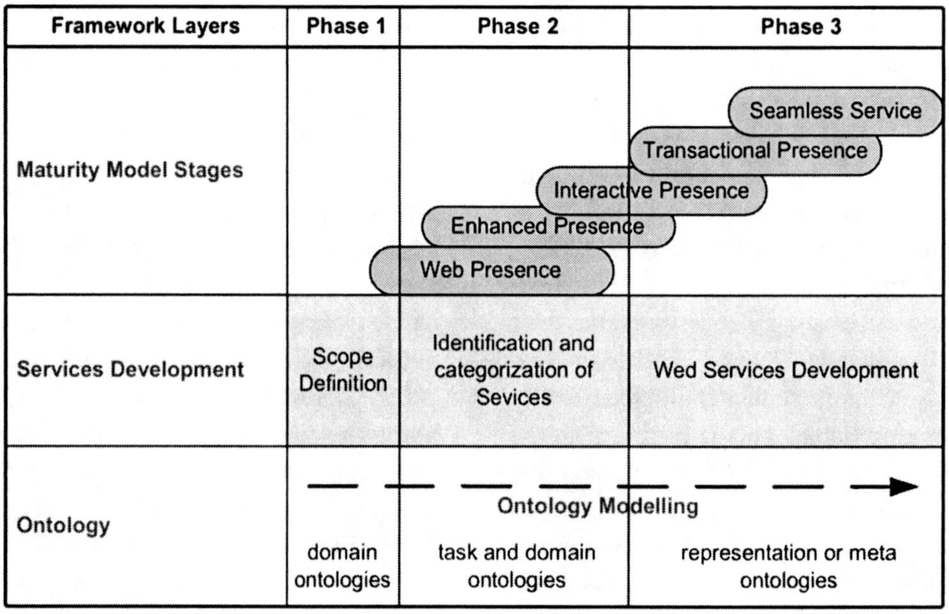

the integration and interoperability of e-Services towards one-stop e-Government system (Muthaiyah and Kerschberg 2008).

The framework in Figure 1 comprises three layers namely maturity model stages layer (MMSL), services development layer (SDL) and ontology layer (OL). The MMSL provides various stages for e-Government development as illustrated with the United Nations maturity model stages in Figure 1. Each stage prescribes the Web features that should be implemented and launched on the government Web portal for online interaction with citizens. The stages are complemented with software engineering and Semantic Web tools and techniques at various phases of the framework to enable effective design, implementation and deployment of the prescribed Web features of maturity models. At each phase of the framework, the SDL and OL provides system analysis and design techniques as well as platforms for the implementation and deployment of the required Web features at the corresponding maturity model stage(s). In particular, the SDL provides state-of-the-art software engineering techniques as object-oriented and agile methods for the design and development of e-Services.

Furthermore, if the proposed framework phases may not be followed chronologically or in a linear order in practice, then, agile methods at SDL provide mechanisms for the iterative and incremental development of e-Services through a continuous review of e-Services requirements and prototyping to enable the quick development of required e-Services (Greg et al. 2006). The OL provides various ontology models that capture each phase of the framework the semantic content of e-Services under development; the resulting e-Services ontology models are implemented in Semantic Web ontology languages such as Extensible Markup Language (XML), Resource Description Framework (RDF) and Web Ontology Language (OWL) with Semantic Web platforms to enable their easy composition, matching, mapping and merging and facilitate their integration and interoperability towards one-stop e-Government.

Phasal Specification of Proposed Framework

As shown in Figure 1, the SDL of the framework proposes three phases of e-Government application development namely: scope definition, identification and categorization of services, and Web services development (See SDL in Figure 1). The scope definition phase is the analysis phase in which the scope of the e-Government project has to be circumscribed. This could be done by identifying the key functions of the corresponding government department or agency that will be concerned by a move to electronic public services, the intellectual and technological resources needed, and the laws or legislations regulating the domain. After the scope of the e-Government project has been delimited, the services identification and categorization commences. At this phase, each domain function identified previously should be analysed and designed into potential electronic services; related services across different functions should be grouped into the same category. The grouping of services should be done according to the ultimate goal of achieving the electronic accomplishment of the related functions. The Web services development phase deploys the required resources (programming platforms and technologies) to effectively realize the electronic delivery of the intended services. This phase does not end; it continues throughout the remaining stages of the maturity models and continuously improves the level of sophistication of e-Services (interactivity, transaction, seamless services) required by the maturity models.

Specification of the Semantic Content of the Framework

It is suggested that domain ontology (Gomez-Perez and Benjamins 1999; Beck and Pinto 2003) be constructed in the first phase of the proposed e-Government application development framework (See OL in Figure 1). The domain ontology will capture the relevant vocabularies about the concepts and their relationships, as well as the activities and the laws or regulations that govern the related functions of the corresponding government department or agency (Gomez-Perez & Benjamins, 1999). The domain ontology at this stage should be written in an informal language (Uschold 1996; Gangemi *et al.* 1999). An example of domain ontology for development programmes monitoring (OntoDPM) in a developing country is depicted in Figure 2.

The OntoDPM was built in Fonou-Dombeu and Huisman (2010b) as a proof of concept in the methodology framework. In fact, in Fonou-Dombeu and Huisman (2010b), a framework adopted from the Uschold and King (1995) ontology building methodology is employed to define the purpose, delimit the scope, gather the concepts and activities of the domain and build the OntoDPM as in Figure 2. This provide a useful example of how a domain ontology could be built in a particular phase of the proposed methodology framework. The OntoDPM in Figure 2 shows the key concepts of the domain (people, stakeholder, financier, monitoring indicator, reporting technique, etc.), the activities carried out in the domain (training, discussion, fieldwork, visit, meeting, etc.) and the relationships between the constituents of the domain.

Figure 2. OntoDPM domain ontology

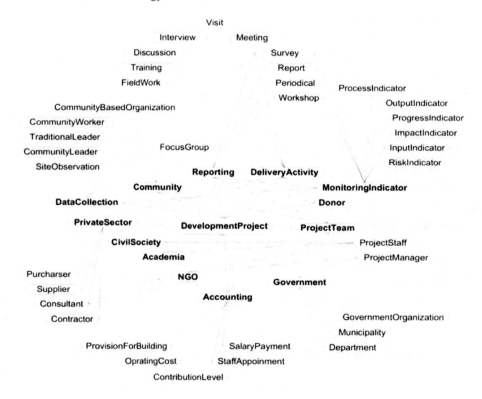

Domain and task ontologies are suggested in the second phase (See OL in Figure 1). This means that domain ontologies could be constructed to describe particular services and one or many task ontologies to demonstrate how the corresponding services could be achieved in the real world interaction with citizens and stakeholders. At this phase, it is suggested that domain and task ontologies be realized in the semi-formal language (Uschold, 1996). The semi-formal versions of the OntoDPM domain ontology in UML and Description Logic were written in Fonou-Dombeu and Huisman (2011a, 2011c) respectively, as a proof of concept in the framework; these studies describe in detail how one can transform domain ontology into its semi-formal version at a particular phase of the framework.

In the Web services development phase (third phase in Figure 1) of the framework, e-Services will need to be automatically composed, mapped, matched and merged to facilitate their semantic integration and interoperability towards one-stop e-Government portals. Therefore, the domain and task ontologies created previously should be rewritten in a more advanced formalism as provision for their integration and interoperability. This ensures that the representation or Meta ontologies are appropriate at this phase (Uschold 1996; Gomez-Perez and Benjamins1999; Gangemi et al. 1999). Once more, it was created as a proof of concept, the formal versions of the OntoDPM in OWL and RDF in Fonou-Dombeu and Huisman (2011a, 2011b) respectively, using state-of-the-art Semantic Web ontology development platforms including *Protégé* and *Java Jena API*. The issue of effective integration of e-Services is out of the scope of this chapter; some techniques for integrating or mapping the resulting formal ontologies at the third phase of the framework are described in (Yannis & Marco 2003; Chen *et al.*, 2007).

ENGINEERING SUPPORT TOOLS

In order to realise the practicality of the proposed framework in an e-Government domain, other engineering support tools need to be clearly outlined. An example of engineering support tools such as business process model and the alignment matrix.

Business Process Model of the Framework

As shown in Figure 1, the service development layer (middle layer) provides the names of the framework phases: scope definition, identification and categorization of services, and Web services development. It represents the process of e-Services development, from the requirements of a government's business domain to the effective e-Services implementation. Figure 3 depicts the business process model (BPM) of the framework in Figure 1 and describes the incremental and iterative engineering process for realizing the Web features prescribed by the maturity models stages, at each phase of the framework. The variables used in the BPM are defined as follows.

- np: Number of framework phases (1 to 3)
- ns: Maturity model's number of stages
- max: Maximum number of phases or stages
- WF: Web features
- MM: Maturity model
- OM: Ontology model

The incremental and iterative process in Figure 3 follows the agile software development paradigm (Greg et al. 2006; Clutterbuck et al. 2009). It commences with the selection of a maturity model. This means that, at the beginning of an e-Government project, a maturity model has to be chosen. The chosen maturity model will provide the stages of development as well as guidelines

Figure 3. Business Process Model of the framework

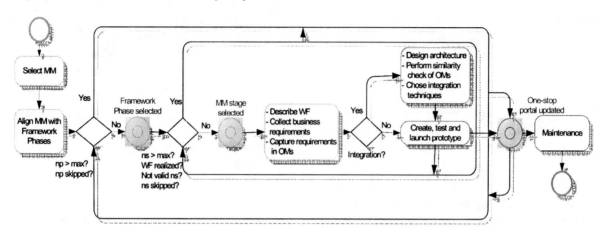

for the planning and implementation of the system from a simple Web presence to a one-stop portal.

Further, each maturity model will provide the Web features required at each stage of e-Government growth. After having chosen the appropriate maturity model, its stages need to be aligned to the framework as described later in this study. Thereafter, the iteration starts with the first phase of e-Services development (see the outer loop in Figure 3). At each phase of development an iterative process is performed (see the inner loop in Figure3) to realize and launch the Web features required by the maturity model stages aligned to the corresponding phase of the framework; at each iteration of the process (see the inner loop in Figure3), the Web feature under development should be described, its requirements collected in consultation with end-users who are the citizens and civil servants, and its semantic content captured with the prescribed semantic ontology models. Thereafter, if an integration is needed i.e. a government Web portal exists and the e-Service being developed is to be integrated with the components of this existing system, the architecture of the integration must be designed, a similarity check of the e-Services ontology models (those of the current system and the new e-service) performed and the mechanisms and

techniques (composition, mapping, merging, etc.) for the integration chosen.

In all the cases (whether integration is needed or not), a prototype has to be developed, tested and launched onto the government Web portal or the resulting prototype from the previous iteration has to be improved and tested. The iterative process is performed until the required Web features are realized at that particular phase, or the required Web features are to be completed in the next phase of the framework as shown in Figure 1 with the United Nations maturity model stages. After all the Web features or changes required by the maturity model stages aligned to the current framework phase have been realized, the iterative process continues to the next phase of the framework.

The requirements of the e-Government business domain are revisited during iterations (see the inner loop in Figure3) to ensure that the prototype systems developed meet the requirements of users who are the citizens and civil servants. The process is repeated until all the Web features or changes prescribed by the maturity model are realized i.e. until a complete one-stop portal is implemented. The phases of the framework might not be followed in a linear order in practice; then, the business process model in Figure 3 allows a direct selection of a particular phase in order to implement and launch a desired Web feature on the government Web portal.

Alignment Matrix of Maturity Models Stages with the Phases of Proposed Framework

As mentioned earlier, several maturity models or 'stage of growth' models have been proposed for e-Government planning and development. These maturity models include: Layne and Lee (2001), Howard (2001), Deloitte and Touche (2001), Moon (2002), United Nation (2003), West (2004), Zarei et al. (2008), Bri (2009), and many more. A maturity model or 'stage of growth' model is designed as a sequence of stages of e-Government growth and constitutes a guiding and benchmarking tool for e-Government planning and development. Each maturity model stage prescribes a list of Web features that are needed online or mechanisms required to create changes at that particular stage of e-Government development.

Although the maturity model stages layer (MMSL) of the framework has been illustrated with the United Nations maturity model stages as in Figure 1, its alignment with other maturity models is feasible. From Figure 4, one can see that the stages of maturity models share the same features (Cortes et al. 2006); for instance, at the first stage, all the maturity models, except the Asia Pacific (2004) model, require a static Web presence and a one-way communication between government and citizens. Therefore, the first stage of these maturity models could be aligned in the framework similar to the first stage of the United Nation maturity model (see MMSL in Figure 1).

Similarly, Figure 4 shows that at the second stage, the maturity models including Baum and Maio (2000), Chandler and Emanuel (2002), United Nations (2003), West (2000), Hiller and Blanger (2001), Moon (2002), Deloitte and Touche (2001) required an enhanced Web presence

and two-way communication between government and citizens. The rest of the maturity models that encompass Layne and Lee (2001), Howard (2001), and World Bank (2003) prescribe a dynamic Web presence and on-line transaction at the second stage. Only the Asia Pacific (2004) maturity model is still at the state of static Web presence and one-way communication at the second stage. Once again, the second stages of other maturity models could be aligned at the second phase of the proposed e-Government application development framework, the same as the second stage of the United Nations maturity model at the MMSL in Figure 1. Such similarities of e-Government Web features at different stages of maturity models (Cortes et al. 2006) is found in Figure 4. Based on this, Table 1 shows the alignment matrix of the maturity models stages with the three phases of the framework as in Figure 1. An alignment matrix *AM* is formally defined as in equation (1) below.

Table 1. Alignment matrix of maturity model stages with the framework

Maturity Models	Maturity Model Stages					
	1	2	3	4	5	6
	Alignment with Framework Phases					
United Nations (2003)	1,2	2,3	2,3	3	3	
Layne & Lee (2001)	1,2	2,3	3	3		
Baum & Maio (2000)	1,2	3	3	3		
Chandler & Emanuel (2002)	1,2	2,3	3	3		
West (2000)	1,2	2,3	3	3		
Hiller & Blanger (2001)	1,2	2,3	3	3		
Moon (2002)	1,2	2,3	3	3	3	
Asia Pacific (2004)	1	2	2,3	3	3	3
Deloitte & Touche (2001)	1,2	2,3	3	3	3	3
Howard (2001)	1,2	3	3			
World Bank (2003)	1,2	3	3			

Figure 4. Summary of eleven existing e-Government maturity models

	1st stage	2nd stage	3rd stage	4th stage	5th stage	6th stage	Model
	Cataloging - static website - one-way communicatiom	Transaction - dynamic websites - on-line transaction - two-way communisation	Vertical Integration - services automation and transformation - functions integration	Horizontal Integration - systems integration - Seamless services			Layne and Lee (2001)
	Web Presence - static websites - one-way communication	Interaction - enhanced web features - two-way communication	Transaction - dynamic websites - on-line transactions	Transformation - processes integration - processes unification and personalization			Baum and Maio (2000)
	Information - static website - one-way communication	Interaction - enhanced web features - Two-way communication	Transaction - dynamic websites - on-line transaction	Integration - horizontal and vertical services integration			Chandler and Emmanuel (2002)
	Emerging presence - static websites - one-way transaction	Enhanced presence - enhanced web features - one-way communication	Interactive presence - dynamic websites - two-way communication	Transaction presence - on-line transaction	Networked presence - functions and systems integration - e-participation facilities		United Nations (2001)
	BillBoard - static website - one-way communicatiom	Partial Service Delivery - enhanced web features - on-way communication	Full Integrated Service Delivery - functions and systems integration	Interactive democracy with public outreach and accountability - e-participation facilities - seamless services			Darral west (2000)
	Information Dissemination - static websites - one-way transaction	Two-way Communication - enhanced web features - two-way communication	Service and Financial Transaction - on-line transactions	Vertical and Horizontal Transactions - systems integration	Political Participation - e-participation facilities		Hiller and Blanger (2001)
	Information Publishing - static website - one-way transaction	Official-two way Transaction - enhanced web features - two-way communication	Multipurpose Portail - single access point to web services	Portal Personalization - features for portal customization	Clustering of Common Services - services and processes clutering	Full Integration and Enterprise transaction - services enhancement and integration	Deloitte and Touche (2001)
	Publishing - static website - one-way communicatiom	Interacting - dynamic websites - on-line interaction - two-way communisation	Transacting - on-line transaction				Howard (2001)
	Publishing - static website - one-way communicatiom	Interactivity - dynamic websites - on-line interaction - two-way communication	Completing Transaction - on-line transaction				World bank (2003)
	One-way Communication - static websites - one-way transaction	Two-way Communication - enhanced web features - two-way communication	Transformation - on-line transactions	Vertical and horizontal Integration - systems integration	Political Participation - e-participation facilities		Moon (2002)
	Setting up an Email System and Internal Network - internal communication through email	Enabling Inter-organizational and Public Access to Information - inter-organization electronic communication - static websites - one-way communication	Allowing Two-way Communication - enhanced web features - two-way communication	Allowing Exchange of value - on-line transactions	Digital Democracy - e-participation facilities	Joined-up government - services integration - seamless services	Asia Pacific (2004)

Increase stage and Complexity

$$AM(m,s) = \begin{cases} (x,y) \\ x \end{cases} \qquad (1)$$

where, m is a maturity model, s a stage of the maturity model m and $1 \leq s \leq 6$ in this study. In equation (1), x and y are the methodology framework's phases to which s is aligned; then, as it is drawn in Figure 1, a stage s of a maturity model m could be aligned either to 1 (x as in equation (1)) or 2 (x and y as in equation (1)) phases of the framework. In other words, the implementation of a Web feature required by a maturity model stage s could start at the phase x and end at the phase y of the framework or it can simply start and end at phase x.

In Table 1, the intersection of column 1 and the United Nations maturity model contains the couple (1, 2); meaning that, the first stage of the United Nations maturity model is aligned to both the first and the second phases of the proposed framework. In other words, the stage starts at the first phase and ends at the second phase of the framework. Similarly, the intersection of column 3 and the Asia Pacific maturity model contains the couple (2, 3); meaning that, the third stage of the Asia Pacific maturity model is aligned to both the second and the third phases of the framework i.e., the third stage of the Asia Pacific maturity model commences at the second phase and ends at the third phase of the framework.

From the fourth column, only the number 3 is appearing in the cells of Table 1. This signifies that, all the stages of maturity models from the fourth stage onwards are aligned to the third phase of the framework which is the Web services development phase. It can be concluded that, although the maturity models studied in this research are of at most six stages, a maturity model with more than six stages will still be aligned conveniently to the framework phases. In fact, advanced stages will be aligned to the third phase of the framework, as the main activity at these stages is Web services development.

Weighting Matrix of Ontology Activities at various Phases of the Framework

Based on the alignment Matrix in Table 1, Table 2 constructs the weighting matrix of the framework phases and corresponding output ontologies with the maturity models stages. A weighting matrix WM is formally defined as in equation (2) below.

Table 2. Weighting matrix of the framework phases and maturity model stages

Framework Phases and Output Ontologies	Maturity Model Stages						Weight
	1	2	3	4	5	6	
Scope Definition, **Domain Ontology**	1						1
Identification and Categorization of Services, **Domain and Task Ontologies**	1	1	1				3
Web Services Development, **Representation or Meta Ontology**		1	1	1	1	1	5

$$WM((x,y),s) = \begin{cases} 1 (s \text{ is aligned to } x) \\ 0 \ (s \text{ is not aligned to } x) \end{cases} \quad (2)$$

where, x is a framework phase, y an ontology model prescribed at x and s a maturity model's stage. Equation (2) specifies that, an entry of the weighting matrix WM is either 1 or 0. It is a 1 if the stage s ($1 \leq s \leq 6$) of all the maturity models (11 maturity models used in this study as in Figure 4 and Table 1) is aligned to the framework phase x ($1 \leq y \leq 3$) with ontology model y. It Is a 0, if the stage s of all the maturity models are not aligned to the x phase of the framework.

A digit 1 in a cell of Table 2 under the maturity model stages columns means that the corresponding stage of all the maturity models is aligned to the corresponding phase of the framework. The weight of a particular phase of the framework is then obtained as the number of stages that are aligned to it (see the rightmost column of Table 2). The weight of a phase can also be obtained from Table 1 by counting the number of columns containing the corresponding framework phase number (1, 2 or 3).

Figure 5 shows the chart of maturity models' stages aligned to the framework phases and corresponding output ontologies. Figure 5 also shows that, the framework prescribes more practice of semantic activities at the advanced phases for easy

Figure 5. Chart of the intensity of semantic activities per phase of the framework

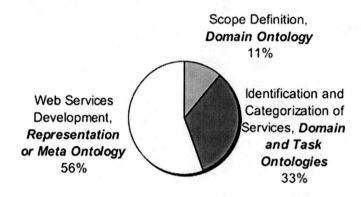

services integration, maintenance, and interoperability. The percentages displayed in Figure 5 represent the intensity of ontology activities at each phase of the framework.

DISCUSSION AND FUTURE TRENDS

This chapter has presented a framework for the semantic-driven development of future e-Government systems. The framework provides guidelines for

1. Gathering the requirements of government services to be deployed online,
2. Designing e-Government services,
3. Semantically integrating newly designed e-Services with existing e-Government systems, and
4. Iteratively and incrementally developing a one-stop portal e-Government system.

For the sake of flexibility and adaptability, the framework specification does not prescribe any specific software engineering methodologies to be employed for requirements gathering, analysis and design of e-services, any specific platforms (open-sources or proprietary) or any contractual arrangement such as in-house of outsource agreements for implementing the e-Services. The choice

of these methodologies, contractual agreements and platforms are left to the e-Government project management teams. Similarly, the framework does not prescribe any specific deployment and access techniques of the resulting one-stop e-Government system; various deployment and access methods such as personal computers, mobile/Smart phones, community access centres such as kiosks, personal digital assistant (PDA), iPad, etc. are subject to parameters such as (1) technological advancement, (2) political will, (3) regulations governing e-Government development, etc. of a given country. Moreover, the political, institutional, legal, social, cultural and linguistic specificities of each country might be dealt with by the e-Government development teams during requirements collection at various iterations of the framework and materialized through specific designs and deployments of e-Government services as well as the development of multilingual contents for the resulting one-stop system.

Finally, despite the intensive empirical validation of the framework through parts and experimental studies presented at conferences (Fonou-Dombeu and Huisman 2010a, 2011a) and published in journals (Fonou-Dombeu and Huisman 2010b, 2011b, 2011c), the specification of the semantic content of the methodology framework needs to be further expanded. This further expansion will provide more insights on the mechanisms and algorithms for e-Services integration, as well as the storage and query of semantic ontology models describing e-Services during iterations, at various phases of development. Further, the proposed framework need to be applied in a real world e-Government development processes in a given country to ascertain its feasibility. These will be the focus of the next stage of research.

CONCLUSION

A framework which provides stages, tools and techniques for the semantic-driven implementation of e-Government systems at various phases of development was presented in this chapter. Features are gathered from maturity models, software engineering, and semantic Web domains to build the framework. The structure of the framework is specified around three axes including: its layers, phases and semantic content. The specification of the layers of the framework explains how features of maturity models stages, software engineering tools and techniques, and semantic Web technologies and mechanisms can be combined or mixed to effectively develop a semantic-driven e-Government system. The software engineering process for identifying, collecting the requirements, designing and implementing e-Government services is provided in the specification of the framework phases. The semantic content of the framework specifies the semantic Web technologies that are needed to semantically represent and model e-Government services at various phases. These include: domain, task and representation/meta ontologies, and semantic Web ontology languages for developing ontologies.

Due to the fact that the framework phases might not always be applied chronologically or in a linear order, its business process model (BPM) was developed to enable the iterative and incre-

mental development of e-Government systems. The BPM explains how (1) maturity models could be selected in e-Government projects and aligned to the framework phases, (2) the requirements of e-Government services to be developed can be collected in conjunction with end-users who are the citizens and civil servants, at each iteration of the development process, (3) various integration scenario (with an existing e-Government system or a one-stop portal built from previous iterations) could be achieved and (4) prototype systems could be built at each iteration and phase of the framework. The BPM is generic and does not prescribe any specific platforms (open-source or proprietary) for building and deploying the resulting semantic-enabled e-Government systems. Therefore, the platforms for implementing the semantic-enabled systems are left to the choice of the e-Government development teams. Similarly, various means of deployment and access of the resulting Web applications through the Internet such as personal computers, mobile/Smart phones, community access centres such as kiosks, Personal Digital Assistant (PDA), iPad, etc. are subject to the technological advancement of a given country. Furthermore, the political, institutional, legal, social, cultural and linguistic specificities of each country might be captured by the development team during requirements collection at various iterations of the BPM and materialized through specific designs and deployments of e-Government services as well as the provision of multilingual content of the resulting Web applications.

Finally, the chapter would particularly be of interest to e-Government project teams of developing countries where little or no progress has been made towards the development of one-stop portals for seamless online services delivery to citizens.

REFERENCES

Apostolou, D., Stojanovic, L., Lobo, T. P., Miro, J. C., & Papadakis, A. (2005a). Configuring e-government services using ontologies. *IFIP International Federation for Information Processing, 189*, 1571–5736. doi:10.1007/0-387-29773-1_10

Apostolou, D., Stojanovic, L., Lobo, T. P., & Thoensen, B. (2005b). Towards a semantically driven software engineering environment for e-Government. *IFIP International Federation for Information Processing, 3416*, 157–168.

Arif, M. (2008). Customer orientation in e-government project management: A case study. *Electronic Journal of E-Government, 6*(1), 1–10.

Beck, H., & Pinto, H. S. (2003). *Overview of approach, methodologies, standards, and tools for ontologies. Agricultural Ontology Service.* UN FAO.

Beynon-Davies, P. (2005). Constructing electronic government: The case of the UK inland revenue. *International Journal of Information Management, 25*(1), 3–20. doi:10.1016/j.ijinfomgt.2004.08.002

Bri, F. D. (2009). An e-government stages of growth model based on research within the Irish revenue offices. *Electronic Journal of E-Government, 7*(4), 1339–1348.

Chen, Y. N., Chen, H. M., Huang, W., & Ching, R. K. H. (2006). E-government strategies in developed and developing countries: An implementation framework and case study. *Journal of Global Information Management, 14*(1), 23–46. doi:10.4018/jgim.2006010102

Chen, Y. N., Chen, H. M., Huang, W., & Ching, R. K. H. (2006). E-government strategies in developed and developing countries: An implementation framework and case study. *Journal of Global Information Management, 14*(1), 23–46. doi:10.4018/jgim.2006010102

Choudrie, J., & Weerrakody, V. (2007). Horizontal process integration in e-Government: The perspective of UK local authority. *International Journal of Electronic Government Research, 3*(3), 22–39. doi:10.4018/jegr.2007070102

Clutterbuck, P., Rowlands, T., & Seamons, O. (2009). A case study of SME web application development effectiveness via agile methods. *The Electronic Journal of Information Systems Evaluation, 12*(1), 13–26.

Cortes, E. C., Espinosa, S. J., & Tari, J. J. (2006). E-government maturity at Spanish local levels. In *Proceedings of the European and Mediterranean Conference on Information Systems* (EMCIS). Costa Blanca, Spain: EMCIS.

Deladoss, P. R., Pan, S. L., & Huang, J. C. (2003). Structurational analysis of e-government initiatives: A case study of SCO. *Decision Support Systems, 34*(3), 253–269. doi:10.1016/S0167-9236(02)00120-3

Deloitte & Touche. (2001). The citizen as customer. *CMA Management, 74* (10).

Estevez, E., Janowski, T., & Ojo, A. (2007). *Planning for e-government -A service-oriented agency survey* (Research Report No. 361). Centre for Electronic Government, United Nations University-International Institute for Software Technology (UNU-IIST).

Fonou-Dombeu, J. V., & Huisman, M. (2010a). Integrating e-government services: A stepwise ontology-based methodology framework. In *Proceedings of the 6th International Conference on eGovernment* (ECEG 2010). ECEG.

Fonou-Dombeu, J. V., & Huisman, M. (2010b). Investigating e-government knowledge base ontology supporting development projects monitoring in sub Saharan Africa. *International Journal of Computing and ICT Research, 4*(1), 20–29.

Fonou-Dombeu, J.V., & Huisman, M. (2011b). Combining ontology development methodologies and semantic web platforms for e-government domain ontology development. *International Journal of Web & Semantic technology, 2*(2), 12-25.

Fonou-Dombeu, J. V., & Huisman, M. (2011c). Semantic-driven e-government: Application of uschold and king ontology building methodology for semantic ontology models development. *International Journal of Web & Semantic Technology, 2*(4), 1–20. doi:10.5121/ijwest.2011.2401

Fonou-Dombeu, J. V., Huisman, M., & Szpak, Z. (2011a). A framework for semantic model ontologies generation for e-government application. In *Proceedings of the 5th International Conference on Digital Society*. Gosier, France: Academic Press.

Gangemi, A., Pisanelli, D. M., & Steve, G. (1999). An overview of the ONIONS project: Applying ontologies to the integration of medical terminologies. *Data & Knowledge Engineering, 31*(2), 183–220. doi:10.1016/S0169-023X(99)00023-3

Gomez-Perez, A., & Benjamins, V. R. (1999). Overview of knowledge sharing and reuse components: Ontology and problem-solving methods. In *Proceedings of the IJCAI-99 Workshop on Ontologies and Problem-Solving Methods* (KRR5). Stockholm, Sweden: IJCAI.

Grey, J., Huisman, M., & Goede, R. (2006). *An investigation of the suitability of agile system development methodologies for the development of data warehouses*. (Msc. Dissertation). North-West University, Potchefstroom, South Africa.

Heeks, R. (2006). Implementing and managing e-government: Book review. *Journal of Scientific and Industrial Research, 65*(10), 845–846.

Howard, M. (2001, August). E-government across the globe: How will e change government?. *Government Finance Review*, 6-9.

Janowski, T., Estevez, E., & Ojo, A. (2007). *A project framework for e-government* (Research Report No. 359). Centre for Electronic Governmen, United Nations University-International Institute for Software Technology (UNU-IIST).

Layne, K., & Lee, J. (2001). Developing fully functional e-government: A four stage model. *Government Information Quarterly, 18*(2), 122–136. doi:10.1016/S0740-624X(01)00066-1

Lee, T., Hon, C. T., & Cheung, D. (2009). XML schema design and management for e-government data interoperability. *Electronic. Journal of E-Government, 7*(4), 381–390.

Lofstedt, U. (2005). E-government – Assessment of current research and some proposals for future directions. *International Journal of Public Information Systems, 1*(1), 39–52.

Mnkandla, E. (2009). *About software engineering frameworks and methodologies*. Paper presented at the IEEE Africon Conference. Nairobi, Kenya.

Moon, M. J. (2002). The evolution of e-government among municipalities: Rhetoric or reality? *Public Administration Review, 62*(4), 424–433. doi:10.1111/0033-3352.00196

Muthaiyah, S., & Kerschberg, L. (2008). Achieving interoperability in e-government services with two modes of semantic bridging: SRS and SWRL. *Journal of Theoretical and Applied Electronic Commerce Research, 3*(3), 52–63. doi:10.4067/S0718-18762008000200005

Sabucedo, P., Rifon, L. E. A., Corradini, F., Polzonetti, A., & Re, B. (2010). Knowledge-based platform for e-government agents: A web-based solution using semantic technologies. *Journal of Expert Systems with Applications, 37*(5), 3647–3656. doi:10.1016/j.eswa.2009.10.026

Saekow, A., & Boonmee, C. (2009). A practical approach to interoperability practical implementation support (IPIS) for e-government interoperability. *Electronic Journal of E-Government*, 7(4), 403–414.

Salhofer, P., & Ferbas, D. (2007). A pragmatic approach to the introduction of e-government. In *Proceedings of the 8th Annual International Digital Government Research Conference*, (pp. 183-189). Philadelphia, PA: Academic Press.

Salhofer, P., Stadlhofer, B., & Tretter, G. (2009). Ontology driven e-government. *Electronic. Journal of E-Government*, 7(4), 415–424.

Sanati, F., & Lu, J. (2009). Multilevel life-event abstraction for e-government service integration. In *Proceedings of the 9th European Conference on E-Government 2009* (ECEG 2009), (pp. 550-558). London, UK: ECEG.

Sang, M. L., Tan, X., & Trimi, S. (2005). Current practices of leading e-government countries. *Communications of the ACM*, 48(10), 99–104. doi:10.1145/1089107.1089112

Sang, M. L., Tan, X., & Trimi, S. (2005). Current practices of leading e-government countries. *Communications of the ACM*, 48(10), 99–104. doi:10.1145/1089107.1089112

Siau, K., & Long, Y. (2005). Synthesizing e-government stages models – A meta-synthesis based on meta-ethnography approach. *Industrial Management & Data Systems*, 105(4), 443–458. doi:10.1108/02635570510592352

Teicher, J., & Dow, N. (2002). E-government in Australia: Promise and progress. *Information Polity*, 7(4), 231–246.

United Nations. (2003). *UN global e-government survey 2003*. Retrieved March 28, 2011, from http://unpan1.un.org/intradoc/groups/public/documents/un/unpan016066.pdf

Uschold, M. (1996). Building ontologies: Towards a unified methodology. In *Proceedings of Expert Systems 96, the 16th Annual Conference of British Computer Society Specialist Group Expert Systems*. Cambridge, UK: BCS.

Uschold, M., & King, M. (1995). Towards a methodology for building ontologies. In *Proceedings of IJCAI95 Workshop on Basic Ontological Issues in Knowledge Sharing*. Montreal, Canada: IJCAI.

Vassilakis, C., Laskaridis, G., Lepouras, G., Rouvas, S., & Georgiadis, P. (2002). Transactional e-government services: An integrated approach. *Lecture Notes in Computer Science*, 2456, 276–279. doi:10.1007/978-3-540-46138-8_44

West, D. M. (2004). E-government and the transformation of service delivery and citizen attitudes. *Public Administration Review*, 64(1), 15–27. doi:10.1111/j.1540-6210.2004.00343.x

Wimmer, M. A. (2002). Integrated service modelling for online one-stop government. *Electronic Markets*, 12(3), 149–156. doi:10.1080/101967802320245910

Xiao, Y., Xioa, M., & Zhao, H. (2007). An ontology for e-government knowledge modelling and interoperability. In *Proceedings of IEEE International Conference on Wireless Communications, Networking and Mobile Computing* (WiCOM 2007). Shanghai, China: IEEE.

Yannis, K., & Marco, S. (2003). Ontology mapping: The state of the art. *The Knowledge Engineering Review*, 18(1), 1–31. doi:10.1017/S0269888903000651

Zarei, B., Ghapanchi, A., & Sattary, B. (2008). Toward national e-government development models for developing countries: A nine stage model. *The International Information & Library Review*, 40(3), 199–207. doi:10.1016/j.iilr.2008.04.001

ADDITIONAL READING

Crichton, C., Davies, J., Gibbons, J., Steve Harris, S., & Shukla, A. (2007). Semantic Frameworks for e-Government. *Proceedings of the 1st International Conference on Theory and Practice of Electronic Governance* (ICEGOV), Macau, China, 10–13 December 2007, 30-39.

Sabucedo, L. A., Rifon, L. A., Perez, R. M., & Gagoa, J. S. (2009). Holistic Semantic Framework for the Provision of Services in the Domain of E-Government. *International Journal of Software Engineering and Knowledge Engineering, 19*(7), 961–993. doi:10.1142/S0218194009004490

KEY TERMS AND DEFINITIONS

Business Process: A specific ordering of work activities across time and place, with a beginning, an end, and clearly defined inputs and outputs.

Business Process Model: A graphical representation of various states of a business process. The representation may be done using flow chart or Business Process Modelling Notations (BPMN).

E-Government: Use of information and communication technologies (ICT) for delivering government services to citizens; the ICT facilities and the Internet technologies are used to deploy Web-based applications that support government processes; this support consists of: (1) providing a large range of government information and services (health care, education, social services, community development, taxes return, etc.) online, (2) facilitating online citizens' participation to government processes and decision making, and (3) streamlining and reorganizing government processes.

Framework: A skeleton abstraction of a solution to a number of problems that have some similarities. It is an outline of the steps or phases that must be followed to implement a solution without getting into the details of what activities are done in each phase (Mnkandla, 2009).

Maturity Model: A sequence of stages of e-Government growth that constitutes a guiding and benchmarking tool for e-Government planning and development. Each maturity model stage prescribes a list of Web features that are needed online or mechanisms required to create changes at that particular stage of e-Government development.

Ontology: An explicit specification of a conceptualization. A conceptualization is an abstract and simplified view of a domain of knowledge one wish to represent for certain purposes; the domain could be explicitly and formally represented using existing objects, concepts, entities and the relationship that exists between them (Gruber, 1993).

Semantic Web: The Semantic Web is a mesh of information that is linked up in a way that it can be easily interpreted and processed by machines. It is an extension of the current World Wide Web that aims to represent the Web using the meaning of its content rather that Web links as in the current Internet. The Web is a medium of documents for people rather than for data and information that can be processed automatically by computers. The aim of the Semantic Web is to extend the principles of the current Web from documents to linked data. This requires unique way of specifying data and relationships between data to enable their automatic processing by computers over the Internet. This is achieved using ontology.

Chapter 3
Web 2.0 in Governance:
A Framework for Utilizing Social Media and Opinion Mining Methods and Tools in Policy Deliberation

Lefkothea Spiliotopoulou
University of the Aegean, Greece

Yannis Charalabidis
University of the Aegean, Greece

ABSTRACT

There has been significant research in the private sector towards systematic exploitation of the emerging Web 2.0/Web 3.0 and social media paradigms. However, not much has been achieved with regards to the embodiment of similar technologies. Currently, governments and organizations are making considerable efforts, trying to enhance citizens' participation in decision-making and policy-formulation processes. This chapter presents a novel policy analysis framework, proposing a Web-based platform that enables publishing content and micro-applications to multiple Web 2.0 social media and collecting citizens' interactions (e.g. comments, ratings) with efficient use of Application Programming Interfaces (APIs) of these media. Citizens' opinions and interactions can then be processed through different techniques or methods (Web analytics, opinion mining, simulation modeling) in order to use the extracted conclusions as support to government decision and policy makers.

DOI: 10.4018/978-1-4666-4900-2.ch003

INTRODUCTION

There has been significant research in private sector enterprises focused on the systematic exploitation of the expanding Web 2.0/Web 3.0 social media (Constantinides, 2009 and 2010; Dwivedi et al., 2011; Evans, 2010). In this digital era, social media has experienced a rapid shift from pure Web-based sites to large and ubiquitous interactive communication platforms. Governments on the one hand and organizations on the other have understood the essential role of Social Media and try to use them in an effective way for their specific needs. More precisely, firms focus on understanding how to use social media in order to support various functions such as Research and Development, Customer Relationship Management and Marketing. It is widely recognized that social media already plays a significant role in many organizations and it is going to increase its role enormously in the near future.

As for the public sector, less research has been conducted sorely oriented to the exploitation of the social media (Moreira, 2010; Punie et al., 2009). Government agencies have been trying for more than a decade to take advantage of the information and communication technologies (ICTs)' capabilities in order to acquire a communication channel with citizens and increase their participation in the decision making processes. At the beginning, the tools that were used are mostly traditional channels. Combined with the possibilities brought forth by the Internet, traditional channels have given rise to focus towards the e-Participation research (Barber, 1984; Commission of the European Communities, 2006 and 2010; Loukis et al., 2011; OECD, 2003, 2004a and 2004b; Rowe and Frewer, 2000 and 2004; Saebo et al., 2008; Sanford and Rose, 2007; Timmers, 2007, United Nations, 2008). E-Participation research focuses on research that aims to find out the rate of engagement in a socio-economic discourse by individuals using ICTs as an interaction platform. The first generation of e-Participation contained many 'official' e-Participation spaces operated by government agencies offering information about decisions, policies and plans taken by the government and the ability to citizens to write their opinions or enter a discussion on various topics. The need for increasing the quality led to more structured e-Spaces and required more focused and disciplined discussions. As a result, the groups of people that could take part in such discussions needed be educated and have a great variety of knowledge. Governments, actually, considered that citizens would visit these websites and actively participate in public debates about policy issues and get familiar with the structure, language and rules of the official websites. However, this action had not as much impact as it was expected. (Chadwick, 2009a; Ferro &Molinari, 2010a). Most of these e-Government spaces were unknown to the majority of online users because the promotion cost a large amount of money and there was a slow pace of dissemination. What is more, many of the topics were initiated by government and did not affect at all citizens who seemed having other problems in relation to which were open for discussion. Additionally, many of these e-Spaces were not user-friendly and as a consequence their use was not easy for all. These problems along with the heterogeneity of online users with respect to political - cultural interests and technological – educational skills as well as the simultaneous evolution of Web 2.0 Social Media led the government agencies to exploit the virtual spaces used and adopted by the online users widening the role of e-Participation.

Also, many of the ICT tools used in the websites were not user-friendly and that led citizens to visit other Web 2.0 social media creating online discussions on their own and moving towards a second generation of e-Participation. Some of the topics that are discussed have a political content (Agarwal et al., 2011; Honeycutt and Herring, 2009; Larsson and Moe, 2011; Mergel et al., 2009; Osimo, 2008, Punie, 2009). While government agencies were trying to bring closely citizens, now they move towards citizens in electronic spaces in which citizens have discussions and create content exchanging ideas, perspectives, views, opinions. In these electronic places, governments cannot be absent but present expressing their decisions, policies, actions and listening to citizens. In this way, agencies can gain a better understanding of citizens' needs and expectations and create a communication channel with them. To succeed in this, the government agencies need to overcome many challenges and learn to use the social media in an efficient way promoting public participation and policy making.

The contribution of this chapter is to promote the concept of a platform that enables publishing content and micro-applications to multiple Web 2.0 social media and collecting citizens' interactions with them (e.g. comments, ratings) efficiently using the application programming interfaces (APIs) of these media. Citizens' data from them will be processed through different techniques or methods (analytics, opinion mining, simulation modelling, etc.) in order to use the extracted conclusions as support to government decision and policy makers.

The proposed framework is being developed and tested within the research project PADGETS ('Policy Gadgets Mashing Underlying Group Knowledge in Web 2.0 Media'), (2010) supported by the 'ICT for Governance and Policy Modeling' research initiative of European Commission and an extension of this approach which is based on 'non-moderated crowdsourcing' and on the collection and analysis of policy-related content generated by citizens in different social media. The extension is the research project NOMAD ('Policy Formulation and Validation through non-moderated crowdsourcing'), (2012).

In this chapter, we will first analyze the theoretical background of the proposed framework. The main focus of the chapter lies on the presentation of the architecture of the central platform, its decision support functionality and the extension of the original policy making concept, followed

by resulting solutions and recommendations. Concluding, lessons learned and future research directions in the area of ICT-enabled public decision making are outlined.

BACKGROUND: COMBINING WEB 2.0 AND PARTICIPATIVE POLICY MAKING

Web 2.0 is considered being a set of technologies, applications and values. (O'Reilly, 2005; Osimo, 2008). The new technologies being introduced, such as XML, Open API, Flash, Ajax focus on increasing usability, integration and re-use of Web applications. Based on the aforementioned technologies, applications have already been developed providing the ability to create content, publish content, share information and collaborate. Blogs, Wikis, RSS Feeds, Social Networking Sites, Virtual Spaces are some examples of applications. Applications, on the one hand, build on the user's knowledge and skills and on the other hand, enable user to build both content and services. At the beginning, Web 2.0 was used as a mean for social communication while it was later used by the private sector mostly for advertising and marketing (Constantinides, 2009 and 2010). Recently, there is a shift towards the use of Web 2.0 applications from the public sector not only for public relations but also for more complicated and significant issues such as knowledge management, law enforcement, and public participation.

E-Governance has become a very popular research topic over the years. Many are those that believe that e-Governance and e-Democracy are two concepts very similar to each other regarding consultation and its mechanisms (Marche and McNiven, 2003). A different point of view is reported by Bose and Rashel (2007) who focus on the application of Information and Communication Technologies (ICTs) in delivering Government services, exchanging information and integrating systems. Governance is actually what Government does in the fields of power, policy and management. The concept of E-Governance includes E-Government and in fact contains three fields: e-Administration, e-Government and e-Democracy (Ferro and Molinari, 2010b).

Participation plays an important role in the relation between citizens and government because increasing citizens' involvement, good Governance is improving quality of engagement and decision making (Commission of the European Communities, 2009). According to Rittel and Webber (1973), designing public policy is a 'wicked' problem. This means that over the years the nature of the design problems of public policy is changing due to the different and heterogeneous views of the problems that exist, making urgent the need of newer and more sophisticated methods for addressing them. These problems demand a combination of public participation on the one hand and technocratic analysis on the other (Kunz and Rittel, 1979; Conklin & Begeman, 1989; Conklin, 2003). In many countries governments promote public participation by supporting different types of interactions during the policy-making life cycle (Charalabidis et al., 2011). These types are distinguished in:

- **Information Provision:** Governments produces and delivers the information to citizens ('one-way' relation)
- **Consultation:** Citizens provide governments with opinions on issues that have been raised (asymmetric 'two-way' relation)
- **Active participation:** Citizens propose new policy issues and discussion topics along with those presented by governments helping them formulate the policy agenda (symmetric 'two-way' relation)

More precisely, public participation means consultation of different stakeholders during negotiations in order to formulate a common definition of the problem and the objectives. Having this as base, in the next phase, we can move on the technocratic analysis by experts using mathematical optimization algorithms for the definition of the problem. Additional research on this approach has brought to light that the solution of policy problems can be supported by information systems allowing stakeholders to enter 'topics', 'questions', 'ideas' and 'arguments'. These systems are called 'Issue Based Information Systems' and are able to stimulate a controlled way of reasoning which reveals the arguments (Kunz and Rittel, 1979). The rapid penetration of Web 2.0 social media creates more opportunities for a wider application of these approaches involving more citizens and social groups on a public policy problem that government is facing. Social media allow government agencies to collect content and knowledge based on a public policy discussion in an efficient way and at a low cost.

In many decision making situations, the complexity in all kinds of organizations, public, private or non-governmental exists. The complexity is proportional to the difficulty of a situation and can be addressed through decision support tools that increase the quality of the decision process (Beers et al., 2002; Courtney, 2001; Sterman, 1994). Anthony (1965) in his research described management activities as decisions based on strategic planning, management control and operational control. What is more, Simon (1960) described decision problems as existing on a continuum from repetitive and well-structured to new, novel and difficult to be solved. Gorry and Scott Morton (1971) in their research combined the two previous ones and described decision problems as structured, semi-structured and unstructured. Simon (1960) also described the decision-making process as a set of three phases: intelligence, design and choice. Intelligence means searching the environment for problems which is the fundamental need to make a decision. Design includes all the alternative ways used for solving the problem, and choice consists of the alternatives' analysis and the choice those for implementation. Once the problem is recognized, it is defined with the creation of mathematical models. Alternative solutions are created, and the models are developed in order to analyze the multiple alternatives. The choice is finally made and the appropriate alternatives are implemented. If the solutions presented for the specific problem do not work out, then a new process cycle continues. Even though these systems are used in a great extent in the private sector, they started gaining popularity in the public sector as well, providing either 'vertical' or 'horizontal' solutions. Collective intelligence is considered being a key ingredient of a "distributed problem-solving" system due to the fact that its output is able to enrich the decision support process. Specifically, politics moves towards cooperation in decision making processes (Shim et al., 2002; Brabham, 2008). However, Decision Support Systems (DSS) for decision making are still in narrow circles. Still, the implementation of a DSS in public sector has not become reality yet. In order to enhance the quality of the decision based on knowledge and simulation scenarios, DSS depend on the availability of relevant, timely and accurate information. As a result, the traditional DSS need to be combined with e-participation (Benčina, 2007; Kamel, 1998), in order to bring the needed functionality to the decision maker. After all, e-Governance programs can be successful admitting the existence of DSSs helping decision makers face problems through interaction with data and analytical models.

Opinion mining is considered being an area in which much research has been conducted. It is defined as the advanced processing of sentiments, feelings, opinions and emotions found or expressed in a text (Maragoudakis et al., 2011). Living in the era of "social Web", users through the exploitation of Web 2.0 social media create various types of content most of which are expressed in the form of text and especially in the form of opinions. Users have shown an interest towards this type of content and focusing on opinion expressions, most Internet specialists are able to indicate people's positive, neutral or negative sentiments or feelings on various topics. It first started to appear in the private sector when firms wanted to analyze comments and reviews about their products made from online users in various websites. Analyzing their comments, firms could draw conclusions as to if users like the specific products or not (through sentiment analysis), conclusions about the products' certain features that users have commented (through features extraction) and the comments' orientations (positive, negative or neutral). The content created in the Web is a valuable source of all kind of information (e.g. commercial, political, etc) and our proposed approaches PADGETS and NOMAD use opinion mining methods and techniques in order to analyse the textual feedback of a proposed public policy provided by social media users and help us make conclusions on the general feelings of users on the specific policy and the raised issues on the policy and its main aspects of it that have been commented as positive, negative or neutral.

THE PROPOSED FRAMEWORK

Communicating with Citizens via Policy Gadgets

The proposed methodology of the framework that is going to be presented in a detailed way is based on the aforementioned background and connects two established domains: the mashup architectural approach of Web 2.0 used for the creation of Web applications (gadgets) and the methodology of simulation modelling for the analysis of complex systems behavior. PADGETS main focus is to design and deploy a prototype tool that will offer to policy makers the ability to create graphically micro-applications developed in the Web 2.0 social media platforms in order to relocate messages concerning a specific policy to end users and interact with them. Using knowledge from different gadget applications approaches in

Web 2.0, PADGETS introduces the concept of Policy Gadget (PADGET), presenting a micro Web application that combines a message on a certain policy with underlying group knowledge in social media platforms and interacts with end users in order to forward their input to policy makers.

PADGETS main objectives are to:

- Design and implement an environment for creating and deploying policy campaigns across social media
- Provide architectural design and specification of the platform
- Implement the various components (for context, decision and interface), integrate them together and deploy the entire PADGETS platform to be used as a service over the internet
- Support pilot scenarios by extending PADGETS platform

In particular, a PADGET (Policy Gadget) is composed of four elements as shown below in Figure 1.

A PADGET is composed of:

- A policy message, which can be a public policy at any stage, e.g. a law at its final stage, a legal document under formulation

- An interface, which will allow users to interact with the policy gadget (setup, deploy, keep track of)
- Relevant group knowledge, in the form of relevant content and users' activities that have been produced in external social media (social context)
- A set of decision support services using as input the above data from the interaction of a PADGET with the public

As already mentioned, the methodology for using Web 2.0 media in policy making process is based on a central platform which can publish policy-related content and deploy micro Web applications to multiple social media and collect users' interactions with them (comments, votes, etc.) efficiently using their application programming interfaces (API). The collected data will be processed through advanced methods (analytics, opinion mining, simulation modelling). Government agencies aim to develop political campaigns on topics with policy-related content in order citizens to discuss about it and express their opinions. To succeed this, according to our methodological approach, a set of relevant multimedia content will be initially created (e.g. description, video, images, etc.) and will be distributed to multiple Web 2.0 social media according to the type of content that can host, e.g. videos in YouTube, images in Picasa, description in blogs, etc. The categories of social media that are targeted for exploitation are the following:

- **Platforms for Communications:** Blogs, forums, social networking sites, social network aggregation sites, event sites
- **Platforms for Collaboration:** Social bookmarking sites, social news, opinion sites, wikis
- **Platforms for Multimedia and Entertainment:** Photo sharing, video sharing, live casting, virtual world sites

Figure 1. Basic elements of a PADGET

- **Platforms for News and Information:** Google News, institutional sites with high number of visitors (Human Rights, WWF)
- **Platforms for Policy Making and Public Participation:** Governmental organizations' forums, blogs, petitions

The aim is to create a 'map' with the most popular Social Media Platforms that are used extensively. An initial approach is to categorize the social media platforms based on their main activities (e.g. collaboration, communication, opinions, rating, etc) and purpose of work (business, leisure, democratic engagement). Moreover, an examination needs to be made on the number of their registered users and their main features, the available languages, the type of content, the accessibility, the user engagement and the political representation. As a next step, a classification of the most popular social media platforms is produced based on their number of unique users, type of content, top popularity, multilingual support and political representation (type of political discussion or political content). Based on the above analysis, a list with the most social media platforms is created. From that list, it is essential to separate and select these platforms that provide the best coverage of European users focusing on demographic categories (e.g. income, education, gender, age) and going a little further, select those that are the most popular by category (type of content and main activities), with the largest multilingual support and provide the proper API frameworks for accessing and managing users' profiles.

Each one of these selected social media platforms opens Application Programming Interfaces (API) in the form of Web Services for communicating with it. For examining the feasibility of the already mentioned platforms, the APIs of the most highly popular social are analyzed. In PADGETS, the most popular social media platforms were Facebook, Twitter, YouTube, LinkedIn, Blog-

ger, Delicious, Flickr, Picasa, Digg and Ustream. Foreach one of them we examined the following characteristics:

- Available APIs and types of provided capabilities
- Capabilities for pushing content through their API (e.g. posts, photos, videos, rating, voting, etc.)
- Capabilities for retrieving content through their API (e.g. comments on posts, photos, videos, approved requests, etc.)
- Capabilities for deploying applications (gadgets) and interacting through them with social media users

Analyzing the social media platforms, as a conclusion is derived that that these social media have a specific strategy of becoming more open and accessible and follow API standards attracting third parties to develop applications (Charalabidis et al., (2010). They provide rich functionality through their APIs for posting and retrieving content exposing methods that provide third party developers with a growing set of capabilities. In particular, it contains content push functionality and functionality that supports direct retrieval of different types of user-generated content. What is more, many APIs create, delete, modify and upload such content. However, only few social media allow the deployment of micro-applications in their environment such as Facebook and Twitter.

Moving further to our methodology, there is a need to make a detailed analysis on the technical architecture of the central platform which consists of five areas:

- **Web Front-End:** Responsible for the communications with the policy maker through the Web (login/register, get input for setting up a campaign, present feedback on a campaign, present in a graphical way the results, etc.)

- **Mobile Native Application and Widget Area:** Responsible for supporting all types of communication with a policy maker and providing a channel of accessing the platform, reading the policy-related content and commenting on it
- **Publishing, Tracking and Storing Content Area:** Responsible for publishing the content in multiple social media and in various content types, monitoring citizens feedback on published content and storing all the relevant information (published content, user interactions, social media analytics)
- **Service Discovery:** Composition and Binding Area, responsible for providing the needed infrastructure for service com-

munication internally among platform components and externally among these components with external systems (widgets, social media platforms)
- **Decision Support Area:** Responsible for processing with advanced techniques (analytics, opinion mining, simulation modelling) all the data and providing decision support to the policy maker.

The PADGETS architecture that contains all the above specifications is depicted below in Figure 2.

A typical application of PADGETS methodology in a policy making process would be initiated by a policy maker who would decide about the future of a policy or for possible modifications

Figure 2. PADGETS architecture

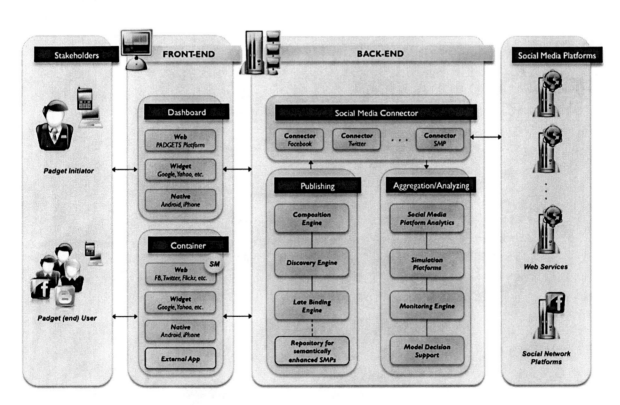

based on the citizens input. The process that needs to be followed consists of four steps shown in Figure 3.

1ˢᵗ Step: The policy maker designs a campaign using platform capabilities through a graphical user interface. He/she can add content to the campaign and publish it in multiple social media. The policy maker can formulate a PADGET application which can contain content and various functionalities (e.g. voting, e-survey) and deploy it in chosen social media.

2ⁿᵈ Step: The beginning of a campaign happens by publishing the above content and deploying the PADGET in the chosen social media according to its purpose.

3ʳᵈ Step: Users interactions take place in various ways in the specific social media with the published content and the PADGET. Specifically, users acquire access on them, are able to see the policy message, can vote either positive or negative oriented, can rate it and can make some comments.

4ᵗʰ Step: The above users' interactions are retrieved from all the used social media and are processed through advanced methods and techniques in order to help the policy maker decide by tracking and analyzing user engagement. This can be the end of a campaign.

Analyzing Citizens' Response

After collecting the data retrieved from multiple Web 2.0 social media platforms that contain users' interaction with the policy messages that have been published in the platforms, as a next step to our methodology, we need firstly to process them and secondly to provide the policy maker with information that will support him/her make a decision. This series of analysis and processing take

Figure 3. Typical application approach of PADGETS methodology

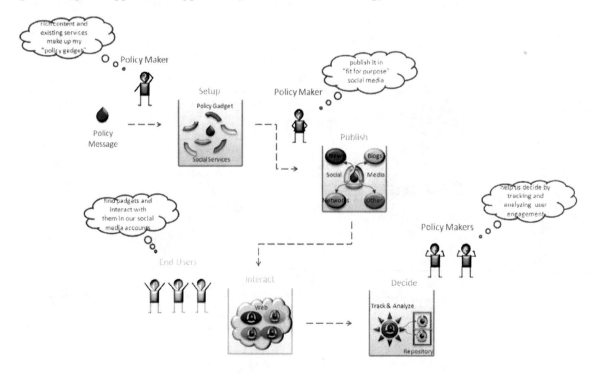

place in the decision support area of the central platform. The inputs of the Decision Support Area come from three different sources:

- Social Media Platforms
- PADGETs
- Policy Maker

The data coming from the social media platforms and the PADGETs can be unstructured (e.g. open text content) or structured (e.g. users' actions and selections). The information from the three different sources will help the policy maker understand the level of interest and awareness that citizens show about a specific policy discussed in multiple social media, the orientation of citizens' opinion indicating if they are positive or negative towards the policy, the elements' definition of the policy through comments, likes or dislikes provided by citizens and last but not least their opinions and suggestions for improvements on a specific policy.

Presenting in more details the architecture of the decision support area in order to acquire a deeper understanding of our proposed methodology, it consists of three layers. Specifically, the first layer is able to collect and process the 'raw analytics' provided by the social media analytics engines either through the user interface or through API methods. From our analysis on the highly popular selected social media platforms and the capabilities that offer, we concluded that there is a very rich variety of raw analytics that can be provided through the continuous evolution and development that is developed at that direction. Furthermore, continuing with the second layer, it provides more advanced analytics that are called 'PADGETs Analytics' that focus on users inputs in the forms of texts (e.g. posts, comments, opinions, etc.) in the chosen social media platforms. It retrieves all the texts that users have posted in the form of comments and opinions based on a

policy message through the social media APIs. The collected data are then processed using opinion mining methods indicating the general sentiment of the policy message (positive, negative or neutral) and the issues raised with their sentiment orientation (Maragoudakis et al. 2011). Finally, the third layer enters the concept of simulation modelling for two specific reasons. First, for identifying the numerous proposals on public policies held under discussion or application and estimating their outcomes and second for depicting the current citizens' interest and awareness in a policy and the level of accepting it. The simulation modelling takes into consideration 'various indicators' produced by the other two aforementioned layers (Charalabidis et al., 2011).

Specifically for the opinion mining methods used in the decision support system, there are three types of problems that need to be addressed (Maragoudakis et al., 2011):

- Classification of an opinionated text which expresses as a whole a positive, negative or neutral opinion (also referred as document-level sentiment analysis)
- Classification of each sentence in a text first if it is subjective or objective meaning if it expresses opinion or not and if it does then if the opinion of the sentence is positive, negative or neutral (also known as sentence-level sentiment analysis)
- Extraction of specific features or subtopics commented by the author of the text and for each feature identify the opinion orientation as positive, negative or neutral (also mentioned as feature-level sentiment analysis)

Based on these conclusions, a basic framework for the opinion mining methods used in the central platform needs to be formulated. It is consisted of five stages:

1ˢᵗ Stage: Classification of each one of the posts on a policy as positive, negative or neutral using document-level sentiment analysis and calculation of relative frequencies as positive, negative o neutral posts.

2ⁿᵈ Stage: Identification of the subjective sentences included in each one of the posts and classification for each one of them as positive, negative or neutral using sentence-level sentiment analysis.

3ʳᵈ Stage: Comparison and integration of findings from the above stages and also findings derived from the analysis of citizens' non-textual feedback. This will lead to make conclusions about citizens' general sentiments either positive or negative about government policies.

4ᵗʰ Stage: Identification of the main raised issues by further process of all posts on a specific policy through feature extraction methods.

5ᵗʰ Stage: Classification of each sentence posted for each issue as positive, negative or neutral using sentence-level sentiment analysis and calculation of the relative frequencies of positive, negative or neutral subjective sentences. This will lead to the identification of the main raised issues and the citizens general sentiments on them (e.g. positive/negative aspects or effects of a policy under discussion or application, improvement suggestions, etc.).

As for the simulation modeling used in the decision support system, we indicate two main approaches, examining the existing approaches in the specific area (Charalabidis et al., 2011):

1ˢᵗ Approach: System Dynamics is considered being one of the approaches with highly promising results for our aforementioned purposes. This approach demands modeling in high/macro level and simulation of complex system in continuous time in order to assess the impacts or policy-related pro-

posals. Complex systems contain multiple individual processes with 'stocks' (employed/unemployed citizens, groups of citizens from various income-education level, etc.) and 'flows' among them influenced by public policies. Thus, this specific approach is suitable for modelling and simulation. Moreover, it has been used with great success in the past meaning that it is no longer is an 'experimental phase'. (Forrester, 1961; Schwaninger et al., 2008).

2ⁿᵈ Approach: Agent-based Modelling and Simulation is an approach used for modelling and simulation at both meso and macro level. It does not demand any definition about the basic structure of the system in order to estimate its meso behavior but it requires us to define the behavior and interaction rules of individual units (e.g. enterprises, personnel, etc.).

Considering that for socio-economic issues it is easier to define the former than the latter, we can predict that Systems Dynamics may be more beneficial than Agent-based Modelling and Simulation. In cases that behavior of individual units is easier to be defined, the Agent-based Modelling and Simulation would be the selected approach. (Epstein, 1999; Ferro et al., 2010)

Taking into account all the above elements that synthesize the PADGETS architecture, we depict in Figure 4 an overview of the graphical representation of the aforementioned PADGETS Platform.

Solutions through a Series of Novelties

From the above analysis of our proposed framework and general approach, a number of dimensions emerges and may vary through the different phases of the policy making cycle. It offers a broader, more inclusive and deeper citizens' e-Participation in the formulation of public policies

Figure 4. PADGETS platform

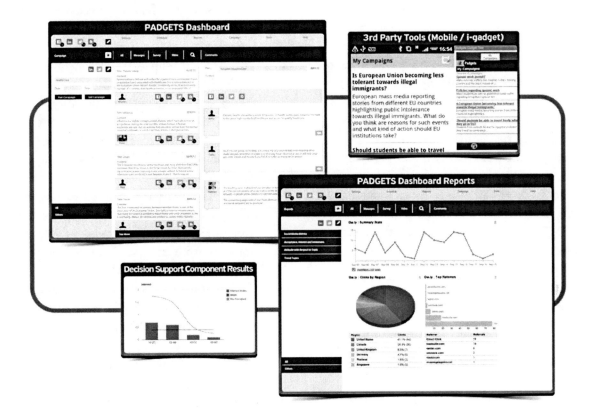

through a systematic exploitation of the emerging Web 2.0 social media and the involvement of multiple groups that usually do not visit government official e-Participation websites. More precisely, it succeeds in bringing government a step towards citizens, using Web locations for interaction with citizens rather than expecting citizens to generate content in their governmental websites. In this way, the distance between policy making and society is reduced in relation to the first generation of e-Participation approaches in terms of time and tools needed. To inform in a better way the decision making process, it offers low cost and efficiency by developing a framework for all the stakeholders' various opinions and multiple priorities. Giving the ability to government agencies to hear directly from citizens their thoughts and concerns in an online space where they feel free to express their opinions and make some suggestions for improvements, enables the agencies to collect, evaluate and decide about society's future using citizens input through an innovative way. Considering that policy design problems are 'wicked', our general approach provides a more intense interaction between stakeholders of a policy under discussion or application and government both in an efficient way and at a low cost. Thus, the problems acquire a better definition and the main objectives become more targeted leading to a more socially-rooted policy.

Moreover, the ability to publish policy-related content to various social media from one point affects time and cost and also the homogeneity of social media presence. The ability of gathering citizens' feedback from different online sources in a single point offers a synthesis of data and a comparison in multiple groups of citizens. Additionally, due to the fact that the civic engagement is developed in various classes of actors, positive externalities are generated from the central platform as well as different benefits for each one of the actors' classes. Specifically, there can be low cost and efficient inputs for the policy makers on the one hand and convenient participation along with balanced policies for stakeholders.

Policy makers also have the ability to start an online campaign during all the phases of policy making cycle and may vary in each phase following the purpose it is created. According to OECD,(2003) the different phases of the policy making cycle are:

- Agenda setting
- Policy analysis
- Policy formulation
- Policy implementation
- Policy monitoring and evaluation

The novelties that PADGETS Platform brought to light can be underlined to the following:

- Decrease of size, quality and frequency constraints in citizens' participation. Stakeholders have the opportunity to participate to any policy process they desire, at any time, providing as much effort as they are willing to give, using the tools that are familiar with
- Integrated social media management. In the PADGETS Platform, a Web dashboard exists in order the policy maker to be able to observe the results of his/her online campaign reducing in this way the complexity and heterogeneity derived from peculiarities in terms of interfaces, functionalities, content when using different social media platforms
- Creation of an "open" decision support system by integrating it with the activity carried out over social media platforms.

This allows the establishment of adirect link between the decision process area and the external world for acquiring updated information

- The decision support component in the PADGETS decision support area offers numerous promising functionalities that generate knowledge in order to inform the decision making process. Specifically, it allows the generation of snapshots in the levels of interest, awareness and acceptance in a specific policy, the creation of possible multiple scenarios of how these levels vary over time and last the display of relevant opinions from the users' interaction with the policy message. PADGETS pilot activities will take place in three different countries and will be focused on two key European Policy subjects. Administration involved in the pilot activities will be the University of the Aegean under the surveillance of the Greek ICT Observatory, supervised by the Ministry of Finance, the Piemont Region in Italy and the Centre of e-governance Development in Slovenia.

Pilots Planning in the Proposed Framework

In order to evaluate PADGETS platform in real life conditions and assess the value derived from the policy gadgets as well as the decision support models in the policy making process, pilot scenarios are created. The scenarios represent needs for policy making. For each specific scenario, the necessary policy gadgets are created and running in various Web 2.0 social media platforms offering to online users the ability to interact and provide significant input to the policy making process. The three Pilotsare provided by University of the Aegean (AEGEAN), the Centre for e-governance Development for South East Europe (CEGD) and Piedmont Region (PIED). In this section, we are going to analyse the Greek pilot case.

PADGETS pilots focus on high priority European Union policies, trying to deliver a combined policy modeling and forecasting model with innovative social networking applications for citizens' participation. The use of PADGETS (policy gadgets) is expected to allow a better communication between government and society and a better policy decision process, providing a clear vision of the different stakeholders' opinions, concerns and priorities. A PADGETS will enable an innovative way to collect, process, evaluate and decide along with society's input.

In order to attract a greater portion of citizens, it was proposed to search for topics with wider acceptance. What is more, more policy makers as end users of the PADGETS usage scenarios were engaged and as a result they are responsible for first formulating decisions, second delivering policies and third utilize PADGETS added value in order to evaluate their policy messages. The topics that were selected to be used were Immigration, Environment and Finance.

Furthermore, concerning the Greek pilot, the team of Policy Makers consists of four Greek members of the European Parliament with their consultants participating in debates and demonstrating their proposals inside the European Parliament. The four members of the European Parliament seem to be the most suitable persons to play the role of the policy makers in the pilot scenarios. Other organisations involved specifically in the Greek pilot are the European Parliament and Greek political parties. The EU legislations, entered into by the European Union require the approval of the European Parliament and the countries concerned. That is the reason why, it is so important the aforementioned groups of people (both policy makers and organisations) to participate in the specific pilot. The four MEPs are responsible for publishing the campaigns, formulating the policy messages and watching the results in order to use them in the policy making process. University of the Aegean team offers essential guidance in the pilot planning.

The pilot will be targeted to Greek citizens between the age of 15 – 75 and the pilot campaigns will be bilingual so that both Greek and European citizens can offer their input. It is expected that all kinds of citizens contribute to the piloting but there are five citizens group that can be distinguished, with the more possibilities to offer feedback during the piloting:

- Academics and Research bodies
- Public sector representatives
- Non – Governmental Organisations (NGOs)
- Private institutions that manage projects
- Journalists and media representatives

It is expected that the pilot campaigns and the online discussions between MEPs and citizens will enhance the outcome of European Parliament's procedures and provide estimations of what people think on a specific policy. A set of metrics can indicate pilot campaigns value proposition for policy makers:

- Level of citizens' willingness to participate in policy formulation
- General public engagement in targeted issues
- Amount of ideas from the general public
- Level of citizens' interest and awareness on various topics
- Rating among European policies under discussion
- Level of acceptance of the proposed actions by citizens
- Amount of opinions shared and feedback to refine initial formulation
- The level of networking and collaboration in cross – border debates
- The valuable insights stemming from a comparative analysis between member states

Overall, the pilot results will help policy makers acquire a more specific point of view on the topics for discussion with the general public both in Greece and European countries. Additionally, estimations will help policy makers identify which of the proposals are preferable and what citizens consider as obstacles in policy actions.

The Greek pilot is based on subjects that attract Greek interest at a specific period of time as well as European emerging issues. The subjects used in pilot campaigns are:

- **Renewable Energy Sources:** A project named "HELIOS" will be implemented and requires the installation of photovoltaic systems for solar energy production on land that is a Greek State property. Its primary objective is the Greek State to export the produced "green" energy to Europe and use this income to decrease the public debt but it has triggered a lot of reactions due to its environmental consequences.

- **Immigration Issues:** European Union develops a common approach when dealing with issues such as the EU Asylum and integration of migrants. The specific EU directive focuses on attracting high qualified migrants and sanctioning employers of irregular migrants. Now is in the stage of draft bill in Greece. In order to acquire a better understanding on Europe's view on this issue, this subject will be common for Greek and Slovenian pilots.

- **Renegotiation of Memorandum Terms**: The consequences of the Memorandum enforcement monopolize Greek citizens and European attention. During the recent elections, candidates of political parties were dealing with the renegotiation of Memorandum terms in order Greece to escape from the financial crisis.

- **Growth Prospects within The Financial Crisis:** this is based on the growth prospects that can emerge under conditions of

financial crisis. This pilot is planned to be a collaborative effort between Greek MEPs with European partners in order to overcome the financial troubles.

The main content of the pilot campaign is a text defining the pilot subject and is used as a central reference for the campaign. The content includes description of the topic for discussion and issues related to the impact of the specific subject, the measures need to be taken and the proposed solutions. Continuing, policy makers and their consultants collaborate in order to create short policy messages related to the subject and attractive enough so that they gain citizens' attention for discussion. Moreover, the Social Media platforms that will be used for the Greek pilot campaigns are Facebook and Twitter. More specifically, facebook and twitter pages will be created for the MEPs involved in the campaigns. Links will be placed to the facebook pages in their official personal websites. Also, their twitter accounts will be connected with other experts' twitter accounts so that an original network can be created and last but not least YouTube will be used as a supplementary mean to support multimedia content presentation.

Extension of the Proposed Framework: Non-Moderated Crowdsourcing

Our proposed framework is extending towards 'non-moderated crowdsourcing'. This means that it would be useful to collect content from multiple social media and analyze it before publishing it on a policy so that it would be easier to identify the problems and issues raised by citizens on a certain domain (e.g. education, immigration, health. etc.). Thus, appropriate policies would be formulated for addressing them. To achieve this, we create four different phases:

1. **Listen:** Listen and monitor what people say, believe, need and think on a certain domain of government activity. To succeed this, NOMAD crawler will be developed searching different sources of information in the Web:
   a. Micro-blogging sites, e.g. Twitter
   b. Blogs
   c. Video Sites, e.g. YouTube, Vimeo
   d. Social Networks, e.g. Facebook, Myspace
   e. Forums
   f. News Sites, e.g.nationa/international
   g. Images Sites, e.g. Flickr

2. **Analyze:** Analyze content, sentiments and other relevant information in order to create a semantically large volume of data to be used in the following phases. Specifically, examine each Web page found by the NOMAD crawler through a set of automated analysis processes:
   a. Language Detection with the use of Natural Language Processing
   b. Opinion and Argument Extraction with the use of semantic similarity measures allowing NOMAD identify content relative to arguments that make up a policy
   c. Sentiment Analysis
   d. Argument Summarization with the use of appropriate algorithms

3. **Receive:** A Position Map of the above extracted clusters of the collected data will be constructed. Using visual analytics, the related data will be presented in graphical forms underlying important features. Data derived from sources like online polls, blogs or government reports will be displayed in a way that will allow make significant conclusions.

4. **Act:** Formulation of the policy agenda by the time the policy maker discovers the opinions on a specific domain of government activity based on argument extraction and visualizations. The policy maker through the use of NOMAD tools will be able to test the policy agenda. A series of tests can be performed using the PADGETS central platform in which we can:
   a. Publish the policy agenda in multiple social media platforms
   b. Collect data on the agenda as future feedback
   c. Analyze it using decision support services
   d. Perform the appropriate modifications to the policy agenda based on the above analysis

CONCLUSION

Public participation has increased over the last few years in the decision and policy making through the emerging exploitation of Web 2.0 social media from citizens, organizations, firms and government agencies. The private sector desires to gain knowledge on how can take advantage of the social media in order to strengthen various functions such as Research and Development, Customer Relationship Management, Marketing, etc. The public sector on the other hand has been trying to create a communication channel with citizens through multiple ways. At the beginning, government agencies created official e-Participation channels in order to interact with citizens and expected that citizens would use these websites in a great extent but this did not come near to their expectations. In contrary, citizens initiated discussions even with political content in other social media non-governmental. Therefore, governments need to organize their presence in multiple social media so that they can express their positions on policies, hear citizens' opinions and finally gain a better understanding of citizens' needs.

Taking these reasons under consideration, it is necessary to acquire knowledge on how social media can be used in order to enhance citizens' participation in the policy making process. In order to achieve this, we developed a framework with two proposed approaches. The first approach is based on a central platform, which can publish content related to a specific policy and micro-applications to social media, gather citizens' interactions with government from the social media platforms using their APIs and finally use advanced processing techniques to the collected data. This approach is part of the research project PADGETS supported by the 'ICT for Governance and Policy Modelling' research initiative of the European Commission. What is more, an extension of this approach is presented, which is based on 'non-moderated crowdsourcing', through the gathering and the analysis of citizen-generated content on a specific domain of government activity in numerous social media platforms. This second approach is part of the research project NOMAD supported by the 'ICT Solutions for Governance and Policy Modelling' initiative of the European Commission.

We presented the theoretical background, continued with the description of the overall architecture of the proposed approach. Specifically, we focused on the decision support area based on the citizens' interaction data processing. As a next step, we mentioned the novelties of our proposed approach and also a description of the extension of the approach was provided in order to acquire a more spherical view. What is more, through the pilots planning, we described how to evaluate PADGETS platform in real life conditions and assess the value derived from the policy gadgets as well as the decision support models in the policy making process.

FUTURE RESEARCH DIRECTIONS

In the previous sections of the chapter, the aim was to present and analyze a framework with two proposed approaches referring to two European funded research projects, specifically PADGETS and NOMAD. The first approach is based on a central platform for which we presented in a great extent through an overview on the overall architecture. We, then, presented an extension of the first approach by proceeding towards the concept of 'non-moderated crowd sourcing'.

The proposed approaches offer a more direct interaction among the different stakeholders of a policy under discussion or application and with the government agencies efficiently and at a low cost defining correctly the problems and objectives which results in more socially-rooted policies. What we should mention at this point is that the application of these approaches considered as a radical change of how government agencies move towards e-participation. This specific approach is based on the development and use of a single e-Participation channel in a form of an official government e-Participation website. Through our proposed framework, this approach will be replaced by a multi-channel using a set of interconnected social media channels with different structure, language, target audience and characteristics.

Nevertheless, this innovative approach will need certain changes in government agencies at three levels; the organizational, human resources and technological level:

- The creation of a new organizational unit in order to manage the presence and profile of the government agency in the multiple channels of e-Participation and to analyze the large volume of structured (e.g. ratings) and unstructured data (e.g. posts in textual form) that will be created by citizens.
- New advanced processes should be established so that the results and the conclusions derived from the analysis of the structured and unstructured data could be integrated in the policy making process of government agencies.
- The human resources of the new aforementioned units must have specialized skills for being able to organize and manage in an ef-

ficient manner the new electronic modes of communication. In particular, government agencies must get familiar with structure, language and style of interaction in the web 2.0 social media, which is in fact quite different in relation to the official e-Participation spaces.

- At the technological level, the analysis of the large volume of the unstructured data provided in the form of text and collected from the multi-channels will need highly specialized ICT-based tools for text analysis and opinion mining. These tools will have to be integrated with the technological infrastructure of the multi-channels and will also need specific language resources, such as lexicons of polar words, synonyms and antonyms.

In order to validate and evaluate the proposed approaches at the political, technological and organizational level, we make some further successful research through the pilot cases of the PADGETS research project. These pilots contain the use of Web 2.0 social media for achieving an extended discussion on significant policies of the three government organizations that we have already mentioned above. Finally, the validation and the evaluation of the proposed extension based on 'non-moderated crowdsourcing' has been arranged to be conducted through the pilots of the NOMAD FP7 project.

REFERENCES

Agarwal, N., Lim, M., & Wigand, R. (2011). *Finding her master's voice: The power of collective action among female Muslim bloggers.* Paper presented at the 19th European Conference on Information Systems. Helsinki, Finland.

Anthony, R. N. (1965). *Planning and control systems: A framework for analysis.* Boston: Harvard University Graduate School of Business Administration.

Barber, B. (1984). *Strong democracy.* Berkeley, CA: University of California Press.

Beers, P. J., Boshuizen, H. P. A. E., Kirschner, P. A., & Van den Bossche, P. (2002). *Decision-support and complexity in decision making.* Paper presented at the 5th Junior Researchers of EARLI Conference. Amsterdam, The Netherlands.

Benčina, J. (2007). Web-based decision support system for the public sector comprising linguistic variables. *Informatica, 31,* 311–323.

Bose, S., & Rashel, M. R. (2007). *Implementing e-governance using OECD model (modified) and gartner model (modified) upon agriculture of Bangladesh.* Paper presented at the 10th International Conference on Computer and Information Technology. Dhaka, Bangladesh.

Brabham, D. C. (2008). Crowdsourcing as a model for problem solving: An introduction and cases. *Convergence: The International Journal of Research into New Media Technologies, 14*(1), 75–90. doi:10.1177/1354856507084420

Chadwick, A. (2009a). The internet and politics in flux. *Journal of Information Technology & Politics, 6*(3-4), 195–196. doi:10.1080/19331680903028743

Chadwick, A. (2009b). Web 2.0: New challenges for the study of e-democracy in an era of informational exuberance. *I/S: A Journal of Law and Policy for the Information Society, 5*(1), 9-41.

Charalabidis, Y., Gionis, G., & Loukis, E. (2010). *Policy processes support through interoperability with social media.* Paper presented at the 5th Mediterranean Conference on Information Systems 2010. Haifa, Israel.

Charalabidis, Y., Loukis, E., & Androutsopoulou, A. (2011). *Enhancing participative policy making through simulation modelling – A state of the art review*. Paper presented at the European Mediterranean Conference on Information Systems 2011. Athens, Greece.

Commission of the European Communities. (2006). *i2010 eGovernment action plan: Accelerating eGovernment in Europe for the benefit of all*. SEC(2006) 511.

Commission of the European Communities. (2009). *European eParticipation summary report*. Retrieved from http://ec.europa.eu/information_society/newsroom/cf//document.cfm?action=display&doc_id=1499

Commission of the European Communities. (2010). *A digital Agenda for Europe*. SEC(2010) 245.

Conklin, J. (2003). Dialog mapping: Reflections on an industrial strength case study. In P. Kirschner, S. Buckingham Shum, & C. Carr (Eds.), *Visualizing argumentation: Software tools for collaborative and educational sense-making*. London: Springer Verlag. doi:10.1007/978-1-4471-0037-9_6

Conklin, J., & Begeman, M. (1989). gIBIS: A tool for all reasons. *Journal of the American Society for Information Science American Society for Information Science, 40*(3), 200–213. doi:10.1002/(SICI)1097-4571(198905)40:3<200::AID-ASI11>3.0.CO;2-U

Constantinides, E. (2009). *Social media/web 2.0 as marketing parameter: An introduction*. Paper presented at the 8th International Congress Marketing Trends. Paris, France.

Constantinides, E. (2010). Connecting small and medium enterprises to the new consumer: The web 2.0 as marketing tool. In *Global perspectives on small and medium enterprises and strategic information systems: International approaches*. Hershey, PA: IGI Global. doi:10.4018/978-1-61520-627-8.ch001

Courtney, J. F. (2001). Decision making and knowledge management in inquiring organizations: Toward a new decision-making paradigm for DSS. *Decision Support Systems, 31*(1), 17–38. doi:10.1016/S0167-9236(00)00117-2

Dwivedi, Y., Williams, M., Ramdani, B., Niranjan, S., & Weerakkody, V. (2011). *Understanding factors for successful adoption of web 2.0 applications*. Paper presented at the 19th European Conference on Information Systems. Helsinki, Finland.

Epstein, J. M. (1999). Agent-based computational models and generative social science. *Complexity, 4*(5), 41–60. doi:10.1002/(SICI)1099-0526(199905/06)4:5<41::AID-CPLX9>3.0.CO;2-F

Evans, L. L. (2010). *Social media marketing – Strategies for engaging in Facebook, Twitter and other social media*. Que Publishing.

Ferro, E., Caroleo, B., Cantamessa, M., & Leo, M. (2010). *ICT diffusion in an aging society: A scenario analysis*. Paper presented at the 9th International Federation for Information Processing, WG 8.5 International Conference on Electronic Government. Lausanne, Switzerland.

Ferro, E., & Molinari, F. (2010a). Making sense of gov 2.0 strategies: No citizens, no party. *Journal of eDemocracy and Open Government, 2*(1), 56-68.

Ferro, E., & Molinari, F. (2010b). Framing web 2.0 in the process of public sector innovation: Going down the participation ladder. *European Journal of ePractice, 9*, 20-34.

Forrester, J. (1961). *Industrial dynamics*. Cambridge, MA: Productivity Press.

Gorry, G. A., & Morton, M. S. (1971). A framework for management information systems. *Sloan Management Review, 13*(1), 55–70.

Honeycutt, C., & Herring, S. C. (2009). *Beyond microblogging: Conversation and collaboration via Twitter.* Paper presented at the 42nd Hawaii International Conference on System Sciences. Waikoloa, HI.

Kamel, S. (1998). *Decision support systems and strategic public sector decision making in Egypt.* Retrieved June 13, 2013 from http://www.sed. manchester.ac.uk/idpm/research/publications/wp/ igovernment/documents/igov_wp03.pdf

Kunz, W., & Rittel, H. (1979). *Issues as elements of information systems. Berkeley, CA.* Berkley: Institute of Urban & Regional Development, University of California.

Larsson, A., & Moe, H. (2011). *Who tweets? Tracking microblogging use in the 2010 Swedish election campaign.* Paper presented at the 19th European Conference on Information Systems. Helsinki, Finland.

Loukis, E., Macintosh, A., & Charalabidis, Y. (2011). Editorial of the special issue on e-participation in southern Europe and the Balkans: Issues of democracy and participation via electronic media. *Journal of Balkan and Near East Studies, 13*(1), 1–12. doi:10.1080/19448953.2011.550814

Maragoudakis, M., Loukis, E., & Charalabidis, Y. (2011). *A review of opinion mining methods for analyzing citizens' contributions in public policy debate.* Paper presented at the 3rd International Federation for Information Processing, Conference on e-Participation. Delft, The Netherlands.

Marche, S., & McNiven, J. D. (2003). E-government and e-governance: The future isn't what it used to be. *Canadian Journal of Administrative Sciences, 20*(1), 74–86. doi:10.1111/j.1936-4490.2003. tb00306.x

Mergel, I. A., Schweik, C. M., & Fountain, J. E. (2009). *The transformational effect of web 2.0 technologies on government.* Retrieved March 12, 2013 from http://ssrn.com/abstract=1412796

Moreira, A., Gerhardt, G., & Ladner, A. (2010). *Impact of web 2.0 on political participation.* Paper presented at the Electronic Government and Electronic Participation, Ongoing Research and Projects of International Federation for Information Processing eGOV and ePart 2010. New York, NY.

NOMAD. (2012). *Policy formulation & validation through non-moderated crowd-sourcing.* Retrieved February 20, 2013 from http://www. nomad-project.eu/

O'Reilly, T. (2005). *What is web 2.0? Design patterns and business models for the next generation of software.* Retrieved December 13, 2012, from http://www.oreilly.com/lpt/a/6228

Organization for Economic Co-Operation & Development. (2003). *Engaging citizens online for better policy-making.* Paris: OECD Publication.

Organization for Economic Co-Operation & Development. (2004a). *Evaluating public participation in policy making.* Paris: OECD Publication.

Organization for Economic Co-Operation & Development. (2004b). *Promise and problems of e-democracy: Challenges of online citizen engagement*. Paris: OECD Publication.

Osimo, D. (2008). *Web 2.0 in government: Why and how?* Luxembourg: Office for Official Publications of the European Communities.

PADGETS. (2010). *Policy gadgets mashing underlying group knowledge in web 2.0 media*. Retrieved February 20, 2013 from http://www.padgets.eu/

Punie, Y., Misuraca, G., & Osimo, D. (2009). *Public services 2.0: The impact of social computing on public services. JRC Scientific and Technical Reports*. European Commission, Joint Research Centre, Institute for Prospective Technological Studies.

Rittel, H. W. J., & Weber, M. M. (1973). Dilemmas in a general theory of planning. *Policy Sciences*, *4*(2), 155–169. doi:10.1007/BF01405730

Rowe, G., & Frewer, L. J. (2000). Public participation methods: A framework for evaluation. *Science, Technology & Human Values*, *25*(1), 3–29. doi:10.1177/016224390002500101

Rowe, G., & Frewer, L. J. (2004). Evaluating public-participation exercises: A research agenda. *Science, Technology & Human Values*, *29*(4), 512–557. doi:10.1177/0162243903259197

Saebo, O., Rose, J., & Flak, L. S. (2008). The shape of eParticipation: Characterizing an emerging research area. *Government Information Quarterly*, *25*(3), 400–428. doi:10.1016/j.giq.2007.04.007

Sanford, C., & Rose, J. (2007). Characterizing eParticipation. *International Journal of Information Management*, *27*(6), 406–421. doi:10.1016/j.ijinfomgt.2007.08.002

Schwaninger, M., Ulli-Beer, S., & Kaufmann-Hayoz, R. (2008). Policy analysis and design in local public management a system dynamics approach. In *Handbook of transdisciplinary research* (pp. 205–221). Springer. doi:10.1007/978-1-4020-6699-3_13

Shim, J. P., Warkentin, M., Courtney, J. F., Power, D. J., Sharda, R., & Carlsson, C. (2002). Past, present, and future of decision support technology. *Decision Support Systems*, *33*(2), 111–126. doi:10.1016/S0167-9236(01)00139-7

Simon, H. A. (1960). *The new science of management decision*. New York: Harper Brothers. doi:10.1037/13978-000

Sterman, J. D. (1994). Learning in and about complex systems. *System Dynamics Review*, *10*(2-3), 291–330. doi:10.1002/sdr.4260100214

Timmers, P. (2007). *Agenda for eDemocracy – An EU perspective*. Brussels: European Commission.

United Nations. (2008). *United Nations e-government survey 2008*. New York: UN.

ADDITIONAL READING

Borshchev, A., & Filippov, A. (2004, July). *From system dynamics and discrete event to practical agent based modeling: Reasons, techniques, tools*. In Proceedings of the 22nd International Conference of the System Dynamics Society, Oxford, England.

Charalabidis, Y., Gionis, G., Ferro, E., & Loukis, E. (2010). Electronic Participation. In Tambouris E., Macintosh A., Glassey O. (eds.). Towards a systematic exploitation of web 2.0 and simulation modeling tools in public policy process. ePart 2010, LNCS, 6229, 1–12, Springer (2010).

Choi, Y., Breck, E., & Cardie, C. (2006). *Joint extraction of entities and relations for opinion recognition.* In Proceedings of the Conference on Empirical Methods in Natural Language Processing (EMNLP), Association for Computational Linguistics Stroudsburg, PA, USA.

Curtis, G. G. (2006, July). *Issues and Challenges - Global E-Government/E-Participation Models, Measurement and Methodology - A Framework for Moving Forward.* Prepared for the United Nations Department of Administration and Development Management, Budapest, Hungary.

Davis, J., Eisenhardt, K., & Bingham, C. (2007, April). *Developing theory through simulation methods.* Paper presented at Academy of Management Review, 32(2), p480.

Dooley, K. (2002). Simulation Research Methods. In J. Baum (Ed.), *Companion to Organizations* (pp. 829–848). London: Blackwell.

Girle, R., Hitchcock, D. L., McBurney, P., & Verheij, B. (2003). Decision Support for Practical Reasoning: a theoretical and computational perspective. In C. Reed, & T. J. Norman (Eds.), *Argumentation Machines. New Frontiers in Argument and Computation* (pp. 55–84). Dordrecht: Kluwer Academic Publishers. doi:10.1007/978-94-017-0431-1_3

Godbole, N., Srinivasaiah, M., & Skiena, S. (2007, March). *Large-scale sentiment analysis for news and blogs.* In Proceedings of the International Conference on Weblogs and Social Media (ICWSM), Colorado, USA.

Held, D. (1988, March). Social Psychology Quarterly. In Skvoretz J. (Ed.). Models of Participation in Status-Differentiated Groups, 51(1), 43-57.

Homer, J. B., & Hirsch, G. B. (2006, March). System Dynamics Modeling for Public Health: Background and Opportunities. *American Journal of Public Health, 96*(3), 452–458. doi:10.2105/AJPH.2005.062059 PMID:16449591

Law, A. M., & Kelton, W. D. (2000). *Simulation Modeling and Analysis* (3rd ed.). New York: McGraw-Hill Higher Education.

Lévy, P. (1997). *Collective intelligence: Mankind's emerging world in cyberspace.* Cambridge, MA, USA: Perseus Books.

Liu, B., Hu, M., & Cheng, J. (2005). *Opinion observer: Analyzing and comparing opinions on the Web.* In Proceedings of 14th Conference WWW Conference, ACM, New York, 342-351.

Liu, C. Y., & Wang, W. T. (2005). *System Dynamics Approach to Simulation of Tax Policy for Traditional and Internet Phone Services.* In Proceedings of the 23rd International Conference of the 12 System Dynamics Society (J. D. Sterman, N. P. Repenning, R. S. Langer, J. I. Rowe and J. M. Yanni Eds.), System Dynamics Society, Boston, USA.

Lo, Y. W., & Potdar, V. (2009). *A Review of Opinion Mining and Sentiment Classification Framework in Social Networks.* In Proceedings of the 3rd IEEE International Conference on Digital Ecosystems and Technologies (DEST). (Ok. Kaynak and M. Mohania Eds), IEEE, 396-401.

Loukis, E., & Wimmer, M. (2010). *Analysing different models of structured electronic consultation on legislation under formation.* In Proceedings of 4th International Conference on Online Deliberation – OD 2010. (F. De Cindio, A. Macintosh, C. Peraboni Eds.), University of Leeds, UK, Universita degli Studi di Milano, Italy, 14-26.

Macintosh, A. (2004). *Characterizing E-Participation in Policy Making.* In Proceedings of the 37th Hawaii International Conference on System Sciences (HICSS'04), Track 5, Vol. 5, p. 50117.1 Hawaii.

Misuraca, G. (2010, February). *Literature Review: Multi-level Governance and ICTs.* EXPGOV Project Deliverable D.3 - DRAFT V.1.0, European Union, IPTS.

Nonaka, I. (1994). A Dynamic Theory of Organizational Knowledge Creation. *Organization Science*, 5(1), 14–37. doi:10.1287/orsc.5.1.14

O'Reilly, T. (2005). What is Web 2.0? Design patterns and business models for the next generation of software. Retrieved December 13, 2012, from http://www.oreilly.com/lpt/a/6228.

Pang, B., & Lee, L. (2008). Opinion mining and sentiment analysis. *Foundations and Trends in Information Retrieval*, 2(1-2), 1–135. doi:10.1561/1500000011

Teekasap, P. (2009). *Cluster Formation and Government Policy: System Dynamics Approach*. In Proceedings of the 27th International Conference of the System Dynamics Society (An. Ford, D. N. Ford and Ed. G. Anderson Eds.), System Dynamics Society, Albuquerque, New Mexico, USA.

Wiebe, J., & Cardie, C. (2005). Annotating expressions of opinions and emotions in language. *Springer Language Resources and Evaluation*, 39(2-3), 165–210. doi:10.1007/s10579-005-7880-9

Xenakis, A., & Loukis, E. (2010). An Investigation of the Use of Structured e-Forum for Enhancing e-Participation in Parliaments. *International Journal of Electronic Governance*, 3(2), 134–147. doi:10.1504/IJEG.2010.034092

Zamanipour, M. (2009). *A System Dynamics Model for Analyzing the Effects of Government Policies: A Case Study of Iran's Cell Phone Market*. In Proceedings of the 27th International Conference of the System Dynamics Society, Albuquerque, New Mexico, USA.

KEY TERMS AND DEFINITIONS

Decision Support Systems: A type of Information Systems that contributes in the organization of decision-making actions. These systems are used in great extent from Business Enterprises.

E-Governance: Application of Information and Communication Technologies (ICTs) to help government agencies make decisions based on citizens' input and enhance citizens participate in the policy making process.

E-Participation: The use of Information and Communication Technologies (ICTs) for enabling citizens take part in the decision making process.

NOMAD: A technological platform which allows a decision maker to collect citizen's' data on a specific policy that is still under formation from multiple social media platforms, analyze them through fully automated techniques, identify the problems, use appropriate citizens suggestions for improvement and make a decision about the specific policy based on citizen's' gathered data.

PADGETS: A technological platform which allows a policy maker to develop an online campaign on a policy, publish it in multiple social media platforms, retrieve citizens' data through APIs, process them through methods and techniques and finally make a decision on a policy based on the results from citizens' collected data.

Social Media: Internet-based applications that allow users to create, share and exchange content, information and ideas.

Web 2.0: Internet technology that allows the creation of multiple applications (e.g. blogs, social networking sites, virtual world sites, etc.), in which users communicate and interact.

Chapter 4
Ontology Development and the Role of Knowledge in E-Government Project Management:
A Lesson for Developing Countries

Bongani Ngwenya
Solusi University, Zimbabwe

ABSTRACT

The literature suggests that the elaboration of ontology contributes to the standardization and classification of concepts and terminologies, and it has been happening in some sectors, such as software engineering, e-Government services implementation, and project management. In the area of e-Government, knowledge plays a critical role in the development of e-Government transformation project management ontology, which aims at adopting and customizing the existing project management approaches according to the specific challenges encountered in the e-Government environment. It is in this context that this chapter presents an ontological representation of the concepts of e-Government project management in one of the developing countries in southern Africa. The chapter further intends to collaborate in the excellence and productivity of the management of the e-Government project process. This will also enable the interoperability and knowledge reuse between all factors and stakeholders related with the implementation of such types of projects as a lesson for developing countries. The data was collected by use of an interview protocol or schedule, and the researcher interviewed relevant employees of the two ministries, the Ministry of Information Technology and the Ministry of Information and Communication. The data was then analyzed qualitatively to draw a model that the Zimbabwean government is adopting.

DOI: 10.4018/978-1-4666-4900-2.ch004

INTRODUCTION

Middleton (2007) suggests that e-Government is an idea raised by former U.S. vice president (Al Gore), within his vision of linking the citizen to the various agencies of government for getting all kinds of government services in an automated and automatic way, using information and communication networks to reduce costs, improve performance, speed of delivery and effectiveness of implementation. E-Government program seeks to achieve greater efficiency in government performance, through raising the performance of services for beneficiaries and investors from all segments of society easily, accurately and efficiently, to become a new type of performance of official government transactions. Online interactive services may include such facilities as petitioning, rate paying, licensing or information queries. There continues to be a diversity of implementation quality and levels for such services (Middleton, 2007). To achieve this requires utilizing the latest means of technology, communications and followup to the rapid global developments and analyZING the reasons for the failure and the success of e-Government programs and to encourage the use of technology and effectively increase the number of users of computers and Internet tools. All this cannot be achieved without proper knowledge on ontology development in e-Government projects management, and this outlines this chapter's focus.

Sarantis and Askounis (2010) suggest that there is a unanimous view among politicians, decision makers, public administration officials, e-Government researchers and information technology practitioners that knowledge is an important driving force in government transformation. According to Lin *et al.,* (2004) communication and knowledge exchange between project teams comprising members from within information systems vendors, external consultants and different public organizations is often hampered by, among other things, confusion in terms of vocabulary. Extended collaboration, such as joint private and public sector ventures, will raise the difficulty and complexity of communication between the cooperating stakeholders. One of the main technical issues is the knowledge management problem when processing shared implicit and explicit knowledge within different systems (Sarantis & Askounis, 2010).

The authors emphasize that collaboration in e-Government projects faces knowledge conflict during knowledge sharing and project development. Prudent knowledge management is critical because poor knowledge management by involved parties can mislead the project processes and cause serious wastage of resources, lack of best practices exploitation and even the failure of the project.

In order for e-Government project management to be properly understood and successfully applied, it needs to be more comprehensively conceptualized. Conceptualization involves a need to address a variety of concerns beyond the existing hard rational Information Technology project management approaches (Sarantis & Askounis, 2009). However e-Government is a detailed and complex development that is difficult to conceptualize and what is known and understood is mostly of a descriptive and anecdotal nature. The bottom line is that e-Government implementations have yet to realize the upper stages of maturity particularly in developing countries and that the understanding and knowledge of the area is still in the process of formation. The development of ontology expands the practitioner's ability to generate information by using search methods beyond simple keywords. If only keywords are used in e-Government project management process, then information that is retrieved will often lack the precision necessary for generating quality information. Therefore, in order to retrieve quality information more quickly and accurately, a broader and more extensive ontology development is required (Lin *et al.,* 2004).

So, the assumption is building an e-Government project Ontology for common understanding within the group of all project stakeholders during the project management will improve the definitions of goals and finally the rate of success of projects. In this chapter, the author proposes electronic Government Transformation Project Management (eGTPM) ontology which is specifically targeting the challenges that are encountered in e-Government project cases. The remainder of this chapter introduces the reader to some e-Government definitions and critical issues on e-Government before concentrating on the main focus of the chapter. The main focus of the chapter presents the proposed e-Government project management ontology adopted by the government of Zimbabwe. The chapter covers the implementation of the ontology as well as the validation procedure. The methodology employed in the study is comprehensively outlined, followed by solutions and recommendations. Finally, the author suggests future research directions and draws conclusions from the foregoig discussions..

INSIGHTS FROM THE LITERATURE AND CONCEPTUAL FRAMEWORK

A comprehensive insight into literature that on what e-Government entails with a focus to knowledge and ontology is presented in this section, before a concentration on the main focus of the chapter. Covered in this section of literature review is the question, what is e-Government? definition of e-Government, maturity of e-Government, challenges and opportunities for developing a successful e-Government. Also covered is knowledge management and ontology methodology literature related to e-Government project management and ontology and information semantics.

The Definition of E-Government

Pardo (2000) suggests that for one to understand e-Government, must first understand government in general. Government is actually a dynamic mixture of goals, structures and functions (Pardo, 2000). E-Government is more than a website,

email or processing transactions via the internet. E-Government becomes a natural extension of the technological revolution that has accompanied the knowledge society. The e-Government added new concepts such as: transparency, accountability, citizen participation in the evaluation of government performance (Mohammad, 2009).

Like other contemporary concepts, there are multiple definitions of e-Government emanating from different researchers and specialists from different contextual settings, but most of them agree to define electronic government as government use of Information Communication Technologies (ICTs) to offer for citizens and businesses the opportunity to interact and conduct business with government by using different electronic media such as telephone touch pad, fax, smart cards, self-service kiosks, e-mail/ Internet, and EDI (Mohammad, 2009). It is about how government organizes itself: its administration, rules, regulations and frameworks set out to carry out service delivery and to co-ordinate, communicate and integrate processes within itself. Another definition of e-Government was presented by United Nation's website to be "e-Government refers to the use of information and communication technologies (ICT) - such as Wide Area Networks, the Internet, and mobile computing - by government agencies". While OECD (2003) noted that electronic government refers to the use of information and communication technologies, and particularly the Internet, as a tool to achieve better government. From a maturity perspective, like any other phenomenon, e-Government practice can also be measured in terms of maturity levels. Borrowing the business language, this would be equivalent to a business cycle or a product life cycle.

E-Government Maturity

According to Mohammad (2009), the concept of government in general, as well as of e-Government, can be distinguished between 3 groups': citizens, businesses and services, and governmental departments of the country. And uses of abbreviations such as (G2C) refer to the relationship between government and citizen, (G2B) denote the transaction between the government and businesses and industrial departments, and (G2G) indicate the relationship between different government units. Most of the governments begin to provide information across direct on-line, but the public needs require more quick services and usually take this form gradually. E-Government becomes more widespread; one is beginning to see the progress through six stages. Not all governments will reach all stages, and there will be much diversity within a government, with different agencies at different stages. The stages are:

1. Using internal network and setting up an email system;
2. Enabling inter-organizational and public access to information;
3. Allowing 2-way communication;
4. Allowing exchange of value;
5. Digital democracy; and
6. Joined-up government.

Implementing e-Government is a continuing process, and most often the development is conceptualized in stages. The widely known maturity model suggested by Layne & Lee (2001) (sited by Almarabeh & AbuAli, 2010) who sees e-Government as an evolutionary phenomenon, from which e-Government initiatives should be derived and implemented. They assume four stages of a growth model for e-Government: (1) Cataloguing, (2) Transaction, (3) Vertical integration, and (4) Horizontal integration as shown in Figure 1 below.

This model is developed by increasing the level of complexity and integration from (1) to (4). Andersen & Henriksen (2006) complement the maturity model with strategic ambitions of governments' use of IT, and present what they

call the Public Sector Process Rebuilding (PPR) model. They argue that the Layne and Lee model build on the same rationale that have dominated the traditional motives for IT adoption; increase in information quality, and efficiency and effectiveness. The PPR model expands the e-Government model.

The major difference between the Layne and Lee model and the PPR model is the activity and customer centric approach rather than the technological capability. The proposition of the researcher in this chapter is that all this argument above can be hampered by the serious challenge of knowledge. Hence the need to understand the role knowledge plays on ontology in e-Government project management. Before delving into the main focus of the chapter, the researcher endeavors to highlight some of the critical challenges and opportunities for developing a successful e-Government, knowledge and ontology methodology and ontology and information semantics.

Challenges and Opportunities for Developing a Successful E-Government

The role of knowledge on ontology development in e-Government project management is a major challenge especially for developing countries like Zimbabwe. This leads to overall and general problems when it comes to e-Government initiatives that are aimed at raising the level of government performance in general, where the proper application of these initiatives lead to upgrade the governmental services provided to citizens and the private sector and enhance the effectiveness of government work internally, in addition to broadening the participation of citizens in decision-making process. However, many studies indicate that a large proportion of initiatives to implement e-Government around the world did not succeed in achieving these promised goals. There

Figure 1. The maturity models of e-Government development(Andersen & Henriksen, 2006).

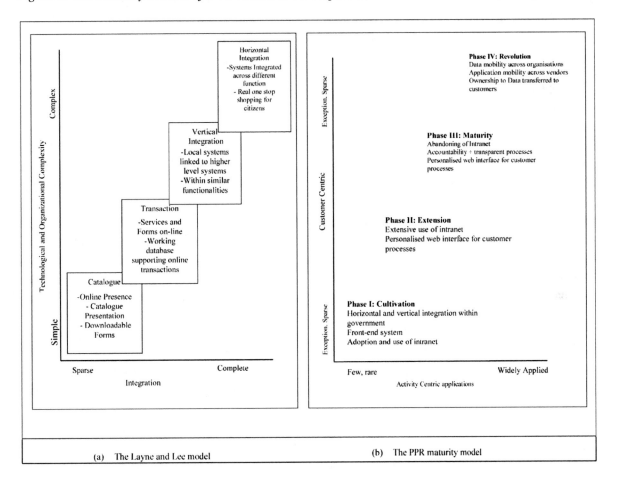

is, in fact, a global consensus on the existence of the need for deeper studies to understand the real reasons behind this failure, but in spite of higher percentage e-Government projects that failed to achieve its goals globally, the world is witnessing a comprehensive consensus that recognizes the possibility of e-Government initiatives to fulfill their promises. The underlying potential of these initiatives will only be achieved when there is better understanding of the obstacles faced. The most challenges that are expected to be faced during the implementation of an e-Government program have been summarized from the e-Government handbook of developing countries (Center of Democracy and Technology, 2002).

Knowledge and Ontology Methodology Literature related to E-Government Project Management

In this section, the knowledge management and ontology methodology literature related to e-Government project management is reviewed. A specific emphasis is focused on methodological considerations that shed light on how one might construct an ontology process that could be used in the e-Government environment. Knowledge is defined as reliable information which is accumulated by knowledge workers. For a public organization to be successful, it must have a structure to manage these invisible assets (Rowe, 2005; Johannes *et* al., 2002). From a decision science perspective, knowledge management may be viewed as the transformation of data to information and then information into knowledge (Johannessen*et al.,* 2002; Hult, 2003; Wang & Ariguzo, 2004; Yim *et al.,* 2004; Gottschalk, 2007). There are several processes and objectives that comprise the knowledge management function in all types of organizations. Figure 2 shows the subsystems that comprise knowledge management. Knowledge management involves the internal management of data and information flows into, and throughout of the organization. These activities include the following: generating information, disseminating information, selecting knowledge, deploying knowledge, creating unique value, and organizing information.

Ramal *et al.,*(2002), work contains an identification of various knowledge domains connected with software maintenance. The domains identified are computer science, application and general common sense knowledge. Research re-

garding ontologies in the area of software maintenance process has been conducted from Derrider (2002), Dias*et al.,* (2003) and Kitchenham *et al.,*(1999). Works have also been published in relation to their use in the maintenance process, included in the taxonomy, along with development, in the engineering processes category. Ruiz *et al.,* (2004), work is concentrated in defining an ontology to assist in the management of software maintenance projects. This ontology includes some elements such as product, activity, process, agent, measure and some dynamic aspects such as workflow. In the case of software management processes, Nour *et al.,* (2000) developed ontology based techniques and tools that allow recovery of the acquired experience in previous software projects to be applied to new projects.

Capability Maturity Model Integration (CMMI) is used to guide mapping, description, standardization and change of software processes in an organization. Therefore, several authors took CMMI as an inspiration for an ontology that should

Figure 2. Knowledge management subsystems

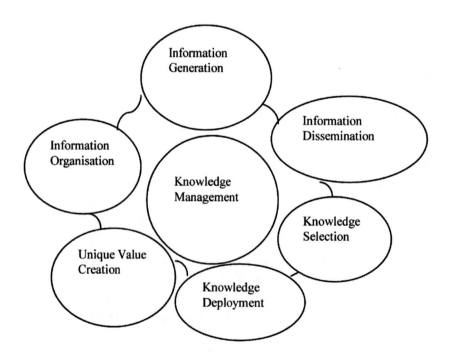

help an information system to support process planning, process definition, process control and management and process change in an organization (Shang &Lin, 2009). Liao *et al.*, (2005) for example, define an ontology which models the CMMI in processes and practices. Both, processes and practices can be atomic or composite. Processes can be further classified to user defined categories. Various process areas from CMMI, such as the requirements management or configuration management, are then modeled as subclasses of the composite or fundamental processes depending on whether they can be further decomposed. They propose that the CMMI-based ontology can be used in a tool which supports software process definition and evaluation.

By examining these ontologies, the researcher is posits that the ontologies are characterized by a purely software engineering and technology perspective, since they have been created mainly for supporting the development of software artifacts and information systems, in order to be used by persons with software engineering skills and education. However, they lack project management perspective (problems/solutions-oriented), so they do not support the search for an exchange of knowledge concerning the specific needs and challenges of e-Government project management. Apart from ontologies, in order to include the project management fundamental principles, the researcher examined the most often used methods and techniques applied in e-Government project management. Prince2 is a project management methodology covering the organization, management and control of projects, developed and maintained by the UK National Computing Centre (2005). PMBOK (2008) is a framework describing the sum of knowledge within the profession of Project Management in an attempt to document and to standardize generally accepted project management information and practices. HERMES is an open method for the uniform and structured management of projects in Information and Communication Technologies (ICT) implemented from Swiss government. Common characteristic of the above approaches is that they are generic ones, not covering the specific features and demands of e-Government projects.

Even though several stimulating approaches with exploitable results exist, regarding ontologies existence in adjacent areas (software management, e-Government service provision, project management), a gap is detected regarding the area of e-Government project management that suits developing countries' like Zimbabwe`s context. Also, project management is characterized by specific needs and challenges such as goal orientation, high complexity and multiple dimensions, politics driven, many stakeholders with different concerns and also different views and perceptions of the problem.

Ontology and Information Semantic

Sarantis & Askounis (2010) suggest that Ontology from philosophical perspective is the science of studying beings Dias*et al.*, (2003). Philosophical Ontology handles the precise utilization of words as descriptors of entities; it gives an account for those words that belong to entities and those that do not Kitchenham *et al.*,(1999). In both computer science and information science, ontology is a representation of a set of concepts within a domain and the relationships between those concepts Ruiz *et al.*,(2004). Ontology in some context is a dictionary of terms formulated in a canonical syntax and with commonly accepted definitions to be shared by different information systems communities Nour *et al.*,(2000). Ontologies are used in many fields such as: artificial intelligence, software engineering, the semantic web, biomedical informatics, library science, information architecture, and as a form of knowledge representation about the world or some part of it. Ontologies enhance collaboration, communication, and knowledge sharing. They contribute in reducing gaps among researchers created by conceptual confusion (Gottschalk, 2007; Shang & Lin, 2009; Liao *et al.*,2005).

According to Sarantis & Askounis (2010), the semantic Web initiative, led by W3C (2005), has changed the ontology landscape, through the initiative, researchers and developers join forces to provide standard semantics markup languages based on XML, ontology management systems, and other useful tools. People rediscover the value of ontology in other important applications such as information and process integration (PMBOK, 2008; Akman *et al.*, 2005). Ontologies have been widely used during the last years in the area of e-Government. Balzer has started advocating the benefits of underlying ontologies of precise and formal specifications, notably for checking a specification adequacy through prototyping (Finger & Pécoud, 2003), others used ontology to propose multi-paradigm frameworks to combine multiple languages in a semantically meaningful way so that different facets can be captured by languages that fit them best (Andersen *et al.*, 2004). Kim (1999) proposes a formal model of enterprise quality, called "Ontology of enterprise quality modeling". Kim's measurement ontology contains many concepts that can be applied within the context of E-Government applications. Under this perspective, Kim's proposal mainly focuses on targets-and-goals, including concepts such as "quality requirement","entity", "enterprise model of quality", and "measured attribute".

Ontologies constitute abstract conceptual models of particular domains, which identify the kinds of entities existing in a particular domain and the kinds of relations among them, being acceptable from a group of people dealing with this domain (Nuseibeh&Easterbrook, 2000). Domain ontology establishes a common vocabulary for the group of people dealing with this domain, in order to create, exchange, combine, retrieve and reuse knowledge. According to Uschold and Grunninger (1996),

ontologies are of critical importance for knowledge acquisition and exchange. Before developing our ontology, we studied the literature on relevant knowledge-based approaches to software management, project management and e-Government areas. Contributions in Software Engineering have been made toward using ontologies. Devedzic has argued that ontologies are needed in all phases of software engineering life cycle, each of which must have knowledge, whether about data structure, methods and domain (Perrott, 1996). This makes ontologies everywhere and they make possible to smoothly integrate artificial intelligence with other software disciplines (Perrott, 1996). Martin & Olsina, (2003), Wand&Weber (1993), Garcia*et al.*, (2005), showed that there is a lack of consensus on the concepts and terminologies that are used in this field.

This chapter is building ontology concepts to capture the conceptualization knowledge about Requirements Engineering Process in E-Government Applications (REPEA). Ontology shows enormous potential in making software more efficient, adaptive, and intelligent. It is recognized as one of the areas, which will bring the next breakthrough in software development (Kayed & Colomb, 2000; Kayed & Colomb, 2005; Rumbaugh *et al.*, 1991; Kim, 1999). The idea of ontology has been welcomed by visionaries and early adopters. Recently, the semantic Web initiative, led by W3C, has changed the ontology landscape completely, through the initiative, researchers and developers join forces to provide standard semantics markup languages based on XML, ontology management systems, and other useful tools. Also, the Web provides interesting applications of ontology critical to daily life such as search and navigation. In addition, people rediscover the value of ontology in other important applications such as information and process integration (Kayed & Colomb, 2000; Kayed & Colomb, 2005; Rumbaugh *et al.*, 1991; Kim, 1999).

ZIMBABWEAN E-GOVERNMENT CONTEXT

Most governments worldwide, Zimbabwe included, face serious challenges to transform their systems to deliver efficient and cost effective services through information and communication technologies. Developing countries in general have a challenge of requirements engineering which is a crucial activity and critical component in systems development process, especially in the development of large scale systems such as e-Government applications. There are also inconsistencies and terminology conflicts that are hindering many e-Government applications. This chapter traces the development of e-Government project management ontology (mainly concepts) in the domain of requirements engineering process for e-Government applications by the Zimbabwean government. This contributes to enabling software engineers, particularly in developing countries, to find out shared-understandable and common concepts to describe requirements for different domain models used in developing ontology on e-Government project management applications. This requires the role of knowledge and several documents related to e-Government requirement need to be collected and the main concepts and relationships extracted and refined. The main theme of this chapter is to provide common concepts and understanding of the requirements for knowledge on ontology in e-Government project management.

Project Management Ontology for E-Government

In the section on literature review above we noted that some literature suggest that in both computer science and information science, ontology is a representation of a set of concepts within a domain and the relationships between those concepts (Ruiz *et al.,* 2004). Ontology in some context is a dictionary of terms formulated in a canonical syntax and with commonly accepted definitions to be shared by different information systems communities (Nour,*et al.,* 2000). This section seeks to discuss e-Government project management ontology as an issue in e-Government implementation projects. In order to define a suitable classification scheme an analysis of e-Government implementation projects from a macro perspective has to take place to identify the essential determining characteristics. We have to appreciate that issues of e-Government projects are manifold and raise varied problems and controversies. To clarify the phenomenon of e-Government project implementation, it is useful to understand which issues describe the e-Government project itself. The analysis of literature brings to light at least three specific aspects, reflecting in turn the e-Government project nature and the management of the project perspectives. The question is: how does knowledge come in, in the equation?

Figure 2 presents knowledge as organized around three different aspects: that is, (1) knowledge about the e-Government project type's domain, (2) knowledge about the e-Government management procedure, and (3) knowledge about the e-Government stakeholders. Each of these three aspects is described in sub-ontology. The section that follows gives a summary of e-Government domain sub-ontology, which is diagrammatically represented in Figure 3.

The E-Government Domain Sub-Ontology

Sarantis &Askounis (2010)'s e-Government transformation project management (egtpm) ontology model presented in Figure 2 presented a structural framework for adoption by the Zimbabwe e-Government project managers and experts. E-Government project management requires a thorough knowledge about the e-Government project types, which is intuitively fundamental to e-Government project management. The sub-ontology is pictured in the upper part in Figure 2.

Figure 3. E-Government transformation project management (EGTPM) ontology (Adopted from Sarantis & Askounis (2010))

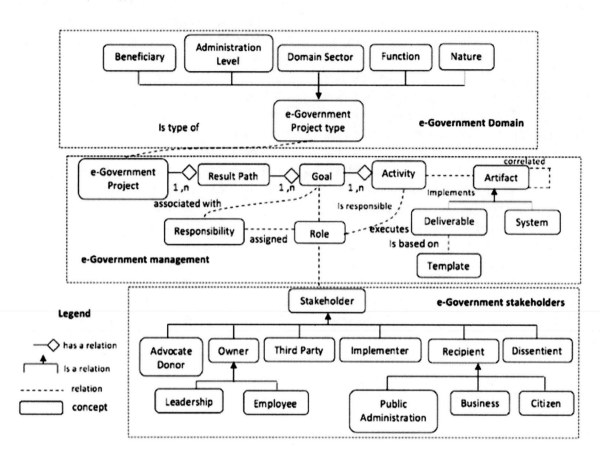

The competency questions for the e-Government domain sub-ontology are: what are the fundamental types of e-government projects? How do they relate to e-government dimensions? Answering these questions led to a decomposition of the e-Government project type in five different concepts. These are: beneficiary, administration level, domain sector, function and nature. Each of these concepts is described in details in the following subsections with direct references made to how each is essentially manifested in the experience of e-government project implementation.

Beneficiary: Based on the e-Government literature, beneficiaries can be classified in four major groups. They are government (G2G), business (G2B), citizen (G2C), international government

(G2I) (Akman *et al.,* 2005). This approach to the cataloguing of beneficiaries insures that the organisations will be fully cognizant of who is to be gained. It should be noted that a large number of e-Government projects particularly in developing countries, Zimbabwe included, perform poorly because of the irrelevance to beneficiaries and stakeholders.

Administration Level: Overall government structures are naturally reflected in most of the developed countries such as Australia, Germany, and USA etc. by their e-Government structures themselves. There are three distinct levels of government in these countries (Finger & Pécoud, 2003), there is the Federal Government on the national level, each state or prefecture is an independent unit of government and there are a number of local governments. According to Finger & Pécoud (2003) an e-Government project can cover the whole country (national level), a part of it (regional level) or a municipality (local level) in such a way determining its administration coverage. On top of those, there are collaborative initiatives among countries (international level) in order to provide interoperable services to citizens and businesses. That is Government to Business initiatives (G2B).Realizing that Information Communication Technologies (ICTs) are not limited by borders, e-Government strategies are formulated and implemented at national, regional and local levels. The policy and implementation procedure depends on each country's political system and administrative structure and regional and local e-Government projects are undertaken in such a way that they link and are compatible to national policy and simultaneously address regional communications policy, financing and regulatory issues in a way that promotes harmonization(Finger &Pécoud, 2003).

Domain Sector: Akman*et al.,* (2005) defines the domains as (interior, finance, social security, agriculture, education etc.) refers to a large extent welldefined areas of the public sector where the tasks to be performed in relation to citizens and businesses are delivered by several different authorities cutting across tiers of authority. The domains can consist of parts of or one or more ministries and municipal and regional spheres of responsibility. In the individual domain sectors action plans are drawn up, ensuring coordinated, efficient and targeted digital development. The link between the individual domain and the national level is achieved by articulating action plans for the respective domains and implementing them within the framework of the overall strategy for digitalizing the public sector.

Function: An e-Government project could provide a system that is extroversive offering services through a public interface (front office systems) or introvert interoperating with other systems in the background (back office systems). Introvert systems are defined as the systems and procedures that mainly computerize the public administration operations, particularly in the back office. In the e-Government context, the "front office" would be the user interface, such as a web site (Sarantis and Askounis, 2010).

Nature: Sarantis and Askounis (2010) depict project nature as being able to provide more precise specifications on projects which present similar problems and for which similar results can be expected. Based on their scope e-Government projects are divided in policy and technical oriented nature. Those two fields are the first level classification of nature concept. They can be further analyzed in a more detailed structure decomposing in more levels the nature of the e-Government project.Following is the second aspect of knowledge organisation.

The E-Government Management Sub-Ontology

According to Sarantis and Askounis (2010) e-Government management sub-ontology attempts to develop e-Government project management field beyond its current conceptual base connecting it more closely to the specific challenges of e-Government projects. E-Government management sub-ontology provides a sound basis forproject management in e-Government area, being a result-oriented approach to project management and offering a radical departure from the more traditional project management methodologies (PMI, Prince2 etc.), focusing on what must be achieved, the goals (Andersen *et al.,* 2004), rather than on trying to predict timescales and resources for activities. E-Government management sub-ontology provides a knowledge rich environment for planning, organizing and monitoring e-Government projects, satisfying the specific e-Government project challenges. The management sub-ontology includes several elements with relationships with each other:

- **E-Government Project:** An e-Government project is a finite endeavour consisting of a set of processes undertaken to create a unique product or service that meets all the requirements established by the stakeholders at the beginning of the development and brings beneficial change or added value to the public. An e-Government project is divided in a number of result paths that covers all the dimensions established at project initiation level.

- **Result Path:** An e-Government project usually addresses several needs or purposes in an organization; it usually has a composite goal and the plan is therefore multidimensional. Each result path defines a specific dimension that the e-Government project should cover.

- **Goal:** A Goal is defined as a practical and tangible step within the project described as a state, which must be reached to meet the final objective. A goal consists of a set of coordinated activities, performed in sequence or in parallel.

- **Activity:** Activity is a specific task that must be done or a decision that must be made, stated in a verb. It describes how to reach the defined goal.

- **Artefact:** An artefact is any kind of material element that can be created, used, or updated during the project implementation. There are two types of artefacts: deliverables, and systems. It is a piece of work that has to be done as part of the project. The granularity of the result depends on the nature and scale of the project and may range for example from producing a particular software module (system), installing a specific type of equipment (system) or producing a paper deliverable (deliverable).

- **System:** An information system project result (software, hardware etc.).

- **Deliverable:** A paper type of deliverable (study, report etc.).

- **Template:** The template intends to function as a guide during the deliverable implementation and sometimes it could be adapted to each project specific situation.

- **Role:** A general name for a set of responsibilities (political leadership, project manager, service modeller, data modeller, security expert, key user etc.) in an e-Government project that can be executed by one or more participants. A role is assigned to one or more stakeholders that have a common set of capabilities and skills. Each role can perform an activity or be responsible for a goal. Responsibility: The nature of the assignment in a specific goal or activity (executes the work, decides, manages progress, must be Informed, available to advise, provides training etc.).Following is the third and last aspect of knowledge organisation.

The E-Government Stakeholders' Sub-Ontology

Sarantis and Askounis (2010) suggest that the complex nature of information system implementation in government outlines areas in which a multitude of potential stakeholders can have a direct or indirect impact in the project result (Grant et al., 1991; Perrott, 1996).Many of the challenges faced by public sector agencies are organizational issues associated with the introduction of new technologies and work processes (Al-Kibisi*et al.,* 2001; Jorgensen&Cable, 2002). The development of citizen-centred services further requires cooperation and technical compatibilities that may be difficult to engineer given the prevalence of institutional conservatism and risk aversion that characterizes the public sector (Bellamy &Taylor, 1998). The political context of the public sector highlights not only the multiple agencies that are involved in the implementation of e-Government, but also the potential impact each can have to the successful development of e-Government (Chan*et al.,* 2003; Adelakun &Jennex, 2002).To support the implementation of e-Government therefore, the process of identifying and managing a broad range of constituent stakeholders must be considered to ensure that the implementation processsencompasses all levels of stakeholders (Chan*et al.,* 2003; Pardo&Scholl, 2002).

Stakeholder theory has been identified as useful and appropriate for the public sector (Tennert &Schroeder, 1999) and has been further developed to determine stakeholder requirements in e-Government projects (Chan*et al.,* 2003; Pardo&Scholl, 2002; Scholl, 2001)to support the process of managing stakeholder relations, reduce the risk of stakeholder conflict and aid the process of e-Government implementation (Scott, *et al.,* 2004). It is clear that all governmental programs and initiatives have multiple stakeholders, that is people or organizations that care about the idea and how it affects them or other things they care about. The users or customers of services are key stakeholders and most efforts to use information on their behalf take them into account. Stakeholder considerations go far beyond this group to include (1) those who are directly involved in the process of designing, delivering, and paying for the system or service and (2) those who are indirectly affected, either by the outcome of the initiative or by the competition for resources that could have gone to a different effort that they value. Stakeholder analysis needs to identify both positive and negative impacts on all these groups. While it is important to understand how certain stakeholders can benefit, it is equally important to know who must contribute and who can be hurt and how (Sharon, 2008). At the strategic level, stakeholder communication needs to be clear, consistent, focused on the essentials, and delivered in plain language (Sarantis and Askounis, 2010).

Sarantis and Askounis (2010) reiterate that strategy is not conveyed in a detailed work plan,

but rather ahigh level statement that tells stakeholders and observers what kind of project to expect. The two authors go further to emphasise that strategy answers key questions such as: What is the goal? Will the approach be incremental or more radical? How long will it take? Who will do the work? Who is the leader? What roles do users and other stakeholders play? Who pays for what? What kind of technology will be used? What are the major result paths or goals? The definitions of each concept of the specific sub-ontology are as follows:

- **Stakeholder:** The e-Government project stakeholders which are affected positively or negatively from the results are identified.
- **Advocate-Donor:** Those who are pushing the project forward; often they will be from outside the implementing agency, and they may well be providing key funding for the project.
- **Owner:** The organization or department that owns and uses the system, who is ultimately responsible for the project result.

Implementation of Ontology

In order to implement the ontology, the researcher discovered that the project managers to adoptedthe Protégé version 4.0 due to its extensibility, and that it provides a plug-and-play environment that makes it a flexible base for rapid prototyping and application development. Protégé ontologies can be exported into different formats including RDF Schema (RDFS) and Web Ontology Language (OWL). Particularly, the eGTPM Ontology was implemented in OWL. The first challenge during this task was how to transform the UML diagram from conceptualization phase into the OWL formalism. This task was hard and time consuming. Modelling in OWL implied to transform composition relations into bidirectional relations. In addition, some concepts modelled as classes in UML were properties in ontology. And not all relations in UML were modelled in ontology but only those relations that were necessary to answer competence questions and would be Zimbabwe situation specific. OWLViz graphics was used to compare the ontology implementation with its conceptualization. Ontoviz plug-ins were generated and compared with UML diagrams. On the one hand, OWLViz enables the class hierarchies in OWL Ontology to be viewed, allowing comparison of the asserted class hierarchy and the inferred class hierarchy. With OWLViz primitive and defined classes can be distinguished, computed changes to the class hierarchy may be clearly seen, and inconsistent concepts can be highlighted. OntoViz generates a graphics with all relations defined in the ontology instances and attributes. It permits visualizing several disconnected graphs at once. These graphs are suitable for presentation purposes, as they tend to be of good clarity with none overlapping nodes. Besides, these graphics are very useful for analysing when a concept must be modelled as a class and when must be modelled as an attribute.

The following are suggested stake holders for ontology implementation.

- **Third party:** Others who could have an important influence on the project or on whom the project will have an important effect.
- **Implementer:** Those who analyse design and implement the e-Government system including the builders/suppliers of the hardware, software and networks.
- **Recipient:** Those to whom data or services are delivered by the specific e-Government project. Sometimes the recipients are divided into primary recipients, who get the data/services directly; and secondary recipients, who only get the data/services indirectly via the primary recipient.
- **Leadership:** The people politician or high ranked public official who have the politi-

cal responsibility regarding decision making of the project.
- **Employee:** Those from the owner organisation who carry out the activities that make the e-Government system work; not just clerical staff, but may also be managers and technical maintenance staff.
- **Validation of Ontology**: After defining ontology, it was validated it in two ways: validation of the quality of the ontology itself (how clear it is, how complete, concise, etc.), and validation of the usefulness of the concepts for e-Government project management. In the next section the researcher presents how the validation of ontology was done in these different ways (Gruber, 1995; Gómez-Pérez, 1995).

Assessment for Quality: To validate the quality of the ontology the following six desirable criteria were considered(Gruber, 1995; Gómez-Pérez, 1995):

- Consistency, referring to the absence (or not) of contradictory information in the ontology;
- Completeness, referring to how well the ontology covers the real world (e-Government project management for us);
- Conciseness, referring to the absence (or not) of needless information or details;
- Clarity, referring to how effectively the intended meaning is communicated;
- Generality, referring to the possibility of using the ontology for various purposes inside the domain fixed (e-Government project management); and
- Robustness, referring to the ability of the ontology to support changes.

To evaluate these criteria, about five experts were involved to study the ontology and fill a quality assessment report composed of questions for each criterion. These people were chosen for their large experience in e-Government project management or for their academic background in the area. The evaluation results were satisfactory; on a scale of 0 to 5 no criterion has an average below 3.5. This evaluation was useful in pointing out specific problems. For example, there was no inclusion of a relation to specify that activities may interact between themselves, some definitions were not clear, or some restrictions were not expressed. Besides the expert assessments experiment, also checked was the completeness and conciseness of the ontology by instantiating the concepts from the documentation of a real e-Government project. For example the project of the implementation of the Greek e-Government Interoperability Framework (e-GIF) was used to instantiate eGTPM ontology (Sarantis & Askounis, 2010). All the concepts from the ontology were instantiated.

Assessment for Usefulness: Representation of the knowledge useful to e-Government project management was one of the main objectives of the ontology. In this section a validation of the usefulness of the concepts for e-Government project management is presented. To do so, the researcher presented the instantiated knowledge to the e-Government project managers and asked them what concepts they used. For the first experiment the researcher used an approach called think-aloud where the managers were asked to say everything they did and why they did it. The sessions were recorded and later transferred on paper to be analysed. During the analysis, the researcher tried to identify the kind of knowledge that the e-Government project managers were using at each moment based on the defined ontology. The ontology was presented and explained to the project managers and they were asked to fill in a questionnaire on the concepts they used. This form consisted of all the concepts that had been instantiated previously and the list of their instances (as they were identified). The e-Government project managers were simply asked to tick the instances

they had used during the managing procedure. They could not add new instances. The experiment was done with four project managers. They filled 8 forms corresponding to 8 different e-Government projects. The results of the assessment are given in Table 1. The table shows the number of concepts that were instantiated for the eGTPM ontology during the two different assessment procedures (interview, questionnaire). One may observe that there are a lot fewer concepts used in the first one than in the second. One reason for this is that there were fewer sessions in the first experiment and interviewees had less time to respond and the responses were more spontaneous. All uses of concepts detected in the first experiment were also found in the second one, it did not bring in any new instances.

METHODOLOGY

The research methodology used in the Zimbabwean case study was semi-structured interviews and a questionnaire for selected specialists in e-Government project management in the two Ministries: Ministry of Information and Publicity and Ministry of Information Technology and Communication. For each one of the sub-ontologies the researcher defined competency questions, captured the necessary concepts to answer these

Table 1. Number of concepts used in assessment

	Ontology	Interview		Questionnaire	
	Concepts number	Con. number	%	Con. number	%
e-Government domain sub-ontology	12	9	75	11	91.7
e-Government management sub-ontology	8	6	75	7	87.8
e-Government stakeholders sub-ontology	14	11	78.6	12	85.7
Total	34	26	76.5	30	88.2

questions, established relationships among the concepts, described the concepts in a glossary and validated them with experts within the two ministries that were studied. Building such ontology is a significant work. The researcher spent three months to define the ontology. The researcher`s first difficulty was to define clearly what was to be the focus of the ontology. This was solved defining scenarios for the use of the knowledge. A second difficulty was to review the relevant literature in search of definitions and validation of the concepts. In this phase, it was deemed important to base each and every concept on independent sources from the literature.

The e-Government program was launched in late 2009 and the researcher conducted interviews during the spring of 2012 with a total of 18 project managers. The interviews were semi-structured and lasted for about an hour on average. All interviews were recorded and written word-by-word. The analysis of the interviews was made by contents analysis. The investigation, conducted basically followed the Case Studies methodology as, according to Tellis (1997): "Case study can be

seen to satisfy the three tenets of the qualitative method: describing, understanding, and explaining". A questionnaire was designed for a selected few specialists in the field of e-Government project management in Zimbabwe. These were four managers out of a total of 18 targeted respondents. These were specialists in the role of knowledge on ontology in e-Government project management. The goals of this study included an exploration of the proposed objectives of the study as they are detailed in Table 2 below. Corresponding to the objectives in the table is a sample of a few selected grand questions that comprised the interview protocol. Table 2.

The section that follows out lines solutions derived from this study and recommendations thereto.

Solutions and Recommendations

EGTPM offered some substantial benefits when compared to traditional project planning and management techniques. The use of eGTPM helped to ensure that eGIF project was in line

Table 2. Chapter objectives and Interview protocol sample questions

Objectives	Questions
1. To help e-Government designers in developing countries understand what Ontology application and platforms are likely to work given their context. 2. To provide a reference source for both researchers and academics concerning current and emerging research trends in technology designs of e-Government applications. 3. To explore the role of Knowledge on Ontology Development in e-Government Project Management. 4. To advance knowledge that knowledge of Ontology Development in e-Government Project Management can institutionalize and diffuse into Developing Countries as well in their context.	What knowledgeshould be taken into account when considering e-Government initiatives? Why is knowledge on ontology development fundamental to e-Government project management? How should you deal with each stakeholder? Which are the essential parts of the designed e-Government projects? What is the relation between specific types of projects and particular Stakeholders? What will be the expected results of the project? What kind of knowledge is most Important? What are the fundamental aspects of domain ontology implementation? What different domain models do you use in developing ontology on e-Government project management applications? What are the fundamental types of e-Government projects? How do they relate to e-Government dimensions? Managers were asked to say everything they did and why they did it? E-Government project managers were asked what concepts they used?

with the public organization's business plan, that the project team was committed to a realistic plan in which they had some ownership, and that the roles and responsibilities of project team members were clearly defined and linked to activities and goals. Organization's final aim for the project was reflected on specific intermediate goals. EGTPM is currently being used in e-Government projects aimed at measuring the performance of development projects by the Zimbabwean government. The researcher intended to demonstrate how to convert an e-Government project into the eGTPM ontology and demonstrate the benefits that can be reached with it. Furthermore, a comparison of different metrics in order to measure the practical applicability of eGTPM was made. The study revealed that, an eGTPM method would also require some tools support, so that the knowledge base can be extended and populated; not to mention support for the actual use of the toolset in real projects.

The major benefit for public organizations derived from this study is to have a chance to re-use experiences, to be guided in the implementation, to join a community of people involved in e-Government projects, to discuss and share problems and solutions. This is envisaged to be a lesson for developing countries. Specific aims ofeGTPMderived from this study are:

- Improvement of the management performance of the public organization in terms of efficiency, transparency and quality as a result of thetransparent and configurable flow of information.
- Enhancement of the public reputation of the organization through well organized and technically functional internal management processes.
- Provision of a knowledge repository with reusable components.
- Standardization of the participating roles in e-government projects.
- Provision of visibility to e-government resources in terms of results and templates.

- Provision of visibility to the variety of projects and approaches on e-Government implemented in different areas and in different organizations.

The study recommends that knowledge management and its activities are in this context not considered as a separate task, but as an integral part of the organizational procedures of e-Government project design and implementation, and hence an integral part of e-Government project management. This research is intended to be the base of a long term project aiming at building a knowledge-based environment to help successful implementation of e-Government projects.

FUTURE RESEARCH DIRECTIONS

Future work includes:

- Better evaluation of the usefulness of the concepts contained in the ontology (by conducting further validation experiment).
- Investigating the possibility of designing manual procedures (process) to populate the ontology.
- Population of the ontology real data.
- Investigating the possibility of creating (semi-)automated tools to assist in populating the ontology from existing e-government projects.
- It could be the base of studies to answer questions as: what knowledge should be taken into account when considering e-government initiatives? Which are the essential partsof the designed e-Government projects? How should we deal with each stakeholder? What is the relation between specific types of projects and particular stakeholders? What will be the expected results of the project? What kind of knowledge is most important?

CONCLUSION

This study provides a reference ontology framework for public sector decision makers and e-government practitioners during knowledge sharing and development in a government transformation project. This work adopts an ontological approach to analyze knowledge management processing in e-government projects. This defined ontology would be useful as a framework to guide future research trying to improve e-government project management using knowledge engineering techniques. Our ontology was based both on expert experience and a study of the relevant literature. Egtpm ontology is created in order to support stakeholders in keeping in contact, sharing resources, approaches, solutions and problems occurring in the implementation of e-government projects. The study concludes that knowledge management and its activities are in this context not considered as a separate task, but as an integral part of the organizational procedures of e-government project design and implementation, and hence an integral part of e-government project management. This research is intended to be the based on a long term project aiming at building a knowledge-based environment to help successful implementation of e-government projects.

REFERENCES

Adelakun, O. M. (2002). Stakeholder process approach to information systems evaluation. In *Proceedings of the Eighth Americas Conference on Information Systems*. IEEE.

Akman, I., Yazici, A., Mishra, A., & Arifoglu, A. (2005). E-government: A global view and an empirical evaluation of some attributes of citizens. *Government Information Quarterly*, 22(2), 239–257. doi:10.1016/j.giq.2004.12.001

Al-Kibisi, G., de Boer, K., Mourshed, M., & Rea, N. (2001). Putting citizens on-line, not inline. *The McKinsey Quarterly*, (2): 64.

Andersen, E. S., Grude, K. V., & Hague, T. (2004). *Goal directed project management*. Kogan Page.

Bellamy, C., & Taylor, J. A. (1998). *Governing in the information age*. Buckingham, UK: Open University Press.

Chan, C. M. L., Shan-Ling, P., & Tan, C. W. (2003). Managing stakeholder relationships in an e-government project. In *Proceedings of Ninth Americas Conference on Information Systems*. Academic Press.

Deridder, D. (2002). A concept-oriented approach to support software maintenance and reuse activities. In *Proceedings of 5th Joint Conference on Knowledge-Based Software Engineering*. IEEE.

Dias, M. G. B., Anquetil, N., & Marcal de Oliveira, K. (2003). Organizing the knowledge used in software maintenance. *Journal of Universal Computer Science*, 9(7), 641–658.

Fensel, D. (2004). *Ontologies: A silver bullet for knowledge management and electronic commerce*. Berlin: Springer.

Finger, M., & Pécoud, G. (2003). From e-government to e-governance? Towards a model of e-governance. *Electronic. Journal of E-Government*, 1(1), 1–10.

Gómez-Pérez, A. (1995). Some ideas and examples to evaluate ontologies. In *Proceedings of 11th Conference on Artificial Intelligence for Applications*, (pp. 299-305). AI.

Gottschalk, P. (2007). Sharing knowledge in law firms. *International Journal of Innovation and Learning*, 4(3), 255–273. doi:10.1504/IJIL.2007.012381

Grant, T. S., Wix, T. S., Whitehead, C. J., & Blair, J. D. (1991). Strategies for assessing and managing organisational stakeholders. *The Academy of Management Executive*, 61–75.

Gruber, T. R. (1995). Toward principles for the design of ontologies used for knowledge sharing. *International Journal of Human-Computer Studies*, *43*(5/6), 907–928. doi:10.1006/ijhc.1995.1081

Heeks, R. (1999). *Re-inventing government in the information age: International practice in IT enabled public sector reform*. London: Routledge. doi:10.4324/9780203204962

Hult, G. T. (2003). An integration of thoughts on knowledge management. *Decision Sciences*, *34*, 189–195. doi:10.1111/1540-5915.02264

Johannessen, J.-A., Olaisen, J., & Olsen, B. (2002). Aspects of a systemic philosophy of knowledge: From social facts to data, information and knowledge. *Kybernetes*, *31*(7/8), 1099–1120. doi:10.1108/03684920210436363

Jorgensen, D. J., & Cable, S. (2002). Facing the challenges of e-government: A case study of the city of Corpus Christi, Texas. *S.A.M. Advanced Management Journal*, *67*(3), 15.

Kayed, A., & Colomb, R. (2000). Extracting ontological concepts for tendering conceptual structures. *Eng.*, *40*(1), 71–398.

Kayed, A., & Colomb, R. (2005). Using BWW model to evaluate building ontologies in CGs formalism. *Information Systems*, *30*(5), 379–398. doi:10.1016/j.is.2004.03.002

Kim, H. (1999). *Representing and reasoning about quality using enterprise models*. (PhD thesis). Dept. of Mechanical and Industrial Engineering, University of Toronto, Toronto, Canada.

Kim, V. A., & Henriksen, H. Z. (2006). E-government maturity models: Extension of the Layne and Lee model. *Government Information Quarterly*, *23*(2), 232–245.

Kitchenham, B. A., Travassos, G. H., Mayrhauser, A., Niessink, F., Schneidewind, N. F., & Singer, J. et al. (1999). Towards an ontology of software maintenance. *Journal of Software Maintenance: Research and Practice*, *11*(6), 365–389. doi:10.1002/(SICI)1096-908X(199911/12)11:6<365::AID-SMR200>3.0.CO;2-W

Layne, K., & Lee, J. (2001). Developing fully functional e- government: A four stage lmodel. *Government Information Quarterly*, *18*(2), 122–136. doi:10.1016/S0740-624X(01)00066-1

Liao, L., Qu, Y., & Leung, H. K. N. (2005). *A software process ontology and its application*. Paper presented at the ISWC2005 Workshop on Semantic Web Enabled Software Engineering. New York, NY.

Lin, H. K., Harding, J. A., & Shahbaz, M. (2004). Manufacturing system engineering ontology for semantic interoperability across extended project teams. *International Journal of Production Research*, *42*(24), 5099–5118. doi:10.1080/00207540412331281999

Nour, P., Holz, H., & Maurer, F. (2000). *Ontology-based retrieval of software process experiences*. Paper presented at the ICSE Workshop on Software Engineering over the Internet. New York, NY.

OECD. (2003). *The e-government imperative*. Paris: OECD.

Office of Government Commerce. (2005). *Managing successful projects with PRINCE2: The PRINCE2 manual*. Stationery Office Books.

Pardo, T. A., & Scholl, H. J. (2002). Walking atop the cliffs: Avoiding failure and avoiding risk in large scale e-government projects. In *Proceedings of Hawai'i International Conference on System Sciences*. IEEE.

Perrott, B. E. (1996). Managing strategic issues in the public service. *Long Range Planning, 29*(3), 337–345. doi:10.1016/0024-6301(96)00030-1

Project Management Institute. (2008). *A guide to the project management body of knowledge (PMBOK Guide)* (4th ed.). PMI.

Ramal, M. F., Meneses, R., & Anquetil, N. A. (2002). Disturbing result on the knowledge used during software maintenance. In *Proceedings of Working Conference on Reverse Engineering*, (pp. 277-287). Richmond, VA: IEEE.

Rowe, J. (2005). Process metaphor and knowledge management. *Kybernetes, 34*(6), 770–783. doi:10.1108/03684920510595481

Ruiz, F., Vizcaíno, A., Piattini, M., & García, F. (2004). An ontology for the management of software maintenance projects. *International Journal of Software Engineering and Knowledge Engineering, 14*(3), 323–349. doi:10.1142/S0218194004001646

Rumbaugh, J., Balha, M., & Premelani, W. (1991). *Object oriented modeling and design*. Upper Saddle River, NJ: Prentice Hall.

Sarantis, D., & Askounis, D. (2009). Electronic criminal record in Greece: Project management approach and lessons learned in public administration. *Transylvanian Review of Administrative Sciences, 25* (E), 132-146.

Sarantis, D., & Askounis, D. (2010). Electronic government interoperability framework in Greece: Project management approach and lessons learned in public administration. *Journal of US-China Public Administration, 7*(3).

Scholl, H. J. (2001). Applying stakeholder theory to e-government. In *Towards the e-society: e-commerce, e-business and e-government*. Boston: Kluwer Academic Publishers.

Scott, M., Golden, W., & Hughes, M. (2004). Implementation strategies for e-government: A stakeholder analysis approach. In *Proceedings of the 12th European Conference on Information Systems*. Turku, Finland: IEEE.

Shang, S. S. C., & Lin, S. F. (2009). Understanding the effectiveness of capability maturity model integration by examining the knowledge management of software development processes. *Total Quality Management & Business Excellence, 20*(5), 509–521. doi:10.1080/14783360902863671

Sharon, D. (2008). *Introduction to digital government research in public policy and management, digital. government*. Academic Press.

Tennert, J. R., & Schroeder, A. D. (1991). *Stakeholder analysis. American Society for Public Administration. Center of Democracy and Technology. (2002). The e-government handbook for developing countries*. Author.

Uschold, M., & Grunninger, M. (1996). Ontologies: Principles, methods and application. *The Knowledge Engineering Review, 11*(2). doi:10.1017/S0269888900007797

Wang, S., & Ariguzo, G. (2004). Knowledge management through the development of information schema. *Information & Management, 41*, 445–456. doi:10.1016/S0378-7206(03)00083-1

Yim, N.-H., Kim, S.-H., Kim, H.-W., & Kwahk, K.-Y. (2004). Knowledge based decision making on higher level strategic concerns: System dynamics approach. *Expert Systems with Applications, 27*, 143–158. doi:10.1016/j.eswa.2003.12.019

Zhao, G., Gao, Y., & Meersman, R. (2004). An ontology-based approach to business modeling. In *Proceedings of the International Conference of Knowledge Engineering and Decision Support*. IEEE.

ADDITIONAL READING

Brazier, F., Jonker, C., & Treur, J. (1998). Principles of Compositional Multi-agent System Development. In J. Cuena (ed.), *Proceedings of the 15th IFIP World Computer Congress, WCC'98, Conference on Information Technology and Knowledge Systems*, IT&KNOWS'98, 347-360.

Floridi, L. (Ed.). (2003). *Blackwell Guide to the Philosophy of Computing and Information. Preprint version of chapter Ontology* (pp. 155–166). Oxford: Blackwell. doi:10.1111/b.9780631229193.2003.00013.x

Girardi, R., & Faria, C. (2004). An ontology-based technique for the specification of domain and user models in multi-agent domain. *CLEI Electron. J.* 7(1).

Greenspan, S., Mylopoulos, J., & Bordiga, A. (1994). On formal requirements modeling languages: RML revisited. *Sixth international conference on software engineering (ICSE-6)*, ACM.

Gruber, T. (2008). Ontology, The Encyclopedia of Database Systems.Ling Liu and M. Tamer Özsu (Eds.), Springer-Verlag.

Lamsweerde, A. (2000). Requirements engineering in the year 00: a research perspective. *Proceedings, 22nd International Conference on Software Engineering (ICSE'00)*, Limerick, Ireland, 5-9th June, 2000, 5-19. IEEE Computer Society Press.

Liao, L., Qu, Y., & Leung, H. (2005). *A software process ontology and its application.* In ISWC2005 Workshop on Semantic Web Enabled Software Engineering.

Nuseibeh, B., & Easterbrook, S. (2000). Requirements Engineering: A Roadmap. *In Finkelstein A. (Ed.), The Future of Software Engineering, (Companion volume to the proceedings of the 22 nd International Conference on Software Engineering, ICSE'00).* IEEE Computer Society Press.

Randell, B., & Naur, P. (1968). *Software Engineering.* Report on a conference sponsored by the NATO Science Committee, Garmisch, Germany, 7th to 11th Oct.

Samhan, A. (2008). *Master Thesis: Towards Ontology for Software Product Quality Attributes.* Middle East University for Graduate Studies, Amman Jordan.

Scacchi W. Jensen C, Noll J., &Elliott M. (2006). Multi-Modal Modeling, Analysis and Validation of Open Source Software Requirements Processes, *Internatioanl Journal of Information Technology and Web Engineering, 3(1).*

Smith, B., & Welty, C. (2003). Ontology: Towards a New Synthesis. [ACM.]. *FOIS, 01*(October), 17–19.

Sommerville, I. (2007). Software Engineering. Pearson Addison Wesely, Seventh Ed., ISBN: 020139815, 2007.

Zhao, G., Gao, Y., & Meersman, R. (2004). An Ontology-based Approach to Business Modeling. *In Proceedings of the International Conference of Knowledge Engineering and Decision Support.*

Zhiyuan, F. (2002). E-Government in Digital Era: Concept, Practice, and Development, *International Journal of The Computer. The Internet and Management, 10*(2), 1–22.

KEY TERMS AND DEFINITIONS

E-Government: The practice of putting government information and data on the Web, so that users access it on line.

Knowledge: Divergent, or opposing roles.

Ontology Development: Means the assimilation of organisational practices that have been adopted from elsewhere.

Ontology Implementation: A general lack of access to the internet.

Ontology Validation: Lack of knowledge of information about the other party by the other party.

Project Management: When organisational practices have attained a full buy-in within all organisational structures and functions, it is referred to have been institutionalized.

Sub-Ontology: Social and economic improvement of standards of living.

Chapter 5
Design Principles for Public Sector Information and Communication Technologies

Liam Church
Escher Group Ltd., USA

Maria Moloney
Escher Group Holdings Plc., Ireland

ABSTRACT

This chapter addresses the design challenge of providing Information and Communication Technology(ies) ICT(s) systems for public e-Service provision. Public sector services differ qualitatively from private sector services in that they aim to provide not just value for money but also public value. Generally speaking, public value is created when public organizations successfully meet the needs of citizens. Therefore, public sector ICTs have unique requirements that are not all thoroughly supported by traditional ICTs and their respective design theories. This chapter presents a design theory to guide developers of public sector ICTs on how to produce systems that provide public e-Services through secure and inclusive information systems. These systems will, in turn, create public value by tackling digital inequality and easing citizens' online privacy concerns. The design theory was created while designing and deploying a digital postal system. By abstracting from the experience of building the system, a design theory for ICTs providing public e-Services was formulated. This new design theory is an important theoretical contribution because it provides guidance to developers and sets an agenda for IS research into public sector information systems design. It achieves this by articulating theory-based principles outlining how public value can be created through the development of appropriate ICTs. The design principles outlined by the theory are also subject to empirical, as well as practical, validation.

DOI: 10.4018/978-1-4666-4900-2.ch005

INTRODUCTION

Twenty first century society is fast becoming digital. A major challenge now facing governments is to create public value not only for traditional society but also for digital society. A common method for governments to create public value is to provide *inclusive* public services. If we consider existing public services like the public education system, the public transport system, and the public waste disposal system, all of these are *inclusive* in that they are available to all members of society. It should follow then that providing inclusive public e-Services will also create public value. For the purposes of this research, the concept of public e-Service is defined as:

Deeds, efforts or performances whose delivery is mediated by information technology, including the Web, information kiosks and mobile devices, and are performed for the benefit of the public or its institutions. Such public e-Services include both customer support and service, and service delivery.

The term e-Inclusion is defined by the European Union (2010) as both inclusive ICT and the use of ICT to achieve wider inclusion objectives. It focuses on participation of all individuals and communities in all aspects of the information society. Europe's e-Inclusion policy, therefore, aims at reducing gaps in ICT usage and promoting the use of ICT to overcome exclusion, and thus improve economic performance, employment opportunities, quality of life, social participation and cohesion.

The new digital age, while hugely beneficial to society, also poses many challenges. Firstly, governments have not yet put in place adequate structures to ensure e-Inclusion in the digital world. This has contributed to the development of a phenomenon called the *digital divide,* which is evident even in developed societies like Europe and the US (Hsieh, Rai, & Keil, 2008). Secondly,

literature shows that a high level of concern has grown among members of society regarding the protection of their personal information when interacting in digital society (Whitley, 2009).

In light of these challenges, this chapter presents a design theory to guide governments when designing ICT systems for public e-Service provision. It is argued that in so doing, digital inequality can be more easily tackled and privacy concerns of individuals can be alleviated. We contend that our design theory is a contribution to the IS literature because it represents an important class of design situations that have not yet been adequately served by existing systems and their associated design theories. Additionally, the design theory contributes to the e-Government literature by providing guidance to practitioners on how to design and develop public e-Services ICTs while ensuring the value orientations of the public sector, namely lawfulness, impartiality, and incorruptibility (Van Der Wal, De Graaf and Lasthuizen 2008), are not compromised. Moreover, by providing these guidelines, it is hoped that this research contributes towards addressing digital inequality and reducing information privacy concerns of citizens.

The next section discusses the theoretical conceptualisation of the design theory. The design theory is then presented as a set of principles that offer guidance to designers of public e-Service systems. Finally, conclusions and an agenda for future research are outlined.

THEORETICAL CONCEPTUALIZATION OF THE PUBLIC E-SERVICE (PES) ICT DESIGN THEORY

Two decades ago, New Public Management (NPM) was proposed for the first time by Hood (1991) as an alternative to what had often become, by that time, costly and bureaucratic public services. NPM sought higher levels of efficiency in the use of resources and of effectiveness in achieving organisational objectives (O'Flynn 2007). It was believed that implementing higher levels of competition in providing public services would lead to greater efficiency and competition, which would in turn benefit the citizen (Aman, 2005; Cordella & Willcocks, 2010). Since that time, NPM has been one of the main drivers of reform within the public sector in the hope of improving upon the existing model of public administration (Spano, 2009). However, in recent times, some weaknesses of the NPM approach have begun to emerge. It was found that very often the adoption of these competitive regimes did not bring about true competition and a market-style approach to management often failed to increase efficiency (O'Flynn 2007). Additionally, this approach was seen to be responsible for a reduction in accountability and emphasised cost efficiency and cost reduction rather than paying attention to public value creation (Spano 2009). However, regardless of the effects of NPM on public service provision, it can be argued that it paved the way for a new form of thinking, or a new "post-competitive" paradigm which places less of an emphasis on results and efficiency and more on the achievement of a broader political goal of public value creation (O'Flynn, 2007).

This new paradigm, first articulated by Moore (1995; 2003), represents a way of thinking which is both post-bureaucratic and post-competitive. It shifts the focus of public service benefit towards the creation of value for society as opposed to the market versus government approach which dominated NPM thinking. Public value has been described as a multi-dimensional construct created not just through 'outcomes' but also through processes which may generate trust or fairness between the citizenry and the government (Alford & O'Flynn, 2008). It has also been defined as 'the value created by government through services, laws, regulation and other actions' (Kelly, Mulgan, & Muers, 2002, p. 4). Moore (1995) argues that the creation of public value is the central activity of public managers, just as the creation of private

value is at the core of private sector managers' action. Such a distinction is supported by Hefetz and Warner (2004) who argue that unlike their private sector counterparts, public managers do more than steer a market process; they balance technical and political concerns to secure public value.

Public value often comes in the form of public e-Services . Services of any kind, be it private or public services, have four characteristics; (1) intangibility, (2) inseparability, (3) heterogeneity, and (4) perishability (Lindgren & Jansson, 2013). Services are intangible in the sense that they are performances rather than objects. This makes them difficult to count, measure, test or verify most services in advance of sale/use to assure quality. The inseparability characteristic refers to the fact that production and consumption of many services cannot be separated from each other. This means that the quality of a service emerges only as the service is delivered, typically when the customer and the service provider interact. The heterogeneity characteristic refers to the fact that services often vary from one producer to another, from one customer to another, and over time. The perishibility characteristic refers to the fact that services cannot be stored, which means that demand is critical, i.e services must be available to the right customers at the right time, place, and for the right price (Grönroos, 2008). The quality of a service is ultimately judged by the customers, and different customers might have different perceptions of what constitutes a good service. Furthermore, it is not only the outcome of a service that is judged by the customer, but also its delivery (Lindgren & Jansson, 2013). Zeithaml et al. (1990) investigated potential causes of low service-quality and identified service-quality gaps that customers may perceive. These gaps concern situations where there is a divergence between customers' expectations and the service delivered. In order to ensure quality services and avoid discrepancies between what the customers expect and what the service delivers, Zeithaml et al. state that the supplier of a service must (1) research the customers' expectations, (2) specify the service according to these expectations, (3) ensure that employees follow these service specifications, and (4) communicate information about the service to the customers that sets realistic expectations.

It follows from the definition provided in the introduction that an electronically mediated service can be perceived of as actions mediated through the use of information technology. In the e-Service context, the e- typically refers to Internet-mediated technology, such as an Internet webpage. When viewing an e-Service as being a technological system and as being connected to other technologies, two additional sets of actors and users become relevant, the actors that design and supply the technology and the users of the e-Services. Two critical issues that currently exists in digital society and that are relevant to these actors (designers and users of e-Service systems), and that would provide significant public value by improving the quality of public e-Services if they were resolved is, firstly, the matter of digital inequality, and secondly the issue of citizenry concern for the protection of their personal information in digital form. Both the private and public sectors have devoted tremendous resources to addressing both of these issues but the results, to date, remain inconclusive (Federal Trade Commission, 2010; Hsieh, Rai, & Keil, 2008). Digital inequality continues to prevent socio-economically disadvantaged citizens from exploring digital opportunities (Hsieh, Rai, & Keil, 2008; Sims, 2011). Literature on digital inequality has shown that, while technology access and creating favourable conditions for initial technology use do not resolve the issue of digital inequality, they are the first step in creating an environment for *continued intention to use ICT* (Davis, 1993; Hsieh, Rai, & Keil, 2008).

The second critical issue regarding the concern for informational privacy experienced by users of ICTs is a complex and multi-dimensional problem. A constant challenge for privacy professionals is that the very definition of privacy is constantly being examined and redefined. One interesting development in IS privacy research, is that there is a growing recognition that an individual's understanding of what constitutes the modern concept of privacy includes having *control* over their personal data (Whitley, 2009). In addition, there is growing recognition among governments worldwide that a secure Internet that respects privacy will promote sustainable innovation (Federal Trade Commission, 2010; The White House, 2010). It is argued, here, that in order to truly develop e-Inclusive systems the issue of data protection in ICTs that provide public e-Services is a central one.

DERIVING THE PUBLIC SECTOR DESIGN PRINCIPLES: A CASE STUDY

Traditionally, the objectives and core values of the public sector have differed considerably from the profit-driven values of the private sector (Van Der Wal, De Graaf, & Lasthuizen, 2008) Consequently, when designing public sector ICTs developers must adhere to a diverse set of requirements than those used for private sector ICTs. They must take into account values such as equality, impartiality, communal good and public service, to produce effective and efficient systems which are accessible and accepted by citizens across all socio-economic groups. This is a considerable challenge and a design theory for public sector ICT could help direct designers and developers when developing such complex applications in an ever changing digital environment.

Having conducted an extensive literature review on design science and design theory (Gregor & Jones, 2007; Hevner, March, & Park, 2004; Walls, Widmeyer, & Sawy, 1992; Markus, Majchrzak, & Gasser, 2002; Butler, Feller, Pope, Emerson, & Murphy, 2008; Iversen, Mathiassen,

& Nielsen, 2004; Pries-Heje & Baskerville, 2008; Shin, 2006; Carlsson, 2010; Cross, 2001), electronic postal systems (Tauber, 2010; Teinowitz, 2011; Commission for Communications Regulation, 2008; Aspray, Bromley, Campbell-Kelly, P.E., & Williams, 1990; De Reuck & Joseph, 1999; Del Gallo, 2009; Dobbins, 2007; Mägli, Jaag, Koller, & Trinkner, 2010; Lesur, 2007) and designing IS artefacts for the provision of e-Government (Shin, 2006; Meneklis & Douligeris, 2010; Esteves & Joseph, 2008; Fedorowicz & Dias, 2010; Grant & Chau, 2005) no such set of guidelines or public e-Service design theory exists. Some interesting and relevant articles were found, Fedorowicz and Dias (2010) provide an overview of design science research in digital government literature over a period of ten years from 2000-2010. Meneklis and Douligeris (2010) had a similar objective to the current research and proposed a set of guidelines for the analysis and design of e-Government information systems. However, the guidelines that are formulated are very general and not specific to the public sector. The e-Government framework outlined by (Grant and Chau (2005) is comprehensive but is too wide in scope, encompassing all sections of e-Government. The aim of the current research is more specific and concentrates on the provision of public e-Services .

None of the research examined make any mention of perpetuating the values underpinning public services provision or of creating public value for citizens through the development of ICTs for public e-Services . Esteves et al. (2008) emphasizes the importance of public value creation in e-Government projects, but it does not mention the design of ICTs. This gap in the public administration and e-Government literature was indentified during the development of a digital postal system entitled Transmission Exchange (TrEx). During the development lifecycle of this product, the researcher identified the need for a design theory for ICTs providing public e-Services .

Research Methodology

It was concluded during the RiposteTrEx project that in order to achieve the goals of the project, namely, alleviate (1) digital inequality, and (2) online privacy concern, the following needs to be realized:

1. Access to the digital world should be freely available to all members of society,
2. Control of personal information should be, at least in part, given to the producer of that personal information, the citizen.

The RiposteTrEx system was to provide a more comprehensive approach to secure transfer of personal information and to create public value through sustaining posts' Universal Services Obligations (USO) in digital form for the benefit of all citizens. It aimed to provide every citizen of the country with a digital postal address. The digital address could be accessed from a citizen's home via their computer or from their local post office via access points installed on site.

As the project developed, it became clear that there was a need for a general architecture which allowed citizens to interact with digital society either privately and securely or openly according to situational privacy needs. Guidelines for developing such an architecture were also needed. In light of this, the action research methodology was adopted for the project.

According to Walls et al. (1992) an appropriate research methodology for design science is action research and diverse design science studies have employed this methodology (Markus, Majchrzak, & Gasser, 2002; Iversen, Mathiassen, & Nielsen, 2004). Generally, the action research process starts with requirements derived from kernel theories and hypothesized design and development principles that meet these requirements (Moore, 1995). The hypothesized principles are then used as the basis for specifying system features. Once developed and deployed, the use and impacts of the system can be observed. If the results are not as expected, new hypothesized principles are generated, a system version instantiating the new principles is developed, deployed, and evaluated, and the cycle is repeated. The action research process for the TrEx project started with devising a provisional set of product requirements derived from the literature on public administration, public value creation and the postal service, combined with the knowledge gathered through the retrospective sense-making exercise conducted at the beginning of the project. This provisional set of requirements was then used as the basis for specifying system features. Once these product requirements were finalized, the first prototype of the product was developed. Then over a period of twelve months, the development team, the product testers and the IS researchers worked together to define, refine, develop and deploy prototypes which tested various features of the system and observed how users responded to the features and iterated.

As a result of the lack of available guidelines within the literature regarding how to design public ICTs which both enable public value creation and embed the core public values of lawfulness, impartiality and incorruptibility into their design, the project members were obliged to independently conceptualise (1) the requirements of the product design process (2) the features of the system to adequately support the provision of public e-Services, and (3) the process of developing the system according to the values orientation of the public sector. The complexity of the project demanded a variety of research methodologies be employed.

During the early stages of the project, a series of twenty one interviews were conducted to ascertain the views of the public regarding such a system, what e-Services such a system should provide, and how best to provide them. An email was sent to 50 randomly selected employees from the University which took part in this case study. This email requested volunteers to take part in semi-structured interviews for an ongoing collaboration project between academia and industry. Twenty one individuals volunteered for the interviews. Each participant was asked a set of questions concerning the benefits and drawbacks of the Internet, their main activities on the Internet and their attitudes to online privacy when interacting online with government, private companies and public-private partnerships. Finally, they were asked to give possible solutions to the challenge of protecting citizens' online privacy while still providing personal information to the government for the benefit of the public in general. Tables 1-4 show the key results.

From the interviews, it was found that these individuals who all proclaimed to be either concerned about or aware of the challenge of safeguarding their online privacy, all agreed that the benefits they have experienced from using the Internet have outweighed the costs. Thus, even though they have online privacy concerns their experiences on the Internet have been positive. Additionally, it was found from the interviews that private companies were perceived as a greater threat to these individuals' online privacy than government or public-private partnerships. Just two people from the twenty that were interviewed believed that private companies had more of an incentive to protect personal data than the

Table 1. Question 1

Question 1	Yes	No
Do the benefits of the Internet outweigh the costs?	100%	0%

Table 2. Question 2

	Gov.	Public-Private Partnership	Private Companies
Who do you trust more with your personal information?	40%	50%	10%

Table 3. Questions 3-5

Question 3	Yes	No
It has often been said that when you submit your data online, it gets used for other purposes than the ones you are told about. Do you believe this to be true: In general		
For government	20%	80%
For public-private partnership	15%	85%
For private company	90%	10%
Question 4	**Yes**	**No**
Even though it is more or less common knowledge that there is risk to your information once you submit it online, do you feel that you still retain sufficient control over your personal information online?	60%	40%
Question 5	**Yes**	**No**
Who should have control over your data online? Yourself	100%	0%

Table 4. Question 6

Question 6	Gov.	Public-Private Partnership	Private Companies
If it is not possible to control your own data, who would be your second choice?	10%	85%	5%

other two options. Question three shows that even though the interviewees were sceptical by nature of their personal information being correctly used online, they were more willing to believe that government and public-private partnerships had more of a responsibility to safeguard their personal information. These findings are supported by several peer-reviewed studies which also found that a stronger threat to privacy, in the past, has come from the private sector rather than from the public sector (Laudon, 1997; Dinev, Hart, & Mullen, 2008; Varian, 1996). This trend has been referred to as the privacy paradox (Etzioni, 1999). It was also found that the private sector, rather

than the public sector, has been attributed with making consumers, as distinct from citizens, vulnerable (Dinev, Hart, & Mullen, 2008; Marx, 2003; Noam, 1997). The events of September 11th 2001 appear to have shifted the concern back onto the public sector. However, a recent report from the European Commission found evidence that supported the argument that the public sector is using a variety of approaches to effectively cooperate with data controllers to increase the deployment of privacy enhancing technologies (PETs). This support can range from the endorsement of certain technologies by public bodies to active support of the development of PETS, official certification and pioneering deployment by public bodies. The case studies in the report showed that, with the right incentives, data controllers work effectively together with public bodies to spread PETs deployment (London Economics, 2010). Additionally, government initiatives to improve national security have a direct influence on citizens' Internet usage with regard to imparting their personal information. The relationship between a citizen's perceived need for government surveillance and their willingness to disclose personal information suggests that users perceive government security initiatives as important and, arguably, tolerable only if government security-related initiatives are not perceived as intrusive. Public support for government security initiatives declines only when these initiatives are perceived to undermine government efforts to increase protection for the public (Dinev, Hart, & Mullen, 2008).

Interestingly, from the interviews, it was found that when the users interacted with public-private partnerships, they felt more in control of their data than when they interacted with either government or private enterprise. This would suggest that using a public-private partnership to protect private information online would help to reduce online users' privacy concerns. With the completion of the interviews, the design of the system started in earnest.

According to Walls et al. (1992) an appropriate research methodology for design science is action research and diverse design science studies have employed this methodology (Markus, Majchrzak, & Gasser, 2002; Iversen, Mathiassen, & Nielsen, 2004). Generally, the action research process starts with requirements derived from kernel theories and hypothesized design and development principles that meet these requirements (Markus, Majchrzak, & Gasser, 2002). The hypothesized principles are then used as the basis for specifying system features. Once developed and deployed, the system is observed. If the results are not as expected, new hypothesized principles are generated, a system version instantiating the new principles is developed, deployed, and evaluated, and the cycle is repeated. The action research process for the Riposte TrEx project started with devising a provisional set of product requirements derived from the literature on public administration, public value creation and the postal service. This provisional set of requirements was then used as the basis for specifying system features. Once these product requirements were finalized, the first prototype of the system was developed. Then over a period of twelve months, the development team, the product testers and the IS researchers worked together to define, refine, develop and deploy prototypes which tested various features of the system and observed how users responded to the features and iterated.

As a result of the dearth of literature available to guide the development of such a system, the following needed to be independently conceptualised: (1) the requirements of the product design process (2) the features of the system that adequately support the provision of public e-Services and (3) the process of developing the system according to the values orientation of the public sector. Therefore, during the early stages of the project and in addition to action research, a series of twenty one interviews were conducted to ascertain the views of the public regarding such a system, what e-Services such a system should provide, and how best to provide them. Additionally, once the proof of concept stage was complete, eight focus groups, each with eight members of the public, across various sections of society were also carried out. All groups were shown the product and asked to provide feedback, by way of group discussion, about their impressions of the product. The data gathered by these qualitative methods were reviewed by IS researchers and useful suggestions and insights were used to improve and refine the set of design principles which are outlined in the next section.

DESIGN PRINCIPLES FOR PUBLIC SECTOR ICTS

This section describes the Public e-Service ICT (PeSICT) design theory as a set of four main design and development principles. The main aim of this design theory is for the production of inclusive ICTs to provide public e-Services . Governments around the world are beginning to recognise that digital inclusion is an increasingly important social issue (Infoxchange Australia, 2011; European Commission, 2010a). The UK government in their action plan for achieving greater digital inclusion argues that digital exclusion is an increasingly urgent social problem because digital technologies pervade every aspect of modern society (Dept. for Communities and Local Government, 2008). Additionally, 17 million citizens in the UK still do not use computers and the research showed that there was a strong correlation between digital exclusion and social exclusion.

The design principles are categorized into *social media system* principles and *software system* principles. A social media system in this context refers to a computer system which facilitates social interaction in digital form. Examples of a social media system would be a social networking website like Facebook or even a smart phone. These systems provide functionality which allows users to interact in an informal manner. A software system refers to any system that consists of several separate computer programs and associated configuration files and documentation, that operate together (Sommerville, 2007). The term is often used in relation to large and complex software, as it focuses on the major components of that software and their interactions.

In turn, both of these principles, social media system principles and software system principles, are supported by specific public sector principles. Figure 1 highlights these public sector principles and their interdependencies.

Public Social Media System Principle 1: Surrendering of Control from the Public Service Provider (SP) to the Service Consumer

The fundamental motivation behind the design and development of Riposte TrEx was to give control of one's personal information back to the individual, and thus help reduce online privacy concerns. In order to achieve this central principle, four sub-principles need to be satisfied.

Secure and Private Data Storage Units (SPDSU)

Each user of the Riposte TrEx system is allocated a secure and private data storage unit (SPDSU) for storing their personal information. When providing public e-Services, it is essential to ensure all private information that passes through the system is securely transferred and stored. This is particularly relevant for public e-Services provision as the data processed and stored within the system can often be regarded as extremely sensitive i.e. financial and health information, and if compromised has real potential for harm to the owner of the information. There are three levels of security that need to be implemented to ensure comprehensive, effective security, (1) access security, (2) communication security, (3) data security.

Figure 1. Requirements for e-inclusive public systems

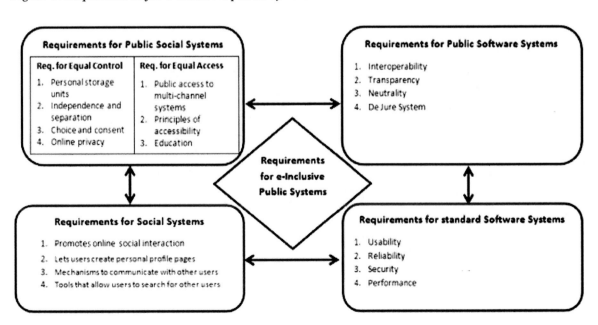

85

- Access security entails ensuring that access to the data storage units are secure. With Riposte TrEx, there is only one service that can access the SPDSUs and this is done at the application level of system. All users access the Riposte TrEx Interface which then accesses the SPDSUs via SSL. These units can be stored within the Riposte TrEx infrastructure or can be stored at other locations provided by other service providers (SPs). Access to the SPDSUs is always achieved through the Riposte TrEx Interface. Figure 1 shows this configuration.

- Communications security is achieved by ensuring all communications, between Riposte TrEx and (1) users, and (2) other SPs, are run through the Secure Sockets Layer (SSL) of the system.

- Data security is achieved by ensuring compliance with industry standards such as the PCI Data Security Standard (PCI DSS). This standard provides an actionable framework for developing a robust

payment card data security process. This includes prevention, detection and appropriate reaction to security incidents. For further details on this compliance process see (PCI Security Standards Council, 2010). The principles of data minimisation and minimal retention should also be applied to any personal data stored within the system. For a detailed account of these principles please see (Goold, 2009).

Once a SPDSU has been set up for a citizen within the system, there is no need for additional SPDSUs to be set up, for that user, by any other public sector that joins the network at a later stage. The same SPDSU, unless otherwise specified by the individual, can serve as a storage unit for all information, pertaining to that user, transferred and stored within the system. There is an option to compartmentalise the data within SPDSU according to the wishes of the individual and to provide greater security and privacy. Figure 2 shows the security architecture for Riposte TrEx.

Figure 2. Security architecture for Riposte TrEx

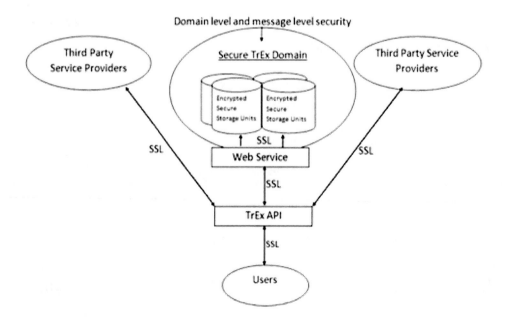

Independence and Separation

The system must be transactional and message-based in nature in order to ensure each user's interactions are separate and independent of each other. In this way, every user of the system has an historical record of their actions and transactions, unlike when users visit websites. The website owners can track the movements and transactions of the user but the user has no equally comprehensive record of their own movements or transactions. By ensuring the system is message-based and transactional, equal records of any actions taken are available to both parties.

Choice and Consent to Citizens Regarding rheir Personal Information

Control of citizens' personal information should be in the hands of the owner of that information, i.e. the citizen to which the information pertains. Citizens should be able to access, process, store and transfer their personal information irrespectively of the SP. Part of this requires that citizens be able to:

- Choose their preferred location for storing their private data storage unit. Various other (private) SPs should be allowed to compete for storing these units in their systems, provided they meet all the requirements for ensuring the appropriate transfer and storage of personal information, this would include receiving consent from the citizen to use their personal information for any reason;
- To retain copies of all their transactions carried out through the system. In this way, citizens, can extract meaningful information regarding their online activities such as monthly financial expenditure.
- Such public e-Service systems should allow for other SPs to inter-operate with the system. It is hoped that as the system grows, agreements can be devised between

governments and third party SPs so that private sector SPs offering appropriate storage facilities and extra value-added services can partner with governments to extend the service offering to citizens. Provided these SPs follow the choice and consent guidelines outlined above.

Informational Privacy Assurance

Akin to the privacy of correspondence in the paper world, users of a public e-Service (PeS) system may require that the content of messages are not altered and are solely disclosed to the recipient. Citizens are entitled to this service to safeguard their democratic right to freedom of speech. Riposte TrEx supports an optional end-to-end encryption (E2EE), thus ensuring confidentiality between the sender and the recipient so that no third party can access the message content.

Protection should be assured for (1) personal data and (2) unique national identifiers, to ensure adequate levels of anonymity for the user and his/her location. In de jure systems the handling of sensitive data is regulated by national laws. This includes disclosing personal data through lookup services within the system as well as the disclosure of personal data to third parties during the course of data transfer and storage (Tauber, 2010). It is of primary importance that PeS systems are not open to security attacks. In the digital world of private email, spammers exploit search engines and use Trojan horse programs for digital identity theft or to collect email addresses and send illicit advertising mail (SPAM) to users of the system. This must be prevented in the context of PeS systems through legal, technical and organizational provisions (Tauber, 2010).

Public Social Media System Principle 2: Ensuring Accessibility to the PeS System

The concept of accessibility within this research can be broken down into three categories:

Public Access to Multi-Channel Systems

In previous times, access to public services like library services, public telephones and public business directories (delivered to homes) was equally available to all members of a community. Increasingly, as we move into the digital world, paying for such services is becoming commonplace. Devices for reading ebooks such as iphones, androids and kindles are expensive. Public telephones are being phased out and replaced by personal mobile phones, and search engines are now the common tool for finding appropriate business services. All of these require a certain amount of financial strength through possessing equipment like computers, mobile phones or other electronic devices. Digital exclusion is routinely reinforced as, in order to continue to enjoy all the benefits of digital society, these devices need to be frequently updated (DiMaggio & Hargittai, 2001).

With the system that Riposte TrEx provides, every citizen will be provided with an official digital address, which will be validated by using a pin number posted to the citizen's address. Once set up on the system, for a small fee, all citizens will be able to securely email, make phone calls or pay bills either at home or if they do not have adequate access at home, at their local post office on access kiosks that are regularly updated. It is hoped that eventually other public access kiosks will be available at public libraries or even local supermarkets. These public access kiosks will be made available in post offices primarily for citizens unable to afford or keep up with the cost of electronic devices.

Principles of Accessibility

The term *accessibility* is defined in this research as the degree to which a system is available to and usable by individuals with disabilities (Las-

kowski, Autry, Cugini, & Yen, 2004). A set of user interface design principles were formulated during the Riposte TrEx project, the following standards were used as guides for developing these principles (ISO, 1999; ISO, 2003). The principles were formulated to guide both developers and testers of Riposte TrEx when assessing the system for accessibility. Tests were routinely completed during the development process.

Education of Citizens

Citizens who have had no training in electronic devices can also avail of the public access points in post offices. Training courses on how to use the PeS system can be provided by post office clerks. It is planned that once Riposte TrEx is commercially viable, these access point will be rolled out in a four phase roll-out schedule. For more proficient users of technology, Riposte TrEx will also be available via mobile phones.

Public Social Media System Principle 3: Ensuring Standard Social Media System Requirements are Met

The term 'Social Networking Services' has been defined by the European Union as online services that combine the following features (O'Connell & Read, 2009)

- A platform that promotes online social interaction between two or more persons for the purposes of friendship, meeting other persons, or information exchange;
- Functionality that lets users create personal profile pages that contain information of their own choosing, such as the name or nickname of the user, photographs placed on the personal page by the user, other personal information about the user, and links to other personal pages on the service of

friends or associates of the user that may be accessed by other users or visitors to the service;

- Mechanisms to communicate with other users, such as a message board, electronic mail, or instant messenger; and
- Tools that allow users to search for other users according to the profile information they choose to make available to other users (O'Connell & Read, 2009).

Public Software System Principle 1: Ensuring the Public Value System is Upheld

Interoperability and Transparency

Service architectures, protocols and interfaces should be standardized to ensure interoperability, transferability and reusability with other systems. This facilitates the deployment of an integrated PeS system and allows new public departments wishing to provide public e-Services to easily integrate into the system. By using standards in system design, the private and public sector can be more easily encouraged to collaborate on development efforts so as to provide increased and improved services for citizens. It is hoped that this will lead to an increased level of system up-take by citizens. Open standards also ensure transparency and freedom of choice. This can be beneficial when considering cross-border interoperability. The ETSI Registered E-mail Standard (REM) defines a common format for developing certified electronic mailing systems to ensure system interoperability with standardized XML, CMS or PDF files (ESTI, 2009). Riposte TrEx uses the SOAP web service specification with backwards compatibility to ensure connectivity for legacy systems (Web Services Interoperability Organisation, 2007).

Neutrality: Managed in an Impartial and Unbiased Manner

It is essential that public service providers do not exploit the users of their services. Research has shown that given the profit-driven and competitive nature of our digital society and individuals' concerns surrounding issues like the protection of their personal information, individuals prefer to entrust their personal information to familiar and trusted brands (Kim & Prabhakar, 2000). The challenge now facing governments and the public sector is to develop this trust to encompass an inclusive, affordable and high-quality *electronic* public service. The semi-structured interviews and focus groups conducted for this research showed that not all potential users of the system were happy to allow a government body to store their personal information. Therefore, a requirement of a PeS system must be to ensure users can decide where their personal information is located i.e. either within the system of a private SP like a bank, with a public/private company like the post or with a governmental department like the department of Public Administration. Provided all SPs meet the legal requirements needed to protect personal information within the system. The Riposte TrEx system will be managed by a national postal operator.

A De Jure System

This means that the system has been developed in the context of e-Government and therefore operates under particular national laws. De jure systems provide services for Non-Repudiation of Submission (NRS) and Non-Repudiation of Delivery (NRD). The former provides public authorities with evidence of the delivery of a mail item having taken place at a certain point in time. The latter provides public authorities with evidence that a recipient has collected the delivery at a certain point in time.

Implementation guidelines concerning non-repudiation protocols are specified by the standards ISO/IEC (ISO/IEC, 1996; ISO/IEC, 1998; ISO/IEC, 1989). Riposte TrEx is built upon an existing postal architecture which has been used for over a decade by post offices globally to electronically interact with each other. All these de jure services have already been developed and tested and are easily transferable to the Riposte TrEx product.

Public Software System Principle 2: Ensuring Standard Software System Requirements are Met

Basic systems requirements must be implemented in addition to the specific requirements of a PeS system.

Continually Improving and Developing Security

An audit process for ensuring a PeS system is secure at all times on an ongoing basis is essential to inspire confidence in the system. In addition to an audit process, the system designers of Riposte TrEx are working with an FP7 project which is developing an open source agent-based credential system. The FP7 funded project is entitled ABC-4Trust (ABC4Trust Project, 2009). Every time the ABC4Trust credential system is updated, so too will the credential system within Riposte TrEx be updated. Additionally, antivirus software will be installed throughout the system.

Reliability and Performance to Ensure Minimal Disruption

Ensuring system reliability and performance entails various checks for hardware, software performance and reliability, as well as performances and reliability of interaction between hardware and software, and between the system

and the operator. As stated above, Riposte TrEx has been developed on an existing, tried and tested architecture entitled Riposte which has provided performance and reliability to postal operators globally for over a decade.

Usability

Usability is defined as a measure of the effectiveness, efficiency, and satisfaction achieved by a specified set of users performing specified tasks with a given product (ISO, 1998). A set of user interface design principles were formulated during the TrEx project, the standards in Table 5 were used as guide for developing these principles (ISO, 1999; ISO, 2003). The principles were formulated to guide both developers and testers of Riposte TrEx when assessing the system for usability.

CONCLUSION AND FUTURE RESEARCH

The chapter presents a design theory for the provision of public e-Services in the digital world. The theory attempts to tackle digital inequality

Table 5. Outline of design principles for the PeSICT design theory

Design Principles	Sub-Principles
Surrendering of control: from the public service provider to the public service consumer	Secure and private data storage units Independence and separation Choice and consent regarding personal information Informational privacy assurance
Ensuring Digital Accessibility to the PeS system	Public Access to multi-channel systems Principles of Accessibility Education of citizens
Ensuring standard social media system requirements are met	User-based and interactive Community and relationship driven Emotion over content
Ensuring values system of public sector is upheld	A de jure system Interoperability and transparency Neutrality
Ensuring standard system requirements are met	Reliability and performance Security Usability

and reduce online privacy concerns through the design of inclusive ICTs. The authors, however, recognize the limitations of this research in that the design theory outlined in this chapter is not a complete solution to resolving digital inequality and online privacy concerns. However, we argue that it is a step in the right direction. In order for this 'step' to be fully realized, is it essential that governments and the public are supportive of such systems and regulation is implemented to ensure their full functionality as De Jure systems. While every effort has been made during the RiposteT-rEx project lifecycle to gauge the opinions of the public, a thorough expert evaluation and survey of user trials must be applied at a future date to gain a deeper understanding of public attitudes towards such systems. These are planned for the future as the project is on-going and is currently undergoing live pilots in various locations across the country.

Finally, the complexity of public service provision in the material world would seem to indicate that as we move further into the digital world, provision of public e-Services that create public value will require a program of research rather than a single study. Further research could conduct investigations into what categories of public e-Services are more salient to the design theory presented here and what categories perhaps require a more refined or adapted version of it.

REFERENCES

ABC4Trust Project. (2009). *ABC4Trust*. Retrieved March 23rd, 2011, from http://abc4trust.de/

Alford, J., & O'Flynn, J. (2008). Public value: A stocktake of a concept. In *Proceedings of Twelfth Annual Conference of the International Research Society for Public Management*. Barcelona: IRSPM.

Aman, A. C. (2005). Privatization, prisons, democracy, and human rights: The need to extend the province of administrative law. *Indiana Journal of Global Legal Studies*, *12*(2), 511–550. doi:10.1353/gls.2005.0000

Aspray, W., Bromley, A., Campbell-Kelly, M., & Williams, M. R. (1990). *Computing before computers* (W. Aspray, Ed.). Ames, IA: Iowa State University Press.

Butler, T., Feller, J., Pope, A., Emerson, B., & Murphy, C. (2008). Designing a core IT artefact for knowledge management systems using participatory action research in a government and a non-government organisation. *The Journal of Strategic Information Systems*, *17*, 249–267. doi:10.1016/j.jsis.2007.10.002

Carlsson, S. A. (2010). Design science research in information systems: A critical realist approach. In A. Hevner, & S. Chatterjee (Eds.), *Design research in information systems* (pp. 209–233). New York: Springer. doi:10.1007/978-1-4419-5653-8_15

Commission for Communications Regulation. (2008). *Postal strategy statement (2008-2010)*. Dublin: Commission for Communications Regulation.

Cordella, A., & Willcocks, L. (2010). Outsourcing, bureaucracy and public value: Reappraising the notion of the 'contract state'. *Government Information Quarterly*, *27*(1), 82–88. doi:10.1016/j.giq.2009.08.004

Cross, N. (2001). *Keynote speech: Design/science/research: Developing a discipline*. Paper presented at the 5th Asian Design Conference. Seoul, Korea.

Davis, F. D. (1993). User acceptance of information technology: System characteristics, user perceptions and behavioural impacts. *International Journal of Man-Machine Studies*, *38*(3), 475–487. doi:10.1006/imms.1993.1022

De Reuck, J., & Joseph, R. (1999). Universal service in a participatory democracy: A perspective from Australia. *Government Information Quarterly, 16*(4), 345–352. doi:10.1016/S0740-624X(00)86839-2

Del Gallo, U. (2009). *The lynchpin of integrated communications: A new paradigm for postal operators.* Retrieved May 20th, 2011, from http://www.accenture.com/SiteCollectionDocuments/PDF/Accenture_Postal_Lynchpin_of_Integrated_Communications.pdf

Dept. for Communities and Local Government. (2008). *Delivering digital inclusion: An action plan for consultation.* London: Communities and Local Government Publications.

DiMaggio, P., & Hargittai, E. (2001). *From the 'digital divide' to `digital inequality':Studying internet use as penetration increases.* Princeton, NJ: Princeton University.

Dinev, T., Hart, P., & Mullen, M. R. (2008). Internet privacy concerns and beliefs about government surveillance – An empirical investigation. *The Journal of Strategic Information Systems, 17,* 214–233. doi:10.1016/j.jsis.2007.09.002

Dobbins, T. (2007, November 14th). *Industrial relations in the postal sector - Ireland.* Retrieved October 20th, 2010, from http://www.eurofound.europa.eu/eiro/studies/tn0704018s/ie0704019q.htm

Esteves, J., & Joseph, R. C. (2008). A comprehensive framework for the assessment of eGovernment projects. *Government Information Quarterly, 25,* 118–132. doi:10.1016/j.giq.2007.04.009

ESTI. (2009). *Directive 2009/140/EC of the European parliament and of the council.* Retrieved September 2, 2011, from http://www.etsi.org/website/document/aboutetsi/ec_directives/2009_140.pdf

Etzioni, A. (1999). *The limits of privacy.* New York: Basic Books.

European Commission. (2010). *e-Inclusion.* (E. I. Society, Producer). Retrieved September 19th, 2011 from http://ec.europa.eu/information_society/activities/einclusion/index_en.htm

European Commission. (2010a). A digital agenda for europe (COM(2010) 245 final/2). Brussels: European Commission.

Federal Trade Commission. (2010). *Protecting consumer privay in an era of rapid change: A proposed framework for businesses and policymakers.* Washington, DC: Federal Trade Commission.

Fedorowicz, J., & Dias, M. (2010). A decade of design in digital government research. *Government Information Quarterly, 27,* 1–8. doi:10.1016/j.giq.2009.09.002

Goold, B. J. (2009). Building it In the role of privacy enhancing technologies (PETs) in the regulation of surveillance and data collection. In B. J. Goold, & D. Neyland (Eds.), *New directions in surveillance and privacy* (pp. 18–38). Cullompton, UK: Wilan Publishing.

Grant, G., & Chau, D. (2005). Developing a generic framework for e-government. *Journal of Global Information Management, 13*(1). doi:10.4018/jgim.2005010101

Gregor, S., & Jones, D. (2007). The anatomy of a design theory. *Journal of the Association for Information Systems, 8*(5), 312–335.

Grönroos, C. (2008). Service logic revisited: Who creates value? And who co-creates? *European Business Review, 20*(4), 298–314. doi:10.1108/09555340810886585

Hefetz, A., & Warner, M. (2004). Privatization and its reverse: Explaining the dynamics of the government contracting process. *Journal of Public Administration: Research and Theory, 14*(2), 171–190. doi:10.1093/jopart/muh012

Hevner, A. R., March, S. T., & Park, J. (2004). Design science in information systems research. *Management Information Systems Quarterly, 28*(1), 75–105.

Hood, C. (1991). A public management for all seasons? *Public Administration, 69*, 3–19. doi:10.1111/j.1467-9299.1991.tb00779.x

Hsieh, J. J.-A., Rai, A., & Keil, M. (2008). Understanding digital inequality: Comparing continued use behaviour models of the socio-economically advantaged and disadvantaged. *Management Information Systems Quarterly, 32*(1), 97–126.

Infoxchange Australia. (2011). *Technology for social justice.* Retrieved from www.infoxchange.net.au

ISO. (1998). Ergonomic requirements for office work with visual display terminals. *ISO 9241-11.*

ISO. (1999). Human centred design processes for interactive systems. *ISO 13407.*

ISO. (2003). ISO/TS 16071 ergonomics of human-system interaction. *Ergonomics of Human-System Interaction.*

ISO/IEC. (1989). ISO/IEC 7498-2:198. *Information processing systems-Open systems interconnection.*

ISO/IEC. (1996). ISO/IEC 10181:1996. *Information technology - Open systems interconnection.*

ISO/IEC. (1998). ISO/IEC 2788:1998. *Information technology-Security techniques.*

Iversen, J., Mathiassen, L., & Nielsen, P. (2004). Managing process risk in software process improvement: An action research approach. *Management Information Systems Quarterly, 28*(3), 395–434.

Kelly, G., Mulgan, G., & Muers, S. (2002). *Creating public value: An analytical framework for public service reform.* Retrieved Nov 2, 2009 from http://www.cabinetoffice.gov.uk/strategy/seminars/public_value.aspx

Kim, K., & Prabhakar, B. (2000). Initial trust, perceived risk, and the adoption of internet banking. In *Proceedings of International Conference on Information Systems* (pp. 537 - 543). Brisbane, Australia: Association for Information Systems.

Laskowski, S. J., Autry, M., Cugini, J., & Yen, W. K. (2004). *Improving the usability and accessibility of votingsystems and products.* Washington, DC: National Institute of Standards and Technology.

Laudon, K. (1997, June). Extensions to the theory of markets and privacy: Mechanics of pricing information. In *Privacy and self-regulation in the information age.* Retrieved February 10th, 2011 from http://www.ntia.doc.gov/reports/privacy/privacy_rpt.htm

Lesur, M. (2007). *Digital opportunities for the postal industry.* Microsoft Corporation.

Lindgren, I., & Jansson, G. (2013). Electronic services in the public sector: A conceptual framework. *Government Information Quarterly, 30*, 163–172. doi:10.1016/j.giq.2012.10.005

London Economics. (2010). *Study on the economic benefits of privacy-enhancing technologies (PETs).* London: European Commission.

Mägli, M., Jaag, C., Koller, M., & Trinkner, U. (2010). *Postal markets and electronic substitution: Implications for regulatory practices and institutions in Europe.* Zürich: Swiss Economics SE AG.

Markus, M. L., Majchrzak, A., & Gasser, L. (2002). A design theory for systems that support emergent knowledge processes. *Management Information Systems Quarterly, 26*(3), 179–212.

Marx, G. (2003). A tack in the shoe: Neutralizing and resisting the new surveillance. *The Journal of Social Issues, 59*(2), 369–390. doi:10.1111/1540-4560.00069

Meneklis, V., & Douligeris, C. (2010). Bridging theory and practice in e-government: A set of guidelines for architectural design. *Government Information Quarterly, 27,* 70–81. doi:10.1016/j.giq.2009.08.005

Moore, M. H. (1995). *Creating public value: Strategic management in government.* Cambridge, MA: Harvard University Press.

Moore, M. H. (2003, May). *The public value scorecard: A rejoinder and an alternative to strategic performance measurement and management in non-profit organizations by Robert Kaplan.* Retrieved August 2011, from http://oueli.voinovichcenter.ohio.edu/alumni/public_value_scorecard.pdf

Noam, E. M. (1997). *Privacy and self-regulation: Markets for electronic privacy.* Retrieved February 10th, 2011, from http://www.citi.columbia.edu/elinoam/articles/priv_self.htm

O'Connell, R., & Read, V. (2009). *Safer social networking principles for the EU.* London: The Home Office Internet Task Force.

O'Flynn, J. (2007). From new public management to public value: Paradigmatic change and managerial implications. *The Australian Journal of Public Administration, 66*(3), 353–366. doi:10.1111/j.1467-8500.2007.00545.x

PCI Security Standards Council. (2010, October). *Payment card industry (PCI) payment application data security standard: Requirements and security assessment procedures.* Retrieved September 08, 2011, from https://www.pcisecuritystandards.org/documents/pa-dss_v2.pdf

Pries-Heje, J., & Baskerville, R. (2008). The design theory nexus. *Management Information Systems Quarterly, 32*(4), 731–755.

Shin, D.-H. (2006). Effective design in the development of public information infrastructure: A social constructionist approach. *Information Polity, 11,* 85–100.

Sims, J. (2011, April). *Tolbert traces cause of digital inequality to lack of skills and money.* Cambridge, MA: Harvard Kennedy School.

Sommerville, I. (2007). *What is software?* (8th ed.). Reading, MA: Addison-Wesley.

Spano, A. (2009). Public value creation and systems management control systems. *International Journal of Public Administration, 32*(3-4), 328–348. doi:10.1080/01900690902732848

Tauber, A. (2010). Requirements and properties of qualified electronic delivery systems in egovernment: An Austrian experience. *International Journal of E-Adoption,* 45–58. doi:10.4018/jea.2010010104

Teinowitz, I. (2011). *Trust of government agencies drops, but folks still love the USPS.* AOL Inc.

Van Der Wal, Z., De Graaf, G., & Lasthuizen, K. (2008). What's valued most? Similarities and differences between the organisational values of the public and private sector. *Public Administration, 86*(2), 465–482. doi:10.1111/j.1467-9299.2008.00719.x

Varian, H. R. (1996, December 6th). *Economic aspects of personal privacy in US dept of commerce privacy and self-regulation in the information age.* Retrieved February 10th, 2011 from http://people.ischool.berkeley.edu/~hal/Papers/privacy/

Walls, J. G., Widmeyer, G. R., & Sawy, O. A. (1992). Building an information systems design theory for vigilant EIS. *Information Systems Research, 3*(1), 25–59. doi:10.1287/isre.3.1.36

Web Services Interoperability Organisation. (2007, December 25). *Basic profile version 2.0.* Retrieved September 14, 2011 from http://www.ws-i.org/Profiles/BasicProfile-2_0(WGD).html

White House. (2010). *DRAFT national strategy for trusted identities in cyberspace: Creating options for enhanced online security and privacy.* Washington, DC: The White House.

Whitley, E. A. (2009). *Informational privacy, consent and the control of personal data.* London: Elsevier. doi:10.1016/j.istr.2009.10.001

Whitley, E. A. (2009). Perceptions of government technology, surveillance and privacy: The UK identity cards scheme. In N. Daniel, & B. Goold (Eds.), *New directions in privacy and surveillance* (pp. 133–156). Cullompton, UK: Willan.

Zeithaml, V. A., Parasuraman, A., & Berry, L. L. (1990). *Delivering quality service: Balancing customer perceptions and expectations.* New York, NY: The Free Press.

ADDITIONAL READING

Mills, L., & Brail, S. G. (2004). UToronto working paper series. New media in the new millennium: The Toronto Cluster in Transition. Retrieved February 11, 2011 from www.utoronto.ca/isrn/publications/Working Papers/Working00/Mills00_NewMedia.pdf.

Mimicopoulos, M. G. (2004). *E-Government funding activities and strategies. Department of Economic and Social Affairs, Division for Public Administration and Development Management.* New York: United Nations.

Minow, M. (2010). *Policy considerations - what are the legal risks?* Retrieved April 5, 2011 from www.egovflorida.org/pdfs/E-GovernmentServicesinFloridaPublicLibraries-Final.pdf.

Misra, D. C. (2007). Ten guidling principles for knowledge management in e-Government in developing countries. *First International Conference on knowledge Management for Productivity and Competitiveness,* New Delhi, 1-13. Retrieved February 12, 2011 from www.unpan1.un. org/intradoc/groups/public/.../UNPAN025338.pdf.

Mitchell, E. S. (1986). Multiple triangulation: A methodology for nursing science. *ANS. Advances in Nursing Science, 8*(3), 18–26. doi:10.1097/00012272-198604000-00004 PMID:3083764

KEY TERMS AND DEFINITIONS

E-Government: This entails utilization of Information and Communication Technologies in delivering public services to citizens and as platforms for doing business with the business organisations.

ICT: This is an acronym that stands for Information and Communication Technologies – listing technology tools and platforms that are used for information interchange.

Interoperability: This is the ability of two independent systems to exchange information and applications or interfaces in a bid to access common resources.

NPM: This is an acronym that stands for New Public Management - the force that revitalized the way public services are perceived and done at the moment.

Public Service: This a service that the government in any region provides to its citizens and businesses for the greater social benefit.

Chapter 6
Designing E-Government Platforms using Systems Thinking Perspectives and Performance Measurement Frameworks

Samuel C. Avemaria Utulu
University of Cape Town, South Africa & Redeemer's University, Nigeria

Kosheek Sewchurran
University of Cape Town, South Africa

ABSTRACT

This chapter intends to present information systems philosophies on design of affluent e-Government platform design. The chapter looks at e-Government platform design in two ways. First, it looks at it as a prevailing concept and philosophy that emanate through the combination of literature in the academic disciplines of government and governance, ICT and information society, and e-Business. Hence, the chapter argues that these fields of study provided the theoretical basis influencing e-Government platform design. Second, the chapter proposes that if the philosophies embedded in the literature dealing with systems thinking and performance measurement are included as part of the theories for e-Government conceptualization, this may culminate into developing a new philosophy. This philosophy may be based on asking relevant and appropriate socio-cultural questions that may facilitate the design of better e-Government platforms. The chapter proposes a model for incorporating the said philosophical standpoints into actual e-Government design. The anticipation is that such a platform may culminate into e-Government platforms that may meet social requirements necessary for requisite e-Government platforms.

DOI: 10.4018/978-1-4666-4900-2.ch006

INTRODUCTION

Academic fields such as information systems, computer science and information technology (IT) management are confronted with the challenge of meeting organizational and societal IT needs in the most efficient and effective manner. This is the reason why several questions have been raised and answered in the literature regarding organizational performance, quality benchmarks and organizational thinking when developing plans to implement any IT solution (Neely, Adams & Kennerley, 2002; Kaplan & Norton, 1996; Waring, 1996; Ridway, 1956). Consequently, we think that despite the fact that issues that relate to performance management and systems thinking have been well integrated into the operations and design of organizations, its tenets and principles can also be appropriately adopted to suit and improve on non-commercial business processes, products and services. This will allow the conceptualization of new strategies which non-commercial entities can adopt to attain organizational efficiency and effectiveness. A very good example of this is the adoption of performance management and systems thinking philosophies to the design of e-Government platforms. This is proposed because the design of IT artifact such as e-Government platform requires that the wants and needs of all the stakeholders for whom it is designed must be identified, assessed and satisfied.

In the literature, systems thinking has been conceptualized as a management perspective that deals with understanding complex social and technical phenomena. Systems thinking perspective allows an actor dealing with a complex situation to assess it from a holistic perspective, that is, to assess the relationship that exist between the parts that formed the whole system as the possible source of the social and technical complexity. According to Aronson (1998) systems thinking is fundamentally a management approach towards analyzing, understanding and solving problems. In his words, systems thinking "focuses on how

the thing being studied interacts with the other constituents of the system-a set of elements that interact to produce behavior-of which it is a part" (p. 1). If we consider revelations from the study carried out by Matavire, Chigona, Roode, Sewchurran, Davids, Mukudu and Boamah-Abu (2010) in which they found out that the following; leadership, project fragmentation, perceived value of information technology, citizen inclusion and task coordination constitute major setbacks hindering e-Government implementation in South Africa, we would then agree that e-Government platform design requires a system thinking approach. This is on the one hand. On the other hand, performance management has been defined as the identification and the management of the measures of factors considered important to the success of any organization. The academic fields dealing with performance management have brought immense transformation into its conceptualization which resulted to the transformational development of about five performance measurement frameworks (Neely, *et al.*, 2005). While all the five frameworks have different philosophies and tenets through which they judge the performances of organizations, Kaplan and Norton's (1992) balanced scorecard and Neely, Adams and kennerley's (2002) performance prism are by far the most popular in business circles.

According to Kaplan and Norton (1996) balanced score card is a balanced presentation of both financial and operational measures in contemporary business management which results to asking and providing answers to four basic questions regarding customers, internal processes, innovation and learning, and financial perspective. These consist of question such as: how do customers see us? What must we excel at? Can we continue to improve and create value? How do we look to shareholders? Neely et al. (2002) on the other hand put forward that performance prism is "a second generation measurement framework designed to assist performance measurement selection…It is a comprehensive measurement framework that addresses the key business issues to which a wide variety of organizations… will be able to relate (p. 6)." The performance prism consists of five facets: stakeholders, strategies, processes, capabilities and stakeholders' contribution and begins with a primary question: who are our stakeholders and what do they want and need? In true sense, both performance prism and balanced score card have underlying philosophies that can be adopted to address the kind of questions and thinking an e-Government platform designer would require to ask and have in order to be able to produce an e-Government platform that has the capability to meet stakeholders' (everybody-individuals, organizations and including government itself) needs and wants. We consider the question in both the balanced score card and performance prism as a philosophical basis for the development of performance assessment questions for e-Government platform designers.

Consequently, we contributed this chapter in order to provide another philosophical lens for interrogating social aspects of IT design that may have been considered important by e-Government platform designers. We did this with the hope that the philosophical lens will help them look more appropriately into social aspects, that is, the human need and want aspects, of e-Government platform design. Our claims were derived by relating the concepts in the literature dealing with governments and functions of government with the concepts in the e-Business, systems thinking and performance measurement literature. We specifically chose to relate conceptual frameworks in the e-Business, systems thinking and performance measurement literature with those in the literature dealing with government and its functions because e-Business, systems thinking and performance measurement literature have contributed to how corporate organizations develop appropriate understanding of their own needs and that of their stakeholders by appropriately asking, properly analyzing and answering relevant questions. We related concepts emanating from these three fields of study to

questions e-Government platform designers will need to ask and answer if they are to achieve the design of formidable, relevant and appropriate e-Government platforms. We adopted a model that is based on constructs derived from the literature to describe the concepts and principles embedded in our e-Government platform design claims. In the end, readers (most of whom we assume to be e-Government platform designers) of this chapter would be able to understand the concepts of e-Business, systems thinking and performance management frameworks and how they can be used to sieve out and analyze social factors that are very fundamental to the design and implementation of e-Government design platforms.

BACKGROUND

Government has always existed as a mechanism and institution for governance. This therefore, means that the concepts, government and governance have different connotations and meanings. While government stands for the actor, governance stands for the action. However, both concepts have existed before the invention of information technologies (ITs), whose use by government for administration and governance led to the evolution of the concepts of electronic (e) government and electronic (e) governance. In trying to explain the use of the two terms, King and Kendell (2003) pointed out that the increase in the conceptualization of government activities as governance is as a result of the increase in the number of those that accept the conception that government in "modern state is an enabling rather than an owning state (p. 129)." In contemporary time, government is made up of public, private and intergovernmental agencies that collaborate to steer socio-political, cultural and economic changes. In our context and as in most contexts, public agencies are believed to be established by government, while private agencies are believed to be established by individuals or groups in the form of non-governmental agencies. The third type of agency is the intergovernmental agencies which are established by collaborating governments. These three agencies, when put together, form the core of the social machinery that steer the evolution and implementation of public policies that define the ways public resources are allocated and managed.

The conception that government is an enabling agency is also supported by Pierre and Peters (2000) (cited in King and Kendell, 2003). Pierre and Peters used governance in place of government as the concept for describing the processes of social and political coordination in territorial states. Their conceptualization mirrors more of government being a socio-political machinery for achieving public good. Indeed contemporary scholars prefer to view government as a process (governance) rather than a state or an institution. This as it were shows that there is thin line between what have been conceptualized as government and governance in the literature. The tin line arises because a government that is on the verge of doing its government business is involved in governance. So governance is government functions put into actions, while government is the entity that is functioning by putting into action some functions that are believed to be its functions. In other words, the term government is a representation of a public institution and not a socio-political process of deploying all the machineries required for governing, that is, achieving public socio-political, cultural and economic goals. We can, for example, say government of Namibia or government of Nigeria, and governance in Namibia and governance in Nigeria. While government in the two politically defined territories is defined by institutions, governance defines the ways the two political institutions choose to carry out their government businesses. This is the reason why we agree that the concepts, e-Government and e-Governance are distinct.

However, one major uprising that influenced government and governance in the recent past is the evolution of the information society. Castells (1996) argued that the information society is distinct from the industrial society and hence, defined it as the society where human activities-socio-political, cultural and economic- take place in technological paradigm that is primarily evoked by information and communication technologies (ICTs). Most commentators on the history of the information society allude that its beginning can be traced to the aftermath of the Second World War in the 1940s, when the exponential increase in the production and use of information and knowledge was observed. Prominent among these commentators was Peter Drucker who traced and tried to define the switch in the ways human activities were being carried out in his book *The age of discontinuity: guidelines to our changing society* (Drucker, 1969). We borrow Drucker's title to say that 'the age of discontinuity and changing society' did not only impact on business oriented private organizations, it also impacted on public institutions and agencies. By 1995 the information society which was at its embryonic stage as of the time Drucker wrote about the age of discontinuity has evolved, and therefore influenced Tapscott (1995) to proclaim that:

Today, we are witnessing the early turbulent days of a revolution as significant as any other in human history. A new medium of human communication is emerging one that may prove to surpass all previous revolutions-the printing press, the telephone, the television, the computer-in its impact on our economic and social life (p. xiii)

The information society syndrome also impacts on the art and act of government, especially in the ways government communicates and transacts businesses with the governed.

Although e-Business began with the use of ICT for management and commercial purposes, it later spilled over into other areas of the human existence such as government, public administration, education and social life and healthcare.

However, governments' adoption of information society philosophies and principles to carry out their businesses did not just occur. People who requested that government programs should impact on the lives of the general public backed their arguments for better deliver of government services by comparing private business organizations' improved business communication and transaction styles with the bureaucratic and bottle-necked communication and transaction styles of government. Specifically, this led to the demand for government to adopt the kind of change that mimics e-Business initiatives and consequently led to the adoption of e-Business principles and practices in government circles. The spillover has been tagged by some commentators as the spillover of e-commerce into a variety of non-commercial (socio-political and cultural) activities of government (Homburg, 2008). The literature however, distinguishes between e-Business and e-commerce in principle. A good example is Bidgoli (2002) who drew a distinction in his definition of the two concepts thus: "E-Business is any electronic transaction (e.g., information exchange), which subsumes e-commerce (p. 5)." The major difference between the two concepts is normally deduced from e-Business being about all the activities (which however, also include commercial activities) such as those that are related with management and transfer of data, information and knowledge. On the other hand, e-commerce is all about commercial (buying and selling) activities. We therefore prefer to say that e-Government originated from e-Business activities since government activities such as the transfer and receiving of data, information and knowledge and other publicly mediated commercial activities go beyond the scope of e-commerce.

The literature has shown how the idea of 'business of government' helped the proponents of e-Government to develop the concept 'e-government.' We have tried to unfold our argument of how the literature showed that government existed right from time and that its operations were impacted upon by the historic transformation of the contemporary society. The impact had manifested in the popularity of the use of ICT for businesses which had to be imbibed by government due to the pressure that arose from pressure groups who agitated for improved delivery of government services to the public. These services manifest in the functions of government which may include, from a broad sense, laying claim to a defined territory, protecting such a territory, making laws within such territory, implementing the laws and interpreting the laws when the need arises. Consequently, we have conceptualized e-Government platform design as the design of an IT based platform through which a government as an institution can perform all required administrative functions that constitutes the totality of government functions towards itself as an institution and towards the people as the governed. We agreed that like e-Business which encompasses e-commerce, e-Government encompasses e-governance.

To effectively do the design of e-Government platform, information systems (IS) designers have over the years relied on existing theoretical views which are primarily drawn from four conceptual frameworks namely, concept of government and its functions, concept of information society, concept of ICT and the concept of electronic business. This is represented in Figure 1.

Great deal of quality theoretical contributions has emerged from approaching e-Government platforms design from the perspective shown in the Figure above. Available e-Government platforms are designed by paying more attention to functional needs while less attention is focused on practices that constitute processes and social needs which deal with answering questions that go beyond the platform itself into issues that have to do meeting stakeholders needs. Example of currently models are shoun in Yuan (2011), Drigas and Koukianakis (2009), Maheshwari, Kumar, Kumar and Sharan (2007) and Bwalya and Healy (2010). We however, reflected on Bidgoli (2002) advice that "To design and implement a success-

Figure 1. Conceptual framework for defining and explaining e-government (authors)

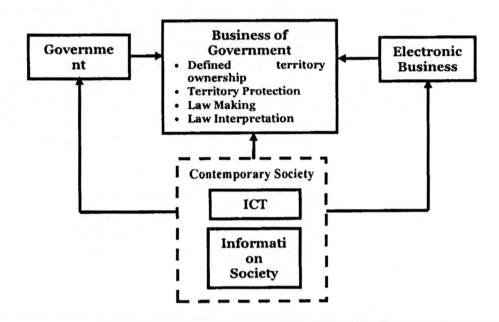

ful…[platform], a number of theories, applications, and technologies must be carefully analyzed and understood (p. 5)," and therefore, decided to expand the theoretical framework that can provide the lens through which we can assess a good design of e-Government platform. We retained existing framework without questioning, but brought to bear the need for incorporating the theories embedded in systems thinking and performance management. We take systems thinking and performance management as management philosophies and thereby tried to convince IS designers that they can achieve better IS design outcomes when designing e-Government platforms if they derive their design and implementation plans from a wider framework that includes the philosophies embedded in systems thinking and performance management. We will use the remaining segments in this chapter to properly present and defend our claims before presenting the extended model in the end of this chapter.

EXTENDED THEORETICAL FRAMEWORK FOR E-GOVERNMENT PLATFORM DESIGN

Electronic Business

There is not doubt that ICT revolutionalized the growth of e-Business in both commercial and non-commercial business circles. This fact showed in Gartner Group's (2000) definition of e-government: "the continuous optimization of service delivery, constituency participation, and governance by transforming internal and external relationships through technology, the internet, and new media." The idea of optimizing service delivery, constituency participation and governance can be likened to the ideas developed by for-profit business entities meant to up their competitiveness, productivity and profit. We can lay claim to this view from the following description of e-Business found in McKay and Marshall (2004):

E-Business takes on a much broader meaning and include the use of Internet-based technology and other information technology to support commerce and improve business performance...an e-Business therefore is a business that creatively and intelligently utilizes and exploits the capabilities of IT and Internet technologies to create efficiencies, to achieve effectiveness gains such as flexibility and responsiveness, and to create strategic opportunities through competitive uses of IT to alter market and industry structures (p. 5).

Very similar to McKay and Marshall's conceptual description of e-Business is Amor's (2000) conceptual description in which he postulates that "E-commerce is just one aspect of e-Business like e-franchising, e-mailing, e-marketing. E-Business is about using the convenience, availability and world-wide reach to enhance existing business or creating new virtual business (p. 7)." One of the points that we tried to clarify so far is that e-Business translates to e-Government, while e-commerce translates to e-Governance and therefore means that we agree that e-Government subsumes e-governance.

IBM, where the term e-Business was coined in 1997 defined it as "a secure, flexible and integrated approach to delivering differentiated business value by combining the systems and processes that run core business operations with the simplicity and reach made possible by Internet technology (quoted in Amore, 2000, p.7)." It follows that e-Business was conceptualized based on the capabilities of IT and the strategic thinking patterns of managers in contemporary business organizations who sought to strategically improve on their business performance. As shown in the definitions above, e-Business simply is the adoption of IT to carry out, in a flexible manner, business functions that have always been carried out in business organizations. However, it is very important to note that the competitive edge business organizations sought for which was eventually actualized through the adoption of IT

resulted because of the evolution of IT. Invariably, e-Business was pre-dated by the use of IT for handling business functions such as data management, transaction record inputting, data analysis and business trend analysis among others. While most businesses use available IT to carry out these business functions, many of them did not foresee the socio-economic impact it will later result into. The emergence of high competitiveness, ability of managers to project into business future using analyzed business data, and the demand by shareholders for higher profit were the unforeseen end products of IT adoption, which eventually led to the evolution of e-Business .

Space constraints do not permit the use of one more example <- one more case will strengthen the arguments)

If we relate our argument with Porter's approach to the development of business strategy which was postulated in 1980 (what is the company doing now? What is happening in the environment? What should the company do next?) we would agree that e-Business evolved when the available competitive tool for achieving contemporary business goal was IT. We may then ask: is e-Business a creative business phenomenon or a natural business progression? The answer to this question may be both in the affirmative or not. While e-Business may be a creative business phenomenon in some societies of the world, especially those societies where the technologies to implement them are creatively invented, it may be a natural business phenomenon in societies where e-Business development in other societies forced the adoption of e-Business initiatives. The force resulted because e-Business assumed the effective and efficient way of ensuring that they remain in business either directly with their customers or directly with their business collaborators. We can say this if we agree that adopting what others do to succeed is not necessarily a way of being creative. This claim is however, not a one-off claim as the scenarios may occur in a single society, especially if we consider terms such as market leaders, market followers, early technology adopter and late technology adopters which describes those who adopt an IT initiative early enough and those who later adopted it after they have confirmed its value-adding potentials.

Irrespective of if e-Business is a creative business phenomenon or a natural business phenomenon, Amor (2000) posited that the reason why business organizations adopt e-Business initiatives may include to expand business reach, attain higher level of market visibility, increase responsiveness, design and deliver new services, strengthen business relationships, reduce cost and to prevent or resolve channel conflicts. Harmon *et al.* (2001) provided four strategies which may spur business organizations into adopting e-Business . They are namely, cost leadership, differentiation, niche specialization and examples of niche specialization. There is no doubt whatsoever about the fact that e-Business adoption is all about increasing competitiveness, productivity and profit. As mentioned earlier, e-Government proponents relied mainly on the theoretical conceptualization of e-Business as a way of justifying the premise upon which e-Government strategies would be based. What they were able to achieve in order to propagate their claim was to prove that government, despite its type (democratic and non-democratic) normally seeks competitiveness, productivity and profit. The question that may arise based on this assertion is: how does a government seek competitiveness, productivity and profit? To answer this question we can adopt Brooker's (2009) proposition in which he says that "political anachronisms can continue to survive through continual modernization, whether they be non-democratic rule, hereditary monarchy or even armed rebellion (p. 4)." Governments device various competitiveness, productive and profit strategies in order to sustain identified political anachronisms most of which are targeted at domestic relations and international diplomacy meant for their acceptance and legitimacy. Gardhi (2010) also wrote that "While in power dictators may have substantive goals they

seek to fufill…[they] seize power to extinguish leftist threats…wanted to lead modernization of their…state (p.82)." While it may be difficult to accept that non-democratic regimes can seek competitiveness, productivity and profit for their states, democratic regimes have been accepted as a political regime that seeks people's support, based its legitimization on people involvement in governance and the implementation of people oriented policies and programs which we may say clearly explains the ways government seek competitiveness, productive and profit.

It is in the desire to drive changes and lead modernization programs that contemporary governments develop claims to support their adoption of e-Business principles and practices. Since this is the case with both democratic and non-democratic governments[1], both types of government seek to attain their goals through e-Business as may have been visible across the globe in the recent past. Governments adopt extended resource planning type of philosophy used in e-Business as a way of enhancing their ability to bring together different agencies, attain agency collaboration and also manage agency relationship such that will allow smooth coordination of government programs across various levels of governmental administrations (Ho, 2002). Several authors have carried out and reported in the literature empirical studies of how contemporary governments use e-government. Hiller and Belanger's (2001) e-Government framework provide a basis for analyzing types of e-government, the stages that they are made up of and the types of services that they can be used to offer. Accordingly, they posited that there are six types of e-government:

- Government to individual (services)
- Government to individual (political)
- Government to business (citizen)
- Government to business (market place)
- Government to employee, and
- Government to government

Their framework (see Hiller and Belanger, 2011, p. 16) shows five evolutionary stages of e-Government namely, information, two-way communication, transaction, integration and political participation. A careful assessment of Hiller and Belanger's e-Government framework reveals the array of entities that make up e-Government platform stakeholders. Intrinsically, it includes government itself and make it easier for us to say that the idea of systems thinking is quite relevant to the design of e-Government platform.

Ho (2002) in a study recognized that local governments have reinvented themselves by giving up traditional bureaucratic paradigm to emphasize standardization, departmentalization and operational cost efficiency which manifests in designing websites that encourage external collaboration and networking to achieve their development goals. Jaeger and Bertot (2010) analyzed how e-Government was used as tool for differentiation by the Obama administration in the United States of America. The differentiation was achieved through the adoption of e-Government initiatives for achieving transparency and therefore showed how e-Government can be used to achieve transparency and access to government information and services. Markaki, Charilas and Ashoums (2010) opined that e-Government services that are meant for both citizens and businesses may include for citizens- tax declaration and notification, job search, social security benefits, personal documents, building permission documents, certificates, enrolment for education, and health related services. Their list of e-Government services for business include social contributions to employees, corporate tax declaration and notification, company registration, custom services, and public procurement. There are several e-Government services that contemporary government provides by using e-Government platform. The successes recorded on the use of e-Government platform for the delivery of government services is dependent on so many factors, primary among which is the level of efficiency and effectiveness

which the e-Government platform designer was able to incorporate into the functioning of the e-Government platform during design. In this chapter our aim is to provide a theoretical prove of how e-Government service delivery challenges that may occur as a result of the level of performance of e-Government platform can be avoided or fixed using the philosophies embedded in systems thinking and performance management. The next segment will therefore be used to elucidate the concept of systems thinking and how its underlying philosophies can be appropriately adopted for e-Government platform design.

Systems Thinking

There cannot be a better way to start ruminating on the importance of systems thinking to e-Government platform design than quoting directly the first paragraph written by Robert Lilienfield in his book The Rise of Systems Theory. Lilienfeld (1978), while trying to do an introduction of the historic evolution of the systems theory wrote thus:

A number of disciplines have emerged in the twentieth century that can be classified under the general heading of "systems thinking." These originally separate disciplines include the following:

1. The biological philosophy of Ludwig von Bertalantty, and his concept of the "open system";
2. Norbert Wiener's formulation of cybernetics and W. Ross Ashby's related work on machines that are claimed to think and to learn, and stemming form the work, the concept of *feeback* and *automation*;
3. Information and communication theory, based on the work of Shannon, Weaver and Cherry and others, on the theoretical, mathematical, and linguistics problems involved in the transmission of messages over message-carrying circuits;

4. Operations research, which first emerged full-fledged in England during the war of 1939-1945 under the leadership of E.C. Williams, and has since been institutionalized by the founding of the Operations Research Society of America and the Operational Research Society in Great Britain;

5. The games theory of von Neuman and Morgenstern;

6. The techniques for stimulating social and environmental processes by computers, advocated by Jay Forrester and many others (p. 1).

The quotation above is very relevant to our discussion in two ways. First, it points out that systems thinking has been in existence for as long as we may have imagined, especially as it point to the evaluation and address of social, technical (or both social and technical which we normally referred to as socio-technical in IS), scientific, engineering and humanistic problems from diverse angles; where such diverse angles are defined by disciplinary or paradigmatic differences. Secondly, it show that major fields, science, technology, engineering, social sciences, and humanities have all, in one way or the other, adopted systems thinking for evaluating and addressing problems that cut across the spheres of their disciplines. This assertion is shown in Jackson' (2003) definition of systems stated below:

...a system is a complex whole functioning of which depends on its parts and the interactions between these parts. Stated like this, it is clear that we can identify systems of very different types:

- Physical, such as river systems;
- Biological, such as living organisms;
- Designed, such as automobiles;
- Abstract, such as philosophical systems;
- Social, such as families;
- Human activities, such as systems to ensure the quality of products (p.3).

The major problem proponents of system thinking face while trying to convince other thinkers to adopt its philosophical thinking is its reductionist nature. By reductionist nature we mean that by the very nature of systems thinking, its paradigm is based on reducing an entity into chunks that make up the entire entity. The primary challenge in trying to make people who do not understand the reductionist theory to reduce, say an e-Government platform to chunks, is that on the surface, e-Government platform like most other IS based platforms, do not look as if they are made up of chunks. By chunks we mean sub-systems that are put together to form a single functional e-Government system. A more general example is the human body which looks to anyone who has not taken a course in the biology of human body systems, like a single functional entity, whereas it is composed of various sub-systems of the body like circulatory, digestive, reproductive, respiratory, etc. Consequently, the idea of reducing entities into the sub-systems that they are composed of, as a way of facilitating a better understanding of its functioning, is referred to as reductionism in the IS literature (Jackson, 2003; Waring, 1996; Weinberg, 1975).

Reductionists see all entities as systems that are made up of sub-systems and as a result, evaluate entities they are confronted with from the perspectives of the sub-systems that make them up. This emanates from their belief that the existence and functioning of any entity is only made possible by the federating sub-entities. This also allows them to develop perspectives in which they propound the belief that problems that affect an entity which may be caused by any of the interrelated functioning of the sub-components did not just occur but may have been caused by the functioning of any of the sub-components. Hence, when a problem occurs within a system, reductionist prioritizes the reduction of the system in question to its basic sub-systems from where they can begin to systematically trace the sub-system where the problem is occurring, the causal or influencing relationship the sub-system has with other systems, and how the problem can be fixed. Interestingly, systems thinking perspective is not only relevant to IS analysts during problem-shooting, it is also relevant to IS designers and analysts during the stages of the design and the implementation of IS. The philosophy of system thinking, either when used by IS practitioners for trouble-shooting or for designing a system such as e-Government platform, is the same. Systems thinking allows systems designers to approach the design of any information system by identifying the needs and wants of five key stakeholders namely, the designers, the owners, the system, the environment and the intended users.

The array of stakeholders named above may have endeared Waring (1996) to point out that a system is made up of two kinds of components namely, structural and process components. Waring however, warned that a system encompasses various components which may not be obvious to systems designers or analysts. He noted that a system should be made to include "necessary components (i.e. those which are essential to any system of its type) and additional components which vary according to the situation and the view of the analyst (pp. 22-23)." In other word, systems components should be determined in three ways: conventional, contextual and personal perspectives. While conventional perspective allows the system designer or analyst to base his judgment of how to come up with a good system based on what is in the books regarding the kind of system in question, contextual perspective requires that he should understand the social context (most importantly social processes and practices within the social context) in which the system would be used. This permits the systems designer to base his judgment of a good IS design on social and contextual applicability. A systems designer's personal perspective refers to a situation in which he evokes his professional expertise and experience when deciding on the components that are relevant to the system he is designing and/or analyzing.

The reason why an IS designer is permitted to evoke his personal perspective (together with conventional and contextual perspective) is because it is assumed that his training and experience with previous design, implementation and trouble-shooting would have equipped him with necessary knowledge, experience and expertise that will aid his judgment when deciding on factors that are necessary for the successful design of, say an e-Government platform. It is important to note that the adoption of systems thinking perspective does not, so to say, make the job of an e-Government platform designer easier in all ways. The systems thinking perspective definitely requires bringing into bear broader perspective which may make requirements and specifications phases more complex and tedious at the initial stage of the design. However, it is certain that systems thinking perspective will make the e-Government platform designer's job of coming up with appropriate socio-technical requirements and specifications that will lead to the design of an e-Government platform which is able to more effectively and efficiently replicate in real life, the functions for which an ideal e-Government platform is designed to performance. If this is achieved extended cost such as cost of trouble shooting, reassessment of specialization and design, lost of confidence and psychological dissatisfaction resulting from not being personally fulfilled, would have been averted.

Consequently, the implications of adopting systems thinking during the choice of structural and process components for an e-Government platform is very enormous and also important to achieving the design of an efficiently and effectively functional e-Government platform. While at the superficial level the structural component seems to consist of only technical sub-components, if well assessed using systems thinking, it contains both social and technical structural sub-components. Our argument is derived from the fact that the social environments where the e-Government platform is intended to be used have structures.

For instance, governments have physical organizational structures that may be classified into two sub-structures: physical environment and social environment. The physical structure is the physical open space which is conditioned in the case of an organization by buildings, locations of offices, open spaces outside buildings and road networks within the organizations' premises. The social structure has to do with social interaction among people (staff, customers, suppliers, contractors, etc.) that are involved in the business of the organization. Wilson's (1984) definition of structure: "Structure are defined as those features related to physical layout, power hierarchy, reporting structure, and the pattern of formal and informal communication (p. 66)" can be used to put our argument into perspective.

With regard to process Wilson (1984) also posited that "Process is related to the on-going activities of conversion of raw material into products, monitoring, decision making, and controlling (p. 66)." The major point we are making is that both structures and processes are socio-technical in nature and requires that an e-Government platform designer must be careful in identifying, selecting and integrating those structures and processes that are vital to the design of the e-Government platform in question into his design. His ability to do this identification, selection and integration will determine the extent to which the e-Government platform which he has designed will perform against parameters that are used to evaluate e-Government platform performance. We represent this in the Figure below:

We argue that e-Government platform is not just the artifact as always been postulated in the literature, but that it include artifact, structure, process and people. In the next segment we will elucidate the concept of performance management and how the philosophies that are embedded in it can be appropriately adopted by e-Government platform designers when designing e-Government platforms.

Performance Measurement

The opening paragraph in Neely, Gregory and Platts (2005) contained the quotation of Lord Kelvin's (1824-1907) statement regarding performance measurement. The quotation goes thus: "When you can measure what you are speaking about, and express it in numbers, you know something about it… [otherwise] your knowledge is of a meager and unsatisfactory kind, it may be the beginning of knowledge, but you have scarcely in thought advanced to the stage of science (Neely, *et al.*, 2005, p.1228)." It therefore follows that the social activities that make up man's ways of life are characterized by measurement, although many people may not be conscious of this. Everything man does, ranging from schooling, working, playing, resting, existing, and even knowing God is being measured in one way or the other. The school system which is made up of primary, secondary and tertiary institutions is a broad way of measuring schooling. When we here people talk about part-time and full-time work, it is also a way of measuring work. In places, say school or work environment or even in the home, where people talk about play time and break time, they are indirectly talking about a measure of the time to be devoted to playing, which is also synonymous with resting which may be measured by smoking or coffee/tea breaks. Everybody has a date of birth which is actually a way of measuring their existence in time term and can also be told if they are devoted or non-devoted Christians, Muslims or Buddhists or atheist. In a nutshell, the social system that people create either permanently or temporarily pay very good attention to measurement, which unfortunately is always taken for granted due to unconscious over-familiarization. In IS, a great deal of study and research time has been devoted to gaining knowledge about IS failure and success rates. If this thought is put in another way, IS study of IS failures and successes is all about IS performance measurement. In other word, there has always been the tendency to measure performances, either through a deliberate effort carefully put together or through a natural taken-for-granted effort. This also points us to the fact that e-Government platform designers may have had different ways in which they measured the performances of the platforms they design.

However, the primary aim of the academic field of performance measurement is to create and explain the science of performance measurement. Neely *et al.* (2005) revealed that all that performance measurement does is to measure the internal and external performance of organizations. They used the concept of efficiency and effectiveness to push forward their argument about the fact that all organizations seek both internal and external performance. In the context of this work, if we say that an e-Government platform designer's major performance target is to be able to design an e-Government platform that is both efficient and effective, we mean that by efficiency the platform designer judges his performance by measuring the resources that has been put to use during the course of the platform design. It is natural that the e-Government platform designer will seek to use lesser resources, that is, the resources should not be more than the resources that are considered appropriate amount of resources required to achieve a stated level of e-Government quality. This is what Neely and his colleagues referred to as internal performance measurement. They conceptualized this way of measuring as internal performance measurement because of the fact that organizational resources are considered as internal variables, that is, variables (which must be carefully identified, assessed and defined) that are directly owned and put to use by the organizations. This is one the one hand. On the other hand, another principal goal which the e-Government platform designer seeks to meet is meeting users' requirements. When an e-Government platform is designed its users actually judge its performance based on the extent to which it meets all their requirements, and these requirements can vary across different users. Because e-Government platform users are external to the organization where the designers work, the extent to which users' requirements are met is what Neely and his colleagues referred to as external performance. In Neely's words, "Effectiveness refers to the extent to which customer requirements are met, and efficiency is a measure of how economically the organization's resources are utilized when providing a given level of customer satisfaction (Neely, 1998, p. 5)."

Declaring that all that the science of performance measurement deals with is internal and external performance measurement makes it looks like the scholars that are devoted to studying the performance measurement science have very little to contribute to organizational performance management and less still to e-Government platform designing. However, right from the time in the 1950s when Drucker (1954) and Ridgway (1956) wrote about the consequences of wrong measurement and the arguments that followed in the literature written by Chandler (1977), Hayes and Abernathy (1980), Johnson and Kaplan (1987) and Ittner and Larcker (2003), the business of performance measurement, be it in business organizations or as a philosophy to derive the design of better IS platforms such as e-Government platform, is a delicate endeavor that requires care, expertise and deep analytical sense. It has always seem that performance measures change as the society changes. In other word, the performance measures that are used to asses e-Government platforms are not static, they transform over time and space. Consequently, the paradigm change that performance measurement experienced in the wake of the 21st Century has been expressed by Neely and his colleagues severally. On one occasion they declared that:

The days when companies could survive and prosper by focusing on the wants and needs of one stakeholder-the shareholder- are long gone...

Now-and increasingly in the future- the best way for organizations to survive and prosper in the long term will be to think about the wants and needs of all their important stakeholders and endeavor to deliver value to each of them (Neely, et al., 2002, p. 1).

If we retrace the fact that performance measurement deals with internal and external performances of organizations in the light of the declaration made by Neely and his colleagues above we will begin to come to term with the fact that it would take proper analytical sense to derive all the internal and external performance measures that may be required to accurately determine how both the organization and stakeholder will measure the performance of an organization and its products and services. This is also applicable to e-Government platform designers understanding of what constitutes high performance to both itself and the intended users of e-Government platforms. It shows that answering questions such as what is our stakeholders' wants and needs, how do our stakeholders see us, what level of process improvement and learning do we need to achieve our goal? may be more complex than may have been imagined.

To be able to easily scale through the complexities that may arise because of the nature of performance measurement, three concepts that normally come to bear when discussing performance measurement needs to be defined. These concepts are namely, performance measurement, performance measure and performance measurement system. Neely *et al.* (2005) defined the concepts thus:

- Performance measurement can be defined as the process of quantifying the efficiency and effectiveness of action.
- A performance measure can be defined as a metric used to quantify the efficiency and/or effectiveness of an action.

- A performance measurement system can be defined as the set of metrics used to quantify both the efficiency and effectiveness of actions.

Questions that arise as a result of the definitions given above are: what constitute efficiency and effectiveness of action in the context of the design and the use of e-Government platform? Another question is: what matrixes are appropriate for the quantification of efficiency and effectiveness of e-Government platform design? The third question is: in what way(s) can identified matrixes be put together in order to form an appropriate performance measurement system that can appropriately measure e-Government platform efficiency and effectiveness? Knowing and understanding what to measure have become a long time debate in the field of performance measurement. Kaplan and Norton (1992) once wrote that "What you measure is what you get...measurement system strongly affects the behavior of managers and employees (p. 71)." We know, based on observation and practical experiences with the use of e-Government that the measures which may have been used to measure their performances do not only influence the behaviors of managers and employees working in government institutions, but that it also affects the behaviors of the users.

It is important to note that what we have been pushing for is the measurement of social aspects of e-Government platform design. Although, IS claims that it deals with IT, organizations and society using social science paradigms and methodologies, IS is still far from providing strong theoretical basis from which scholars and practitioners can come up with solutions to social challenges that are plaguing the design and use of IS platforms such as e-Government platform. This does not mean that IS has not performed well in its chosen trade of proffering solutions to phenomena that arise due to the interaction between IT, organizations and society. Major IS theories have been used in the recent past to assess why IS which share the same characteristics with e-Government fail or succeed. Popular among the theories that have been used in IS studies are such as technology acceptance model (TAM) Davis (1989), theory of reasoned action (TRA), Dillion and Morris (1996), and the unified theory of acceptance and use of technology model (UTAUT), Venkatesh, Morris, Davis and Davis (2003) and Tibenderana and Ogao (2008). The outcomes of e-Government research that adopted these theories are synonymous with the outcomes of major IS research that dealt with some other kinds of IS failures and successes. Bwalya (2010) summarized the outcome of such theoretical evaluation to include failure factors such as leadership failures, poor technical design, work place and organizational inflexibility, financial inhibitors, digital divides and choices, poor coordination and lack of trust.

The truth of the matter is that IS research that take this form normally provide excellent theoretical explanation that have very little practical substances that are not enough to impact dramatic change in IS design practices. This is because of the concreteness of the measures that were adopted as means to express in numerical form the performances of e-Government platforms. In other to be able to talk about the fluid, lucid, heuristic and flexible variables that may affect the performance of e-Government platform that may arise as a result of faulty design, the measures to adopt must take into consideration the variables proposed by Ittner and Larcker (2003). Ittner and Larcker termed the variables non-financial measures because of their lucid, fluid, heuristic, flexible and social nature, and opined that they include, set the right performance target, measure correctly, link measures to strategy, and validate link between measures and strategy. The duo concluded that linking the four variables together can be achieved if those interested in measuring performance "base decision making on well-established *series of links* (Ittner and Larcker, 2003, p. 94). We emphasized series of link in the

quotation above to bring us back to the complementary nature of our proposed theoretical shift in the way e-Government platform designers think and approach e-Government platform design. We proposed that the theoretical shift should be rooted in the theory of systems thinking and performance measurement. We devote the next segment to explaining the theoretical shift which is occasioned by including systems thinking and performance measurement into the theoretical foundation of e-Government platform design.

E-Government Platform Design from the Perspectives of Systems Thinking and Performance Management

We have identified four variables namely, artifact, structure, process, and people as important variables to the theoretical shift we are advocating. What we are saying is that if these four variables are appropriately interrogated with the theories of systems thinking and performance management that the likelihood that there will be an improvement in the designs done by IS practitioners that design e-Government platforms would be have improved. We have said it earlier during the course of presenting the arguments in this chapter that systems thinking adopts the reductionist approach when dealing with socio-technical phenomena. This therefore, means that each of the variables identified will be taken and interrogated as a unit, which formed the basis for separating them in Figure 2. It is only after the unit based interrogation has been concluded on the four variables that the causal or influence relationship will be interrogated. Put more clearly, we advocate that artifact will we taken first of all separately from the other three variables and interrogated with the theories embedded in systems thinking and performance measurement using the following questions: what are the sub-systems that comprise e-Government artifact and what are the measures that can be used to measure identified sub-systems performance?

Figure 2. Dynamics of e-Government platform design (authors)

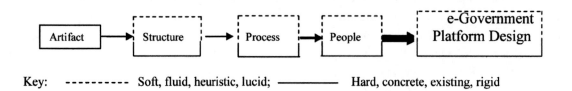

Key: ---------- Soft, fluid, heuristic, lucid; ——————— Hard, concrete, existing, rigid

When this kind of interrogation has been done and concluded on each of the remaining three variables then the causal and influence relationship will then be carried out. These stages of interrogation allows for better understanding and the attainment of a holistic view of the e-Government platform to be designed. It will show how people or structure factor, can impede or enhance the performance of an e-Government artifact and verse-versa. Figure 3 shows how systems thinking and performance measurement philosophies can lead to a holistic interrogation of what contemporary society needs and wants from an e-Government platform using artifact, structure, process and people as variables. Below figure should be used as Figure 3

However, it is important to appreciate that e-Government platform design strategy which is represented in Figure 3 are not universally the same. This results because of the variations in the variables-structure, process and people that are inherent in different societies and government agencies. There might be a generic e-Government platform where everybody is expected to access government services and products but the possibility of having a gigantic e-Government platform where all government services and products are provided is slimmer than the specialized platforms meant to provide specific services and products that are meant for specific classes of people. Hiller and Belanger (2011) framework has provide a strong basis for arguing that the likelihood to have a specialized e-Government platform is quite higher than that of having a generic platform that can serve everybody's wants and needs, say a given country or countries com-

bining to form a region. However, the framework which we have provided which comprises of e-Government platform structure, process and people and how these variables can be manipulated to design artifacts, is therefore, not meant to be a static all-encompassing framework. The framework is designed to be elastic and situation specific, which again is the kind of e-Government platform that will evolve if designers assess firstly, the kind of structure that the design would be operated in; secondly, the nature of the process that is available to run it and thirdly, the kind of people for which it is designed. This helps in the integration of technical, geographical, social and cultural differences that may exist in different setups where the e-Government platform to be designed is expected to be used.

The framework we proposed helps us to provide the basis for asking very fundamental questions that will allow e-Government platform designers to approach their design using systems thinking and performance measurement philosophies. The constructionist philosophy of the framework provides it with flexibility, comprehensiveness and elasticity required of a system that deals with social designs. Hence so many questions ranging from what kind of e-Government platform do we want to design, what are the stakeholders needs and wants that led to its proposed design, will it be stand-alone platform or meant to compliment an already existing e-Government platform, what exactly are the needs and wants of the public that led to the request to have it designed, what exactly are the needs and wants of the government that led to the request to have it designed, what expertise

Figure 3. Emergent of systems thinking and performance measurement in e-government platform design (authors)

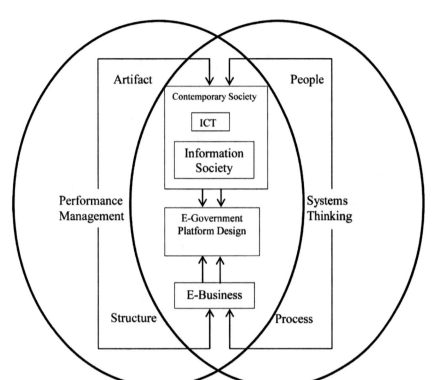

do we need to successfully design the e-Government platform in such a manner that it will meet stakeholders requirements? The questions to ask can go on and on and can also be made to emerge as e-Government platform designers begin their designs. The advantage of this kind of approach and thinking is that it prepares the e-Government platform designers to succeed. It provides them with a list of needs and wants and automatically with a list of resources and requirements that can make the project to succeed. Fundamentally, it provides them with required thinking that is necessary for setting performance benchmarks for the proposed e-Government platform. It has been noted earlier in this chapter that the approach may be complex and tedious at the initial stage of e-Government platform design project, however, as the e-Government platform designers get used to it, it would provide them better assurance for

success. Dealing with social aspects of IS design has never been easy, this it the reason why most IS failures have been ascribed to some sought of social carelessness on the part of IS analysts and designers.

FUTURE RESEARCH DIRECTIONS

There has been a great deal of effort put into research focusing on e-Government platform design. This research has helped to shape the current thinking which was discussed in the early part of this chapter. We have argued that research that precede this chapter dealt with the concatenation of government and governance, ICT and e-Business as means to the formation of principles and practices of e-Government as presently been practiced by e-Government platform designers. With the new thinking based on systems thinking and performance management, several avenues for new research directions have emerged. The position proposed in this chapter is based on an extensive review of the literature covering government and governance, ICT and information society, e-Business, systems thinking, performance measurement, and IS design, together with the combination of lived observation of e-Government platform usages. As such, there is a need for empirical studies that will use the theoretical positions provided in this chapter as a basis for interrogating practical aspects of e-Government platform design in appropriate empirical contexts where e-Government platforms are designed and used. Apart from looking at e-Government platform design, the theories provided in this chapter can also be used to interrogate the reasons why available e-Government platform fail or succeed. This will help to put the theoretical argumentation provided in the chapter in perspective. In its currently shape the arguments provided in this chapter is still lucid and fluid and will therefore require that it is used in empirical contexts for empirical research that will provide it with required level of externalization and validation.

There is no doubt about the fact that the IS fields need more socially oriented research regarding IS design, adoption, use, success, and failure. The theoretical position in this chapter is applicable to any kind of assessment that may need to be carried out on any IS design endeavor. This is more so as it touches the development of appropriate philosophies and approaches which will help in providing better ways for interrogating and assessing IS designs. Our argument in this chapter is multi-disciplinary in nature as a result of its combination of various academic fields. Precisely, government and governance as academic disciplines form a minute parts of the arguments that have been unfolding both theoretically and practically in the field of performance measure-

ment. This chapter therefore takes credence as few of available theoretical postulations that evokes the theoretical doctrines of performance measurement with the purpose of linking it with political performance. The chapter therefore, provides an avenue for the disciplines of performance measurement, IS and politics to develop research questions that are necessary in providing answers to how the three disciplines can combine to produce theories and practical knowledge that is capable of aiding socio-cultural development across the globe. We agree that the main aim of research is to bring about better understanding of social phenomena that constitute barriers to socio-political, cultural and economic development of the human society. The research directions that may emanate from this chapter are as numerous as the number of stakeholders that may be identified during the use of the tenets of the theories proposed in this chapter. This is because each stakeholder exists as a fundamental part of the systemic nature of the e-Government platform design strategy being proposed in this chapter.

CONCLUSION

We conclude that it is very relevant to adopt the principles available in the theory of systems thinking and performance measurement for improving the current practices evidence among e-Government platform designers. We agree to this because of the role systems thinking and performance measurement can play in making available the philosophies that are relevant to sieving out social factors that are necessary for successful design and implementation of e-government. We conclude that the future of e-Government design lies on the ability of e-Government platform designers to be able to understand and interrogate e-Government platform as an IT artifact, structure and process.

REFERENCES

Amor, D. (2000). *The e-business (r) evolution: Living and working in an interconnected world.* Upper Saddle River, NJ: Prentice Hall PTR.

Bidgoli, H. (2002). *Electronic commerce: Principles and practice.* San Diego, CA: Academic Press.

Bothma, C. (2000). *E-commerce for South African managers.* Irene: Interactive Reality.

Brooker, P. (2008). *Non-democratic regimes.* Hampshire, UK: Palgrave Macmillan.

Bwalya, K. (2010). E-government adoption landscape Zambia: Contexts, issues and challenges. In C. G. Reddick (Ed.), *Comparative e-government* (pp. 241–258). New York: Springer.

Bwalya, K. J., & Healy, M. (2010). Harnessing e-government adoption in the SADC region: A conceptual underpinning. *Electronic Journal of E-Government, 8*(1), 23–32.

Castells, M. (1996). *The rise of the network society.* Malden, MA: Blackwell.

Chandler, A. (1977). *The visible hand – Managerial revolution in American business.* Boston: Harvard University Press.

Davis, F. (1989). Perceived usefulness, perceived ease of use, and user acceptance of information technology. *Management Information Systems Quarterly, 13*(1), 319–340. doi:10.2307/249008

Dillon, A., & Morris, M. (1996). User acceptance of information technology: Theories and models. In *Annual review of information science and technology* (pp. 3–32). Medford, NJ: Information Today, Inc.

Drigas, A., & Koukianakis, L. (2009). Government online: An e-Government platform to improve public administration operations and services delivery of the citizens. In *Proceedings of WSKS,* (pp. 523-532). WSKS.

Drucker, P. (1954). *The practice of management.* New York: Harper.

Drucker, P. (1969). *The age of discontinuity: Guidelines to our changing society.* London: Pan Book Ltd.

Gartner Group. (2000, May 23). Key issues in e-government strategy and management. *Research Notes, Key Issues.*

Hayes, R., & Abernathy, W. (1980, July-August). Managing our way to economic decline. *Harvard Business Review,* 67–77.

Hiller, J., & Belanger, F. (2001). *Privacy strategies for electronic government.* Arlington, VA: The Pricewaterhouse Coopers Endowment for the Business of Government.

Ho, A. (2002). Reinventing local governments and the e-government initiative. *Public Administration Review, 62*(4), 434–444. doi:10.1111/0033-3352.00197

Homburg, V. (2008). *Understanding e-Government: Information systems in public administration.* Oxon, UK: Routledge.

Ittner, C., & Larcker, D. (2003, November). Coming up short on non-financial performance measurement. *Harvard Business Review,* 88–95. PMID:14619154

Jackson, M. (2003). *Systems thinking: Creative holism for managers.* West Sussex, UK: John Wiley & Son Ltd.

Jaeger, P., & Bertot, J. (2010). Transparency and technological change: Ensuring equal and sustained public access to government information. *Government Information Quarterly, 27,* 371–376. doi:10.1016/j.giq.2010.05.003

Johnson, H., & Kaplan, R. (1987). *Relevance lost – The rise and fall of management accounting.* Boston: Harvard Business School Press.

Kaplan, R., & Norton, D. (1996, January-February). Using the balanced scorecard as a strategic management system. *Harvard Business Review*, 3–13.

King, R., & Kendall, G. (2003). *The state, democracy & globalization*. Hampshire, UK: Palgrave Macmillan.

Maheshwari, B., Kumar, V., Kumar, U., & Sharan, V. (2007). E-government portal effectiveness: Managerial considerations for design and development. In *Proceedings of International Congress of E-Government*. E-Government.

Markaki, O., Charilas, D., & Askoumis, D. (2010). Evaluation of the impact and adoption of e-government services in the Ballrans. In *Comparative e-government*. New York: Springer. doi:10.1007/978-1-4419-6536-3_5

Matavire, R., Chigona, W., Roode, D., Sewchurran, E., Davids, Z., Mukudu, A., & Boamah-Abu, C. (2010). Challenges of e-government project implementation in South African context. *The Electronic Journal of Information Systems Evaluation, 13*(2), 153–164.

McKay, J., & Marshall, P. (2004). *Strategic management of business*. Milton, UK: John Wiley & Sons.

Neely, A. (1998). *Measuring business performance*. London: Profile Books Limited.

Neely, A., Adams, C., & Kennerley, M. (2002). *The performance prism: The scorecard for measuring and managing business success*. London: Prentice Hall.

Pierre, J., & Peters, B. (2000). *Governance, politics and the state*. London: Macmillan.

Porter, M. (1980). *Competitive strategy*. Cambridge, MA: Harvard Business School.

Ridgway, V. (1956). Dysfunctional consequences of performance measurements. *Administrative Science Quarterly, 1*(2), 240–247. doi:10.2307/2390989

Tapscott, D. (1995). *The digital economy: Promise and peril in the age of networked intelligence*. New York: McGraw Hill.

Tibenderana, P., & Ogao, P. (2008). Information and communication technologies acceptance and use among university community in Uganda: A model for hybrid library services end-users. *International Journal of Computing and ICT Research, 1*(1), 391–410.

Venkatesh, V., Morris, M., Davis, G., & Davis, F. (2003). User acceptance of information technology: Toward a unified view. *Management Information Systems Quarterly, 27*(3), 425–478.

Waring, A. (1996). *Practical systems thinking*. Hampshire, UK: Canage Learning.

Weinberg, G. (1975). *An introduction to general systems thinking*. New York: John Wiley & Sons.

Wilson, B. (1984). *Systems: Concepts, methodologies and applications*. Chichester, UK: John Wiley & Son.

Yuan, M. (2011). A design of e-government SMS platformbased on web. *International Conference on Management and Artificial Intelligence*. Retrieved March 1, 2011, from http://www.ipedr.com/vol16/24-A10019.pdf

ADDITIONAL READING

Modinis. (2007). Breaking Barriers to e-Government: *Overcoming obstacles to improving European public services*. Retrieved April 10, 2011 from www.egovbarriers.org/downloads/deliverables/solutions_report/Solutions_for_e-Government.pdf.

Mohd-Suki, N., & Ramayah, T. (2011). Modelling Customer's Attitude Towards e-Government Services, *International Journal of Human and Social Sciences*, 6(1). Retrieved March 18, 2011 from www.waset.org/journals/ijhss/v6/v6-1-4.pdf.

Moon, J. W., & Kim, Y. G. (2001). Extending the TAM for a world-wide-web context. *Information & Management*, *38*, 217–230. doi:10.1016/S0378-7206(00)00061-6

Moon, M. J. (2002). The evolution of E-Government among municipalities: Rhetoric or Reality? *Public Administration Review*, *62*(4), 424–433. doi:10.1111/0033-3352.00196

Moon, M.J. (2010). Shaping M-Government for emergency management: Issues and challenges, *Journal of e-Governance*, 33, 100-107.

Muir, A., & Oppenheim, C. (2002). National Information Policy Developments Worldwide in Electronic Government. *Journal of Information Science*, *28*(3), 173–186. doi:10.1177/016555150202800301

Mulozi, D. L. (2008). Rural access: options and challenges for connectivity and energy in Zambia, International Institute for Communication and Development (IICD thematic report. Retrieved September 10, 2010 from www.iicd.org/files/Zambia-Rural-Access-Report.pdf.

Mutula, S. M. (2010). Deploying Development Informatics in Bridging the Digital Divide: Challenges & Opportunities. *11th DIS Annual Conference 2010*, 2-3 September, Richardsbay, University of Zululand, South Africa. Retrieved August 17, 2011 from www.lis.uzulu.ac.za/research/conferences/2010/DIS%20 conferenceFP%20 Mutula%20Sept%20%2025%20final.pdf.

KEY TERMS AND DEFINITIONS

E-Business: Takes on a much broader meaning and include the use of Internet-based technology and other information technology to support commerce and improve business performance

E-Government: This entails the use of ICTs in public service value chains with a goal for an improved (efficient and effective) service delivery.

ICTs: This is an acronym that stands for Information and Communication Technologies – technology platforms or tools that are utilised for information interchange.

Systems Thinking: This is a conceptual underpinning that is based on inter-connected sets of activities towards a common goal. The results of a process are postulated through contributions of each individual entity in the information exchange value chain.

ENDNOTES

[1]   Our postulation about democratic and non-democratic government does not express our sentiment in favour of any of the two types of government.

Chapter 7
An Agile and Modular Approach for Developing Ontologies

Baby A. Gobin
University of Mauritius, Mauritius

ABSTRACT

Ontologies are used to represent human knowledge in a machine-understandable format. Knowledge exists in all domains and the proper capture and utilization of the knowledge is very important. Many ontology engineering methodologies are available for the development of ontologies. However, they suffer from their heavy weight nature and make the development process tedious. In addition, the resulting ontologies are monolithic ontologies and are not easy to reuse. Therefore, an agile and modular method is proposed to develop ontologies. The ease of use of the method is tested by a group of 68 inexperienced ontology engineers who compare it with Ontology 101 by developing ontologies in the e-Government domain using both methods.

INTRODUCTION

With knowledge being considered as a key asset, knowledge management principles are now being adopted by many countries. Knowledge management research focuses on developing concepts, methods and tools to support human knowledge (Jurisdisca et al., 2004). With respect to this, ontologies have been developed in the field of computer science to be able to represent the human knowledge so that machines can be used to interpret this knowledge. Computer systems, which use this knowledge for decision making, can then be developed. Ontology is a term borrowed from philosophy where ontology means a doctrine about existence in which general foundations, principles of existence, its structure and laws are studied. Gruber (1999) defines 'ontology' as 'a formal, explicit specification of a shared conceptualization', and definitions in Gruberian spirit are

DOI: 10.4018/978-1-4666-4900-2.ch007

still accepted by most ontological engineers. This definition is based on the idea of conceptualization i.e. a simplified version of the real world that we want to represent. They provide a shared and common understanding of a domain that can be communicated across people and application systems.

In these recent years, much work has been done with regards to the development of ontologies for e-Government (Salhofer et al., 2009; Hinkelmann et al., 2010; Dombeu et al., 2011). Different projects have been initiated in many countries and e-Government ontologies have been developed. However, small island developing states (SIDS) still lag behind in this field, Mauritius being one of them. In Mauritius, the field of Knowledge Management and Engineering is still in its infancy and the IT industry is more geared towards software development. However, to cope with this situation, a module in ontology development is being proposed in the IT curriculum at University of Mauritius. However, while working on ontology projects, it has been seen that final year students, face a lot of difficulty when they are requested to use ontology engineering methodologies or ontology development methods like Ontology Development 101. Some of the reasons were as follows: the heavy-weight nature of the ontology engineering methodologies, high learning curve associated to the development methodologies and the method and the reluctance of Domain Experts to participate. Therefore, these problems motivated the need for a new approach to the development of ontologies and this is how the Agile and Modular Method for Ontology Development (AMOD) was developed. This method is based on two concepts namely agile software development and ontology modules.

Agile methodologies (Vijayasarathy & Turk, 2008) use iterative and incremental approach to software development which is performed by a group of people with different functional expertise working towards a common goal. These methodologies have been proposed as an alternative to

traditional heavyweight software development methodologies. They are particularly helpful when requirements are not very well defined at the beginning of the project. Through the different iterations and releases, high quality software which also meets the client's requirements are developed in a cost effective and timely manner. Extreme Programming (Beck, 2000) is perhaps the best known and most widely used agile method. It takes an 'extreme' approach to iterative development. Here, the developer prioritizes what to do first on the basis of client requirements. This approach can be used to develop domain ontologies, whereby the Domain Expert becomes part of the development team and with the Knowledge Engineer both embark on the development process. The ontology is developed into phases based on the different user stories.

The second concept is, modular ontologies, which is inspired by software modules. Ontology modularisation is the process of defining a module which is the subset of the main ontology (Doran, 2009). The aim of developing a module is to make the ontology smaller so that it can be used for a particular application. A large ontology is not easy to understand and use and as such the use of module simplifies the task of those developing intelligent systems. Ontology modules being smaller also promote re-use and increases understandability. The concept of modules is used in the proposed development ontology, with the difference that instead of extracting modules, different modules are merged together to form the final domain ontology. Each module is developed bearing in mind the different applications that can be developed using these ontologies.

These two concepts are investigated upon and integrated together to produce a method for ontology development as will be seen in the different sections of this chapter. Up-to now, they have been considered separately. We merge these two concepts to develop the proposed method in this chapter. The different steps of the method are discussed in this chapter as well as the validation process. To validate the method, 68 novice ontology engineers were requested to use this method to develop ontologies in the e-Government domain. They also compared it with the Ontology Development 101 and explained the difficulties faced and their preferences. It is hoped that this new approach for ontology development can then be adopted by other countries especially SIDS.

BACKGROUND

From a philosophical perspective, 'ontology' means a doctrine about existence in which general foundations, principles of existence, structure and laws are studied. It is used to describe things that exist in the world. This concept has been re-adapted to the world of computers where ontologies are used to model common entities which can be used to achieve a certain task. As stated by Stevens et al., (2010), in Computer Science, ontology represents a shared background knowledge for a community of Domain Experts. There is a clear distinction between 'Ontology' from the philosophical discipline and the 'ontology' from the computer science and informatics field. 'Ontology' deals with the nature of the entity and the description of the world, while 'ontology' denotes its use in knowledge based systems (Guarino1998).

Gruber (1993) defines 'ontology' as 'a specification of a shared conceptualization', and definitions in Gruberian spirit have been and still are accepted by most ontological engineers. This definition is based on the idea of conceptualization i.e. a simplified version of the real world that needs to be represented. According to Gruber, a 'conceptualisation' is the understanding of concepts and the relationships that exist between them. Conceptualisation provides for a shared and common understanding of a domain that can be communicated across people and application systems (Sureephong et al., 2008). On the other hand, a 'specification' is how the knowledge within a domain, which has been agreed upon by the Domain Experts and which is shared among them, is represented (Dillon et al., 2008).

Alternatives to this definition are normally considered as refinements of Gruber's definition (Doran, 2009). Borst (1997) states that ontology should be formal, agreeing, with the general notion above. Studer et al.,(1998) extend this by stating that the ontology must be explicit i.e. explicitly defined resulting in a "formal, explicit, specification of a shared conceptualization". Formal ontologies imply that the meaning of the ontology is unambiguous to avoid misunderstanding. Formal languages are used to specify the different entities in the ontology. The heart of any knowledge representation system is the ontology (Chandrasekaran et al., 1999). Since knowledge cannot be represented if the ontology is not built, then ontology analysis is primordial to allow the building of an effective knowledge representation system. This is why it is very important to have a good understanding of concepts around ontologies and differentiate it with other domain models.

In computer science, ontologies are classified in different categories (Sanchez et al., 2007). Guarino (1998) classifies ontologies by their level of generality: top-level ontologies, task and domain ontologies and application ontologies while van Heijst et al. (1996) classifies them based on their use as follows: terminological ontologies, information ontologies and knowledge modelling ontologies. Domain ontologies define concepts of a particular domain (Kharbat & Ghalayini, 2008). It specifies the concepts in a particular subject area, and the relationships between these concepts (Boyce & Pahl., 2007). For example, an Urban Domain Ontology is an ontology modelling the urban domains and the knowledge about individuals and their relationships in their spatial context (Finat et al., 2010) whilst a Budgetary and Financial Domain Ontology models all the information particular to budgeting and finance (Brusa et al., 2006). Most ontology engineering methodologies focus on the development of such type of ontologies. A team consisting of Domain

Experts and knowledge/ontology engineers is set up to develop domain ontologies. The purpose of these ontologies is to allow knowledge about a particular domain to be re-used. For example, when developing knowledge-based applications the same domain ontology can be used for different applications.

Ontology Engineering Methodologies

Many approaches have been developed for creating ontologies. The approaches were built by reflecting on practical experience in the construction of specific ontologies and are therefore relatively immature for the general purpose (Knublauch, 2002). Some of the methodologies are: Uschold and King's Methodology (Uschold and King, 1995), Gruninger and Fox's methodology (Gruninger and Fox, 1995) and Methontology (Fernández-López, 1997). All these methodologies cater for project management processes, development processes and integral processes (Kehagias et al., 2008).

Uschold and King's Methodology: Enterprise

The main steps in Uschold's methodology are: 1) identifying of the purpose of ontology 2) building the ontology (capture, coding and integrating with existing ontologies), 3) evaluating the ontology and 4) documentation. The purpose and key concepts and relations are identified. They are then captured in an unambiguous textual form. A terminology is agreed upon and the concepts and relations are coded using a formal language and integrated with existing ontologies. The ontology is then evaluated and documented.

Gruninger and Fox's Methodology

As for Gruninger and Fox's methodology, it consists of formulating competency questions out of the problems of the partners, defining terminology: objects, attributes, relations, working on definitions and constraints on terminology, finally going through the Completeness theorem to test correctness.

Methontology

Methontology adopts a waterfall approach and caters for management, development and support activities. The development process iterates through the following phases: specification, conceptualisation, formalisation, implementation and maintenance. It is more complex than the previous mentioned methodologies.

NeON Methodology

NeOn is a framework that has been proposed to develop network ontologies. It provides for methodological guidelines to carry out processes and activities related to ontology development. Nine scenarios for building ontology networks have been identified and guidelines are provided for the different scenarios.

Ontology Development 101

Apart from these heavy-weight ontology engineering methodologies, there are other ontology development methods that have been proposed. Ontology Development 101 (Noy and McGuiness, 2001) is one of the most popular methods and is normally used by novice ontology engineers. It provides for eight main steps in the development process which are as follows:

1. **Determine Scope:** Domain ontology represents a specific domain and there is no correct ontology for a domain. A series of basic questions help to define the scope. The questions range from the domain that the ontology will cover, what is ontology is going to be used for, what are the questions that the ontology should provide answers for and who will be using and maintaining the ontology.

2. **Consider Reuse:** Building large ontologies from scratch can be very tedious and resource intensive(Bontas et al., 2005). Ontology reuse is to a certain extent help in decreasing complexities where instead of starting from scratch, ontology engineers can use available ontologies as input. Many ontology engineering methodologies advocate the reuse of ontologies. However, it is not very clear how to go about this process especially for novice engineers. Ontology 101 only recommends looking for ontologies that are publicly available and import them.

3. **Enumerate Terms:** During this phase, ontology engineers are required to list the different terms identified in the particular domain. There are obtained from answers of competency questions. Ontologies should be able to answer the competency questions. Identified nouns eventually map onto classes and attributes while verbs are used to identify relations between the different classes.

4. **Define Taxonomies:** Taxonomy is a classification of different information/knowledge components in a certain order, mostly in a hierarchical structure.Uschold and Gruninger(1996) proposed three approaches to build the ontology hierarchy namely, the top-down approach, the bottom-up approach and a combination of both approaches. The top-down approach focuses on specializing concepts by starting with a general concept. On the other hand, the bottom-up approach supports the grouping of concepts with common attributes in a more general concept. A combination of both approaches consists of developing the hierarchy using the top-down and bottom approach.

5. **Define Properties:** The remaining terms are used to define the properties of the different classes. Properties can either be attributes of the classes or relationships between the different classes. Inverse properties are also identified.

6. **Define Facets:** This step involves defining the different constraints e.g. cardinality constraints, disjoint constraints and so forth. The domain and range for each property is also defined.

7. **Define Instances:** Instances are defined for each class by putting values to each property. Instance creation is normally not done manually. They are retrieved from databases or extracted from a text corpus.

THE NEED FOR AGILITY AND MODULARITY FOR ONTOLOGY DEVELOPMENT

Agile Ontology Development

Agile methodologies are based on an iterative and incremental approach to software development which is performed by a group of people with different functional expertise working towards a common goal. These people contribute to produce high quality software in a cost effective and timely manner and also meeting the client's requirements. In addition, the methodology helps to increase productivity and is useful especially when there is no a clear idea of the client's requirements. There are several methods by which agile methodology can be implemented. Table 1 shows the difference between agile methodologies and traditional methodologies.

Table 1. Difference between agile and traditional methodologies (M.A.Awad, 2005)

	Agile Methods	**Traditional Methods**
Approach	Adaptive	Predictive
Success Measurement	Business value	Conformation to plan
Project Size	Small	Large
Management Style	Decentralized	Autocratic
Perspective to change	Change adaptability	Change sustainability
Culture	Leadership-collaboration	Command-control
Documentation	Low	Heavy
Emphasis	People-oriented	Process-oriented
Cycles	Numerous	Limited
Domain	Unpredictable/Exploratory	Predictable
Upfront Planning	Minimal	Comprehensive
Return on Investment	Early in project	End of project
Team Size	Small/Creative	Large

XP is perhaps the best known and most widely used agile methods (Beck, 2000). It takes an 'extreme' approach to iterative development. Here, the developer prioritizes what to do first on the basis of client requirements. It advocates frequent releases which are delivered to the customer every two weeks. All tests must be run for every build and the build is only accepted if tests run successfully.

An agile approach to ontology development can be very beneficial to novice ontology engineers as it helps the decrease complexities attached to it. As such existing heavy weight ontology methodologies have their degree of complexity, are resource intensive and time consuming. Hristozova (2003) argues that these methodologies are the results of efforts to build large-scale ontologies, without a specific narrow domain of purpose. It also enhances collaboration between the Domain Experts and the ontology engineers. This is very important since understanding the domain of interest can be very difficult for the ontology engineers. Agile approach promotes proximity and interaction since it puts more focus on people rather than process. There are already existing works whereby the XP methodology has been readapted to build agile methodologies for the development of ontologies.

The first is the XP.K methodology proposed by Knublauch (2002). It is an agile methodology for the development of knowledge based systems. It follows the same values of XP but generalises the value of Communication to Community which includes Humility. This implies that the teams should build and nurture collaboration infrastructure and must also be humble enough to acknowledge their limited knowledge, especially when dealing with Domain Experts. They must respect the attitudes, background, languages of their other team members. XP.K relies on the XP practices for development of inference engines, user interfaces, and database access or acquisition tools. For ontology development, additional practices are applied. The ontology design is done jointly i.e. both the Domain Expert and the ontology engineer participate in the modelling and design process together. Modelling standards are adopted during the modelling phase and tests are also carried out after the modelling sessions.

EXPLODE (Extreme Programming for Lightweight Ontology Development) is a methodology proposed by Hristozova (2003) for the agile development of lightweight ontologies. The method is based on XP and has a set of rules and practices to be used when creating ontologies. Below is an overview of changes made to XP to create the new methodology. XP user stories are replaced by competency questions (CQ), and requirements for the ontology are extracted from these questions and systems constraints.

During planning, each CQ is discussed and the time to add concepts and relations pertaining that question to the ontology is estimated. Users co-operate with the ontology engineers to come to an agreement about each CQ. The baseline ontology focuses on the architectural and usage requirement. The goal of the baseline is to reduce the risk of a technical problem and also increase the reliability of the answers of the CQs. Each iteration consists of three steps 1) testing the CQs, 2) iteration planning and 3) implementation. The CQs are tested against the baseline ontology since CQs may often overlap and even subsume each other. If this is the case then the next CQ is considered. Once a CQ has been selected, the iteration is planned. The two inputs to this phase are CQs and results acceptance tests. Once these are obtained, the iteration may start. Continuous integration detects compatibility problems with other environments. Small releases of the ontology, helps in this process. Maintenance and support are done immediately after the first release just like XP iteration.

RapidOWL (Auer and Herres, 2006) is another methodology which promotes collaborative Knowledge Engineering. It is inspired by XP.K and at the same time has concepts from Wiki used for collaborative text editing. It differs from XP.K as it focuses on the development of generic knowledge bases whereas the development of the knowledge base in XP.K is subject to a particular scenario. The knowledge base is refined, annotated and structure through iterations. Ontologies are developed jointly whereby the Domain Experts turn into part-time knowledge engineers. It does not provide for a lifecycle though.

All the three methodologies propose the development of a large monolithic ontology at one go. The concept of reuse is not present and this will also impact on the maintenance of the ontology. Ontology modularization can, to a certain extent, help to solve these problems.

Ontology Modularization

The idea of ontology modules evolved from the concept of software modules in software engineering. An ontology module is normally a section of a large monolithic ontology which has been extracted for a particular purpose. An ontology module can be considered as a loosely coupled and self-contained component of an ontology maintaining relationships to other ontology modules, hence making the ontology module an ontology (d'Aquin et al., 2006). The need for modularizing large monolithic ontologies has been felt due to problems in terms of reuse, maintenance and reliability. Ontology modularization enables ontology developers to include only those concepts and relations that are relevant for the application they are modelling an ontology for (Doran, 2009).

There are many advantages of using ontology modularization. First, it facilitates knowledge reuse across various applications (Abbes et al., 2012, Doran 2009). It enhances understandability and reusability (Ensan, 2010, Ozacar et al., 2011). Since the modules are smaller, ontology engineers have a better understanding of the ontology and this increases the chances of the ontology being reused. Due to its size and scope, ontology modules are also easier to build and maintain as compared to a large monolithic ontology. The ontology engineer will focus only on the most relevant part. Managing modules is also more effective and updating smaller ontologies is a less tedious and complex task. Division of labour, scalability and broadened participation are other benefits identified by Ozacar et al., (2011). An ontology module can be assigned to the expert who better understands the sub-domain such that different experts will be working on different ontology modules. An ontology module is more scalable and is easier to edit and maintain as compared to a large monolithic ontology which will have higher computational cost and memory requirements. User participation is easier and a large number of users can easily contribute to the ontology modules without compromising its quality.

There are two approaches to ontology modularization (Abbes, 2012). Modularization of ontologies can be seen as either extracting modules from a large ontology or integrating several modules that have been developed separately to form a new large ontology with respect to a specific domain. The first approach is the most common one and a lot of work and tools have been developed for this purpose. This approach can be split into two distinct tasks: ontology partitioning and ontology module extraction (Doran, 2009). Ontology partitioning involves the breaking down of a large ontology into smaller ontologies based on a particular partitioning algorithm. The union of all modules should be same as the large ontology that has been partitioned. Work addressing this issue is covered by Grau el al. (2005), Stuckenschmidt and Klein (2004) and Schlicht and Stuckenschmidt(2008). Ontology module extraction on the other hand is the task of extracting a module from a large ontology based on a specified signature Sig (M). In the second approach, the modules are initially identified in the design phase itself by bringing together different concepts based on certain criteria. It is this approach that is used in the proposed development framework. Ozacar et al., (2011) proposed ANEMONE, a methodology for the development of modular ontologies, whereby an ontology module network behaves like a monolithic global ontology. The global ontology is organised into modules as follows:

- **Base Ontology Module**: The module stores domain-free knowledge units and abstract concepts. They will be directly or indirectly imported by other modules.
- **Higher-Order Domain Ontology Modules**: These modules contain common concepts shared by domain modules.
- **Domain Ontology Modules**: A domain ontology module defines knowledge related to a particular domain. They will import higher-order domain ontology modules.
- **Local Ontology Modules**: The local ontology module stores two kinds of knowledge: localised domain concepts and assertion domain knowledge.

These modules should be considered when designing e-Government applications.

AN AGILE AND MODULAR METHOD FOR ONTOLOGY DEVELOPMENT (AMOD)

AMOD is an agile method which enables the development of ontologies by merging ontology modules. These ontology modules can exist independently and used with respect to a certain application or merged to form a large monolithic ontology which will be generic in nature. The method is not a methodology but if compared to the development processes of existing agile ontology engineering methodologies, it does have additional elements which contribute to enhancing the development process. One of them is expert stories. Expert stories are stories that are written by the Domain Expert, which describes a particular scenario with the domain of interest. It also provides clear steps (Figure 1) on how to go about the development process which are described in this section. To illustrate the ideas around each task, we give extracts of the development process of an ontology for the social integration domain.

Figure 1. AMOD development processes

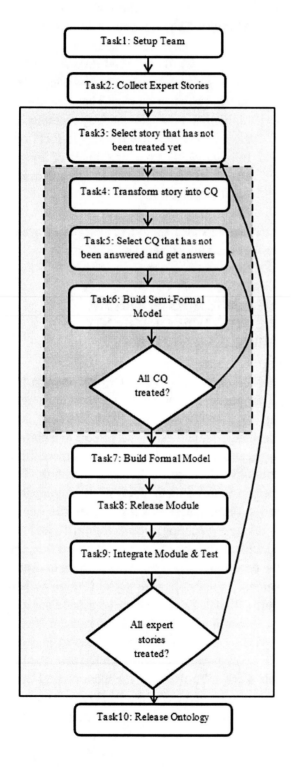

Task 1: Setting up the Team

The development process of the ontology starts with knowledge engineers and Domain Experts coming together and discussing the aim of the project. Normally, Domain Expert will not have much knowledge about the role of knowledge engineers and what is expected from them. Domain Experts play a crucial part in the development of the ontology and will contribute a lot in the knowledge acquisition/capture process. As for knowledge engineers, they need to have a better understanding of the domain of interest. During this phase they will get a better overview of the objectives, the problem to be tackled and also become familiar with terms being used with the domain. The outcome of the phase is a collaborative environment and an understanding between the Domain Experts and the knowledge engineers. The working environment to be shared and the way of proceeding through the project will be agreed upon.

Task 2: Collect Expert Stories

During this stage, the Knowledge Engineer will write stories based on the information gathered during interview sessions with Domain Experts. This involves the write up of real life scenarios from which facts can be obtained which will be used to build the ontology. The stories are given priorities and relationships between them are identified. Each story is depicted using a small card and is written in simple English. The Domain Experts are then requested to validate the stories so as to make sure that whatever has been written by the Knowledge Engineer is in line with the Domain Expert. Stories can be added at any point in time of the project e.g. a requirement that has not been identified from the beginning can be written. Figure 2 is an example of a story card for needs assessment carried out by case workers to identify the needs of households who are below the poverty threshold.

Figure 2. Needs assessment story card

Title	Needs Assessment
Depends On	None
Description	Case workers visit potential beneficiaries identified to perform a needs analysis. Various questions are set to the head regarding the household. This will include questions on demographics, education, health, employment, training interest and housing facilities.
Priority	High
Actors	Case Workers, Beneficiaries
Supporting Documents	Needs Assessment Form of Mr X
Impact on other stories	No

Task 3: Select a Story that has not been Treated Yet

Two Knowledge Engineers select a story that has not been dealt with and will focus on it for the next iteration. A new wiki page is created based on the information on the card. The pairs enter in development iteration and will not work on any other story until this one is complete.

Task 4: Transform the Story into Competency Questions

The pair processes the story on the wiki page and adds competency questions to be answered by them with the help/clarification from Domain Experts. Feedback from Domain Experts is very important at this point. The story is split into simple sentences which are then transformed in CQs. For example for the needs assessment form some CQs obtained are shown in Table 2.

Task 5: Select a CQ which has not been Treated Yet and Get Answers Related to It

The answers from the competency questions are obtained from different sources ranging from interviews of Domain Experts, forms, policy papers, excel sheets, reports and other documents.

Table 2. Competency questions for story card "Needs Assessment"

	Competency Questions
Q1	Which details are kept for about each household?
Q2	What are the details kept for each household member?
Q3	What relation a household member can share with the head of the household?
Q4	Give the different marital status identified.
Q5	What are the different health issues noted for each household?
Q6	Are schooling details recorded for each member?
Q7	What are the training options that a beneficiar ycan have?
Q8	Can a beneficiary have hisown house, or rent a house?
Q9	What are the different pieces equipment/furniture recorded for each person being assessed?
Q10	What are existing public utilities available?

The answers need to be validated by the Domain Expert and appropriate changes should be done. Examples of answers to CQs are found in Table 3.

Task 6: Build/Add to Semi-Formal Model

During the task, a semi-formal model is developed using natural language. Each RS (Requirement Story) will have its own semi-formal model. The semi-formal model associated to an RS is built using the first CQ and is updated based on the answers of different CQs after each iteration. There are different subtasks associated to the

Table 3. Answers to competency questions

CQ	Answers
Q1	Age, Gender, Disabilities, Education, Marital Status, Occupation, District, Village/Town, Housing Facilities, Utilities
Q2	Name, Date of Birth, NIC, Address (head only), Relation with head, Contact Number (head only), Place of birth, Marital Status
Q3	Wife, Son, Daughter, Stepson, Stepdaughter, Grandson, Granddaughter, Mother, Father, Grandmother, Grandfather, Husband
Q4	Marital Status: Married Religiously (MR), Married Civilly(MC), Married Religiously & Civilly (MRC), Widowed (W), Divorced (D), Separated (SEP), Single (S)
Q5	Health Issues: Diabetes(Db), High BP(HBP), Asthma (Asth), Scabies (Sc), Cardiac Problem(Cp), Epilepsy(Ep), None, Other

Table 4. List of terms

Term	Link	Term
aHousehold	isfound	in aPovertyPacket
aHouseholdMember	ISA	Person
aHouseholdMember	has	a Marital Status
aHousehold Head	isresponsible	of a Household
Diabetes	ISA	Health Issue

Table 5. Concepts and Taxonomies

Concepts	IS-A Relationship
RelationToHead	Wife, Husband, Son, Daughter, Stepfather, Stepmother Stepson, Stepdaughter, Grandson, Granddaughter, Mother, Father, Grandmother, Grandfather, Father-in-Law, Mother-in-Law, Niece, Nephew, Uncle, Aunt, Cousin
MaritalStatus	MarriedReligiouslyOnly, MarriedCivillyOnly, Married, Widowed, Divorced, Separated,Single
HealthIssues	Diabetes, HighBP, Asthma, Scabies, CardiacProblem, Epilepsy, None,Other
Schooling	NeverAttendedSchool, AttendedSchool, AttendingSchool, CNYS
EducationLevel	Primary, Secondary, Tertiary

development task which are shown in Figure1. During these subtasks, KE will define the classes, taxonomies, attributes, relations which exist between the different classes, constraints and rules required to check the different constraints. A glossary of terms is also the obtained after having completed these tasks.

Task 6.1: Identify All Terms

During this phase the different terms which will be used to create the different concepts, relations and attributes of the ontology are identified (see Table 4). The relations that exist between the different terms are also described. This will help to build taxonomies and define the attributes.

Task 6.2: Define Concepts

After having identified all terms, the list of concepts and the taxonomy is built (Table 5). The concepts obtained for the needs analysis ontology are defined in the table below. The ontology engineer checks whether the concepts are found in other modules. If so, then the concepts will not be created during the development of the formal model. They will be imported.

Task 6.3. Define Attributes of Each Concept

The attributes of each concept as well as the relations between the different concepts are then listed. The attributes and relations are already identified during the term identification phase but it is in this phase that they are well defined. Table 6 shows some the attributes identified for some of the concepts. Similarly the relations are also defined in Table 7.

Table 6. Concepts and attributes

Concepts	Attributes
District	DistrictName,
Cluster	ClusterNo, HasHousehold
PovertyPacket	PovertyPacketNo, PovertyPacketType
Household	HouseholdNo,ResidentialAddress, ContactNo, Householdstatus, Case-WorkerNo, HouseholdHead, HouseholdMembers
HouseholdMember	RelationtoHead, Age, Gender, DOB, Place of Birth, Marital status, HealthIssues, Schooling, Level of Education, EmploymentStatus, Occupation, Income, Disability, ReceivingSocialAid, ProblemNoted,

Table 7. Concepts and relations

Concepts	Relation	Concepts
District	hasCluster	Cluster
Cluster	hasPovertyPacket	PovertyPacket
PovertyPacket	hasHousehold	Household
Household	hasMember	HouseholdMember
Household-Member	hasHead	HouseholdMember

Task 6.4: Describe Business Rules and Categorize Them

The different business rules are identified and these will become the constraints on the different classes of the ontologies. These constraints are written in natural language so that they can be vetted by the Domain Expert.

Task 6.5: Describe Instances

Instances are normally required when building the knowledge base. Still a few instances for each concept are identified so that it can be used for testing purposes.

Task 7: Build/Add to Formal Model

The formal model is developed using OWL formal language. The Protégé 2000 software is used for creating the ontology. The different concepts are created as per the list built as well as the attributes and relations. Axioms and SWRL rules are used to represent the different business rules. Existing modules can be imported to develop new modules.

Task 8: Release the Module

During this phase the module is tested and then released so that it can be reused to develop other modules.It will also be integrated to form part of a monolithic ontology. The module can also be used later when developing knowledge-based applications. Tests carried out are consistency checking, concept hierarchy tests, attributes and relations tests. In our case since we are using the Protégé 2000 editor,the Pelletreasoner is used to check the consistency, while the remaining is done manually. All concepts, attributes and relations are verified and validated against the semi-formal model.

Task 9: Integrate, Test and Fix

When integrating the module with the existing ontology, consistency checks have to be done. This is done using the Pellet reasoner. Redundancy also needs to be checked. This is done manually and changes are done.

Task 10: Release the Ontology

The version of the ontology is updated and the module is released.

EVALUATING AMOD AMONG NOVICE

68 Mauritian novice ontology engineers (all final year students in Computer Science and Information Systems) were requested to test AMOD by using it to build ontologies. They were grouped into 16 teams (14 teams of 4 and 2 teams of 6). They had no prior knowledge about ontology engineering. The ontology development was done over 15 weeks. The first week concepts on Semantic Web and OWL were explained. A brief overview of Ontology Development 101 (OD101) was also given during the practical sessions. The practical session also covered the use of Protégé 2000. Six weeks were allocated to the development of ontologies using OD101 and the remaining weeks for the development ontologies using the agile and modular approach. The different teams studied the domain of e-Governance and each team was requested to develop different ontologies. The different ontologies covered domain ranging from agriculture to tourism. They were to study different pages on the e-Government portal

and also identify Domain Experts based on their initial understanding of the domain.

They were first asked to develop the ontology using the Ontology Develop 101 guideline first. The level of difficulty for each step was then assessed. Figure 3 gives a summary of the results obtained. 11 teams considered defining scope of the ontology as a moderate-difficult activity. Lack of experience and complexity of the domain were the main reasons behind this score. Students found it difficult to define questions since they felt that the scope was vast and required an in-depth understanding. The output from the interaction with Domain Experts was quite minimal and did not contribute much for defining the scope since the Domain Expert he did not provide a proper answer. It is to be noted that many Domain Experts were not IT conversant and had no basic IT knowledge. Hence most of the Domain Experts asked the students to refer to the Mauritian E-Government Portal. The students therefore tried to define a scope based on the content found on the portal.

As shown in Figure 3, 11 teams considered reusing ontologies and looked for ontologies that could be used by searching on the ontology search

Figure 3. Survey results for Ontology Development 101

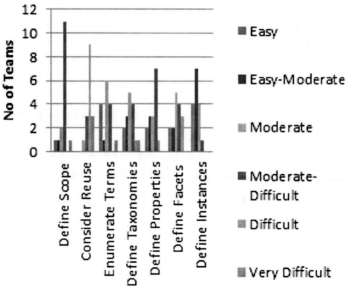

engine Swoogle. However they find this activity difficult as they had to analyse each ontology obtained after the search.

The ontologies have been often not relevant or if partially relevant the student would have had to extract that part. Thus this task proved to be very tedious for them and hence they all opted to develop their ontologies from scratch. Some did not find appropriate ontologies which could be reused.

Enumerating terms are considered to have a moderate level of difficulty by the teams. The main difficulty faced here was to understand terms that were specific to the domain. The students extracted the terms from the website and consulted Domain Experts for clarifications. Also the main problem faced by students was how to group the different concepts in a hierarchy. Since they had a large set of concepts, finding the link between them was quite difficult. As such many made mistakes when grouping the concepts despite having been given clear guidelines on how to group the concepts. 7 teams out of 16 found the task of defining attributes moderate to difficult, the main reason of this score being that the domain is complex to understand. Defining facets and instances on the other hand seems to be easier for the students as per the figures obtained.

Figure 4 gives an overview of the results obtained with regards to AMOD guidelines. 8 teams out of 16 found the process of collecting ES moderate in terms of complexity. Some minor problems faced was essentially in terms of interaction with Domain Experts. It was sometimes difficult to separate the stories and assign priorities. The input of the Domain Expert was very important. However this exercise did help them to have a better understanding of the domain of interest and also determine the scope of the project. The majority of the teams found the transformation of ES into CQs easy to moderately easy. The main difficulties faced here was that new CQs could crop up while answering certain CQs. As for the other steps here also the majority found it easy to moderately easy. As per results in Figure 5

Figure 4. Ontology reuse results

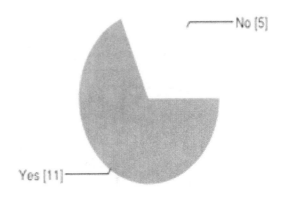

Look for ontologies to reuse

No [5]

Yes [11]

the students preferred the approach of AMOD to OD101 for identifying terms, concepts, properties and building and testing the ontology (Figure 6). Some minor difficulties are faced by some students but they pointed out that they preferred AMOD as it was more focused and provided a starting point. Stories help them to better understand the domain and it was easier to communicate with the Domain Expert since the Domain Expert felt involved in telling the stories and hence more committed. Also the answers helped the students to get detailed insight of the domain. They were able to build better hierarchies as it was done gradually with concepts being added after each story. The same was felt when defining properties, constraints and instances.

Table 8 gives an idea of the size of the ontologies developed. The size is defined as the number of concepts and properties of the ontology. An indication of the number of modules is also given. It is to be noted that the quality of the ontologies created has not been evaluated. As can be seen both from the table and Figure 7, the size of the ontologies is bigger for AMOD as compared to OD101. When queried about this, participants justified this by the fact that by using AMOD they had been able to identify additional concepts and properties which they had missed initially.

Figure 5. Survey results for AMOD Guidelines

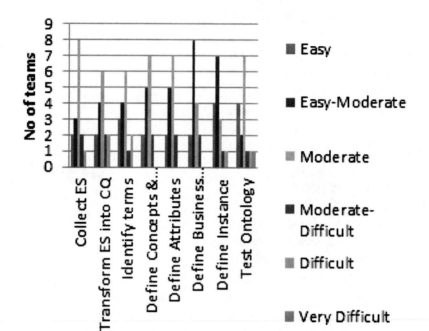

Figure 6. AMOD Preference over OD101

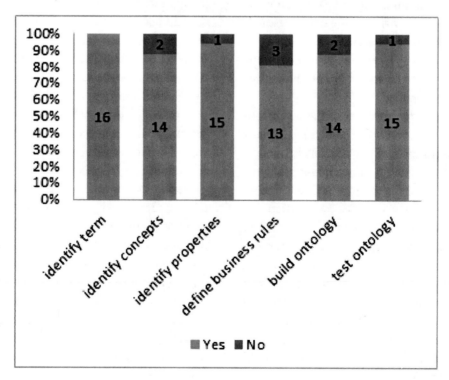

Table 8. Ontology size comparison

Team	Ontology	OD101	Agile & Modular Approach	
		Size of Ontology	No of Modules	Size of Ontology
Team1	Health Ontology	140	13	300
Team2	Land and Housing Ontology	75	9	110
Team3	Law and Order Ontology	110	10	250
Team4	Passport&Immigration Ontology	73	13	100
Team5	Public Utilities Ontology	109	9	171
Team6	Social welfare ontology	219	23	272
Team7	Taxation ontology	100	14	234
Team8	Security & Welfare	230	10	256
Team9	Commerce	80	7	99
Team10	Environment ontology	331	10	365
Team11	Agriculture ontology	120	9	159
Team12	Arts ontology	65	6	79
Team13	Education	176	11	243
Team14	Social Security & Welfare	40	6	97
Team15	Sports and youth	294	16	345
Team16	Tourism and Travel	311	13	336

Figure 7. Ontology size comparison

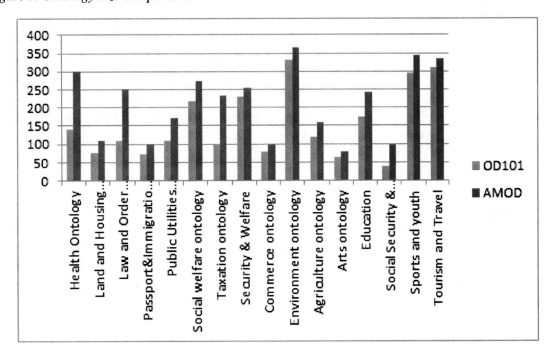

FUTURE RESEARCH DIRECTIONS

The next step is to develop a complete methodology which will integrate the AMOD method. The aim is to have a full-fledge agile methodology which can be easily used by ontology engineers especially inexperienced ones so that they can build both ontology modules and large monolithic ontologies. The methodology will provide the proper lifecycle, tools and a validation framework in addition to the existing development process. As the methodology will be developed, ontology testing and evaluation methods will also be investigated upon and tools also need to be provided. In AMOD, some tests are proposed and done manually. Automating these tests can help improve the development process. Also, no mention on ontology evaluation is done in AMOD since it focuses mainly the tasks required to construct the ontology. Much work has been done in the field of ontology evaluation. This will be integrated in the methodology. Automatic population of the instances of the ontology is another field that needs to be investigated.

CONCLUSION

Many ontology engineering methodologies and methods are available to develop ontologies so that knowledge can be captured, easily shared and reused. However, ontology development remains a very tedious task. It may be a big challenge for new and inexperienced ontology developers, especially for those who belong to SIDS, who have limited resources as compared to developers in big developing countries. In an attempt to help in the development process, a method which uses an agile and module approach to ontology development has been developed. The method has been successfully welcomed among the young and first generation of Mauritian ontology engineers due to its agile and modular nature. It is hoped that this method can be used, improved and re-adapted to help more ontology developers. Still, there is a lot that remains to be done. The development of a whole methodology around this method will indeed provide for better project management capabilities and also evaluation strategies.

REFERENCES

Abbes, S. B., Scheuermann, A., Meilender, T., & d'Aquin, M. (2012). *Characterizing modular ontologies*. Paper presented at the International Conference on Formal Ontologies in Information Systems (FOIS). Graz, Autriche.

Auer, S., & Herre, H. (2006). Rapid OWL - An agile knowledge engineering methodology. In *Proceedings of at Sixth International Andrei Ershov Memorial Conference - Perspectives of System Informatics PSI'06*. Novosibirsk, Russia: PSI.

Awad, M. A. (2005). *A comparison between agile and traditional software development methodologies*. Retrieved May 20, 2013 from http://pds10.egloos.com/pds/200808/13/85/A_comparision_between_Agile_and_Traditional_SW_development_methodologies.pdf

Beck, K. (2000). *Extreme programming explained: Embrace change*. Reading, MA: Addison Wesley Longman, Inc.

Bontas, E. P., Mochol, M., & Tolksdorf, R. (2005). Case studies on ontology reuse. In *Proceedings of the 5th International Conference on Knowledge Management IKNOW05*. IKNOW.

Borst, W. N. (1997). *Construction of engineering ontologies for knowledge sharing and reuse.* (PhD thesis). Centre for Telematica and Information Technology, University of Twente, Twente, The Netherlands.

Boyce, S., & Pahl, C. (2007). Developing domain ontologies for course content. *Journal of Educational Technology & Society*, *10*(3), 275–288.

Brusa, G., Caliusco, M. L., & Chiotti, O. (2006). A process for building a domain ontology: An experience in developing a government budgetary ontology. In *Proceedings of the Second Australasian Workshop on Advances in Ontologies*, (Vol. 72). IEEE.

Chandrasekaran, B., Josephson, J. R., & Benjamins, V. R. (1999). Ontology of tasks and methods, (acrobat), Banff knowledge acquisition workshop. *IEEE Intelligent Systems*, *14*(1), 20–26. doi:10.1109/5254.747902

Cuenca-Grau, B., Parsia, B., Sirin, E., & Kalyanpur, A. (2005). Automatic partitioning of OWL ontologies using e-connections. In *Proceedings of the 2005 International Workshop on Description Logics* (DL-2005). DL.

d'Aquin, M., Sabou, M., & Motta, E. (2006). Modularization: A key for the dynamic selection of relevant knowledge components. In *Proceedings of First International Workshop on Modular Ontologies*, ISWC2006. Athens, GA: ISWC.

Dillon, T., Chang, E., Hadzic, M., & Wongthongtham, P. (2008). Differentiating conceptual modelling from data modelling, knowledge modelling and ontology modelling and a notation for ontology modeling. In *Proceedings of the Fifth Asia-Pacific Conference on Conceptual Modeling*. Australian Computer Society Inc.

Dombeu, J. V. F., Huisman, M., & Szpak, Z. (2011). A framework for semantic model ontologies generation for e-government applications. In *Proceedings of the Fifth International Conference on Digital Society*, (pp. 152-158). ICDS.

Doran, P. (2009). *Ontology modularization: Principles and practice.* (PhD Thesis). University of Liverpool, Liverpool, UK.

Ensan, F. (2010). *Semantic interface-based modular ontology framework.* New Brunswick, Canada: The University of New Brunswick.

Fernandez-Lopez, M., Gomez-Perez, A., Pazos-Sierra, A., & Pazos-Sierra, J. (1999). Building a chemical ontology using methodology and the ontology design environment. *IEEE Intelligent Systems & Their Applications*, *4*(1), 37–46. doi:10.1109/5254.747904

Finat, J., Delgado, F.J., Martìnez, R., Hurtado, A., Fernández, J.J., San José J.I., & Martìnez, J. (2010). Constructors of geometric primitives in domain ontologies for urban environments. *Journal of Information Technology in Construction*.

Gruber, T. R. (1993). A translation approach to portable ontology specifications. *Journal of Knowledge Acquisition*, *5*(2), 199–220. doi:10.1006/knac.1993.1008

Gruninger, M., & Fox, M. S. (1995). Methodology for the design and evaluation of ontologies. In *Proceedings of Workshop on Basic Ontological Issues in Knowledge Sharing*. Montreal, Canada: IEEE.

Hinkelmann, K., Thonssen, B., & Wolff, D. (2010). Ontologies for e-government. In *Theory and applications of ontology: Computer applications* (pp. 429–461). IEEE. doi:10.1007/978-90-481-8847-5_19

Hristozova, M. H. (2003). *EXPLODE: Extreme programming for lightweight ontology development*. (MSc Thesis). University of Melbourne, Melbourne, Australia.

Ikeda, M., Seta, K., Kakusho, O., & Mizoguchi, R. (1998). Task ontology: Ontology for building conceptual problem solving models. In *Proceedings of ECAI98 Workshop on Applications of Ontologies and Problem-Solving Model,* (pp. 126-133). ECA.

Jurisdisca, I., Mylopoulos, J., & Yu, E. (2004). Using ontologies for knowledge management: An information systems perspective. *Knowledge and Information Systems Archive*, 6(4), 380–401. doi:10.1007/s10115-003-0135-4

Kehagias, D., Kontotasio, D., Mouratidis, G., Nikolaou, T., Papadimitriou, I., & Kalogirou, K. … Normann, I. (2008). *Ontologies, typologies, models and management tools*. OASIS Deliverable. Retrieved March 16, 2013 from www.oasis-project.eu%2Fdocs%2FOFFICIAL_DELIVERABLES%2FSP1%2FD1.1.1%2FOASISDeliverableD1_1_1_version_4%25205.doc&ei=LOvfUb6wHayr0gXmw4HADg&usg=AFQjCNE4ZcnK1XU_G02SdgCFKLwgEDZlnA&bvm=bv.48705608,d.d2k

Kharbat, F., & El-Ghalayini, H. (2008). *Building ontology from knowledge base systems, data mining in medical and biological research*. InTech.

Knublauch, H. (2002). *An agile development methodology for knowledge-based systems including a Java framework for knowledge modeling and appropriate tool support*. (PhD Thesis). University of Ulm, Ulm, Germany.

Nicola, G. (1998). Formal ontology in information systems. In *Proceedings of FOIS'98*. Amsterdam: IOS Press.

Noy, N. F., & McGuinness, D. (2001). Ontology development 101: A guide to creating your first ontology. *Stanford Knowledge Systems Laboratory Technical Report KSL-01-05 and Stanford Medical Informatics Technical Report SMI-2001-0880*.

Ozacar, T., Ozturk, O., & Unalir, M. O. (2011). ANEMONE: An environment for modular ontology development. *Data & Knowledge Engineering*, 70(6), 504–526. doi:10.1016/j.datak.2011.02.005

Salhofer, P., Stadlhofer, B., & Tretter, G. (2009). Ontology-driven e-government. *Electronic. Journal of E-Government*, 7(4), 415–424.

Schlicht, A., & Stuckenschmidt, H. (2008). A flexible partitioning tool for large ontologies. In *Proceedings of the 2008 IEEE/WIC/ACM International Conference, on Web Intelligence and Intelligent Agent Technology*. IEEE.

Stuckenschmidt, H., & Klein, M. C. A. (2004). Structure-based partitioning of large concept hierarchies. In *International semantic web conference (LNCS)* (Vol. 3298, pp. 289–303). Berlin: Springer.

Suarez-Figuearoa, M. C., & Dellschaft, K. E. Montiel-Ponsoda, Villazon-Terrazas, B., Yufei, Z., Aguado de Cea, G., … Sabou, M. (2008). *NeOn deliverable, NeOn Methodology for building conceptualised ontology networks*. NeOn Project. Retrieved May 20, 2013 from http://www.neon-project.org

Sureephong, P., Chakpitak, N., Ouzrout, Y., & Bouras, A. (2008). An ontology-based knowledge management system for industry clusters. In *Proceedings of International Conference on Advanced Design and Manufacture* (ICADAM 2008). Sanya, China: ICADAM.

The Protégé Ontology Editor and Knowledge Acquisition System. (2013). Retrieved May 20 2013 from http://protege.stanford.edu/

Uschold, M., & Gruninger, M. (1996). Ontologies: Principles, methods and applications. *The Knowledge Engineering Review*, *11*(2), 93–155. doi:10.1017/S0269888900007797

Uschold, M., & King, M. (1995). *Towards a methodology for building ontologies*. Paper presented at the 'Workshop on Basic Ontological Issues in Knowledge Sharing' held in Conjuction with IJCAI-95. Retrieved July 10, 2013 from http://www1.cs.unicam.it/insegnamenti/reti_2008/Readings/Uschold95.pdf

Vijayasarathy, L. R., & Turk, D. (2008). Agile software development = a survey of early adopters. *Journal of Information Technology,* 1-8. Retrieved May 17, 2013 from http://www.aom-iaom.org/jitm_pdfs/jitm_08/article3.pdf

ADDITIONAL READING

Finger, M., & Pécoud, G. (2003). From e-Governmente-Government to e-Governance? Towards a model of e-Governance, Electronic. *Journal of E-Government*, *1*(1), 1–10.

Jorgensen, D. J., & Cable, S. (2002). Facing the Challenges of e-Government: A Case Study of the City of Corpus Christi, Texas. *S.A.M. Advanced Management Journal*, *67*(3), 15.

Karen Layne., & Jungwoo Lee. (2001). Developing Fully Functional e- Government: A Four Stage lModel. *Government Information Quarterly*, *18*(2), 122–136. doi:10.1016/S0740-624X(01)00066-1

Kitchenham, B. A., Travassos, G. H., Mayrhauser, A., Niessink, F., Schneidewind, N. F., & Singer, J. et al. (1999). Towards an Ontology of Software Maintenance. *Journal of Software Maintenance: Research and Practice*, *11*(6), 365–389. doi:10.1002/(SICI)1096-908X(199911/12)11:6<365::AID-SMR200>3.0.CO;2-W

Liao, L. Qu, Y., & Leung, H.K.N. (2005). *A\ Software Process Ontology and Its Application*. ISWC2005 Workshop on Semantic Web Enabled Software Engineering.

Ruiz, F., Vizcaíno, A., Piattini, M., & García, F. (2004). An Ontology for the Management of Software Maintenance Projects. *International Journal of Software Engineering and Knowledge Engineering*, *14*(3), 323–349. doi:10.1142/S0218194004001646

Rumbaugh, J., Balha, M., & Premelani, W. (1991). *Object Oriented Modeling and Design*. Prentice Hall.

Sarantis, D., & Askounis, D. (2009). Electronic Criminal Record in Greece: Project Management Approach and Lessons Learned in Public Administration, *Transylvanian Review of Administrative Sciences,* 25 (E), 132-146.

Sarantis, D., & Askounis, D. (2010). Electronic Government Interoperability Framework in Greece: Project Management Approach and Lessons Learned in Public Administration. *Journal of US-China Public Administration*, *7*(3).

Scott, M., Golden, W., & Hughes, M. (2004). Implementation Strategies for E-Government: A Stakeholder Analysis Approach. *In the 12th European Conference on Information Systems, Turku, Finland,* 203-215.

Shang, S. S. C., & Lin, S. F. (2009). Understanding the effectiveness of Capability Maturity Model Integration by examining the knowledgeknowledge management of software development processes. *Total Quality Management & Business Excellence*, *20*(5), 509–521. doi:10.1080/14783360902863671

Yim, N.-H., Kim, S.-H., Kim, H.-W., & Kwahk, K.-Y. (2004). Knowledge based decision making on higher level strategic concerns: system dynamics approach. *Expert Systems with Applications*, *27*, 143–158. doi:10.1016/j.eswa.2003.12.019

Zhao, G., Gao, Y., & Meersman, R. (2004). An Ontology-based Approach to Business Modeling. *In Proceedings of the International Conference of Knowledge Engineering and Decision Support.*

KEY TERMS AND DEFINITIONS

Agile Ontology Development: Lightweight ontology development based on agile practices from software engineering.

Competency Questions: Questions that need to be answered by the ontology.

Expert Stories: stories written based on what the Domain Expert. Each expert story is mapped on a module.

Ontology: It is a shared conceptualisation of a domain.

Ontology Engineering: Construction of ontologies.

Ontology Engineering Methodologies: Methodologies used to construct ontologies.

Ontology Modularization: Breaking down of large monolithic ontologies into smaller ontologies. The monolithic ontology can be constructed back from the ontology modules.

Chapter 8
The Promise of Open Source Systems/Software in Developing Requisite E-Government Solutions for the Developing Countries:
A Review of Literature

Adeyinka Tella
University of Ilorin, Nigeria

Adetayo O. Tella
University of Ibadan, Nigeria

ABSTRACT

E-Government open source system is now becoming commonplace. The e-Government open system requires at each review stage the relevant official input, the date, and the time when each application is processed. Free access to the status of an application makes applicants realize that there is no need to contact officials or to provide a bribe to complete the process. No doubt, e-Government open system is a very useful system currently being used by a majority of governments in developing world countries. However, extant review of literature has shown that some developing countries governments are now also making frantic effort to implement the open system although the practice seems to have gone farther in developed nations. In light of this, this chapter discusses e-Government open source system in developing countries and compares this to what is happening in the developed countries, examines the role OSS/SF has played in developing e-Government solutions or applications in the developing world, identifies the benefits and challenges of OSS/SF in the developing countries' context, and discusses possible ways forward. The chapter posits that open source plays a significant role in designing e-Government applications.

DOI: 10.4018/978-1-4666-4900-2.ch008

INTRODUCTION

The revolution brought about by the information communication technologies touches nearly every areas of human endeavor including governance. Not long ago, governments in most countries around the word realized the potential of Information Communication Technologies (ICTs) to enhance and improve their governance and ensure that government is brought closer to the people. These governments have created Web portals and government online services/platforms in order to ensure citizens directly and easily access government services and employees. Furtherance to the above is to increase citizens' participation in governance. Similarly, (Webe, 2003) testified to this pointing out that many governments around the world have begun to consider the use of open source software as a key part of their strategic thrust in information technology, requiring that its use be considered when it provides a feasible alternative to proprietary software. Developing countries in particular, with the resource constraints they have, view open source software (OSS) as a means of reducing the cost of IT investment and increasing its productivity. The imperative to adopt OSS in these countries particularly in the public sector is also motivated by a desire for independence, a drive for security and autonomy and a means to address intellectual property rights enforcement.

Bruggink (2003) describes open source/free software (OSS/FS) as the software which may be copied and used freely. Open source/free software is often available free of charge on the Internet so it can be acquired only at the cost of downloading it or obtained on CDs at packaging cost. The most popular open source software is the GNU/Linux operating system. Unlike proprietary software, OSS/FS can be copied, used, studied, modified, distributed with few or no copyright restrictions (Backus, 2001).

According to (Baguma, 2005), users of free and open source software have four kinds of freedom: the freedom to run the program, for any purpose; the freedom to study how the program works, and adapt it to their needs; access to the source code is a precondition for this, hence the open source concept; the freedom to redistribute copies so they can help their neighbor; the freedom to improve the program, and release their improvements to the public, so that the whole community benefits (Skidmore, 2005). Similarly, Gnu.org, the official home of the free and open source software movement, upholds that: "Free software" is a matter of liberty, not price. To understand the concept, you should think of ``free'' as in "free speech'," not as in "free beer'." This is in relation to the associated freedoms to free software (David & Michael, 2004).

Open source software play significant roles in e-Government. For instance, an open source tool, provides a secure method for system administrators to instantly access and manage the servers located in remote local government offices, e-Governance is the most effective way of reducing costs in running public affairs from the lower levels of government to the central government.

E-Government (short for electronic government, also known as digital government, online government, or connected government), refers to digital interactions between a government and citizens (G2C), government and businesses/Commerce (G2B), government and employees (G2E), and also between government and governments / agencies (G2G). Within each of these interaction domains, four kinds of activities take place. These are: Pushing information over the Internet (for example: regulatory services, general holidays, public hearing schedules, issue briefs, notifications, etc.); two-way communications between the agency and the citizen, a business, oranother government agency (In this model, users canengage in dialogue with agencies and post problems, comments, or requests to the agency); conducting transactions (for example: Lodging tax returns, applying for services and grants); governance (for example: online polling, voting, and campaigning). The most important anticipated benefits of e-Government in a developing country is that these technologies can serve a variety of different ends: better delivery of government services to citizens, improved interactions with business and industry, citizen empowerment through access to information, or more efficient government management. The resulting benefits can be less corruption, increased transparency, greater convenience, revenue growth, and/or cost reductions.

E-Government (e-Government or e-Gov) refers to the use of Internet technology as a platform for exchanging information, providing services and transacting with citizens, businesses, and other arms of government (UN e-Government survey, 2004, 2005, 2008). According to Dode (2007), e-Governance is a democratic practice that is gradually gaining universal acceptance and applicability. It refers to a governmental type aimed at achieving effective service delivery from government to citizens, moving governance from traditionalist bureaucratization to modernist participatory administration. The UNESCO definition of e-Governance is: "E-Governance is the public sector's use of information and communication technologies with the aim of improving information and service delivery, encouraging citizen participation in the decision-making process and making government more accountable, transparent and effective. E-Governance involves new styles of leadership, new ways of debating and deciding policy and investment, new ways of accessing education, new ways of listening to citizens and new ways of organizing and delivering information and services. E-Governance is generally considered as a wider concept than e-Government, since it can bring about a change in the way citizens relate to governments and to each other. E-Governance can bring forth new concepts of citizenship, both in terms of citizen needs and responsibilities. Its objective is to engage, enable and empower the citizen."[www.unesco.org]. E-Government may be applied by the legislature, judiciary, or administration, in order to improve internal efficiency, the delivery of public services, or processes of democratic governance. However, the primary delivery models are Government-to-Citizen or Government-to-Customer (G2C), Government-to-Business (G2B) and Governmentto- Government (G2G) and Government-to-Employees (G2E).

Many open source now available that allow e-Government to run. Open source/free software (OSS/FS) is the software where users have the freedom to run, copy, distribute, study, modify and improve the software, and the source code is freely available. The adoption of open source software for e-Government, where substantial claims are made about efficiency and effectiveness of Governance and the responsiveness of Government to its citizens, would have strategic and operational implications of great significance. The goals of security and independence and others would be secured more effectively in managing information flows in Government with the adoption of open source software. Thus, within the broad policy framework of software procurement for the public sector, specific strategies should be in place to deal with situations where the aforesaid considerations become paramount.

No doubt, the use of e-Government open source system has now become a commonplace. E-Government is a general term describing the use of technologies to facilitate the operation of government and the disbursement of government information and services. The term is an abbreviation of the phrase "electronic government," and it deals heavily with Internet applications to aid governments' activities. However, observations have shown that use of e-Government open source is more pronounce in the developed than the developing countries. It is on this note that this chapter discussed e-Government open source system in terms of what operate in developed and developing countries, the benefits open source in e-Government, the challenges developing countries are facing using open source in e-Government and the possible way forward.

E-GOVERNMENT EVOLUTION

Electronic or digital government and open government or what is sometimes called Government 2.0, are the common concepts used interchangeably. Revolutions in ICTs directly influence the development of the concepts all over the world with unprecedented speed by changing traditional understanding of these and other related paradigms such as public administration, governance, democracy, accountability and transparency of governments, etc. In this respect, the development of Web-technologies as a part of the process influences the emergence of various concepts and their constant transformation in accordance with the latest achievements in the ICT sphere, especially those related to the organization of interactions between government and citizens. For instance, during the advent of the Internet era in the 1990s, the introduction of the e-Government idea was regarded as a necessary process in the modernization of public administration from the traditional paper-based (Khan et al., 2012) system of organization to the digital one, with a one-way process of realization mainly through directives and limited feedback from people (Chun et al. 2010). At that time, therefore, e-Government was conceptualized as a governmental system based on providing information-based online services to citizens. The emergence of various social media technologies and eventually their active use in the public sector during the next decade led to new generalizations and concepts, e.g. theWeb 2.0-based government concepts such as Government 2.0 or open government (Khan et al. 2012; Harrison et al. 2011; Chun et al. 2010; Mergel, 2010). Open government is thus regarded today as a governmental system based on providing interactivity-based online services to citizens via new technologies such as social media, mashups, open data platforms, interactive television, interactive mobile platforms, etc. Moreover, notwithstanding being today an integral part of the e-Government paradigm, the open government concept has a more political meaning, since the ultimate goal of the idea is transparency and accountability of the public sector as well as collaboration within civil society, i.e. it is a two-way process based on harnessing the collective knowledge of people or citizen-sourcing, for example, via social media tools and mobile applications (Khan et al. 2012), interactive open data platforms and mapping (Mergel, 2010). Thus, it is not only a technology driven process in transformation of the public sector but also a new social phenomenon which requires collaborative efforts from people at local, national and even international levels.

E-Government Open Source System in Developing Countries

Baguma (2005) pointed out that traditionally, the interaction between a citizen or business and a government agency took place in a government office. He explained that that with emerging information and communication technologies (ICTs), it is possible to locate service centres closer to the clients. It is on this note that Backus, (2001) defines e-Governance as the use by government agencies of information technologies (such as wide area networks, the Internet, and mobile computing) that have the ability to transform relations with citizens, businesses, and some arms of government.

According to Kamara and Onsrad (nd) many developing nations are currently actively considering policies to support or enforce the adoption of open-source software by public institutions especially the government (Dravis, 2002). Based on this, some arguments were levied in favor of adoption by public institutions include (Ghosh et al., 2002):

- **Lower cost:** Adoption of personal computers based on open-source software for public use can reduce initial entry cost by as much as 50 percent. Easier replication of solutions is also possible. Large-scale public projects can greatly benefit from having a prototype developed and tested that can then be replicated across the country with no additional software costs.

- **Independence from proprietary technology:** Many governments are increasingly concerned with overdependence in some important markets on a small number of vendors.
- **Security:** Governments and governmental agencies are becoming aware of the risks they are subject to when adopting proprietary software solutions in sensitive areas, such as e-Government, e-procurement, elections, and public finance.
- **Availability of efficient and low-cost software:** The virtuous examples of some products (such as Linux and Apache) have encouraged statements about the widespread availability of open-source software for public use.
- **Ability to develop custom applications and to redistribute the improved products:** Given the open nature of open-source software, skilled local programmers could adapt the software to fit local needs and thus increase the efficiency of the services provided by the improved products.

There is a huge demand for end-user applications in developing nations, especially in the public sector. However, from observation, corporations dominate open-source software development. These corporations will develop software based on their strategic interests, which are unlikely to include the full range of end-user applications needed by developing countries. Therefore, if governments in developing nations aim to profit from the potential benefits of open source, they must intervene and dedicate a substantial amount of public funds to support the establishment and long-term maintenance of open-source software

projects (Camara and Onsrad, nd). These authors added that the benefits of this strategy could be substantial. They gave the example of the case of urban cadastral systems based on a spatial database for medium-size cities. The typical base cost of a commercial spatial database solution for one city is $100,000. From their analysis, If 10 cities were to adopt such a solution in a given year, there would be a saving of $1 million per year on licensing fees, which could finance local development and local adaptation.

There is also a substantial additional benefit of investing in qualified human resources. Government strategies for supporting indigenous open-source software development and adaptation would result in a learning-by-doing process. Such processes, as opposed to learning-by-using, are credited with fostering innovation in the developed world (Landes, 1999), and the same lessons could apply to those nations supporting emerging economies. As an example of government-funded projects, a group of research and development institutions in Brazil is currently developing TerraLib,4 an open-source GIS library that enables quick development of custom-built applications for spatial data analysis. As a research tool TerraLib aims to enable the development of GIS prototypes that would include recent advances in geo-information science. On a practical side TerraLib enables quick development of custom-built applications using spatial databases. Projects such as TerraLib show that open-source GIS projects can make substantial contributions to the spatial information community by providing a platform for innovation and collaborative development (Câmara et al., 2000). The mechanism of e-Government is regarded today as a universal tool which may be used by any nation to address common issues in a new technological manner. However, this does not emanated spontaneously. The journal begins somewhere. On this note, the next section discusses the evolution of e-Government.

E-Government Open Source Initiatives: Examples from Developing Countries

While the open source phenomenon is indeed truly open in the sense of being open to all in the world, contributing developers are surprisingly concentrated in the developed world. Recently, however, the economic benefits of open source technologies have attracted a growing move towards adopting open source software (OSS) options in developing countries to a point that now the developing world is leading the developed world in open source adoption. It is noteworthy that governmental interest and activismis global and not aligned by geographic area, economic group or political philosophy. The following are examples of current governmental initiatives in various stages of review or implementation from the developed and the developing nations of the world (Dravis, 2002).

Venezuela adopted an official policy in 2002 for the use of OSS/FS in their government based on the principle: "Open Source whenever possible, proprietary software only when necessary". This arose from the concern that 75% of the funds for software licences went to foreign nations, 20%to foreign support agencies and only 5% to Venezuelans.

India: The Indian government has launched the Linux India Initiative that focuses on developing resource centers, special interest groups, pilot projects, assisting in the localization of Open Source software and to support the development of research studies.

Malaysia: The government is establishing a national OSS reference center directed by the Malaysian Administrative Modernization and Management Planning Unit. Among the activities to be carried out are the management of OSS implementation through the provision of consultancy, support and audit, formulation of policies and standards, certification and training, and OSS research and knowledge building. In October 2003, The Ministry of Finance announced its plan allocate funds to the Malaysian Venture Capital

Philippines: The Philippine government has initiated an effort to develop a package of open source software products as well as a support mechanism for government agencies, schools, and small businesses. The Advanced Science and Technology Institute (ASTI), which falls under the Philippines' Department of Science and Technology (DOST) has released a simplified version of Linux called Bayanihan Linux (bayanihan.asti.dost.gov.ph). ASTI is also developing enhanced thin client and embedded solutions using OSS. The DOST has also funded an OSS based information system that is being implemented by the National Computer Center for use by more than 3,000 local governments.

Pakistan: The Government has announced that Linux and Open Source products are at the forefront of its initiatives to curb piracy and protect intellectual property. TReMU, Pakistan's Technology Resource MobilizationUnit, has created a task force it calls "Linux Force," to review the value these offerings can provide to their computing needs.

Coming down to Africa, Heeks (2003) cited in Baguma (nd) highlighted a number of case studies of e-Governance implementations in Africa. They include the following among others:

Nigeria: In Nigeria, an SMS Helpdesk Application (SMS blackbox) developed with open source is in use to provide helpdesk functionality to citizens in Lagos. Ahmed (2004) documents that in India, Delixus, Inc., a private IT company, implemented, the Delixus e-Governance Platform 2004 edition in 2004 that leverages the strengths of Linux to provide improved services to widows, pensioners and poor farmers in the Indian state of Karnataka. The Delixus e-Governance Platform addresses the needs of millions of rural poor citizens in India who receive widow or pension cheques through services provided by local government offices. Ahmed says that the reasons why Linux was selected as the technology of choice for the Delixus e-Governance Platform include:

- It best satisfied technical and legal requirements.
- More specifically, Linux servers provided an optimal level of security and cost effectiveness, as well as supported the local language requirements.
- The support for open standards enabled Linux to serve an interoperable e-Governance application that is accessible from Linux, Windows and other desktop operating systems.
- It provides great benefits to the government operations and to citizens (widows, pensioners and farmers).

South Africa: In South Africa, the government approved the proposal that when proprietary and open source are equal, open source will be given preference owing to the improved returns on investment associated with the elimination of licensing and the endless maintenance agreements that lock government into expensive long-term contracts. In January 2003, the government's report "Using OpenSource Software in the South African Government" recognizes the educational and commercial benefits of Open Source development and recommends that partnershipsbetween academic, industry and governmentinstitutions be implemented. The report proposes that 1) "discrimination and prejudice will be avoided in softwareprocurement procedures, making choices basedon merit, thus giving OSS and proprietary software (PS) equal opportunities to be selected" and 2) "as OSSoffers significant indirect advantages, opting for OSSwill be preferable where the direct advantages anddisadvantages of OSS and PS are equally strong, andwhere circumstances in the specific situation do notrender such preference inappropriate."

In July 2003, Geraldine Fraser-Moleketi, South African Minister of Public Service and Administration provided the following comments on OSS: "Support - As long there is a market for support, the open source code allows anybody to provide

it, whereas proprietary software (PS) support is dependent on the development company. If that company goes out of business, the support can disappear with it".

It is obvious from the various case studies and initiatives on e-Government open source system enumerated above that e-Government open source is more prominent in the developed nations particularly in Europe and some countries in Asia. However, very limited evidence of adoption of e-Government open source exists in Africa. In line with this, (Song, 2006:33) listed the names of countries that can be benchmark for e-Government as:

- **Anglo-America**: United States, United Kingdom, Canada, Australia.
- **Continental**: France, Germany, Japan, Austria, Italy.
- **Nordic**: Sweden, Norway, Finland and Denmark; and;
- **Asian**: Republic of Korea, China, Singapore, India.

It is clear from the list that Africa which houses a considerable number of developing countries was conspicuously missing. Therefore, something need to be done as this might continue to broaden the digital divide between the technology have and have not. Relevant information is the situation in Figure 1 below, which shows regional comparison chart for e-Government based on 2008 to 2012 survey. Africa again pulled the lowest value 0.2780, followed by Oceania and Asia the three regions that feature most developing countries of the world. This is a confirmation that developed regions Americas and Europe have gone far ahead of others in e-Government open source adoption.

It clear from the figure above that the Europe (0.7188) shows the highest e-Government development followed by the Americas. Figure 1 highlight that despite considerable strides towards bridging the digital divide, infrastructure and human capital limitations in several parts of the

Figure 1. Regional average in e-Government (Source: United Nations e-Government survey 2012 http://unpan1.un.org/intradoc/groups/public/documents/un/unpan048065.pdf.

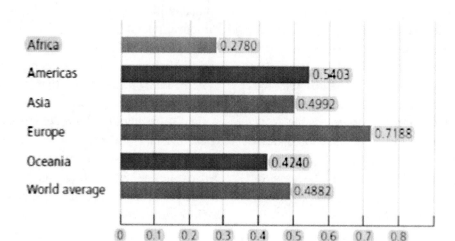

world impinge upon the ability of governments to spread and the citizens to partake of the benefits of information technology in the delivery of services. With a history of high levels of functional education and wide spread telephony infrastructure, Europe and the Americas as a whole remain far ahead of the rest of the world regions. Asia, which is home to around three-fifths of the world citizens, has nevertheless only around 70% of the level of e-Government in Europe while the level services in Africa barely squares off a 40% of those in Europe. Within any region, countries at the lower percentile of e-development do not fare well either. This is especially true of the lower income countries in booth Asia and Africa. The 10 least e-ready countries in Asia have barely 37 per cent of the level of e-Government in Europe while in Africa the figure is little more than 20 per cent.

Regional comparison of e-Government development index value and advances in the last decade was provided by United Nations. From the report, Africa is lagging behind other continents in e-Government development and advancement. It is sad to note that Africa is very far below world average (Figure 2). Even other developing regions such Asia and Oceania have better value compare to Africa though not comparable to what obtained on the developed regions such as Europe and Americas.

THE BENEFITS OF E-GOVERNMENT OPEN SOURCE IN DEVELOPING COUNTRIES

Much has been said and written about the potential use of information and communications technology (ICT) by government agencies to transform relations with citizens and businesses. Increased transparency, less corruption, better delivery of government services, greater government responsiveness and accountability, and empowerment of citizens especially poor ones are commonly cited among the possible benefits of electronic government (e-Government) (World Bank, 2004, 2005).

E-Government has demonstrated that it can make the difference in the way government provides goods and services to its citizens in an efficient and responsive way. In the execution of

Figure 2. Advances in regional e-Government development in the last decade - Regional comparison chart - (Source: United Nations E-Government Survey 2012 http://unpan1.un.org/intradoc/groups/public/ documents/un/unpan048065.pdf.

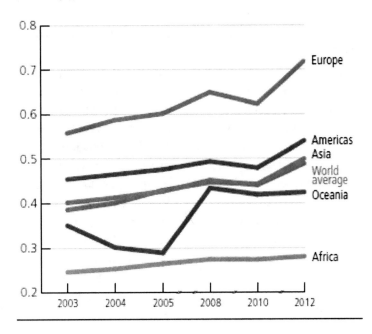

E-Government strategies, open standards primarily and open source software in that order would be critical to an effective implementation strategy. Thus, outside of any reduction that may arise in IT investment cost through theOSS, the "open model" becomes the very bedrock on which these initiatives are executed (Baguma, 2005). On the one hand, it is necessary that a rigorous approach to e-Government software architecture is adopted in the context of competing technologies and current developments in the area; on the other, it is imperative that security and independence are considered in their proper perspective with OSS viewed not merely as a product choice but in a more fundamental and strategic context of the production, flow and control of information in the economy and the process by which the rules that governs such flows are managed.

Baguma (2005) identified two major benefits of open source for e-governance. These are low initial cost and flexibility. It was explained that open source can be obtainedfree of charge or at a far cheaper cost, where a manufacturer charges for the packaging/distribution. The author explains that one pays for the physical CD, with or without an additional cost of packing additional tools. When it is downloaded from the Internet, the cost incurred is for connectivity. Relevant to this, Ahmed (2004) asserts that using Linux for e-Governance benefits both government operations and the citizens by:

- Lowering the cost of operations.
- Providing scalability for future growth.
- Following open standards for interoperability with other applications.
- Providing a robust and stable system to support ongoing government operations, a vital requirement for reliable e-Governance systems.
- Simplifying system maintenance and management.

Flexibility and security: Since the source code is accessible and based on public standards, technically inclined users can see how the software works and modify it to suit their needs as long as they continue to comply with the open source definition. Baguma (2005) used the example of Uganda, where a Luganda Web browser called "Kayungirizi" translated from the open source Mozilla browser was released in Sept. 2004 by Luganda ICT Translations. He pointed out that efforts are still under way to get it into other languages, such as Runyakitara and Swahili. An Open Office Swahili version called *jambo* has been developed too for use across East Africa including Rwanda, Burundi and DRC. South Africa also already has a Zulu version of Open Office. With the unique challenges in the South such as very low literacy levels and agrarian-based economies, OSS/FS is a huge opportunity for local customisations and tailoring of software beyond language to widen ICT usage and relevance which is a pre-requisite for effective e-governance.

Other OSS/FS benefits to e-Governance include: The global open source community provides opportunities for South-North and South-South collaboration and knowledge-sharing, meaning that there is always someone out there sharing or ready to share experiences with bug-fixing, troubleshooting network problems and developing updates, which means a reliable functional environment for e-Government systems managed by even not so technically competent staff.

OSS/FS works well with older computers compared to proprietary software where upon the release of a new type of software, e.g. operating systems, means more processing power, RAM, and storage space than the previous version. Specifications sufficient for Windows 95 need to be doubled for an efficient windows XP installation. This means continuous costly hardware upgrades for e- governance systems set up on proprietary software.

Aside of the above, (Kassen, 2013) summarized the benefits of e-Government open source

e-Government to include economic benefits, technological benefits, and political benefits. These are discussed in details as follows:

Economic Benefits

There is no doubt that the world continues suffering from an unprecedented financial and economic crisis and many countries resort to unpopular austerity measures, the idea of e-Government and the unification of platforms and realization procedures under single open-source codes could result in saving substantial financial and intellectual resources that many governments have been spending on the creation and development of various e-Government projects. Kassen explained that it is a very attractive and inspiring impetus for potential members to join the initiative. Moreover, many countries have realized that e-Government is a time- and money-consuming, therefore undertaking it is more reasonable as it will lead to the development of universal e-Government realization mechanisms together.

Technological Benefits

The major technological benefit of open source in e-Government for developing nations is the standardization of procedures in e-Government realization on a global scale. In addition, active promotion of open data and open-source software for e-Government platforms could potentially boost the development of related industry in the free market by independent software developers and freelancers. The situation is reminiscent of the development of non-proprietary operating systems and related applications and programs for touch-screen computers in recent years (Kassen, 2013). The emergence of open-source Android-based software facilitates citizen-sourcing in the independent development of related applications are good examples. This can be considered a tangible result of the global technological cooperation of people from many countries. Relevant to this,

(Jaeger and Thompson, 2003: 392) attest to this by pointing out that study of theprojects from ''different parts of the world offers amethod to share knowledge about e-Government''

Environmental Benefits

E-Government will reduce the amount of paper used in public services because the use of electronic forms will lessen the need for hardcopy forms (Dezayas, 2008). The United States government utilizes a website (http://www.forms.gov) to provide internal government forms for federal employees and thus produce significant savings in paper.

Political Benefits

It is now clear that the emergence of open source in e-Government as an important agenda in the international arena and being supported by many countries has made the open government idea becomes truly a universal value. Moreover, participating in the open government politics, all eligible nations could improve the realization of their national e-Government projects by harmonizing them with a single internationally approved conception, which in turn will lead to the promotion of civic engagement globally, since participation in this collaborative movement is a good incentive for many developing countries to improve the quality of their governance in accordance with established universal open government procedures. Therefore, the initiative has a great potential to unify the world under one idea of making governance transparent and accountable.

In addition, e-Government open source benefits can be realized in the following ways (Kamar and Ongo'ndo, 2007):

1. The citizens get connected to the government more easily using electronic means of communication. This results in better efficiency in public service delivery through faster dissemination of government information to a larger audience.

2. A reduction in corruption cases as accountability and transparency is increased. This derives from the limited physical contact between citizens and government service providers and their activities can be easily monitored.

3. Equal opportunity is given to all to access information irrespective of the person's physical location or disability and the elimination of the bureaucracy experienced in government offices.

4. The interdepartmental exchange of information and merger of related services is enhanced between government agencies with an accompanying reduction of transaction costs, time, space and manpower.

Furthermore, for the citizens that have access to Internet and are computer literate, e-Government eliminates the necessity for physical travel to government agents sitting behind a desk and allows interactions with the government to take place at any time and from any location. The management of information and the access to information are improved (improved record keeping and accounting, access to forms and information) because the information is stored in databases that can be easily queried and not in hardcopies stored in different locations. There are some categories of people with mobility problems that now can be active in governance from the comfort of their home, like individuals with disabilities or conditions.

The Challenges of Open Source in Developing Countries

Bruggink, (2003) notes that a research study carried out in 2003 in Uganda, Tanzania and Burkina Faso identified a number of systematic obstacles to the widespread adoption of open source in African organisations, they are:

- Limited availability. There are few resellers of OSS/FS. Although it's available on the Internet, unreliable connections and the high cost of the Internet in developing countries makes it difficult and expensive to download software from the Internet.

- Lack of technical expertise by certified support personnel. Few certification programmes exist for computer and network support professionals specialising in open source software. Most ICT training programmes are preparing students to work with the most commonly used proprietary software packages such as Microsoft.

- Information on migrating from proprietary to open source systems is hard to find, and there is need for decision-making tools specifically geared to the needs of African organisations.

- In Burkina Faso, it was noted that large hierarchical organisations are more hesitant to use open source software owing to risk the prevalence of aaverse organisational culture.

- Finally, researchers found that there is a widespread perception that the Linux operating system is the only real open source application and that this type of software is less user friendly than proprietary alternatives.

Baguma (2005) listed other obstacles to include:

- Making a large-scale switch from one type of software to another can be costly and complex for the organisation, especially if there is lack of experience, support and information.

- Some proprietary software is not compatible with open source. Sharing files with outside organisations can be more difficult for the individual user. The development community is addressing this progressively; Linux (Suse9.3) has addressed the compatibility problem between Open Office and MS Office.

- Bias about OSS/FS as hard to set up and later work with, Grass Root Organising, a USA CBO supported by the Low Income Networking and Communications Project (LNC, 2003); sharing their experience when they switched to OSS/FS, they say, they found this to be a far cry from reality. What it means is just a different way of working, not harder, not more technical, and just different. "The challenge wasn't in the actual work but it was in getting over our habits."

In addition to the above, the following factors have been identified by (Kamar and Ongo'ndo, 2007) as barriers to effective E-Government implementation in developing countriesas supporting evidence of challenges to amassing the full value of OSS/FS:

A reluctance to share information which has resulted in policies that deny access to information and the creation of "empty" government ministries websites with information of little value.The government being faced with management challenges in the implementation of E-Government. The uncoordinated E-Government activities result from low level of public administration of E-Services as well as low quality and insufficient E-Content information from grassroots levels. Low information technology literacy in developing countries is perceived as slowing down the process of E-Government. The uneven distribution of Internet facilities, high cost of connection and in some cases low penetration of high speed connectivity to the Internet. Digital Divide which is experienced between the urban rich and poor, the rural and urban citizens, the IT literate and the IT illiterate. This manifests also in the language in which Web site content is delivered which can only be understood by a minority elite.Insufficient allocation of financial resources due to financial constraints and mixed government policies which has slowed down the rate at which e-Government is introduced. E-Government implementations failing due to a mismatch between the current and future systems resulting from the large gap between physical, social, cultural, economic and other contexts between the software designers and the place in which the system is being implemented.

Principles for Ensuring Fuller Utilisation of OSS/FS

There is need to provide strategic and technical information geared to the needs of IT decision-makers about e-Government open source in relation to the following:

- Supporting decision-makers with decision models, toolkits and casestudies relating to choice of technology and system migration in differentcontexts.
- Getting the message across that Linux and open source software in generalare increasingly user-friendly and easy to install.
- IT training institutions should also incorporate in the curriculum OSS/FStraining to increase the support skill base for OSS/FS.
- E-Government should reach all the people who need government services regardless of their location, age, status, language, or access to the Internet.
- The e-Government global survey is a means by which governments can assess their level of preparedness for the provision of services to their citizens using modern ICT and telecommunication techniques. This can be achieved by the provision of adequate ICT infrastructure, improving online services and citizens' access to these services and dedicating itself to improving the country's literacy level.
- Developing countries will benefit if they critically examine their present state and then identifies those areas that needs to be

improves. Most developing countries still need to improve further on its ICT services and telecommunications systems.

- Mobile telephony holds some promise for increasing access for marginalized sectors of the population and there has been an exponential growth in mobile subscriptions and all developing countries now have some form of mobile coverage, however, there are still millions of Africans for example with limited or no access to ICT services due to lack of network infrastructure. ICT infrastructure cannot work without a regular source of electrical power. More effort should be devoted to improving most developingcountries epileptic power supply.
- Some developing countries still needs to commit more resources into the development of its Human Capital, address the internal digital divide between the literate and illiterate citizens, while the nation's websites set up by government and private agencies should be integrated and reviewed to make them e-service compliant within the context of a national portal.
- There must be unification of e-Government platforms based on open-source codes which requires harmonization of legislation in many developing countries.
- Lastly, there is need for a strong commitment by national governments in developing countries to e-Government services. These should be designed in such a way as to be available to all citizens. There should be telecommunications policy frameworks that ensure that the needs of all and sundry irrespective status and location are part of the national structure.

ICT training should be organized for all the citizens with affordable connectivity and safe, convenient centers where they can use computers (telecenters, post offices, community centers, etc.). Moreover, there is need for clearly designed content in local languages; and feedback mechanisms that allow all citizens to have input into e-Government.

FUTURE RESEARCH DIRECTIONS

This chapter so far has examined through review of literature covering the open source systems/software in developing requisite e-Government solutions for the developing countries. The future researcher should consider empirical investigation of similar study with particular reference to developing countries so that outcomes could serve as model that can be adopted by any developing country trying to put e-Government systems in place.

CONCLUSION

This chapter has examined through literature review the e-Government open source system in developing countries and with a comparison of what is obtaining in the developed countries. The chapter also discusses the role OSS/SF has played in developing e-Government solutions or applications in the developing world and identifies the benefits and challenges developing countries are faced with with regards to e—Government system development and deployment. The chapter posits that open source plays a significant role in e-Government application and its benefits are overwhelming as it results to less corruption, increased transparency, greater convenience, revenue growth, and/or cost reductions. However, it adoptions is not without challenges. These may include the fact that e-Government is not easy to implement because it involves taking computer-based technologies and combining them with human-based administrative processes to create

new ways of serving citizens. Similarly, ICTs exist in a broader context; it is not only challenging for organizations to understand computer systems, it is also challenging to understand the business, legislative and political processes that makeup the day-to-day operations of all types of government institutions. Many of the processes involve numerous steps and procedures that have evolved in form of a peculiarity to conform to legislation, mandates, and norms based on the formal bureaucratic structure and informal employee practices of each ministry.

REFERENCES

Ahmed, A. S. (2005). *Automating government with e-governance*. Retrieved April 15, 2013, from http://www.linuxjournal.com/article/7591

Backus, M. (2001). *E-governance and developing countries: Introduction and examples. International Institute for Communication and Development*. IICD.

Baguma, R. (2005). *Affordable e-governance using free and open source software*. Retrieved March 12, 2013 from http://cit.mak.ac.ug/iccir/downloads/SREC_05/Rehema%20Baguma_05.pdf

Bruggink, M. (2003).Open source in Africa: Towards informed decision-making. *IICD Research Brief, 7*.

Camara, G., & Onsrud, H. (n.d.). *Open-source geographic information systems software: Myths and realities*. Academic Press.

Câmara, G., Souza, B. R., Pedrosa, B., Vinhas, L., Monteiro, A., Paiva, J., et al. (2000). *TerraLib: Technology in support of GIS innovation*. II Workshop Brasileiro de Geoinformática, GeoInfo2000, InstitutoNacional de PesquisasEspaciais, São Paulo.

Chun, S. A., Shulman, S., & Sandoval, A. R. (2010). Government 2.0: Marking connections between citizens, data and government. *Information Polity, 15*(1–2), 1–9.

David, M., & Michael, B. (2004). Usability and open source software. *First Monday.*

Dezayas, H. (2008). *So, how much paper does our local government use?* Penn-Trafford Star.

Dravis, R. (2002). *Open source software: Perspective for development.* InfoDev, TheDravis Group. Retrieved April 15, 2013, from http://www.infodev.org/en/Document.21.pdf

Ghosh, R. A., Krieger, B., Glott, R., & Robles, G. (2002). *Open source software in the public sector: Policy within the European Union.* Maastricht, The Netherlands: International Institute of Infonomics, University of Maastricht.

Harrison, T. M., Santiago, G. G., Burke, B., Cook, M., Cresswell, A., & Helbig, N. ... Pardo, T. (2011). Open government and e-government: Democratic challenges from a public value perspective. In *Proceedings of the 12th Annual International Conference on Digital Government Research.* College Park, MD: DGR.

Heeks, R. (2001). *Understanding e-governance for development' paper no.11.* Manchester, UK: Government Working Paper Series, Institute for Development Policy and Management, University of Manchester, UK.

Jaeger, P. T., & Thompson, K. M. (2003). E-government around the world: Lessons, challenges, and future directions. *Government Information Quarterly, 20*(4), 389–394. doi:10.1016/j.giq.2003.08.001

Kamar, N., & Ongo'ndo, M. (2007). *Impact of e-government on management and use of government information in Kenya.* Paper presented at the World Library and Information Congress: 73rd IFLA General Conference and Council. Durban, South Africa.

Kassen, M. (2013). *Globalization of e-government: Open government as a global agenda, benefits, limitations and ways forward.* Retrieved 17 April 2013 from http://idv.sagepub.com/content/early/2013/01/18/0266666912473620

Khan, G. F., Young, H. Y., & Park, H. W. (2012). Social media use in public sector: a comparative study of the Korean & US government agencies. In *Proceedings of the 8th International Conference on Webometrics, Informatics and Scientometrics & 13th COLLNET Meeting.* Retrieved 17 April, 2013 from http://collnet2012.ndsl.kr/wsp/submission/submitted.jsp

Landes, D. S. (1999). *The wealth and poverty of nations.* New York: W. W. Norton & Co.

Low Income Networking AndCommunications Project. (2003). *Building an open source office: GRO case study part II, 2003.* Welfare Law Center.

Mergel, I. (2010). Government 2.0 revisited: Social media strategies in the public sector. *American Society for Public Administration, 33*(3), 7–10.

Skidmore, D. (2005). *Governance of open source software projects.* Melbourne, Australia: Center for Public Policy, University of Melbourne.

Song, H. J. (2006). E-government in developing countries: Lesson learnt from the republic of Korea. Bangkok: United Nation Educationa, Scientific and Cultural organization, UNESCO.

UN Global E-Government Readiness Report. (2004). *Towards access for opportunity*. New York: United Nations Department of Economic and Social Affairs/Division for Public Administration and Development Management, UN-PAN/2004/11.

UN Global E-Government Readiness Report. (2005). *From e-government to e-inclusion*. New York: United Nations Department of Economic and Social Affairs/Division for Public Administration and Development Management, UN-PAN/2005/14.

United Nations. UN Global E-Government Survey. (2008). From e-government to connected governance. New York: United Nations Publication.

United Nations. UN Global E-Government Survey. (2010). Leveraging e-government at a time of financial and economic crisis. United Nations.

Weber, S. (2000). *The political economy of open source software*. Berkeley, CA: University of California.

World Bank. (n.d.). *Definition of e-government*. Retrieved 12 July, 2011 from http://go.worldbank.org/M1JHE0Z280

ADDITIONAL READING

AlAwadhi, S., & Morris, A. (2008).The use of the UTAUT model in the adoption of e-Government services in Kuwait. Proceedings of the 41st Hawaii International Conference on System Sciences - 2008, Kona, HI.

Carter, L., & Belanger, F. (2005). The utilization of e-Government services: citizen trust, innovation and acceptance factors. *Information Systems Journal*, *15*, 5–25. doi:10.1111/j.1365-2575.2005.00183.x

Harrison, T. M., Santiago, G. G., Burke, B., Cook, M., Cresswell, A., Helbig, N., et al. (2011). Open government and e-Government: democratic challenges from a public value perspective. Proceedings of the 12th Annual International Conference on Digital Government Research. June 12 – 15, 2011. College Park, Maryland.

Herrera, L., & Gil-Garcia, R. J. (2011). Implementation of e-Government in Mexico: The case of Infonavit. In S. Assar et al. (Eds.), *Practical studies in e-Government best practices from around the world* (pp. 29–47). New York: Springer. doi:10.1007/978-1-4419-7533-1_3

The Open Government Partnership. (2012). Outcome documents of the World Summit on the Information Society (2006) Geneva: ITU: 95 p. Retrieved June 15, 2013 from http://www.opengovpartnership.org/country commitments.

Tinati, R., Halford, S., Carr, L., & Pope, C. (2012). Using mixed methods to track the growth of the Web: tracing open government data initiatives. Retrieved September 13, 2012 from http://eprints.soton.ac.uk/335270/1/WWW12_Web_Science_Track_-_Tracing_Open_Government_Data_Initiatives.pdf

United Nations. (2008). *UN e-Government Survey 2008: From e-Government to Connected Government. UNPAN*. New York: United Nations.

KEY TERMS AND DEFINITIONS

Developing Countries: A developing country, also called a less-developed country (LDC), is a nation with a low living standard, underdeveloped industrial base, and low Human Development Index (HDI) relative to other countries. A developing country is one in which the majority lives on far less money with far fewer basic public services than the population in highly industrialized.

Digital Government: Refers to the "umbrella term that comprises all uses of information and telecommunication technologies in the public sector" (Garson 2006 18).

E-Governance*:* Refers to the use of ICTs for organization of political activity within and beyond nation states. E-Governance "is one of a wide range of competing terms pertaining to use of new communications technologies, such as the Internet and mobile telephony, for political and governmental purposes. Other widely used terms that have overlapping meaning include: electronic democracy (e-democracy), online democracy, cyber-democracy, virtual democracy, online governance, teledemocracy, e-participation and e-deliberation" (Chen 2008).

E-Government: The terms digital government, electronic government (e-Government) and electronic governance (e-Governance) are used widely to represent the use of information and communication technologies in public sector organizations. It is one aspect of digital government. E-Government refers to the provision of governmental services by ICTs, particularly over the Internet.

Governance: Is the act of governing. It relates to decisions that define expectations, grant power, or verify performance. It is the set of policies, roles, responsibilities, and processes that you establish in an enterprise to guide, direct, and control how the organization uses technologies to accomplish business goals.

Information Communication Technologies: ICTs encompass all those technologies that enable the handling of information and facilities different form of communication among human, between human beings and electronic systems. It is the electronic means of capturing, processing, storing and communicating information.

Internet: The Internet is a global system of interconnected computer networks that use the standard Internet protocol suite (TCP/IP) to serve billions of users worldwide. It is a means of connecting a computer to any other computer anywhere in the world via dedicated routers and servers.

Open Source Systems/Software: open source/free software (OSS/FS) is the software which may be copied and used freely.

Section 2
Design and Use of E-Government Applications

Chapter 9
Geospatial Technology-Based E-Government Design for Environmental Protection and Emergency Response

Tianxing Cai
Lamar University, USA

ABSTRACT

Fast development of geospatial technologies has made it possible to integrate existing user operational information and value-added services in a single harmonized infrastructure. This has made it possible to utilize geospatial technologies in the e-Government context. The emerging technologies have made it possible for natural disaster monitoring and mitigation for early warning in order for effective actions under emergency situation, such as natural disaster and chemical accident, to be taken. Natural disasters may include fires, explosions, leakages, or releases of toxic or hazardous materials that can cause people illness, injury, disability, or death. With emerging geospatial technology capabilities and applications such as Google Earth, GIS, and GPS, computer modeling and simulation can provide the inverse identification of emission profile and location. The modeling result can further present the forward prediction of the likely impact of any disaster event. Therefore, the community can acquire the situation in time to form spontaneous emergency response planning, which will also help the other stakeholders such as government and responsible community team. This modeling tool can form a virtual e-Government solution requisite for effective monitoring and mitigation. This chapter highlights the current research trends and future prospects with regards to integrating technologies for managing spatio-temporal information with e-Government conceptualization.

DOI: 10.4018/978-1-4666-4900-2.ch009

INTRODUCTION AND BACKGROUND

E-Government research is becoming a hot topic in many governments in the world. According to the definition from United Nations Department of Economic and Social Affairs, "E-Government' (or Digital Government) is defined as 'The employment of the Internet and the world-wide-web for delivering government information and services to the citizens.' (UNDESA, 2012). E-Government should enable anyone visiting a city website to communicate and interact with city employees via the Internet with graphical user interfaces (GUI), instant-messaging (IM), audio/video presentations, and in any way more sophisticated than a simple email letter to the address provided at the site" (Deloitte Research, 2000). And "the use of technology to enhance the access to and delivery of government services to benefit citizens, business partners and employees" (

Transparency and Open Government, 2012). The e-Government has traditionally been understood as being centered on the operations of government, e-Governance is understood to extend the scope by including citizen engagement and participation in governance. As such, following in line with the OECD definition of e-Government, e-Governance can be defined as the use of ICTs as a tool to achieve better governance.

E-Government describes the use of technologies to facilitate the operation of government and the dispersion of government information and services. It deals heavily with Internet and non-Internet applications to aid in governments. By the application of electronics in government as large-scale as the use of telephones and fax machines, as well as surveillance systems, tracking systems such as RFID tags, and even the use of television and radios to provide government-related information and services to the citizens.

In the USA, the Office of E-Government and Information Technology (E-Gov), headed by the Federal Government's Chief Information Officer (CIO), develops and provides direction in the use of Internet-based technologies to make it easier for citizens and businesses to interact with the Federal Government, save taxpayer dollars, and streamline citizen participation (Brown, 2003).

The ever-increasing dominance of ICTs in human lives cannot be overemphasized as seen in President Barack Obama regarding the same: "I want us to ask ourselves every day, how are we using technology to make a real difference in people's lives." On January 21, 2009, newly elected President Obama signed one of his first memorandums – the Memorandum for the Heads of Executive Departments and Agencies on Transparency and Open Government. In the memo, President Obama called for an unprecedented level of openness in Government, asking agencies to "ensure the public trust and establish a system of transparency, public participation, and collaboration". The memo further "directs the Chief Technology Officer, in coordination with the Director of the Office of Management and Budget (OMB) and the Administrator of General Services (GSA), to coordinate the development by appropriate executive departments and agencies and to take specific actions implementing the principles set forth in the memorandum." (Shailendra, Jain, & Sushil, 2007).

Recent government policy updates have seen a shift away from e-Government towards a much more radical focus on transforming the whole relationship between the public sector and users of public services. This new approach is referred to as Transformational Government. Transformation programs differ from traditional e-Government programs in four major ways: they take a whole-of-government view of the relationship between the public sector and the citizen or business user; they include initiatives to e-enable the frontline public services: that is, staff involved in direct personal delivery of services such as education and healthcare – rather than just looking at transactional services which can be e-enabled on an end-to-end basis; they take a whole-of-government view of the most efficient way managing the cost base of government; they focus on the "citizen" not the "customer". That is, they seek to engage with the citizens as owners of and participants in the creation of public services, not as passive recipients of services. With the continuous development of the primary delivery models of e-Government, it can thus be divided into: Government-to-Citizen or Government-to-Consumer (G2C), Government-to-Business (G2B), Government-to-Government (G2G) and Government-to-Employees (G2E). Within each of these interaction domains, four kinds of activities take place (Atkinson & Castro, 2008; UNDESA, 2012): pushing information over the Internet (e.g.: regulatory services, general holidays, public hearing schedules, issue briefs, notifications, etc); two-way communications between the agency and the citizen, a business, or another government agency(in this model, users can engage in dialogue with agencies and post problems, comments, or requests to the agency); conducting transactions (e.g.: lodging tax returns, applying for services and grants); governance (e.g.: to enable the citizen transition from passive information access to active citizen participation by informing the citizen, representing the citizen, encouraging the citizen to vote, consulting the citizen and involving the citizen.

The ultimate goal of e-Government is to be able to offer an increased portfolio of public services to citizens in an efficient and cost effective manner. E-Government allows for government transparency. Government transparency is important because it allows the public to be informed about what the government is working on as well as the policies they are trying to implement. Simple tasks may be easier to perform through electronic government access. Many changes, such as marital status or address changes can be a long process and take a lot of paper work for citizens. E-Government allows these tasks to be performed efficiently with more convenience to individuals. E-Government is an easy way for the public to be more involved in political campaigns. It could increase voter awareness, which could lead to an increase in citizen participation in elections. It is convenient and cost-effective for businesses, and the public benefits by getting easy access to the most current information available without having to spend time, energy and money to get it. E-Government helps simplify processes and makes access to government information more easily accessible for public sector agencies and citizens. It can also reduce operation cost and improve efficiency, service quality, accessibility of public services, operation transparency and accountability (Harding, 2006) .

However, it should be noted that the current attentions of e-Government development focus on the business operation and management. Actually, e-Government can also play an important role in environmental protection and emergency response. By nature, national environment and emergency response have always been regarded as two of the main management responsibilities in each country's government. The fast development of geospatial technologies has made it possible to integrate existing user operational information and value added services in a single harmonized infrastructure. Natural disaster monitoring and mitigation will be integrated together to help the government to achieve early warning and take effective actions under emergency situation such as natural disaster and chemical accident. Therefore, it should also be observed that the greatest impact of such kind of accident to the local environment will always result in the release of a substance or substances hazardous to human health and/or the environment in the short or long term. Such events include fires, explosions, leakages or releases of toxic or hazardous materials that can cause people illness, injury, disability or death. The public need to get the dispersion scenario for such kind of hazards release event. Actually, the application of geospatial technologies can satisfy this requirement. With the aid of Google Earth, GIS and GPS, the computer modeling and simulation can provide the inverse identification of emission profile and location. The modeling result can further present the forward prediction of the event impact. Therefore, the community can acquire the situation in time to form the spontaneous emergency response planning, which will also help the other stakeholders such as government and responsible community team. However, we already have a great amount of information and monitor data while we are lack of the automatic and accurate decision making process implemented by the computers which can take the advantage of available information to get the optimal solution automatically and smartly.

Thus, the integration of geo-technology, modeling and simulation can be a successful e-Government design. If done successfully, it may provide a platform for practitioners to share their experiences with emphasis on technological design and how to map technology to the unique characteristics of systems. This will further complement the work of international committees in order to achieve a common interoperable technology solution for the design of virtual environment protection agency or virtual emergency response agency regardless of whether it is implemented in a developed or resource-constrained economy because the modeling tool can form a virtual e-Government to take the above responsibilities.

This chapter provides an introduction to current research progress on this topic and its future role for the application of spatio-temporal information in the design of virtual e-Government to provide environment protection service and response planning under the emergency situation.

The whole chapter has been separated into five sections. In the first section, the topic focuses on the government's responsibility for environment protection and emergency response. The practice for environment and emergency response from multiple countries is presented. In the second section, the current geo-spatial technology and the related information system is introduced, which has included Google Earth, GIS, GPS and other tools. In the third section, the application of geo-spatial technology to construct the virtual e-Government

which will behave to take the responsibility of government monitor and management for the environment protection and emergency response is discussed. The main attention and introduction focuses on the theoretical/conceptual design and methodology framework . In the fourth section, the chapter provides application illustration with virtual case studies. In the last section, the chapter outlines the author's view point and expectation for the future role of this technology based on the current research progress.

CONTENT

Part 1: Government's Responsibility for Environment Protection and Emergency Response

Discussion concerning environmental protection often focuses on the role of government, legislation and law enforcement. However, in its broadest sense, environmental protection may be seen to be the responsibility of all people and not simply that of government. Decisions that impact the environment will ideally involve a broad range of stakeholders, including industry, indigenous groups, environmental group and community representatives. Gradually, environmental decision-making processes are evolving to reflect this broad base of stakeholders and are becoming more collaborative in many countries (USEPA, 2012). In the USA, the U.S. Environmental Protection Agency (EPA or sometimes USEPA) is an agency of the United States federal government which was created for the purpose of protecting human health and the environment by writing and enforcing regulations based on laws passed by Congress (Google Earth, 2012). The agency is led by its Administrator, who is appointed by the president and approved by Congress. The EPA has its headquarters in Washington, D.C., regional offices for each of the agency's ten regions, and 27 laboratories. The agency conducts environmental assessment, research, and education. It has the responsibility of maintaining and enforcing national standards under a variety of environmental laws, in consultation with state, tribal, and local governments. It delegates some permitting, monitoring, and enforcement responsibility to U.S. states and Native American tribes. EPA enforcement powers include fines, sanctions, and other measures. The agency also works with industries and all levels of government in a wide variety of voluntary pollution prevention programs and energy conservation efforts (Google Earth, 2012). Each year, more than 20,000 emergencies involving the release (or threatened release) of oil and hazardous substances are reported in the United States, potentially affecting both communities and the surrounding natural environment. Emergencies range from small scale spills to large events requiring prompt action and evacuation of nearby populations. EPA coordinates and implements a wide range of activities to ensure that adequate and timely response measures are taken in communities affected by hazardous substances and oil releases where state and local first responder capabilities have been exceeded or where additional support is needed. EPA's emergency response program responds to chemical, oil, biological, and radiological releases and large-scale national emergencies, including homeland security incidents. EPA conducts time-critical and non-time-critical removal actions when necessary to protect human health and the environment by either funding response actions directly or overseeing and enforcing actions conducted by potentially responsible parties. In carrying out these responsibilities, EPA coordinates with other EPA programs (including the Superfund remedial program), other federal agencies, states, tribes, and local governments.

The emergency situation will include not only the environment and safety issue but also the problems caused by the disasters such as local energy shortage and infrastructure damage. For natural disasters, the national agency's primary purpose is to provide Disaster mitigation, preparedness, response, recovery, education, and references. They coordinate the response to a disaster that has occurred and overwhelm the resources of local authorities. In recent years, the increasingly frequent occurrences of extreme events, such as U.S. southern storm and tornado (2011), Japan earthquake and tsunami (2011), and India power shortage (2010), have rang the world an alarm on reexamining whether current rescue policies are effective or efficient enough for a speedy recovery of the suffered areas. These disasters have caused tremendous damages to local areas in terms of economy, people's health and safety, transportation, as well as the energy and the living infrastructures. To restore the functionality and capability of these damaged systems, the recovery of energy system is one of the most important because all the other recovery operations have to be supported by enough available energy. On the other hand, if the local energy shortage caused by a disaster cannot be effectively restored, the local areas will be at risks of rescue delay, widespread power outages, economic losses, and even public safety threats. Therefore, the recovery time minimization of a suffered energy network system should be a top priority of an emergency rescue plan.

Nowadays, energy supply is characterized by its diversity, including traditional energy such as fossil fuels, nuclear power, as well as renewable energy such as solar, hydroelectric, geothermal, biomass, and wind energy. It also involves a complex network system composed of energy generation, energy transformation, energy transportation, and energy consumption. The network does provide the great flexibility for energy transformation and transportation; meanwhile, it presents a complex task for conducting agile energy dispatching when extreme events have caused local energy shortages that need to be restored timely. Conceivably, any type of dispatched energy under certain emergency condition has its own characteristics in terms of availability, quantity, transportation speed, and conversion rate and efficiency to other types of energy. Thus, different types of energy should be dispatched through a superior plan. For instance, energy sources such as petroleum or coal can be directly transported to a suffered area. Meanwhile, they can also be converted to electricity in a source region and then sent to the suffered area through an available electricity network. Sometimes, even the transportation of the same type of energy may have different alternative routes for selection, which needs to be optimally determined from the view point of the entire energy dispatch system.

Part 2: Current Geo-Spatial Technology and Related Information System

Geo-spatial technology is the discipline of gathering, storing, processing, and delivering geographic information, or spatially referenced information. It includes the tools and techniques used in land surveying, remote sensing, cartography, geographic information systems (GIS), global navigation satellite systems (GPS, GLONASS, Galileo, Compass), photogrammetry, geography and related forms of earth mapping. The application of geo-spatial technology involves multiple areas: air navigation services, archaeological excavation and survey for GIS applications, coastal zone management and mapping, criminology, disaster informatics for disaster risk reduction and response, the environment Infrastructure management, land management and reform, natural resource monitoring and development, seismic interpretation sociology, subdivision planning, urban planning, oceanography meteorology, resource management and climate change/environmental monitoring.

The commonly used geo-spatial technology based software and information system are Google Earth, GIS and GPS. Google Earth is a virtual globe, map and geographical information program that was originally called Earth Viewer 3D, and was created by Keyhole, Inc, a Central Intelligence Agency (CIA) funded company acquired by Google in 2004 (see In-Q-Tel). It maps the Earth by the superimposition of images ob-

tained from satellite imagery, aerial photography and GIS 3D globe. It was available under three different licenses, two currently: Google Earth, a free version with limited function; Google Earth Plus (Google Earth, 2012), which included additional features; and Google Earth Pro, which is intended for commercial use (Google Earth, 2012). The product, re-released as Google Earth in 2005, is currently available for use on personal computers running Windows 2000 and above, Mac OS X 10.3.9 and above, Linux kernel: 2.6 or later (released on June 12, 2006), and FreeBSD. Google Earth is also available as a browser plugin which was released on May 28, 2008 (Media Coverage of Geospatial Platforms, 2007). It was also made available for mobile viewers on the iPhone OS on October 28, 2008, as a free download from the App Store, and is available to Android users as a free app in the Google Play store. In addition to releasing an updated Keyhole based client, Google also added the imagery from the Earth database to their web-based mapping software, Google Maps. The release of Google Earth in June 2005 to the public caused a more than tenfold increase in media coverage on virtual globes between 2004 and 2005, (Official Google Blog, 2012) driving public interest in geospatial technologies and applications. As of October 2011 Google Earth has been downloaded more than a billion times (Axetue Team, 2012). Geographic information system (GIS) is a system designed to capture, store, manipulate, analyze, manage, and present all types of geographical data. The acronym GIS is sometimes used for geographical information science or geospatial information studies to refer to the academic discipline or career of working with geographic information systems (GIS, 2011). In the simplest terms, GIS is the merging of cartography, statistical analysis, and database technology. A GIS can be thought of as a system—it digitally creates and "manipulates" spatial areas that may be jurisdictional, purpose, or application-oriented. Generally, a GIS is custom-designed for an organization. Hence, a GIS developed for an application, jurisdiction, enterprise, or purpose may not be necessarily interoperable or compatible with a GIS that has been developed for some other application, jurisdiction, enterprise, or purpose. What goes beyond a GIS is a spatial data infrastructure, a concept that has no such restrictive boundaries. In a general sense, the term describes any information system that integrates, stores, edits, analyzes, shares, and displays geographic information for informing decision making. GIS applications are tools that allow users to create interactive queries (user-created searches), analyze spatial information, edit data in maps, and present the results of all these operations (Clarke, 1986). Geographic information science is the science underlying geographic concepts, applications, and systems (Goodchild, 2010). The Global Positioning System (GPS) is a space-based satellite navigation system that provides location and time information in all weather conditions, anywhere on or near the Earth where there is an unobstructed line of sight to four or more GPS satellites. The system provides critical capabilities to military, civil and commercial users around the world. It is maintained by the United States government and is freely accessible to anyone with a GPS receiver. The GPS project was developed in 1973 to overcome the limitations of previous navigation systems (National Research Council, 2011), integrating ideas from several predecessors, including a number of classified engineering design studies from the 1960s. GPS was created and realized by the U.S. Department of Defense (DoD) and was originally run with 24 satellites. It became fully operational in 1994. Roger L. Easton is generally credited as its inventor. Advances in technology and new demands on the existing system have now led to efforts to modernize the GPS system and implement the next generation of GPS III satellites and Next Generation Operational Control System (OCX) (Factsheets, 2011) Announcements from the Vice President and the White House in 1998 initiated these changes. In 2000, U.S. Congress authorized the modernization

effort, referred to as GPS III. In addition to GPS, other systems are in use or under development. The Russian Global Navigation Satellite System (GLONASS) was developed contemporaneously with GPS, but suffered from incomplete coverage of the globe until the mid-2000s. There are also the planned European Union Galileo positioning system, Chinese Compass navigation system, and Indian Regional Navigational Satellite System (Cai, Zhao, & Xu, 2012).

Part 3: Theoretical/Conceptual Design and Methodology Framework

The operation of environment protection and emergency response can be regarded as a problem of network operation across different regions or even different countries. No matter what industry it is, there are some common characterizations in its network: 1. The attention of network analysis is aimed to examine the structure of relationships among multiple entities (network nodes). These entities may be groups and organizations such as manufacturing sites and suppliers. 2. The optimization of network solution involves finding an optimal way of combinatorial optimization. Examples include network flow, shortest path problem, transport problem, transshipment problem, location problem, matching problem, assignment problem, packing problem, routing problem, Critical Path Analysis and PERT (Program Evaluation & Review Technique).

Different government responsibilities will have their own operation network based on its own characterization such as energy transmission network in the energy industry, supply chain network in the field of industrial operation management and communication network in the field of mass media. Coupled with the continuous development in the field of operation research and management, the requirement for operation optimization in large scale network has provoked more interest in the research field of all the subjects.

Among all the industries, the chemical industry and the energy industry have higher opportunity to meet with the abnormal and emergency situations due to their own industry characterization. The chemical industrial sector is highly heterogeneous encompassing many sectors like organic, inorganic chemicals, dyestuffs paints, pesticides, special chemicals, etc. The risks associated with the chemical industry are commensurate with their rapid growth and development. Apart from their utility, chemicals have their own inherent properties and hazards. Some of them can be flammable, explosive, toxic or corrosive etc. In chemical industry, chemical facilities, where toxic or hazardous chemicals are manufactured and housed, present a high potential of hazards emission during manufacturing operation, such as the upset operations. These are usually caused by various factors of equipment failure, operation, or extreme conditions such as earthquake, tsunami, hurricane, transportation accidents, or terrorist attack. Therefore, chemicals have the potential to affect the nearby environment also. Chemical industrial regions have a high concentration of many chemical plants, whose emissions may cause highly localized and transient air pollution events violating national ambient air quality standards. Many chemical plants are spatially located in an industrial region. Their startup flare emissions exhibit significant temporal variability under extreme meteorological conditions. Such variability may cause an unexpected coincidence of flare emissions and local air quality problems. Therefore, from the emission control point of view, the best practice to improve regional air quality should integrate both efforts on plant-wide emission minimization at every industrial point source, and regional-wide multi-plant emission variability control, which can be regarded as emergency response planning to the extreme weather condition.

In the energy industry, energy shortage is a very serious problem in the world with the continuous growth of global population and rapid exhaust of energy resources on earth. Besides this, extreme

conditions, such as earthquake, tsunami, and hurricane will result in the consequence of short-time energy shortage, which may cause local areas to suffer from delayed rescues, widespread power outages, tremendous economic losses, and even public safety threats. In such urgent events of local energy shortage, agile energy dispatching through an effective energy transportation network, targeting the minimum energy recovery time, should be a top priority.

Therefore, the common characterization of these problems is that they are both about the network solutions: Firstly, the chemical industrial regions are networks composed of multiple nodes of chemical plants while the energy network has multiples nodes to conduct the energy generation, energy conversion and energy consumption; secondly, there is the mutual relationship between the nodes in chemical industrial network and energy network; thirdly, the objective in the optimization of network solution is to satisfy each node's requirement with the minimal time for energy network dispatch optimization under energy shortage and minimal delay time for multiple chemical plants' startup to meet environment requirement. The methodologies will support to give aid in emergency response planning and proactive risk assessment in the above two industries. Compared with the traditional way to take the remedial measure after the occurrence of the emergency event or abnormal situation, the current operation control calls for more proactive risk assessment to set up early warning system and comprehensive emergency response planning. The introduced methodology can benefit both aspects. The prediction modeling will identify the potential problem whether some nodes in the network will be in abnormal situation due to the change or disturbance (energy shortage or high pollutant concentration in the atmosphere). Then if the model predicted result can satisfy the node criteria, there is no need to optimize the network solution; otherwise, the optimization model will be adopted to realize the rapid and effective response to solve the problem. The overall strategy to evaluate the network solution for emergency response planning and proactive risk assessment has been generalized in below methodology framework.

1. At the first stage, the network solution is characterized. The network characterization, network scope and node distribution should be quantitatively described and mapped. Since GIS/GPS only provides the longitude and latitude data for the geological locations, a systematic way can been applied by obtaining the coordinate information.

2. Afterwards, in the second stage, the normal situation should be identified before the occurrence of change or disturbance. The quantitative and qualitative property (criteria, capacity, quantity, and availability) in each node will be determined. The condition of whether the connection or interaction is feasible between nodes should also be identified. The information will be the initial status of prediction and optimization model.

3. In the third stage, under emergency situation with the input information of change or disturbance, the initial condition for each node of the studied network will be evaluated and estimated. This is the prediction of change trend of each node with the occurrence of change or disturbance. The predicted condition is generally an update of scenarios from the second stage, affected by the emergency events case by case. The change or disturbance information such as energy shortage and extreme weather condition should be collected in this stage.

4. Then based on the estimation, in the fourth stage we should judge and conclude whether the network optimization should be made: if the criteria can be satisfied in all the nodes, there is no need to further proceed model construction while if there is some nodes under unsatisfactory condition, the developed model needs to be run to get optimization strategy in a timely way.

5. In the fifth stage, the developed optimization model will integrate information of input and output of initial node condition and interaction status between nodes. This should be a general optimization model, which can cover all the scenarios of node relationship. Available commercial solver can be employed to solve the model and obtain the global optimal solution. The optimal solution is obtained based on the node information of the network. Uncertainties in the quantitative properties of nodes or connections within the network system have to be addressed during the decision making. They can affect the optimality and even feasibility of the obtained solution. Thus, the sensitivity analysis of objective function to uncertainty parameters should be taken. One way is to do that is to characterize this quantitative relationship by partitioning the entire space of uncertainty parameters into multiple subspaces. For each of the partitioned subspaces, the objective value with respect to the uncertainty parameters within the subspace has the same representation function. An algorithm has been developed for this purpose. It actually discloses a roadmap of uncertainty impacts to objective variables, based on which in-depth analysis can be conducted to support decision making in network solution.

6. In the next step, after iteration for all the scenarios of abnormal situations in the network solution, the optimization strategies can be collected to form the comprehensive emergency response planning for the respective industry.

7. Continuous review should be conducted regularly to verify whether the current emergency response planning system has been sufficient to comply with the potential risk. Then the systematic risk assessment will be an input to check the quality of response planning system.

8. If the risk assessment step has demonstrated that there is new abnormal dimension or the abnormal quantity has been out of scope in our previous model consideration, then the new information of change or disturbance should be input and returned to step 3 for the newly evaluate the network condition and proceed step 4-6 accordingly. Then all these steps has constructed a closed loop for the set-up and continuous improvement in the comprehensive EWS(early warning system) and ERPS(emergency response planning system) which can be integrated to be an integrated EMS(emergency management system) for the each industry.

The developed methodology integrates the optimization of MINLP(Mixed Integer Nonlinear Programming) or MILP(Mixed Integer Linear Programming) with geo-spatial technology to provide the decision making. Mathematical optimization involves the selection of best values for decision variables from available alternatives. It consists of maximizing or minimizing an objective function by manipulating decision variables from a constraint domain space. The generalization of optimization model can be represented by below formula. Here, the objective function is to minimize our targets in environment protection and emergency response and the values of decision variables need to satisfy both the inequality constraints and equality constraints. They should also belong to the interval between the lower bound and the upper bound.

$$
\begin{aligned}
\min_{x}/\max \quad & J = f\left(x,u\right) \\
s.t. \quad & g_i\left(x,u\right) \leq 0, \quad \forall i = 1,2,\cdots,p \\
& h_j\left(x,u\right) = 0, \quad \forall j = 1,2,\cdots,q \\
& x \in \left[x^L, x^U\right] \\
& u \in \left[u^L, u^U\right]
\end{aligned}
$$

The e-Government design is based on our previous research of mathematical modeling and optimization for environment management and emergency response. The theoretical/conceptual design has been briefly introduced below to achieve the responsibility of e-Government and more detailed illustrations will be presented in the next part of this chapter.

Emergency Response for Energy Shortage Recovery (Cai, Wang, & Xu, 2013)

The consequence of short-time energy shortage under extreme conditions, such as earthquake, tsunami, and hurricane, may cause local areas to suffer from delayed rescues, widespread power outages, tremendous economic losses, and even public safety threats. In such urgent events of local energy shortage, agile energy dispatching through an effective energy transportation network, targeting the minimum energy recovery time, should be a top priority. The novel methodology is developed for energy network dispatch optimization under emergency of local energy shortage. It includes four stages of work. First, emergency-area-centered energy network needs to be characterized, where the capacity, quantity, and availability of various energy sources are determined. Second, the energy initial situation under emergency conditions needs to be identified. Then, the energy dispatch optimization is conducted based on a developed MILP (mixed-integer linear programming) model in the third stage. Finally, the sensitivity of minimum dispatch time with respect to uncertainty parameters is characterized by partitioning the entire space of uncertainty parameters into multiple subspaces. The developed methodology is the first prototype in the field of energy dispatch optimization under emergencies. Although it is based on some simplifications and assumptions, it has built a solid foundation for future in-depth study and real applications.

The study considers a region containing multiple living areas (e.g., towns or cities). To support these areas, energy production and consumption must exist in this region. This can be considered as an energy distribution and exchange network, where each living area is considered as a node having its own energy generation, transformation, consumption, and storage system; meanwhile, multiple energy dispatch infrastructures are available, such as highway, railway, power line, and petroleum pipelines, which enable the distribution of multiple energy sources among those energy nodes. The energy transportations between two nodes are also called connections. Note that in such an energy dispatch network, each node has limited capacities of storage for different types of energy source, energy generation, and energy transformation; meanwhile, each energy transportation connection also has a restrained capability.

Under extreme conditions of natural disaster and accidents, both energy nodes and connections of a given energy dispatch network may suffer from potential damages. The damages may be reflected as the breakdown of transportation pipeline, losses of energy source materials, or failure of energy transformation equipment (e.g., the damage of power station can fully or partially disable the electricity generation from coal or petroleum fuels). In such a damaged energy network, some nodes may suddenly be in the trouble of energy shortage. To recover the energy supply as soon as possible, the entire region should be motivated to support the energy shortage areas, i.e., through available infrastructure, dispatching various energy or energy source materials from other areas to the in need areas timely. Note that different energy sources have different dispatch ways and speeds based on an available infrastructure. To minimize the energy recovery time, optimal decisions will be made to determine how to select appropriate energy sources and conduct smart dispatching methods, which involves an optimization problem.

This methodology has included four stages as shown in Figure 1. In the first stage, the energy

Figure 1. General methodology framework

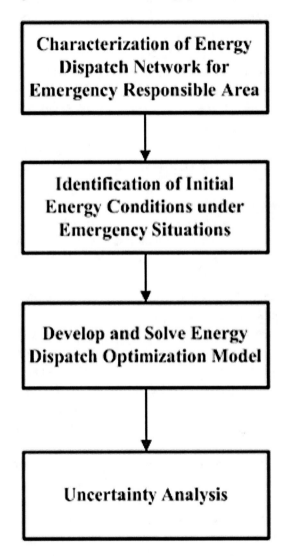

network for emergency responsible area is characterized. The capacity, quantity, availability, and the convertibility of various energy sources in each energy node will be determined. The considered energy sources may include petroleum, nuclear electric power, natural gas, coal, and the renewable energy (solar energy, geothermal energy, biomass, and wind energy). In the second stage, under emergency of local energy shortage, the energy initial condition for each node of the studied energy network will be evaluated and estimated. The energy initial condition is generally an update of energy scenarios from the first stage, affected by the emergency events case by case. Energy shortage information should be collected in this stage.

Based on the estimated energy initial conditions, in the third stage energy dispatch optimization based on a developed MILP model will be conducted, which will integrate information of input and output of energy resource, energy demand, inventory, and transformation and transportation methods to minimize the recovery time for local energy restoration. It is a general energy dispatch model, which can cover all the energy dispatch scenarios (e.g., $1 \rightarrow 1$, $1 \rightarrow n$, $n \rightarrow 1$, or $n \rightarrow n$). Available commercial solver, such as CPLEX, can be employed to solve the MILP model and obtain the global optimal solution. Since the optimal energy dispatch solution is obtained based on the damage evaluations of the energy network. Uncertainties, such as energy loss percentage and energy supply to the network system, have to be addressed during the decision making. They can affect the optimality and even feasibility of the obtained dispatch solution. Thus, the sensitivity of minimum dispatch time to uncertainty parameters is characterized by partitioning the entire space of uncertainty parameters into multiple subspaces in the fourth stage. For each of the partitioned subspaces, the minimum dispatch time with respect to the uncertainty parameters within the subspace has the same representation function. An algorithm has been developed for this purpose. It actually discloses a roadmap of uncertainty impacts to energy dispatch solutions, based on which in-depth analysis can be conducted to support energy dispatch decisions.

Environment Protection through Multiple Plant Operation Scheduling (Cai, Wang, & Xu, In Press)

Chemical plant concentrated regions may suffer localized and transient air pollution events that violate national ambient air quality standards (NAAQS). Flaring emissions, especially intensive start-up flaring emissions from chemical plants, have potentially significant impacts on local air quality. Thus, when multiple plants in an industrial zone plan to start-up within a same time period, their start-up plans should be evaluated and optimally controlled so as to avoid unexpected air-quality violations in any air-quality concern regions (AQCRs). Our developed general systematic methodology for multi-plant start-up emission evaluation and control has been developed. The methodology starts with collecting regional meteorological information such as wind speed and temperature; geographical information of all of the involved chemical plants and AQCRs; as well as plant operation data such as the start-up time window, start-up duration, and estimated emission profile. Next, a regional air-quality evaluation based on Gaussian dispersion model will be conducted. If any air quality violation is predicted to an AQCR, a multi-objective scheduling problem will be generated and solved to optimize the start-up sequence and start-up beginning time for all chemical plants. The scheduling model minimizes the overall air quality impacts to all of AQCRs as well as minimize the total start-up time mismatch of all plants, subject to the principles of atmospheric pollutant dispersion. This study may provide valuable quantitative decision supports for multiple stake holders, including government environmental agency, regional chemical plants, and local communities.

Based on the aforementioned, the study will firstly evaluate the feasibility (in terms of any air quality violation to an AQCR) of the original start-up schedule for a given list of chemical plants in an industrial zone, who coincidently plan to start-up in an overlapping time period; meanwhile generate the same concerned air pollutants that may jeopardize air quality in AQCRs. If the feasibility evaluation for the original start-up plan is negative, an optimal startup schedule needs to be identified in the second stage. The objective function of this optimization problem is to minimize the overall air quality impact to all AQCRs as well as the total start-up time mismatches for all the plants.

This developed general methodology framework is shown in Figure 1. It contains two stages of work. In the first stage, the start-up beginning time proposed by each plant is filed as an original multi-plant start-up schedule, which will be evaluated to check if all the plant emissions by following this schedule would cause air quality violations to any AQCRs during a considered time horizon. To conduct this potential air-quality risk analysis, a Gaussian dispersion model will be employed based on the necessary model parameters and initial conditions. The model inputs include geographical information (e.g., every plant location and every AQCR location), air quality constraints, predicted meteorological conditions (e.g., wind direction and speed, atmospheric stability) during the considered time horizon, the original start-up plan (e.g., planned start-up beginning time,

flexible time window of the start-up beginning time, and start-up duration), and emission source properties (e.g., emission rate, stack height and exit diameter, and outlet temperature).

Based on Gaussian dispersion modeling results, if the predicted air quality (i.e., pollutant concentration) in all AQCRs can meet the environmental criteria during the considered time horizon, it means the original multi-plant start-up schedule is already good enough and can be safely implemented; otherwise, any potential air quality violation at an AQCR suggests the original multi-plant start-up schedule is infeasible and a new optimal schedule needs to be identified. Thus, in the second stage an optimization model will be firstly setup, which employs similar model parameters and initial conditions from the first stage of work, except that the start-up beginning time of each plant will be optimized instead of given as an input (Figure 2). Next, the scheduling

Figure 2. Methodology framework

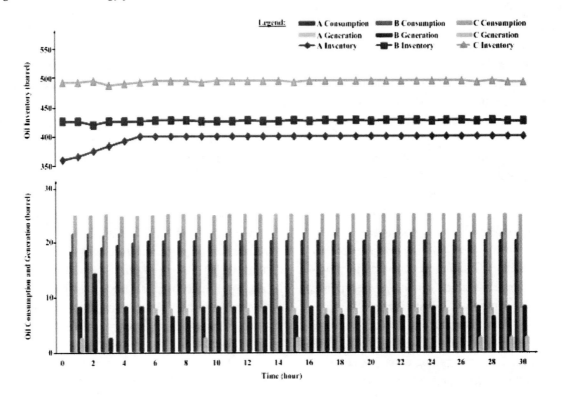

model will be solved and the optimization results need to be validated through virtual simulations. After validation, the optimal solution strategy for multiple chemical plant start-ups will be identified, which may provide quantitative decision support relevant decision makers.

Part 4: Application Illustration with Virtual Case Studies

To demonstrate the efficacy of the developed methodology, two case studies for energy shortage recovery and air quality optimization have been conducted and discussed.

Emergency Response for Energy Shortage Recovery (Cai, Zhao, & Xu, 2012)

An energy network composed of three cities (A, B, and C) was influenced by an extreme weather event, the infrastructure of city A got partially damaged and is currently experiencing energy shortage. The other two cities (B and C) are not affected by the event and thus are able to provide energy and source materials to support city A. By following the first two stages of the proposed methodology, the energy initial conditions of this case study are summarized in Table 1, which gives all the parameters used in the energy dispatch model. Beside the listed parameters, the efficiency of electricity transportation is approximated as 0.95, suggesting 5% loss during electricity network transmission; the hourly energy consuming index is 0.05, suggesting 5% of the available inventory energy will be consumed from the network. Meanwhile, there is no time retention for electricity transmission between cities while the transportation time for source material is two hours between two different cities.

During the emergency situation, assume all types of energy suffer 10% loss in city A, meanwhile there is no energy loss damage to the other cities. Note that the optimization is performed to

deal with an MILP problem. Because the number of variables and constraints involved is not large, the global solution optimality can be guaranteed by employing the commercial solvers such as CPLEX used in this study. Based on the developed energy dispatch model with GAMS [18], the optimization result shows that the minimum dispatch time for this energy restoration of city A is 26 hours. The dynamic profiles for the energy dispatch within the network are presented in Figures 3 through 11.

Figures 3 through 6 show the dynamic energy inventory (represented by bar chart) and energy consumption (represented by trend curves) of petroleum oil (see Figure 3), coal (Figure 4), natural gas (Figure 5), and electricity (Figure 6) in different cities during the energy dispatch period. Figures 3 through 5 indicate that the energy sources of petroleum oil, coal, and natural gas in city A have reached the required quantity within 6 hours. However, electricity recovery picks up slowly because: i) during the first 6 hours, the electricity source materials are insufficient and unstable to fully support electricity generation; and ii) three cities all have small electricity generation capacity, even surplus electricity generated from cities B and C are fully transmitted to city A already. Figure 6 shows that the electricity restoration time in city A is 26 hours.

From Figures 3 through 6, energy profiles in cities B and C only experience small upsets during the energy dispatch period; while those of city A change a lot because it suffers from energy shortage. Especially from Figures 4 through 6, the energy source consumption for electricity generation in city A changes dramatically. This is because city A needs to use the most efficient and available energy sources to generate electricity, so as to accomplish electricity restoration as soon as possible. Thus, in the first two hours city A is with insufficient energy sources for electricity generation. City A uses large quantity of natural gas for electricity generation in the 3rd hour (see Figure 5) because of the high conversion

Table 1. Given data of the case study

Description	Parameter	Energy Source	Unit	i / j		
				A/B or C	B/A or C	C/A or B
Electricity Conversion Efficiency from Other Energy Sources (k: electricity)	$\eta_{i,l,k}$	l: Petroleum Oil	MWh/Barrel	0.55	0.51	0.62
		l: Natural Gas	MWh/Million ft³	0.12	0.125	0.11
		l: Coal	MWh/Short Ton	1.5	1.2	1.6
Hourly Electricity Generation Limit from Source Materials (k: electricity)	$EG^u_{i,l,k}$	l: Petroleum Oil	MWh/hr	75	65	90
		l: Natural Gas	MWh/hr	500	400	600
		l: Coal	MWh/hr	50	40	45
Hourly Limit of Transportation Input from City j to City i	$EI^u_{j,i,k}$	k: Petroleum Oil	Barrel/hr	0.03	0.03	0.03
		k: Natural Gas	Million ft³/hr	0.2	0.2	0.2
		k: Coal	Short Ton/hr	0.01	0.01	0.01
		k: Electricity	MWh/hr	0.05	0.05	0.05
Hourly Limit of Transportation Output from City i to City j	$EO^u_{i,j,k}$	k: Petroleum Oil	Barrel/hr	0.03	0.03	0.03
		k: Natural Gas	Million ft³/hr	0.2	0.2	0.2
		k: Coal	Short Ton/hr	0.01	0.01	0.01
		k: Electricity	MWh/hr	0.05	0.05	0.05
Required Energy Inventory Amount for City i	$RE_{i,k}$	k: Petroleum Oil	Barrel	400	426	493
		k: Natural Gas	Million ft³	500	700	600
		k: Coal	Short Ton	314	346	396
		k: Electricity	MWh	1600	1550	1600
Hourly Energy Supply for City i	$S_{i,k,t}$	k: Petroleum Oil	Barrel/hr	27.45	29.25	27
		k: Natural Gas	Million ft³/hr	135	180	225
		k: Coal	Short Ton/hr	27	22.5	27
		k: Electricity	MWh/hr	0	0	0

efficiency; and thus the natural gas inventory has decreased a lot in the 3rd hour. After that, because the natural gas inventory needs to pick up, petroleum oil and coal consumptions for electricity generation in city A increase (see Figures 3 and 4). Starting from the 6th hour, all the energy sources are consumed in full capacity for electricity generation in city A.

Figure 7 gives a 3D view of the accumulative transportation amount of various energy resources between any pair of cities. The three coordinates represent the accumulative transportation amounts of petroleum oil, coal, and natural gas, respectively. As time elapses, the accumulative transportation amount is always non-decreasing. Thus, arrows

of each curve indicate direction of change with respect to dispatching time. It shows that the accumulative transportation amounts of various energy resources from city A to city B and from city A to city C keep zero until the inventory quantity in city A has been satisfied; while the transportation amounts from cities B and C to A are most significant, although the mutual transportations between B and C are also nontrivial. Furthermore, Figure 7 shows that the hourly transportation amounts from both cities B and C to A are in their full capacities until the near end of the time period. Therefore, both accumulative transportation increments are changing linearly in a wide range in the 3D plot.

Figure 3. Dynamic profiles of petroleum oil inventory and consumption in different cities

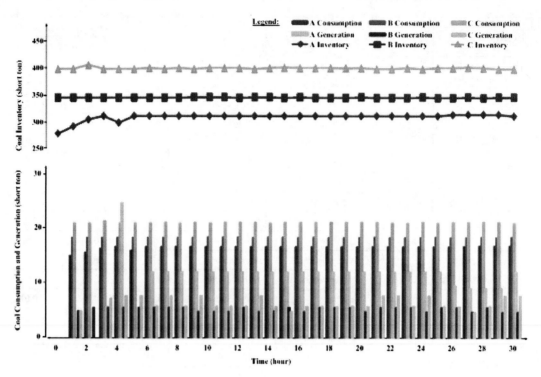

Figure 4. Dynamic profiles of coal inventory and consumption in different cities

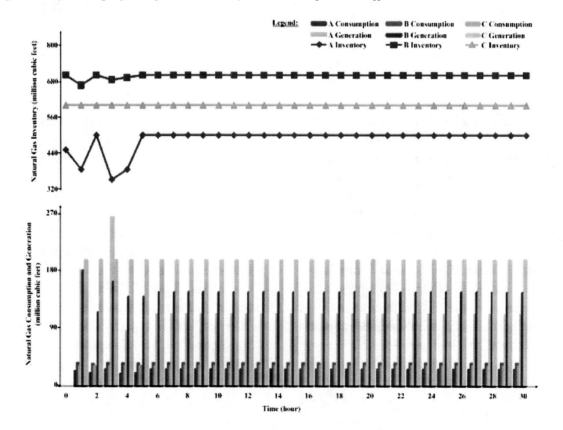

Figure 5. Dynamic profiles of natural gas inventory and consumption in different cities

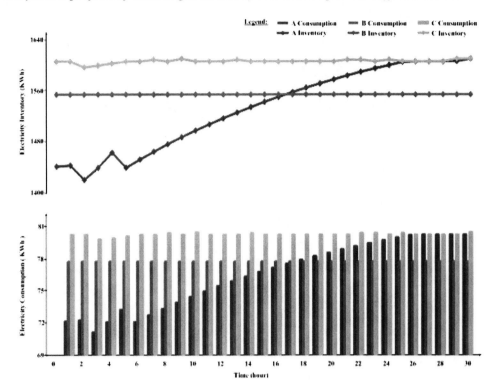

To disclose more details of energy source transportation between each pair of cities, Figures 8 through 10 show accumulative transportation amounts of the petroleum oil, natural gas, coal, and electricity, respectively. Because the energy source materials dispatched from one city to another will take two hours to reach the destination, the curves in Figures 8 through 10 (respectively addressing petroleum oil, natural gas, and coal) clearly show such a transportation time delay. Note that the time delay during electricity transportation (see Figure 11) between two cities has been ignored; however, it costs 5% loss during the transportation. Thus, the electricity arrival and departure curves between two cities are always in 95% proportion in Figure 11. Figures 8 through 11 also show no energy output from city A because of its energy shortage. Cities B and C are dispatching the energy material with the highest loading to city A, which is consistent with the previous analysis based on Figure 7. After the 26th hour when city A has

restored all energy, the energy dispatch activity from the other two cities reduces.

In this case study, two parameters, the energy loss for coal and electricity in city A, are estimated before the energy dispatch optimization. They are actually typical uncertainties that should be investigated to disclose their impact to the final energy dispatch optimization results. Assume they can vary within the range from 0 (no energy loss) to 0.3 (30% energy loss). Then based on the proposed algorithm of uncertainty space partition, a two-dimensional uncertainty space has been constructed, where uncertainties θ_1 represents the energy loss fraction of coal ($0 \leq \theta_1 \leq 0.3$) and θ_2 represents the energy loss fraction of electricity ($0 \leq \theta_1 \leq 0.3$). Figures 12 and 13 show the partitioning result with the total of 46 critical regions (CR1~CR46). The detailed regressed functions for the optimal dispatch time with respect to θ_1 and θ_2 as well as the validation results are

Figure 6. Dynamic profiles of electricity inventory and consumption in different cities

Figure 7. Accumulative transportation amount of various energy resources between cities

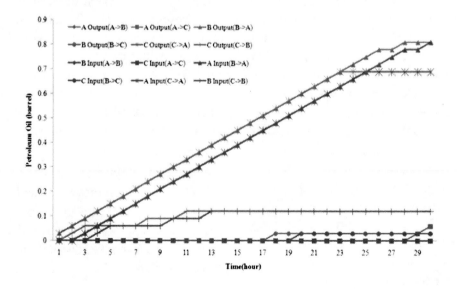

Figure 8. Accumulative transportation amount of petroleum oil between cities

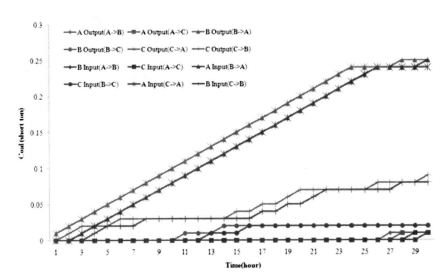

Figure 9. Accumulative transportation amount of coal between cities

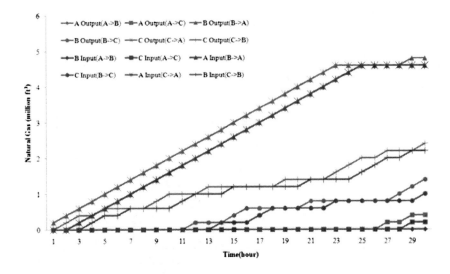

shown in Table 3, where the standard criteria (SC) of derivative percentage is set as 1.5% to identify the approximation performance of function regression.

Note that the 3D profile in Figure 13 is not a smooth surface although it looks like. Together with Table 2, they characterize the relation between the optimal energy dispatch time and the studied two uncertain parameters. They provide decision makers a reference manual for the easy lookup of the possible impact from uncertainties and thus help conduct right decisions. For example, the 3D surface generally shows the less coal and electricity shortages will result in less energy recovery time. As its 2D projection on the uncertainty space as shown in Figure 14, any emergency case specified by coal and electricity shortage for City A corresponds to a point (say point S) in the plane.

Figure 10. Accumulative transportation amount of natural gas between cities

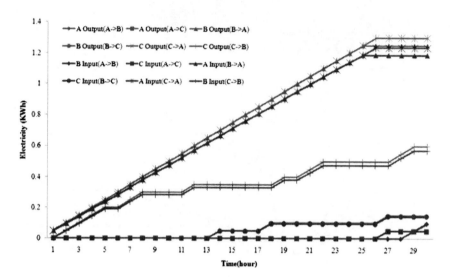

Figure 11. Accumulative transportation amount of electricity between cities

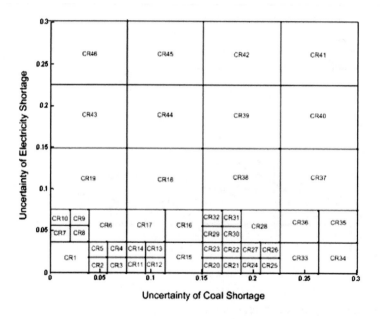

The energy dispatch behaviors among the network are actually moving the point S to finally reach the left-bottom corner point. It should be known that any movement in a short time period can be decomposed into two directions: one is toward the iso-time direction that does not reduce energy recovery time at all; the other is gradient direction perpendicular to the iso-time direction, which represents the shortest energy recovery time and smart move direction. For illustration, the iso-time and gradient directions at a point S (with 20% electricity and 15% coal shortages respectively)

Figure 12. Uncertainty space partitioning for the case study

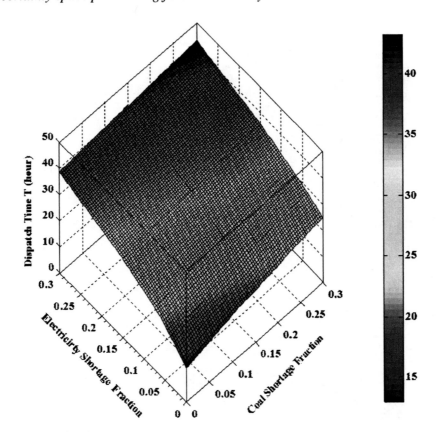

are demonstrated in Figure 14. Based on such information, the dynamic impact of different energy dispatch strategies can be evaluated, which will help decision makings under uncertainties.

Environment Protection through Multiple Plant Operation Scheduling (Cai, Wang, & Xu, 2013)

The presented three case studies share the same emission sources and AQCRs distributed in a squared region (30 km×30 km) as shown in Figure 15. The entire region is gridded and the edge length of each grid cell is 1 km, which includes an industrial zone where the emission sources of three chemical plants (E1, E2, and E3 represented by red dots in Figure 15) planning to start-up in a similar time period; and the rest gridded cells

colored in pink are all considered as AQCRs. The surface wind blows from the southwest to northeast as shown in Figure 15. The three plants are expected to have startup durations for 1 hr, 2 hrs and 3 hrs, respectively. According to the original start-up plan, the start-up beginning time of all three plants is set at 08:00 and thus their start-up completed time will be 09:00, 10:00, and 11:00, respectively. Sulfur dioxide is the major emission during three plants' start-ups. The NAAQS of SO2 is 75 ppb. The plume and stack parameters of three plants are given in Table 1. When potential risk analysis and optimal scheduling are conducted, the spatial computational resolution is 0.01 km for both X direction (along the wind direction) and Y direction. The temporal computational resolution is 0.1 hr.

Table 2. Uncertainty space partitioning results for the case study

Region	Vertex	θ1	θ2	M(θ)	A(θ)	Dispatch Time T	AVG θ1	AVG θ2	M(θ)	A(θ)
CR1	P1	0	0	13	13	$T = \frac{160}{3}\theta_1 + 160\theta_2 + 13$	0.01875	0.01875	17	17
	P2	0.0375	0	15	15					
	P3	0.0375	0.0375	21	21					
	P4	0	0.0375	19	19					
CR2	P1	0.0375	0	15	15	$T = \frac{160}{3}\theta_1 + 160\theta_2 + 13$	0.046875	0.009375	17	17
	P2	0.05625	0	16	16					
	P3	0.05625	0.01875	19	19					
	P4	0.0375	0.01875	18	18					
CR3	P1	0.05625	0	16	16	$T = \frac{160}{3}\theta_1 + 160\theta_2 + 13$	0.065625	0.009375	18	18
	P2	0.075	0	17	17					
	P3	0.075	0.01875	20	20					
	P4	0.05625	0.01875	19	19					
CR4	P1	0.05625	0.01875	19	19	$T = \frac{160}{3}\theta_1 + \frac{320}{3}\theta_2 + 14$	0.065625	0.028125	21	21
	P2	0.075	0.01875	20	20					
	P3	0.075	0.0375	22	22					
	P4	0.05625	0.0375	21	21					
CR5	P1	0.0375	0.01875	18	18	$T = \frac{80}{3}\theta_1 + \frac{400}{3}\theta_2 + 14.75$	0.046875	0.028125	20	20
	P2	0.05625	0.01875	19	19					
	P3	0.05625	0.0375	21	21					
	P4	0.0375	0.0375	21	21					
CR6	P1	0.0375	0.0375	21	21	$T = \frac{80}{3}\theta_1 + \frac{320}{3}\theta_2 + 16$	0.05625	0.05625	23	23
	P2	0.075	0.0375	22	22					
	P3	0.075	0.075	26	26					
	P4	0.0375	0.075	25	25					
CR7	P1	0	0.0375	19	19	$T = \frac{80}{3}\theta_1 + \frac{400}{3}\theta_2 + 14.25$	0.009375	0.046875	21	21
	P2	0.01875	0.0375	20	20					
	P3	0.01875	0.05625	22	22					
	P4	0	0.05625	22	22					
CR8	P1	0.01875	0.0375	20	20	$T = \frac{160}{3}\theta_1 + \frac{320}{3}\theta_2 + 15$	0.028125	0.046875	21	21
	P2	0.0375	0.0375	21	21					
	P3	0.0375	0.05625	23	23					
	P4	0.01875	0.05625	22	22					
CR9	P1	0.01875	0.05625	22	22	$T = \frac{160}{3}\theta_1 + \frac{320}{3}\theta_2 + 15$	0.028125	0.065625	24	24
	P2	0.0375	0.05625	23	23					
	P3	0.0375	0.075	25	25					
	P4	0.01875	0.075	24	24					
CR10	P1	0	0.05625	22	22	$T = \frac{320}{3}\theta_2 + 16$	0.009375	0.065625	23	23
	P2	0.01875	0.05625	22	22					
	P3	0.01875	0.075	24	24					
	P4	0	0.075	24	24					
CR11	P1	0.075	0	17	17	$T = \frac{80}{3}\theta_1 + \frac{400}{3}\theta_2 + 15.25$	0.084375	0.009375	19	19
	P2	0.09375	0	18	18					
	P3	0.09375	0.01875	20	20					
	P4	0.075	0.01875	20	20					
CR12	P1	0.09375	0	18	18	$T = \frac{160}{3}\theta_1 + \frac{320}{3}\theta_2 + 13$	0.103125	0.009375	20	20
	P2	0.1125	0	19	19					
	P3	0.1125	0.01875	21	21					
	P4	0.09375	0.01875	20	20					

The first case study involves a sunny spring day with the strong radiation of 20 K/km lapse rate and the surface wind speed of 1.8m/s at 10 meter height and the ambient temperature of 20 °C. Firstly, the potential risk analysis has been conducted to examine the original start-up plan, which assume all the plants initiate their startups at the same time (08:00). Figure 16 shows the spatial and temporal distribution of the cumulative concentration of SO2 emissions. At the initial three

Table 3. Plume and stack parameters for each emission source

Chemical Plant	E1	E2	E3
Stack Height h_i (m)	80	110	95
Stack Exit Temperature $T_{S,i}$ (K)	480	400	460
Stack Exit Velocity $V_{S,i}$ (m/s)	17.5	13.0	15.6
Stack Exit Diameter (m)	1.6	1.9	1.5
Startup Emission Parameter γ_i (mg/s)	330000	320000	310000
Time Difference of PS_i - TS_i (hr)	0.5	0.5	0.5
Peak Duration Time DT_i (hr)	1	2	3
Normal Emission Coefficient α_i	0.05	0.04	0.03

Figure 13. Minimum energy dispatch time with respect to uncertainties

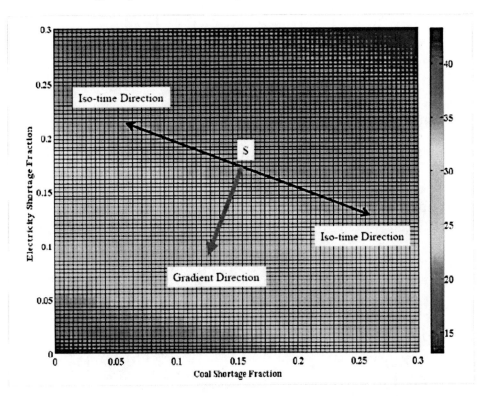

Figure 14. Application analysis based on uncertainty space partitioning

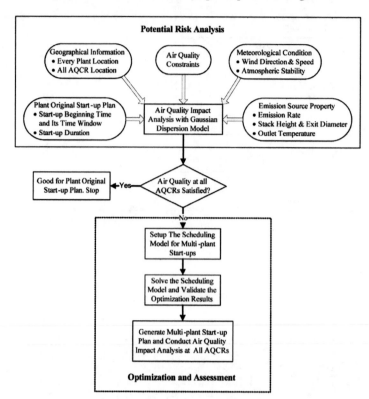

Figure 15. Illustration of an industrial zone and AQCRs

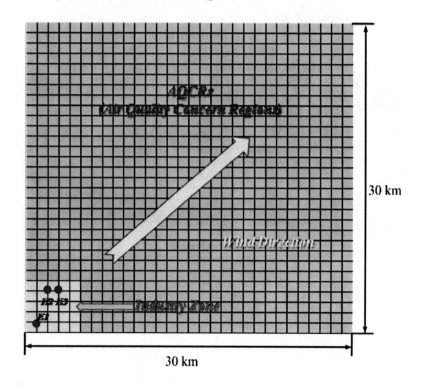

Figure 16. Spatial and temporal distribution of SO$_2$ emissions for case study

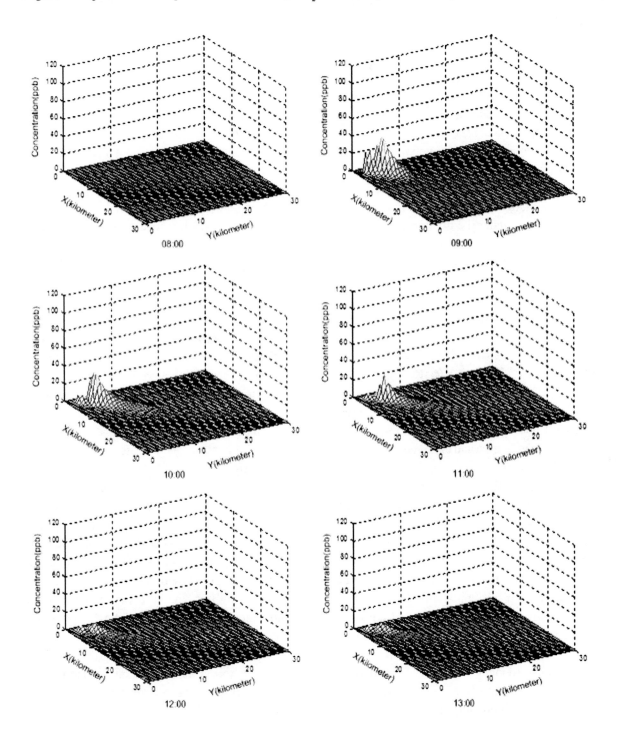

hours, the peak concentration will reach 45 ppb and maintain for one hour. The three concentration peaks in the emission profile at 09:00 has been reduced to two at 10:00 because one plant (plant E1) has completed its start-up and its emission rate at normal condition has trivial impacts on the superposed emission profile. Since 11:00, the maximum emission concentration will be gradually reduced to be less than 5 ppb, although the emission affected area is increasing due to continuous dispersion. It can be seen from Figure 16 that the original plant start-up plan will not cause air quality problem under the given meteorological conditions. Since the simultaneous startup will not have potential impact on the local environment, there is no need to perform further optimization on multi-plant start-up scheduling according to the developed methodology.

Part 5: Discussion for Findings and Future Work

The current geospatial technologies will facilitate the timely and scientific decision making for environment protection and emergency response. It will help the government to achieve early warning and take effective actions under emergency situation. Up to now, the optimization algorithm and geospatial technologies have already been available while there is still a long way to go to realize the seamless integration between these two elements. Both the government and the public will benefit from this application by capability expansion for Google Earth, GIS and GPS, the computer modeling and simulation. The modeling result can further present the forward prediction and the backward identifications, which will also help the other stakeholders such as government and responsible community team. This potential

modeling tool can form a virtual e-Government to take the above responsibilities.

CONCLUSION

This chapter has demonstrated the potential application of geo-spatial technology based e-Government design for emergency response and environment protection. It has provided the introduction of current research progress of this topic and its future role for the application of spatio-temporal information in the design of virtual e-Government to provide environment protection service and response planning under the emergency situation. The fast development of geospatial technologies has made it possible to integrate existing user operational information and value added services in a single harmonized infrastructure. It is the first systematic study in this area and it may provide proactive and quantitative decision supports for multiple stake holders, including government environmental agency, regional chemical plants, and local communities. The public need to get the dispersion scenario for such kind of hazards release event. Actually, the application of geospatial technologies can satisfy this requirement. With the aid of Google Earth, GIS and GPS, the computer modeling and simulation can provide the inverse identification of emission profile and location. The modeling result can further present the forward prediction of the event impact. Therefore the community can acquire the situation in time to form the spontaneous emergency response planning, which will also help the other stakeholders such as government and responsible community team. This modeling tool can form a virtual e-Government to take the above responsibilities.

REFERENCES

Atkinson, R. D., & Castro, D. (2008). *Digital quality of life: Understanding the personal & social benefits of the information technology revolution.* The Information Technology and Innovation Foundation. Retrieved March 28, 2013 from http://www.innovationfiles.org/

Axetue Team. (2011, October 12). *Google Earth gets a billion downloads.* Retrieved August 16, 2012 from http://www.axetue.com/2011/10/12/google-earth-billion-downloads

Cai, T., Wang, S., & Xu, Q. (2013). Scheduling of multiple chemical plant start-ups to minimize regional air quality impacts. *Computers & Chemical Engineering, 54,* 68–78. doi:10.1016/j.compchemeng.2013.03.027

Cai, T., Zhao, C., & Xu, Q. (2012). Energy network dispatch optimization under emergency of local energy shortage. *Energy, 42,* 132–145. doi:10.1016/j.energy.2012.04.001

Clarke, K. C. (1986). Advances in geographic information systems. *Computers, Environment and Urban Systems, 10,* 175–184. doi:10.1016/0198-9715(86)90006-2

EPA. (n.d.). *Our mission and what we do.* US EPA. Retrieved August 16, 2012 from http://www.epa.gov/aboutepa/whatwedo.html

ESRI. (2011). *Geographic information systems as an integrating technology: Context, concepts, and definitions.* Retrieved March 24, 2013 from http://www.colorado.edu/geography/gcraft/notes/intro/intro.html

Factsheets: GPS Advanced Control Segment (OCX). (n.d.). Retrieved November 6, 2011 from http://www.losangeles.af.mil/library/factsheets/factsheet.asp?id=18676

Goodchild, M. F. (2010). Twenty years of progress: GIScience in 2010. *Journal of Spatial Information Science, 1,* 3–20.

Google Discontinues Google Earth Plus. (n.d.). Retrieved August 16, 2012 from http://www.techpluto.com/google-earth-live/

Google Earth. (n.d.). *Meet the browser.* Retrieved from http://google-latlong.blogspot.com/2008/05/google-earth-meet-browser.html

Google Earth Plus Discontinued. (n.d.). Retrieved August 16, 2012 from http://www.gearthblog.com/blog/archives/2008/12/google_earth_plus_discontinued.html

Google Earth Product Family. (n.d.). Retrieved August 16, 2012 from http://earth.google.com/products.html

Harding, R. (2006). Ecologically sustainable development: Origins, implementation and challenges. *Desalination, 187*(1-3), 229–239. doi:10.1016/j.desal.2005.04.082

Media Coverage of Geospatial Platforms. (2007). Retrieved September 17, 2013 from http://www.geospatialweb.com/figure-4

National Research Council (U.S.), Committee on the Future of the Global Positioning System, National Academy of Public Administration. (1995). *The global positioning system: A shared national asset: Recommendations for technical improvements and enhancements.* Washington, DC: National Academies Press. Retrieved November 6, 2011 from http://books.google.com/books?id=FAHk65slfY4C

Official Google Blog. (2011). *Google Earth downloaded more than one billion times.* Retrieved from http://googleblog.blogspot.com/2011/10/google-earth-downloaded-more-than-one.html

Shailendra, C., Jain, P., & Sushil, S. S. (2007). *E-government and e-governance: Definitions/domain framework and status around the world.* ICEG. Retrieved March 28, 2013 from http://www.iceg.net/2007/books/1/1_369.pdf

United Nations Department of Economic and Social Affairs. (2012). United Nations e-government survey 2012. New York: UN. Deloitte Research. (2000). Public sector institute at the dawn of e-government: The citizen as customer. Author. Transparency and Open Government. (2012). Retrieved from whitehouse.gov Brown, M.M. (2003). Electronic governmen. In J. Rabin (Ed.), Encyclopedia of public administration and public policy. Marcel Dekker.

United Nations Department of Economic and Social Affairs. (2012). *United Nations e-government survey 2012*. New York: UN.

ADDITIONAL READING

Mutula, S. M., & Van Brakel, P. (2006). An evaluation of e-readiness assessment tools with respect to information access: Towards an integrated information rich tool. *International Journal of Information Management*, 26(3), 212–223. doi:10.1016/j.ijinfomgt.2006.02.004

Naidoo, G. (2004). Introduction of E-governance and its implications for developing countries. In Gupta. M.P. (ed.) Towards E-Governance Management Challenges, 145-154. New Delhi. India. Tata McGraw Hill Publishing Company.

Naidoo, G., & Van Jaarsveldt. (2004). Electronic government: Strategies and Implementations: E-governance in South Africa: A perspective on initiatives, readiness and development issues. In Gupta, M.P. (ed.). *Towards E-governance Management Challenges*, 138-144. New Delhi. India. Tata McGraw Hill Publishing Company.

Nanayakkara, C. (2007). A Model of User Acceptance of Learning Management Systems: a study within Tertiary Institutions in New Zealand. Retrieved October 30, 2010 from www.caudit. edu.au/educauseaustral asia07/authors_papers/ Nanayakkara-361.pdf.

Napoli, J., Ewing, M. T., & Pitt, L. F. (2008). Factors Affecting the Adoption of the Internet in the Public Sector. *Journal of Nonprofit & Public Sector Marketing*, 7, 77–88. doi:10.1300/ J054v07n04_07

Navarra, D. D., & Cornfcrd, T. (2007). The state, democracy and the limits of new public management: Exploring alternative models of e-Government. *Presented at the e-Government Workshop '06 (Egov06) September 11 2006, Brunel University, London, UB8 3PH*, 1-14. Retrieved August 14, 2011 from is2.lse.ac.uk/wp/ pdf/wp155.pdf.

Ndou, V. D. (2004). E-Government for developing countries: opportunities and challenges, *The Electronic Journal on Information Systems in Developing Countries (EJISDC)*, 18(1),1-24. Retrieved May 17, 2010 from citeseerx.ist.psu. edu/viewdoc/download?doi=10.1.1.127.

KEY TERMS AND DEFINITIONS

E-Government: This entails the use of ICTs in different government business value chains in order to foster effectiveness and efficiency in the bid to interact with citizens and businesses.

Emergency: This is any natural or human endeavour that requires urgent and immediate attentention in order to avoid its repercutions.

Geospatial Technologies: These are technology platforms or tools that may be utilized to capture spatial and temporal information of any place in the world.

ICTs: These are technology tools or platforms that are used for managing or interchange of different information resources. The acronym ICTs stands for Information and Commnication Technologies.

Public Service: This is a not-for-profit service usually given by elected government to its citizens and businesses. Such kind of business is usually devoted towards achieving a public good.

Chapter 10
Anti-Corruption Capabilities of Public E-Procurement Technologies:
Principal-Agent Theory

Arjun Neupane
University of Southern Queensland, Australia

Jeffrey Soar
University of Southern Queensland, Australia

Kishor Vaidya
University of Southern Queensland, Australia & University of Canberra, Australia

ABSTRACT

Public procurement is an important area warranting further attention in government reform, as electronic systems for procurement have enormous potential to help reduce corruption. Public e-Procurement is the use of an Internet or Web-based system by government institutions for the acquisition of goods and services, which can improve transparency and accountability. This chapter discusses different types of e-Procurement technologies with case examples from different countries that demonstrate how the e-Procurement technologies have great potential as the anti-corruption technologies. The chapter reviews the Principal-Agent Theory and discusses other relevant theories including Transaction Cost Theory, Fraud Triangle Theory, Diffusion of Innovation Theory, and the Technology Acceptance Model. Following a discussion of the potential of e-Procurement systems in mitigating corruption, a theoretical research model is proposed for identifying public e-Procurement anti-corruption capabilities.

DOI: 10.4018/978-1-4666-4900-2.ch010

INTRODUCTION AND BACKGROUND

Governments across the globe have been increasing the adoption of information and communication technologies (ICTs) as tools to enhance transparency and accountability in government (McCue & Roman, 2012; Neupane &Soar et al., 2012). Public e-Procurement is an e-Government tool with the potential to help reform the government procurement systems

(Filho & Mota, 2012) and enhance efficiency, improve the speed and quality of procurement processes, and, importantly, to enhance transparency and accountability (Brun et al., 2010; Wen & Wei, 2007).

Public e-Procurement is defined as the use of ICT such as Internet or web-based systems by government institutions in conducting procurement-related tasks, such as the acquisition of goods, services, and the allocation of work to bidders (Davila,Gupta & Palmer, 2003; Leipold et al., 2004). Vaidya (2007) defined public e-Procurement as an Internet based inter-organisational information system that integrates and automates any parts of procurement processes in order to improve transparency and accountability.

Corruption in public procurement is believed to be rapidly increasing, especially in developing countries. It is a global threat to economic and human development of all nations (Neupane,Soar & Vaidya, 2012a). Public procurement accounts for almost 10 to 15 percent of Gross Domestic Product (GDP) in developed countries and almost 20% of GDP in developing countries (GTN, 2003). The basic principle of public procurement is to acquire the right item at the right time, and at the right price. Developing countries are more vulnerable to fraud and corruption and there is a need for procurement processes to be more transparent and accountable. There are many related aspects of corruption such as unjustified or hidden procurement planning, lack of assessment, political pressure, lack of monitoring capacity, inconsistent cost estimates, and weak professionalization of the bureaucracy of the country (Del Monte & Papagni, 2007; Kolstad & Wiig, 2009; Neupane andSoar et al., 2012; Pellegrini & Gerlagh, 2008; Subedi, 2006; Ware et al., 2012).

Public procurement processes have different phases and each phase has a potential risk for corruption. The three main phases of the public procurement process have been illustrated by Matechak (2002): procurement planning and budgeting, procurement solicitation, and contract award and performance. Szymanski (2007) proposed five stages for setting up structures to fight corruption in public procurement, these were: procurement planning and needs assessments, product design and document preparation, tender processes, contract award and implementation, and accounting and audit. Szymanski identified the most vulnerable areas of corruptions that need assessments as: project specification, bid evaluation, and sub-contracting. Szymanski suggested that the major risks for corruption arise from a lack of transparency, limited access to information, a lack of accountability and a lack of control at each stage of the public procurement process.

The main propose of this Chapter is to expand the existing Body of Knowledge about anti-corruption capabilities of public e-Procurement and to discuss relevant organizational theories, particularly Principal-Agent theory, Technology Acceptance Model, and Transaction Cost theory to identify and explain the relevant variables. The Principal-Agent Theory is considered the most relevant theory to understand the dynamics behind public procurement processes between government and their bidders. The theories of anti-corruption capabilities (Constructs) discusses and justifies why these characteristics play significant and positive roles in order to improve transparency and accountability in public procurement as to reduce the chances of corruption.

The Chapter is structured as follows. Firstly, it discusses the different types of e-Procurement technologies. Secondly, an overview of theoretical concepts in relation to perceived benefits of public e-Procurement has been presented. Next, capabilities of anti-corruption of public e-Procurement based on the theoretical constructs have been presented. Following the discussion of anti-corruption capabilities, the research model is presented. A discussion of the findings and the conclusion is presented in the final section.

TYPES OF E-PROCUREMENT TECHNOLOGIES

Currently, there are different types of e-Procurement technologies used by governments or private organisations, including e-MRO (Maintenance, Repair, and Operating), Web-based ERP (Enterprise Resource Planning), e-Tendering, e-Sourcing, e-Auction, e-Informing, e-Ordering, e-Markets, e-Exchange, e-Intelligent, and e-Contract management (Chang, Tsai & Hsu, 2013; Croom, 2000; De Boer et al., 2002; Walker & Brammer, 2012). Each type of system is built for special purposeS and has its own specific functionality and characteristics. Table 1 demonstrated the most common types of public e-Procurement and their explanation.

Different countries have already implemented and practiced public e-Procurement in public and private levels with different names. E-Procurement has been popular in advanced countries like Australia, UK, and USA as well as in governments in emerging economies including China, India, Mexico, South Korea, and Brazil, which are imple-

Table 1. Types of e-procurement systems

E-Procurement System	Description	Authors(S) & Year
e-Informing	Gathering and distributing purchasing information both from and to internal and external parties using InternetInternet technology.	(Boer, Harink & Heijboer, 2001; De Boer et al., 2002; Essig & Arnold, 2001)
e-Sourcing	Process of identifying new suppliers for specific categories of purchasing requirements using Internet technology.	(Chang et al., 2013; De Boer et al., 2002; Fuks, Kawa & Wieczerzycki, 2009; Knudsen, 2003)
e-Tendering	The process of sending requests for information and prices to suppliers and receiving the response using Internet technology.	(Betts et al., 2010; De Boer et al., 2002)
e-Reverse auctioning	Internet based reverse auction technology which focuses on the price of the goods and services auctioned.	(Carter et al., 2004; Teich, Wallenius & Wallenius, 1999)
e-MRO and Web based ERP	The process of creating and approving purchasing requisitions, placing purchase orders and receiving the goods or services ordered via a software system based on Internet technology, e-MRO deals with indirect items (MRO), web-based ERP deals with product-related items.	(Bruno et al., 2005; De Boer et al., 2002; Fink, 2006; Gunasekaran et al., 2009)
e-Ordering	The use of Internet to facilitate operational purchasing process, including ordering (requisitioning), order approval, order receipt and payment process.	(Harink, 2003; Reunis, Santema & Harink, 2006)
e-Markets	E-Markets are meeting venues for component suppliers and purchasers, who use exchange mechanism to electronically support the procurement process.	(Block & Neumann, 2008; Fuks et al., 2009)
e-Intelligence	Management information system with spend analysis tools	(Eakin, 2003; Harink, 2003)
e-Contract Management	The use of information technology for improving the efficiency and effectiveness of contracting processes of companies.	(Angelov & Grefen, 2008; Yang & Zhang, 2009)
E-Submission	It is the process of online submission of electronic document like tender document that is specially designed to facilitate the bidders' submissions of their bids through e-submission.	(Neupane & Soar et al., 2012a; Salin & Abidin, 2011)

menting e-Procurement initiatives (Vaidya & Hyde, 2011).

One of the most highly-regarded examples of e-Procurement is the South Korean government systems that integrates e-Procurement solutions with other electronic government operations, including financial management systems, company registrations, and tax systems. It uses the Korea Online e-Procurement system (KONEPS) which links seventy-seven external systems to share any necessary information, and provides one-stop service, including Internet banking. It is interesting to note that in year 2010 over 60 precent Korea's total public procurement (124 billion USD) was conducted through KONEPS (Chang, 2011). Other countries that have introduced public e-Procurement systems include Costa Rica, Vietnam, Pakistan, Mongolia, and Sir Lanka collaboration with the Korean government (KONEPS system) (Chang, 2011). To conclude, these systems have improved transparency and efficiency including public access to procurement information, reduced the contracting officer's arbitrary discretion, and minimised face-to-face contract in entire public procurement processes.

In another example, in the year 2000, Singapore implemented Government Electronic Business (GeBIZ); a one-stop e-Procurement portal. All public sector quotations and tenders are posted on this system and the supplier can easily access procurement information anywhere and anytime with just an Internet connection, download tender documents, and submit their bids online. Currently, there are about fifty-five thousand local and foreign suppliers registered as 'GeBIZ' (Kunakornpaiboonsiri, 2013). Government of the Singapore has numerous benefits after implementing e-Procurement system including work efficiency through the integration of the procurement activities, easy access of public procurement information, increase transparency, and fair competition.

In Australia, the New South Wales (NSW) government eTendering system has implemented Web-based tender management system that offers a wide range of solutions for all the buyers and suppliers to assist the end-to-end contract management system, efficiency, and reduces the tender processes. Currently, there are more than one hundred thousand register suppliers in this system. E-Tendering is also popular in many nations for the process of sending requests for information and prices to suppliers and receiving the response using Internet technology (Betts et al., 2010; De Boer et al., 2002).

Similarly, from supplier perspective, it increases sales productivity, accuracy orders, fast receipt of orders, reduces time for receiving payment, real time order status information. These benefits can be linked to different factors such as real time order status link to transparency, effective monitoring linked to lack of control, improved contract compliance linked to lack of accountability, increase information on suppliers to limit access to information. Therefore, it is a powerful technology among the government agencies for ensuring the transparency (Doyle, 2010), enhancing efficiency, increasing accountability, and economic performance of the country.

Yet in another example, China established a government procurement system in 1996. After implementation of the system, procurement efficiency increased rapidly from about $3.1 billion in 1998 to $213.57 billion in 2004, an average increase of 88.78 percent per year (UN, 2006). This government procurement system has improved the efficiency of financial expenditure, limits corruption and encourages efficient administrative operations (UN, 2006). This technologies plays an important role to national productivity growth in the removal of non-value added activities in procurement process (Sherah Kurnia & Rahim, 2007). Similarly, Asian and Pacific countries have increasingly adopted ICT systems in order to enhance government services and business transaction (Wescott, 2001). The Government of Andra Pradesh (India) is another example offering all the procurement activities through e-Procurement with transparent manner and reduces the opportunities for the corrupt parties (Bikshapathi et al., 2006). The government of Nepal has also developed a master plan with the main objective being the building of the more efficient, productive, transparent, and responsible value added quality services through ICT. For example, the recent study (Neupane & Soar et al., 2012a; Neupane Soar & Vaidya, 2012b) has pointed out that the implementation the e-Procurement system solved eighty percent of problems of manual tendering in Department of Road Nepal and completely avoid the human interference in public tendering processes.

OVERVIEW OF THEORIES LINKING ANTI-CORRUPTION TO TECHN OLOGIES

Why theories? Theories provide guidelines that govern research and provide a structure to the concepts and relationships between constructs, that collectively present logical, systematic, and coherent explanation of phenomenon of the interest with some assumption (Bacharach, 1989). No single theory provides the explanations of all social or natural phenomena. There is research about the attributes or qualities of good theories, including logical consistency and technological artefacts, meaningful explanations and exploratory powers, being open to scientific evaluation, and the stimulation of new thinking and research (Bacharach, 1989; Bhattacherjee, 2012; Gregor,2006). Different theories can explain the different types of behaviours, using a set of construct, propositions, boundary conditions, assumptions, and underlying logic.

In this work, we discuss the different theories and their exploratory powers in the anti-corruption role of public e-Procurement. Diffusion of Innovation theory (Rogers, 1995) discusses technological innovation including technology's potential benefits such as relative advantages and the compatibility of information technology. Technology Acceptance Model (TAM) (Davis, 1989) is based on two beliefs of technology used perceived usefulness, and perceived ease of use. Fraud triangle theory (Cressey, 1953) describes the three factors perceived pressure, perceived opportunity, and rationalisation that are present in every situation of fraud.

Principal-Agent Theory

Agency theory can be considered as one of the most significant theoretical foundations because it constructs relationships in terms of Principal and Agent problems (Singh & Sirdeshmukh, 2000) and it has been used in different areas of research including business management and information systems, organisational economics, and public procurement. It is also known as Principal-Agent Theory, and is concerned with resolving two problems that can occur in agency relationships between two parties: the Principal and the Agent, the Agent being the one who makes the decision or takes any action on the behalf of the Principal (Eisenhardt, 1989; Jensen & Meckling, 1976). To use this concept, it is assumed that the Government is the Principal body that provides public services to the people, and the Agents are the bidders (Contractor, supplier) who work for the Government and are providers of goods and services. The main role of Principal or Government authority is itsresponsibility for formulating policy options to help in the regulation and development of public procurement, the monitoring of the various procurement activities, the regulation and maintenance of standards of procurement, capacity-building and professional development, information mangement and dissemination. Agents' roles are to bid for the government work and services, comply with all statutory, legal and award requirements relative to the work and services, complete all tasks within agreed cost structures, maintain quality and also complete all the tasks within the designated time frame. In this regard, the main contribution of Principal-Agent Theory is to explain the risk of corruption in public procurement processes between two parties - Principal and Agent - and also examine contractual problems to determine the most efficient contract type that will satisfactorily govern the Agency relationship (Whipple & Roh, 2010).

Based on the above discussion, principal-agent theory can be considered to help the design of the most effective types of e-Government application tool such as e-Procurement technology for examine contracting problems to determine the most efficient contract type that will satisfactory govern the agency relationship (Whipple & Roh, 2010). Principal-agent theory deals with moral hazard, information asymmetry, monopoly of power, shrinking, hidden action, and trust. These construct are playing very important role to analyse the corruption in government procurement processes. Therefore, the principal-agent theory provides a very influential theoretical approach for the design of the incentive e-Government application.

Transaction Cost Theory

The concept of the Transaction Cost Theory supposes that the organisation tries to minimise transaction costs including information costs, negotiation costs, and monitoring costs (Williamson, 1981). In economics and other disciplines, a transaction cost is a cost of incurred in making an economic exchange. In broad terms, the Transaction Cost Theory identifies the services specific characteristics that affect the effectiveness in contracting or procurement processes and these costs are playing significant role in stages of public procurement processes like project planning, project design and documentation, tender processes, contract award, and accounting and

auditing. Hobbs(1996) illustrates an example of such costs in the context of supply chain management: search and information costs are costs that arise in search of information about products and services, prices and inputs. Negotiation or bargaining is the costs that result from the physical act of the transaction, such as negotiating and writing, or paying the services of an intermediary of transaction (such as an auctioneer, or a broker). Monitoring or the enforcement costs arise after an exchange has been negotiated. This may involve monitoring the quality of goods and services from the suppliers or monitoring the behaviour of the supplier to ensure that all the pre-agreed terms of the transaction are met.

Previous scholars have conducted studies in the area of e-Commerce and public e-Procurement research using transaction cost theory to explain organisational and individual issues. For example, Vaidya et al. (2008)used transaction cost theory in assimilation of public procurement innovation and study found the association between transaction cost uncertainties and e-Procurement assimilation. Similarly, Parker and Hartley's (2003) study developed a framework for assessing public private partnership based on Transaction Cost Theory and an understanding of the roles of reputation and trust in contracting in the UK defence sector. In addition, the case study has highlighted the potential of transaction costs in defence procurement and illustrated reduce costs, contractor to generate profits, and building partnerships and trusts. Kauffman and Mohtadi (2004) focussed on the information technology adoption behaviour of organisation in the presence of transaction costs, agency costs and information uncertainty. Kauffman and Mohtadi study suggested that two guidelines emerged for practitioners: the adoption of standard e-Procurement platforms that must be understood in terms of controllable trade-offs, and gauging the business value impacts of exogenous shocks are critical to decision-making. At the end, reducing transaction cost is also one of the main benefits of implementing e-Procurement technologies so the concept of transection cost theory is an important ingredient in the approach of design of e-Government application. Many scholars have identified that transaction cost theory can be used in assimilation of the public procurement innovation (Vaidya et al., 2008)as well as the buyer-seller interaction.

Fraud Triangle Theory

Fraud Triangle Theory describes the three important factors present in every situation of fraud, namely perceived pressure, perceived opportunities, and rationalisation (Cressey, 1953). In an organisation, employees face many kinds of perceived pressure. Most of the pressures involve financial need, also non-financial pressures, such as the need to report results that paint a better picture than actual performance, frustration of work, or even a challenge to beat the system, and this can also motivate fraud (Albrecht, Albrecht & Albrecht, 2004). Similarly, perceived opportunities to commit management fraud include weak Boards of Directors, inadequate internal controls, and separation of duties. Rationalisation is a crucial component of most fraud, because most people need to reconcile their behaviour with the commonly-accepted notions of decency and trust. Matthew, Patrick and Denise(2013) pointed to two factors that influence fraud and corruption in public procurement, namely: motivational factors, and organisational or environmental factors and perceived factors. Fraud Triangle Theory represents a ground-breaking model for explaining the necessary conditions within which fraud occurs.

Diffusion of Innovation Theory

The Diffusion of Innovation (DOI) Theory has potential application to information technology ideas, artefacts, and technique, and has played a significant role as the theoretical foundation for information system research. Rogers (1995) draws upon comprehensive work in the field of information system research and he identified the five main characteristics of innovation that influence the potential adopters' perception of accepting the innovation, including observability, relative advantage, compatibility, trialability, and complexity. DOI theory is not suitable for this research's theoretical foundation because it is not concerned with the effect of technology and is not able to extrapolate upon the relationship between two groups. The relative advantage of technology can be considered, but all perceived advantages of technology are identified by another theory known as the Technology Acceptance Model.

Technology Acceptance Model

Technology Acceptance Model (TAM) is widely accepted model in electronic commerce research (Li & Huang, 2009). The TAM model specified two main important key beliefs, namely: perceived usefulness, and perceived ease of use (Davis, 1989). It is considered to be a robust model in predicting determinants of users adopting or using of new technology. Many researchers test this model in the context of the intention to use technology and found there to be a positive and significant relationship between perceived usefulness, and perceived ease of use. For example, Aboelmaged (2010)applied TAM and Theory of Planned Behaviour in predicting the e-Procurement adoption in the United Arab Emirates. His study revealed the practical implications to the procurement professional and system developers for the useful adoption model that demonstrates the significance of the perceived usefulness of e-Procurement systems in influencing adoption decisions. Similarly, Chu et al's (2004) study explored the key success factors of the electronic tendering system in Taiwan through the behavioural perspective of the end users. Rahim (2008) applied TAM model and identified factors affecting acceptance of e-Procurement systems in an Australian City Council. This study is concerned with how to relate the public e-Procurement technology benefits with anti-corruption factors when used as strategy to combat corruption. TAM supports the theoretical foundation for constructing our research model. The concept of the TAM features can be utilized to investigate the perception of the user on the overall performance of the technology adoption. This might help government agency or policy maker for future design of public e-Procurement technologies.

FACTORS OF ANTI-CORRUPTION CAPABILITY OF PUBLIC E-PROCUREMENT

Information Asymmetry

Amagoh (2009, p. 6) stated that information asymmetry is a core component of the Principal-Agent Theory. In Agency relationships, information asymmetry occurs due to information gaps like incomplete information, incompleteness of contract, problems with monitoring mechanisms, the cost of configuration of the project in the contracting process between Principal and Agent when the Agent has more information than the Principal does or vice versa (Amagoh, 2009; Finkle, 2005; Gauld, 2007; Taylor, 2005). Singh and Sirdeshmukh (2000: 152) revealed different examples that demonstrated how the existence of asymmetrical information increases the probability of opportunistic behaviour. Similarly, Hao and Qi (2011: 39) showed that asymmetrical information leads to collusive behaviour, and incomplete supervision in procurement activity. The above arguments lend weight to the view that information asymmetry is a main cause of problems of corruption in Principal-Agent Relationships. In this regard, ICT tools such as public e-Procurement can be the best tools to avoid an information asymmetry problem in public procurement processes. Xinzhang and Yonggang(2011) reveal that electronic government enhanced transparency, accountability, economic performance, efficiency

and mitigate the asymmetric information. Teo, Lin and Lai (2009) demonstrated that sharing more information helped to reduce information asymmetry thereby also to reduce corruption. As a result, this study has identified that reducing information asymmetry through the use of public e-Procurement is an important contribution to the reduction corruption in Principal-Agent relationships. This study has pointed out that the perceived benefits of public e-Procurement help to reduce information asymmetry, as e-Procurement contributes to greater competition, openness, and fairness in contracting processes, up-to-date information, consistency in procurement processes, and is more transparent than paper-based systems. In summary, the above factors have helped to reduce the information gap between Principals and Agents as well as in reducing the chances of corruption in public procurement.

Monopoly of Power

In public procurement processes, government officers are key persons who play significant roles to supply the Government with goods and services in an efficient and transparent way. Government officers' roles include identifying the need to purchase, selecting suppliers or bidders, contracting, and placing orders for goods and services. in some situations, corruption occurs where the public officials use public power for private benefits, for example, by assigning public contracts and/or tenders to favoured contractors or bidders, or accepting a bribe in exchange for granting a tender (OECD, 2010). In some instances, government officials create shortages of goods and services in the market in order to create opportunities for bribery. Klitgaard (1988) emphasised that the three most critical factors bearing upon opportunities for corruption including the monopoly upon power of officials, the degree of discretion that officials are permitted to exercise, and the degree to which there are systems of accountability, and transparency within an institution. Our study also emphasised that monopoly of power of government officials (Principal) is a critical factor of corruption in Principal Agent relationships and that public e-Procurement is the best option to reduce the monopoly of power provision on goods and services of government officers in procurement processes. The significant key elements of public e-Procurement that help to reduce the monopoly of power of government officers in Principal and Agent relationships include: (a) auditing capabilities with real-time procurement information of public e-procurement; (b) automation processes of procurement management, efficiency and quality; (c) facilitate accounting controls thereby reducing likelihood of fraud or accounting errors by enabling the electronic machine of requisition, purchase orders, invoice and receipts; and (d) fixed price contracts for all buyers and sellers. These factors are linked to a reduction the chances of corruption in public procurement.

Trust

The concept of trust has garnered great attention in the existing pool of scholarly research. More importantly, many researchers have demonstrated that it is the most fundamental elements for e-Commerce and information security. Trust has been identified as an important factor that determines the intention, behaviour, attitude, belief of user to adopt any inter-organisational information systems (Bachmann & Inkpen, 2011; Dubelaar, Sohal & Savic, 2005; Ngai,Lai & Cheng, 2008) for instance e-procurement. In fact, lack of trust has been touted as one of the main reasons for consumers not engaging in e-Commerce (Keen, 1999). Security of e-Commerce transactions is also an important concern of users or consumers when making online financial transactions(Pi,Liao & Chen, 2012). On the other hand, maintaining trust in Principal-Agent relationships ensures beneficial outcomes for both exchange partners such as Government and bidders (Singh & Sirdeshmukh, 2000).

In this study, our assumption is that the potential of public e-Procurement benefits increases the trust in Principal-Agent relationships that minimises the risk of corruption. In this regard, increasing the trust between Government and bidders is one of the most important anti-corruption factors (Neupane & Soar et al., 2012a). Neupane et al's. (2012a) study revealed that trust factors are highly significant and arecorrelated with the intent to adopt e-procurement. Similarly, another study Tran (2009) pointed that trust factors can minimise the risk of corruption. Consequently, several studies pointed out that trust played a prominent role in helping the public to overcome the perception of risk and uncertainty (McKnight,Choudhury & Kacmar, 2002). As a result, information and communication technology tools are the important bridge to established a trust in governance towards effectiveness and positive results (Cordella, 2005). This study reveals how trust is an important anti-corruption factor that contributes to both Government and bidders to increase their mutual levels of trust. Most importantly, public e-Procurement benefits comprise security of transaction, fair competition among bidders, user-friendly environment among buyers and/or suppliers in public tendering processes, anywhere anytime bidding e-Procurement platform services, and monitoring and tracking of documents these factors played a significant role in reducing the chances of corruption in public procurement.

Perceived Usefulness and Perceived Ease of Use

The main purpose of these two variables, namely perceived usefulness and perceived ease of use,helpsto explain the perception of users affects their tendencies either to use or not to use an application such as technology, and the extent of use of such tools to the extent they believe it will help them perform their job satisfactorily or if they believe it is useful (Davis, 1989). Theoretically, the importance of perceived usefulness and perceived ease of use is to determine the user behaviour, attitudes, and intentions as it relates to the adoption of any applications or technology. These two constructs reveal the perceived benefits technology-based tools can have on user perceptions. The main reason for selecting these constructs in this study is to identify the potential for perceived benefits of public e-Procurement such as the reduction of paper work,

user-friendliness, ease of access of public information (e.g. tender document), reduction of administration cost, increase in buyer and seller productivity, shorter order cycle, clearer and more transparent communication between Government and citizens, minimisation of human errors as well as more efficiency and transparency (Brun et al., 2010; Gunasekaran et al., 2009; Panayiotou, Gayialis & Tatsiopoulos, 2004; Ronchi et al., 2010; Teo et al., 2009).Other studies(Croom & Brandon-Jones, 2007) have found that based on an eighteen month examinationof e-Procurement deployment within a UK public sector organisation, "*the reputation of public procurement function and the general disposition of an organization towards e-Procurement is strongly influenced by users' perceptions of internal service*". In addition, the main practical implication is that the manager can force individuals to use e-procurement. Another study conducted by Neupane et. Al (2012a) identified that perceived usefulness and perceived ease of use are useful anti-corruption factors within public e-Procurement for reduced corruption. Similarly, Bwalya et al. (2012) study concluded that the willingness to adopt e-Government may help to improve the governance and fight against corruption. Therefore, this study also revealed that the benefits of technology are driving the economic growth of the country as well as enhancing good governance.

Transaction Cost

The benefits of online or web-based technology for the effectiveness and efficiency of the day-to-day operations of government reflect the impact of electronic government procurement on the cost of transaction and value for money (Leipold, 2007). The potential impact of implementing or adopting ICT tools like e-Procurement systems in an organisation are to reduce the cost of transaction and produce significant time savings including information cost, monitoring cost, and coordination cost (Kachwamba, 2011; Ojha,Palvia & Gupta, 2008; Tai,Ho & Wu, 2010). The automation of procurement processes helps the bidders who no longer have to travel in order to submit the bids or tender documents, and this helps to avoid potential for physical threats from other potential bidders. This situation most commonly happens in developing countries due to the corruption. Bidders can save huge amounts of time and money in each step of procurement processes such as bid preparation or bid submission. Buyers and/or suppliers can easily search the information about goods and services prices and inputs. There are some examples of studied impacts of transaction costs to reduce corruption in procurement, such as reducing exchange costs in, reducing the total number of transactions (Shah, 2006), best price and open auctions(Tran, 2009). Therefore, this study is concerned with the potential benefits of public e-Procurement and its potential to reduce transaction costs and eliminate corruption in procurement. In this regard, there are valid arguments that public e-Procurement has played a positive role in Principal-Agent relationships that can help to reduce transaction costs, including shorter procurement cycles, increased availability of information, common management framework, centralisation and consistency of procurement processes, more competition and pricing in auction or bidding processes, and improved capacity within an organization to monitor their partner's behaviour. By way of conclusion, reducing transaction costs is an important anti-corruption factor to reduce the potential for corruption in procurement processes.

Based on the above discussion of perceived anti-corruption factors in public e-procurement, Figure 1 depicts the proposed research framework for understanding the anti-corruption capabilities of public e-Procurement in the context of three academic theories' variables, namely an independent construct and intent to adopt public e-Procurement as a dependent construct. The model focuses on the Principal Agent-based approach in public procurement processes as a relationship between Government and bidders. Intent to adopt public e-Procurement technology is a dependent construct of this study that demonstrates adoption and use of ICT tools as way to transform or reform the government system. Government institutions can do their all procurement activities through their e-Procurement web portal, such as procurement planning, tendering, and the awarding of contracts that help to make these processes more transparent and accountable, as well as reducing opportunities and incentives for fraud. Bidders can easily access all of the procurement information online, and submit their bids online anytime and anywhere. This helps to avoid physical threats to other potential bidders, and has many other benefits.

DISCUSSION AND IMPLICATION FOR FUTURE RESEARCH

In this Chapter, there was a review of different types of the e-Procurement with different countries case example, different IS theories and their constructs that explain the anti-corruption capability role within the Principal Agent relationship in public procurement processes. The main contribution of this Chapter is to demonstrate to Government institutions, academic, and procurement practitioners that the perceived benefit of adopting public e-Procurement technology to reduce the likelihood of corruption in procurement processes. The main aim of the Governments of most countries in implementing public e-Procurement is to make processes more transparent and accountable, encouraging greater openness, and availability of public information.

This work is significant for researchers, government agencies, and public procurement practitioners in providing a better understanding of the anti-corruption potential of public e-Procurement in procurement management. From an academic perspective, this study provides theoretical

Figure 1. The proposed research framework for anti-corruption capabilities

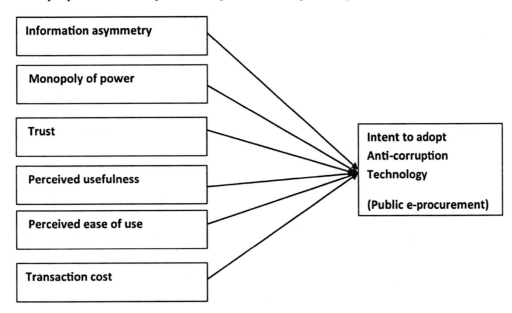

foundations by integrating the anti-corruption construct of different theories within a Principal Agent relationship model. This model provides an understanding of the role of public e-Procurement in reducing corruption in public procurement processes. In addition, this research reveals the Principal-Agent Theory as a core theory for procurement research that evaluates the technology's perceived benefits in order to reduce information asymmetry, monopoly of power, and increase in trust. TAM model demonstrates two key beliefs: perceived usefulness, perceived ease of use which in turn helps to enhance understanding and use of perception of technology. Reducing transaction costs is another prominent anti-corruption factor for reducing corruption, and future work should attempt to apply rigorous methodologies such as survey, interview, and focus group discussion for validation of the research model.

From a government and public procurement practitioner's perspective, the implementation or adoption of public e-Procurement for good governance is an urgent and necessary part of procurement management reforms. This study suggests that Governments should promote e-Procurement as part of an anti-corruption agenda, use public e-Procurement initiatives to drive government administrative reforms, and develop, and implementation of perceived benefits of e-Procurement strategy at the planning level.

CONCLUSION

The literature presented in this Chapter includes the discussion of the different types of e-Procurement, the review of five IS theories and explores the various anti-corruption issues in Principal-Agent relationships. This study has identified Principal-Agent Theory, Transaction Cost Theory, and Technology Acceptance Model as important theories for this field of research. Based on the literature

survey, the findings of this study indicated that information asymmetry, monopoly of power, trust, perceived usefulness, perceived ease of use, and transaction costs were significant factors influencing the intent-to-adopt public e-Procurement in the context of a Principal-Agent relationship. All of these factors were perceived to make an important contribution to reducing corruption and the misuse of power in public procurement. This study result helps Government agencies and public procurement practitioners in enhancing their understanding of the perceived anti-corruption benefits of public e-Procurement to reduce corruption and to enhance transparency and accountability. This research is of great interest and applicable for Government departments, which provide public services for multinational organisations such as the United Nations, Transparency International, the World Bank, the Asian Development Bank, and the Organization for Economic Co-operation and Development. Future research should include a strong empirical component to valid the factors influencing successfully e-Procurement systems design and deployment as identified in this study.

REFERENCES

Aboelmaged, M. G. (2010). Predicting e-procurement adoption in a developing country: An empirical integration of technology acceptance model and theory of planned behaviour. *Industrial Management & Data Systems, 110*(3-4), 392–414.

Albrecht, W. S., Albrecht, C. C., & Albrecht, C. O. (2004). Fraud and corporate executives: Agency stewardship and broken trust. *Journal of Forensic Accounting, 5*(1), 109–130.

Amagoh, F. (2009). Information asymmetry and the contracting out process. *The Innovation Journal: The Public Sector Innovation Journal, 14*(2), 1–14.

Angelov, S., & Grefen, P. (2008). An e-contracting reference architecture. *Journal of Systems and Software*, *81*(11), 1816–1844. doi:10.1016/j. jss.2008.02.023

Bacharach, S. B. (1989). Organizational theories: Some criteria for evaluation. *Academy of Management Review*, *14*(4), 496–515.

Bachmann, R., & Inkpen, A. C. (2011). Understanding institutional-based trust building processes in inter-organizational relationships. *Organization Studies*, *32*(2), 281–301. doi:10.1177/0170840610397477

Betts, M., Black, P., Christensen, S. A., Dawson, E., Du, R., & Duncan, W. et al. (2010). Towards secure and legal e-tendering. *Journal of Information Technology in Construction*, *11*, 89–102.

Bhattacherjee, A. (2012). *Social science research: Principles, methods, and practices* (2nd Ed.). Reterived February 5, 2013 form http://scholarcommons.usf.edu/oa_textbooks/3/

Bikshapathi, K. RamaRaju, P., Bhatnagar, S., & Ahmedabad, I. (2006). E-procurement in government of Andhra Pradesh India. Washington, DC: World Bank.

Block, C., & Neumann, D. (2008). A decision support system for choosing market mechanisms in e-procurement. In *Negotiation, auctions, and market engineering* (pp. 44–57). Berlin: Springer. doi:10.1007/978-3-540-77554-6_3

Boer, L., Harink, J., & Heijboer, G. (2001). *A model for assessing the impact of electronic procurement forms*. Paper presented at the 10th International Annual IPSERA Conference. Jönköping, Sweden.

Brun, A., Ronchi, S., Fan, X., & Golini, R. (2010). What is the value of an IT e-procurement system? *Journal of Purchasing and Supply Management*, *16*(2), 131–140. doi:10.1016/j. pursup.2010.03.013

Bruno, G., Esposito, E., Mastroianni, M., & Vellutino, D. (2005). Analysis of public e-procurement web site accessibility. *Journal of Public Procurement*, *5*(3), 344.

Bwalya, K. J., Zulu, S. F., Grand, B., & Sebina, P. M. (2012). E-government and technological utopianism: Exploring Zambia's challenges and opportunities. *Electronic Journal of E-Government*, *10*(1), 16–30.

Carter, C. R., Kaufmann, L., Beall, S., Carter, P. L., Hendrick, T. E., & Petersen, K. J. (2004). Reverse auctions--Grounded theory from the buyer and supplier perspective. *Transportation Research Part E, Logistics and Transportation Review*, *40*(3), 229–254. doi:10.1016/j.tre.2003.08.004

Chang, H. H., Tsai, Y.-C., & Hsu, C.-H. (2013). E-procurement and supply chain performance. *Supply Chain Management: An International Journal*, *18*(1), 34–51. doi:10.1108/13598541311293168

Chang, K.-S. (2011). *Enhancing transparency through e-procurement*. Retrieved February 12, 2013 from http://www.oecd.org/dataoecd/47/30/49311011.pdf

Christenses, S., & Duncan, W. (2006). Maintaining the integrity of electronic tendering by government-reflections on the capacity of the Australian legal framework to meet this challenge. *eLaw Journal, 13*(8).

Chu, P. Y., Hsiao, N., Lee, F. W., & Chen, C. W. (2004). Exploring success factors for Taiwan's government electronic tendering system: Behavioral perspectives from end users. *Government Information Quarterly*, *2*(2), 219–234. doi:10.1016/j.giq.2004.01.005

Cordella, A. (2005). *The role of information and communication technology in building trust in governance: Towards effectiveness and results*. Washington, DC: Inter-American Development Bank.

Cressey, D. R. (1953). *A study in the social psychology of embezzlement: Other people's money.* Glencoe, IL: Free Press.

Croom, S., & Brandon-Jones, A. (2007). Impact of e-procurement: Experiences from implementation in the UK public sector. *Journal of Purchasing and Supply Management, 13*(4), 294–303. doi:10.1016/j.pursup.2007.09.015

Croom, S. R. (2000). The impact of web-based procurement on the management of operating resources supply. *Journal of Supply Chain Management, 36*(1), 4–13. doi:10.1111/j.1745-493X.2000.tb00065.x

Davila, A., Gupta, M., & Palmer, R. (2003). Moving procurement systems to the internet: The adoption and use of e-procurement technology models. *European Management Journal, 21*(1), 11–23. doi:10.1016/S0263-2373(02)00155-X

Davis, F. D. (1989). Perceived usefulness, perceived ease of use, and user acceptance of information technology. *Management Information Systems Quarterly, 13*(3), 319–340. doi:10.2307/249008

De Boer, L., Harink, J., & Heijboer, G. (2002). A conceptual model for assessing the impact of electronic procurement. *European Journal of Purchasing & Supply Management, 8*(1), 25–33. doi:10.1016/S0969-7012(01)00015-6

Del Monte, A., & Papagni, E. (2007). The determinants of corruption in Italy: Regional panel data analysis. *European Journal of Political Economy, 23*(2), 379–396. doi:10.1016/j.ejpoleco.2006.03.004

Doyle, T. (2010). *Information and communications technology procurement for border management.* Washington, DC: Border Management Modernization.

Dubelaar, C., Sohal, A., & Savic, V. (2005). Benefits, impediments and critical success factors in B2C E-business adoption. *Technovation, 25*(11), 1251–1262. doi:10.1016/j.technovation.2004.08.004

Eakin, D. (2003). Measuring e-procurement benefits. *Summit: Canada's Magazine on Public Sector Purchasing.*

Eisenhardt, K. (1989). Agency theory: An assessment and review. *Academy of Management Review, 14*(1), 57–74.

Essig, M., & Arnold, U. (2001). Electronic procurement in supply chain management: An information economics based analysis of electronic markets. *Journal of Supply Chain Management, 37*(4), 43–49. doi:10.1111/j.1745-493X.2001.tb00112.x

Filho, J. R., & Mota, F. P. B. (2012). Public e-procurement implementation: Insights from the structuration theory. In K. Vaidya (Ed.), *Interorganizational infromation systems and business management: Theories for researcher.* Hershey, PA: IGI Global.

Fink, D. (2006). Value decomposition of e-commerce performance. *Benchmarking: An International Journal, 13*(1/2), 81–92. doi:10.1108/14635770610644592

Finkle, A. (2005). Relying on information acquired by a principal. *International Journal of Industrial Organization, 23*(3-4), 263–278. doi:10.1016/j.ijindorg.2004.12.001

Fuks, K., Kawa, A., & Wieczerzycki, W. (2009). *Improved e-sourcing strategy with multi-agent swarms.* Paper presented to Computational Intelligence for Modelling Control & Automation, International Conference. Vienna, Austria.

Gauld, R. (2007). Principal-agent theory and organizational change. *Policy Studies, 28*(1), 17–34. doi:10.1080/01442870601121395

Gregor, S. (2006). The nature of theory in information systems. *Management Information Systems Quarterly, 30*(3), 611–642.

GTN. (2003). *Centre for international development at Harvard University: Government procurement.* Retrived February 14, 2013, form http://www.cid.harvard.edu/cidtrade/issues/govpro.html

Gunasekaran, A., McGaughey, R. E., Ngai, E. W. T., & Rai, B. K. (2009). E-procurement adoption in the southcoast SMEs. *International Journal of Production Economics, 122*(1), 161–175. doi:10.1016/j.ijpe.2009.05.013

Hao, X., & Qi, P. (2011). Analysis on corruption and collusive behaviors in government procurement in a game theory perspective. *Journal of Management and Strategy, 2*(2), 38. doi:10.5430/jms.v2n2p38

Harink, J. H. A. (2003). *Internet technology to purchase.* (PhD thesis). University of Twente, Twente, The Netherlands.

Hobbs, J. E. (1996). A transaction cost approach to supply chain management. *Supply Chain Management: An International Journal, 1*(2), 15–27. doi:10.1108/13598549610155260

Jensen, M. C., & Meckling, W. H. (1976). Theory of the firm: Managerial behavior, agency costs and ownership structure. *Journal of Financial Economics, 3*(4), 305–360. doi:10.1016/0304-405X(76)90026-X

Kachwamba, M. A. (2011). Impact of e-government on transaction cost and FDI Inflows: A proposed conceptual framework. *International Journal of Business and Management, 6*(11), 285. doi:10.5539/ijbm.v6n11p285

Kauffman, R. J., & Mohtadi, H. (2004). Proprietary and open systems adoption in e-procurement: A risk-augmented transaction cost perspective. *Journal of Management Information Systems, 21*(1), 137–166.

Keen, P. G. W. (1999). *Electronic commerce relationships: Trust by design.* Englewood Cliffs, NJ: Prentice-Hall.

Klitgaard, R. (1988). *Controlling corruption.* Berkeley, CA: University of California Press.

Knudsen, D. (2003). Aligning corporate strategy, procurement strategy and e-procurement tools. *International Journal of Physical Distribution & Logistics Management, 33*(8), 720–734. doi:10.1108/09600030310502894

Kolstad, I., & Wiig, A. (2009). Is transparency the key to reducing corruption in resource-rich countries? *World Development, 37*(3), 521–532. doi:10.1016/j.worlddev.2008.07.002

Kunakornpaiboonsiri, T. (2013). *GEBIZ: Enhancing Singapore procurement system.* Alphabet Media Pte Ltd. Retrieved February 1, 2013, from http://www.futuregov.asia/articles/2013/feb/28/gebiz-enhancing-singapore-procurement-system/# Leipold, K. (2007). *Electronic government procurement (e-GP) opportunities and challenges.* Retrieved February 18, 2013, from http://www.uncitral.org/pdf/english/congress/Leipold.pdf

Leipold, K., Klemow, J., Holloway, F., & Vaidya, K. (2004). The World Bank e-procurement for the selection of consultants: Challenges and lessons learned. *Journal of Public Procurement, 4*(3), 319–339.

Li, Y. H., & Huang, J. W. (2009). Applying theory of perceived risk and technology acceptance model in the online shopping channel. *World Academy of Science. Engineering and Technology, 53*(29), 919–925.

Matthew, K., Patrick, K., & Denise, K. (2013). The effects of fraudulent procurement practices on public procurement performance. *International Journal of Business and Behavioral Sciences, 3*(1), 17–27.

McCue, C., & Roman, A. V. (2012). E-procurement: Myth or reality? *Journal of Public Procurement, 12*(2), 212–238.

McKnight, D. H., Choudhury, V., & Kacmar, C. (2002). Developing and validating trust measures for e-commerce: An integrative typology. *Information Systems Research, 13*(3), 334–359. doi:10.1287/isre.13.3.334.81

Neupane, A., Soar, J., & Vaidya, K. (2012). Evaluating the anti-corruption capabilities of public e-procurement in a developing country. *The Electronic Journal on Information System in Developing Countries, 55*(2), 1–17.

Neupane, A., Soar, J., & Vaidya, K. (2012b). The potential of e-procurement technology for reducing corruption. *International Journal of Information Technology and Management, 11*(4), 273–287.

Neupane, A., Soar, J., Vaidya, K., & Yong, J. (2012). *Role of public e-procurement technology to reduce corruption in government procurement.* Paper presented to 5th International Public Procurement Conference (IPPC5). Seattle, WA.

Ngai, E., Lai, K. H., & Cheng, T. (2008). Logistics information systems: The Hong Kong experience. *International Journal of Production Economics, 113*(1), 223–234. doi:10.1016/j.ijpe.2007.05.018

OECD. (2010). *Policy rounddables: Collusion and corruption in public procuremnet.* Retrieved February 12, 2013, from http://www.oecd.org/daf/competition/cartelsandanti-competitiveagreements/46235884.pdf

Ojha, A., Palvia, S., & Gupta, M. (2008). A model for impact of e-government on corruption: Exploring theoretical foundations. In J. Bhattacharya (Ed.), *Critical thinking in e-governance.* New Delhi: Gift Publishing.

Panayiotou, N. A., Gayialis, S. P., & Tatsiopoulos, I. P. (2004). An e-procurement system for governmental purchasing. *International Journal of Production Economics, 90*(1), 79–102. doi:10.1016/S0925-5273(03)00103-8

Parker, D., & Hartley, K. (2003). Transaction costs, relational contracting and public private partnerships: A case study of UK defence. *Journal of Purchasing and Supply Management, 9*(3), 97–108. doi:10.1016/S0969-7012(02)00035-7

Pellegrini, L., & Gerlagh, R. (2008). Causes of corruption: A survey of cross-country analyses and extended results. *Economics of Governance, 9*(3), 245–263. doi:10.1007/s10101-007-0033-4

Pi, S. M., Liao, H. L., & Chen, H. M. (2012). Factors that affect consumers' trust and continuous adoption of online financial services. *International Journal of Business and Management, 7*(9), 108–119. doi:10.5539/ijbm.v7n9p108

Rahim, M. M. (2008). Identifying factors affecting acceptance of e-procurement systems: An initial qualitative study at an Australian city council. *Communications of the IBIMA, 3*(2), 7–17.

Reunis, M. R. B., Santema, S. C., & Harink, J. H. A. (2006). Increasing e-ordering adoption: A case study. *Journal of Purchasing and Supply Management, 12*(6), 322–331. doi:10.1016/j.pursup.2007.01.006

Rogers, E. M. (1995). *Diffusion of innovations.* New York: Free Press.

Ronchi, S., Brun, A., Golini, R., & Fan, X. (2010). What is the value of an IT e-procurement system? *Journal of Purchasing and Supply Management, 16*(2), 131–140. doi:10.1016/j.pursup.2010.03.013

Salin, A. S. A. P., & Abidin, Z. Z. (2011). *Information and communication technologies and local governance trend–A case study of a smart city in Malaysia*. Kuala Lumpur, Malaysia: IACSIT Press.

Shah, A. (2006). *Corruption and decentralized public governance*. Washington, DC: World Bank. doi:10.1596/1813-9450-3824

Singh, J., & Sirdeshmukh, D. (2000). Agency and trust mechanisms in consumer satisfaction and loyalty judgments. *Journal of the Academy of Marketing Science, 28*(1), 150–167. doi:10.1177/0092070300281014

Stamer, R. T. (2006). *Reducing costs of exchange by combating corruption in procurement*. Paper presented to 10th ISNIE Conference. Boulder, CO.

Subedi, M. S. (2006). Corruption in Nepal: An anthropological inquiry. *Dhaulagiri Journal of Sociology and Anthropology, 1*(0), 110–128. doi:10.3126/dsaj.v1i0.283

Szymanski, S. (2007). *How to implement economic reforms: How to fight corruption effectively in public procurement in SEE countries*. Paris: OECD.

Tai, Y.-M., Ho, C.-F., & Wu, W.-H. (2010). The performance impact of implementing web-based e-procurement systems. *International Journal of Production Research, 48*(18), 5397–5414. doi:10.1080/00207540903117915

Taylor, P. (2005). Do public sector contract catering tender procedures result in an auction for lemons? *International Journal of Public Sector Management, 18*(6), 484–497. doi:10.1108/09513550510616724

Teich, J., Wallenius, H., & Wallenius, J. (1999). Multiple-issue auction and market algorithms for the world wide web. *Decision Support Systems, 26*(1), 49–66. doi:10.1016/S0167-9236(99)00016-0

Teo, T. S. H., Lin, S. J., & Lai, K. H. (2009). Adopters and non-adopters of e-procurement in Singapore: An empirical study. *Omega-International Journal of Management Science, 37*(5), 972–987. doi:10.1016/j.omega.2008.11.001

Tran, A. (2009). *Can procurement auctions reduce corruption? Evidence from the internal records of a bribe-paying firm*. Cambridge, MA: Harvard University.

UN. (2006). *E-procurement: Economic and social commission for Asia and the Pacific Asian development bank institute public procurement service of the Republic of Korea*. New York: United Nations Publication.

Vaidya, K. (2007). *Electronic procurement in the Australian public sector: The organizational assimilation process and its impact on public procurement performance*. University of New England.

Vaidya, K., & Hyde, M. (2011). Inter-organisational information systems assimilation: An empirical evaluation in light of the diffusion of innovation theory. *International Journal of Business Information Systems, 7*(3), 247–268. doi:10.1504/IJBIS.2011.039330

Vaidya, K., Sajeev, A., Johnston, J., & Cox, M. A. (2008). *Assimilation of public procurement innovation: An empirical analysis in light of transaction cost theory*. Paper presented to Annual Conference of International Purchasing and Supply Education and Research Association. Perth, Australia.

Walker, H., & Brammer, S. (2012). The relationship between sustainable procurement and e-procurement in the public sector. *International Journal of Production Economics, 140*(1), 256–268. doi:10.1016/j.ijpe.2012.01.008

Ware, G. T., Moss, S., Campos, J. E., & Noone, G. P. (2012). Corruption in procurement. In A. Graycar, & R. Smith (Eds.), *Handbook of global research and practice in corruption*. Chichester, UK: Edward Elgar Publishing.

Wen, W., & Wei, L. (2007). *Decision-making analysis of e-procurement with the rough set theory*. Paper presented to International Conferenceon Wireless Communications, Networking and Mobile Computing. Shanghai, China.

Wescott, C. G. (2001). E government in the Asia pacific region. *Asian Journal of Political Science*, 9(2), 1–24. doi:10.1080/02185370108434189

Whipple, J. M., & Roh, J. (2010). Agency theory and quality fade in buyer-supplier relationships. *International Journal of Logistics Management*, 21(3), 338–352. doi:10.1108/09574091011089781

Williamson, O. E. (1981). The economics of organization: The transaction cost approach. *American Journal of Sociology*, 87(3), 548–577. doi:10.1086/227496

Xinzhang, C., & Yonggang, W. (2011). *E-government, government procurement and the development of e-commerce: Korean experience and its implications*. Paper presented to E -Business and E-Government (ICEE). Shanghai, China.

Yang, J., & Zhang, R. (2009). The research and analysis of e-procurement for iron and steel enterprises. In *Proceedings of Information Management, Innovation Management and Industrial Engineering*. IEEE. doi:10.1109/ICIII.2009.158

De Pablos, P. O., & Tennyson, R. D. (2013). *E-Procurement Management for Successful Electronic Government Systems*. Hershey, PA: Information Science Reference.

Kaliannan, M., & Awang, H. (2008). ICT to enhance administrative performance: a case study from Malaysia. *International Journal of Business and Management*, 3(5), 78.

Kim, S., Kim, H. J., & Lee, H. (2009). An institutional analysis of an e-Government system for anti-corruption: The case of OPEN. *Government Information Quarterly*, 26(1), 42–50. doi:10.1016/j.giq.2008.09.002

Mahmood, S. A. I. (2010). Public procurement and corruption in Bangladesh confronting the challenges and opportunities, *Journal of public administration and policy research*, 2(6), 103-111.

Singh, G., Pathak, R., Naz, R., & Belwal, R. (2010). E-governance for improved public sector service delivery in India, Ethiopia and Fiji. *International Journal of Public Sector Management*, 23(3), 254–275. doi:10.1108/09513551011032473

Thai, K. V., & Piga, G. (2007). *Advancing Public Procurement: Practices, Innovation, and Knowledge Sharing*. PrAcademics Press.

Vaidya, K. (2011). *Inter-organizational information systems and business management*. Hershey, PA, USA: IGI Global. doi:10.4018/978-1-60960-768-5

Vaidyanathan, G., & Devaraj, S. (2008). The role of quality in e-Procurement performance: An empirical analysis. *Journal of Operations Management*, 26(3), 407–425. doi:10.1016/j.jom.2007.08.004

Yusoff, W. S., Islam, M. A., Abas, Z., & Yusuf, D. H. (2010). Electronic government procurement adoption behavior amongst Malaysian SMEs. *International Business Research*, 4(1), 100.

ADDITIONAL READING

Burton, R. A. (2005). Improving integrity in public procurement: the role of transparency and accountability, *Fighting Corruption and Promoting Integrity in Public Procurement*, 23-28.

KEY TERMS AND DEFINITIONS

Information Asymmetry: Information asymmetry is another key terms of public e-Procurement and it arises in the public contract when the public officers have more information than contractors or bidders or vice versa.

Intent-to-Adopt E-Procurement Technology: Adoption and use of public e-Procurement as a way to change traditional procurement processes in order to modernise public procurement processes, to improve government performance, and narrow the digital gap. Government can conduct their procurement processes and transactions through the online systems that help to make these transactions far more transparent and fair for the purposes of reducing opportunities and incentives for fraud.

Monopoly of Power: Monopoly of power is one of the important terms in public procurement and it identifies the power of government officers in the provision of goods and services.

Perceived Usefulness and Ease of Use: Perceived usefulness and ease of use predicts the attitude towards use of a technology.

Procurement Processes: Procurement processes are the process of procurement project planning, project design and implementation, tender processes, contract award, and accounting and auditing.

Public E-Procurement: Public e-Procurement is defined as the use of information and communication technology (ICT) such as Internet or web-based system systems by government institutions in conducting their procurement activities in order to improve efficiency, quality, and transparency in government procurement.

Public Procurement: Public procurement is the process whereby the public sector organizations acquiring of goods, services, works, and other supplies from the other parties.

Trust: Trust is an important key facilitator of e-Commerce to explain the inter-organizational relationship and creates positive attitudes towards trust between government and bidders in the contracting processes.

Chapter 11

Smartphone–Based Digital Government Model:
The Case of the Beyaz Masa (White Table) App in Turkey

Ronan de Kervenoael
Sabanci University, Turkey & Aston Business School, UK

Egemen Sekeralp
Pordiva Bilisim Teknolojileri A.S., Turkey

ABSTRACT

M-Government services are now at the forefront of both user expectations and technology capabilities. Within the current setting, there is growing evidence that interoperability is becoming a key issue towards service sustainability. Thus, the objective of this chapter is to highlight the case of "Beyas Masa" – a Turkish application for infrastructure repair services. This application requires different stakeholders from different cultural background and geographically dispersed regions to work together. The major aim of this chapter to showcase experiences in as far as implementation and adoption of m-Government is concerned in the case of Turkey. The study utilizes the co-creation literature to investigate the factors influencing successful implementation of the Beyas Masa. This study reveals that initiatives are fragmented due to differences in the characteristics of the targeted audience, the marketing strategy, technology supply, distribution, and media utilized to promote its awareness. The chapter posits that in order to have affluent m-Government implementation in Turkey, it is important that many of the standalone applications are integrated to encourage interoperability and that socio-cultural behaviours should be re-shaped to encourage active engagement and interactive government service provisions that unlock the power of ICT.

DOI: 10.4018/978-1-4666-4900-2.ch011

INTRODUCTION

In the last few years, a shift has occurred both in the public and private sector towards an entrepreneurial approach that emphasises a change from service management to service competence (Cova et al, 2011; Schilling, 2010). As stated by Cordella (2007: 265), 'the dominant literature has seen e-Government as a next step in the rationalization of government activities along the line of new public management'. In turn, m-Government is often presented as a reflection of the evolution in Information Communication Technology (ICT) from desktop to wireless devices that echoed the changes from Web 1.0 that represented an early non-interactive version of the Internet whereby users could only view WebPages, simply acting as consumers of content. Today, with Web 2.0 (and the emerging Web 3.0), users interact and collaborate with each other as well as brands through media including videos, audio and photos. In a wireless world, a series of technological artefacts (Smartphones, tablets, and netbooks) allows access and feedback in real time (the ubiquity and pervasiveness of mobile devices) in addition to leveraging new tools such as digital cameras, GPS and mapping. Yet, new radical logics, challenges and opportunities may force a total reshaping of the understanding of e-Government in practice. Through an unpacking of detailed and often practical issues, m-Government is encouraging a move from macro issues such as democracy and access to micro practical voicing to what once was local governments' competence area. M-Government is also becoming more fully interactive with citizens pushing information towards government agencies and requesting actions rather than the one way information flow (from e-Government officials), which often requests citizens to take certain actions. Organizational boundaries are thus being contested both by local civil servants (they need access to these new ICT tools, training and authority to use them) and citizens now re-shaping the

order of priority and revealing the evolution of their preferences by constantly re-voting.

Simultaneously, a key difference in the environment is appearing as citizens, who may have once been perceived as homogenous, now come into light as fragmented in their day-to-day needs. These individuals are revealing their wants, needs and more importantly, priorities. The concept of m-Government, in sum, is thus moving government from an ideological macro position to a localised producer of services. This is especially important in emerging market conditions where budget constraints are strong and technologies often leapfrog traditional cycles (greater usage of wireless devices than traditional PCs). Thus, emancipated civil servants and citizens, since the emergence of new public management, take the functional performance of a service for granted and expect far more than simple consumption of government services (De Kervenoael et al, 2010; De Kervenoael & Koçoğlu, 2011). First, a knowledge sharing potential has been identified that can develop both new management innovations models and technologies for digital government. Knowledge sharing potential consists of the creative combination of individuals and collective knowledge transfer (co-creation) (Thompson & Malaviya, 2012; Gronroos, 2011; Payne et al, 2008, Zwick et al, 2008, Cova and Dalli, 2009). Second, the Smartphone as a technological artefact and social media tool can be leveraged to enable broad real time participation in public policy making as well as delivery. While traditional town hall meetings, radio call-in and surveys have shaped the policy conceptualization, Smartphone and social media add a set of new, instant and dynamic (augmented reality, 3D imaging) dimension with easy access for all via apps (DePriest, 2012; Connolly et al, 2010; Yonck, 2008; Gervautz & Schmalstieg, 2012). Consequently, interoperability design choices tacitly embedded in a technology will have an important impact and will encourage or deter citizen engagement and behaviour (Fisher and Smith, 2011). It is also important at this point to note that Turkey, like many other countries, is desperate to make budget ends meet. Currently, the universally accepted 'quick fix' seems to be across the board 5%, 10% or even 25% funding cuts. However, it is reasonable to expect that citizens and business are unwilling to accept drastic reductions to public services and that politicians dislike compromising key public outcomes – 'social goods' such as better health, education and care; hence, the leveraging of the Smartphone.

Previous research has demonstrated that interoperability is concerned primarily with technical factors such as data semantics and process standardization (e.g. computer readable format, specific type of unit) as well strategic issues including legal, political, and social aspects (e.g. what to do with the data they receive in the exchange) (Ford et al, 2007). Interoperability is defined as: 'the ability of disparate and diverse organizations to interact towards mutually beneficial and agreed common goals, involving the sharing of information and knowledge between the organizations via the business processes they support, by means of the exchange of data between their respective information and communication technology (ICT) systems'. (European Communities 2008, p. 5). It provides many benefits in the long term, including improved efficiency (data exchange), transparency (audit login, monitoring), accountability (activity level), and access, as well as coordination of services at lower costs. However, the cycle of government election timing often sacrifice long-term approaches to short-term political gains. In this chapter, particular attention is paid to the second aspect of interoperability namely strategic issues including legal, political, and social aspects. Figure 1 summarizes the literature on interoperability models

Figure 1. E-Government interoperability model. Source: http://www.sei.cmu.edu/reports/11tn014.pdf.

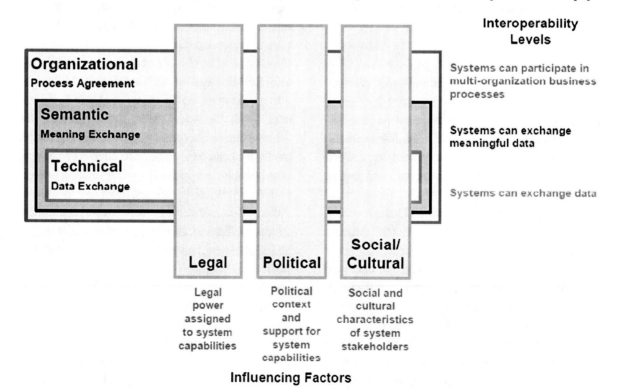

To better understand the socio-political setting of the case, a review of the Turkish situation contextualizes our discussion. Deloitte's second Global Mobile Consumer Survey (2012), which provides insight into the mobile consumer behaviour of 26,960 respondents across 15 countries, reports that Turkey leads in mobile internet connectivity with 91% of Smartphones connected. However, penetration of unlimited packages is very low: 72% of Turkish people prefer prepaid subscriptions. Still, when Turks were asked what they would like to own in the coming 12 months, 35% answered a Smartphone and 37% said tablets. Indeed, Turkish people spend an average of 209.3 minutes per month on their mobile phones, putting the country in third place among European countries in mobile call duration. Some 77.7% of total call traffic consists of mobile-to-mobile calls. Furthermore, some 59% of mobile phone subscribers use a 3G connection in Turkey, almost double the rate in Europe (30%). The total number of 3G subscribers in Turkey has surpassed 40 million, according to the latest data from the Information and Communication Technologies Authority (BTK).

An interesting comment by Apple cofounder Steve Wozniak, verified by data, also reveals that the faster 3G connection in Turkey is better than the USA's 4G. The Turkish market is also proven to be very dynamic and competitive. With the introduction of number portability in 2009, a total of 18.7 million people have switched their mobile operators as of Aug. 9. 2012. Regarding network providers, 2012 statistics indicate that Turkcell has a 55.1% share of all subscribers; Vodafone, 26.2%; and Avea, 18.6%. The combined first quarter revenues, in 2012, for Turk Telekom and Turkey's mobile operators, Turkcell, Avea and Vodafone Turkey were up 6.4% accruing to 5.68 billion Turkish Liras (BTK, 2012). In the first three months of 2012 40.4 billion mobile SMS messages were sent in Turkey, an increase of 1.7% from the previous quarter. According to these figures, the average mobile phone user sends seven SMS messages daily. Regarding access, many initiatives are present. For example, in 2010 Vodafone unveiled its new "Vodafone 840," a cell phone selling for just one Turkish Lira, with unique characteristics such as easy access to social networks including Facebook, Twitter, MSN, e-mails and TFT touch screen features.

Concerning the use of mobile phone apps to pay bills, this service in Turkey reached 500 million Turkish Liras in 2012. Among the country's working age population of 46 million people, 16 to 20 million do not deal with banks at all. Mobile finance is perceived as an important tool in reaching the segment that does not use banking services. Turkcell's involvement in studies of Near Field Communication (NFC) with Garanti Bank and Akbank over the last two years led Turkcell to consider offering commercial use of the mobile wallet toward the end of 2012. One other interesting development to date is the change in use during the last 12 months, with highest growth rate in apps and mobile web (See Figure 2 and 3).

In addition, almost all Turkish politicians now have Facebook/Twitter/Youtube pages, which are increasingly used as channels of communication with their domestic constituency. Twitter statistics confirm that President Abdullah Gül has over 2.3 million followers, followed by Prime Minister Recep Tayyip Erdoğan with close to 2 million followers, and the chair of the main opposition Republican People's Party (CHP), Kemal Kılıçdaroğlu, approaching 1 million followers (Hurriyet Daily News, 2012). When one government service hears of an incident, tweeting rather more traditional methods is preferred. That tweet is then linked back to the local authority blog/website, where people can obtain additional information. This communication chain is reported to be an efficient information disseminator to citizens as well as side stepping calls' inundation. Citizens in turn want to see more openness and information in real time. As such, modern government is described, in practice, as not only transparent, but also collaborative and participa-

Figure 2. Service penetration

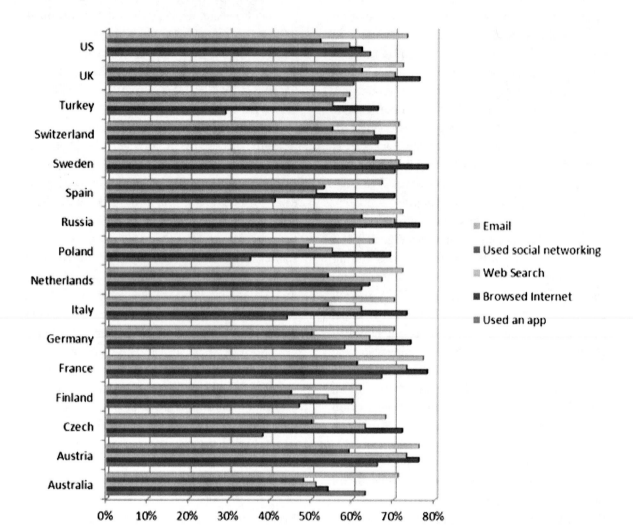

tory. This notion speaks directly to the concept of citizen engagement. Involvements in government empower citizen ownership and agency over the city affairs and ultimately trust in government activities.

Turkey recognizes that mobile phones will become the primary point of contact between a government agency and its citizens because of the devices' greater accessiblty at a lower cost. In the long term, the key benefit of the citizen-engagement phenomenon is that the government to treat constituents less as citizens and more as colleagues (as is already the case elsewhere). In

Australia, as quoted in the Herald, 'future public servants will need to learn a "very new set of skills" as collaborators, mobilisers and community curators "rather than managers in a hierarchical system" pushing many of them out of their comfort zone (The Herald, 2012).

Progress is still needed on the regulatory front. Turkey's new e-trade draft code, for example, has yet to be finalized. The new code does not create a sufficient base for securing consumer identity information or providing alternative communication channels for various sectors, according to senior legal advisers. Soon in Parliament, voting

Figure 3. Smartphone penetration. Source: http://txt4ever.wordpress.com/2011/12/30/1715/ Compiled from Comscore (Oct 2011), Google/IPSOS (ourmobileplanet.com), Informa and Netsize 2011 guide.

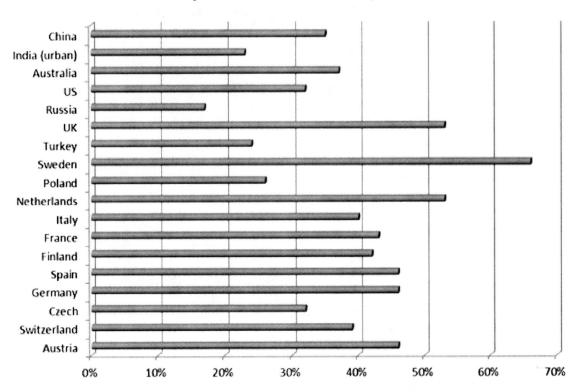

will occur on new e-legislation to curb spamming via e-mail and SMS messages from companies to be sent without customer consent. In addition, a supervising body, similar to the Information Commissioner's Office in the United Kingdom, is expected to regulate such e-trade cases in Turkey.

Furthermore, according to Kerem Alkin, head of the Mobile Service Provider Businessmen Association (MOBİLSAD), the Turkish government may also be losing potential revenues as no tax income has been received from the $200 million worth of applications downloaded from the Internet over the last four years. In addition, according to the Turkish Phonographic Industry Society (MÜYAP), the growing digital music sales have yet to reach a sufficient level to compensate producers' losses from lower sales due to piracy and illegal online sharing. Lastly, too few apps in

Turkish exist; this situation can be remedied with simple language applications. .

Vis-à-vis the information communication technology applications and services landscape described above, the specific objectives of this paper are:

1. This chapter's primarily aims to re-define the potential of Smartphone and apps for m-Government purpose in the case of Turkey.
2. A second issue underlined in the case and the discussion is related to enabling m-Government systems to interoperate. The case of the m-Government application "Beyaz Masa" (White Table) is presented and analyzed.

The chapter is structured as follows: It begins by re-defining m-Government at the age of digital media and Smartphone providing a broader backdrop to the present research. A summary review of the literature is then presented. Here, the relevance of the co-creation literature is considered. The presentation of the case study of the 'Beyaz Masa' app then follows. These empirical insights illustrate multi-tasking activity facing m-Government across different levels of ICT knowledge and local circumstances. The paper concludes with a discussion outlining the implications of this study, and its limitations, as well as suggestions for further research.

Re-Defining E/M-Government in the Age of Digital Media and Smartphones

This paper is nested in the traditional Unified Theory of Acceptance and Use of Technology (UTAUT) model that integrates a series of traditional technology acceptance models (Venkatesh et al, 2003). These include: the theory of reasoned action (Davis et al. 1989), the technology acceptance model (Davis, 1989), the motivational model (Davis et al., 1992), the theory of planned behaviour (Ajzen, 1991), Taylor and Todd (1995) framework that combine TAM and TPB, Thompson et al., (1991) Personal Computing utilization model, the innovation diffusion theory (Rogers, 2003), and the social cognitive theory (Compeau and Higgins, 1995; 1999).

The term e-Government and m-Government traditionally refers to all information communication technology applications and services usually offered by a centrally organized government platform to inform and interact with citizens and firms (Irani et al, 2007; Weerakkody and Dhillon, 2008). E-Government efforts aim to benefit from the use of the most innovative forms of information communication technologies, particularly Web-based Internet applications in improving governments` fundamental functions (Kuschu

2007). As a second step, mobile government (m-government) is defined as "a strategy and its implementation involving the utilization of all kinds of wireless and mobile technology, services application, and devices for improving benefits to the parties involved in e-Government including citizens, businesses and all government units" (Kuschu and Kuscu, 2003 in Kuschu 2007 p2). This definition emphasises the spatial aspects of most services with any given location. Mobility allows different choices regarding technologies and a wider participation in emerging market condition. As such, new platforms need to be designed along different processes adapted for a wireless, wifi world. Some authors have in this regard argued that mobile government strategies need to provide an "efficient utilization of all wireless devices" (Zalesak, 2003 in Kuschu 2007 p61) or the development of "a functional subset of all-inclusive e-Government" services specially adapted to Smartphone increasing capabilities (Arazyan, 2002 in Kuschu 2007 p61).

In other words, experts concur on the point that more attention must be paid to the list of apps characteristics. One the one hand, apps are described as convenience and fun, task-based, quick and effective. They provide a sense of ownership and being "close at hand" icons, apps have a home on users device (Baker, 2011). Apps also encourage discoverability, innovation and are a clear distribution channel for developers allowing for monetization of the channel. On the other hands, drawbacks do exist, including device and platform specificity(s), little if any interoperability across devices or platforms, highly centralized model; gatekeepers who block app and content creators from reaching users; requires permission at many levels — centralization allows a few App Store owners to control business model, pricing, relationships; learning helplessly: if there isn't "an app for that" then it's not worth trying to do something and lastly, too often apps and web experiences live in separate silos.

As implied by the term 'mobile government', m-Government aims to bring mobility to e-Government processes. Regarding mobility in particular, three levels are analyzed in the literature: (a) social, (b) physical, and (c) virtual with the introduction of information and communication technologies. Further characteristics need to be underlined including: (a) spatial mobility referring to the extensive movement of citizens in their local environment allowing real time information to be produced and the mobility of objects including evolution of the environment (weather, planned physical work, unplanned incidents); (b) temporal mobility referring to the urgency of time in the eye of the beholder, the moving of time according to prioritisation and expectation for answers/solution/task completion; (c) asynchronous time communication (email, SMS) allowing a re-arranging of task in a dynamic rather than traditional fashion. Further questions arise regarding device access, type of devices, service provision and the ability to provide one-to-one or one-to-many services. As such, m-Government denotes the use of mobile technologies for digital governmental services. The focus lies on both, the enrichment of existing e-Government services, as well as the development of new approaches using mobile technologies.

The devices themselves are of great advantage for governments. They are always on and usually personal. The simplicity of mobile devices can improve processes in terms of efficiency and reduce learning/change fears. Mobile devices support different types of interaction (voice, text, audio, mapping applications and video). From a network perspective, they do not require large infrastructure investment; legal frameworks are already in place in most country with private and often global providers competing. Yet, for most devices, the situation is more complicated than it is in traditional web access. Modern Smartphones or other comparable mobile devices such as tablets are usually equipped with a web browser but that browser is run by many different operating systems. While some devices have a large hardware capacity including memory, many still lack standardized functions. It is also important to note that many citizens may be unaware of the quality/shortcoming of their devices (also echoed by civil servants as many new devices are priced beyond their resources if not provided fee of charge). Other areas vary greatly, including screen size and quality, input ergonomic capabilities and services offered by the different operators. In most emerging markets, a browsing download limit is imposed upon most users in their contract, making exceeding it prohibitive (data transfer rate may also be an issue on 3G networks). Charging and battery life may also be a concern. In addition, the frequent release of new models with wider capability may also be beyond m-Government competences (interoperability issues). Lastly, mobile device may be more prone to signal interception and security breaches.

Furthermore, citizen engagement is paramount making m-Government service comparable to the traditional concept of co-creation. A conceptual summary of the co-creation, co-production and co-opetition (collaboration and completion) is now undertaken and illustrated to provide a clearer backdrop to the case. Co-creation is defined as a type of business approach that underlines the production of mutual firm-customer value (Rowe and Frewer, 2000). The main difference with traditional value creation is that the firm or government only offers a value proposition. Citizens then capitalize (or not) on the offer, thus creating value in use. In so doing, many will appropriate and re-shape the original offer to better fit local and personal conditions (Macintosh and Whyte, 2008). Co-creation and co-destruction practices further shape and re-shape the market place as forums and communities where active stakeholders (firms, governments, NGOs, individual) voluntarily share, combine and renew resources and capabilities to create more relevant value through new forms of interaction, services and learning mechanisms. Co-created value emerges from the personalized, unique experiences of citizens (value-in-use) often at the point of consumption. Value is co-created with citizens, allowing them to foster particular agendas, re-arrange priorities and overall tailor generic services into actionable day to day tasks. As such, m-Government is attempting to co-opt citizens' knowledge sharing capabilities, competences and experiences (Prahalad and Ramaswamy, 2000). In other words, co-creation is a process whereby government agencies create goods, services and experiences in close cooperation with experienced and creative citizens, tapping into their intellectual capital and, in exchange, giving them a direct say in (and rewarding them for) what actually gets produced, developed, designed, serviced, or processed (Warkentin et al, 2002). These initiatives have also been termed/ referred to as 'civil servant professional empathy' preventing 'turf wars'. Indeed, for decades, citizens have been saving up their insights and rants about the government services they consume, simply because they didn't have adequate means to interact, group together and really influence outcomes. As societies evolve, a gradation is found in the level of government connectedness. Figure

4 identifies key stages that demonstrate a need for evolution in term of overall interoperability and specifically infrastructure development, content delivery, business re-engineering, data management, security and customer management.

Some issues remain challenging. Co-creation pre-supposes a conceptual level in which civil servants (internal) and citizens (external) want or need to work together (cutting across organizational 'silos'). This is no easy task since co-creation's very nature requires mobilizing people across departments, ministries and societal milieus as well as crossing cultural and intellectual boundaries. Indeed many researchers argue that citizens can't express and report their needs to government agencies. Their actual behaviour, however, provides important hints about the range of their unmet needs. Storytelling on m-Government platforms could help communicate solutions to a diverse set of stakeholders, particularly across, as is the case in many developing countries, language and cultural barriers. At the very least, m-Government platforms could create the conditions for dialogue by listening, linking up, and empowering social innovators to define clear collaboration and

Figure 4. E-Government 5 stages model

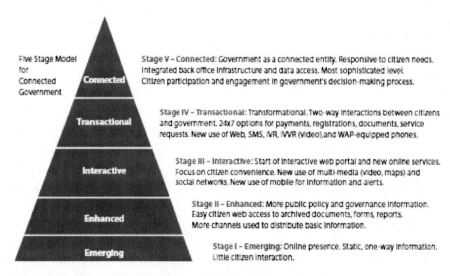

Source: DESA (2010), *E.Government Survey 2010*, United Nations, New York.

interoperability procedures (See figure 5). At this point, it is clear that the role of civil servant is now evolving from expert to facilitator (knowledge driven as opposed to position driven strategy). Unfortunately, most m-Government initiatives are often hurriedly conceived, with a small budget, and often lack any planning or cross-organizational mobilization to encourage a learning attitude among users (and shared responsibilities). Other characteristics can also been underlined such as tolerance to failure, being less bound by rules and hierarchical decision making process. Ignoring the above characteristics often results in a disjointed flow of mediocre ideas, rendering a large number of social projects already 'dead' on arrival.

This evolving set of models, moreover, requires new ways to manage stockholders' expectations and interoperability moving from (a) representative democracy to participatory democracy; (b) disciplinary base design to trans-disciplinary design; (c) getting from top down design to bottom-up transparent media led strategies that will in the medium to long term re-shape society as a whole. There are several unanswered questions. Firstly, the government mobile project will need to figure out how to keep the large and diverse set of participants engaged (repeat visit, contribution, participation and action). Second, how to share the risks (priorities social good vs. individual needs) and value of innovation (digital divide)? Third, how to manage the complex interoperability of this system without too many legal con-

Figure 5. Example of m-Government organizational chart

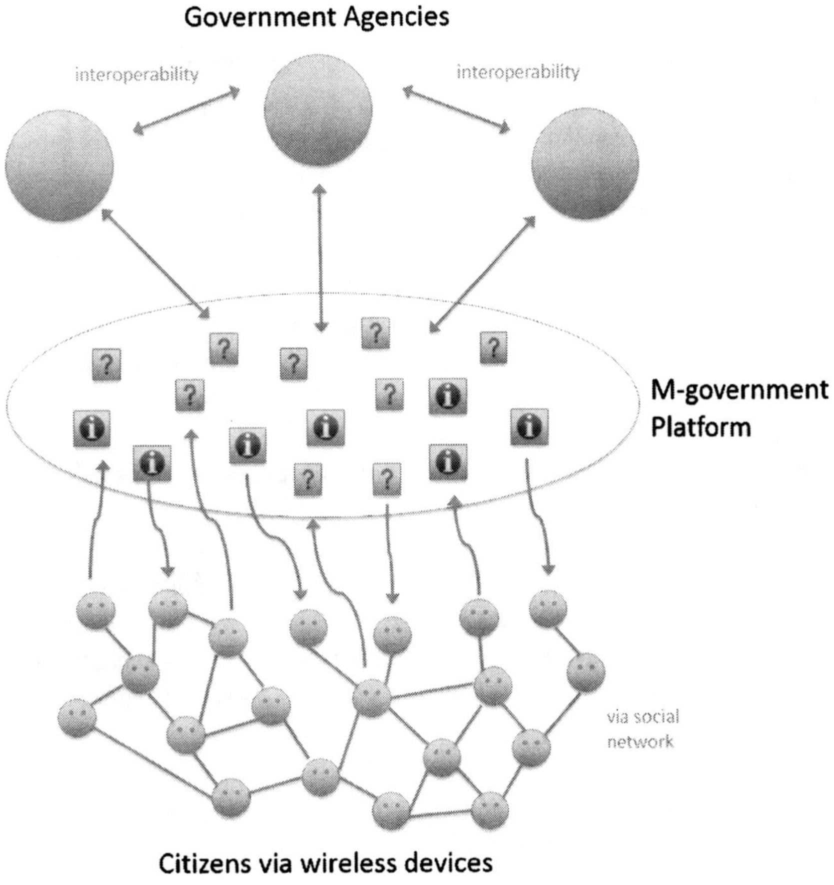

Government Agencies

interoperability   interoperability

M-government Platform

via social network

Citizens via wireless devices

straints? And fourth, how to manage the flow of information and activity across the boundaries where the degree of trust is yet to be established?

Regarding the last pillar of interoperability, three further areas of concern are often highlighted in the media including: (a) the fear of 'citizen dictators', (b) questions regarding citizen involvement and resources – won't it take too long, and won't it be too expensive, (c) citizen involvement creates unrealistic expectations and (d) are local authorities going to rule the central government? Many scholars have indeed commented on the potential big brother effect of m-Government services. Yet, the McKinsey Global Institute's (2012) report for the private sector argues that unlocking value and productivity through social technologies platforms, including crowdsourcing and co-creation, could improve productivity of high-skilled knowledge workers by 25%. Furthermore, this change could contribute between $900 billion to $1.3 trillion per annum across four commercial sectors: consumer packaged goods, retail financial services, advanced manufacturing and professional services.

Moreover, the media have also emphasized timing. Is the m-Government initiative trying to deal with angry citizens? Are the community leaders confident that the government is genuinely trying to change? How will the initiative be sustained and what will be considered success? Lastly, will politicians try to capture or control the process of change? While action is required, it is important to underline how authority is constituted, who gets to act and on what basis, and how people in power are held accountable to their publics. What's more, these initiatives require re-tool or re-train actors to the emerging reality and new ecosystem. The innovation of existing services is another underestimated, but key aspect of interoperability.

Consequently, instead of seeing m-Government as a subset of e-Government limited to mobile and wireless technology, this chapter conceptualizes the changes above as a paradigm shift from offering offline traditional service to social network base participatory models. A case study follows on the so-called "white table"- an app specially designed in Turkey to solve roadwork issues. We demonstrate that some services and functions can only be competently delivered by mobile devices. This case study/Beyaz masa, we contend, does not depict a simple extension of e-Government but, more broadly, the emergence of a new and distinct model of governance.

The Case of "Beyaz Masa" (White Table) Mobile Application for Istanbul Municipality

From a methodological perspective, the case is analysed using a qualitative approach based on the factors outlined in the literature review above. We aim to provide a condensed and broad description of the situation. Content analysis, developing procedures of inductive category development, is employed as there are few previous studies dealing with the phenomenon and findings are fragmented (Krippendorff, 1988). The outcome of the analysis is a set of categories describing m-Government and apps' practices. In moving services a mere click away from their constituents, governments are finding themselves contemplating many new different business models. Some do internal development; others, outsource part or all the services technical, content and management. Beyaz Masa, "White Table" in Turkish, embodies the new ideological standing of the Turkish government regarding: (a) transparency in government service provision and (b) its response to citizens' request for public work to be conducted. This model outsources its services to Pordiva A.Ş. one of the founder members of "Mobil Server Business Provider Businessman Association" (MOBİLSAD). As such, this new application on the cutting edge of technology overhaul traditional processes and systems, turning them inside out from agency-centric to customer-facing systems that span agency silos.

The objective of the app and services is to have a system that would systematically record citizens' demands and queries (automatically placing the request into queue) about infrastructure problems (e.g. reporting of potholes, graffiti, traffic accidents, open manhole covers, abandoned or illegally parked cars, trash problems) so as to offer clear responses and updates of a task. The app function informs municipal agencies so that they can operate more efficiently. Citizens now perform the role of 'first first responders'.

At the macro level, this type of app also generates much meta-data that enables agencies, in time, to automate their response to a service request without the need to physically verify the problem and create trend patterns maps through geo-spatial analysis. The overall process is faster and recorded with a tracking number. Geo-tagging the data also will enable future local government services to transmit warnings based on citizen registration and location relative to an incident, thus, for example, reducing panic, as in the case of earthquakes (a common occurrence in Istanbul).

This particular service was initiated in 1997 by the Turkish Government and supported by traditional communication methods, including mail, email, and telephone. Data collection, extraction, consolidation and evaluation of priorities were difficult to track and manage. Figure 6 summarizes the traditional system. A set of difficulties were identified:

1. Location of the infrastructure work that needed attention was gathered via often approximate address, and location description was not always accurate.
2. The organization of task in clear categories emerging from many non-standardized forms and different sources under many data bases was complicated,
3. The organization of the appropriate response in view of human, time and financial resources were inefficient
4. The feedback to citizens about progress and completed work was complex.

Figure 6. Traditional organizational model

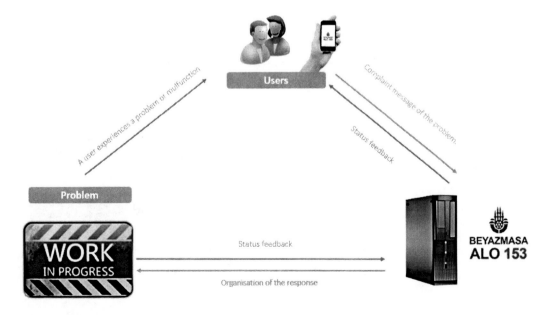

In 2012, a smart phone app was designed for the Istanbul Municipality to solve the above problems with the newest technological developments in mobility and Smartphones. In practice, the new Beyas Masa applications involve: still image, video, streaming, file transfer, web browsing, collaborative working (updating) and regarding the back end of services, tasks include job dispatch, remote monitoring, SMS and vehicle positioning.

Figure 7 summarizes the rationale for the development of the new services. The new services leverage the interactive aspect of Smartphones all organized under one database.

The Beyaz Masa smart phone application operates on all mobile devices such as Smartphones and tablets that use the two most popular operating systems in Turkey-- ios (apple) and android based operating systems. As of February, 2013, the application does not work on the Blackberry 10 platform or Windows phone 8. The app is free. Adoption was unexpectedly quick (within 3 months, Android downloads: 4595; Iphone downloads: 8284 Photo files; 2576 Video files: 5869 and 80 Audio files were received). Citizens not only downloaded but also used the app with strong motivation. People happily engaged with local government authorities as they provided information/ warning about appropriate services and problems as they appeared on a daily basis. The application was described as the combination of a user friendly interface, efficient data processing and automated communication properties blended with the benefits of mobility. Citizens are requested to help in the classification of their reporting. Eight categories have been created to speed up classification: development, human resources, environment, transportation, social support, health, infrastructure, other.

Subsequently responses are provided by the relevant agencies. Table 1 describes some of the communication. Here, the issues linking back to interoperability are concerns with detail, aggregation, and/or summarization, sophistication and availability of data, as well as automation of responses as citizens tends to interpret information in slightly different ways having different goals. As such, interoperability is found to account for context-dependent situations. Figures 10 to 12 portray the user interface and the various functions. A specific strategy has been put in place involving a series of steps (stage 1 and 2 in Figures 8 and 9, respectively) and options (photos, video,

Figure 7. New system model

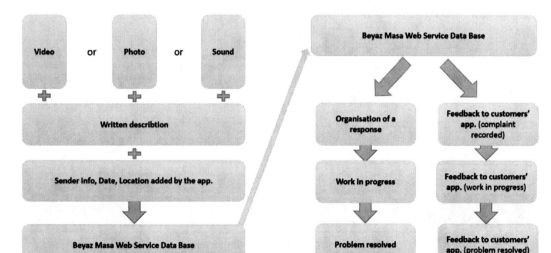

Table 1. Examples of warning/reply messages

Voice	"It is very nice that citizens' voice can be heard. The best advantage of the mobile application is the ability to report on the spot. I got reply in a short time for a complaint that I reported. My request was sent to highway authority and necessary changes were made. Thanks." https://play.google.com/store/apps/details?id=tr.gov.ibb.beyazmasa&hl=tr. 31st October 2012
Interactivity	"This is a great bridge between people and municipality. Transparent and sufficient. This is an application that needs to be an example to many other institutions." https://play.google.com/store/apps/details?id=tr.gov.ibb.beyazmasa&hl=tr 31st October 2012
Technological Leadership	"This is a well thought application, everybody who are on the streets also become an inspector. The municipality cannot sleep on problems anymore" HTC https://play.google.com/store/apps/details?id=tr.gov.ibb.beyazmasa&hl=tr 21 April 2012
Very Helpful	"From now on there won't be any keeping quiet after witnessing a problem."
Still Some Problems are Present	
Uploading	"A name called Emeah Billur appears when I select address. I tried twice but could not upload my complaint. It was a complaint with photographed, documented complaint. Besides that the idea behind the application is very nice." Samsung Galaxy Tab https://play.google.com/store/apps/details?id=tr.gov.ibb.beyazmasa&hl=tr 21st May 2012
Compatibility	"It gives error on Galaxy S3 while loading the address on the map. Still, this is a nice application with detailed thinking. The application should have a survey on user satisfaction regarding the replies given to the reported complaints. Besides that, application visuals do not switch to horizontal when you hold the phone horizontally. Even with all these missing features, it deserves 5 stars just because it makes complaint reports possible for people who use this platform. I hope these feedbacks are considered." Samsung Galaxy S3 https://play.google.com/store/apps/details?id=tr.gov.ibb.beyazmasa&hl=tr 23 August 2012
Fixed or Not?	"Application is nice but what good is it if the problems won't get fixed? The problems I reported a month ago are still not resolved. I got no response or no feedback from anybody. If you did this application to listen to our complaints and solve them, then take a step to resolve them as well." iphone 21 April 2012
Fear	"I am a new user and worried that it has some sort of virus in it, what do you say my friends?" SEMC Xperia S https://play.google.com/store/apps/details?id=tr.gov.ibb.beyazmasa&hl=tr 12 September 2012
Competence	District municipalities are incompetent "The application is nice but the problem does not get solved, the road collapsed more and no one bothers" Samsung Galaxy S https://play.google.com/store/apps/details?id=tr.gov.ibb.beyazmasa&hl=tr 20 July 2012

Own translation messages issued from Jan 2013 to February 2013

audio) that can be managed by the users. Various levels of precision (map, address) are then made available depending on the user's actual knowledge. Finally information sharing is available to all users in various formats (text, pin on various maps option).

Overall, the new application provides:

1. A central data base from which data are aggregated logically,
2. A wider spread of information whereby no un-noticed malfunctions in infrastructure were left unanswered,
3. An efficient response team was created as tasks were assessed and prioritized accordingly,
4. Lower operating costs as team time, skills and machinery used more efficiently,
5. Rapid progress *in situs* for smaller tasks encourages further reporting of issues that can be solved rapidly; thus, boosting confidence in the services (as well as timing out requests when work was completed).

The spatial and descriptive power of this technology is of primary importance in minimizing

Figure 8. Stage 1: In progress

Figure 9. Stage 2: Resolved or completed

errors and speed-up responses. The appropriate government units are immediately contacted. Smartphone's standard photograph, video and sound recording capabilities are used along with location tracking system to identify the location of the problem. During complaint submission, citizens provide personal information to allow for follow up feedback when a situation is resolved. In addition, at a collective level and to limit duplication, the location of the problem submitted is visible to all users. The description of the complaint and the possibility to see and comment on the government's response helps governments restore public trust by coping with corruption, inefficiency, ineffectiveness, and policy alienation. The description of the government's response message includes the problem's reference number, date and time, start dates of repair the

current state of the problem and alterative solution, if appropriate.

From a technical perspective, the app is directly connected to the web service of the Istanbul Municipality. The data used in the system is open to public; therefore no special system security was deemed necessary. In order to eliminate false or irrelevant complaints, the system requires the Smartphone identification number of the user. "WCF (Windows Communication Foundation) and ".Net Framework" was used for the development of the web service side. On the mobile side "Native SDK" was used for Android and Ios. No open source system (such as TOGAF) was used in the development and at the moment cannot be modified by other parties. However, the application is open to further modifications if existing codes are presented. The system works

Figure 10. Application console 1

Figure 11. Application console 2

Figure 12. Application console 3

as instant upload; its speed is limited to 3G data transfer speed. The data and information that is sent is first categorized by the application in to 8 different categories such as

1. Development
2. Human resources
3. Environment
4. Transportation
5. Social support
6. Health
7. Infrastructure
8. Other

Information is then distributed to the related departments according to the categories are filtered manually. No semantic automatic filtering is used at this stage.

Limitations relevant to the interoperability issue are still worth noting: (a) the app requires during the first connection that the user allow GPS data to be downloaded. Some privacy issues may be present when the service is not used but the phone is on with GPS location abilities enabled; (b) during subsequent connections, the user phone ID is directly recognized to prevent a long log-in procedure. This pre-supposes that users are happy to share their phone ID with government services. (c) while the system is normally calibrated to limit duplications (no need for other citizens to waste time reporting the same incident) in practice questions have been raised in review comments. (d) the services are only available in Turkish. User range, especially the large expat population living in Istanbul, is thus restricted. (e) Istanbul municipality traffic density map and that of Beyas Masa are yet to be integrated. Nevertheless, Beyas Masa still gives, depending on location, some traffic information such as malfunction of traffic lights and other infrastructure. Users need to navigate between various apps for a full picture of traffic. (f) the daily news service is also unfocused and unfiltered: any information is provided (e.g. art, music events, income information from museum

visits, future projects). It is noted that apps are deigned mainly from a client perspective with users in mind rather than fully integrated and leveraging users' history towards providing only the relevant information.

Analysing further the service potential, Mr. Kadir Topbaş, the Mayor of Istanbul Metropolitan Municipality and the president of United Cities and Local Governments (UCLG) describes the new app service as follows:

Citizens/Residents are Our Eyes and Ears

With this system, everybody will gain a voice and be able to hear about the city. Because we live in a metropolis of 15 million residents everybody's fate (future) is linked to each other. We all interdependently use the city infrastructure and all infrastructures run at 100% capacity. The problem is on part affecting even other countries. With this project, citizens will be our eyes and ears. This is the conception (understanding) of citizenship in a modern city. From now on, you don't call and say 'hello', you take a picture or video of the problem and send it right away to the municipality (Aksam newspaper, 2012)

One recognition of the Turkish government is citizen's preference to interact with their government online versus traditional means. It is often easier and more convenient for them to do so. While many citizens complain about their experiences in dealing with the local government, especially when related to the social good shared by all (this is also referred to as 'the commons', 'common goods') (e.g. road needing maintenance) rather than personal issues, data also demonstrate that (a) engagement is greater online and (b) frustration is less of an issue. Proactiveness is recognized as essential if government agencies desire to improve. Thus, if a government service waits for traditional feedback to determine where to focus their priorities, it risks losing engagement with and trust of citizens because of unmet expectations and needs.

Moreover, as with any new technologies, feedback is encouraged. Some comments, positive and negative are presented and analysed below. An analysis of the main themes positive and negative is reported for a period covering 10 weeks in 2012. Four positive macro categories are found including: voice, interactivity, technological leadership and helpfulness. Four negative categories are also uncovered: uploading, compatibility, fixing the problem and fear of technology.

Some issues emerge from this feedback: (1) organizational issues including accessibility and availability, (2) technological issues including system integration, (3) social issues including security, privacy and training and (4) political issues including legislation and support and commitment to resolves issues. While the development of Smartphone technologies has created a new venue for governments services to reach out to a much greater number of people than ever before, it has also brought citizens previously unimaginable opportunities to communicate both positively and more importantly negatively with government services and among each other in a convenient way together with an official recording of tasks/discussion that need attentions. Cheap and ready-for-use apps are removing technology related psychological barriers and are empowering citizens to connect and voice their views to individual governments' services in a number of policy areas where they had previously little input.

Consequently, m-Government should not be perceived as eliminating existing on-line and off-line service access, but as a complementary channel that increases access to existing services and leverages new technologies such as mapping and photography. By empowering a new type of citizens, m-Government is improving the quality of life of all citizens within the metropolis of Istanbul. Specifically, reporting faulty infrastructures allow the powers of the masses to pressure government services bring a new momentum towards sorting issues rapidly and transparently. This new model allows a dispersed private sector knowledge and expertise to be communicated in real time to the public sector, backed by tangible data access, and offer relevant solutions.

Managerial, Public Policy, Telecommunication Policy Implications

Citizens are using government services for many reasons reflecting the different types of expectations and groups in the society. While over the years a fatalistic tendency that government will not be able to cope with any demand was wide spread, ICT and Smartphone via apps, in particular, are radically changing the ecosystem. The multiple provisions of services are creating a greater choice of access, leading to more patronage of services and feelings of social accomplishment for many participants-- both civil servants and citizens alike. With apps services governments cannot no longer remain passive. New online behaviors encourage the positive voicing but also negative of involved citizenry.

As such harnessing apps to boost public sector performance is an imperative that no government can ignore. In Turkey, the model emerging seems, at the moment, to favor third party providers using closed proprietary system rather than open source or a system based on agreed global standards. However, in the case of many emerging market economies, open standards are not always the solution. There will always be domains where open standards do not yet exist. Governments must de facto trust often a local single company that is in return expected to keep abreast of the latest innovations and tends. An advantage of ignoring detailed standards leads emerging market government to create more innovative feature and services rather than imitate the already more mature markets' experiences. This feature is also relevant to keep up with the speed of new wireless devices that are offered to citizens. The central issue in this model for Istanbul municipality is to ensure that various services are not developing and creating custom made apps that will prevent interoperability. As seen in the case app, Beyaz Masa is yet to be fully integrated with other similar services such as road traffic maps.

'Beyaz Masa' and Pordiva have demonstrated that citizens desire involvement and look forward to participation. In turn, many other apps (in native language) can be expected in area such as taxes, health (especially with an ageing population), unemployment benefits, fire and police department, education etc. The modularity approach allowing development of services and best practices to be observed and benchmark is noticed as one additional positive effect. As such, priorities can be organized in a better fashion depending on geographical component, type of work etc.

The case also draws attention to the increasing significance of policies directed at changing behavior of both service providers and service users in the new welfare settlement. While these ideological and practical reforms are recent and continuing, they point out at the fact that well design apps are able to harness the plurality in society in an appropriate direction. Citizens are also able to reflect on the trade off facing local services between multiple tasks that require a response. Drawing on the work of Gintis et al (2005: 8) we also confirm that citizens 'are often neither self regarding nor altruistic' but rather 'strong reciprocators: conditional co-operator). The design of institutional access and the type of technology used hence frame choice and patterns of motivation to engage or not with government services. As underlined by Taylor-Gooby (2008: 178) these issues 'raise the question of whether a transition from state or voluntary provision to the market nexus introduces a different frame of reference for making choice'. One outcome is 'as provision of services via apps and Smartphone is reframed in the context of quasi-market, a more critical caveat emptor consumerism emerges among users' (Talor-Gooby, 2008: 180). In other words, citizens are encouraged to differentiate between immediate self interest and promoting a longer term, socially oriented set of behaviors to

create a better metropolis. Equally, a risk is found regarding the compatibility of the civil service values and a certain type of citizen based real time interactions that may reinforce certain patterns of existing exclusion (Selwyn, 2002). Once again it is necessary to assess the importance of the policy signal in itself while using new ICT services such as apps.

Regarding interoperability in particular, it will achieve better decision, better services delivery and overall better governance. One of the key issue emerging in the case of m-Government is time related with long vs. short term objectives. Second the data required to make advanced decisions are often more qualitative (ground in the socio-cultural environment) rather than quantitative (technical automation). As such, interoperability's main aim could be to re-shape government towards more transformative rather than just a tool for service delivery. Emerging market government in particular, must reflect about the need to set standards and get the architecture right in advance. At the same time such governments must allow innovation and flexibility required by the local ecosystem, to succeed through the use of ICT. It is important to note that standards follow a life cycle of emergence to obsolescence. Yet, as underlined in the literature Turkey as yet to formally adopt a Government Interoperability Framework (GIF) that will represent a set of minimum standards and guidelines to specify preferences for its agencies, citizens and partners to interact. Nor has Turkey debated the need to encourage a National Enterprise Architecture (NEA) framework as a strategic planning forum that relates and aligns government ICT with the governmental functions that it supports (Guijarro, 2007). Other issues have yet to be addressed in the case such as scalability to the whole country, security and privacy as underlined in the GPS geo-localization tool, and market support for further apps development beyond the first wave of services that usually aim at a broad audience. In this chapter the broader case of international interoperability also remain beyond the scope.

CONCLUSION AND FUTURE RESEARCH

Without a doubt, Web 2.0 technologies and Smartphone as technological artifact will continue to play an increasingly important role in digital government strategy. Smartphone apps are creating, as demonstrated above in the case of Beyaz Massa, specific opportunities that leverage their increasing abilities (GPS, Video). Indeed, the capacity to integrate collaborative tools in digital government will further unlock the potential of crowdsoucing, co-creation of knowledge, and citizen participation to create better government. As such, the issue of interoperability is yet again flagged as key to long term sustainability. Governments have no choice but to clearly develop strategies that foster interoperability between an increasing long list of actors both internal (other government functions) and external (technology providers). Assessment of digital government success in the future and future research agenda should, hence, develop new tools that capture the level of interoperability in practice as a yardstick for initiative success or failure. Lastly, as hinted in the case interoperability should also not only be examined from a technical perspective but also from a cultural perspective.

REFERENCES

Ajzen, I. (1991). The theory of planned behavior. *Organizational Behavior and Human Decision Processes*, *50*, 179–211. doi:10.1016/0749-5978(91)90020-T

Akşam. (2012). *Fotoğrafı çek büyükşehire yolla yönetime ortak ol*. Retrieved February 13, 2013 from http://www.aksam.com.tr/guncel/foto-grafi-cek-buyuksehire-yolla-yonetime-ortak-ol/haber-109272

Anatolia News Agency. (2010). *Turkcell sees future in mobile wallet*. Hürriyet Daily News Economy Er-Sectors - HDN ISTANBUL. Retrieved February 13, 2013 from http://www.hurriyetdailynews.com/turkcell-sees-future-in-mobile-wallet.aspx?pageID=438&n=turkcell-sees-future-in-mobile-wallet-2010-05-12

Anatolia News Agency. (2010). *Turkey on the phone for long talks*. Hürriyet Daily News, Economy Er-National, Ankara. Retrieved February 13, 2013 from http://www.hurriyetdaily-news.com/turkey-on-the-phone-for-long-talks.aspx?pageID=438&n=turkey-on-the-phone-for-long-talks-2010-08-12

Anatolia News Agency. (2012). *Turks surpass EU citizens in using mobile internet*. Hürriyet Daily News, ANKARA. Retrieved February 13, 2013 from http://www.hurriyetdailynews.com/turks-surpass-eu-citizens-in-using-mobile-internet.aspx?pageID=238&nID=35715&NewsCatID=344

Anatolia News Agency. Istanbul. (2012). *Turkey fails to tax mobile internet applications*. Hürriyet Daily News. Retrieved February 13, 2013 from http://www.hurriyetdailynews.com/turkey-fails-to-tax-mobile-internet-applications.aspx?pageID=238&nID=25913&NewsCatID=344

Armitage, C. (2012). *Council uses phone apps to give power to the people*. Herald, Newcastle. Retrieved February 13, 2013 from http://www.theherald.com.au/story/409807/council-uses-phone-apps-to-give-power-to-the-people/

Baker. (2011). *The app. model and the web*. Retrieved February 13, 2013 from https://blog.lizardwrangler.com/2011/08/09/

Chui, M., Manyika, J., Bughin, J., Dobbs, R., Roxburgh, C., Sarrazin, H., et al. (2012). *The social economy: Unlocking value and productivity through social technologies*. Retrieved June 27, 2013 from http://www.markleweeklydigest.org/2012/07/the-social-economy-unlocking-value-and.html

Compeau, D. R., & Higgins, C. A. (1995). Computer self-efficacy: Development of a measure and initial test. *Management Information Systems Quarterly*, *19*(2), 189–211. doi:10.2307/249688

Compeau, D. R., Higgins, C. A., & Huffs, S. (1999). Social cognitive theory and individual reactions to computing technology: A longitudinal study. *Management Information Systems Quarterly*, *23*(2), 145–158. doi:10.2307/249749

Comscore. (2011). *Google/IPSOS (ourmobileplanet.com), informa and netsize 2011 guide*. Retrieved February 13, 2013 from http://txt4ever. wordpress.com/2011/12/30/1715/

Connolly, C., Chambers, C., Eagleson, E., Matthews, D., & Rogers, T. (2010). *Augmented reality effectiveness in advertising*. Retrieved July 6, 2013 from http://edgd.asee.org/conferences/ proceedings/65th%20Midyear/Connolly_Chambers_Augmented_Reality_%20Effectiveness%20 in%20Advert.pdf

Cova, B., & Dalli, D. (2009). Working consumers: The next step in marketing theory? *Marketing Theory*, *9*(3), 315–339. doi:10.1177/1470593109338144

Cova, B., Dalli, D., & Zwick, D. (2011). Critical perspectives on consumers' role as 'producers': Broadening the debate on value co-creation in marketing processes. *Marketing Theory*, *11*(3), 231–241. doi:10.1177/1470593111408171

Davis, F. D. (1989). Perceived usefulness, perceived ease of use, and user acceptance of information technology. *Management Information Systems Quarterly*, *13*(3), 319–339. doi:10.2307/249008

Davis, F. D., Bagozzi, R. P., & Warshaw, P. R. (1992). Extrinsic and intrinsic motivation to use computers in the workplace. *Journal of Applied Social Psychology*, *22*(14), 1111–1132. doi:10.1111/j.1559-1816.1992.tb00945.x

De Kervenoael, R., & Koçoğlu, I. (2011). E-government strategy in Turkey: A case for m-government? In *Handbook for e-government in emerging economies – Adoption, continuance, usage, e-participation and legal frameworks*. Hershey, PA: IGI Global Publishing.

De Kervenoael, R., Palmer, M., & Cakici, N. M. (2010). Exploring civil servant resistance to m-government: A story of transition and opportunities Turkey. In *Mobile information communication technologies adoption in developing countries: Effects and implications*. Hershey, PA: IGI Global Publishing. doi:10.4018/978-1-61692-818-6.ch010

DePriest, D. (2012). The fifth dimension: How augmented reality is launching worlds within our world. In *Proceedings of TCC*. TCC.

Desa. (2010). *E-government survey 2010*. Retrieved February 13, 2013 from http://books.google. com.tr/books?id=IPsnu3nBeksC&pg=PA28& lpg=PA28&dq=%22desa+2010+e.governmen t+survey+2010%22&source=bl&ots=RbnJT iBwT_&sig=22jJP9oCD61-dEVIxbgvDAVIJ 6I&hl=tr&sa=X&ei=4dwwUaWFCs3Zsgb-6YDwDA&ved=0CDcQ6AEwAg#v=onepage-&q=%22desa%202010%20e.government%20 survey%202010%22&f=false

European Communities. (2008). *Draft document as basis for EIF 2.0*. Official Publications of the European Communities. Retrieved February 13, 2013 from http://ec.europa.eu/idabc/servlets/ Docb0db.pdf

Ford, T. C., Colombi, J. M., Graham, S. R., & Jacques, D. R. (2007). A survey on interoperability measurement. In *Proceedings of the 12th International Command and Control Research and Technology Symposium*. Retrieved February 13, 2013 from http://www.dtic.mil/ cgibin/GetTRDoc?Location=U2&doc=GetTR Doc.pdf&AD=ADA481314

Gervautz, M., & Schmalstieg, D. (2012). Anywhere interfaces using handheld augmented reality. IEEE Computer Society, 26-31.

Gintis, H., Bowles, S., Boyd, R., & Fehr, E. (2005). *Moral sentiments and material interest*. Cambridge, MA: MIT Press.

Guijarro, L. (2007). Interoperability frameworks and enterprise architectures in e-government initiatives in Europe and the United States. *Government Information Quarterly*, *24*(1), 89–101. doi:10.1016/j.giq.2006.05.003

Guler, E. (2012). *Obama versus Turkish politicians: Who fares better on social media?* Hürriyet Daily News, Ankara. Retrieved February 13, 2013 from http://www.hurriyetdailynews.com/obama-versus-turkish-politicians-who-fares-better-on-social-media-.aspx?pageID=238&nid=33906

Hürriyet Daily News. (2010). *Vodafone Turkey presents cell phones for 1 TL*. Retrieved February 13, 2013 from http://www.hurriyetdailynews.com/vodafone-turkey-presents-cell-phones-for-1-tl.aspx?pageID=438&n=vodofone-presents-cell-phones-for-one-lira-2010-07-23

Hürriyet Daily News. (2011a). *Turkish marketing world discusses e-trade draft law*. Retrieved February 13, 2013 from http://www.hurriyetdailynews.com/turkish-marketing-world-discusses-e-trade-draft-law.aspx?pageID=438&n=turkish-marketing-world-discuss-e-trade-draft-2011-01-28

Hürriyet Daily News. (2011b). *Digital sales not making up for losses over piracy*. Retrieved February 13, 2013 from http://www.hurriyetdailynews.com/digital-sales-not-making-up-for-losses-over-piracy.aspx?pageID=238&nID=7924&NewsCatID=345

Hürriyet Daily News. (2012a). *Revenues for Turkey's telecom firms up 6 pct*. Retrieved February 13, 2013 from http://www.hurriyetdailynews.com/revenues-for-turkeys-telecom-firms-up-6-pct.aspx?pageID=238&nID=21623&NewsCatID=345

Hürriyet Daily News. (2012b). *Turkey's 3G faster than US 4G: Reports*. Retrieved February 13, 2013 from http://www.hurriyetdailynews.com/turkeys-3g-faster-than-us-4g-reports.aspx?pageID=238&nID=34452&NewsCatID=374

Irani, Z., Elliman, T., & Jackson, P. (2007). Electronic transformation of government in the UK: A research agenda. *European Journal of Information Systems*, *16*(4), 327–335. doi:10.1057/palgrave.ejis.3000698

Krippendorff, K. (1980). *Content analysis: An introduction to its methodology*. Thousand Oaks, CA: Sage Publications.

Kushchu, I. (2007). *Mobile government: An emerging direction in e-government*. Hershey, PA: Idea Group Publishers. doi:10.4018/978-1-59140-884-0

Lallana, E. (2008). *e-Government interoperability*. Retrieved February 13, 2013., from http://unpan1.un.org/intradoc/groups/public/documents/UN-OTHER/UNPAN032094.pdf

Lallana, E. C. (2007). e-Government interoperability: A review of government interoperability. New York: United Nations Development.

Louise, P., Nordstokka, U., Friesen, C., Sigaloff, C., Moerbeek, K., & van Loon, L. (Eds.). (2011). *Co-creation guide: Realising social innovation together*. Retrieved February 13, 2013 from http://www.euclidnetwork.eu/resources/doc_view/158-co-creation-guide-realising-social-innovation-together.html

Macintosh, A., & Whyte, A. (2008). Towards an evaluation framework for eparticipation. *Transforming Government: People. Process and Policy*, *2*(1), 16–30.

Novakouski, M., & Lewis, G. A. (2012). *Interoperability in the e-government context.* Software Engineering Institute. Retrieved February 13, 2013 from http://www.sei.cmu.edu/reports/11tn014.pdf

Payne, A., Storbacka, K., & Frow, P. (2008). Managing co-creation of value. *Journal of the Academy of Marketing Science, 36,* 83–96. doi:10.1007/s11747-007-0070-0

Prahalad, C. K., & Ramaswamy, V. (2000). Co-opting customer competence. *Harvard Business Review, 78*(1), 79–87.

Rogers, E. (2003). *Diffusion of innovations.* New York: Free Press.

Rowe, G., & Frewer, L. J. (2000). Public participation methods: A framework for evaluation. *Science, Technology & Human Values, 25*(1), 3–29. doi:10.1177/016224390002500101

Schilling, M. A. (2010). *Strategic management of technological innovation.* Columbus, OH: McGraw-Hill.

Selwyn, N. (2002). E-stablishing and inclusive society? Technology, social exclusion and UK government policy making. *Journal of Social Policy, 31*(1), 1–20. doi:10.1017/S0047279402006487

Taylor, S., & Todd, P. A. (1995). Assessing IT usage: The role of prior experience. *Management Information Systems Quarterly, 19*(2), 561–570. doi:10.2307/249633

Taylor-Gooby, P. (2008). Choice and values: Individualised rational action and social goals. *Journal of Social Policy, 37*(2), 167–185. doi:10.1017/S0047279407001699

Thompson, D., & Malaviya, P. (2012). *When co-creation backfires: The effects of disclosing consumers source on advertising persuasiveness.* Academic Press.

Thompson, R. L., Higgins, C. A., & Howell, J. M. (1991). Personal computing: Toward a conceptual model of utilization. *Management Information Systems Quarterly, 15*(1), 124–143. doi:10.2307/249443

Venkatesh, V., Morris, M., Davis, G., & Davis, F. (2003). User acceptance of information technology: Toward a unified view. *Management Information Systems Quarterly, 27*(3), 425–478.

Warkentin, M., Gefen, D., Pavlou, P., & Rose, M. (2002). Encouraging citizen adoption of e-government by building trust. *Electronic Markets, 12,* 157–162. doi:10.1080/101967802320245929

Weerakkody, V., & Dhillon, G. (2008). Moving from e-government to t-government: A study of process reengineering challenges in a UK local authority context. *International Journal of Electronic Government Research, 4,* 1–16. doi:10.4018/jegr.2008100101

Yonck, R. (2008). The future of advertising and you. *Mensa Bulletin,* 32-33.

Zwick, D., Bonsu, S. K., & Darmody, A. (2008). Putting consumers to work: ''Co-creation'' and new marketing govern-mentality. *Journal of Consumer Culture, 8*(2), 163–196. doi:10.1177/1469540508090089

ADDITIONAL READING

NeGP Report. (2007). Draft Report of the first phase of NeGP Impact Assessment Study. Ahmedabad: Indian Institute of Management, Ahmedabad. Retrieved November 6, 2008 from mit.gov.in/.

Ngulube, P. (2007). *The Nature and Accessibility of E-Government in Sub Saharan Africa, Internation Review of Information Ethics* (Vol. 7). IRIE.

Ngulube, P. (2010). Mapping mixed methods research in library and information science journals in Sub-Saharan Africa: 2004-2008, *The International Information & Library Review. Elservier*, *42*, 252–261.

Ngulube, P., Mokwatlo, K., & Ndwandwe, S. (2009). Utilisation and prevalence of mixed methods in library and information research in South Africa 2002-2008. *South African Journal of Library and Information Science*, *72*(2), 105–116.

Noh, Y. K. (2009). ICT development in Korea. Retrieved October 2010 from www.tiaonline.org/gov.../Young_Noh_Presentation.ppt.

Nour, M., & AbdelRahman, A., & FadlAllah, A. (2008). A Context-Based Integrative Framework for e-Government Initiatives. *Government Information Quarterly*, *25*, 448–461. doi:10.1016/j.giq.2007.02.004

NOVOSEC. (2008). Authentication in E-Government, Authentication mechanisms and areas of application. Retrieved April 8, 2011 from https://www.bsi.bund.de/SharedDocs/Downloads/EN/BSI/ Egovernment/4_Authen_en_pdf.pdf?__blob=publicationFile.

Nurdin, N., Stockdale, R., & Scheepers, H. (2011). Examining the Role of the Culture of Local Government on Adoption and Use of E-Government Services. Retrieved August 6, 2012 from www.swinburne.edu.au/ict/research/riso/publications/Examining%20the%20Role.pdf.

KEY TERMS AND DEFINITIONS

Co-Production: This describes the sub-production chain of a main production. Co-Production supports the actives enthroned in the major production processes.

ICTs: This entails the different technologies and tools that are utilised in managing diverse information resources. The acronym stands for Information and Communication Technologies.

Interoperability: This entails the ability of two or more independent technology platforms or systems to share information or digital resources through common application interfaces.

M-Government: M-Government stands for mobile government i.e. the use of mobile technologies in delivering public services.

Public Services Culture: This describes the general work culture accepted in different public service delivery value chains.

Chapter 12
Stages of E-Government Maturity Models:
Emergence of E-Governance at the Grass Roots

Hakikur Rahman
University of Minho, Portugal

Isabel Ramos
University of Minho, Portugal

ABSTRACT

E-Government and e-Governance are the two terms within the governance system that need to be attended through clarity, distinctness, and justification. No matter how the stages of the governance system evolve, where they have been applied, and in which stages they are at a present moment, these two prominently distinct elements of the governance systems are yet to be watched closely and minutely. After synthesizing existing e-Government maturity models and exploring relevant literature, this chapter proposes a new model that may guide e-Government implementation in a developing world context. It is expected that the proposed model would assist researchers, academics, and policy makers in establishing sustained e-Government model in emerging and developing economies.

INTRODUCTION

E-Government is now widely regarded as an essential element of the governance system to reform, modernization and improvement of the government (Foley and Ghani, 2005; OECD,

2007). It has been characterized by the utilization of information and communication technologies (ICTs), and particularly the Internet, as a tool to achieve better government (OECD, 2003). However, the real costs of and benefits of e-Government have rarely been thoroughly and systematically evaluated. One may notice that during the 'dot. com' boom, e-Government has enjoyed a healthy

DOI: 10.4018/978-1-4666-4900-2.ch012

level of political and financial support across the world, and ICTs and e-Government were largely seen as key tools for modernizing public administrations and providing better government. It has been observed that, in many countries, despite many years of initiatives and efforts, the stage of maturity in e-Government is likely to require further investment in terms of the development of services and systems whose benefits often seem less readily apparent to politicians and policy makers, and to the public. This means that vigorous evaluation and monitoring of the costs and benefits of e-Government needs to be incorporated into e-Government planning and investment. This is commonly referred to be the need of the moment for the deployment of the e-Government, and must be supported by a strong business case in terms of availing financial aspects and sustainability. Without this, e-Government implementers find it increasingly difficult to obtain support for making the investments required to enable them to achieve the objectives that governments set for them. This chapter looks at some aspects of maturity in e-Government models across the world following an exploratory review (OECD, 2007)

Information and communication technologies (ICTs) serve as a mean to connect within and across government, businesses, communities, and individuals; to handle complex business processes; and facilitate effective communication, interaction and innovation, for improving efficiency, transparency, responsiveness, competitiveness, and empowerment. Because of these benefits, ICTs have been applied to and integrated with a wide range of human development activities (ADB, 2009). However, studies indicate that countries vary enormously in their overall e-Government performance across the regions. West (2008) observes that, in terms of technology utilization, the United States has fallen behind countries, such as South Korea and Taiwan. In their study, they find that the most highly ranked e-Government nations are South Korea, Taiwan, the United States, Singapore, Canada, Australia, Germany,

Ireland, Dominica, Brazil and Malaysia, while countries such as Tuvalu, Mauritania, Guinea, Congo, Comoros, Macedonia, Kiribati, Samoa and Tanzania barely have a web presence.

E-Government is meant to serve various customers, each with differing service needs. In the early days of inception of the e-Government, an international information technology consulting firm, Gartner, Inc., presented its concept of e-Government at a conference sponsored by the State of Wisconsin for state and local government officials in June 2001. This firm presented the development and use of e-Government in four phases, such as developing an Internet presence; providing interaction between local government and the public by e-mail and information; allowing individuals to conduct business with the local government; and re-engineering of a local government's business practices because of increased use and functions of e-Government (Thieme, 2001). Evidently, this concept has become a benchmark of e-Government initialization in many countries.

E-Government offers the prospective to bring citizens closer to their governments. Regardless of the type of political system that a country has, the population at large benefits from interactive features of the e-Government system that facilitates communication between citizens and government (West, 2008, and an effective e-Governance provide an efficient solution for most of the problems in many government and public sectors (Monga, 2008). This study thus further discusses about various features of e-Government in terms of its benefits and emergence of e-Governance at the grass roots; discusses about various stages of e-Government maturity models as developed by researchers, agencies and various institutions; synthesizes various maturity models of e-Government; and proposes a newly established framework. However, before going to the next section, to clarify the concept of e-Government and e-Governance, a few basic points are being discussed next. The study is a lateral evaluation of available maturity models of e-Government carried out through a longitudinal literature review (Barker and Barker, 2012; Olbrich, 2012; Rahman, 2013), including extant and classic literatures and expected to contribute to e-Government research and development, especially in developing and emerging economies.

E-GOVERNMENT AND E-GOVERNANCE

Before going to further exploration, one may need to understand in detail about the format of the government and various forms of the governance system so that they are easily accessible to the people at large (by people at large, authors meant about the common people of the society). With the advent of ICTs, this has made it possible to reach almost all the stakeholders through various tools and techniques. Furthermore, utilizing effective methods, models and frameworks government around the world has implemented various forms of government models based on electronically depended communication tools, in a way popularly known as the electronic government or e-Government. Along this route of enhanced and effective governance, ICT dependency has increased the awareness, availability, and accessibility at the level of the end user, which can be seen as electronic governance or e-Governance. In this aspect, e-Government is heralded as the pioneering way forward for the public sector in both developed and developing countries. There are success cases around the globe on how this form of government leads to increased rates of development and allows for greater democracy, and how it can be successfully implemented in countries across the world (Krishna and Walshan, 2005; Bhatnagar, 2002).

In simple terms, e-Government has been seen as "the use of information technology to support government operations, engage citizens, and provide government services"[1] (Scholl, 2003: p. 2). Broadly defined, "e-Government can include

virtually all information and communication technology (ICT) platforms and applications in use by the public sector" (UN, 2002: p.8). Another definition of e-Government was presented by United Nation's website referring e-Government as the use of ICTs, such as Wide Area Networks, the Internet, and mobile computing, by government agencies (Almarabeh and AbuAli, 2010). While, OECD recorded e-Government as the use of ICTs, especially the Internet as a tool to accomplish better government (OECD, 2003: p. 23). According to the World Bank web site (2012),

E-Government refers to the use by government agencies of information technologies (such as Wide Area Networks, the Internet, and mobile computing) that have the ability to transform relations with citizens, businesses, and other arms of government. .. The resulting benefits can be less corruption, increased transparency, greater convenience, revenue growth, and/or cost reductions.[2]

Given the aforementioned definitions, it is apparent that e-Government is not simply the computerization of a government system, but leads to the maturity of technology-lead-policy to achieve high levels of improvement in various areas of government, thus transforming the nature of policies and politics, including the relations between governments and citizens (Dada, 2006).

Furthermore, following these definitions, one can refer e-Government as the delivery of national, state/regional or local government information and services via the web based Internet, or intranet, or other digital mediated means to citizens, businesses, civil societies, non-governmental agencies or other governmental agencies as a one-stop gateway. E-Government turns to facilitate the provision of providing relevant government information in electronic form in a timely manner; offer better service delivery with improved quality; empower the grass roots population of the society or people at large through ease of access to information without any bureaucracy or restriction; improve the productivity, efficiency and cost savings in doing business with suppliers and customers of government; improve the relationships among the stakeholders, and foremost actively participate in public policy, decision-making and democratic processes (Fang, 2002; Palvia & Sharma, 2006; Rahman, 2010; 2011) While definitions of e-Government may vary widely, but there is a common theme in terms of the utilization. E-Government entails utilization of ICTs, and especially the Internet, to improve the delivery of government services to its stakeholders, and thus enables citizens to act, interact and receive services from the federal, state, division, region, district or local governments twenty four hours a day, seven days a week.

Literatures outline more or less eight different potential types or models in an e-Government system that is useful to define scope of e-Government studies, such as interactions among Government-to-Citizen (G2C); Citizen-to-Government (C2G); Government-to-Business (G2B); Business-to-Government (B2G); Government-to-Government (G2G); Government-to-Nonprofit (G2N); Nonprofit-to-Government (N2G); and Government-to-Employee (G2E) (Fang, 2002). For sake of the progressive relationship among its stakeholders, these eight models may seem sufficient for the time being, but another emerging potential section of the society is teaming up, namely the civil society, and acting as advocate or enabler or catalyst in various government policies and legislations in relation to e-Government and thus e-Governance. They could be termed as Government-to-Civil Society (G2CS), and Civil Society-to-Government (CS2G) (Rahman, 2012).

On the other hand, E-Governance refers to how administrators, managers, supervisors and facilitators utilize ICTs and the Internet to execute their functions of supervising, planning, organizing, coordinating, supporting and staffing effectively (Palvia & Sharma, 2006). E-Governance, is seen as the 'electronic form of governance' that is utilizing ICTs at all the levels of the government and the public sectors and beyond, for the purpose of enhancing overall governance (Okot-Uma, 2000; Bedi, Singh & Srivastava, 2001; Holmes, 2001). According to Keohane and Nye (2000: p. 12),

Governance implies the processes and institutions, both formal and informal, that guide and restrain the collective activities of a group. Government is the subset that acts with authority and creates formal obligations. Governance need not necessarily be conducted exclusively by governments... Private firms, associations of firms, nongovernmental organizations (NGOs), and associations of NGOs all engage in it, often in association with governmental bodies, to create governance; sometimes without governmental authority.

Evidently, this definition suggests that e-Governance is not only limited to the public sector, but also implied to administer, manage, support, and facilitate policies and procedures in the private sector as well (Palvia & Sharma, 2006).

E-Governance in a broader term includes transformation of the government at various levels. Firstly, it involves the rigorous transformation of the businesses of the government (e-Government, as mentioned above). Secondly, it entails a transformation in the operational definitions of the principles upon which governance is founded, thus shifting towards increased participation, openness, transparency, and interaction (Schiavo-Ocampo & Sundaram, 2001). Thirdly, it incorporates a transformation in the interactions among government and its (internal and external) clients, classified as government-to-citizen (G2C), government-to-business (G2B), government to its internal employee clients (G2E), government to other government institutional clients (G2G), citizen-to-citizen (C2C), and other stakeholders (Csetenyi, 2000; Stiglitz, Orszag & Orszag, 2000; Heeks, 2001). Fourthly, it accelerates the interactions among its stakeholders through effective and interactive communication channels (Rahman, 2011). Finally, it involves a transformation of the society itself, through the emergence e-societies, made up of networks of relationships like citizen-to-citizen connections, as well as relations among NGOs and other agencies, built and sustained through utilization of electronic means for grass root e-Governance (Dinsdale, Chhabra & Rath-Wilson, 2002; Pablo & Pan, 2002; Rahman, 2011)

In terms of its applications, e-Governance comprises the utilization of ICTs to support public services, government administration, democratic processes, and relationships among citizens, civil society, the private sector, and the state. Developed over more than two decades of technology innovation and policy rejoinders, and progressing through various maturation stages, the evolution of e-Governance can be examined in terms of the following interrelated objectives, such as a policy framework, enhanced public services, high-quality and cost-effective government operations, citizen engagement in democratic processes, and administrative and institutional reform (Dawes, 2008). Moreover, included within the perception of e-Governance is another emerging conception, such as e-democracy, which deals with how the citizen interacts with the government and influence the legislative or public sector process. It strives to engage the citizen with governments and their legislatures through the use of the new ICTs. It is this new dynamic that is developing between the citizen and the government that concurrent researches explore, and evaluate what impact, if any, the new ICTs are having on the participation

of the grass roots communities in the government decision-making processes (Riley, 2003).

E-Governance differs from e-Government in many aspects. The latter constitutes the way public sector institutions use technology to apply public administration principles, conduct the business of the government, and enhance the delivery of its existing services (Okot-Uma, 2000). E-Governance is more than just a government website on the Internet. The strategic objective of e-Governance is to sustain and abridge governance for all parties; government, citizens and businesses. The utilization of ICTs can connect all three parties and support processes and activities. In other words, e-Governance is the electronic means to reinforce and stimulate good governance. Therefore, the objectives of e-Governance are analogous to the objectives of good governance. Good governance can be seen as an exercise of economic, political, and administrative authority to better administer affairs of a country at all levels (Basu, 2004).

In this aspect, an effective e-Governance system can be seen as the focus and centricity model, as shown in Table 1, where emphasis has been given towards achieving grass roots e-Governance.

However, one may have to understand that e-Government and e-Governance cannot be used interchangeably. Of the two, e-Government, for many may be seen as a narrower term, just by referring to the transformation of the businesses of a government (processes, operations, and transactions) driven primarily by ICTs. One may contest this argument, but authors feel that is not

Table 1. Focus and centricity model (adopted from Marche, 2003)

Centricity Dimension	Government/Governance Dimension	
	Quadrant-1 E-Government (administrative) Citizen-Centric	**Quadrant-2** E-Governance (policy, legislation and power) Citizen-Centric
	Quadrant-3 E-Government (administrative) Organization-Centric	**Quadrant-4** E-Governance (policy, legislation and power) Organization-Centric

the mere transformation of the traditional government to make it electronics form. Effective e-Governance require many other facets of the governance systems. Aiming towards an effective e-Governance, the transformation could be both external (through simplified, enhanced government-client interactions via online services, no longer limited to the traditional boundary of fixed office hours and physical office premises) and internal (through streamlined government administration processes for greater efficiency and effectiveness) (Backus, 2001; Dinsdale, Chhabra & Rath-Wilson, 2002). Therefore, a people oriented e-Governance needs to focus on a defined framework blending available means of interactions from the perspective of inside or outside approaches, which has been shown in Table 2.

From the above discussions, it is evident that e-Government and e-Governance have emerged as specialized subject of research and to achieve their effective success, much attention need to be taken at the national level in each country of their implementation. Ranging from mere transformation of the government processes, these paradigms

incorporate each and every aspect of a society, community and nation. While, e-Government applications vary from country to country, society to society and culture to culture, this chapter has tried to synthesize a few popular maturity models through an exploratory study.

CHRONOLOGY OF VARIOUS E-GOVERNMENT MODELS

Varying from technology, management, administration, policy, studies, researches, demands and services e-Government maturity models varies across continents, countries, and communities. A few of them are being discussed below in terms of their maturity and diversification.

Four Stages of Quirk Model (2000)

Quirk (2000) presented four staged model (Table 3) that is based on quantitative study of the characteristics of 20 local government web sites in Victorian council, UK. The model identifies

Table 2. Palvia and Sharma (2006) Framework for e-Government versus e-Governance (modified by authors)

		Focus	
		Outside	Inside
Type of Organization	Public sector- Government agencies	e-Government (extranet and Internet)	e-Governance (intranet)
	Private sector- SMEs, MNCs	Inter-organizational systems- (extranet and Internet)	e-Governance (intranet)
	Civil society- NGOs, other agencies	Intra-and-inter-organizational- (extranet and Internet)	e-Governance (intranet and Internet)

Table 3. Four stages of quirk model for local authorities

Stages	Activities
e-Services	Interface with customers
e-Commerce	Cash transactions
e-Management	Improved management of people
e-Democracy	Political dialogue with citizen and community

common features of web sites and provides some indication of the maturity levels of those studies websites. To investigate the content and level of maturity of different aspects of Victorian council web sites, a context matrix was developed and basic features like quality of basic information, email facilities and the ability to make a payment online were examined (Quirk, 2000; Shackleton, et al., 2005; Nawaz, et al., 2007).

Four Phases of Gartner Model (2000)

As an early leader, Gartner group (Baum & Maio, 2000) developed an e-Government maturity model to measure progress for e-Government initiatives and establish a road map to achieve the desired levels of constituency service. The study classifies e-Government into four distinct phases, as:

- **Web Presence:** This is the initial stage where government provides website content (mainly, static) with necessary information that the citizen can easily access.
- **Interaction:** This is the second stage where government provides website content (static and dynamic) with various capabilities like, search engines, downloading forms, email contact, and facilities for interactions between parties involved.
- **Transaction:** The transaction stage enables citizens (users) to initiate and complete transactions, like paying for license renewals online, paying taxes or fees, or submitting bids for procurement contracts. In effect, buyers (citizens) and sellers (government) can conduct complete on-line transactions at this stage.
- **Transformation:** This is the highest stage where all government operational processes are integrated, unified and customized, which is most closely aligned with the concept of governance that involves a reinvention of how government functions are conceived and organized (Al-Hashmi & Darem, 2008; Karokola & Yngström, 2009, Rahman, 2011).

West's Four Stage Model (2000)

As one of the earlier e-Government model, West (2000) proposed a four stage model considering the evolutionary approach of information technology and its applications towards a citizen centric e-Governance. The stages are:

- **Billboard:** This is the first stage where websites (with static content) are used for information display, such as basic information, reports and publications.
- **Partial Service Delivery:** At this second stage government starts to set services online for citizen to access and websites have more capabilities and functionalities, such as sorting and searching of information.
- **Full Integrated Service Delivery:** At this stage a one stop centre is created (online portal) with full integrated online services from where citizen can easily access government and agencies information.
- **Interactive Democracy with Public Outreach and Accountability:** This is the final stage of e-Government development where government website develops into a system wide political transformation with executable and integrated on-line services through customized service delivery (Tolbert and Mossberger, 2003; Karokola & Yngström, 2009; Kaisara & Shaun, 2009).

Deloitte and Touche's Six Stage Model (2001)

To promote grass roots e-Governance through sustained e-Government, Deloitte and Touch (2001) presents a six stage model. The stages are:

- **Information Publishing:** At this stage government sets up websites (static) for providing information to citizen through one-way communication.

- **Official-Two Way Transaction:** This is an advanced stage where information are transacted and exchanged between citizen and government.
- **Multipurpose Portal:** Government uses a single portal as a single entry point providing services to its departments, agencies and citizen.
- **Portal Personalization:** At this stage government provides with the opportunity to customize the portal based on the demand at the grass roots.
- **Clustering of Common Services:** This is the fifth stage where all government services and operational processes are clustered along common lines to provide unified and seamless services.
- **Full Integration and Enterprise Transaction:** This is the final stage where government changes its structure and provides more sophisticated, integrated and personalized services (Siau & Long, 2004; Zhou & Hu, 2008; Karokola & Yngström, 2009).

Hiller and Blanger's Five Stage Model (2001)

Considering political dynamics and following Gartner's model, Hiller and Blanger (2001) proposed a model with five stages, as:

- **Information Dissemination:** This is the initial stage of the government to disseminate information to the citizen by posting it on the website (static) through a one-way communication.
- **Two-Way Communication:** Similar to other models, such as Chandler and Emanuel (2002), at this stage government uses enhanced websites with various capabilities, like emails and downloadable forms to interact with citizen.

- **Service and Financial Transaction:** This is the stage where government offers online services including financial transaction to citizen.
- **Vertical and Horizontal Integration:** At this fourth stage government integrates various systems at various levels vertically and horizontally.
- **Political Participation:** As an important and essential stage, here government involves citizen in political participation and other activities, like online voting and discussion forums. (Moon, 2002; Karokola & Yngström, 2009).

Howard's Three Stage Model (2001)

Similar to other models, Howard (2001) developed a three stage one, such as:

- **Publishing:** As the initial stage of e-Government development where information about activities of government is made available online.
- **Interacting:** At this stage citizens have the ability to do simple interactions with governments through chat rooms, and/or filling and sending forms, or sending e-mail.
- **Transacting:** In this model, this is the highest stage of e-Government development where citizens are able to conduct online transactions, such as purchasing / paying for licenses and permits (Karokola & Yngström, 2009; El-Qawasmeh, 2011).

Layne & Lee's Four Stage Model (2001)

Layne and Lee (2001) provided a four stage e-Government development model and propose a 'stages of growth' version to assist public administrators and other involved organizations for a fully functional e-Government. These are:

- **Cataloguing:** The first stage has been termed as cataloguing, where initial efforts of state governments are focused on establishing an on-line presence of the government.
- **Transaction:** In the second stage, e-Government initiatives should focus on connecting the internal government system to on-line interfaces and allowing citizens to transact with government electronically. In this stage, users are actively interactive through those interfaces.
- **Vertical Integration:** Vertical integration refers to local, district, state, regional and federal governments connected for different functions or services of government through integration of concerned departments. This stage provides the possibility of linking to web sites related to the system´s complete functionality at different levels, such as municipal, provincial, national and international.
- **Horizontal Integration:** This stage focuses on systems integration among all levels and functionalities for providing a unified and seamless service. The vertical integration across different levels within similar functionality is posited to precede the horizontal integration across various functions (Al-Hashmi & Darem, 2008; Karokola & Yngström, 2009; Rahman, 2011).

Wescott's Six Stage Model (2001)

With a view of sustained e-Government program in the Asia Pacific region, Wescott (2001) proposed a six stage e-Government model. These are:

- **Setting up an email system and internal network:** This is the initial stage where government focuses on providing basic administration functions, like email and electronically available payroll.

- **Enabling inter-organizational and public access to information:** This is the second stage where government assists in managing workflow from paper based to electronic form, and provides access to citizen through Internet.
- **Allowing 2-way communication:** At this stage government encourages citizen to establish a two-way communication by publishing telephone numbers, fax numbers, email addresses through web sites and citizen are able to interact with the government.
- **Allowing exchange of value:** This is the fourth stage where government allows citizen to conduct business with the government through online services, like making tax assessment, visa application, or renewal of license in more flexible and convenient ways.
- **Digital democracy:** By taking one step ahead, this stage enables citizen to take part in the democratization of the government system through empowerment and participation in the policy making processes.
- **Joined-up government:** This is the final stage where a one-stop web portal provides seamless services by integrating all the departments and agencies needed for a particular service through both vertical and horizontal integration (Wescott, 2001a; 2001b; Karokola & Yngström, 2009).

United Nation's Five Stage Model (2001)

In 2001, United Nations Division for Public Economics and Public Administration initiated a series of reports, "Benchmarking E-Government: A Global Perspective, Assessing the Progress of the UN Member States" (this was the first one and later on they are transformed into benchmarking of e-Government readiness), which identifies five stages for quantifying progress of e- government in a country. Those stages are:

- **Emerging web presence:** This is the initial stage where government web sites provide mostly basic and limited static information.
- **Enhanced web presence:** This is the second stage where government web sites provide frequently updated static content as per the requirement of the citizen that are reflected to the dynamic nature of the web sites, where features like search facilities, on-line help, and site-maps are included.
- **Interactive web presence:** In addition to the dynamic nature of the web site, users are able to download forms, interact respective officials through emails or feedback forms, able to make appointments and requests. solve problems either virtually or physically faster than before.
- **Transactional web presence:** In this stage a two-way communication channel is being established to initiate, and complete on-line transactions depending on the services.
- **Seamless/Networked web presence:** This is the final and the most sophisticated stage of e-Government service delivery, where all services and functions of all government levels are integrated and citizens can easily access any kind of services or facilities from any place and at any time (Szeremeta, 2002; UN, 2002; Al-Hashmi & Darem, 2008; Karokola & Yngström, 2009, Rahman, 2011).

Chandler and Emanuel's Four Stage Model (2002)

Chandler and Emanuel (2002) developed a four stage model. They are similar to the Gartner´s

model, however, for sake of illustration, the stages are being described below:

- **Information:** This is a preliminary stage where most of government services delivery is made available on-line, and citizen can access government information over a website (static) through a one-way communication between government and citizen.
- **Interaction:** This is the advanced stage of the first one where simple interaction between citizens and governments occur through various website features and functionalities, such as search, and emails through a two-way communication.
- **Transaction:** This is the third stage that enables transactions between citizen and government to complete various services, like paying taxes, or submitting forms on-line.
- **Integration:** This is the final stage where vertical and horizontal integration (Gartner´s model) of services across government and relevant agencies occurs, and citizen can access information on-line from a one stop service centre. (Irani et al., 2006; Al-Hashmi & Darem, 2008; Aykut, 2008)

Moon's Five Stage Model (2002)

Similar to Hiller and Blanger (2001), Moon (2002) developed a five stage model, namely One-way communication, Two-way communication, Transformation, Vertical and horizontal integration, and Political participation. Apart from the first stage, which they termed as One-way communication where government disseminates information to the citizen by posting on the website, other four stages are largely similar to the five stage model of Hiller and Blanger (2001) (Nygren, 2009; Karokola & Yngström, 2009).

Three Phases of World Bank Model (2002)

To assist policymakers in devising their own plans and initiatives, Center for Democracy and Technology (2002) incorporates a three phase e-Government model. These phases are not dependent on each other, nor need one phase be completed before another commences, but conceptually they offer three ways of thinking about the goals of e-Government. These phases are:

- **Publishing:** This is the first stage where government disseminates information about government to reach as wide an audience as possible by serving as the leading edge of e-Government.
- **Interactivity:** At this stage government interacts with citizen through two-way communications, starting with basic functions like email contact information for government officials or feedback forms allowing users to submit comments on legislative or policy proposals.
- **Transaction:** This is the final stage of e-Government development where citizens are allowed to obtain government services or transact business with the government online. A transact website offers a direct link to available government services, available at any time (World Bank 2001; 2003; Al-Hashmi & Darem, 2008; Karokola & Yngström, 2009; Rahman, 2011; Kowalski & Yngstrom, 2011).

IBM's Four Phase Model (2003)

E-Government transformations have to be flexible, adaptable, and outcome-focused so that citizens can be inclusive in the learning and at the same time, governments can develop on demand capabilities. On demand environment requires an open and scalable infrastructure, new technologies, and appropriate and targeted implementations of reengineered processes (IBM Business Consulting Services, 2003). As per IBM's study, the overall e-Government evolution has been divided into four stages. These are:

- **Automation:** In this initial phase the focus is on citizens and relatively straightforward web presence.
- **Enhancement:** Governments do not have to make many changes to existing applications or policies but requires the stage of enhancement.
- **Integration:** This phase is relatively complex and requires serious planning in transformation of business processes and integration.
- **On demand:** Transformation towards this phase incorporates three paths: business model transformation, infrastructure transformation, as well as cultural transformation (Al-Hashmi & Darem, 2008; Rahman, 2011).

SYNTHESIS OF THE STAGES OF E-GOVERNMENT MODELS

Most of the discussed models include access to information, interaction, transaction and integration, which are being synthesized in Table 4. But, majority of them at that timeline (or time period) did not incorporate the participation of the people at large (effectual participation of the common people of the society or community) in the government decision making processes, which is an essential aspect of e-Government model to improve the grass roots e-Governance. Unless the people has voice and active participation in the nation building processes, the government system remains out of reach to the common people of the society or community, and at the same time the citizens need to be empowered through these tools and utilities. However, most of these studied models are found to be static and do not include the evolving information dynamics and its utilization in various stages of governance around the globe. Furthermore, Quirk´s (2000) model directs the four stage maturity model towards e-services, e-management, e-commerce and e-democracy at the very inception period of e-Government concept across the world. West´s (2000) five stage model also includes interactive democracy with public outreach and accountability as the final stage of his e-Government model. Also, apart from the four commonly adopted stages, Hiller and Blanger (2001) emphasize on political participation of citizen as an important and essential stage of grass roots e-Governance. In addition to these, Wescott´s (2001) six stage model highlighted setting up of the infrastructure and digital democracy, which are yet very fundamental to many developing nations, where e-Government models are in transitional stage. Similarly, Deloitte and Touche´s (2001) six stage model emphasizes on customized multipurpose portals in their third and fourth stages of e-Government model. Finally, IBM´s (2003) model highlighted ´On demand´ nature of e-Government model, which is important for people´s participation.

Proposed Model (Namely, Rahman's Six Stage Model, 2011)

Majority of the maturity models have been developed during the early years of e-Government inception, but the revolutionary ideas and contexts made them to be followed in many countries around the world. Majority of the countries in the developed and emerging economies are gaining the benefits of e-Government, and having better e-Governance. However, a few countries from the developing world are yet to gain the momentum and reap the benefits out of e-Government systems. This research, proposes a six stage model deducting from studies models. The stages are:

- **Awareness raising and strategy development:** Firstly, despite e-Government and e-Governance being talked in many platforms through the years, but this researcher has observed that in developing countries, especially in South Asia and Africa, awareness among the common population is not sufficiently supported by this sort of national effort. For this reason, participation of people at large is not satisfactory. Secondly, logistic support is meager due to

Table 4. Various stages of the studied models

Stages with Activities:	Models Developed by:
Easy access to relevant information and free flow of information	Gartner, 2000; West, 2000; UN, 2001; Howard, 2001; Deloitte and Touche, 2001; Layne and Lee, 2001; Hiller and Blanger, 2001; Wescott, 2001; World Bank, 2002; Chandler and Emanuel, 2002; Moon, 2002; IBM, 2003
Interaction with citizen without any bureaucracy	Gartner, 2000; West, 2000; UN, 2001; Howard, 2001; Deloitte and Touche, 2001; Layne and Lee, 2001; Hiller and Blanger, 2001; Wescott, 2001; World Bank, 2002; Chandler and Emanuel, 2002; Moon, 2002
Transaction with citizen with trust, responsiveness and security	Gartner, 2000; West, 2000; UN, 2001; Deloitte and Touche, 2001; Layne and Lee, 2001; Hiller and Blanger, 2001; Chandler and Emanuel, 2002; Moon, 2002
Integration of all government department and agencies for a one stop service	Gartner, 2000; West, 2000; UN, 2001; Deloitte and Touche, 2001; Layne and Lee, 2001; Hiller and Blanger, 2001; Chandler and Emanuel, 2002; Moon, 2002

the nature of the social discrepancies, perhaps food, shelter, education (though they are the basic component of governance) take major share of the budget, Thirdly, lack of appropriate strategies make them as failed project, including lack of proficient personnel, sustained support from the higher authority, and transparency. Finally, all these cause abrupt, or constricted flow of finance at the appropriate stage at the appropriate time;

- **Web presence and technology management:** In terms of e-Governance at the grass roots, especially in developing countries, infrastructure is one of the main elements that has been ignored by policy makers or professionals behind this sort of projects. It is obvious that mobile technologies have enhanced the infrastructure in many countries, but lack of applications and technology management, web presence is not seen at the local level of the population. Furthermore, the web presence needs to be understood by all, which demand that the web sites should be bilingual (English and the local national language);

- **Web interaction and transparent management:** With bilingual web sites the interactivity will certainly increase, however, effort should be given for cost reduction, not at the end of the supplier (the government), but also at the end of receiver (the citizen). Transparent management can enhance this situation. Somehow, population at large has to be taken under this platform gaining their confidence on trust, transparency and cost;

- **Transaction through Portal and legal issue implementation:** Even in developed world, many of the citizens would not feel comfortable in presenting private information through the web or the Internet. This could be due to awareness about the security, or legal issue, or understanding about

the nature of transaction, especially when they involve finance. These issues need to be clarified among the stakeholders, making them also bilingual citizens involvement could be enhanced further. Further, appropriate legal issues need to be taken and to be made clear at the local level of the population;

- **Dynamic transformation of Portal and demand driven expansion:** E-Government, or e-Governance in a country where it is running successfully for many years cannot be replicated in another country just by replicating the model. The model needs to be customized as per the demand of the socio-economic and cultural aspects of the community or nation; and

- **Citizen´s participation and e-democracy:** Though it could be the final stage of these six stages, but nobody knows where the next revolution of the Internet stops, or when another evolution of the Internet begins. However, peoples´ participation in the national policy making processes are the ultimate aim of e-Governance, so that the population at large feel comfortable that they are not being bypassed, or ignored during their national building agendas. This way, the days will pass; more and more of the population will be attracted towards this form of electronically maintained governance initiatives.

FUTURE WORKS

By far there have not been much improvements among the mentioned maturity models that have been mentioned in this study. It may happen due to many reasons beyond the scope of this research. There may be a few that e-Government models could be stagnant in many countries, or reached at such a maturity level that further improvement is not distinctly visible, or may be due to the fact that many of the developing countries are still experimenting with the e-Government transformations, not by having the real benefits out of their implementations. This may happen due to lack of vision, awareness among the grass roots stakeholders, or limitations at the policy initiation level (Rahman, 2011). There are quite good number of studies that have been carried out periodically by the UNDP under their e-Government readiness reports, or e-Government readiness ranking. Future research may be carried out by utilizing the archived data from these reports (and other available reports) and carry out an empirical study on the implication e-Governance in the developing and emerging economies by focusing variour e-Government maturity models.

CONCLUSION

E-Governance is to be seen to be beyond the scope of e-Government. While e-Government is objected towards the delivery of government services and information to the citizen using electronic means, e-Governance allows citizens' direct participation of constituents in political activities going beyond government that includes e-democracy, e-voting, and active participation political of political activities. In broad sense, concept of e-Governance covers government, citizens' participation, political parties and civil societies in parliament and judiciary functions (Bhatnagar, 2004).

Furthermore, e-Government and e-Governance are independent of each other, but at times, or places many misses out the major distinction between e-Government and e-Governance.

This study has tried to evaluate various e-Government maturity levels that are available through this exploratory longitudinal literature review and thus has also tried to develop a new model, where emphasis has been to incorporate the common people of the community for whom the e-Governance is in reality has to be developed and by whom the system has to be utilized. Also, it has

been proposed that the model should be dynamic and adaptable to the demand at the grass roots.

Hence, the study concludes that in devising, designing, developing, administrating e-Government its evolution and maturity of various models need to be understood clearly. The study further concludes that not replicating conceptual models, e-Government models need to be customized according to the demand and evolution at the local level of the government. Finally, it concludes that peoples' active participation is a prerequisite to establish grass roots e-Governance, especially in developing economies.

REFERENCES

ADB. (2009). *Improving public services through information and communication technology (Technical Assistance Report)*. Asian Development Bank.

Almarabeh, T., & AbuAli, A. (2010). A general framework for e-government: Definition maturity challenges, opportunities, and success. *European Journal of Scientific Research, 39*(1), 29–42.

Aykut, A. (2008). Assessment of the Turkish local e-governments: An empirical study. *International Journal of Human Sciences*. Retrieved from http://ssrn.com/abstract=1259378

Backus, M. (2001). E-governance in developing countries`. *IICD Research Brief, 1*(1).

Barker, D. R., & Barker, L. L. (2012). Criteria for evaluating models of intrapersonal communication processes. In *Communication Yearbook 15*. London: Routledge.

Basu, S. (2004). E-government and developing countries: An overview. *International Review of Law Computers & Technology, 18*(1), 109–132. doi:10.1080/13600860410001674779

Bedi, K., Singh, P. J., & Srivastava, S. (2001). *Government net: New governance opportunities for India*. New Delhi: Sage.

Bhatnagar, S. (2002). Egovernment: Lessons from implementation in developing countries. *Regional Development Dialogue, 24*, 164–174.

Center for Democracy and Technology. (2002). *E-government handbook*. Washington, DC: World Bank.

Center for Technology in Government. (2012). *Definition of e-government*. Retrieved March 12, 2012 from http://www.ctg.albany.edu/publications/reports/future_of_egov?chapter=2

Chandler, S., & Emanuels, S. (2002). Transformation not automation. In *Proceedings of 2nd European Conference on EGovernment*. Academic Press.

Csetenyi, A. (2000). Electronic government: Perspectives from e-commerce. In *Proceedings of the 11th International Workshop on Database and Expert Systems Applications* (DEXA'00). IEEE Press.

Dada, D. (2006). The failure of e-government in developing countries: A literature review. *Electronic Journal of Information Systems in Developing Countries, 26*(7), 1–10.

Dawes, S. S. (2008, December). The evolution and continuing challenges of e-governance. *Public Administration Review*, 86–102. doi:10.1111/j.1540-6210.2008.00981.x

Deloitte & Touché. (2001). The citizen as customer. *CMA Management, 74*(10), 58.

Dinsdale, G., Chhabra, S., & Rath-Wilson, J. (2002). *A toolkit for e-government: Issues, impacts and insights*. Canadian Centre for Management Development.

El-Qawasmeh, E. (2011). Assessment of the Jordanian e-government: An empirical study. *Journal of Emerging Trends in Engineering and Applied Sciences, 2*(4), 594–600.

Fang, Z. (2002). E-government in digital era: Concept, practice, and development. *International Journal of the Computer, the Internet and Management, 10*(2), 1-22.

Foley, P., & Ghani, S. (2005). *The business case for e-government*. Paris: OECD.

Heeks, R. (2001). *Understanding e-governance for development*. Retrieved March 12, 2012 from http://www.sed.manchester.ac.uk/idpm/research/publications/wp/igovernment/igov_wp11.htm

Holmes, D. (2001). eGov: eBusiness strategies for government. London: Nicholas Brealey.

Howard, M. (2001). E-government across the globe: How will 'e' change government?. *Government Finance Review*, 6-9.

IBM Business Consulting Services. (2003). *How e-government are you? e-Government in France: State of play and perspectives*. Retrieved March 30, 2012 from http://www-07.ibm.com/services/pdf/bcs_egovernment.pdf

Irani, Z., Al-Sebie, M., & Elliman, T. (2006). Transaction stage of e-government systems: Identification of its location & importance. In *Proceedings of the 39th Hawaii International Conference on System Sciences*. IEEE.

Kaisara, G., & Pather, S. P. (2009). *E-government in South Africa: e-Service quality access and adoption factors. Informatics & Design Papers and Reports*. Cape Peninsula University of Technology.

Karokola, G., & Yngström, L. (2009). Discussing e-government maturity models for developing world – Security view. In *Proceedings of the 8th ISSA 2009 Conference on Information Security*. Johannesburg, South Africa: ISSA.

Keohane, R. O., & Nye, J. S. Jr. (2000). Introduction. In *Governance in a globalization world*. Washington, DC: Brookings Institution Press.

Kowalski, S., & Yngström, L. (2011). Secure e-government services: Towards a framework for integrating it security services into e-government maturity models. Information Security South Africa, 1-9.

Krishna, S., & Wlashan, G. (2005). Implementing public information systems in developing countries: Learning from a success story. *Information Technology for Development*, *11*(2), 123–140. doi:10.1002/itdj.20007

Layne, K., & Lee, J. (2001). Developing fully functional e-government: A four stage model. *Government Information Quarterly*, *18*, 122–136. doi:10.1016/S0740-624X(01)00066-1

Marche, S. (2003). E-government and e-governance: The future isn't what it used to be. *Canadian Journal of Administrative Sciences*, *20*(1), 74–86. doi:10.1111/j.1936-4490.2003.tb00306.x

Monga, A. (2008). E-government in India: Opportunities and challenges. *JOAAG*, *3*(2), 52–61.

Moon, J. M. (2002). The evolution of e-government among municipalities: Rhetoric or reality? *Public Administration Review*, *62*(4), 424–433. doi:10.1111/0033-3352.00196

Nawaz, M., Issa, M., & Hyder, S. I. (2007). e-Government services maturity models. In *Proceeding of the 2007 Computer Science and IT Education Conference*, (pp. 511- 519). IEEE.

Nygren, K. G. (2009). The rhetoric of e-government management and the reality of e-government work- the Swedish action plan for e-government considered. *International Journal of Public Information Systems*, *2*, 135–146.

OECD. (2003a). *Implementing e-government in OECD countries: Experiences and challenges*. Paris: OECD.

OECD. (2003b). *The e-government imperative*. Paris: OECD.

OECD. (2007). *Good governance for development (GfD) in Arab countries*. Paris: OECD.

Okot-Uma, R. W. O. (2000). *Electronic governance: Re-inventing good governance. Londo*. Commonwealth Secretariat.

Olbrich, S. (2012). Reflecting ten years of e-government: A plea for a multimethodological research agenda. In *Transformational government through egov practice: Socioeconomic, cultural, and technological issues*. London: Emerald.

Pablo, Z. D., & Pan, S. L. (2002). A multidisciplinary analysis of e-overnance: Why do we start? In *Proceedings of the 6th Pacific Conference on Information Systems* (PACIS 2002). Tokyo, Japan: PACIS.

Palvia, S. C. J., & Sharma, S. S. (2006). *E-government and e-governance: Definitions/domain framework and status around the world, foundations of e-government*. New Delhi: Computer Society of India.

Quirk, B. (2000). *From managing change to leading transformation*. Paper presented at the E-Government Summit. London, UK.

Rahman, H. (2010). *Developing successful ICT strategies: Competitive advantages in a global knowledge-driven society. Hershey, PA. USA*: Idea Group Inc.

Rahman, H. (2011). *e-Governance framework at the local government level: Empowerment of community people and improvement of e-governance at the grass roots*. (PhD Thesis). Empresarial University of Costa Rica, Costa Rica.

Rahman, H. (2012). Preface. In *Cases on progressions and challenges in ICT utilization for citizen-centric governance*. Hershey, PA: IGI Global.

Rahman, H. (2013). Data mining technologies to improve early warning systems in the Bay of Bengal: A Bangladesh perspective. In *Ethical data mining applications for socio-economic development*. Hershey, PA: IGI Global. doi:10.4018/978-1-4666-4078-8.ch004

Riley, C. G. (2003). *The changing role of the citizen in the e-governance & e-democracy equation*. Commonwealth Center for E-Governance.

Schiavo-Ocampo, S., & Sundaram, P. (2001). *To serve and preserve: Improving public administration in a competitive world*. Manila, Philippines: Asian Development Bank.

Scholl, H. J. (2003). E-government: A special case of ICT-enabled business process change. In *Proceedings of the 36th Hawaii International Conference on System Sciences* (HICSS'03). Waikoloa, HI: IEEE.

Shackleton, P., Fisher, J., & Dawson, L. (2005). *From dog licences to democracy: Local government approaches to e-service delivery in Australia*. Paper presented at the Thirteenth European Conference on Information Systems. Regensberg, Germany.

Siau, K., & Long, Y. (2004). A stage model for e-government implementation. In M. Khosrow-Pour (Ed.), *Innovations through information technology*. Hershey, PA: Idea Group Inc.

Stiglitz, J., Orszag, P., & Orszag, J. (2000). *The role of government in a digital age*. Retrieved March 12, 2012 from http://www.ccianet.org/digital_age/report.pdf

Szeremeta, J. (2002). *Benchmarking e-government: A global perspective*. Paper presented at the International Congress on Government Online 2002. Ottawa, Canada.

Thieme, J. (Ed.). (2001). *A best practices review: Local e-government services*. Madison, WI: Legislative Audit Bureau.

Tolbert, C., & Mossberger, K. (2003). The effects of e-government on trust and confidence in government. In *Proceedings of the 2003 Annual National Conference on Digital Government Research*. Digital Government Society of North America.

UN. (2002). *Benchmarking e-government: A global perspective - Assessing the UN member states*. New York: United Nations Division for Public Economics and Public Administration.

Veenstra, A. F. V., Bram, K., & Marijin, J. (2009). Barriers for transformation: Impediments for transforming the public sector through e-government. In *Proceedings of ECIS 2009*. ECIS.

Wescott, C. G. (2001a). e-Government in the Asia-Pacific region: Progress and challenges. *Systemics. Cybernetics and Informatics*, 3(6), 37–42.

Wescott, C. G. (2001b). *E-government in the Asia-Pacific region*. Asian Development Bank.

West, D. M. (2004). E-government and the transformation of service delivery and citizen attitudes. *Public Administration Review*, 64(1), 15–27. doi:10.1111/j.1540-6210.2004.00343.x

West, D. M. (2008). *Improving technology utilization in electronic government around the world, 2008*. Washington, DC: Government Studies at Brookings, The Brookings Institution.

World Bank. (2001). *Issue note: E-government and the World Bank*. Washington, DC: World Bank.

World Bank. (2003). *World development indicators*. Washington, DC: World Bank.

World Bank Web Site. (2012). *Full definition of e-government*. Retrieved March 12, 2012 from http://web.worldbank.org/WBSITE/EXTERNAL/TOPICS/EXTINFORMATIONANDCOMMUNICATIONANDTECHNOLOGIES/EXTEGOVERNMENT/0,contentMDK:20507153~menuPK:6226295~pagePK:210058~piPK:210062~theSitePK:702586~isCURL:Y,00.html

Zhou, Z., & Hu, C. (2008). Study on the e-government security risk management. *International Journal of Computer Science and Network Security*, *8*(5), 208–213.

ADDITIONAL READING

Markellos, K., Markellou, P., Panayiotaki, A., & Stergianeli, E. (2007). Current State of Greek e-Government Initiatives, *Journal of Business Systems. Governance and Ethics*, *2*(3), 67–88.

Marshall, G. W., & Stamps, M. B. (2005). Sales force use of technology: Antecedents to technology acceptance. *Journal of Business Research*, *58*, 1623–1631. doi:10.1016/j.jbusres.2004.07.010

Masrom, M. (2007). Technology Acceptance Model and E-learning, *12th International Conference on Education,* Sultan Hassanal Bolkiah Institute of Education, Brunei Darussalam, 21-24.

Mbeki, T. (2000). Keynote address of the President of the ANC to the National General Council. Available from www.anc.org.za/ancdocs/speeches (Accessed 15 December 2008).

McClure, D. L. (2000). Statement of David L McClure, US General Accounting Office, before the subcommittee on Government Management, Information and technology, committee on Government reform, House of Representatives. Retrieved March 12, 2012 from www.gao.gov.

Michel, H. (2005). E-Administration, e-Government, e-Governance and the Learning City: A typology of Citizenship management using ICTs, *The Electronic Journal of e-Government*, *3*(4), 213-218. Retrieved March 12, 2012 from www.ejeg.com.

Ochara-Muganda, N., & Van Belle, J. P. (2010). A Proposed Framework for E-Government Knowledge Infrastructures for Africa's Transition Economies, Journal of e-Government Studies and Best Practices, 9p. Retrieved March 12, 2011 from www.ibimapublishing.com/journals/JEGSBP/2010/ 303226/303226.pdf.

OECD. (2004). E-Transformation Turkey Project: Turkish Case for e-Government, OECD Meeting of Senior Officials from Centres of Government on Using New Tools for Decision-Making: Impacts on Information, Communication and Organisation, 7-8 October 2004, Istanbul, Turkey. Retrieved October 18, 2010 from unpan1.un.org/intradoc/groups/public/documents/UNPAN/UNPAN025638.pdf.

OECD. (2007). *Table E-9. Volume of electronic commerce. OECD Science, Technology and Industry Scoreboard 2007*. OECD.

KEY TERMS AND DEFINITIONS

Developing Economy: Also called Less-Developed-Country (LCD), a developing country has low living standards, underdeveloped industrial base and low Human Development Index (HDI).

E-Governance: The operationalization of ICTs in enforcing government's mandate at various stages of the governance hierarchy.

E-Government: The use of ICTs in the government's business value chains with a goal achieving efficient and effective public service delivery.

Emerging Economy: Unlike developing countries, emerging economies have active social or business activities and are in the process of rapid growth and industrialization.

Grass Roots E-Governance: Entails governance inititiatives at the community levels of the socio-economic hierarchy.

Maturity Model: is a representation of the different stages that e-Government follows through on its growth path.

ENDNOTES

[1] http://www.ctg.albany.edu/publications/reports/future_of_egov?chapter=2. Retrieved April 28, 2013.

[2] http://web.worldbank.org/WBSITE/EXTERNAL/TOPICS/EXTINFORMATIONANDCOMMUNICATIONANDTECHNOLOGIES/EXTEGOVERNMENT/0,,contentMDK:20507153~menuPK:702592~pagePK:148956~piPK:216618~theSitePK:702586,00.html. Retrieved April 28, 2013

Chapter 13
M–Governance:
Use of Technology in Water Service Delivery in Kenya

Hilda Moraa
iHub Research, Kenya

Anne Salim
iHub Research, Kenya

Albert Otieno
iHub Research, Kenya

ABSTRACT

iHub Research conducted a study on 896 citizens to establish whether citizens raise alarm when faced with problems related to water. The study aimed to ascertain the communication channels they use to forward complaints to relevant authorities and the level of satisfaction obtained by the citizens after their complaints have been received. The study found that 68% of the respondents had faced challenges while trying to access their main source of water and were not able to complain to anyone about the problems affecting them due to inexistence of appropriate communication channels. A lack of understanding with regards to whom or where to complain was cited as one of the major reasons as to why most respondents do not complain about the water service levels. Majority of the citizens interviewed use face-to-face communication to raise their water grievances. Levels of satisfaction were found to vary when it comes to rating the action taken on water complaints raised. This study opines that with the emergence of Information and Communication Technologies (ICTs) this scenario is poised to change. The study participants revealed that they are motivated to utilise ICTs to air their complaints with regards to their levels of service satisfaction. Emerging ICT applications, especially those accessible on mobile devices, provide a lot of promise for enhancing water service delivery in Kenya because feedback on water/service quality can be received ubiquitously.

DOI: 10.4018/978-1-4666-4900-2.ch013

INTRODUCTION

Poverty is one of the many problems faced by many developing countries. It is a stumbling block to the development of any economy in the world, Kenya inclusive. The Government of Kenya (GoK) has been undertaking a series of reforms aimed at enhancing quality, efficiency and transparency in service delivery by public sector institutions in an effort to alleviate poverty. There are opportunities through Kenya's current Development Framework, Millennium Development Goals (MDGs) and Vision 2030, which aims at transforming Kenya into a newly industrialized middle-income country providing a high quality life to all its citizens by the year 2030. The elimination of poverty is pegged on improved access to water supply and appropriate sanitation whose achievement is hinged on good governance, accountability, feedback, action and transparency. Since poverty is a multi-dimensional phenomenon, it is assumed that reducing or eliminating it should also employ a multi-dimensional approach. Therefore, in addition to the poverty-reduction-strategies being implemented by the GoK, the use of ICTs in public service delivery channels shows a pronounced positive promise.

iHub Research conducted a study covering urban and rural areas of the three counties (Kiambu, Migori, and Makueni) in Kenya. The methodology used to conduct this study involved literature review, development of study framework tools, mapping, field data collection and analysis. In-depth interviews were conducted with a total of 896 people and key informant discussions with 9 stakeholders in the water sector in the three counties in Kenya. The main objective of the study was to explore Use of Technology (herein ICTs) in escalating citizen complains and satisfaction in water service delivery. This was achieved by understanding: if citizens raise their water issues, who and where they complain to, whether they receive any feedback or action after complaining and if they were satisfied with the service they received. Citizens were also asked if they were aware of some mobile technology tools that have been created to enable them communicate with water service providers and government as well.

This chapter intends to highlight the challenges faced in effecting a quality water service delivery in Kenya and thereafter outline the prospects of utilising ICTs with a view to provide a participatory service. The chapter looks at mobile applications which are being implemented in Kenya in the realm of m-Government (The use of mobile ICTs to improve public service delivery). It can be seen from this chapter that there are a lot of prospects brought about by the emerging mobile technology platforms. In the water sector, citizens may be accorded an opprotunity to engage with the water service providers in a bit to improve the overall service delivery.

The chapter is arranged as follows: the next section presents the background which outlines the general conceptualisation of ICT usage in the water sector and outlines prospects brought about by the emerging technologies. Thereafter, the study context and findings are outlined and presented. The chapter then presents the recommendations (which are not recommendations per se but pointers which may aid effective mainstreaming of ICTs, among other things, towards an improved water service delivery framework). After that, a future research section is presented outlining the future works both from the research and practical perspective. The last section is the conclusion which provides a recap of what has been discussed in this chapter.

Background

Effective water governance goes beyond ensuring that policies and institutions are in place and rather captures issues of access to resources, information and affordable technology while participating in the decision making process that affects the management and effectiveness of service provision (UNDP, 2007). Water governance entails the upholding of policies, strategies and legislation where water service providers have to develop and manage water resources in an effective and efficient manner while being accountable to the recipients of the water services (Ibid). This ultimately means that for governance in the water sector to work in a mutually beneficial way, citizens need to be aware of their rights, and also need to be accorded a mechanism where they can communicate and complain when they feel that their rights are not being fully met.

Kenya is limited by a renewable fresh water supply of only 647 cubic meters per capita and is classified as a water scarce country (Momanyi & Lee, 2005 & MOW Strategic Plan, 2009). The country therefore faces serious challenges with regards to protection of water resources and provision of water supply and sanitation services. More so, quality service delivery and accountability in ensuring democratic governance becomes harder to achieve.

Water supply and service delivery in Kenya is largely affected by lack of integrity and low performance of water utilities and informal water service providers. The urban and rural poor often have no way to advocate for their basic needs for water and sanitation because their problems are invisible to higher levels of planning and policymaking. Funders together with Water, Sanitation and Hygiene (WASH) Non-Governmental Organizations (NGOs) often do not have the resources to track continued functioning of their projects once they are built and handed over to communities. Water utilities and governments often lack information on the specific needs of the populations they serve, and are not held accountable for planning and budgeting decisions. This could be due to the lack of information on the state of water resources—both in terms of water quantity and quality. In the absence of a "single water manager," there is no one place for information to be collected or shared in ways that can promote better management of water supply and over-extraction results (mWASH, 2012).

Kenya is in the verge of promoting a cleaner government through e-Government. According to a study conducted by university of Nairobi school of computing and informatics, *'E-Government in Kenya: A Conceptual Framework to Increase Public Participation'* showed that **GoK** has been making significant attempts to make its services and information on the Internet available to all citizens. In the past, the government relied on traditional ways in storing, communicating and distribution of information. Now, the trends have changed and the GoK has also invested heavily in initiatives to foster and make public government data accessible and transparent to the people of Kenya. Moreover, the Government has worked to improve public resources, accountability and public participation in the areas of sensitive issues such as water and sanitation. The information on water on the open government site (https://opendata.go.ke/) includes: reports largely on sanitation by District and census on households. The available information is not the most updated as the most recent data sets are for 2009. In an interview conducted to the Information and Communication Permanent Secretary, *Dr. Bitange Ndemo* told the *Sunday Nation* that the ministry was getting frustrated because of the low amount of data supplied by organizations. "There is no reason at all why anyone should hold on to information and claim to own it. Even university research papers should be dispatched as public information to help improve lives of Kenyans and aid planning. This will also improve performance of the open learning initiative," said Dr Ndemo.

The water information available for citizens is dependent on the organization providing the service. Most of the water information available is on websites owned by parastatals of the government of Kenya, or private water companies. The biggest concern has been has been whether the available information is sufficient to promote transparency to citizens and other stakeholders concerned in accessing the water information to make decisions.

These are still low amounts of data in the different governance thematic areas, water inclusive. Most of the ministries are still in the process of digitizing their information. This has accounted for the low supply of information to governmental portals accessible by citizens. There is, therefore, need to explore more on transparent instruments and tools to allow citizens both in urban and rural areas to view actionable data in the water sector. Appropriate ICTs come in handy regarding the disseminatiion and capture of water services information. This is further compounded with the emerging Internet-enabled mobile phones / technology platforms on the African market which can allow ubiquitous access and usage. The use of ICTs will ensure there are equal opportunities for citizens from both rural and urban areas to exercise their right of equal access to water-related information.

Education is key in helping citizens understand and become aware of where they can access information. Shockingly, of the average 74% (N=532) of respondents who said they have no access to any kind of water information, 76 of the respondents also have no access to formal education. The same trend was observed with respondents who have primary education with correspondingly higher inaccessibility rates compared to the ones who had post primary education.

Public education and awareness remains an important milestone towards promoting transparency and openness of public information in order to eliminate the myriad digital divide implications and create a socio-economic well being through reliable, available and actionable information.

It cannot be denied that ICTs are pegged to enhance access to information on water and related issues. Reports written by different Non-Governmental Organisations (NGOs) and Civil Society Organisations (CSOs) indicate that several software applications (mobile, Web, stand-alone) have been developed to solve water issues (mWASH, April 2012). Collecting, aggregating, and analyzing data from remote regions and making the data

available in a transparent way can help identify where investments are most urgently needed and can improve the long-term project monitoring.

There are a few mobile technologies that are being used in the water sector to solve some water issues. Some of the applications developed are designed to receive complaints from Citizens and present them to the relevant authorities. Others are used to create awareness of where water can be located or if the water is safe for consumption. Such applications, in the context of Kenya, include Huduma, Mmaji, MajiVoice, mWater among others. Although these applications exist, majority of the citizens interviewed were not aware of them (Moraa et al, 2012).

Ensuring transparent information for citizens to interact with will then allow them to engage actively in local decision and policy making. The success of the Kenyan efforts for e-Government (and/or m-Government) depends to a great extent; on how well the targeted users i.e. the citizens in general make use of the services and information. Therefore, it is important that local governments seek new and interesting ways to engage their citizens.

STUDY SETUP AND EMPIRICAL RESULTS

The Kenyan government, just like many other governments in the world, has paid considerable attention to the use of ICTS as a means of improving the delivery of public services. Enhanced communication capability provides the prospect of distance-independent delivery of service, and particularly the capacity to improve the delivery to rural and remote locations.

In Kenya, water is a problem that cuts across both rural and urban dwellers and that the problems are not limited to water supply and sanitation services (USAID 2010). Research conducted by Huduma in Langata and Embakasi constituencies showed that the majority of people demanded rights on water-related issues. Water issues are worsened when citizens have no clue where to get information and the people they should approach to solve their problems.

The iHub Research study sought to establish whether citizens raise alarm when they are faced with problems related to water, the communication channels they use to put up their complaints, and the satisfaction level citizens get out of the attention accorded to them. This section therefore seeks to answer questions on access to water information, how the citizens went about their water issues, feedback mechanism and the level of satisfaction they got and why other citizens never complained when faced with problems related to water.

Access to Water Information

Access to water information is still a huge gap faced by citizens. Only an average of 26% of the interviewed citizens (N=896) have access to water information leaving an average of 74% with no access to any kind of water information. Out of the population with no access to any kind of water information, 73% are from the rural areas, mostly in Makueni County, followed by Kiambu, then Migori. Despite the fact that Kiambu has more developed constituencies, it is still faced with high rates of inaccessibility to water information.

The study points to an indication that literacy levels dictate the kind of information currently accessed by the citizens. The study participants who have no formal education had access to other kinds of water information that included water treatment, preservation, conservation and water related diseases. On the other hand, citizens with a primary (O level) education had access to information on water availability updates, which was accessible through informal groups such as water vendors. The respondents with more than primary level of education had more access to variety of water information via e-Government platforms such as government websites. Sadly, on 12% of the citizens in rural areas had access to water price information and 3% raised complains

raised on water issues. It is the mandate of the water service providers (WSPs) to ensure tariff schedule is accessible to citizens. WSPs should maintain affordable tariffs in order to maximize efficiencies in the provision of water services and the satisfaction and safety of water consumers by acting as agents to escalating their complaints to higher boards such as Water Services Regulatory Board (WASREB).

Only 5% of the citizens mentioned that they had received invitations to give opinions by participating in decision-making process on water issues in their area. Another 2% from the rural area did not know what kind of information they had ever accessed. This can be explained due to ignorance traits portrayed by some of the household members.

Other information like water news, water related diseases, water charges/bills and where to raise water complains were equally expressed as important information that both the rural and urban respondents desired to be informed about. 10% of respondents did not want to be informed on any water information and 1% did not know what they wanted to be informed about. This can be attributed to the fact that they were ignorant or had low literacy levels hence did not bother whether the information was available or not.

Citizens' Complaints

Out of the total number of respondents, of the 68% who had faced challenges while trying to access their main source of water, only 39% said that they have complained about their problems (Figure 1). Majority (46%) of the people complaining were coming from the urban areas. 97% of the urban folks had attained post primary education while 91% of the rural folks had at least post primary education. This, therefore, confirms that while education may influence responsiveness in raising alarm, the impact is not much. The responsiveness could as well be triggered by among other factors campaign awareness and quick access to information in the urban areas.

Figure 1. Did household complain based on counties

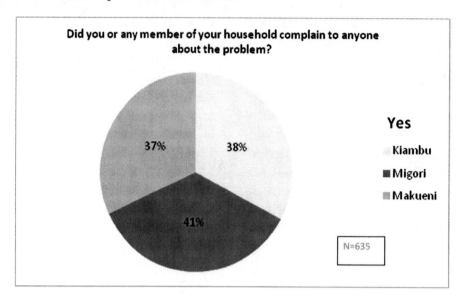

A total of 68% of the respondents had faced challenges while trying to access water and never complained to any one of the problems affecting them. The study affirmatively learned that the lack of idea on whom or where to complain was the major reason as to why most respondents did not complain. A further 61% did not know who or where to complain and majorities were from the rural area (urban, 57% and rural 62%). It was also observed that 1% complained that the people to complain to are too far away.

In terms of counties, Makueni County topped the list with highest number (78%) of respondents (N=305) unaware of where/who to complain to when faced with water related challenges. If the respondents knew where or rather who to complain to then they would not hesitate to raise alarm when faced with the challenges in trying to access water. "I can complain if I know to whom I should address the complaint to," stated one respondent.

15% of the respondents who never complained cited reluctance on the part of the authorities to act on the complaints from the citizens. They felt that it is needless to complain since no one listens to their pleas, "Complaining is like wasting time

because nobody is bothered about the complaints", said one middle aged man from Kiambu county.

There is a feeling among the citizens that only those who have money are entitled to complain. 10% of the respondents stated lack of ability or courage to face the authority as the reason for not complaining; "I am poor, I cannot complain", posed one respondent. He went further and said that even if he complains, no one would listen to him. Others (especially those who lived in rental houses) felt that it is not their mandate to complain, but rather the responsibility of the landlord/landlady. At times, it is the landlord/landlady who rations the water and if the tenants complain they risk being ejected from their rentals.

Time is another crucial factor: 2% had to suffer in silence since they could not get time to go to the authorities in charge to put across their complaints. Many of whom are either held up at work or businesses until late hours when the offices are closed.

It is said that necessity is the mother of invention. The necessity to overcome some of the water problems affecting the citizens has prompted a number of citizens to come up with other alternatives. 9% of the respondents did not complain when faced with problems simply because they had invented other alternatives. For instance, water rationing and constant water shortages have led some citizens to digging wells and boreholes that would help them have water all the time without being controlled.

At the same time, 2% of the respondents said that they were used to the problem and saw no need to complain. It is either they had accepted the problem to be part of them or felt that no amount of effort can help change the situation. "I don't think it can be solved, it is a natural disaster", said a middle-aged man (Table 1).

Water Complaints Handling

It is the mandate of the Ministry of Water and Irrigation to ensure that each and every citizen has access to water. With this in mind, 22% of the citizens interviewed when faced with water challenges go to the ministry docket in charge of water. A total of 55% complain to other authorities who include landlord/caretakers and employees or officers of water supply in the region also fall under the Ministry of Water and Irrigation to. In Kiambu County for instance, the highest number of complaints (39%) were directed to the Ministry

of Water and Irrigation. However, this is not true for Migori and Makueni.

Counties (Migori and Makueni) with the highest number of complaints (32% and 26% respectively) were directed to the Public Administration Officer (e.g. chief, D.O) at an average of 21%. This could be driven by the proximity and accessibility of the nearest authority to the citizens; Public Administration Officers especially the chiefs are very close to the people more so in the rural set ups which Migori and Makueni are highly inclined to.

Despite the fact that more of the rural folks (27%) preferred going to the public administration officers (e.g. chief, D.O), it still emerged that Ministry of Water & Irrigation and public administration officers are the top two receivers of citizens' water-related complaints. The proximity with which the public administration officers are to the citizens probably is the contributing factor and therefore making them the champions of information that the citizen would desire to have.

Youth/women groups also have a role with regards to water issues affecting both the rural and urban residents. 5% and 7% of the urban and rural residents respectively said that they have complained to the youth/women groups when they had issues with water. Other channels that

Table 1. What were your reasons for you not complaining?

Reasons	County			Area of interview		Total
	Kiambu	Migori	Makueni	Urban	Rural	
I don't know who/where to complain	48%	58%	78%	57%	62%	61%
Am always busy	2%	2%	2%	2%	2%	2%
We have alternatives	14%	5%	5%	7%	10%	9%
I can't complain to anybody; it's a natural disaster	1%	1%	2%	1%	1%	1%
No one listens/acts; so it's needless to complain	14%	26%	7%	16%	14%	15%
Am used to the problem	2%	3%	1%	3%	1%	2%
I have no ability/courage to complain	19%	3%	5%	14%	9%	10%
People we can complain to are far away	0%	2%	1%	0%	1%	1%
Total	100%	100%	100%	100%	100%	100%

were used by the urban respondents are media channels at 2%. Surprisingly, church leaders (1%) were not highly placed when it came to escalating citizens' voices. Friends and relatives were also placed among the last options at 2%.

It is important to note that majority of respondents prefer to raise their complaints face to face to either the water providers or landlord/caretaker and not necessarily the Ministry of Water & Irrigation. It has to be understood that some of the complaints relate to the water providers or landlord/caretaker, e.g. if it is a water hike issue, it makes sense to complain to the landlord first as the chain of complaints is clear rather than go to the ministry first. There seems to be a channel that is followed as the issues may relate first to the people they choose to complain to. In fact the highest number of citizens (44%) raised complaints to officers or other employees of the water projects in their respective areas. The second largest receiver of complaints (30% of the respondents) was landlord/caretaker.

Politicians also have a role as far as issues affecting citizens are concerned. About 10% of the respondents feel that their elected leaders should help solve the water issues affecting them. A number of citizens are affected with not only the problems of water scarcity or price exploitation but also with health issues that come along with contaminated water and it is for this very reason that it is not surprising to observe a number of complaints being directed to the Ministry of Health and to the companies that offload sewage to the rivers and lakes. It is not a surprise that a noticeable number of people (about 1 out of every 100 people) complain to Kenya Power & Lighting Company (KPLC) since the problems affecting the citizens are diverse and need different attention at different levels and probably the need of electricity to aid in communication their issues through the phones or other media (TV/Radio).

Person Complained To

A number of citizens do not mind whether the receiver of their complaints is the right person or not, what matters is the action taken against their concerns. Approximately 7% of the respondents interviewed could not tell whether the person they complained to is the right person to address their issues or not, while 12% out rightly knew that whoever they complained to was not the right person. This could probably be based on the position of the person complained to, where the person works or the action taken by the person complained to.

From the findings, there is a clear indication that there is need for the government, media, the civil society organizations and or Water Action Groups (WAGs) to enlighten the citizens on the right channels to use to address issues related to water affecting them so as to be assured of positive feedback. Addressing issues to the wrong person could be the possible reason as to why citizens fail to receive response or action on matters raised.

Platforms Citizens Used to Complain

As earlier mentioned, a big percentage of citizens access information related to water through face-to-face. It is therefore not a surprise that the majority of the respondents (approximately 9 out of every 10) use the same platform to air out their grievances. 11% of the respondents used mobile phone (3% used SMS while 8% made phone calls) to let the authorities know of their problems.

Urban residents make calls and send SMS more frequently than their counterparts in rural areas, it is therefore not surprising to note that a higher percentage of urban residents communicate their problems more often using mobile technology than the rural folks (Figure 2). It is, however, a very slight difference with 14% of the urban residents

Figure 2. Platform used to make complaints

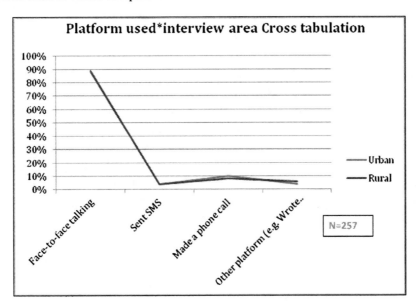

and 12% of the rural residents communicate their problems using mobile technology. This shows that there is potential to use of mobile technology in complaints handling to ensuring accountability from the service providers.

ACTION AND FEEDBACK

It is proven that access to information and communication in its own right plays an important role in promoting good governance (Coffey, 2007). Further, information delivery to the public is a key task of government and it is their responsibility to keep citizens informed of what is happening around them. It is therefore crucial that for any communication to be considered effective there must be a well-organized system of relaying the feedback. In the study conducted in the three counties in Kenya, it was established that many of the citizen's concerns go unattended to.

Citizens were asked whether someone acted on their concerns related to water issues and about 43% of the respondents calmly stated that no one bothered to take action on the matters they raised.

57% of the respondents said that someone acted on their issues. Despite getting attention, the question of duration, on how long it took to get a response on the complaint was raised. In some instances it took up to over one year to get the reply. The promise of ICTs usage in raising alarm for water service quality problems is that responses can be obtained instantaneously.

Citizen Satisfaction

Communication motivates and stimulates how citizens view the organizational structure towards meeting their demands. It is an important part that helps manage complaints and feedback from the citizens, making sure that citizens are satisfied with the outcome of their complaints. The study therefore sought to understand the levels of citizens' satisfaction with respect to the complaints raised. Levels of satisfaction were found to vary with the county when it comes to rating the action taken on water complaints raised. When asked whether citizens complained to the right person to handle their issues, a majority of respondents answered in the affirmative (especially in Migori County which recorded the highest percentage of people) (see Table 2). Ironically, the highest number of dissatisfied citizens was again recorded in Migori County at 65%. This was despite acknowledging that persons complained to were rightly placed. Makueni followed this with 40% and lastly Kiambu at 30%.

The study established that there exists a slight difference in the level of satisfaction between the urban residents and the rural residents. 40% of the respondents in urban areas and 41% of those in rural areas stated to have been dissatisfied with the action taken on the problems raised. This clearly shows that the challenges affecting the citizens cuts across and does not necessarily depend on the area of residence.

Proper responsive feedback mechanisms need to be put in place. Enforcing stakeholders to citizens reporting will be a guide to ensuring citizens complains are solved and that citizens remain satisfied with public service delivery.

There is need for further research in defining suitable approaches in ensuring effective citizen participation in decision-making and citizen satisfaction with e-governance tools and platforms.

Use of Mobile Technology by Citizens

The study also sought to understand how the citizens generally use their phones and if they would be interested to use them to communicate with water stakeholders. Majority of the respondents indicated that SMS would be the best technological platform for them to use to receive water information. 31 respondents indicated that they would prefer to use the internet to receive water information. This response highlighted a clear gap in the sector where despite majority of the water related information being provided on websites, on 31 respondents preferred it as an option. Another puzzling finding from the research was that very few respondents preferred the use of social media as a platform to raise their water issues.

It is important to highlight that currently in Kenya, mobile subscriptions are on the rise. In their April report, the Communication Commission of Kenya (CCK) reported that the number of mobile subscriptions rose to 30.7million. This represents 78% of the population. The number of internet subscribers also rose to above 14million

Table 2. How satisfied were you on the action taken on the matter you raised?

% within County				
	County			
Level of satisfaction	Kiambu	Migori	Makueni	Total
Strongly satisfied	19%	11%	18%	17%
Satisfied	23%	18%	23%	22%
Somewhat	25%	5%	20%	19%
Dissatisfied	16%	16%	20%	17%
Strongly dissatisfied	14%	49%	20%	24%
I don't know	3%	0%	0%	2%
Total	100%	100%	100%	100%

a growth attributed to the growth of demand for internet services and competitive tariffs from the mobile operators. This rise in use of mobile technology and internet should be leverage to attempt to solve some of the communication issues citizens are facing.

SOLUTIONS AND RECOMMENDATIONS

Recommendations from the Researchers to the Stakeholders e.g. Government, Civil Society in Water Sector

Citizen Participation

Based on the preceding key facts, it is clear that citizen participation and inclusion remains a big challenge in many parts of the country. It is essential that champions of information at the county level be identified in each and every part of the country to help educate the citizens on their roles in governance and provide them with other necessary information. Technology can play a potential role in ensuring effective communication in accessing information on water and enhance transparency. Use of technology might also be a challenge in implementation of online citizen participation as many people in the rural settings have basic phones that could send/receive SMS and phone calls. In addition, not many have the literacy of technology hence starting with the champions at the county level will be the best approach. Active citizen participation helps ensure that the governmental decisions and policies reflect the public interest.

Public Education

Public education and awareness remains an important milestone towards promoting transparency and openness of public information in order to eliminate the myriad digital and data divide implications and create a social and economic well being through reliable, available and actionable information. It is true that not everyone can read and write. This might pose a challenge in embracing online civic education. It is therefore recommended by the citizens interviewed that people should be assisted, educated and sensitized on the use of technology in combating water issues. Trainings and workshops should be organized in various parts of the country to educate and sensitize the citizens on their roles and how they can use mobile technology in ensuring effective governance.

Effective Feedback Mechanisms in Place

Immediate response should be guaranteed and network boosters be improved so as to wash out fears of possible delays and failure of getting timely response. Good governance is all about effective communication and transparency. For effective communication to be achieved proper feedback mechanisms need to be put in place; citizens' concerns need to be tackled in accordance to the required attention and communication be relayed even if there is no action taken on the matter. The water stakeholders need to approach feedback and complaint handling as part of their broader commitment to accountability, which promotes information sharing, transparency, participation and learning with the communities. The implementation of this recommendation can pose challenges such as ensuring timely responses, managing citizens' expectations when they complain and capacity/staff to handle the complains. Hence these challenges can be improved through increasing local capacity to handle the complaints and emphasize of accountability within line management.

Accountability in Water Services

Accountability is about being answerable for what is done, and requires the ability of citizens, civil society organizations (Non-Governmental Organizations (NGOs), Community-Based Organizations (CBOs), media) and the private sector to scrutinize public institutions and governments and hold them to account (Rethinking Governance In Water Services, 2007). Accountability in water governance requires the government to understand the processes, tools and objectives for improved accountability. While much focus on accountability is placed on the government, the other stakeholders e.g. civil society also play a key role especially in education the citizens about their rights and importance of raising their issues. This requires understanding on civic education and incentive mechanisms through creative engagement with local communities and government. Most of all, government and other water stakeholders need to ensure responsiveness in acting to citizens' water issues. This can be done by ensuring equity in the development of water services, including concerns on women rights and access. Pro-poor policymaking and implementation and the integrity of public officials in fulfilling their roles and responsibilities to citizens is needed to build responsive regulations in ensuring water quality.

Government Effectiveness

Access to public services still remains a big hole with government still not acting in a timely manner and being reachable in ensuring service delivery. There is need for government to cultivate decentralization, effective public administration and participatory planning and budgetary at the county level. Strengthening the local capacity and citizen empowerment at the county level to hear and respond to citizens' problems can further enhance this.

Ensuring Transparency

Despite the fact that initiatives such as open data portals and e-governance frameworks being implemented by the local government, there is still high need for them to ensure openness across all sectors though providing up to date and actionable data or information that citizens can use and re-use to make informed decisions. Using mobile phones and other creative virtual tools to provide the information can be a starting point in making the information closer to the rural communities.

Media should also play a key role in escalating citizens complains and water information at county level. An example of existing application is M-Maji that has been designed to give citizens in Kibera transparent information in their village of where they can find clean water from water vendors near their landmarks. Other mobile applications that are being deployed to provide platforms to complain as well as water information include Huduma and MajiVoice. Platforms such as these should be well marketed to the citizens especially in the rural areas so that they can be made aware of them in order to encourage usage.

Advocacy and Capacity Building There is need for the government to partner with other water stakeholders, including the civil society, media, non-governmental organizations and academia in promoting awareness. Also developing capacity through training people is important so that they can act as spokesmen in ensuring citizens are made aware of water information, quality sources, management, and corruption impact. This can be achieved through continuous research and development, workshops, trainings on water management and protection, and building local skilled citizens that can educate and inform their households and community at large.

Recommendations from the Researchers to the Citizens

For transparency and accountability to prevail it is important that each and every player participates effectively. Governance is a collective responsibility of each and every person(s) involved; citizens should understand that it is not the role of government alone but that the government is just one of the actors. In view of this, citizens need to take into account the following considerations:

Stay Informed

Effective governance of water resources and water service delivery requires a combined commitment of citizens, government and various groups in the civil society, especially at the community level. Citizens should therefore not sit back and wait for the government to act, but should make efforts to understand what is taking place and where or how they can access water related information. They can do this through accessing the information from their mobile phones, through calling, browsing the internet or social media to communicate with their water service providers and government.

Citizen Participation

Citizens have a role to play when it comes to ensuring water quality, management and transparency. Citizens need to be the champions of ensuring good governance in water sector is reached. They can achieve this through participating in water monitoring programs, water conservation and management and serve as advisors to decision-makers. Active citizens' participation in water and sanitation initiatives is crucial to ensure sustainable improvements in water services for the poorest. More so, citizens need to lower their expectations when amplifying their complaints as most of them complain to the wrong people or do not cooperate with authorities.

Positive Mind Set

Citizens feel a sense of hopelessness with regards to their water problems and as such perceive that no one will help them out or give them feedback if they complain. This results in citizens losing faith in the feedback system thus resulting in the citizens not articulating issues on the quality of water, or obtaining of the existing available water information. Hence such individuals believe there is no need to articulate their complaints, ensure quality water, or learn from already available water information. Citizens' diminished hope with the other stakeholders can be linked to negative mindset to the lack of action when they complain, the fact that they may seem far away from the citizens or some corrupt cases. It is high time citizens change their mindset and look at the problems they face, as challenges that can be solved to make sure they have an improved living standard. Citizens should think of themselves as agents by amplifying their voices and reporting on water issues as their right. They should therefore build trust and confidence in the feedback process.

FUTURE RESEARCH DIRECTIONS

Future research should focus on looking at how citizens' complaints can be escalated effectively though immediate feedback and action from the respective stakeholders using accessible tools and approaches. This should look into efforts being made to encourage use of technology through addressing the above mentioned challenges. More so, the research should focus on developing an effective feedback mechanism and complaints systems among citizens and other stakeholders. This looks very possible given the emerging ICTs.

Recommendation to the next book's theme can focus on approaches to ensuring effective feedback mechanisms and case studies to how it has been implemented in different countries using different technologies e.g. Mobile for others to learn from their experiences through running models and programs. This will help to learn from models that already work and have established improvement in feedback and complaint systems. Most important, how e-Government and mobile government (m-Government) can be blended in approaching the steps in ensuring proper feedback systems and accountability within line managers.

CONCLUSION

Governance is the exercise of economic, political and administrative authority to manage a country's affairs at all levels. It comprises of the mechanisms, processes, and institutions, through which citizens and groups articulate their interests, exercise their legal rights, meet their obligations and mediate their differences (United Nations Development Programme, 2005). Mobile government is the extension of eGovernment to mobile platforms to help make public information and government services available "anywhere, anytime" using the ubiquity of mobile devices. The strategy and its implementation through using all kinds of wireless devices to provided services to the public has a high potential to provide several benefits to the citizens involved

Inclusiveness, accountability, participation, transparency, predictability and responsiveness are some of the vital ingredients that make up good governance in water sector. Even though a series of reforms and e-governance frameworks aimed at enhancing quality, efficiency and transparency in service delivery by water sector institutions have been rolled out by the government, there is still a long way to go.

These are still low amounts of data in the different governance thematic areas, water being one of them that has limited supply of information. Most of the ministries are still working to digitize their information, hence the low supply of transparent information that can be accessed by citizens from a single portal. There is therefore need to explore

on more transparent instruments and tools to allow citizens both urban and rural to view actionable data in the water sector. This has made it a challenge in the development to technological tools as without information; it is difficult to champion this change in mGovernance.

Good governance is all about effective communication and transparency, for effective communication to be achieved proper feedback mechanisms need to be put in place; citizens' concerns need to be tackled in accordance to the required attention and communication to be relayed even if there is no action taken on the matter.

From this research, it seems evident that technology has great potential to escalating citizens' complaints and ensuring satisfaction in the water service delivery. However, the practical uses of technology as a tool in solving the current water complaints handling and feedback on the ground still remains fully untapped. Citizens are still unfamiliar with use of certain technologies, as most of them (90%) still prefer to use face to face in amplifying their complains. 11% of the respondents used mobile phone (3% used SMS while 8% made phone calls) to let the authorities know of their problems. Hence there is need for civic education in technological tools in complains management and other tools they can use.

If properly developed and the right stakeholders involved at each level, technology can be used in solving and improving water transparency needs through creative ways. This can be through solving the existing water challenges faced by citizens, e.g. access to water information, amplifying their complaints, etc. Improved water governance can also be achieved by involving the users and the right stakeholders through each stage of development and implementation.

There is ample evidence that access and transparency helps ensure accountability and delivery in water provision as well as boosts effectiveness since water is now enshrined as a human right in Kenya constitution. The promise of technology in ensuring a successful service delivery especially with the emerging global adoption of mobile technologies and Internet-enabled mobile phones is unimaginable.

REFERENCES

About MWater. (2012). MWater. Retrieved July 9, 2013 from http://mwater.info/Site/About_mWater.html.

ADDITIONAL READING

Coffey International Development (CID). (2007). *The role of communication in governance: Detailed analysis*. Retrieved March, 15, 2009 from http://www.icdev.info/portal/documents/GovernanceSummaryPaper_003.pdf

Communication Commission of Kenya (CCK). (2012). *Quarterly sector statistics report fourth quarter of the financial year 2011/12, April- June 2012*. Retrieved December 12, 2012 from http://cck.go.ke/resc/downloads/sector_statistics_report_q3_11-12.pdf

Huduma. (2013). *About Huduma*. Retrieved January 25, 2013, from HTTP://huduma.OR.KE

MAJIDATA. Retrieved July 9, 2013 from http://www.majidata.go.ke/index.php?MID=MQ==.

Ministry of Water and Irrigation. December (MWID). (2008). Ministerial strategic plan. Author.

MMAJI. (2013). *MMAJI water application: About MMAJI*. Retrieved February 2, 2013, from HTTP://MMAJI.WORDPRESS.COM

Momanyi, L. (2005). An analysis of water governance in Kibera, Kenya (2004/2005). Academic Press.

Moraa, H., Otieno, A., & Salim, A. (2012). *Technology in solving society's water problems*. Academic Press.

Nexleaf Analytics. (2012). *Mobile phone applications for the water, sanitation and hygiene sector*. Author.

Plummer, J., & Slaymaker, T. (2009). *Rethinking governance in water services*. Academic Press.

UNDP. (2007). *WGF: A mapping and baseline report, improving water governance in Kenya through the human rights based approach*. Retrieved June 26, 2013 from http://ebookbrowse.com/baseline-report-hrba-kenya-pdf-d107548951

Watex System. (2012). Kenya Turns to Satellite Technology to Quench Thirst for Water. *HumanIPO*. Retrieved June 9, 2013 from http://www.humanipo.com/news/493/Kenya-turns-to-satellite-technology-to-quench-thirst-for-water.

World Bank. (2012). *Kenya: About MajiVoice*. Retrieved July 1, 2013 from WWW.MAJIVOICE.COM

KEY TERMS AND DEFINITIONS

CCK: This is the commission in Kenya mandated for regulating all communication-related issues.

CSOs: This is an acronym that stands for Civil Society Organizations – organisations mostly mandated to advance the social discourse.

ICTs: This is an acronym that stands for Information and Communication Technologies. It details the technology tools and platforms that are used to effect appropriate information resource management and interchange.

mWASH: Acronym for a mobile technology application in Kenya standing for mobile Water, Sanitation and Hygiene.

NGOs: This is an acronym that stands for Non Governmental Organizations – organizations geared towards rectifying one or more social ills in a community or setup.

UNDP: A United Nations agency mandated to deal in issues of development programme in different nations of the world.

WAGs: This is an acronym that stands for Water Action Groups – detailing groups at different levels of the socio-economic hierarchy that aim to advance the water sanitation and availability agenda.

Chapter 14
Government 2.0:
Innovation for E–Democracy

Malgorzata Pankowska
University of Economics in Katowice, Poland

ABSTRACT

E-Government and e-Democracy system development is enabled by Internet technology. The implementation of Information and Communication Technologies (ICTs) accelerates the transformation of government institutions and their methods of operations. The use of ICTs at municipality institutions not only opens up possibilities for improving services to citizens and businesses, but also increases their involvement in local community governance. The general objective of this chapter is to reveal, at the municipality level, the opportunity for local community development and stronger citizen involvement in governing processes (e-Democracy). The chapter aims to present the new sources of knowledge, particularly through the involvement of individuals in local government development. The chapter aims to understand challenges in developing open information infrastructures that support municipality innovation and development. The chapter utilizes extensive literature reviews and the analysis of the content of selected e-Government portals to inform its positions.

INTRODUCTION

European Union agencies are particularly interested in supporting the creation of innovative Europe. Innovation is understood as comprising the renewal and enlargement of a range of products and services and their associated markets; the establishment of new methods of design, production, supply and distribution; the introduction of changes in management, work organization, and working conditions and skills of the workforce. There are different forms of innovation e.g., technological, non-technological and organizational innovation. The main purpose of this chapter is to highlight the different open innovations in public

DOI: 10.4018/978-1-4666-4900-2.ch014

administration at the municipal level and attempt to understand how these innovations are developed.

E-Government is defined as the use of ICTs in public administration business value chains. It encompasses organizational change and new skills in order to improve public services and democratic processes in a bid to strengthen support for public policies. The advantages of e-Government on the public service delivery landscape are grandiose: For example, it improves the development and implementation of public policies and helps the public sector to cope with conflicting demands of delivering more and better services with fewer resources. Public administration agencies are looking for innovative solutions that facilitate citizen-oriented strategy realization. E-Government is not an objective *per se*, it has to be seen more as means in organizing public governance for better serving citizens and enterprises. E-Government concerns the whole scope of administrative actions and the connected political processes because ICTs are an enabling force that will enhance effectiveness, quality and efficiency of public actions as well as its legitimacy. In the contemporary world, e-Government is placed at the core of any meaningful public service management modernization efforts towards a more responsive and a service more alienated towards public value. The creation of public value encompasses various democratic, social, economic, environmental and administrative roles of governments. The particular examples of the roles cover the provision of public administration services, implementation and evaluation of policies and regulations, the guarantee of democratic political processes (Centeno et al., 2004).

In e-Government, two complementary perspectives are of equal importance i.e. cooperation and knowledge. Support of computer-mediated cooperation in a comprehensive manner means that sophisticated tools and multiple media for the contacts are a must. The meeting activities as such may be performed online and via video techniques and improved by tools using multimedia. Prospects for knowledge management in e-Government are

remarkable from the point of demand: nearly all administrative tasks are informational in nature, decision-making is a public task, and for any agency, its particular domain knowledge is an asset of key importance.

Generally, innovation is usually related to the first instance of using a new technology. A technical innovation is defined as the first commercial application or production of a new process or product and innovation is defined as a change of decision rules to fit with the surrounding requirements (Pedersen & Pedersen, 2006). Innovation in many organizations is not a luxury, but a critical means of keeping up with changing circumstances and opportunities. Innovations are made in the context of institutional embeddings. That is, the object of innovation does not stand alone, but is set within an economy, within cultural and business practices. The circumstances in a particular context determine the unique development of innovation. The true value of innovation hinges on the ability of an organization to exploit tacit knowledge from both internal and external sources in order to improve organizational and competitive performance. According to B. Roberts, innovation is an invention plus its exploitation (Gaynor, 2002) and at least one must be brilliant, modern and unique. Innovation is the practice of creation, conversion and commercialization of services and products. Innovative practices rely very much on existing knowledge networks in communities and on how such networks are converted to allow for knowledge management in new and meaningful ways (Justesen, 2004).

E-Participation must be seen as an activity depending on the concept of full participation, not only by the engaged citizens, but also by the staff and politicians who are intended to get involved in preparing, supporting and maintaining the community of citizens. Methods supporting e-Participation must therefore support a system of social relations. E-Participation must be rooted in important experiences and in work practices related to the contextual dimensions to future development (Kolsaker & Lee-Kelley, 2006). E-Democracy is the use of Information and Communication Technologies (ICTs) by governments, international government organizations, elected officials, the media, political parties, non-governmental organizations, and citizen or other interest groups in the political processes of local, regional, state, and national communities, up to the global level (Parlak & Sobaci, 2006). The relevance of e-Democracy to public political processes is important because citizens must have the opportunity to participate in the public arena. Otherwise, they will force the government to resign. In order to improve its interaction with society, governments should constantly improve spaces for participation, in addition to the involvement and commitment of citizens to its government. The notion of spaces includes the cyberspace and electronic platform for citizens' communication.

The chapter consists of three main parts. The first part presents background analysis of municipal information systems and e-Government systems. Next, the main focus of the chapter covers the analysis of open innovations to support e-Participation and e-Democracy at municipality level. The last part includes considerations for further ICT development for municipalities.

Background

The e-Government vision is placed at the core of public management modernization and reform, where technology is used as a strategic tool to modernize structures, processes, the regulatory framework, human resources, and the culture of public administrations to provide better government, and ultimately increased public value. Creation of public value covers concrete examples: the provision of public administration and public services (i.e., health, education, social care) the development, implementation and evaluation of policies and regulations, the management of public finance, social inclusion and personal security,

the management of environmental sustainability and sustainable development of communities. In order to create public value for the citizen, governments must better understand and address the citizen's needs and understand to what degree they should empower users of e-Government. Governments must also take account of business needs, and consider the increasing importance of intermediaries i.e., private, social and public partners in the delivery of public services and in the exercise of democratic governance (Centeno et al., 2004). The European Union (EU) will in the next decade go through a number of social and economic transitions (such as increasing cultural and religious diversity, aging population and changing living, working and consumption patterns) posing new challenges for the delivery of public services.

The emerging vision for e-Government in the European Union (EU) requires a shift in governance. Some emerging trends in public service provision include the following:

- Personalized service addressing the different needs of different citizen groups;
- Government pro-active services;
- Access to public sector information;
- Services enabling the democratic participation of EU citizens; and
- Cross-border services (e-Health, e-Education and internal market).

For the service accessibility, citizens require the provisions of multi-channel access mix, with a variety of contact points, availability of the necessary access infrastructure, round the clock provision of the services, ensuring inclusiveness across a diversity of human beings, having different psychological and physical capabilities. Public services for citizens are expected to concern the following problems (e-Governance, 2004, Halfawy et al., 2004, MAIS, 2012,):

1. **Employment and training:**
   a. **Job search:** Search a job database containing job opportunities drawn from several sources, including the city's employment department, integrating legacy systems and data;
   b. **Training support:** Emphasizing training opportunities in relation to a job opportunity and the requester's current skills, providing detailed information on the training courses, including locations and schedules, legacy services can be enriched by adding data sources and by linking with other third party services (e.g., Geographical Information System, GIS, mobility);

2. **Accessible services (Government to Customer, G2C, Business to Customer, B2C):**
   a. **Media service:** Provide easy access to TV channels, video on demand, internet and government information through TV set, using simple menus and navigation;
   b. **Business services to the citizen:** Tele (T) shopping, T-learning, Ticketing, enabling access of small traders and the disabled into online marketing and inform citizens to purchase local goods and services online;

3. **Mobility:**
   a. **Informobility services:** Transfer of data about tourism information, points of interest of the city and municipal services;
   b. **Traffic management:** Traffic and public transport management through real time monitoring of traffic and public bus transport and citywide road signage;

4. **Land use information management:**
   a. Geoservice integration and application platform for an interoperable geospatial information management in cities;
   b. Geoservices based connection of legacy GIS desktop applications to the platform;
   c. Geo-participation that provides interactive and dynamical access for citizens to distributed and heterogeneous public sector geoinformation and data sources within participation procedures, including: search service catalogue, viewing and creating maps by combining layers/ themes from several map servers, viewing and analyzing attributive data, spatial analyzing – online – statements referring to planned land use changes and other public or private projects or plans;
   d. Geo-content and data provided for external service partners and customers of city administrations, integration of all kinds of distributed heterogeneous geo sources (databases, geo services, GIS);
   e. Web maps based on geo data sources.
   f. Strategic environmental assessment (SEA) plan for monitoring land use change with support of remote sensing;
   g. Urban regeneration cross border monitor and integration of data from different municipalities, different GIS, and decentralized datastore; and

5. **Regeneration planning:**
   a. Allowing the citizens to report geo-referenced environmental problems, such as abandoned vehicles, illegal refuse dumping, criminal incidents;
   b. Building scanning and building data integration and analysis for property professionals and building designers;
   c. Creating and maintaining customer's personalized real estate objectives, preferences and evaluation criteria, participation of various stakeholders in joint determination of criteria defining real estate, market signaling,

providing device-based data about the indoor microclimate, searching for real estate alternative and making an initial negotiation table, completing a multiple criteria analysis of alternatives, making electronic negotiations based on real calculations, determining the most rational real estate purchase variant and completing an analysis of the loan alternatives offered by certain banks;

d. **Environmental simulation:**
   i. Air pollution;
   ii. Planning visualization of redevelopment projects including 3D buildings and simulation results using color coding for noise and pollution concentration levels.

Various e-Government initiatives at the municipality levels provide legislative information for the needs of people working in legislative organizations or needing the information outside the organizations. Legislative information includes information about the ongoing and past legislative processes in a country, documents and other content created in the processes, as well as information about human and organizational actors participating in the processes. The information is important to legal experts, politicians, media, various interest groups, and laypersons. Following legislative processes and finding information about them requires both knowledge about these processes and about various information sources and services important to the local communities.

The above mentioned services require not only the abilities to perform them accurately, consistently and in time, but also the interaction between users and service providers' employees, users, and the website and among peer users. It is affected by the knowledge and courtesy of employees and their ability to convey trust and confidence. Moreover, it is also linked to the degree of personalization of the service and facilities

such as message boards and chat rooms the site may provide (Papadomichelaki et al, 2006). The e-Government information should on one hand be characterized by the accuracy, correctness, reliability, timeliness, completeness, relevancy, and ease of understanding of data and the number and quality of hyperlinks the site offers. On the other hand, the presentation part consists of the website's structure, design and appearance, search facilities, easiness of navigation and an easy to remember URL. The e-Government system should contain quality dimensions such as availability, accessibility, system integrity, performance, reliability, interoperability, and last but not least security.

E-Government system could be supported by the adoption and implementation of ICT such as Enterprise Resource Planning (ERP) system to improve operational efficiencies of public sectors. However, it requires the undertaking of a more radical transformation of the municipality organizational model and accompanying business processes. Business Process Reengineering (BPR) is the principal practice for radical transformation of organization and the fundamental pre-requisite for integrated information system implementation. Public sector organizations have included the practice of BPR under the banner of Government Process Reengineering (GPR) to transform the public sector from its traditional hierarchical bureaucratic model to customer-oriented process model (Kassahun et al. 2012).

The ERP systems have been developed to help organizations integrate and better manage information within and also with their business partners, to coordinate many activities such as e-Procurement, HR, project management, finance, and budgeting. ERP data is often spread throughout different government functions such as accounting, project management, purchasing and procurement, and supply logistics. The benefits of ERP are that it enables masses of information, previously dispersed and fragmented, difficult and expensive to bring together manually in a timely way, to be brought together and processed in seconds (Thomson, 2012). Implemented in the e-Government domain, ERP system combines all the government functions together into one single integrated system with a single central database.

This system serves the information needs of all the departments across geographies, while allowing them to communicate with each other (Sahi, 2012). The objective of the integration is to provide efficient services to citizens, to enable organizational processes and workflows. The ERP system improves the quality of public service delivery system and offers these services with optimal effectiveness and transparency. It allows data sharing across different departments, and facilitates the decision making process of top management by delivering the right information at the right time.

Figure 1 covers system architecture of ERP system for municipality management. Generally, the ERP system presents the activities realized in municipal office. The activities are activities are divided into two main parts. The first part includes modules to support the internal management i.e., Human Resources Management, Investment and Procurement, Project Management, Business Intelligence Tools, ICT Tools and Services.

The second part includes modules for evidence and management of external stakeholders i.e., institutions and particular citizens. The Budget Finance and Accounting module seems to be the most important module of the system. Usually, a municipality has some resources i.e., lands, buildings, parks, parking, and roads, which demands investments and maintaining. On the other side, a municipality provides an evidence of its citizens, their taxes, permissions, concessions etc.

The Sustainable development and management of municipal infrastructure assets require the use of reliable and sound information systems that address a wide range of technical, economical, environmental, and social issues. Municipalities typically use, develop and maintain a wide range of information systems to support the multi disciplinary decision making processes. Municipality asset based management strategies require addressing diverse issues in an integrated manner, therefore particularly Municipal Infrastructure Management System (MIMS) seems to be useful. The MIMS is used to store and manage all relevant information on infrastructure assets and to support decision making processes in areas related to asset acquisition, operation, maintenance, and re-

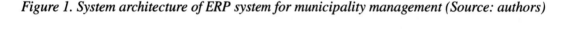

Figure 1. System architecture of ERP system for municipality management (Source: authors)

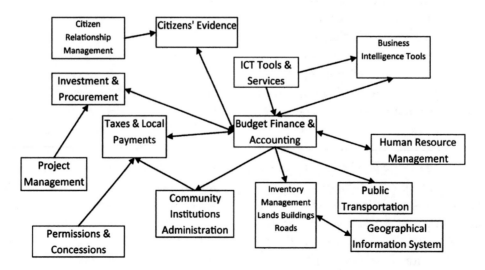

placement. The MIMS systems are usually supplemented by GIS system enabling spatial data management, visualization, and query (Halfawy et al., 2004). Beyond MIMS, there are also other classes of municipal information systems. For example, Municipal Accounting and Information System (MAIS) is a fully integrated system consisting of many modules to meet the managerial needs of local government i.e., accounts payable, accounts receivable, animal licenses, asset management, budgeting, building permits, business license, finance, inventory, online solutions, payroll, sale cash receipting point, property taxation, purchasing, system security and utility billing (MAIS, 2012). The MAIS systems integrate real-time processing of all financial transaction for municipality.

OPEN INNOVATION FOR MUNICIPALITIES

For many authors, e-Government, e-Administration and even sometimes e-Municipalities are considered and developed in separation from e-Democracy and e-Participation. E-Government system development proponents focus so strongly on administrative, managerial and political issues of community authorities that they forget about individual citizens, who should be partners in the governmental processes. According to Orihuela and Obi, e-Government is defined as the usage of ICTs in order to improve the services and information given to citizens, to increase the efficiency and effectiveness of public management. However, they also introduced concept of e-Governance, which is understood by them as using technology to improve public services and democratic processes and to strengthen support to public policies (Orihuela and Obi, 2007). According to Hirst, governance is generally perceived to be an alternative to government (Hirst, 2002). He has noticed the growth of multiple conceptions of governance thus reflecting real changes away from

the central government of the nation state as the principal provider of control and regulation within the national territory. Nowadays, the conventional conception of democracy in modern democratic theories has relied on the notion of the self-governing community. Per analogy to corporate governance, the municipality governance can be considered as a strategy of balancing municipality requirements and environment possibilities. Therefore, governance can be defined as the means by which an activity or a set of activities is controlled or directed, such that it delivers an acceptable range of outcomers according to the established social norms. According to Aziz, e-Governance is a controllership instrument that makes provision of government services and information available to the public by electronic means. Furthermore, electronic government as one part of electronic governance can provide the public and the government itself with public information and services. It can improve internal processes, as well as integrate interactions and interrelations between government and society. E-Democracy as another part of electronic governance can support citizens to participate in public life through forums, meetings, search, referendums, votes, decisions on rules (Aziz, 2011).

Contemporary national and local governments can be supported by different new ICT application i.e., e-Government, e-Democracy, e-Municipalities. They are innovative in their own way, as they support gathering and distribution open innovation through the access to public information and open maps. Public information is all information originating from the field of work of the public sector bodies and occurring in the form of a document, a case, a dossier, a register, a record or other documentary material drawn up by the body, by the body in cooperation with other body, or acquired from other persons. Natural and legal persons can under certain conditions use this information also for commercial or non-commercial reuse (Murray, 2010). E-Democracy provides a mechanism for consulting and respecting the interests involved in decisions. Democracy and e-Democracy are central to governance. The relevance of e-Democracy to public administration and political processes is that, in order for a democratic government to function, citizens must have the opportunity to participate in the public arena. Parlak and Sobaci have noticed that the mere existence of forums for citizen participation does not ensure the development of a deliberative and participative democracy. They have specified a number of factors (i.e., digital inclusion of all community members, deliberation free from disillusion and deception, citizenry and legitimacy, where decisions are made through participation after a period of public deliberation (Parlak & Sobaci, 2010)).

Municipality e-Governance should be understood as a means of achieving public sector goals, as well as the results of local community actions and their impacts on the sector, the city and the overall urban region. However, if e-Governance should help restore and increase the legitimacy of the public sphere, then there is a need for the transformation of government at the very bottom (Cotterill, 2009). Therefore, the success lies in reorganizing the working processes within and between government agencies for integrating the back and front office systems and the service delivery channels as well as in the integration of citizens in governance processes through e-Democracy and e-Participation development support. The engagement of citizenry in the governmental decisions that will impact them is a hallmark of the democratic process. There are benefits of e-Participation for both the citizens and the government agency, including increasing the education and awareness levels of the citizenry, civic engagement, government responsiveness, and citizens' commitment to implementation (Chen & Dorsey, 2009). Innovative Internet-based participation approaches provided by governments, including Geographical Information System (GIS) and e-Government websites, provide additional communication opportunities

for participants for exchange of new ideas. Generally, open innovation for public administration at municipal level is about creating new inbound as well as outbound flows of knowledge to leverage the municipal institution's innovation capabilities. In this process, institutions should look for new sources of knowledge and new outlets for their decisions. For the effective management of local community, the institutions should collaborate with others, including volunteers, non-profit organizations, citizens, academics, religious groups, and business firms. A group of terms has been used to describe the tendency of the openness of innovation activities: open source, open standard, open research, user-driven innovation (see Figure 2). However, in contrast to open source, open innovation typically implies the payment of license fees as well as other financial arrangements.

The degree of openness in innovation models differs, depending on factors such as the importance of the technology, the strategy of the firm, and the characteristics of the industry.

The attractiveness of open innovation understood as a governmental institution strategy is the way to exploit the benefits from ideas outside the institutions and exporting intellectual property. The goal of open innovation is to create a new value for the participating members through the innovation process. The governmental institutions find partners among citizens and any other volunteers in open networks and they can develop alliances. Interorganizational relations, cooperation, and networking are an important dimension of open innovation. With both inbound and outbound flows of technology and knowledge, there must be some sort of cooperation and networking between formal and informal ties and deep and wide ties. Open innovation system requires communication and interaction between all parties involved, namely the institution's internal actors as well as its external stakeholders.

The outside-in processes, individual municipalities have traditionally been receptive to the concept of outside knowledge flowing in than to

Figure 2. Openness for innovation development activities (Source: Based on [Giving Knowledge for Free, 2007])

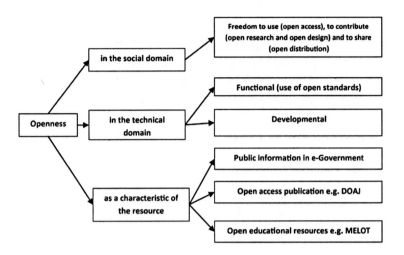

that of internal knowledge flowing out. External knowledge can be used in the development of systems and services and the performance of operational activities, although the willingness to share innovations and experiences are very limited, traditionally, other municipalities can be considered as competitors. In the inside-out processes, the municipality's main task to-date has been to serve the citizens and companies within the municipality, and the exploitation of innovation has been secondary to the operational concerns of organizing and delivering services within budget constraints. For example, eGOV-Forge.org is the Swedish national repository of open source software designed to meet the demand for increased cooperation both between and inside government bodies and provides mechanisms for the conversion of software developed within the public sector into open software, increasing the development of this software and stimulating collaborative development and open formats and standards (Feller et al., 2008).

E-Government definitions have evolved over the last 10 years and efforts result to the conclusion that the usage of ICT and ERP systems implementation are conducted strictly according to the local and regional political rules and financial possibilities of investment. However, through the open innovation the e-Government institutions now shift toward constituencies and stakeholders at all levels to include them in Government 2.0 initiatives. According to Luna-Reyes at al., (2010), the main objectives of Government 2.0 projects are to provide a more efficient user experience as a result of effective design and navigation, to capture core content from the authoritative source in order to reduce duplication and inconsistencies, to conduct systematic client engagement to drive continuous improvement, to ensure that the Internet helps fulfill policy imperatives and client needs, to establish clear accountability, roles, and responsibilities for its Internet sites, to allow for more effective resource investments in its Internet sites, to provide for greater integration of services with partner departments, and to yield more operational efficiency through common processes and technology shared with partners (Luna-Reyes at al., 2010, p.147). However, per analogy to Web 2.0, Government 2.0 can be defined as the common usage of capabilities of open ICT solutions to involve citizens and any other stakeholders in the local or regional governance processes. Although it demands citizens education on Internet skills, connecting government to citizens through the joint websites development, providing Internet access to communities, and creating an appropriate legal framework for e-Democracy and e-Participation. The Government 2.0 project development is supported by the strong development of open source software applications of Web 2.0, such as blogs, microblogs (e.g., Twitter.com, Jaiku.com, Tumblr.com, Plurk.com), mashups, podcasts, Really Simple Syndication (RSS), social networking sites (i.e., MySpace, Facebook, LinkedIn), video sharing, photo sharing (e.g., Picassa Web Albums). The potential of applying Web 2.0 technologies and social media to e-Politics, e-Government, and e-Participation has not gone unnoticed. Web 2.0 and social media tools are going to be very common in political and electoral campaigns as a major platform for enabling interactions and forging relations between politicians and citizens, as it was in President Barack Obama campaign.

Municipality Websites' Review and Analysis

Theories on democracy are numerous. Throughout the centuries, democracy has undergone many changes, as the size of the citizenry has evolved from a narrow, exclusively defined body that participated in a collective will within small city – state (direct democracy) to a universal suffrage system (representative and liberal democracy).

In this chapter, eDemocracy refers to the participation in a government or democratic activity online or to using the internet to express an opinion. It is widely believed that the internet enables people to connect from all over the world who share the same beliefs and principles through websites or e-mail discussion groups and this would result in the changing of government policies. In this way existing communities will be altered and new ones might emerge with new relationships and

new citizenship scopes. E-Democracy encourages radical decentralization in which every municipal unit, citizens' business organizations alike, are involved in the innovation process.

Computer-aided democracy covers the access to politically relevant information (teleconsulting), the availability of pluralistic discussion places (electronic conferences, newsgroups and e-forums), and the possibility for all to intervene in decision making (e-voting, televoting, on-side manifestations). Therefore e-Democracy means that citizens will not only use technology to inform themselves about current events, but will also use it as a voting tool in both their national and local election or administration and as a means for active participation. E-Democracy consists of information provision, deliberation and participation in decision making. Citizens may become more aware of public affairs and when participating in the decision making process, better choices and decision will be taken. However, to be involved in e-Democracy people must be educated. Promoting awareness of the responsibilities that are incumbent on each individual in a democratic society, in particular within the local community, whether as an elected representative, local administrator, public servant and ordinary citizen, must be encouraged (Biasiotii & Nannucci, 2004).

Citizens need knowledge for solving a problem or making a decision. A knowledge service is a service for solving a problem. The important characteristic of knowledge service different from that of data service is the level of knowledge. A data service assumes the same level of knowledge between the provider and the recipient, but knowledge service assumes different knowledge levels between the provider and the client. The question is what knowledge in e-Municipality is transferred among municipal authorities and citizens. In public administration top down flow of knowledge covers rules, regulations, and orders. Bottom up transfer can include comments, suggestions, ideas, initiatives, critiques, and proposals. To evaluate eMunicipalities development in Polish communities, the following criteria have been accepted:

- Online presentation of community office organizational structure.
- Online access to knowledge from governmental sources (i.e., Parliament, Ministries, central agencies) to ensure top down public administration knowledge dissemination.
- Website presentation of legal acts compulsory for citizens .
- Online access to law interpretation portals and websites.
- Online access to training materials on public administration procedures.
- Opportunity to download forms of documents concerning issues dealt with at the office.
- Online access to Citizen Service Office.
- Website presentation of procedures of behavior in emergency cases, alert mechanisms.
- Online access to emergency assistance support systems.
- Online access to databases containing tenders and proposals specifications within e-Procurement system.

A review of over 100 websites of municipalities in Poland allows revealing interesting observations. At municipal level, for e-Democracy development open source software, open contents, open standards are opportunities demanding risk taking to receive benefits. Opportunity utilization is a change of state, exploitation of change as an opportunity for a different business or service. Open source software supported virtual communities may help citizens to revitalize democracy by enabling massive participation in the political processes, but also they may cheat them into buying attractively packaged substitutes of democratic discourses. Virtual communities provide an existing platform for knowledge sharing and relationship building as well as for public participation, which is a growing part of spatial and environmental planning. The main purpose of environmental decision making and thus the main purpose of public participation is to achieve protection, conservation and wise management of the socio-economic and natural environment. The level at which the public is involved varies with the relevant legislation, and the attitude of the other stakeholders. For interactive, collaborative decision making between citizens and politicians, two key elements are required. Firstly, citizens must be prepared to become knowledgeable about current issues and to express opinions (particularly on new initiatives) in order to bring clarity to the decision making process of elected representatives. Secondly, the state must be prepared to provide timely, comprehensive information as well as channels of communication through which the citizens can express their opinions and engage in debate. E-Participation means the ICT supported joint activities in municipality governance processes. Therefore, e-Participation demands the following activities realized online, particularly on municipal portal:

- Presentation of the community mission, vision and strategy.
- Presentation of community history (i.e. people, buildings, calendar of events).
- Access to information from non-governmental sources to create relations and knowledge exchanges.
- Access to land use plans, to Land Information System and to Geographic Information System for citizens and business organizations.
- Availability of search engines, FAQs on websites.
- Providing public opinion questionnaires on websites for citizens, tourists.

- Providing links to commercial and business units, their advertisements, through websites.
- Presentation of the special activities within the community for the physically and mentally impaired, for the unemployed and the homeless on websites.
- Presentation of the special activities of benevolent institutions and charity houses on websites.
- Access through the community website to chat rooms, forums, blogs of citizens, politicians and communities' officers.
- Presenting the information on contests, competitions for citizens and guests.
- Providing e-News containing citizens' comments, questions and suggestions on the community and its website development.
- Presentation of rules and regulations for community, resolutions, meetings' protocols, projects for community, private properties declarations of main officials in municipality.
- Presentation of information on municipality elections, addresses of polling stations and information on opening hours.
- Access to links to political parties websites.
- Access to journals published by municipality office or municipality citizens.

In Poland, the resolution of the Act on Access to Public Information of 6th June 2001 caused rapid development of municipalities' Public Information Bulletin (PIB) and websites. They are linked, although developed separately. 98% of municipalities included in this research have implemented PIB. This electronic journal, according to the requirements included in the Act on Access to Public Information, contains information important to citizens on municipality authorities, organization of municipality offices, electronic forms of documents, administrative procedures mandatory for citizens and for local businesses, declaration of private properties owned by mu-

nicipality authorities, community legal regulations and rules, information on procurements for municipality, invitations to tenders and auctions, municipality budgets and land planning.

Generally, municipalities' websites and PIBs ensure achievement of e-Government strategic goals. They enable transfer of top down administrative information and access to governmental sources of public information, as well as to portals for law interpretation and public administration knowledge dissemination. The citizens have the opportunities to learn about legal acts mandatory for them, to recognize office procedures. They can download forms of documents. They have the possibility to utilize multichannel communication with Citizen Service Office, where an official can use stationary telephone, mobile, emails, or internet application.

The PIBs usually ensure investors and business units access to databases of tenders considering jobs for public institutions. Municipalities' authorities reveal spatial plans on the websites or in PIBs. Obtaining maps including buildings, roads and data on media deliveries and on environment protection from GISs is possible. Municipalities' websites cover links to many non-governmental institutions e.g., charity houses or to private business companies e.g., restaurants, hotels. Municipalities' websites contain information on help for the unemployed and the homeless as well as for others that need social security.

Information included in municipalities' websites is addressed to different info market segments i.e., citizens, tourists, investors, sponsors, business units and non-profit organizations. Citizens have the opportunity of two-way communication with central institutions i.e. State Archive, Central Office of Geodesy and Cartography, European Information, Environmental Protection Inspection, the Institute of National Remembrance, Supreme Chamber of Control, Supreme Administrative Court, National Bank of Poland, President of the Republic of Poland, Supreme Court of the Republic of Poland, Social Insurance etc.

Municipalities sufficiently well utilize Internet as a medium to involve citizens and sponsors to act for community and to promote local activities. Contests, competitions, festivals, fairs, joint actions and projects are well advertised in Internet, therefore it creates a real feeling of belonging to the community and participating in decision making for the community. E-Participation tools i.e., fun games, blogs, video interviews, chats, forums, interface agents are used to engage citizens in discussions, exchange views, and in creation of social relations. Citizens are involved in e-Publishing on local news and problems. Political party elections have been strongly supported by Internet. Politicians have discovered the opportunity to communicate with people through Twitter, Facebook and blogs. They utilize social media as an important political marketing tool. E-News, municipal Internet TV and radio, forums, blogs, e-mails, chats, webinars, webcastings encourage to knowledge creation, externalization, dissemination and reusing. The new media integrate citizens within a virtual community. Municipal agencies understand that virtual communities created around the municipal portal and supported by municipal office or even sponsored by them could help them create their image.

The activities support an idea of open government development, which has been influenced by the open source software movement, and taken on a greater focus for allowing participation in the procedures of government. Open government means government, where citizens not only have access to information, documents and proceedings, but can also become participants in a meaningful way (Lathrop & Ruma, 2010).

The commonly accepted access to the public information at municipal office and the magic of open data enable transparency and support local innovation, as developers build applications that reuse government data in unexpected ways. Taking the idea of citizen self-service, you can imagine government using a platform like Meetup to support citizens in self-organizing to take on major projects that the government would otherwise leave undone. Today, there are thousands of civic-minded meetups around issues like beach, road and waterway cleanups. Citizen self-organization is a powerful concept. It's worth remembering that early, many functions were self-organized by citizens: militias, fire brigades, lending libraries, not to mention roads, harbors and bridges (Lathrop & Ruma, 2010). In supporting citizens different e-Municipality services are provided i.e., computer support services, education, data mining tools to establish for example what stage government debate has reached in a particular legislation change, a charter of rights for citizens, translation tools to allow citizens to understand complex political-legal documents, virtual agents to mediate against functional or procedural complexity, navigation tools to help citizens to find what they need even if they are unaware of how to do this or how it is officially described, user-friendly e-deliberation software, e-alerts to inform citizens when an issue of interest to them is being discussed at government level (Hansen & Reinau, 2006). Particularly useful for citizens are maps and virtual walks in municipal office, enabling them to move easily on-side. The exceptional examples of virtual walks in municipal office building have been implemented in the following Polish municipalities:

- Podkarpacie Virtual Museum, http://www.wmp.podkarpackie.pl/#muzeum=sanok:
- Virtual Walk in Municipal Office in Chorzow, http://www.chorzow.eu/spacer/;
- Space Information Infrastructure Internet Portal of Municipal Office in Bytom, http://sitplan.um.bytom.pl/wu/;
- Virtual Walk at Regional Employement Office in Ostrow Wielkopolski, http://wirtualny-urzad.pup.ostrowwlkp.pl/
- Virtual Officer at Municipal Office in Gdynia, http://www.gdynia.pl/bip/?wu=true

- Kujawsko-Pomorski Regional Office in Bydgoszcz, http://www.bydgoszcz.uw.gov. pl/ws/BudynekA/TourWeaver_budynekA. html
- Buildings and investments in Bielsko-Biala, comments on e-forum, http:// www.skyscrapercity.com/showthread. php?t=424783

Citizen participation in urban planning and development processes is an important exercise that enriches community involvement in the planning and management of their locality. A well designed participatory urban planning system can serve as an enabler for collaborative decision-making and help reduce conflict and mistrust between planning officials and the local community.

The advancement in Geographic Information Systems (GIS) and Planning Support Systems (PSS) technologies has provided the opportunity for planning agencies to adopt innovative processes to aid and improve decision-making (Aikins, 2010). A potential value of e-planning is the use of GIS to assess the economic, fiscal, social, traffic and environmental impacts of urban development projects. Additionally, much of the research on available in Internet GIS has focused on specific aspects of the urban planning process and an accessibility to GIS and geodesy maps in Internet for free to citizens, as well as on investigation how information and telecommunication technology can enhance that participatory processes. Such information availability and accessibility could help to reduce the information asymmetry that plaques the participation process and ensure informed citizen participants in the policy process, including participatory urban planning. For example, generally accessible geoportal for citizens and investors is available at Siemianowice in Poland (see http://siemianowice.geoportal2.pl/ map/www/mapa.php?CFGF=wms&mylayers=+ granice+), where Internet users are able to review town maps, with buildings, roads, and other local investments). GIS systems play an increasingly

important role. This is demonstrated for example by the emergence of Google Earth and Google Maps. Therefore it is not surprising that on neighborhood level experiments with GIS-oriented websites become more and more common. The potential of these initiatives can mostly be found in stimulating location based ways of service delivery and e-Participation. However, open standards implementation and interoperability development are crucial to making an opportunity to integrate geospatial information and geospatial processing with the World Wide Web. For example, the OpenGIS Consortium (OGC) is a global industry consortium responsible for designing the open interfaces and protocols defined by OpenGIS® Specifications, which empower technology developers to make spatial information and services accessible and useful to all kinds of applications. With its OpenGIS® Specification, the Open GIS Consortium, Inc. has undertaken to overcome the non-interoperability of e-Government systems. The OpenGIS Specification for geoprocessing interfaces largely eliminates the need for data format standards and costly batch data conversion (McKee, 2000). Based on standards, open system geoprocessing has important implications for government agencies and municipal departments. Governments manage resources that are distributed spatially. Thus in every municipality area there are a lot of agencies and citizens that could benefit from GIS systems that help collect, manage, and analyze spatial data. The Open Source Geospatial Foundation (OSGeo) (http:// www.osgeo.org/content/foundation/about.html) is a non-profit organization that supports the collaborative development of open source geospatial software and to promote its usage. The organization promotes freely available geodata and the use of open source software in the geoinformation processing. It encourages the implementation of open standards and standards-based interoperability, as well as communication and cooperation between OSGeo communities on different language and operating system platforms.

CONCLUSION AND FUTURE RESEARCH DIRECTIONS

The engagement of citizens in policy development and government mean a certain strengthening of the representative relationship. ICT provides new opportunities to connect citizens to their representatives and governmental authorities, resulting in a less remote system of democratic governance. However, beyond that, ICT and particularly e-Government and Government 2.0 tools should be designed and implemented to learn citizens' responsibilities for their properties and develop their involvement and competencies of self-organizing and self-management for sustainability of their communities. In this chapter, the two different ICT strategies for municipality management have been presented. At first, the strong necessity to manage material and human resources within a municipality encourages municipality board to invest in commercial software i.e., ERP system. The ERP system is applied for management all the municipality resources and for the municipality decision making support. The second strategy covers spontaneous development of Web 2.0 applications. The second strategy is realized by citizens and mostly in their own interests.

Future research directions are strongly related with the further development of ICT applications for municipalities and governmental institutions. However, optimization of governmental institution internal and cross-organizational processes will demand focus on cooperation among different public administrative units in the sense that they need to rationalize their resources and integrate their software assets. Taking into account the citizens' needs, the research should focus on multichannel access of citizens to e-Government services, whether by PC, hand-held devices, WebTV, mobile phones or any other device. Further development of e-Democracy requires changes of legal frameworks as well as providing transparent access to the public services, in the sense that citizens have a reliable opportunity to take part in deliberations on local community problems, be a part in the local government decision making processes and be able to present their achievements of their work for their municipality. An excellent opportunity for Government 2.0 development seems to be the popularization of cloud computing processing, therefore citizens could have wide access to software services to support and promote their activities.

REFERENCES

Aikins, S. K. (2010). Participatory e-planning: Bridging theory and practice through improvements in technology. In Ch.G. Reddick (Ed.), Politics, democracy and e-government, participation and service delivery (pp. 131-150). Hershey, PA: IGI Global.

Aziz, M. (2011). Implementing ICT for governance in a post-conflict nation: A case study of Afghanistan. In D. Piaggesi, K. J. Sund, & W. Castelnovo (Eds.), *Global strategy and practice of e-governance: Examples from around the world* (pp. 185–208). Hershey, PA: IGI Global. doi:10.4018/978-1-60960-489-9.ch011

Centeno, C., van Bavel, R., & Burgelman, J. C. (2004). eGovernment in the EU in the next decade: The vision and key challenges, based on the workshop held in Seville. In Proceedings of eGovernment in the EU in 2010: Key policy and research challenges. Brussels: European Commission, Directorate General Joint Research Centre, EUR 21376.

Chen, Y., & Dorsey, A. (2009). E-government for current and future senior citizens. In C. G. Reddick (Ed.), *Strategies for local e-government adoption and implementation, comparative studies* (pp. 306–322). Hershey, PA: IGI Global. doi:10.4018/978-1-60566-282-4.ch016

Cotterill, S. (2009). Local e-government partnerships. In C. G. Reddick (Ed.), *Strategies for local e-government adoption and implementation, comparative studies* (pp. 105–122). Hershey, PA: Information Science Reference. doi:10.4018/978-1-60566-282-4.ch006

E-Governance Practices, Strategies and Policies of European Cities. (2004). Retrieved October 2012 from http://www.intelcitiesproject.com

Feller, J., Finnegan, P., & Nilsson, O. (2008). Openning public administration: Exploring open innovation archetypes and business model impacts. In L. Gonzalo, A. M. Bernardos, J. R. Casar, K. Kautz, & J. I. DeGross (Eds.), *Open IT-based innovation: Moving towards cooperative IT transfer and knowledge diffusion* (pp. 483–500). New York: Springer. doi:10.1007/978-0-387-87503-3_27

Gaynor, G. H. (2002). *Innovation by design*. New York: American Management Association.

Halfawy, M. R., Vanier, D. J., & Hubble, D. (2004). Integration of municipal information systems for sustainable management of infrastructure assets. *Environmental Informatics Archives, 2*, 375–386.

Hansen, H. S., & Reinau, K. H. (2006). The citizens in e-participation. In M. A. Wimmer, H. J. Scholl, A. Gronlund, & K. V. Andersen (Eds.), *Electronic government* (pp. 70–82). Berlin: Springer. doi:10.1007/11823100_7

Hirst, P. (2002). Democracy and governance. In J. Pierre (Ed.), *Debating governance, authority, steering and democracy* (pp. 13-33). Oxford, UK: Oxford University Press. Retrieved December 2012 from http://fds.oup.com/www.oup.co.uk/pdf/0-19-829514-6.pdf

Justesen, S. (2004). Innoversity in communities of practice. In *Knowledge networks, innovation through communities of practice* (pp. 79–95). Hershey, PA: Information Science Publishing.

Kassahun, A. E., Molla, A., & Sarkar, P. (2012). Government process reengineering, what we know and what we need to know. In S. Chhabra, & M. Kumar (Eds.), *Strategic enterprise resource planning models for e-government, applications and methodologies* (pp. 1–25). Hershey, PA: IGI Global. doi:10.4018/978-1-4666-1740-7.ch086

Kolsaker, A., & Lee-Kelley, L. (2006). Mind the gap: E-government and e-democracy. In M. A. Wimmer, H. J. Scholl, A. Gronlund, & K. V. Andersen (Eds.), *Electronic government* (pp. 96–106). Berlin: Springer. doi:10.1007/11823100_9

Lathrop, D., & Ruma, L. (2010). *Open government, collaboration, transparency and participation in practice*. Sebastopol, CA: O'Reilly Media.

Luna-Reyes, L. F., Pardo, T. A., Gil-Garcia, J. R., Navarrete, C., Zhang, J., & Mellouli, S. (2010). Digital government in North America: A comparative analysis of policy and program priorities in Canada, Mexico, and the United States. In C. G. Reddick (Ed.), *Comparative e-government* (pp. 139–160). New York: Springer. doi:10.1007/978-1-4419-6536-3_7

McKee, L. (2000). *Implications of the OpenGIS® specification for regional science: An open GIS consortium (OGC)*. Retrieved November 2012 from http://www.opengeospatial.org/pressroom/papers

Murray, A. (2010). *Information technology law, the law and society*. Oxford, UK: Oxford University Press.

OECD. (2007). *Giving knowledge for free: The emergence of open education resources, centre for educational research and innovation*. OECD. Retrieved May 2011 from http://www.oecd.org/document/41/0,3343,en_ 2649_35845581 _38659497_1_1_1_1,00.html

Orihuela, L., & Obi, T. (2007). E-government and e-governance: Towards a clarification in the usage of both concepts. In T. Obi (Ed.), *E-governance: A global perspective on a new paradigm* (pp. 26–33). Amsterdam: IOS Press.

Papadomichelaki, X., Magoutas, B., Halaris, C., Apostolou, D., & Mentzas, G. (2006). A review of quality dimensions in e-government services. In M. A. Wimmer, H. J. Scholl, A. Gronlund, & K. V. Andersen (Eds.), *Electronic government* (pp. 128–138). Berlin: Springer. doi:10.1007/11823100_12

Parlak, B., & Sobaci, Z. (2010). A comparative analysis of local agenda 21 websites in Turkey in terms of e-participation. In C. G. Reddick (Ed.), *Politics, democracy and e-government, participation and service delivery* (pp. 75–94). Hershey, PA: IGI Global. doi:10.4018/978-1-61520-933-0.ch005

Pedersen, S. M., & Pedersen, J. L. (2006). Innovation and diffusion of site-specific crop management. In *Contemporary management of innovation* (pp. 110–123). Houndmills, UK: Palgrave Macmillan.

Sahi, G., & Madan, S. (2012). Information security threats in ERP enabled e-governance: Challenges and solutions. In S. Chhabra, & M. Kumar (Eds.), *Strategic enterprise resource planning models for e-government, applications and methodologies* (pp. 158–170). Hershey, PA: IGI Global.

Temple Consulting Group. (2012). *MAIS: Municipal accounting and information system*. Retrieved November 2012 from http://findaccountingsoftware.com/directory/temple-consulting/mais-municipal-accounting-and-information-system/

Thomson, J. D. (2012). E-government management practice, enterprise resource planning. In S. Chhabra, & M. Kumar (Eds.), *Strategic enterprise resource planning models for e-government, applications and methodologies* (pp. 40–55). Hershey, PA: IGI Global.

ADDITIONAL READING

Bhalla G. (2011). Collaboration and Co-creation, New Platforms for Marketing and Innovation, Springer Berlin 2011.

Chesbrough, H. (2003). *Open Innovation: The New Imperative for Creating and Profiling from Technology*. Boston, MA: Harvard Business School Press.

Contini, F. Lanzara G.F. (Ed.) (2009). ICT and Innovation in the Public Sector European Studies in the Making of E-Government. New York, Palgrave Macmillan.

Cordoba-Pachon, J. R., & Ochoa-Arias, A. E. (Eds.). (2009). *Systems Thinking and E-Participation: ICT in the Governance of Society*. Hershey: Information Science Reference. doi:10.4018/978-1-60566-860-4

Gottschalk, P. (Ed.). (2008). *E-Government Interoperability and Information Resource Integration: Frameworks for Aligned Development*. Hershey: Information Science Reference.

Hakikur, R. (Ed.). (2010). *Handbook of Research on E-Government Readiness for Information and Service Exchange: Utilizing Progressive Information Communication Technologies*. Hershey: Idea Group Publishing.

Janssen, M. (Ed.). (2010). *E-Government E-Services and Global Processes*, Joint IFIP TC 8 and TC 6 International Conferences EGES 2010 and GISP 2010 Held as Part of WCC 2010 Brisbane, Australia, September 20-23, 2010 Proceedings. Heidelberg, Springer.

Kavanaugh, P. (2004). *Open Source Software, Implementation and Management*. Amsterdam: Elsevier, Digital Press.

Manoharan, A. Holzer M (Ed.) (2012). E-Governance and Civic Engagement: Factors and Determinants of E-Democracy. Hershey, Information Science Reference.

Mendes, M. J. Suomi R., Passos C. (Ed.) (2004). Digital Communities in a Networked Society e-Commerce, e-Business and e-Government The Third IFIP Conference on e-Commerce, e-Business and e-Government (I3E 2003) September 21–24, 2003, Sao Paulo, Brazil. Boston, Kluwer Academic Publishers.

Norris, D. (Ed.). (2007). *E-Government Research: Policy and Management*. Hershey: Information Science Reference. doi:10.4018/978-1-59904-913-7

Ramon, G.-G. J. (Ed.). (2012). *Enacting Electronic Government Success: An Integrative Study of Government-wide Websites, Organizational Capabilities, and Institutions*. Heidelberg: Springer Heidelberg.

Viscusi, G. (Ed.). (2010). *Information Systems for e-Government: A Quality-of-Service Perspective*. Heidelberg: Springer.

KEY TERMS AND DEFINITIONS

Digital Divide: It refers to the gap between those who have access and those who do not to information technology, digital resources, and online services. It includes any imbalance or disparity in skills, resources, or knowledge needed to make activities in the digital environment.

E-Democracy: The usage of electronic channels for democratic process such as public policy making and voting. It refers to the participation of governments, international government organizations, elected officials, the media, political parties, and non-governmental organizations, as well as citizens and interest groups, in the political processes of local, regional or state, and national communities, up to the global level through the use of the information and communication technologies.

E-Governance: The ways and means of government and organization function using modern information and communication technology such as internet, computers mobile phones to deliver services faster, easier and cheaper to its people and customers.

E-Government: The use of internet technology as a platform for exchanging information, providing services and transacting with citizens, businesses, and other arms of government. E-Government may be applied by the legislature, judiciary, or administration, in order to improve internal efficiency, the delivery of public services, or processes of democratic governance. E-Government is a relevant area of study in public administration because public administration is changing under the influence of rapidly changing ICT.

Geographic Information System (GIS): A system that enables data from a wide variety of sources and data formats to be integrated together in a common scheme of geographical referencing, thereby providing up-to-date information.

Government 2.0: It relates to the increased focus on the demand side for public services, user empowerment and engagement, benefits and impact addressing specific societal issues – like an aging population and increased global competition.

Municipality: A town level organization comprised of the elected representatives and appointed state government staff to look after the civic and social functions of the area and plan and deliver services to the people inhabited in the area. It is a local government working with the directions of the state government.

Political Participation: It is a stage of e-Government that pertains to the political arena. It incorporates different technologies that serve mainly as communication and public relations tools (two-way communication stage) to promote democratic participation in policy-making processes, but also supporting online voting in countries where this is allowed.

Web 2.0: Describes a second generation of the World Wide Web and focus on the ability for people to collaborate and share information online e.g., via social media and networks. Web 2.0 refers to the transition from static HTML Web pages to a more dynamic web. Web 2.0 covers applications of open communication (e.g., blogs, wikis, Web services) with an emphasis on web-based communities of users, and more open sharing of information.

Chapter 15
System Design and ICT Adoption in Agricultural Extension Services Delivery in Tanzania

Camilius Aloyce Sanga
Sokoine University of Agriculture, Tanzania

Siza D. Tumbo
Sokoine University of Agriculture, Tanzania

Malongo R. S. Mlozi
Sokoine University of Agriculture, Tanzania

ABSTRACT

The major purpose of this chapter is to explore the options of Information and Communication Technologies (ICTs) to complement conventional agricultural extension services in Tanzania. Group discussions and meetings were conducted to investigate the role of ICTs in extension services delivery using CATWOE framework of Soft Systems Methodology. The findings of the study reveal that the use of SSM helped the researchers to understand easily the problematic areas of the current situation of agricultural exten-sion services. In addition, it was easy to plan feasible actions to be taken to improve the situation. The framework for the conceptual model towards improving the agricultural extension services in Kilosa District of Tanzania was developed. These results have been used in the development of an ICT-based system (Web- and Mobile-Based Farmers' Advisory Information Systems) to supplement the conventional agricultural extension system. The roadmap developed as the implementation plan for this research can be used in any e-Government project. The need to improve the way agricultural extension is done in Tanzania through integration of relevant and affordable ICTs is well researched. This book chapter presents how this can be done using SSM approach in an action and participatory research. This is the first presentation of SSM intervention in agricultural informatics in Tanzania. The approach used in this study can be adopted by researchers doing any e-Government research.

DOI: 10.4018/978-1-4666-4900-2.ch015

BACKGROUND

Agriculture employs 80% and has significant contribution to the economy of Tanzania. The study by Sicilima (2003) shows it contributes 50% of the GDP but of recently, contribution of agriculture to GDP is less than 50%. The sector accounts for 30% of GDP, 30% of export earnings and 65% of raw materials for domestic industries (URT, 2008). The crops cultivated range from those produced for food and for cash purposes. Examples of food crops are maize, sorghum while cotton and cashew nuts are cash crops. Even though there are large scale farmers, smallholder farmers are main producers of food crops (Scialabba, 2000). Thus, the Government of Tanzania has established various policies and different programs to sustain smallholder farming. Examples of such initiatives are Kilimo Kwanza, Famogata, MKUKUTA, subsidized farm inputs Program, Southern Block Agriculture Development, MKUZA, TASAF etc (MAFSC, 2009). Despite all these initiatives and immense potential for agriculture productivity, agricultural growth rate in Tanzania is not encouraging. According to Eele et al. (2000) the growth rate of agricultural in Tanzania is 4%. Thus, its contribution to food security, poverty reduction and agricultural production and productivity is very minimal.

Factors hindering the growth of agricultural sector are: low farm produce price, inadequate agro-processing, weak cooperative system and limited access of farmers to information pertaining to agricultural innovations and agricultural technologies (Kaaya, 1999; Eele et al., 2000). Agricultural innovations and agricultural technologies are mainly produced from agricultural research institutes (Sanga et al., 2007). Agricultural researchers in Tanzania have developed a number of agricultural technologies and innovations, but very few smallholders' farmers are aware of such developments. Hence, there is a need for looking into how the usage of most agricultural innovations and technologies to farmers can be improved. In principle, agricultural extension officers are used as educational tools in disseminating agricultural technologies and innovations to farmers; but in many countries including Tanzania, they face a number of obstacles. Some of the factors affecting extension services in Tanzania are inadequate extension officers, inadequate working facilities, poor incentives for staff retention and weak link between research- extension and farmers (Sicilima, 2003).

Various studies have shown that traditional way of disseminating agricultural knowledge and information in Tanzania have had limitations in reaching out to many farmers, a situation which prompts to seek for complementary alternatives (Parikh et al., 2007). Thus, this calls for a research to investigate how ICT can strengthen the weak link between researchers, extension officers and farmers. The key question raised during the workshop was: How can an extension service supported by ICT be designed?

More specifically, workshop participants were interested in understanding how the ICTs will link researchers, farmers and other actors in the agricultural value chain. The role of researchers in the value chain is to disseminated knowledge to farmers via extension officers. Hence, researchers must complement the knowledge of agricultural officers and the indigenous knowledge owned by farmers. Given that the study's focus was new ICT options to support extension, existing approaches were deemed insufficient (Sicilima, 2003). Thus, the researchers were required to develop new approaches that would provide enhanced agricultural extension services from alternative viewpoints.

This chapter tries to answer the research question "How can an extension service supported by ICT be designed?" The chapter addresses this question by investigating the ICT led- extension services in Tanzania. The chapter further introduces Soft System Methodology (SSM) concepts and articulates how they are used in analyzing the potential of ICTs in unlocking the fuzzy problems facing the conventional agricultural extension services. From this chapter, it is argued that SSM is a tool to help software developer not only to do analysis and design but also in development of useful systems for different agricultural value chains. In specific, the chapter end with providing the prototypes of the Web- and mobile-based Farmers' Advisory Information Systems developed with the aid of SSM.

RELATED WORK

Swanson and Rajalahti (2010) defined agricultural extension as the function of providing need- and demand-based knowledge in agronomic techniques and skills to rural communities in a systematic, participatory manner, with the objective of improving their production, income and quality of life. Therefore, agricultural extension services transfer agricultural technology from experts to farmers using a wider range of communication and learning activities well organized by professionals for the purpose of improving agricultural production in different value chains.

For this study, Porter's and Kaplinsky's definition of value chain was adopted (Kaplinsky & Morris. 2000; Porter, 1985). It states that value chain is "the full range of activities which are required to bring a product or service from conception, through the intermediary phases of production, delivery to final consumers, and disposal after use". Thus, this calls for the development of systems in an integrated way rather than in an isolated manner. In this study, the applicability of ICTs will be in extension services rather than in integrated agricultural value chains (Appendix B). The applicability of ICT in extension services has been researched by many scholars (Bachu, Polepalli, & Reddy, 2006; Purnomo & Lee, 2010; David, & Asamoah, 2011; Kameswari, Kishore & Gupta, 2011; Ratnam et al., 2006; Colle, 2005; Sanga, Churi, & Tumbo, 2007; Eicher, 2007; Sife et al, 2010; Mtega, 2012; Mtega & Msungu, 2013; Mtega & Malekani, 2009; Sanga, Kalungwizi,

& Msuya, 2013). Its importance in improving agriculture sector in developing countries is well documented by Richardson (2004).

The biggest challenge to the development or adoption of ICTs in agriculture is that many ICTs solutions need to be specific to certain environment (Heeks, 2010). This is due to the fact that each environment has different problems which need different solutions. This is based on Gelb and Bonati (2007) and Gelb and Parker (2007) who stated the need for specific solutions for specific environments. Nevertheless, before ICT solution(s) could be designed and formulated as well as applied; the challenges need to be identified and properly analyzed for the sustainability of whatever effort for improvement is to be put in place (Heeks, 2010). Already there are quite a number of studies which worked toward this objective but what is missing in those researches is that they did not use the research method [that] allow participatory involvement of all stakeholders from the beginning and end of the research (Arokoyo, 2008; Frempong et al, 2006). It is in view of this proposition that this research study was undertaken to fill the gap in knowledge.

RESEARCH METHODOLOGY

The system approach adopted from Kenny and Shannon (2010), soft systems methodology, was used in this study.

How is System Approach Good for This Study?

The system approach which was used in this study is Soft Systems methodology (SSM). Soft systems methodology is defined by Checkland (1981) as 'a system – based means of structuring a debate' about the nature of a problem situation. In order to analyze the problem, it requires those interested in solving a problem to design a system which will operate in both concrete (real) and abstract world (Kline, 1995).

The extension services were conceptualized as a system. The importance of using the system view approach to agricultural extension service was towards easy visualization of different actors involved in the process. The actors of the convectional system of the agricultural extension services consists mainly of farmers, agricultural extension officers, extension materials. In order for any country to have an efficient and effective agricultural extension service smooth interaction of these actors is necessary (Swanson & Rajalahti, 2010).

This study used a system approach model for the analysis, design, development, and implementation of mobile- and Web-based farmers' advisory information system. This paper presents the findings obtained from the phases of software development life cycle (SDLC) which were done as case study in Kilosa District.

Area of Study

The study was conducted in Kilosa District in Morogoro region. Kilosa District is one of the six districts of Morogoro region. It is located on the eastern part of Tanzania, and about 270 km from Dar Es Salaam (Figure 1), and situated between 6 to 100S and 350E, with an altitude ranging between 300-600 meters above sea level. The District covers 14,175 square kilometers, and in 2002 had a total population of about 438,512 people (URT, 2012). Kilosa District comprises nine Divisions, 36 Wards and 132 Villages, with Kilosa town being its administrative headquarters. The District is divided into three ecological and six agro-economic zones. The three ecological zones include the flood plain, the plateau and the mountainous or upland zones. Kilosa is among the Districts in Tanzania that has both crops and livestock.

Figure 1. Map of Kilosa district

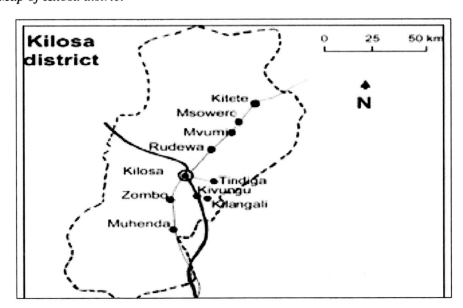

285

Reasons for Kilosa being Chosen as Area of Case Study

The District had a considerable number of inhabitants with personal computers, radio and mobile phones. In terms of other ICTs, the district has two community telecentres, one owned by Districts and another owned by the private sector, Kilosa Rural Services & Electronic centre (KIRSEC) (Mtega, 2012). Also, the district has a community radio. Furthermore, the district has Ilonga Agriculture Institute and Ministry of Agriculture Training Institute – MATI Ilonga (Kilosa). Thus, Kilosa district has been chosen as area of case study by many researchers because it has good rural ICT infrastructure (Lwoga, 2010; Chilimo, Ngulube, & Stilwell, 2011; Sife et al, 2010; Mtega & Msungu, 2013). These enabling environment helped authors to assess how agricultural researchers, extension officers, farmers and other actors in maize value chain can communicate agricultural knowledge using ICTs.

Planning for the Implementation of Soft Systems Methodology

In this research, the stakeholders were all the actors in maize value chains in Kilosa District. After the problem has been identified using SSM then it was tackled using traditional software development methodologies as described by Checkland (1981). As proposed by Checkland and Scholes (1990), the fundamental four issues under SSM are as shown in Figure 2, namely: finding out about the problem situation, formulating models of potential activity to address the problem, test ideas against the real world, and taking action to improve the agricultural extension services' problem situation.

Customizing SSM to Suit the Research Setting

The SSM was customized in cyclic fashion (Figure 3) to address the problem in question by identifying specific tasks for each issue. The output of each phase was used as input for the next phase of

Figure 2. Basic shape of SSM (adapted from Checkland, 1981)

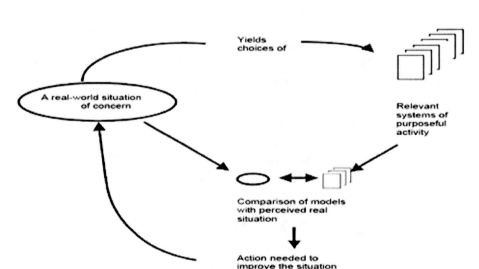

SSM. This helped to inform learning and changes needed in order to improve the agricultural extension services. The general description of different phases of SSM is as described in Figure 3.

Tasks on problem situation consist of description of the current agricultural extension service in Tanzania and detailed description of the information flow in agricultural extension services. Description of the problem situation that requires incorporation of ICT to improve the agricultural extension system initiated other phases of SSM.

The task on model formulation consists of identification of 'what needs to be done', 'how to do it' and 'why do it'. This was addressed by activities which aimed at improving the agricultural extension services using ICT. Then task on testing was done by comparing the conceptual (abstract) model against the real world systems. Finally, task on implementation consists of construction of an action plan for future remedial of the situation in cyclic fashion.

First Cycle of SSM: Stakeholder Analysis

Stakeholder analysis can be defined as an identification of all persons, groups and institutions who may have an interest in a research project and taking steps to manage their interests and expectations so that the project runs as smoothly as possible. The aim of stakeholder analysis was to identify the stakeholders in maize value chain in Kilosa District. In Figure 3, the letter 'a' represents the stakeholder analysis.

Second Cycle: Inception workshop

The objective of inception workshop was to introduce the research to the representatives of the actors and also to give their role. Also it was done to validate the objectives of the research. Furthermore, it was a forum where stakeholders and researchers shared the main areas of focus

Figure 3. How SSM was used to manage the research

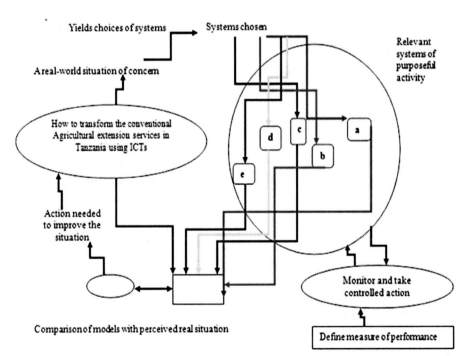

for project assessment. In Figure 3, the letter 'b' represents the inception workshop.

Third Cycle: Conducting Baseline Survey

The baseline survey is an initial point for monitoring and evaluation that provides a comprehensive characterization of a phenomenon in a research project area so that later changes in its attributes can be measured. It provides the actual measurements of certain parameter prior to implementation of a research project. Furthermore, it gives good indicators for comparison after the intervention has been done.

The purpose of baseline survey was to identify the characteristics of farmers, ICT services and devices used by farmers, ICT use in crop productions and constraints that farmers face in using ICTs in agriculture. In Figure 3, the letter 'c' represents the baseline survey.

Fourth Cycle: Implementation of Web Based Farmers' Advisory Information System (W-FAIS)

The aim of this investigation was to develop W-FAIS to supplement the conventional agricultural extension services. In Figure 3, the letter 'd' represents the W-FAIS.

Fifth Cycle: Implementation of Mobile Based Farmers' Advisory Information System (M-FAIS)

The objective of this investigation was to develop M-FAIS. In Figure 3, the letter 'e' represents the M-FAIS.

RESULTS AND DISCUSSIONS

This section presents the results obtained after subjecting SSM to analyze how ICT can be in-

corporated to improve the agricultural extension services in Kilosa district.

First Cycle of SSM: Stakeholders' Analysis

After the relevant activity systems of the conceptual model has been formulated in form of the root definition then comparison was done. The comparison was based on assessing abstract /conceptual/hypothetical world against real world using CATWOE approach. The CATWOE for this study is as shown in Table 1.

This output from the first cycle of SSM helped to get the background information about the research to be undertaken. This was taken as input to the second cycle of SSM where the participants were required to have a consensus on the areas of the research's focus.

Second Cycle: Introducing the Research to Participants

The participants in the inception workshop were divided into seven groups. The groups were formed according to actors of the maize value chain which are namely: farmers, extension officers, processors, trainers, researchers, communication experts and policy makers. Each group identified the key problems, challenges, and their expectation from the project, how could them contribute to the project and other criteria they thought valuable in achieving the research objective. Some of the responses from each group are as summarized below in Tables 2 to 8.

After the problems and challenges facing maize value chain actors from Kilosa have been identified, then baseline survey was conducted in three villages to collect information about farmers' characteristics, ICT used in their agriculture activities and constraints which they face.

Table 1. CATWOE mnemonic

C	Customer	Who Might be the Beneficiaries of the System Be?	Small Scale Farmers
A	Actors	Who are the key players / actors?	farmers, processor, microfinance institution, maize producers' association, input suppliers, Non- Government Organization, Community Based Organization, local government authority, policy makers, middlemen, transporters, international agency, donor, consumers, researchers, community centre, media organizations.
T	Transformation process	What are the input and outputs of the system?	Analysis of the agriculture information flow to different actors in the maize value chain. The input involves the current knowledge and experiences of different actors involved in the agricultural value chains. The expected output is an improved agricultural extension services and its coverage.
W	Worldview	What are the worldviews that makes the activity system meaningful?	The possibility of doing analysis, design and development of an ICT based system to support conventional extension service of farmers in Tanzania. Its essence is on improving the linkages of actors.
O	Owner	Who owns it?	Government and all actors
E	Environment constraints	Real world constraints	ICT resources, maintenance of ICTs owned by farmers and Knowledge Resource Centres, electricity, ICT literacy

Table 2. Problems and challenges facing farmers

Farmers Group	
Problems	**Challenges**
• Low production • Low price especially for maize product • Lack of reliable market • High cost of production and farm inputs for example fertilizers, seeds and pesticides. • Shortage of agricultural extension services especially in rural areas. • Shortage of land; Large portion of land are owned by private organization for example sisal farms. • the prevailing climate change which make it hard for farmers to predict the onset of the raining season	• Inability of most farmers to posses mobile phones • Lack of reliable source of power (electricity) especially in rural areas hinders the information and communication services. • Limited coverage of mobile phones network • High cost to buy and operate mobile phones • Limited coverage of Radio frequency (especially in rural areas) • Most farmers do not posses radio thus can't benefit the programmes aired by Kilosa Community Radio

Table 3. Problems and challenges facing extension officers

Extension Officers	
Problems	**Challenges**
• Shortage of facilities for transport, production and processing • High cost of production and farm inputs especially in maize production • Lack of reliable market • Lack of reliable information and communication infrastructures	• Adverse of Climate change • Farmers do not receive farm inputs on time • Shortage of facilities like transport and production facilities lead to failure in educating most farmers • Increase in forged as well as poor quality (i.e. Counterfeit) farm inputs lead to poor quality of products • Lack of reliable infrastructures for information and Communication Technology (ICT)

Table 4. Problems and challenges facing researcher group

Researcher Group	
Problems	**Challenges**
• Inability to buy and operate mobile phones. This was for the stakeholders who can't own and service mobile phones • Mobile phone network coverage problems; some areas are not covered by mobile phone network. • Wrong information provided by some stakeholders during data collection	• Lack of source of power in some areas especially rural areas • ICTs cannot solve some problems especially real time evaluation and monitoring of the research activities in the field. e.g. Soil research need samples of soil from the particular place (farm) that will be worked out in the laboratory to determine the extent of nutrients. Some farms are located far away such that they cost researchers (i.e. time, money, resources). • Agro-dealers and law agency should be included in this research to facilitate stakeholders in agriculture especially maize value chain to access relevant information on time.

Table 5. Problems and challenges facing communication group

Communication Group	
Problems	**Challenges**
• High operation cost for mobile phones and Internet access • Unreliable source of power • Limited time for advertisement through Radio • Most agriculture stakeholders are not interested to access/listen announcements or agriculture training session which are advertized through radio or uploaded on the Internet. • Lack of knowledge to some agriculture stakeholders on how to use the Internet	• Unreliable network connectivity • Shortage of reliable source of power

Table 6. Problems and challenges facing trainers group

Trainers Group	
Problems	**Challenges**
• Insufficient budget allocated to train stakeholders and improve information and communication services. • Poor communication between trainers and agriculture stakeholders • Wrong information from some stakeholders	• Insufficient ICT facilities to be used by a large number of students available in colleges • High cost required to buy and run ICT facilities like mobile phones • Rapid change of ICT and related facilities • Lack of interest to most Tanzanians to use their mobile phones to search agriculture related information.

Table 7. Problems and challenges facing processors' group

Processors' Group	
Problems	**Challenges**
• Low quality of raw materials produced. • Shortage of reliable infrastructures like roads and source of power • Shortage of specialists.	• Shortage of quality packages • Shortage of processing facilities and skilled manpower in packaging and agro-processing industry • Poor quality of available processing facilities

Table 8. Problems and challenges facing policy maker group

Policy Maker Group	
Problems	**Challenges**
• Most researcher leave their findings in documents, they are not implemented to help the intended group like agriculture stakeholder at Kilosa and other places, something which lead to difficult in decision making, evaluation of improvement and even monitoring. • Improper communication between policy maker and other agriculture stakeholders	• Lack of reliable source of power (electricity) especially in rural areas hinders the information and communication services, this lead to delay in accessibility to information hence affect decision making especially on marketing price and farm inputs • Poor quality of products produced in turn make difficult in price synchronization.

Third Cycle of SSM: Identifying Farmers' Characteristics, ICT used in Agriculture by Farmers and Constraints Facing

Characteristics of Farmers

Respondents' Social-Economic Characteristics

Respondents were asked to state their social-economic characteristics such as age, education, sex and marital status. In total, forty (40) respondents were interviewed and their specific categories were: male headed household heads, female headed household heads, presence of grown up children, and households' heads living with relatives. Of all the respondents, 31 (78% Response Rate (RR)) indicated that they had male household heads, while five (13% RR) had female household heads, two respondents for each indicated that they lived with grown up children and relatives, respectively. Table 9 also shows that of the 40 respondents, 31 (78% RR) males, while nine (23% RR) were females.

The reason for a small number of females during survey could be due to the fact that this

Table 9. Respondent Category (N=40)

Respondents' Category	Frequency	Percent
Male household heads	31	78
Female household heads	5	13
Grown up child	2	5
House heads with relatives	2	5
Total	**40**	**100**
Respondents' sex		
Male	31	78
Female	9	23
Total	**40**	**100**

Source: Survey data, 2012.

study interviewed heads of households, majority of which are male. Most of the female respondents who were married agreed to answer questions just because their husbands were not around.

Respondents' Ages

Of the 40 respondents, 25 (64%) reported that they were aged between 20 and 30 years old, while, eight (18%) indicated as aged between 31 and 40 years old. Also, seven (18%) of the respondents mentioned that they were aged between 51 and 60 years old (Table 10). The fact that two thirds of the respondents (64%) were aged between 20 and 30 years old signifies that agriculture is an important activity in the study area involving young people who are potential users of ICTs.

Respondents' Marital Status

Table 11 shows the respondents' education levels. The study findings show that among the respondents 29 (73%) were married, six (15%) were single, and five 13%) were either separated (5%) or divorced (8%). This meant that over two thirds of the respondents, 73 percent were married, which implied that they had stable families that engaged in farming as a means to ensure food security and income generation, and could be potential users of ICTs.

Further, Table 11 shows that of the 40 respondents, 23 (58%) indicated that they had no formal education, while 14 (35%) reported to had attained primary education level, that is, standard seven. Also, of all the respondents, two (5%) reported

Table 10. Respondents' age groups (N=40)

Age group	Male		Female		Overall	
	n	**%**	**N**	**%**	**n**	**%**
20 – 30	19	48	6	15	25	64
31 – 40	7	18	1	3	8	18
51 – 60	5	13	2	5	7	18
Total	**31**	**78**	**9**	**23**	**40**	**100**

Source: Survey data, 2012.

Table 11. Respondents' marital status and education levels (N=40)

Marital Status	Male		Female		Overall	
	n	%	n	%	n	%
Married	27	68	2	5	29	73
Single	3	8	3	8	6	15
Divorced	1	3	1	3	2	5
Separated	0	0	3	8	3	8
Total	**31**	**78**	**9**	**23**	**40**	**100**
Education level						
No formal education	19	48	4	10	23	58
Standard Seven	9	23	5	13	14	35
Form Four	2	5	0	0	2	5
Form Six	1	3	0	0	1	3
Total	**31**	**78**	**9**	**23**	**40**	**100**

Source: Survey data, 2012.

to had attained Form Four level of education, that is secondary school, one (3%) indicated to had completed high level, that is, Form Six. The study findings implied that most of the respondents had no (58%) or low formal education (35%), which affect the use of ICTs such as computers, mobile phones and other electronics devices which require reading skills to operate them. The other implication is that extended efforts would be needed to educate people in the villages to use ICTs.

Respondents' Main Occupation and Crop Types Grown

Table 12 shows that of the 40 respondents, 30 (75%) reported that their main occupations were crop farming, while, few, three (8%) indicated to keeping livestock. On the other hand, five (13%) of the respondents mentioned that they did business, while two (5%) said that they were involved in mixed farming. In total, most, 55 (88%) of the respondents involved themselves in agricultural activities signifying that that they were potential users of ICTs for communicating agricultural information. Further, Table 12 shows that less than half of the respondents, 19 (48%) reported to growing maize, while 17 (47%) mentioned to growing paddy rice (Table 12). Other minor crops

that respondents reported to grow were sunflower (5%), sesame (3%) and cowpeas (3%). This implied that ICTs should concentrate in developing information contents in maize and paddy rice.

ICT Services and Devices that Respondents Used

Type of ICTs Device Possessed, Internet Access and Use

Table 13 show the type of ICTs that the 40 respondents possessed. Of the 40 respondents, 16 (40%) and 11 (28%) indicated that they possessed mobile phones and television sets, respectively. A quarter of the respondents, ten (25%) reported that they possessed radio, while few, three (8%) mentioned to possessing computers. Less than a third of the respondents possessed mobile phones (43%) implying that they were using them for communicating agricultural information. Low possession of computers (8%) could be due to high cost of buying computers and the lack of power. Generally, there are potentials for using ICTs in the study areas.

Further, Table 13 shows that of the 40 respondents, 28 (70%) denied that their mobile phones could not access Internet. The implication of this

Table 12. Respondents' main occupations (N=40)

Main occupation	Male		Female		Overall	
	n	%	n	%	n	%
Crop farmers	25	63	5	13	30	75
Livestock keepers	2	5	1	3	3	8
Business people	3	8	2	5	5	13
Mixed farming	1	3	1	3	2	5
Total	31	78	9	23	40	100
Crops grown						
Paddy rice	13	33	4	10	17	43
Maize	14	35	5	13	19	48
Sunflower	2	5	0	0	2	5
Sesame	1	3	0	0	1	3
Beans	1	3	0	0	1	3
Total	31	78	9	23	40	100

Source: Survey data, 2012.

Table 13. Type of ICTs device possessed (N=40)

Type of ICT Device Possessed	Male		Female		Overall	
	n	%	n	%	n	%
Computer	2	5	1	3	3	8
TV	9	23	2	5	11	28
Mobile phone	15	38	1	3	16	40
Radio	5	13	3	13	10	25
Total	31	78	9	23	40	100
If mobile phone can access to Internet						
No	21	53	7	18	28	70
Yes	10	25	2	5	12	30
Total	31	78	9	23	40	100
Use of mobile phone with Internet						
To search information	2	5	0	0	2	5
Do not use it at all	29	73	9	23	38	95
Total	31	78	9	23	40	100

Source: Survey data, 2012.

is that over two thirds of the respondents possessed mobile phones with lower capability and had no features to access Internet. Also, of the 40 respondents, most, 38 (95%) reported that they did access Internet using their mobile phones to search for different information or e-mails even for those whom their mobile phones had such capabilities. This might be due to inadequate awareness of Internet services amongst the respondents or cost associated with accessing Internet via mobile phones.

Local Radio Stations that Respondents Listened To

Table 14 shows the radio stations that respondents tuned to. Of the 40 respondents, the most, nine (23% RR) indicated that they tuned to TBC Taifa, followed by eight (20% RR) and seven (18% RR) who mentioned that they listened to Ukweli radio and Radio Maria, respectively. Few, five (12% RR), and two (5% RR) reported that they listened to RFA, Clouds FM and Imam Radio, respectively. Abood and Radio One were reported to be tuned by three (8% RR) and one (2% RR) of the respondents. These results indicate that there is a wide range of radio preference in the study areas and that half (50% RR) of the respondents preferred TBC Taifa, Radio Ukweli and Radio Maria stations. On the other hand, all 40 respondents listened to Kilosa community radio. These radio stations could in the future be the ones to send agricultural messages for broadcasting.

Network Companies that Respondents Accessed

Table 15 shows the network companies that respondents accessed. Of the 40 respondents, a third, 13 (33% RR) reported that accessed Tigo Mobile Phone Network Company, while 12 (30% RR)

mentioned to access Airtel Mobile Phone Network Company. Also, eight (20% RR) and seven (18% RR) of the respondents said that they accessed to Zantel Mobile Phone Network Company and Vodacom Mobile Phone Network Company, respectively. In spite of the coverage mentioned above, two thirds of the respondents, 26 (65% RR) indicated that the mobile phone network coverage was available periodically, while 14 (35% RR) said it was available always. The implication of these results is that the study area was covered by all major mobile phone service providers, an aspect that could in the future aid in dissemination and communication of agricultural information using mobile phones. However, the question of network unavailability could somehow hinder such efforts.

ICT Use in Crop Production

Sources of Information at Start of Season, Rainfall and Markets

Table 16 shows the various sources of information that respondents used. Of the 40 respondents, most, 30 (75% RR) of the respondents indicated that they did not receive any information about agriculture from the agriculture extension agents at the start of the growing season. Similarly, 28 (70% RR) and 26 (65% RR) of the respondents

Table 14. Local radio stations that respondents listened (N=40)

	Male		Female		Overall	
Radio	**N**	**%**	**n**	**%**	**n**	**%**
TBC Taifa	7	18	2	5	9	23
Ukweli	6	15	2	5	8	20
Abood	2	5	1	3	3	8
Radio Maria	5	13	2	5	7	18
RFA	4	10	1	3	5	12
Imam	2	5	0	0	2	5
Clouds FM	4	10	1	3	5	13
Radio One	1	2	0	0	1	2
Total	**31**	**77**	**9**	**23**	**40**	**100**

Source: Survey data, 2012.

Table 15. Network companies that respondents accessed

Network company	Male		Female		Overall	
	n	%	n	%	n	%
Tigo	10	25	3	8	13	33
Airtel	10	25	2	5	12	30
Zantel	6	15	2	5	8	20
Vodacom	5	13	2	5	7	18
Total	**31**	**78**	**9**	**23**	**40**	**100**

Source: Survey data, 2012.

Table 16. Various sources of information (N=40)

Various Source of Information	Male		Female		Overall	
At Start of Growing Season	No	Yes	No	Yes	No	Yes
Extension agents	22	9	8	1	30	10
Meteorological agency - radio	19	12	7	2	26	14
Meteorological agency - TV	20	11	8	1	28	12
Habitual calendar	14	17	8	1	22	18
About rainfall amount						
Extension agent	23	8	9	0	32	8
Meteorological agency - radio	16	15	9	0	25	15
Meteorological agency - TV	19	12	8	1	27	13
About crop markets and prices						
Middlemen	17	14	8	1	25	15
Fellow farmers	19	12	7	2	26	14
Business people	20	11	9	0	29	11
TV	25	6	8	1	33	7
Radio	25	6	8	1	33	7

Source: Survey data, 2012.

reported that they did not receive any meteorological information from the radio and their TVs, respectively at the start of the growing season. On the other hand, of the 40 respondents, 22 (55% RR) of the respondents mentioned that they did not use the habitual calendars as a source of information about agriculture at the start of the crop growing season.

Further, 18 (45% RR) of the respondents agreed that they used the habitual calendars as a source of information about agriculture at the start of the crop growing season. Yet, few, ten (25% RR) of the respondents reported that they received information about agriculture from the agriculture extension agents at the start of the growing season. Similarly, 14 (35% RR) and 12 (30% RR) of the respondents agreed that they received meteorological information from the radio and TV, respectively at the start of the growing season (Table 14).

Of the 40 respondents, 15 (37.5% RR) and 14 (27.5% RR) agreed that they got information about crop markets and prices from the middlemen and fellow farmers, respectively, while 11 (29.5% RR) said that they got it from the business people. TVs and the radio were each mentioned as sources of information about the crop markets and prices by seven (17.5% RR) of the respondents (Table 16).

The implications of this study results is that few respondents use the Tanzania Meteorological Agency (TMA) data via radio or TV as a source of information at the start of the agricultural season. This is to say that farmers had less trust in the TMA weather data forecast, especially information about when the first rains are to come. And because of this, therefore, a significant number of the respondents used the habitual calendar (e.g. when to plant knowing when the rains will start as a source of information at start of the agricultural season.

Respondents' Sources Of Information Used to Improve Agricultural Knowledge

Table 17 shows the sources of information that respondents used to improve their knowledge about agriculture. Of the 40 respondents, 24 (60% RR) reported that their main source of information for improving their agricultural knowledge were the agricultural extension agents. A quarter of the respondents, 10 (25% RR) and few, six (15% RR) mentioned that their sources of information for improving their knowledge about agriculture were the experienced fellow farmers and the TV and radio, respectively. The implication of these findings are that still the agricultural extension

agents is the main source of agricultural information to almost two thirds of the farmers in the study areas. Hence, there is a need to involve them in the dissemination and communication of agriculture knowledge and information through ICTs to smallholder farmers. The low use of TV and radio as sources of agricultural information could perhaps be due to lack of power and their high initial cost to buy them.

Respondents' Limitations to Using ICTs In Agriculture

Table 18 shows the study results of frequencies that respondents gave as aspects limiting the use of ICTs in agriculture. Of the 40 respondents, 16 (40% RR) agreed that illiteracy among farmers was a factor limiting the effective use ICTs in agriculture. The other aspect was poverty, which was agreed by 19 (47.5% RR) of the respondents. On the other hand, of all the respondents, 15 (37.5% RR) agreed that poor ICT infrastructure limited the effective use of ICTs in agriculture. Yet, 11 (27.5% RR) of the respondents agreed that ignorance about ICTs was another limitation to their effective use in agriculture. The implications of these findings is that there is about a half of the population in the study areas that could make use of the ICTs, and so in the District. It is anticipated that such a potential should be utilized for improving the dissemination of agricultural information using ICTs.

Table 17. Sources of information used to improve agricultural knowledge (N=40)

Source of Information	Male		Female		Overall	
	n	%	n	%	n	%
From the agricultural extension agent	19	48	5	13	24	60
From watching TV and listening to radio sessions	5	13	1	3	6	15
From experienced fellow farmer	7	18	3	8	10	25
Total	**31**	**77.5**	**9**	**22.5**	**40**	**100**

Source: Survey data, 2012.

Table 18. Respondents' limitations to using ICTs in agriculture (N=40)

Variable	Male				Female			
	Agree	Strongly agree	Undecided	Disagree	Agree	Strongly agree	Undecided	Disagree
Illiteracy	7	7	14	3	2	0	7	0
Poverty	6	13	11	1	0	0	7	0
Poor ICT infrastructure	9	5	11	6	1	1	7	0
Ignorance on ICTs	4	5	13	9	1	1	7	0

Source: Survey data, 2012.

The general finding from this third cycle of SSM is that most of farmers do possess mobile phones, laptop and desktop computers which have no Internet connection. Also, it was found that there was high need for information and knowledge pertaining to farmers' agriculture. Thus development of a system which will add value to the ICTs they have was very important.

Fourth Cycle of SSM: Development of Web based Farmers' Advisory Information System

What Needs To Be Done?

After the results for third cycle of SSM has been obtained, they were then used as inputs for the fourth cycle of SSM. This means the need for developing concepts to implement the conceptual framework which was already developed (Appendix A and Figure 4). The framework proposes the use of tele-centres equipped with community radios; SMS and Internet to supplement the conventional extension services. In this regard, Kilosa has community centres operated by private sector (KIRSEC) and community radio. Therefore, the missing link which is worked by this research is the ICT enabled system to link farmers and other actors. The proposed extension model (see Figure 4) is a mix of six extension models as identified by Eicher (2007). Eicher (2007) identified six extension models which are being operationized in developing countries, namely: the national public extension model, the commodity extension and research model, the Training and Visit (T&V) extension model, the NGO extension model, the private extension model and the Farmer Field School (FFS) approach (model).

How to Do it?

In order to develop the proposed model an interactive mobile- and Web- based farmers' advisory information system (W-FAIS & M-FAIS) has been developed. With an interactive mobile and Web based system, farmers will be able to submit their request for information / knowledge by SMS and those questions will be stored in a database. The tele-centre officer or agricultural extension officer will answer the questions from farmers. This is for the case when they have an answer, otherwise – if the question is complex the system will forward the question to Knowledge Resource Centres (KRCs). This will be done through Web based system. The experts in KRCs will then answer the farmers' questions directly. These functionalities have been implemented in W-FAIS and M-FAIS.

W-FAIS utilizes the advantages offered by Web based information systems. It contains knowledge and information on important agricultural aspects (Figure 5).

While using this system, farmers can get advice in various agricultural topics such as agronomic practices, post-harvest operations, livestock husbandry, forestry, veterinary services, community development, market and financial support services. Farmers can submit their questions to the system through the Web and the questions will

Figure 4. Conceptual framework to improve extension services in Tanzania

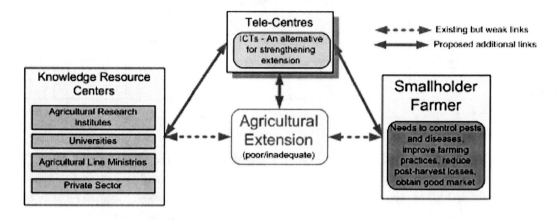

Figure 5. Homepage of W-FAIS

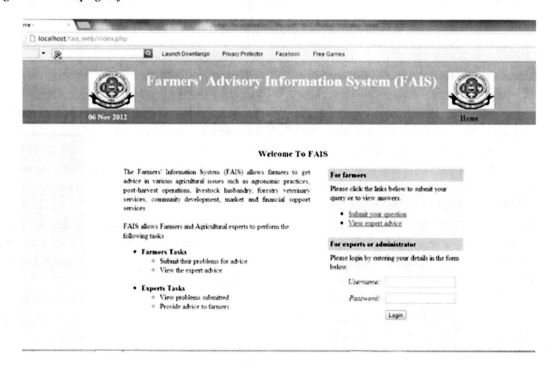

be assigned to relevant well experienced experts to answer them. Answers from the experts are then uploaded to the system to be viewed by farmers and any user who will use the system.

In principle, all functionalities available in W-FAS has been replicated in M-FAIS. The idea behind this is that the user of both systems will have an integrated system which allows the user to access and use it anytime and anywhere (ubiquitously).

Fifth Cycle of SSM: Development of Mobile based Farmers' Advisory Information System

The SMS module for W-FAIS serves as main channel of communication between farmers, administrators and experts via their mobile phones.

Farmer

Farmer sends SMS based question asking the expert about question of his/her interest. This is done in real time. When the farmer asks the question which has already been asked before, the system will provide the desired result (if the question has already been answered). Communication between farmer and the expert is completely done through short message service (SMS). The mobile phone

SMS program is used as input/output device during the conversation. For example: "132#*mahindi yana komaa baada ya miezi miwili na nusu.*"After the message has been sent to the system, the message will be received by the system and forwarded to respective farmer as shown in Figure 7.

The farmer will receive the answer sent to him/her as SMS in his/her mobile phone as normal text messages e.g. *"Mahindi yanakomaa baada ya miezi miwili na nusu"* (Figure 6).

CONCLUSION AND RECOMMENDATION

SSM has been used widely in research studies dealing with information systems, but more commonly for information management, and strategy as well as business analysis than for computer system design (Iivari and Hirschheim, 1996, Mingers, and White, 2010). This chapter has filled this gap in knowledge by presenting how SSM can be used in analysis, design and implementation of information system. The execution of the SSM in five cycles helped to understand the fuzzy and complex problems facing traditional agricultural extension services (Sicilima, 2003). Then stakeholder analysis identified different actors of maize value chain. Some representatives of actors were

Figure 6. Main window for M-FAIS

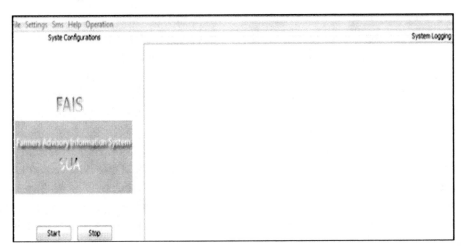

Figure 7. M-FAIS window showing answered SMS

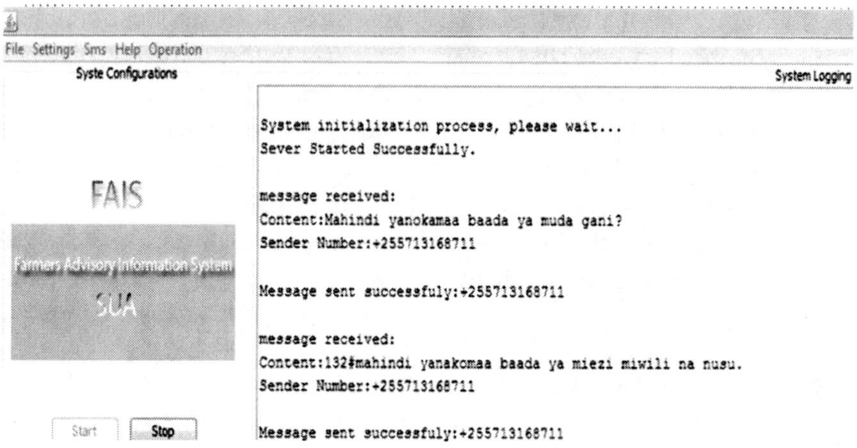

selected purposively to participate in an inception workshop and thereafter, the baseline survey was done. After that, the researchers were able to start development of the Web based farmers' advisory information system and mobile based farmers' advisory information system from the user requirements obtained from end user. Both systems can be used in advisory services to any actors in maize value chain even though its name specified farmers. It was done purposively since farmers are at the epicenter of the sharing process in agricultural knowledge and information system (AKIS).

Furthermore, SSM helped to unpack the activities needed to be implemented to stimulate the desired development of traditional agricultural extension services in Tanzania. The study by Mtega and Msungu (2013) in Kilosa revealed that mobile phones and radio were preferred as communication channels among farmers while researchers and extension staff mentioned to prefer using computers and Internet. Thus, our study has brought the solutions in an action research which fit well the findings of previous empirical researches (Sife et al, 2010; Mtega & Msungu, 2013; Mtega & Malekani, 2009; Sanga, Kalungwizi, & Msuya, 2013).

Future study will be done to probe the efficacy, effectiveness and efficiency of W- FAIS and M-FAIS to different actors in the maize value chain

found in Kilosa District. The proposed future activities to be done will initiate more cycles for SSM which will add an endless debate and learning to researchers and participating users or respondents.

It is anticipated that the induction of the proposed ICTs (W- FAIS and M-FAIS) in the conventional agricultural extension system will bring some desired change to the Tanzania's farmers and other actors. These changes are the ones Checkland (1981) called them "desirable and feasible changes". Examples of such desirable changes expected after the incorporation of ICTs in agricultural extension service in Tanzania are: (i) the increase of knowledge (ii) the introduction of new perception how ICT can improve extension services through improving the linkages between different actors (iii) the altitude / behaviour change in using available ICTs in agriculture especially through improved communication and (iv) the improve of livehood and food security (Sife et al, 2010; Mtega & Msungu, 2013; Mtega, & Malekani, 2009; Sanga, Kalungwizi, & Msuya, 2013).

The developed W-FAIS and M-FAIS should be tested in field and then scaled up to different districts of Tanzania. This will open avenues for future studies to evaluate its impacts in improving the coverage of agricultural extension service in Tanzania.

ACKNOWLEDGMENT

The authors would like to thank Mr. Lupyana Muhiche, Mr. James John Mariki and Mr. Juma Mwidadi for the work done in developing prototype of M-FAIS and W-FAIS. Also, we thank the financial support given to our research group from EPINAV – Sokoine University of Agriculture. Any opinions expressed in this paper are those of the authors alone.

REFERENCES

Annor-Frempong, F., Kwarteng, J., Agunga, R., & Zinnah, M. M. (2006). Challenges and prospects of infusing information communication technologies (ICTS) in extension for agricultural and rural development in Ghana. In *Proceedings of the Annual Conference of the International Association of Agricultural and Extension Education*. Academic Press.

Arokoyo, T. (2008). *ICTs in the transformation of agricultural extension: The case of Nigeria*. Retrieved May 16, 2013 from http://www.cta.int/observatory2003/case_studies/Case_study_Nigeria.pdf

Bachu, V. R., Polepalli, K.R., & Reddy, G.S. (2006). eSagu: An IT based personalized agricultural extension system prototype - Analysis of 51 farmers' case studies. *International Journal of Education and Development using ICT, 2*(1).

Checkland, P. (1981). *Systems thinking, systems practice*. Chichester, UK: John Wiley & Sons.

Checkland, P., & Scholes, J. (1990). *Soft systems methodology in action*. Chichester, UK: John Wiley & Sons.

Chilimo, W. L., Ngulube, P., & Stilwell, C. (2011). Information seeking patterns and telecentre operations: A case of selected rural communities in Tanzania. *Libri, 61*(1), 37–49. doi:10.1515/libr.2011.004

Colle, R. (2005). Building ICT4D capacity in and by African universities. *International Journal of Education and Development using ICT, 1*(1).

David, S., & Asamoah, C. (2011). Video as a tool for agricultural extension in Africa: A case study from Ghana. *International Journal of Education and Development using ICT, 7*(1).

Eele, G., Somboja, J., Likwelile, S., & Ackroyd, S. (2000). Meeting international targets in Tanzania. *Development Review Policy, 18*(1), 1467–7679.

Eicher, C. K. (2007). *Agricultural extension in Africa and Asia*. East Lansing, MI: Michigan State University, Department of Agricultural Economics.

Gelb, E., & Bonati, G. (2007). Evaluating internet for extension in agriculture (1997). In *ICT in agriculture: Perspectives of technological innovation*. Jerusalem, Israel: Hebrew University of Jerusalem. Retrieved June 2, 2013 from http://departments.agri.huji.ac.il/economics/gelb-sum-12.pdf

Gelb, E., & Parker, C. (2007). Is ICT adoption for agriculture still an important issue? In *ICT in agriculture: Perspectives of technological innovation*. Jerusalem, Israel: Hebrew University of Jerusalem. Retrieved March 23, 2013 from http://departments.agri.huji.ac.il/economics/gelb-gelb-parker.pdf.

Heeks, R. (2010). Do information and communication technologies (ICTs) contribute to development? *Journal of International Development, 22*(5), 625–640. doi:10.1002/jid.1716

Iivari, J., & Hirschheim, R. (1996). Analyzing information systems development: A comparison and analysis of eight is development approaches. *Information Systems, 21*(7), 551–575. doi:10.1016/S0306-4379(96)00028-2

Kaaya, J. (1999). Role of information technology in agriculture. In *Proceedings of FoA Conference,* (vol. 4, pp. 315-328). FoA.

Kameswari, V. L. V., Kishore, D., & Gupta, V. (2011). ICTs for agricultural extension: A study in the Indian Himalayan region ICTs for agricultural extension. *Electronic Journal of Information Systems in Developing Countries, 48*(3), 1–12.

Kaplinsky, R., & Morris, M. (2000). *A handbook for value chain research.* Ottawa, Canada: International Development Research Centre.

Kenny, S., & Shannon, P. (2010). Using soft systems methodology to support extension program development in the dairy industry. *Extension Farming Systems Journal, 6*(1), 124–129.

Kline, S. J. (1995). *Conceptual foundations for multidisciplinary thinking.* Palo Alto, CA: Stanford University Press.

Lwoga, E. T. (2010). Bridging the agricultural knowledge and information divide: The case of selected telecenters and rural radio in Tanzania. *Electronic Journal of Information Systems in Developing Countries, 43*(6), 1–14.

Mingers, J., & White, L. (2010). A review of the recent contribution of systems thinking to operational research and management science. *European Journal of Operational Research, 207*(3), 1147–1161. doi:10.1016/j.ejor.2009.12.019

Ministry of Agriculture. Food Security and Cooperatives (MAFSC). (2009). *Ten pillars of Kilimo Kwanza (implementation framework).* Retrieved May 9, 2013 from http://www.tzonline.org/pdf/tenpillarsofkilimokwanza.pdf

Mtega, W., & Malekani, A. (2009). Analyzing the usage patterns and challenges of telecenters among rural communities: Experience from four selected telecenters in Tanzania. *International Journal of Education and Development using ICT, 5*(2).

Mtega, W., & Malekani, A. (2009). Analyzing the usage patterns and challenges of telecenters among rural communities: Experience from four selected telecenters in Tanzania. *International Journal of Education and Development using ICT, 5*(2).

Mtega, W. P. (2012). Access to and usage of information among rural communities: A case study of Kilosa District Morogoro Region in Tanzania. *Partnership. The Canadian Journal of Library and Information Practice and Research, 7*(1).

Mtega, W. P., & Msungu, A. C. (2013). Using information and communication technologies for enhancing the accessibility of agricultural information for improved agricultural production in Tanzania. *Electronic Journal of Information Systems in Developing Countries, 56*(1), 1–14.

Parikh, T. S., Patel, N., & Schwartzman, Y. (2007). A survey of information systems reaching small producers in global agricultural value chains. In *Proceedings of IEEE Conference on Information and Communication Technologies for Development* (ICTD 2007). IEEE.

Porter, M. E. (1985). *Competitive advantage.* New York: Free Press.

Purnomo, S., & Lee, Y. (2010). An assessment of readiness and barriers towards ICT program implementation: Perceptions of agricultural extension officers in Indonesia. *International Journal of Education and Development using ICT, 6*(3).

Richardson, D. (2004). *How can agricultural extension best harness ICTs to improve rural livelihoods in developing countries?* Retrieved May 9, 2013 from http://departments.agri.huji.ac.il/economics/gelb-how-11.pdf

Sanga, C., Churi, A. J., & Tumbo, S. (2007). *Status, opportunities, potential and challenges of technology-mediated open and distance education (Tech-MODE) for agricultural education and improved livelihoods: A case study of Tanzania, July 2007.* Retrieved March 28, 2013 from http://www.col.org/SiteCollectionDocuments/Tech-MODE_report_online.pdf

Sanga, C.A., Kalungwizi, V.J., & Msuya, C.P. (2013). Building agricultural extension services system supported by ICTs in Tanzania: Progress made, challenges remain. *International Journal of Education and Development using ICT, 9*(1), 80-99.

Scialabba, N. (2000). *Factors influencing organic agriculture policies with a focus on developing countries.* Paper presented at the IFOAM 2000 Scientific Conference. Basel, Switzerland.

Sicilima, N. (2003). Strengthening the linkage among researchers, farmers and extension as a means towards enhancing adoption of agricultural technologies. In *Proceedings of the Second Collaborative Research Workshop on Food Security.* TARP II-SUA.

Sife, S. A., Kiondo, E., & Lyimo-Macha, J. G. (2010). Contribution of mobile phones to rural livelihoods and poverty reduction in Morogoro region: Tanzania. *The Electronic Journal of Information Systems in Developing Countries, 42*(3), 1–15.

Swanson, B. E., & Rajalahti, R. (2010). *Strengthening agricultural extension and advisory systems: Procedures for assessing, transforming, and evaluating extension systems.* Washington, DC: World Bank-Agriculture and Rural Development.

ADDITIONAL READING

O'Cathain, A., Murphy, E., & Nicholl, J. (2007). Integration and publications as indicators of 'yield' from mixed methods studies. *Journal of Mixed Methods Research, 1,* 147–163. doi:10.1177/1558689806299094

Ojo, A., Janowski, T., & Estevez, E. (2007). *Determining progress towards e-Government: What are the core indicators? UNU-IIST Report, No. 360, Macao.* International Institute for Software Technology, United Nations University.

Ok, H-Y. (2011). New Media Practices in Korea, *International Journal of Communication,* 5:320-348. Retrieved march 18, 2011 from ijoc.org/ojs/index.php/ijoc/article/viewFile/701/527.

Olson, J. R., & Boyer, K. K. (2003). Factors influencing the utilisation of Internet purchasing in small organisations. *Journal of Operations Management, 21,* 225–245. doi:10.1016/S0272-6963(02)00089-X

Ooh, K. L., Lean, O. K., Zailani, S., Ramayah, T., & Fernando, Y. (2009). Factors influencing intention to use e-Government services among citizens in Malaysia. *International Journal of Information Management, 29*(6), 458–475. doi:10.1016/j.ijinfomgt.2009.03.012

Osterweil, L. J., Schweik, C. M., Sondheimer, N. K., & Thomas, C. W. (2004). Analyzing Processes for E-Government Application Development: The Emergence of Process Definition Languages. *Journal of E-Government, 1*(4), 63–87. doi:10.1300/J399v01n04_05

Othman, J. B., & Mokdad, L. (2010). Enhancing data security in ad hoc networks based on multipath routing. *Journal of Parallel and Distributed Computing, 70*(3), 309–316. doi:10.1016/j.jpdc.2009.02.010

Palvia, S. C. J., & Sharma, S. S. (2007). E-Government and E-Governance: Definitions/Domain Framework and Status around the World. *Foundation of e-Government*, Retrieved January 17, 2010 from www.iceg.net/2007/books/1/1_369.pdf.

Panuwatwanich, K., Stewart, R. A., & Mohamed, S. (2009). Critical pathways to enhanced innovation diffusion and business performance in Australian design firms. *Automation in Construction, 18*(6), 790–797. doi:10.1016/j.autcon.2009.03.001

Papadopoulou, P., Nikolaidou, M., & Martakos, D. (2010). What Is Trust in E-Government? A Proposed Typology. Proceedings of the 43rd Hawaii International Conference on System Sciences (HICSS-43, 2010), Koloa, Kauai, Hawaii.

KEY TERMS AND DEFINITIONS

Extension Programme: In the agricultural field, these are interventions put in place to ensure that best-practices are integrated into the different aspects of agriculture programmes or initiatives.

ICTs: This is an acronym that stands for Information and Communication Technologies – technology platforms and tools used for information interchange.

SDLC: In this chapter, this acronym stands for Software Development Life Cycle – stages that are utilized in the development of software applications.

APPENDIX A

Roadmap for the Project Implementation Plan which was used in ICT Based System to Support Conventional Agricultural Extension Services in Tanzania

Figure 8. The roadmap for the project implementation plan

Begin by surveying and documenting all the existing agricultural extension systems at the study site (i.e. Kilosa District)

Record all ICTs along with its usage, also, record all the information how convetional extension system is done.

We will make reference to the extension service processes that are supported by the technology. The survey needs to be exhaustive, accurate and well-documented.

Research solutions to the deficiencies.

This require some expert knowledge from the fields of ICT and agricultural extension & education. Careful judgment is needed to propose the solutions.

Site assessment may suggest they need some new ICTs and different systems. Investigate different suggestions and draw conclusions about its effectiveness and suitability.

Consult the Organization / Government Strategy and Master Plan documents.

Recommendations should be consistent with strategy documents related to ICT as well as agriculture.

If you make proposals in ignorance of strategy documents you may be at variance with existing standards and that compromises the value of your research.

Propose induction of ICTs in conventional agricultural extension services

Write up your findings and conclusions in a comprehensive document that includes your needs assessment survey, a listing of deficiencies and the effects these have on the organization's function, prototype system, along with suggested recommendations

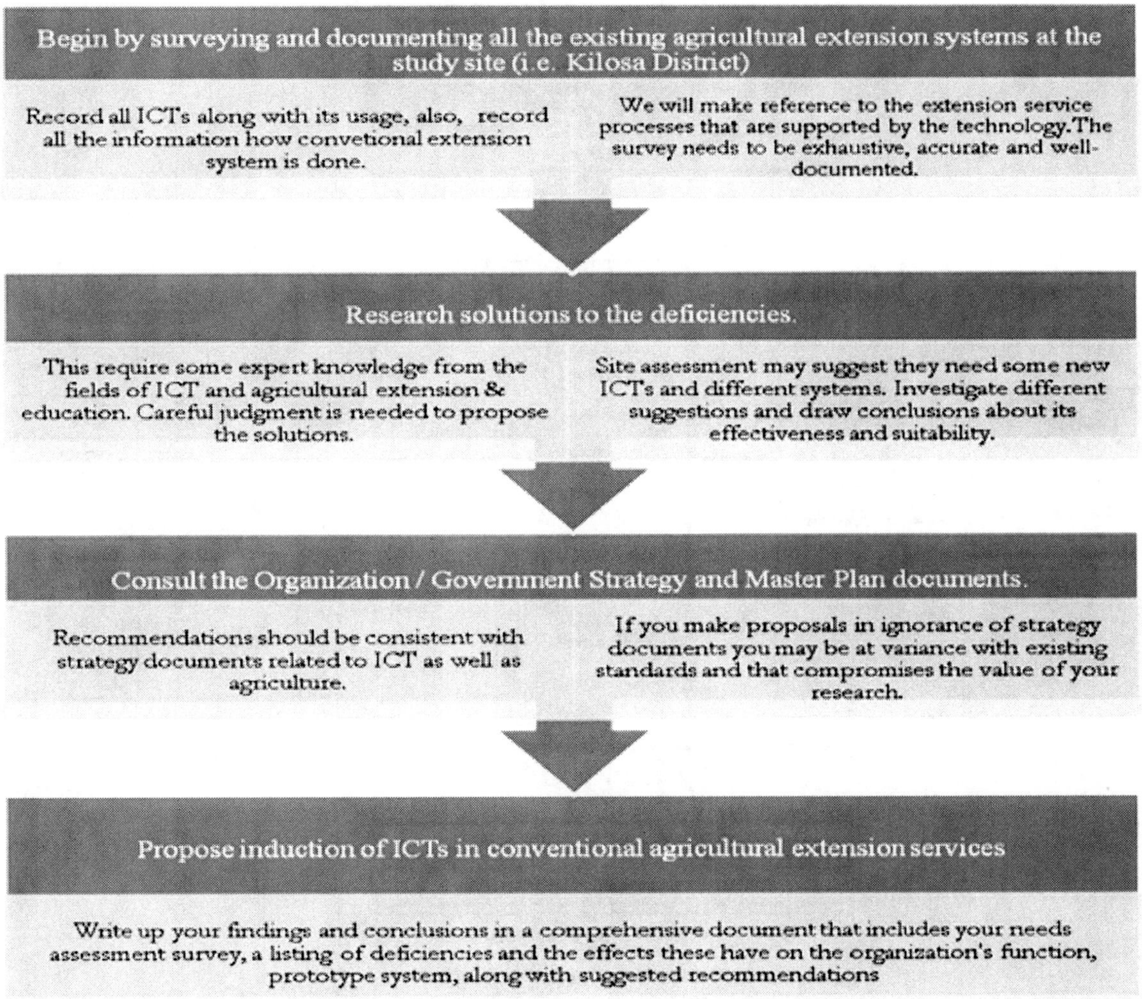

APPENDIX B

Mind Map for Different ICT Needed to Support Agricultural Value Chain

Figure 9. ICTs needed in different phases in agriculture (GFAR, 2012)

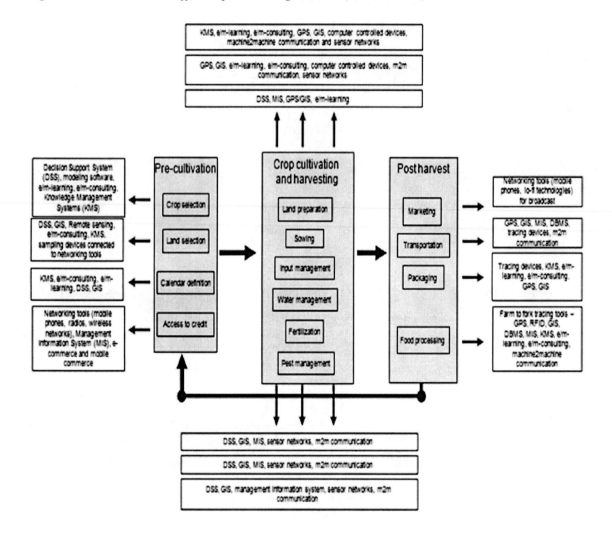

Chapter 16
An Overview of E–Government Technological Divide in Developing Countries

Rafiat A. Oyekunle
University of Ilorin, Nigeria

H. B. Akanbi-Ademolake
University of Ilorin, Nigeria

ABSTRACT

This chapter presents an overview of e-Government technological divide in developing countries. Technological divide here does not consist simply of telecommunications and computer equipment (i.e. ICTs), but it is also e-Readiness (i.e. the available capacity as indicated by workforce capacity to build, deploy, and maintain ICT infrastructure), ICT literacy (using digital technology, communication tools, and/or networks appropriately to access, manage, integrate, evaluate, and create information), e-Inclusion and/or e-Exclusion (i.e. no one is left behind in enjoying the benefits of ICT), etc., which are factors also necessary in order for people to be able to use and benefit from e-Government applications. Most of the currently published works on e-Government strategies are based on successful experiences from developed countries, which may not be directly applicable to developing countries. Based on a literature review, this chapter reveals the status of e-Government technological divide in developing countries and also underscores the challenges associated with e-Government in developing countries, thus bringing to the limelight the factors that influence the growth of the technological divide and different approaches that have been put in place to overcome the divide. In conclusion, this chapter advocates education and training, local content development, enhancing network infrastructure, and capacity building, among others, as ways of bridging the divide.

DOI: 10.4018/978-1-4666-4900-2.ch016

INTRODUCTION

Many governments worldwide are attempting to increase accountability, transparency, and the quality of services by adopting information and communications technologies (ICTs) to revise and change the way their administrations work. Meanwhile e-Government is becoming a significant decision-making and service tool at local, regional and national government levels and the vast majority of users of these governments online services see significant benefits from being able to access services online. The rapid pace of technological development has created increasingly more powerful ICTs that are capable of radically transforming public institutions and private organizations alike. These technologies have proven to be extraordinarily useful instruments in enabling governments to enhance the quality, speed of delivery and reliability of services to citizens and to business (VanderMeer & VanWinden, 2003). However, there is unequal access to ICTs—primarily computers and the Internet—based on income, ethnicity, geography, age, and other factors. Eventually it has evolved to more broadly define disparities in technology usage, resulting from a lack of access, skills, or interest in using technology.

The initiatives of government agencies and departments to use ICT tools and applications, Internet and mobile devices to support good governance, strengthen existing relationships and build new partnerships within civil society, are known as e-Government initiatives. Many government agencies in developed countries have taken progressive steps toward the Web and ICT use, adding coherence to all local activities on the Internet, widening local access and skills, opening up interactive services for local debates, and increasing the participation of citizens on promotion and management of the territory (Yaghoubi, Haghi and Khazaee, 2011). According to Cordella (2007), e-Government is often thought of as "online government" or "Internet-based government," but there are non-Internet "electronic government" technologies that can be used in this context, some of which include telephone, fax, PDA, SMS text messaging, MMS, wireless networks and services, Bluetooth, CCTV, tracking systems, RFID, biometric identification, road traffic management and regulatory enforcement, identity cards, smart cards and other NFC applications.

Adejuwon (2012) stated that governance has undergone important changes in the last decade or thereabout and the emergence of supra-national, inter-state, and private governance mechanisms and practices have also taken place, further challenging the traditional power of national governments (UNDP, 2005). Electronic Governance (e-Governance) is a new way to govern processes in which Information and Communication Technology (ICT) play an active and significant role. The arrival of ICT in the modern years has presented an opening for the central and state governments to change the way organizations control and leverage and value their information assets. Throughout the world, the work of government is being reshaped by two ineluctable trends (Adejuwon, 2012). The first is the movement away from centralized, vertical and hierarchical government machines towards polycentric networks of governance based upon horizontal interactions between diverse actors within complex, dynamic and multi-layered societies. Governance entails government co-governing with a range of organizations, public, private and voluntary, in what Bryson and Crosby have called a shared power, no-one in charge, interdependent world (Coleman, 2008).

Moving away from these assertions, the aim of this chapter is to discuss and analyze the key issues that have brought about e-Government technological divide and the opportunities and challenges that e-Government initiatives present for developing countries.

BACKGROUND

An important component of the factors which interface with the ability of developing nations to harness the use of IT for better and more productive governance as well as delivery of public goods and services is the issue relating to Digital Divide between countries integrating with each other in the total IT environment. This divide is not merely between countries: developed and developing, rich and the poor, English-speaking and non-English speaking but also exists within countries, between one community and another, one race and another, one ethnic group and another. Governments are actively embracing e-Government as a tool for cutting bureaucracy and improving communications with the public. Research has shown that e-Government can enhance access to and delivery of information and services to citizens, partners, employees, cross-agency, and other entities, and can lead to simple, clearly understood, and constantly implied standards regarding government information and services, but only if it is put in place and people can get to it. Without the means to navigate content through non-technical terms, in relevant languages, or in a manner accessible to those with special needs such as Internet connection speeds, physical limitations etc., technology poses a challenge as much as it does a solution. The data from the United Nations e-Government Survey of 2008 clearly reveals that there is a consistent gap across each level of e-Government functionality between developed countries and developing countries (United Nations, 2008).

As with e-Commerce, e-Government represents the introduction of a great wave of technological innovation as well as government reinvention (Fang 2002). Evolution of e-Government has some degree of similarities with the evolution of e-Commerce. Analogous to e-Commerce, which allows businesses to transact with each other more efficiently (B2B) and brings customers closer to businesses (B2C), e-Government aims to make the interaction between government and citizens (G2C), government and business enterprises (G2B), and inter-agency relationships (G2G) more friendly, convenient, transparent and inexpensive. Although ICT is believed to be the backbone for the implementation of e-Government and is referred to as an "enabler", the adaptive challenges of e-Government go far beyond technology, they call for organizational structures and skills, new forms of leadership, transformation of public-private partnerships (Allen, Paquet & Roy, 2001).

E-Government Models

Although the United Nations e-Government survey (2012) states that there is no superior e-Government model, individual countries at different stages of e-Government development, namely emerging stage, enhanced stage, transactional stage, and connected stage, can adopt different models of e-Government in line with the specific needs and wants of their respective constituencies - it is worthy of note to mention some existing models in the literature.

The Onion Ring Model

The Onion Ring Model developed by Heeks (2005) shows the total context of a system for e-development. This model calls for a methodical to e-development where information drives the process and technology does not dominate. The four main components of the model are information, technologies, information systems and environment. It emphasizes the fact that in e-Government implementation, it is important to focus not only on its ICT infrastructure or social enterprise but also the whole surrounding system needs to be adapted to match the situation.

The Gartner Four Phases of E-Government Model

The Gartner four phases of e-Government Model demonstrates the progression of e-Government in the connected environment, and identifies strategy and other factors that contribute to success in each phase. It states that e-governance can be matured through the following four phases:

- **Information – Presence:** E-governance means being present on the Web, providing the public with relevant information;
- **Interaction – Intake processes:** The interaction between the government and the public is stimulated by various applications;
- **Transaction – Complete transactions:** The complexity of technology is increasing, but customer value is also higher. Complete transactions can be done without going to an office – e.g., online services for income tax, property tax, renewal of licenses, visa and passports and online voting;
- **Transformation – Integration and exchange:** All information systems are integrated and the public can get services at one virtual counter.

Technology Enactment Framework

Another notable framework is the Technology Enactment Framework as proposed by Fountain (2001). The TEF is a framework that aims to identify the cardinal factors that are at the centre of technology encapsulation into the different organizational value chains and structures and it is based on the institutionalization theory, governance and bureaucracy. Coupled with the institutionalization theory, the TEF aims to find ways on how technology can be positively be introduced into the government business processes and its acceptance and adoption by government employees in their operations (Bwalya, Zulu, Grand & Sebina, 2012). This framework can be used in diverse environments to understand e-Government adsorption in different organizational contexts.

E-GOVERNMENT IN DEVELOPING COUNTRIES

Although E-Government strategies exist in some developing countries (e.g.: The Republic of Ghana, 2003; Republic of Kenya – Cabinet Office – Office of the President, 2004; Republic of Uganda, 2004) they often repeat general E-Government rhetoric and say little about the actual state of implementation. Other Web analyses show that only ministries and some central authorities have websites.

An e-Government benchmark study conducted by the American Society for Public Administration (UNPA & ASPA, 2001) aimed to categorize the progress made by developed and developing countries in developing an online presence on a five stages scale: Emerging stage; Enhanced stage; Interactive stage; Transactional stage and Seamless stage, revealed that nearly all 32 countries at the Emerging Presence level were among the world's least developed nations, characterized by static and insufficient information that is infrequently updated, few interactive features, and non-existent online services. There were, however, several cases of developing countries that were at the Enhanced Presence stage and Interactive Presence stage, demonstrating their predisposition for e-Government success. The Transactional stage and in particular the Seamless stage were seen as very distant points for both developed and developing countries, with a few exceptions (Singapore, UK, etc) (UNPA&ASPA, 2001).

A 2010 survey carried out by the United Nations reported that although there has been some improvement in the African region, especially in Middle, Northern and Western Africa since the 2008 survey, all the sub-regions in Africa still fall below the world average. Northern Africa leads the region and is closely followed by the Southern Africa. Western Africa lags far behind the other sub-regions and is the lowest scoring sub-region in the 2010 Survey.

According to Schuppan (2009), an exact ranking of sub-Saharan African countries with regard to the implementation of e-Government is difficult because the countries of this region are rarely mentioned – with the exception of South Africa – in relevant studies. This he attributes to the fact that, to date, sub-Saharan Africa has barely registered on the e-Government radar screen and thus hardly any measurable e-Government data available. Schuppan (2009) stated that relevant e-Government studies have been conducted, especially by large consulting firms and also by some universities, but these studies provide little information about the state of Ee-Government implementation in developing countries in general (or in sub-Saharan Africa in particular) and they often show also considerable methodical shortcomings. Thus, e-Government is reduced to the extent to which public service processes are conducted online (Schuppan, 2009). Schuppan (2009) concluded it can be stated without a doubt that, from a global perspective, the countries of sub-Saharan Africa are particularly underdeveloped in the implementation of e-Government, with the exception of South Africa. In these countries, internet access is not sufficient and e-Government services are rare, although some very few advanced individual cases can be found.

Schuppan (2009) gave a report of the success story of Ghana Community Network — GCNet. Prior to GCNet, bureaucratic procedures delayed imports and exports for up to four weeks. The procedure was not only extremely ineffective, but contributed considerably to corruption, because many of the offices involved also expected "acceleration money" (which was usually paid). With the introduction of a newIT system – the GCNet – all customs affairs necessary for the import and export of goods can, to a very large extent, be performed electronically. The GCNet was first used in October 2002 at the Kotoka international airport and was later implemented in Ghana's ports. GCN has two central components: the so-called TradeNet and the customs management system. The TradeNet is a data exchange platform for sending messages and information concerning trade to organizations involved in the transaction. The customs management system automates the issuance of custom declarations as well as the management of import and export licenses. Ministries including the Ministry of Trade and Industry (MoTI), as well as the Bank of Ghana and the Customs and Excise Preventive Service (CEPS), are integrated into the system. From the private sector, the Ghanaian shipping council, the shipping companies, cargo enterprises and banks are involved. For the data exchange and communication between the GCNet and the CEPS, a broadband network created especially for the system is used. By July 2006 the system was implemented in six locations including Tema (the most important port in Ghana). A gradual implementation at all border crossing points was planned. Despite the difficulties implementing the system, acceptance of the project was encouraged by the fact that the system was based upon a similar system in Mauritius, making it a successful example of a south–south cooperation. Furthermore, implementation of the project had been personally and actively accelerated by the Minister, ensuring political support for the project. Implementation and operation of the project is through a Public Private Partnership (PPP) founded in 2000 and consisting of a Swiss investor (60%), the Ghanaian CEPS (20%), the Ghanaian Shippers' Council (10%), and two local banks (5%). A total of seven million U.S. dollars was reported to have been invested. The PPP has concluded a ten-year service contract with the MoTI to provide, among other things, the installation and operation of the system, construction of the infrastructure in the CEPS, and training for employees and users. For every customs declaration executed via the system, the PPP receives a fixed sum from the commercial ministry. As a result of the project, the flow of goods could be substantially accelerated by the system, not just because the interactions between different government offices and contact points for importers were computerized, but also because they were reduced in number. For example, importers no longer need to personally visit the different permitting institutions and authorities because most processes can be executed electronically. In the CEPS, documentation and verification were reduced to fifteen minutes, and the payment of duties (and bank confirmation) occurs within ten minutes. Goods at the airport are dispatched within one day and in the harbor within three days. Ship's idle time, and the resultant demurrage, has been substantially reduced. According to Sudan (2005), tax and duty revenues have increased by up to 50% since the introduction of the system.

Other examples of relatively successful projects in some developing countries according to Coleman (2008) include: Zamlii: the online Zambian legal information portal which is a comprehensive online collection of documents and research relating to Zambian legal and constitutional issues, intended as a legal network for lawyers, judges, academics, students and citizens. The Ugandan Parliamentary Technical Assistance Project introduced in 1998, to assist the Parliament of Uganda with its own modernisation process so that elected members can better represent the interest of their constituents, make better laws and provide more effective oversight of the executive. Features include e-mail addresses for all Mps; an electronic bill tracking system; a parliamentary information database; parliaments own Vsat satellite; and provided training to the IT staff, researchers and MPs. The Mozambique e-SISTAFE which is a standard and computerized system for the administration of public finances, including electronic payment of salaries. The Tanzanian Government Pay role and Human resources System covering 280,000 public servants intended to create more efficient management of government employees. The South African Cape Gateway Portal which provides Web-based information about government services and departments, structured according to users life

events. And the Cameroun Tax Portal, a site that contains tax-related data and guidance, providing citizens and businesses, providing instant information on payment and refund procedures and to undermine opportunities for corrupt officials to charge for such information.

As well, according to the Web measure index from the United Nation's worldwide e-Government readiness report, countries such as Mauritius, South Africa, Uganda, and Ghana are in the upper third scale of the readiness index; while countries including Zambia and Central African Republic do not statistically register on the scale at all (United Nations Department of Economic and Social Affairs, 2005).

THE TECHNOLOGICAL DIVIDE

There are so many examples articulating the differences in telecommunications and computer equipments, e-Readinesse-Readiness, ICT literacy, e-Inclusion and/or e-Exclusion etc. between developed countries and developing countries. In Europe for instance, registering the birth of a child used to involve a visit to the local registry office to make the declaration there, but many hospitals now transfer the baby's details electronically to the registrar, and in some places the parent can now make their declaration on-line, saving a trip (European Commission, 2005). However, citizens of developing countries like Nigeria are yet to benefit from this kind of e-Government service because such facility is not in place – as even manual registration of the birth of a child is not something that all Nigerian citizens carry out, especially rural dwellers.

The lack of infrastructure and education is a serious barrier to e-Government implementation in developing countries. The enabling environment of most developing countries is characterized by irregular or non-existent electricity supplies especially in some rural areas, telephone remains a luxury item and Internet access is available only to the privileged few (UNDESA, 2005). This was also revealed in a study by Ndou (2004) who conducted an empirical, Web-based research of 15 case studies in developing countries (Argentina, Brazil, Chile, China, Colombia, Guatemala, India, Jamaica, Philippines) which had explored and implemented e-Government initiatives. The study found that e-Government offers opportunities for governments; however, the ability of developing countries to reap the full benefits of e-Government is limited and is largely hampered by the existence of a myriad of political, social and economic hindrances. Bhuiyan (2009) argued that the key areas that Africa as a nation must address are the development of information and communications infrastructure; human resources development and employment creation; the current African position in the world economy; insufficient legal and regulatory frameworks and government strategy and fighting corruption like in the situation where a developing country's political landscape is characterized by a political elite who influence the direction of ICT initiatives.

Furthermore, some of the most disturbing gaps can be seen by comparing the access to ICT and performance of isolated and disperse rural communities with those of urban areas. This problem is also present within the urban environment, as evidenced by differences in the quality of the education available to poor and middle-class neighborhoods. These gaps are reflected in the number of the schools and their condition, as well as in the existence and level of complementary resources. In addition, teachers in rural areas usually experience difficult socioeconomic conditions, and have fewer opportunities for professional development to acquire the needed new skills and abilities. The process of urban concentration and rural dispersion – which accelerates throughout the developing world – makes the problem of remote regions more acute and the use of distance technologies indispensable.

Another factor that contributes to the divide is the global economy and new trends in job diversification, with universities in the rich nations at the forefront of scientific and technological research. Nowadays, high technology exports are just as important as manufacturing ones, and in some OECD countries, the creation and diffusion of knowledge generate almost half their gross domestic product (OECD, 2001). There is a synergy between their educational and economic systems, that less developed countries lack. This reinforces the existing international division of labor, and hinders the capacity of developing countries for a more coherent and equitable social development. These countries generally have a very well-educated elite, a small but growing middle class, and a large labor force that has not completed basic education, with hardly any middle-level technicians and professionals.

Chen et. al (2006) highlights the following differences between the developed countries and the developing countries in various aspects of government, this differences contributes to the reason why many developing countries have been left behind:

1. **History and Culture:** The government and economy of developed countries was developed early immediately after independence, their economy is growing at a constant rate, productivity is increasing; there is high standard of living, relatively long history of democracy and more transparent government policy and rule. While the history and culture of developing countries is characterized by government usually not specifically defined; economy not increasing in productivity; economy not growing or increasing productivity; low standard of living; relatively short history of democracy and less transparent government policy and rule;

2. **Technical Staff:** Developed countries have current staff; needs to increase technical abilities and hire younger professionals; have outsourcing abilities and financial resources to outsource; current staff would be able to define requirements for development. On the other hand, developing countries do not have staff or have very limited in-house staff; does not have local outsourcing abilities and rarely has the financial ability to outsource; current staff may be unable to define specific requirements;

3. **Infrastructure:** Developed countries have good current infrastructure and high Internet access for employees and citizens, while the infrastructure in developing countries is currently bad and there is low Internet access for employees and citizens;

4. **Citizens:** In developed countries, there is high Internet access and computer literacy among citizens; there is still digital divide and privacy issues and citizens are relatively more experienced in democratic system and more actively participate in governmental policy-making process. Citizens in developing countries on the other-hand have low Internet access; citizens are reluctant to trust online services; few citizens know how to operate computers and citizens are relatively less experienced in democratic system and less active participation in governmental policy-making process.

Basu (2004) also posits that development of e-Governments is directly proportional to the IT infrastructure that is capable of supporting and enabling the execution of e-Government. An e-Government infrastructure in general comprises network infrastructure, security infrastructure, application server environment, data and content management tools, application development tools, hardware and operating systems, and systems management platform. However, many developing countries do not have the infrastructure necessary to deploy e-Government services throughout their territory.

CHALLENGES OF E-GOVERNMENT IN DEVELOPING COUNTRIES

Introducing e-governance can pose huge challenges to many governments. Difficulties can arise in the development, implementation and updating of e-Government sites (Matavire, Chigona, Roode, Sewchurran, Davids, Mukudu and Boamah-Abu, 2010; Tlagadi, 2007). More serious challenges that can emanate from e-governance are indicated as follows:

1. **Insufficient planning capacity and political instability** (Adejuwon, 2012);

2. **Inadequate infrastructure:** This needs to be addressed before any e-Government project can be successful (Schuppan, 2009);

3. **Privacy:** Many e-Government systems collect, store and use the personal details of those who use their services or visits websites. That can pose a threat to individual privacy (Kroukamp, 2005);

4. **Security:** Governments will need to protect their information and systems from breaches of computer security that threaten not only the integrity and availability of services but also the confidence of users and the general public in the system (Kroukamp,2005);

5. **Economic disparities:** According to the Organisation for Economic Co-operation and Development (OECD, 2003) the economically disadvantaged have the lowest level of access to e-governance (Van Themaat, 2004);

6. **Education:** Educated people are more likely to be the most user of the Internet. As the standard of education rises, so does use of the Internet (Kroukamp, 2005);

7. **Accessibility:** Ensuring accessibility to all members of the society is essential. This must include individuals with disabilities to be able to use e-Government websites (Kroukamp, 2005);

8. **Citizen awareness and confidence:** Creating awareness of the advantages of e-governance and persuading people to become users of the system are bigger challenges (Matavire, Chigona, Roode, Sewchurran, Davids, Mukudu and Boamah-Abu, 2010);

9. **Lack of leadership and management:** Political leadership which lacks the necessary drive to bring about change in the public sector may be the biggest obstacle to development. Leaders who do not see e-Government as priority pay little attention to ensuring that IT policies and programmes are introduced (Matavire, Chigona, Roode, Sewchurran, Davids, Mukudu and Boamah-Abu, 2010);

10. **Bureaucratic government organization:** In many cases the flow of information between governments departments and agencies is developed and operated to meet the needs of government departments and agencies and not citizens (Kroukamp, 2005);

11. **IT impact:** People without access to ICT, would not be able to participate in the e-governance hence causing the domestic divide (Khan, 2010);

12. **Legal framework:** E-governance requires Legal Framework that supports and recognizes digital communication (Tlagadi, 2007);

13. **Technologies and approaches:** The technologies and approaches for building and operating e-Government services are obtained through technology transfer initiatives between developed countries and developing countries. This creates a great problem for developing countries because knowledge and resources are needed to modify software and hardware solutions to fit the local condi-

tions. These modifications may drive up the cost and time to implement e-Government solutions (ITU, 2008).

Furthermore, Kreps and Richardson (2007) identified the following reasons for failures in e-Government in developing countries:

1. Drivers of ICT Project Failures;
2. Systems delivered late;
3. Creeping scope;
4. Software not reliable and robust;
5. Software not delivering the promised functionality;
6. Lack of integration and effective interface with legacy systems;
7. Escalating costs;
8. Lack of consultation with users or stakeholders;
9. Data integrity and confidentiality issues;
10. Poor knowledge of the system and lack of suitable training.

In addition, Kamar and Ongo'ndo (2007) in their own words identified the following as barriers to effective E-Government implementation in developing countries:

1. A reluctance to share information which has resulted in policies that deny access to information and the creation of "empty" government ministries websites with information of little value;
2. The government being faced with management challenges in the implementation of E-Government. The uncoordinated E-Government activities result from low level of public administration of E-Services as well as low quality and insufficient E-Content information from grassroots levels;

3. Low information technology literacy in a country which slows down the process of E-Government;

4. The uneven distribution of Internet facilities, high cost of connection and in some cases low penetration of high speed connectivity to the Internet;

5. Digital Divide which is experienced between the urban rich and poor, the rural and urban citizens, the IT literate and the IT illiterate. This manifests also in the language in which website content is delivered which can only be understood by a minority elite;

6. Insufficient allocation of financial resources due to financial constraints and mixed government policies which has slowed down the rate at which E-Government is introduced;

7. E-Government implementations failing due to a mismatch between the current and future systems resulting from the large gap between physical, social, cultural, economic and other contexts between the software designers and the place in which the system is being implemented.

Ajayi (2007) in his paper outlined unstable power supply, advance fee fraud (419), Internet connectivity problems, high duty and tax regime, cable and facility vandalisation and relatively low consumer purchasing power as challenges of e-Government in Nigeria.

BRIDGING THE E-GOVERNMENT TECHNOLOGICAL DIVIDE

According to the Organization for Economic Co-Operation and Development OECD (2001), OECD countries' policies and programs intended at reducing the digital divide range from general approaches aimed at strengthening and extending the infrastructure, to policies to diffuse access and information more widely and to improve the skills of individuals and workers. Particular

attention is paid to policies to improve access in public institutions (libraries, local and regional government facilities, post offices, etc.) so that individuals can access ICTs at low or no cost, build familiarity and develop skills. Policies for making available low-cost and subsidized access in schools seek to build the future skills base of the workforce and to enhance diffusion. OECD further reported that measures like improving access for underprivileged groups, the disabled and the elderly, and for rural, remote and low-income areas, for reasons of equity and to enhance overall economic efficiency via network effects are steps towards bridging e-Government technological divide. Other steps identified by OECD include support for small businesses which increasingly has a component aimed at increasing the rate of uptake and use of ICTs; government assistance for some regions and rural areas owing to particular problems associated with lagging regions; identifying online delivery of services, information and transfer of government activities and procurement on line as having important demonstration effects as well as improving government efficiency; and multilateral co-operation which is considered important for reducing differences in international digital divides across countries and improving, by learning from others' experience, the efficiency of measures taken by other countries.

In 2006, the 'e-Government road map' was agreed by the Commission together with a group of experts from Member States. The road map directs efforts to ensure Inclusive e-Government develops in the period up to 2010, with the expert group meeting regularly to steer efforts at European level. Stakeholders, in particular from agencies and authorities delivering e-Government services and groups representing vulnerable user groups at risk of exclusion, are also consulted to establish real needs on the ground.

Furthermore, developing countries are being assisted by international organizations for development, through building and encouraging e-strategies and initiatives to address a wide range of economic, social, technological, infrastructural, legal and educational issues. G8 on Digital Opportunities Task Force and UN Task Force on ICT Access (Digital Opportunity Task Force, 2002) have evidenced e-Government as one of the priorities based on the decisive role it would play for ICT accessibility.

Dewan and Kraemer [2000] found that spending on ICT is highly correlated with level of development, and ICT investments are associated with higher output in developed countries, but such investments are not (yet) productive in developing countries. They conducted an analysis of the aggregate impact of ICT investments on national output of developed and developing countries. Estimating a cross-country production function, they find that the two groups of countries differ sharply in terms of the structure of returns on capital investments. ICT capital investments are associated with higher output in developed countries, but non-ICT capital investments are not associated with higher output at the margin. The situation is exactly the reverse for developing countries, where ICT capital investments are not productive, but non-ICT capital investments generate a healthy positive return at the margin. They concluded that developing countries should first concentrate on building out their stocks of ordinary capital investment, before ramping up their investments in ICT capital.

Furthermore, Dewan and Riggins (2005) suggested the cross-border implications of the digital divide, including issues such as technology transfer, tariffs and trade of technology products and services; and the policy implications of the digital divide at the global level, including the key questions of whether to subsidize access to ICT, and how best to promote the skills that are complementary to the productive use of ICT should be examined as steps to bridge the divide.

Finally, it can be deduced from the foregoing that implementation of proper policies and deploy-

ing proper technologies in the right context at the right place in developing countries would go a long way in solving issues surrounding technological divide in e-Government.

Recommendations

Despite the considerably efforts geared towards bridging the technological divide in e-Government, the divide still exists. Thus the following recommendations based on an assessment of the literature are recommended:

1. Government in developing countries needs to overcome social and geographical differences to ensure an inclusive digital society which provides opportunities for all;
2. Government in developing countries should establish a program to enhance local content, in this regard; all productive sectors of the economy are to be encouraged to develop their websites and Government employees to obtain an individual email address;
3. There should be willingness to initiate change within the government sector, this will translate to an effective e-governance because e-Government requires strong political leadership in order to succeed;
4. Security measures should be put in place to safeguard ICT facilities, especially the V-Sat facilities that are sometimes vandalized;
5. Budget for IT related products and services should improve;
6. E-Government deployment should be done hand-in-hand with sustainable strategies to bridge the digital divide for different categories of people, including low-literate populations, non-native English speakers and the disabled;
7. Upgrading of the standard of living of the people of the state through use of IT in all sectors as a tool to enhance productivity,

efficiency and optimum utilization of re-sources, and through full exploitation of the employment potential of the IT sector;

8. Establishment of an information infrastructure comprising a high speed broadband communication backbone, nodes, access network, distributed data warehouses and service locations to cater to the needs of trade, commerce, industry and tourism and also to enhance the delivery of government services to the people;

9. Development of human resources for ICT through increased use of ICT in educational institutions and through academic and training programmers that improve the employability of educated youths in the ICT sector;

10. Facilitation of decentralized administration and empowerment of people through the application of ICT.

CONCLUSION

This study has shown that difference in telecommunications and computer equipments, e-Readiness, ICT literacy, e-Inclusion and/or e-Exclusion are some of the factors that constitute technological divide that still exists in developing countries as far as e-Government is concerned, and bridging the divide is very essential in accelerating the assimilation of more people and countries into the Networked World. This would require translating commitment into action at both national and regional levels and bringing national e-strategies into overall development and governance practices. Even though steps like deregulating the telecommunications market which has improved accessibility and reduced cost, and building and encouraging e-strategies and initiatives to address a wide range of economic, social, technological, infrastructural, legal and educational issues have put in place; developing countries can only realize the potential of e-Government if certain minimum preconditions outlined previously exist in the countries in question.

REFERENCES

Abramson, A. M., & Means, E. G. (2001). *E-government, price water house coopers endowment for the business of government*. London: Rowman & Littlefield Publishers Inc.

Adejuwon, K. D. (2012). From e-government to e-governance: Whither African public administration? *Advances in Arts. Social Sciences and Education Research*, 2(1), 63–75.

Ajayi, L. (2007). *ICT business in Nigeria: Challenges and opportunities*. Retrieved March 12, 2013 from www.nitpa.org/articles/globalit/NCS_Paper.pdf

Allen, A. B., Juillet, L., Paquet, G., & Roy, J. (2001). E-governance and government online in Canada: Partnerships, people and prospects. *Government Information Quarterly*, *18*, 93–104. doi:10.1016/S0740-624X(01)00063-6

Amit, R., & Zott, C. (2001). Value creation in e-business. *Strategic Management Journal*, *22*, 493–520. doi:10.1002/smj.187

Basu, S. (2004). E-government and developing countries: An overview. *International Review of Law Computers & Technology*, *18*(1), 109–132. doi:10.1080/13600860410001674779

Bhuiyan, S. (2009). E-government in Kazakhstan: Challenges and its role to development. *Public Organization Review*, *10*, 31–47. doi:10.1007/s11115-009-0087-6

Bwalya, K., Zulu, S., Grand, B., & Sebina, P. (2012). E-government and technological utopianism: Exploring Zambia's challenges and opportunities. *Electronic. Journal of E-Government*, *10*(1), 16–30.

Chen, Y. N., Chen, H. M., Huang, W., & Ching, R. K. H. (2006). E-government strategies in developed and developing countries: An implementation framework and case study. *Journal of Global Information Management*, *14*(1), 23–46. doi:10.4018/jgim.2006010102

Cordella, A. (2007). e-Government: Towards the e-Bureaucratic. *Journal of Information Technology, 22*, 265–274. doi:10.1057/palgrave.jit.2000105

Dewan, S., & Kraemer, K. L. (2000). Information technology and productivity: Evidence from country-level data. *Management Science, 46*(4), 548–562. doi:10.1287/mnsc.46.4.548.12057

Dewan, S., & Riggins, F. J. (2005). The digital divide: Current and future research directions. *Journal of the Association for Information Systems*. Retrieved March 12, 2013 from http://misrc.umn.edu/workingpapers/fullpapers/2005/0524_120605.pdf

European Commission. (2005). *Inclusive e-government - No citizen left behind*. Retrieved December 20, 2010 from http://ec.europa.eu/information_society/activities/einclusion/policy/egov/index_en.htm

Fang, Z. (2002). E-government in digital era: Concept, practice and development. *International Journal of the Computer, 10*(2), 1–22.

Godse, V., & Garg, A. (2009). *From e-government to e-governance*. New Delhi: Computer Society of India.

Graham, S., & Aurigi, A. (1997). Virtual cities, social polarisation, and the crisis in urban public space. *Journal of Urban Technology, 4*(1), 19–52. doi:10.1080/10630739708724546

Heeks, R. (2005). *Foundations of ICTs in development: The onion-ring model*. Retrieved March 12, 2013 from http://www.sed.manchester.ac.uk/idpm/research/publications/wp/di/short/DIG-Briefing4Onion.pdf

Heeks, R. B. (2001). *Building e-governance for development (iGovernment paper no.12)*. Manchester, UK: University of Manchester.

Information Policy. (2006). *Comparing e-governance and e-government*. Retrieved on January 12, 2013 from http://www.i-policy.org/2006/06/comparing_e-Gove.html

ITU. (2008). *Electronic government for developing countries*. Retrieved on January 12, 2013 from www.itu.int/ITU-D/cyb/app/e-gov.html

Kamar, N., & Ongo'ndo, M. (2007). *Impact of e-government on management and use of government information in Kenya*. Paper presented at the World Library and Information Congress: 73rd IFLA general Confernce and Council. Durban, South Africa.

Kreps, D., & Richardson, H. (2007). IS success and failure - The problem of scale. *The Political Quarterly, 78*(3). doi:10.1111/j.1467-923X.2007.00871.x

Kroukamp, H. (2005). E-governance in South Africa: Are we coping. *Acta Academia, 37*(2), 52–69.

Matavire, R., Chigona, W., Roode, D., Sewchurran, E., Davids, Z., Mukudu, A., & Boamah-Abu, C. (2010). Challenges of e-government project implementation in a South African context. *The Electronic Journal Information Systems Evaluation, 13*(2), 153–164.

Ndou, V. D. (2004). E-government for developing countries: Opportunities and challenges. *The Electronic Journal on Information Systems in Developing Countries, 18*(1), 1–24.

OECD. (2001). *Engaging citizens in policy-making: Information, consultation and policy participation (Puma Policy Brief No. 10)*. Paris: OECD.

OECD. (2002). *ICT and business performance – Empirical findings and policy implications*. Paper presented at the Workshop on ICT and Business Performance. New York, NY.

Organization for Economic Co-Operation and Development (OECD). (2001). *Understanding the digital divide*. Retrieved February 25, 2013 from www.oecd.org/bookshop/

Schuppan, T. (2009). E-government in developing countries: Experiences from sub-Saharan Africa. *Government Information Quarterly, 26*, 118–127. doi:10.1016/j.giq.2008.01.006

Tapscott, D. (1996). *The digital economy*. New York: McGraw Hill.

Tlagadi, P. (2007). *E-governance for improved service delivery*. Paper presented at the Free State SMS Conference. Retrieved on January 12, 2013 from http://www.fs.gov.za/INFORMATION/Events/2007/Premier/SMS%20Conference/Presentations/Tlagadi.pdf

(2003). Towards a definition of electronic government: A comparative review. InGil-Garcia, J., & Luna-Reyes, L. (Eds.), *Techno-legal aspects of the information society and the new economy: An overview*. Badajoz, Spain: Formatex.

UN/ASPA. (2001). *Benchmarking e-government: A global perspective*. Retrieved March 16, 2009 from http://www.unpan.org/e-government/Benchmarking%20E-gov%202001.pdf

UNDESA. (2005). *UN global e-government readiness report 2005: From e-government to e-inclusion*. New York: United Nations Publication.

United Nations. (2008). *UN e-government survey 2008: From e-government to connected government*. New York: United Nations.

United Nations. (2010). *UN global e-government survey 2010: Leveraging e-government at a time of financial and economic crisis*. Retrieved February 25, 2013 from http://www.unpan.org/DPADM/E-Government/UNE-GovernmentSurveys/tabid/600/language/en-US/Default.aspx

Van Themat, C. (2004). The digital divide: Implications for South Africa. *South African Journal of Information Management, 6*(3), 12–19.

VanderMeer, A., & VanWinden, W. (2003). E-governance in cities: A comparison of urban information and communication technology policies. *The Journal of the Regional Studies Association, 37*(4), 407–419. doi:10.1080/0034340032000074433

Yaghoubi, N. M., Haghi, A., & Khazaee, S. (2011). E-government and citizen satisfaction in Iran: Empirical study on ICT offices. *World Applied Sciences Journal, 12*(7), 1084–1092.

ADDITIONAL READING

Park, E. G., Lamontagne, M., Perez, A., Melikhova, I., & Bartlett, G. (2009). Running ahead toward interoperable e-Government: The government of Canada metadata framework. *International Journal of Information Management, 29*(2), 145–150. doi:10.1016/j.ijinfomgt.2008.06.003

Park, H. M. (2008). *Hypothesis Testing and the Statistical Power of a Test*. Technical working paper. The University of Information Technology Services (UITS), Center for Statistical and Mathematical Computing, Indiana University.

Partnership on Measuring ICT for Development. (2009). *Revisions and Additions to the Core List of ICT Indicators*. Background paper for the 7th World Telecommunication/ICT Indicators Meeting, Cairo, Egypt, 3-5 March 2009. New York: United Nations Statistics Division. Retrieved March 10, 2010 from unstats.un.org/unsd/statcom/doc09/BG-ICTIndicators.pdf.

Pascual, P. J. (2003). E-Government. E-Asean Task Force, UNDP-APDIP. A Retrieved October 13, 2009 from www.apdip.net/publications/iespprimers/eprimer-egov.pdf.

Pathak, R. D., & Prasad, R. S. (2006). Role of E-governance in tackling corruption: The Indian Experience. In Raza Ahmad (Ed.), The role of public administration in building a harmonious society. 434-463. Philippines: Asian Development Bank.

Pavlou, P. (2003). Consumer acceptance of electronic commerce: Integrating trust and risk with the technology acceptance model. *International Journal of Electronic Commerce, 7*(3), 101–134.

Pedersen, P. (2005). Adoption of mobile internet services: An exploratory study of mobile commerce early adopters. *Journal of Organizational Computing and Electronic Commerce, 15*(3), 203–222. doi:10.1207/s15327744joce1503_2

Pereira, J. (2009). Zambia Aid effectiveness in the health sector. Publication of the Action for Global Health. Retrieved Decemeber 20, 2010 from www.actionforglobalhealth.eu/fileadmin/user_upload/doc_library/ AE_Zambia_Case_Study_Final_version.pdf.

KEY WORDS AND DEFINITIONS

Digital Divide: The disparity in access to different information brought about by limit access to requisit ICTs.

E-Government: This entails the use of ICTs in government business value chains to promote efficiency and effectiveness.

E-Government Challenges: These are different factors that inhibit affluent development of e-Government in a given environment. The different types of challenges can be categorized into two broader themes: Institutional (organizational environment) and Individual (personal attributes).

ICTs: This is an acronym standing for Information and Communication Technologies – detailing technology platforms used for information interchange.

TEF: This is an acronym standing for Technology Enactment Framework – a theoretical frameworkl used to investigate the integration of technology in different organizational frameworks.

Chapter 17
E–Justice in Administrative Process:
Insights from Lithuanian Landscape

Tatjana Bilevičienė
Mykolas Romeris University, Lithuania

Eglė Bilevičiūtė
Mykolas Romeris University, Lithuania

ABSTRACT

Social technologies are slowly occupying the central place of available and emerging solution for a variety of socio-economic problems. Although not a panacea, it cannot be overemphasized that social technologies have an influence on the social effects of humans, social groups, hierarchical social structures (such as public administrations, local authorities, non-governmental organizations, etc.), and behaviour. Of late, there has been an escalation in the use of social technologies in the legal fraternity. The Lithuanian government has started putting in place interventions that promote the utilization of social technologies into legal administrative processes. This came after the realization that Lithuanian citizens have the right to full and truthful information about administrative law and administrative processes. Using extensive literature reviews, this chapter probes the key success factors that need to be considered in the successful utilization of social technologies in legal administrative processes. The chapter posits that within the e-Government realm, the opportunities to be amassed from the use of Information and Communication Technologies are immense.

DOI: 10.4018/978-1-4666-4900-2.ch017

INTRODUCTION

The need for justice is growing all over Europe. This increases workload on court systems, which often calls for reforms in work methods despite budgetary constraints. The demand for efficient judicial systems has coined the term e-Justice for the growing use of technology to improve access to justice, boost collaboration between jurisdictions, and strengthen the legal system.

E-Justice can be defined as use of Information and Communication Technologies (ICTs) to improve exercising of citizens' right to justice and increase efficiency of judicial activity, i.e., of any activity related to dispute resolution or penal sanctions for a certain activity. Development of e-Justice is one of the most important aspects in modernisation of judiciary systems. E-Justice is related to the broader concept of e-Government and constitutes a separate part of this phenomenon. E-Government refers to application of ICTs in all public administrative procedures. Successful application of e-Justice is dependent on several factors. For example, in the context of Europe, potential area of application of e-Justice is rather wide and its development shall depend on technological advancements as well as on progress in European justice area (Commission of the European Communities, 2008) as posited below:

Union law permeates a wide number and diverse range of activities at national level. Its impact on the daily life of people and businesses is high. It creates rights and obligations, which national courts must safeguard. The national judge has become the front-line judge of Union law. With successive changes to the European Union Treaties, the scope and impact of Union law has increased, access to justice was strengthened. The Lisbon Treaty strengthened Union competences especially in the area of Freedom, Security and Justice. (European Commission, 2011)

The application of ICTs into court administrations opens up opportunities to improve performance of the system of justice, organise legal procedures more rationally, and reduce costs.

By offering standard tools, techniques, and data structures, information sharing becomes easier, quicker, and less expensive for the justice sector. This is all the more important in the current economic climate when most governments are seeking budget savings in the public sector. Public agencies require software that is intentionally designed to facilitate and accommodate new thinking and reform. When professionals in law enforcement — whether judges, prosecutors, defense attorneys, prison officers, or the police — can connect with each other and securely share information, everything changes. Economy, efficiency, and effectiveness are the principal drivers for all justice and citizen safety organizations when making decisions about ICT solutions (Integrated Justice, 2010).

Administrative disputes are conflicts between people and public administration entities or among mutually non-subordinate public administration entities (Lietuvos Respublikos..., 1999). Hearing of administrative cases has two major aims: to ensure protection of administrative subjective rights of a person (protection of human rights from illegal actions by public administration entities, protection of rights of civil servants from license of the administration as well as protection of rights of municipal institutions from illegal actions of state institutions); ensure legitimacy in public activities of government. These aims can be viewed as resonating the major aims of administrative justice (Teisės institutas, 2004).

Contrary to courts of general jurisdiction that hear criminal cases and deal with disputes arising out of civil, family, labour, and other private legal relationships, administrative courts settle disputes arising in the fields of internal and public administration and governance. Therefore, administrative proceeding has close link to public administration and solutions of e-Government.

Administrative law employs general principles of law. One of them is the principle of publicity that, in the context of administrative law, is viewed as legal obligation to announce the passed laws and bylaws, information of society and provision of information, and publication of the administrative decisions that have been made. The Law on Information of the Public of the Republic of Lithuania (Lietuvos Respublikos visuomenės..., 1996) establishes the procedure for collection, preparation, announcement and dissemination of public information as well as rights, obligations, and responsibility of producers and suppliers of public information and of members thereof, journalists, and institutions supervising their activities. It provides that freedom of information enshrined in the Constitution, this and other laws, and international agreements of the Republic of Lithuania are guaranteed in the Republic of Lithuania.

Today, almost every Lithuanian citizen is aware of all their rights at all to build up basic knowledge of legal issues and familiar with operating in the country's legal framework. Understanding of the principles of administrative justice is aggravated by administrative violations of law dealing with pre-trial organizations and the judicial system, and the imperfection of the current laws.

Algimantas Urmonas (2007) argues that the reticence of administrative law, search for solutions in only the legal environment in terms of social technology restricts its ability to enrich it to rely more on other social science information. Development of an optimal institutional framework of administrative justice and the governing legislative framework necessary should implant the advantage of the latest social technologies. The task of technology is not to randomly influence the natural and social processes, but achieve the aims of the state by directing them to human society. Each technology provides the uniformity of its components and the procedures and permanent use of implemented operations and procedures (Kurpuvesas, 2007).

Social technologies are the entirety of available efficient or less efficient reusable methods intended for dealing with tasks for social management and facilitating achievement of the intended goal (result) of activity by exerting social effects upon behaviour of persons, social groups, and hierarchical social bodies (public administration entities, municipal institutions, non-governmental organisations, etc.) (Bughin at al., 2012). Manifestation of social technologies in law is related to condition of social and legal scientific knowledge (factors of science) and to efficiency of social legal activity, which has been determined by sought methods to make decisions towards achievement of social and legal aims in society (factors of social-legal practice). In this regard, for example, area regulated by Lithuanian administrative law abounds with sought methods to make decisions (Urmonas, 2007).

Arūnas Augustinaitis and Rimantas Petrauskas (2010) maintain that in modern society information and communication technologies (ICT) are viewed and practically applied as foundation of any contemporary model of organisation and public management in ever-changing complex environments. Complexity of public relations is now at such a level where major roles (economic, social, and political) start to be played by social interactions and their efficiency. This is the basis of the new economy, which stimulates development of human resources, creativity, innovation, and sustainable development (Chang, Kannan, 2008). Social technologies also express the forms of exchange, arrangement, and interaction of civic information and knowing, which occur as the process of communication and shape various models of civic communication, and communicational mechanisms of their implementation, too.

It follows that the main measures aimed at education of the public about administrative proceeding must be applied in informational space (Velicogna at al., 2011). However, researches show that information available on websites of state institutions and administrative courts is mainly aimed at publicity of the process of hearings at courts. There is almost no information about peculiarities of investigation into administrative contraventions of law.

SOCIAL TECHNOLOGIES IN LAW

Social technologies are instruments to build a model of public communication and create procedures to manage it in complex and multiple environments dominated by ever-increasing influence of technological factors. Therefore, social technologies (in the broad sense) refer to creation and management of competitive forms and methods of communicational organisation of society. Social technologies are phenomenon of the information era and cannot exist without ICT-based development (Augustinaitis, Petrauskas, 2010; Maurer, 2007).

Representatives of social sciences have different views as to application of social technologies in social practice. Contemporary approaches to solving of social legal problems must be based on methodology of creation of social technologies. Methodology of creation of social technologies involves static aspects of theoretical, methodological and procedural modelling of entities. Dynamic aspects of modelling of social technologies are revealed by stages of technologization (Urmonas, 2007; Adler, Henman, 2001):

Administrative law refers generally to the laws and legal principles governing the creation, administration and regulation of government agencies at the federal, state, and local levels. (Salovaara, Augusiak, 2011)

Rule of law and administrative justice is an essential function of the legal means to protect a person from the public administrations of illicit acts or omissions (Kurpuvesas, 2007). Birutė Pranevičienė (2007) states that the fundamental (or otherwise known as generic) Lithuanian administrative law system consists of rule of law, justice, prudence, transparency, control and responsibility. In Lithuania, the mechanisms of social influence and their opportunities and ways to influence the administrative system of processes taking place more frequently seen and treated as public management. Modern administrative law studies emphasize the importance of social relations in the administrative process and procedures (Kargaudienė, 2007).

Standards of freedom of speech and media defined in the constitution and laws of the Republic of Lithuania are based on the same fundamental principles: priority of individual's rights against the state, freedom of expression, right to correct information, prohibition and restriction of harmful information, liability, diversity of opinions (Aleknonis, 2010). Social changes affect Lithuanian legal system and activate new changes in values and norms of administrative law. Qualitative transformation in social relations necessitates search for new models of regulatory environment of administrative law. Search for them by applying legal and non-legal forms (technologies) would facilitate systematic work towards the major aim: to ensure human rights and protection of legitimate interests (Deviatnikovaitė & Kalašnykas, 2007). A need enables a person to understand and identify what he lacks, what he needs, while an interest allows understanding, comprehending, identifying public character of the need. Case law of administrative courts provides that public interest in the light of the Law on Administrative Proceedings should be interpreted as anything objectively important, necessary, valuable for the entire society or a part of it (Trumputis, 2010).

Social technologies in law or law as a social technology have received little attention in Lithuanian jurisprudence. It is often said that law allegedly goes away from people (currently not every person comprehends a text of a legal act, let alone understanding its spirit) and legal institutions are criticised for being too reticent in their activities. Bearing in mind the purpose of law and the duty of every state institution (including judicial ones) to work for people, such a situation should be regarded as unsatisfactory and calling for prompt and wise decisions based on the potential of not only legal but also other sciences. A large gap between law and other social sciences is noticeable, but, on the other hand, interaction between law and social technologies exists as well. The purpose of both law and social technologies is to influence the social environment (Kurpuvesas, 2007).

Lithuania formed contradictions between social cognition and technological forecasting in various spheres of social life. Social breakthrough technology implementation can be described as a social control algorithm is used. Perceived as social technology - a set of cyclic target practices related to social solutions to legal problems in an effort to change the social legal state of the object. These legal changes are implemented in the social order to the expected performance using the methods and techniques as a whole. It helps to identify and use social legal system until now, undisclosed, and therefore unused potential of their development objectives, social norms and legal standards (Urmonas, 2007). Purpose and aims of administrative courts are to ensure exercising of the constitutional provision that governmental institutions work for people, to adjudicate disputes between the state and a private individual, and to stimulate advancements in administrative competences of governmental institutions through the rulings made. As provided by the Law on Administrative Proceedings and other laws, presently in Lithuania the first instance for administrative dispute adjudication is regional administrative courts and the appeal instance is the Supreme Administrative Court of Lithuania. For certain cases, the Supreme Administrative Court is the first and the highest instance. An administrative court does not hear cases assigned to courts of general jurisdiction or other specialized courts. However,

the naming of certain types of cases presupposes overlapping of competences of an administrative court and other courts. Problems with case admissibility between courts of general jurisdiction and institutions performing out-of-court settlement of administrative disputes are not uncommon. So, the complicate system comprise only specialists who understand this system.

Citizens today expect individualized online services. To meet these demands, many justice organizations are improving access to their services through intuitive. Where accurate case records, judicial precedents, or pre-sentencing reports are available electronically, inter-agency cooperation in the justice community improves—information that took days to produce is available in minutes. From a customer perspective, delays in bringing defendants to trial can be reduced and the chances of a conviction or an award of compensation to a victim of crime improved.

Administrative justice institutions should more widely use the public relations and information technology. Allow access to any person interested in information resources to inform their work decisions and processes (without prejudice to the rights and freedoms). This must beprovided for each person (Kurpuvesas, 2007).

The communication *Towards a European e-Justice Strategy* from the Commission of the European Communities (Commission of the European Communities, 2008) describes e-Justice strategy aimed at increasing citizens' trust in the European justice area. The key aim of e-Justice is to make justice more efficient and useful for citizens throughout Europe. Therefore, the priority projects will have to be focused on making positive influence on productivity of work of lawyers and facilitating exercising of citizens' right to justice. Moreover, the projects shall help to implement European legal acts applicable to the area of justice. Should it become necessary, the projects shall include all or most of the member states.

Justice agencies are under pressure throughout the world to become more efficient in delivering public services at less cost to the taxpayer. The principal areas of focus in developing a vision at national level for an integrated justice chain are:

- Improvement in communication among courts, citizens, and organizations;
- Standardization in justice systems with justice data distributed in a common format;
- Modernization of business processes;
- Integration of information systems;
- Meeting the challenge of decreasing budgets and providing value for money.

Lack of integration capabilities across jurisdictions, agencies, and organizations hinders justice — it also means that very often justice agencies fail to provide the right services to the right people. By streamlining the justice enterprise and its connected data transmission, people are safer and have equal access to services. Organizations find that outcomes and performance indicators improve because new tools exist for cases to be solved, and criminals are caught and prosecuted more efficiently and quickly. The latest technology from Microsoft and applications developed by its global partner ecosystem help to improve analytics, shorten the justice process, and reduce time and money previously spent on paperwork.

Effective integrated justice solutions collect, analyze, and circulate information across multiple agencies and organizations in the justice community. Using the latest applications that are designed to work together, electronic data collection is more reliable and cost efficient, freeing up officials to detect and investigate crime, instead of managing paper work. These Web-based solutions—designed to comply with international

standards— ensure easier horizontal and vertical integration and allow interoperability with data management software (Integrated Justice, 2010).

E-JUSTICE AS COMPONENT OF POLICY OF E-GOVERNMENT

Development of Policy of E-Government

2010 saw approval of a new strategy – *A Digital Agenda for Europe* (European Commission..., 2010). This strategy is one of seven major initiatives for the Europe 2020 strategy and defines the most important, incentive function of ICT in ensuring that the EU implements what has been scheduled to be achieved by 2020. Much attention in the strategy is paid to methods and measures to increase possibilities and capabilities for use of public services, boost digital trust, improve compatibility between electronic tools, and implement innovations in ICT. The strategy also refers to use of ICT in the field that initially may seem unrelated to ICT: the environment protection (in order to improve efficiency of consumption of energy and reduce emissions of greenhouse gas). Moreover, it emphasizes the potential for use of ICT in transport in creating next-generation transportation systems. All this shows that ICT policy should not be associated exclusively with public administration.

The European Commission emphasizes that e-Government is first of all a component of public administration, therefore its development should focus on applying ICT for improvement of the system of public administration, increasing of accessibility to and quality in public services, cost reduction, etc. Four focuses of e-Government can be identified:

1. Focus on recipient/user: contact with system of public administration;
2. Focus on processes: reformation of governmental processes;
3. Focus on cooperation: cross-institutional collaboration;
4. Focus on information: knowledge and information management in system of public administration.

As a result of such conception and focus, e-Government is a horizontal-type area of public policy, which involves or is closely related to other areas, such as development of information society, public electronic services, management of information resources of state, electronic signature, information and communication technologies, and security of information technologies. When conducting a comprehensive analysis of policy of e-Government, these areas must be analysed as well (Vyriausybei atskaitingų institucijų..., 2011; Wyld, 2008).

As with any other area of public policy, successfully e. power development requires certain conditions (factors). According to the academic literature (Torres et al., 2005), pronounced that the technological, legal, institutional and social conditions contribute to faster and higher quality e. government development:

1. *Technological development of the country* in the area of ICT must be rather high. Possibilities for citizens and business to use these technologies must be ensured. In addition, appropriate ICT network must be established at state institutions. Developing of such a network requires solving, inter alia, the issues of interoperability and security of technologies, i.e., information systems and networks must be interconnected in such a way that transfer of information is not hampered by restrictions related to data encoding and security.

The mentioned EU strategies provide that for e-Government to be efficient it is necessary to implement measures such as cross-compatible management of electronic identification as well as systems for authentication and e-archiving of electronic documents (Chang, Kannan, 2008):

2. *Regulatory framework* of policy of e-Government must be capable of regulating the ongoing projects of e-Government without restricting their implementation just because certain legal acts have not been passed yet;
3. There is no single, standardized model of *institutional arrangement,* which would facilitate achievement of aims of policy of e-Government. Analysis of foreign practice shows that in the world and European countries leading in e-Government assessment indices coordination of e-Government policy is based on both centralised and decentralised models. In the centralised model, the key role is played by the national government or some ministry with subordinate agencies. In the centralised model, a significant role is played by the Ministry of Finance as well as commissions for horizontal cross-institutional coordination;
4. *Resource-related conditions* refer to the level of certain financial, human, and material resources. Allocation of adequate funding and material resources for development of e-Government must be ensured. As to human resources, not only adequate number of employees, but also their ICT skills are necessary;
5. *Social conditions* in this context reflect readiness of society and business to use services of e-Government. It has been noticed that its success also depends on positive attitude of society and business to implementation of such policy, positive view towards ICT, and trust in public electronic services. Moreover, their skills must be advanced enough to enable use of ICT means (Vyriausybei atskaitingų institucijų …, 2011).

The Lithuanian programme for development of information society for 2011–2019 (Lietuvos Respublikos Vyriausybės..., 2011) has been drawn up with a view that development of information society is a dynamic and rapidly changing process encompassing many areas of societal and state activities and that successful involvement of the public sector in encouraging positive and minimizing negative outcomes of the process would contribute much to sustainable development of information society.

The purpose of the programme is to outline the priorities, aims, and objectives of development of information society so as to achieve best use of social and economic possibilities opened up by information and communication technologies, first of all the internet: a very important tool in economic and social activities, which can be used for providing and receiving services, working, entertainment, communication, and free expression of opinion (Lietuvos Respublikos Vyriausybės..., 2011). The programme is in harmony with the aims laid out in the Communication from the European Commission of 19 May 2010 to the European Parliament, the Council, the European Economic and Social Committee and the Committee of the Regions *A Digital Agenda for Europe* (COM (2010) 245 final) and is compatible with the Communication from the European Commission of 3 March 2010 *Europe 2020. A strategy for smart, sustainable and inclusive growth* (COM (2010) 2020 final). The aim of the programme is to motivate Lithuanian people to gain knowledge and skills they need for successful use of ICT, participation in knowledge-based society, improvement of their life quality, and reducing of social divide (hereinafter referred to as objective of Priority 1), to establish conditions for that (Lietuvos Respublikos Vyriausybės..., 2011).

Implementation of E-Justice in the European Union

Napoleon Xanthoulis pointed that "Following the recently developed ideas of e-governance and e-democracy, it appears inevitable that eventually the concept of "e-justice" will rise as well." (Xanthoulis, 2009).In administration of courts in the European Union ICT are used increasingly more often. The member states run numerous projects to improve informing of legal entities: information on legal systems, legal acts, and case law is made available online; litigant-court electronic communication systems are being created. There are cases when exclusively electronic procedures are used. It is increasingly more common practice to use electronic measures to record testimonies:

Placing information and communication technologies (ICT) at the service of judicial systems creates possible solutions by improving their functioning and contributing to a streamlining of procedures and reduction in costs. "e-Justice" represents an initial response to the threefold need to improve access to justice, cooperation between legal authorities and the effectiveness of the justice system itself. (Commission of the European Communities, 2008)

The European e-Justice system is being created adhering to the principle of independence of judiciary. Technically e-Justice must be compatible with the broader system of e-Government. It is necessary to promote the European Interoperability Framework (EIF) created under the ID-ABC (Interoperable Delivery of pan-European eGovernment Services to Public Administrations, Businesses and Citizens) programme. European work on e-signature and e-identity are especially necessary for judicial activities where validation of authenticity of acts is critical (Council of the European Union, 2008).

The European interoperability framework (EIF) developed within the IDABC programme should be promoted. European work on e-Signature and e-Identity is particularly relevant in judicial matters, where the authentication of acts is essential (Council of the European Unijon, 2008):

Justice approach uses ICT to improve citizens' access to justice and to make legal action more effective, the latter being understood as any type of activity involving the resolution of a dispute or the punishment of criminal behaviour. (Commission of the European Communities, 2008)

E-Justice issues are not related to certain legal areas only. They arise in many areas of civil, criminal, and administrative law. Therefore e-Justice is a horizontal issue for the area of European international cases (Council of the European Union, 2008).

European e-Justice system should be accessible to all citizens, companies, practicing lawyers and judicial institutions, which will use the available modern technologies. European e-Justice is aimed at establishment of European judicial area through the use of information and communication technologies. Therefore, all the European Union member states must be able to participate in the projects related to the field of European e-justice. Providing a platform for efficient and secure exchange of information and specific functionality European e-Justice should also be an instrument available to practicing lawyers and judicial institutions. It is very important to develop European e-Justice in such a way that it directly serves (though a website) citizens of Europe, who can benefit from the value-added offered by e-Justice. When selecting projects or prioritizing them it is necessary to ensure that citizens can quickly start making practical use of the measures of e-Justice (Council of the European Union, 2008).

The EU's action in the area of e-Justice should enable citizens, particularly when they have been the victim of a criminal offence, to access information without being hindered by the linguistic, cultural and legal barriers related to the multiplicity of systems. This action should also support mechanisms promoting cooperation between legal authorities. (Commission of the European Communities, 2008)

Since 2003, the Commission has been developing an internet portal http://ec.europa.eu/civiljustice/ for judicial cooperation in civil and commercial matters. Various organisations of lawyers throughout Europe run highly useful electronic information exchange or conviction data consolidation projects such as association of the councils of state website http://www.juradmin.eu/, common portal of case law of the supreme courts http://www.network-presidents.eu/ or the European testament registry www.cnue.be. The European Union e-Justice activities must enable citizens, especially victims of criminal acts, to get acquainted with information and overcome linguistic, cultural, and legal barriers caused by the variety of systems. Mechanisms encouraging cooperation of judicial institutions must also be supported (Commission of the European Communities, 2008).

The purpose of the European e-Justice portal https://e-justice.europa.eu/ (see Figure 1) is to make it easier for citizens and companies to exercise their right to justice in Europe. Over time, the portal should become a symbol of the European justice area and a part of the common policy of online communication. The portal enables familiarization with case law (civil, criminal, and administrative cases) of different countries of the European Union. The Lithuanian database covers case law of the following courts: the Supreme Court, the Court of Appeal, Vilnius Regional Court, Kaunas Regional Court, Klaipėda Regional Court, Panevėžys Regional Court, Šiauliai Regional Court, the Supreme Administrative

Court, Vilnius Regional Administrative Court, Kaunas Regional Administrative Court, Klaipėda Regional Administrative Court, Šiauliai Regional Administrative Court, and Panevėžys Regional Administrative Court.

National e-Justice systems are an important power for national economies — they represent the space where the most advanced information and communications technology (ICT) makes the administration of justice better, faster, and less expensive for taxpayers (Integrated Justice, 2010). National e-Justice systems are also an important driver for national economies. The European Union (EU) is working on a project to create an EU e-Justice Portal. The aim is to provide a virtual environment where national authorities, relevant private interests, and individual citizens can access information on certain legal topics, which may already exist electronically in national databases. Achieving full cross-border data

and document exchange, as well as interoperability between the courts of EU member states is a very laudable aim, although it may take some time to achieve with support needed for all 23 EU languages. The EU e-Justice portal is due to be launched in stages from 2010 (Integrated Justice, 2010). In future the European e-Justice portal shall be a single electronic place dedicated for topics on justice. The first stage is aimed at helping the citizens by providing information about justice systems in 22 languages and making it easier to seek justice all over the EU.

The third release of the European e-Justice Portal, which had been under preparation since August 2011, went live on 23 October 2012. This release introduced new forms for the European Payment Order and an improved back office content management system. With this system, the Member States will become responsible for managing their links and will be able to update

Figure 1. The European e-justice portal

their content more easily. This release also provides the technical framework necessary for the full migration of the content pages of the European Judicial Network in civil and commercial matters (EJN civil) which is planned for January/February 2013 (Council of the European Union, 2012):

The European e-Justice Portal is a one-stop-shop, targeted at citizens, businesses and legal practitioners. It provides a wealth of information in 22 languages that serves as a reference tool in the context of judicial training. The Portal will be further developed to provide information about training providers and training events, to ensure easy access to legal databases and high quality training material and also to function as an entry point regarding the co-funding possibilities made available by the Commission. (European Commission, 2011)

But this site mostly oriented at information concerning criminal and civil justice. Association of the Councils of State and Supreme Administrative Jurisdictions of the European Union i.n.p.a. - Europe is composed of the Court of Justice of the European Union and the Councils of State or the Supreme administrative jurisdictions of each of the members of the European Union. Webpage of this organization (http://www.juradmin.eu/index.php/en/) provide opportunity to familiarize with system of administrative justice of different EU countries. The interactive map (*Tour of Europe*) presents links to main themes of every EU country:

- **Introduction**: History, purpose of the review and classification of administrative acts, definition of an administrative authority;
- **I:** Organization and role of the bodies, competent to review administrative acts;
- **II:** Judicial review of administrative acts;
- **III:** Non-judicial settlement of administrative disputes;
- **IV:** Administration of justice and statistic data.

E-JUSTICE IN LITHUANIAN ADMINISTRATIVE PROCEEDINGS

System of Administrative Courts of Lithuania

Administrative law deals with cases of violations by the Administrative Commission of the municipal councils, municipal townships in rural areas, elders, district (city) district courts (district courts), the police, the State Inspectorate of the Republic of Lithuania and other laws to authorize the bodies (officials) (Lietuvos Respublikos administracinių...). Administrative courts of Lithuania are a two-tier: 5 regional administrative courts (in Vilnius, Kaunas, Klaipeda, Panevezys and Siauliai) and the Supreme Administrative Court. Administrative courts of Lithuania deals with disputes between civil servants as well as disputes in the environmental, agricultural, health, communications regulation, consumer rights and competition. Can be distinguished, and one quite specific areas of dispute - Disputes arising out of tax relations. In summary, one can say that the administrative courts deal with disputes in which at least one of the parties is a State, municipality or state or local government, institution, office, and those who are subjects of public authority functions (Valančius, 2007).

Under the valid Code of Administrative Offences (CAO) (Lietuvos Respublikos administracinių...) and the Administrative Proceedings Act (Lietuvos Respublikos..., 1999), the administrative courts themselves not impose penalties for administrative violations committed (to be appointed by the authority and general jurisdiction of district courts), but deals with complaints about these or other penalties in cases of procedural decisions taken.

Lithuanian administrative courts hear administrative cases of several types. Pursuant to Lithuanian law, administrative courts also adjudicate disputes over law in public or internal administration, cases regarding legality of normative administrative acts, and administrative offence cases. The procedure of all these cases is regulated by one piece of legislation: the Law on Administrative Proceedings of the Republic of Lithuania (Lietuvos Respublikos administracinių..., 1999), which provides for minor differences in hearing cases of different categories. Obviously, the legal nature of cases of the said types is very different. The procedure of administrative offence cases is particularly outstanding (Valančius, Norkus, 2006).

In Lithuania the administrative courts are officially publishing the statistics of received and examined cases. Statistics on numbers of cases received and settled at administrative courts in Lithuania are released officially. Analysis of statistical data shows that numbers of administrative disputes at administrative courts keep increasing. This indicates that citizens know and understand their rights better. This is natural and results from activities of non-governmental organisations, increased activeness of communities, and intensifying spread of legal awareness through mass media. People begin to realise that they

have certain rights and possibilities and, which is very important, start using and defending them. Figure 2 shows dynamics of the number of cases received and settled at the Supreme Administrative Court of Lithuania in 2005-2010 (Lietuvos vyriausiasis..., 2012).

Complete administrative law proceedings of District courts are presented in Figure 3 (Lietuvos Respublikos teismų..., 2011). It can be argued that these cases represent a wide range of economic topics and range management activities.

Level of IT Application in Lithuania

The main condition of e-Government and e-Justice systems' realization is the level of IT application in the country and computer literacy of citizens (Wyld, 2008).

At the beginning of 2012, 82.7 per cent of state and municipal authorities and agencies provided first-level e-services via the Internet, i.e. information on the functions performed and services provided by the institutions was avail-

Figure 2. Number of in 2005 -2010 received cases of the Lithuanian Supreme Administrative

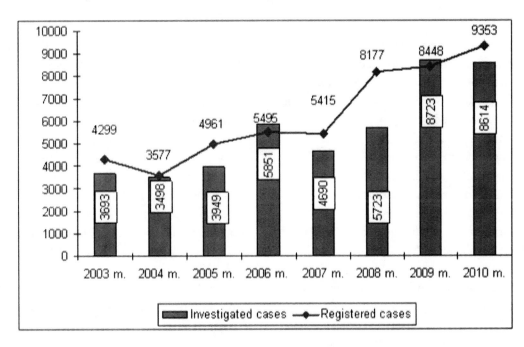

Figure 3. Complete administrative law proceedings of district courts

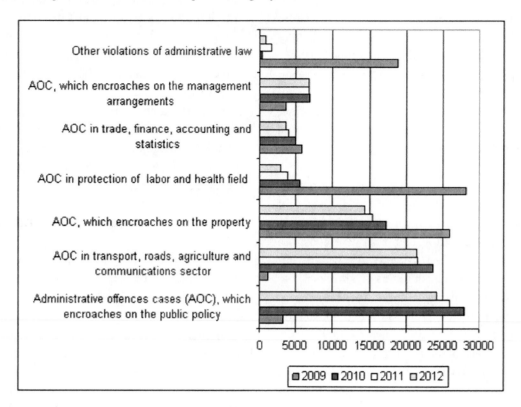

able on their Internet websites. 59.6 per cent of institutions provided a possibility to download various forms, 15.7 per cent – to return filled-in forms. 18.4 per cent of institutions indicated that they had provided an opportunity to perform administrative procedures electronically, i.e. without additional paperwork. 10.2 per cent of institutions automatically (without a request for a separate application) provided certain services of social or economic nature, when providing e-services were using preceding user's registration and data (provided partially prefilled data transfer forms). More than 85 per cent of institutions provided institution's activity-related news, legal information, institution's structure and contact information on their website. 94.5 per cent of institutions provided consultancy services by email, 77.2 per cent – on the website. According to the data of the Information Society Development Committee (ISDC) under the Ministry of Transport and Communications, at the beginning of 2012, the proportion of the main public services moved to the electronic environment in Lithuania stood at 81.5 per cent.

In Lithuania, the following e-services are already provided at the highest possible maturity level: individual income declaration, job search, issue of driving licences, reporting to the police, declaration of the place of residence, declaration of social contributions for employees, declaration of profit and value added taxes, establishment of a new company, submission of customs declarations, execution of public procurement. Based on the data of the ISDC, in the middle of 2011, there were 906 websites of public and municipal authorities and agencies operating in Lithuania. At the beginning of 2012, most (98.4 per cent) institutions were using broadband Internet connection. More than half (60.2 per cent) of institutions had fibre-optic lines, 43.7 per cent – digital subscriber lines (DSL).

At the beginning of 2012, 82.8 per cent of the employees of institutions used computers, 72.2 per cent – the Internet for working purposes. Although most of the institutions have been providing public and administrative services in a traditional manner (by mail, phone or accepting visitors in the institution), electronic servicing via social networks (e.g. Facebook, MySpace) becomes more and more popular. At the beginning of 2012, 9.9 per cent of institutions provided information and consultancy in social networks. At the beginning of 2012, 74.7 per cent of institutions performed electronic exchange of documents with other State and municipal authorities and agencies. In I quarter 2012, 54 per cent of the population aged 16–74 used the Internet to interact with public authorities and made use of electronic public services. 37 per cent of individuals in this age group used the electronic services provided by public authorities and other public service institutions at least once during the year. In 2011, almost all (99.6 per cent) enterprises used the Internet for communication with public authorities (Lietuvos Statistikos departamentas, 2012).

Many people in Lithuania use computer or internet every day: they file tax returns, do online banking, search for work-related information, or simply seek entertainment. However, there are certain groups of people in Lithuania who do not use computer or internet or use them very little. Successful development of information society depends on secure electronic space trusted by its users. If ICT are not reliable, introduction of certain online services such as electronic banking or governmental services will be simply impossible. The following preconditions are crucial for emergence of secure electronic space: creation and use of infrastructure for identity verification, people's abilities to use ICT safely, understanding of potential online risks, and knowledge of how to deal with these threats. It is very important to change the presently prevailing attitude that there are no sanctions for illegal actions online (Lietuvos Respublikos Vyriausybės..., 2011).

Lithuanian Court Information System LITEKO

The first steps towards use of public relations and information technologies in court activities have already been taken. Pursuant to Procedure for Online Publication of Court Rulings, Judgments, Decisions, and Decrees (Teismų taryba, 2005) procedural decisions of courts are made available online in order to inform the society about interpretation and application of law at Lithuanian courts. Procedural decisions of courts and related information are published online through court information system LITEKO. Structural diagram of the system is given in Figure 4.

LITEKO system (http://www.teismai.lt/lt/ LITEKO/) is intended to improve quality in work of courts as organisations and of the entire judiciary, to increase publicity of functioning of the system of courts, to better administration of work at courts and throughout the judiciary, to make work easier for judges and court staff, to provide electronic services in the fields of both justice delivery and information provision to other organisations and the general public.

Chief functions of LITEKO are:

- Storage of electronic information about each case (procedural documents of parties, parties to proceedings, other participants in the proceedings, course of proceedings, procedural documents of court) both at an individual court and in the central database;
- Automatic generation of statistical reports on performance of judges and courts on the basis of the stored information;
- Search for documents and information needed in court proceedings, both in databases of court information system and in external registries and databases;
- Increasing of publicity and transparency of functioning of courts through use of computer programme for allocation of cases,

Figure 4. LITEKO system flowchart

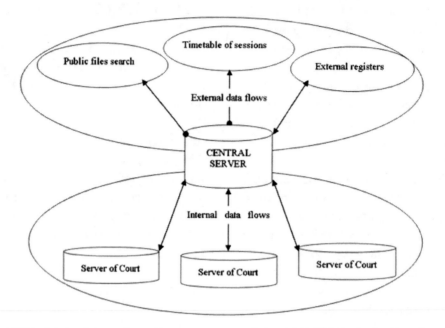

online publishing of schedules of judicial sittings, court rulings, and reports on case hearings;

- Provision of electronic services related to supply of legal information and law enforcement to other institutions and the general public;

- Automation of proceedings for certain cases.

The court order the electronic booking system TĮEUS (http://liteko.teismai.lt/tieus/) allows natural and legal persons to submit an application for a court order for electronic (online). This system facilitates lenders' access to justice; the court is to examine the possible cases of this type. The system is available only to legal entities and natural persons who are qualified electronic signature certificate. The certificate is necessary because without it cannot connect to the system and sent documents to sign.

Development of processes of dissemination of information by modern electronic means is definitely important for the judiciary. Amendment to the Code of Civil Procedure, which has been passed in summer of 2011, provides that starting with the 1 January 2013 procedural documents can be submitted to court by electronic communications facilities. Use of electronic communications facilities shall also be adopted in the managerial process and the bailiff activities, use of information and electronic communication technologies (videoconferencing, teleconferencing etc.) in judicial proceedings shall be made possible. The amendment establishes a list of persons who are obligated to receive procedural documents electronically (after the court has fulfilled its obligation to send documents electronically). This list includes attorneys at law, assistants of attorneys at law, bailiffs, assistants of bailiffs, notaries, state and municipal companies, institutions and organisations, financial companies, and insurance firms. In addition, electronic delivery of documents shall be extended to persons whom laws or contracts with court information system manager obligate to receive procedural documents by electronic communications facilities. A court will be allowed to deliver documents by electronic communications facilities to other persons as well, if such persons requested so and provided appropriate contact information. It must be noted, however, that the said laws do not specify what electronic facilities (e-delivery system, other information systems, or simply email) can be used. This shall be set out by the order of the minister of justice. The order or the draft order has not been publicly announced so far. Hopefully the Ministry of Justice will get everything ready by the end of the year and the innovations will proceed as planned (GLIMSTEDT, 2012).

E-Cases

In response to changes in the Code of Civil Procedure, the laws on courts and on bailiff activities were supplemented by provisions related to management of electronic cases. Starting with the beginning of 2013 information and electronic communication technologies shall be used for management, entering in records, and storage at courts of electronic data related to judicial process cases. In the manner set out by the minister of justice participants in the proceedings will have a right to access the electronic case and get copies of the documents it contains. All the procedural documents made in writing shall be digitized and their digital copies shall be placed in the electronic case. Documents that cannot be digitized shall be stored on paper and this shall be noted in the electronic case. Authenticity and security of the data shall be ensured by electronic signature (GLIMSTEDT, 2012).

Administrative E-Justice Solutions in Lithuania

Lithuania Government Resolution *On general requirements for state and municipal institutions and Web sites describe the approval* (Dėl bendrųjų..., 2003) provides that each site should

be menu *Legal Division*. However, the analysis of the Lithuanian Ministries web site, you may notice that the legislation put in this section are not associated with administrative proceedings. Does not refer to CATL, the Administrative Proceedings Act, there is no case law under the Ministry of topics.

Trust by the society in laws, democratic values, and independent courts in essential condition for survival of a state. Principles such as transparency, publicity, and openness shall contribute to updates to the system of administrative courts, restoration of trust of the public in justice as well as their belief that justice is delivered by transparent, open, and professional courts, that people's constitutional right to fair trial is ensured (Piličiauskas, 2011a).

The following procedural decisions of courts in administrative cases are published online: all effective procedural decisions passed by regional administrative courts and essentially deciding an administrative case or closing it without a ruling, procedural decisions by Supreme Administrative Court of Lithuania made upon essential adjudgment of a case in response to an appeal or a separate complaint, procedural decisions made upon adjudgment of a case regarding legitimacy of a normative administrative act, election case and other cases heard as the sole instance, procedural decisions to close the case without a ruling, procedural decisions made upon adjudication of application for renewal of the process. Subject to a warrant of the judge or judicial panel who made procedural decisions, or such court president, deputy president, or person authorized by the president other effective procedural decisions settling a procedural issue in the case (for example, regarding appointment of expert examination, imposition of claim security measures, stay of proceedings, removal etc.) can also be published online if it is necessary to ensure provision of information to the public about case law at administrative courts.

The edition of the Law on Administrative Proceedings of the Republic of Lithuania (Lietuvos Respublikos administracinių..., 1999), which is scheduled for coming into force on 1 July 2013, provides that participation of participants in the proceedings in court sessions can be ensured by using information and electronic communication technologies (videoconferencing, teleconferencing, etc.). When using these technologies in the manner established by the minister of justice it is necessary to ensure reliable verification of identity of the participants in the proceedings as well as objectivity of submission of explanations, testimonies, questions, or motions. A complaint (a motion) can be sent in electronic form, by electronic communication facilities. A response, a court ruling, and other procedural documents can be received by electronic communication facilities. When sending a complaint (a motion) to an administrative disputes commission by electronic communications facilities a secure electronic signature is used to verify identity of the person. Participants in the proceedings have a right to access case documents, other material (including electronic case) at the court and, subject to court (judge) permission, receive paid copies (digital copies) and extracts of them. Factual data are obtained through the following measures: explanations of parties to the proceedings and their representatives, witness testimonies, explanations from professionals and expert opinions, material evidence, documents, and other textual, electronic, audio and video evidence. Where so specified, subpoena and notifications are delivered by electronic communication facilities. Court delivers subpoena and notifications by electronic communication facilities to attorneys at law, assistants of attorneys at law, bailiffs, assistants of bailiffs, notaries, ombudsmen, public administration entities, state and municipal companies, financial companies, and insurance firms. Where so specified, court rulings and court orders are sent by electronic communication facilities. Having accepted an appeal a court of the first instance forwards the case (electronic case) together with the received appeal and annexes to it to the court of appeal instance within three days. Where so specified, a court of appeal instance sends, by electronic communication facilities, digital copies of the appeal and annexes to it to persons involved in the appeal process.

Decision by the Council of Judges on regulations of provision of the public and the media with information about court activities (Teisėjų taryba, 2007) establishes a procedure for all courts to provide, in accordance with laws and other legal acts of the Republic of Lithuania and in order to ensure publicity of court activities, the public and the media with information on court activities. When publishing information on court activities, which is related to personal data managed at court (schedules of court sessions, court procedural decisions, etc.), to court websites it is necessary to adhere to the principles of expediency and proportionality and ensure protection of confidential personal data. These regulations are mandatory for all courts of general jurisdiction and of special jurisdiction in the Republic of Lithuania. The website of Vilnius Regional Administrative Court contains publicly available Regulations Concerning Provision of the Public and the Media with Information about Activities of Vilnius Regional Administrative Court approved by the Order No. T-25 of 4 March 2010 of President of Vilnius Regional Administrative Court (http://www.vaateismas.lt/lt/aptarnavimo-tvarka/informacijos-teikimo-taisykles.html). Vilnius Regional Administrative Court Regulations Concerning Distribution of Cases among Judges by Means of Information Technologies (Vilniaus apygardos..., 2010) govern allocation of administrative cases and administrative offence cases to judges of Vilnius Regional Administrative Court by means of information technologies. The Regulations govern the process of automated allocation of cases to judges and picking of jury so that cases are allocated to judges by taking into consideration the particularities of activities of the court, its internal procedures, types and peculiarities of cases (e.g., differences in the number of judges in administrative cases: one judge or a jury, etc), and legal acts in force. The Regulations have been prepared in accordance with the Decision of 10 October 2008 of the Council of Judges (Teisėjų taryba, 2008).

In order to enhance openness of the court to the public the Supreme Administrative Court of Lithuania now uses a fully-functional computerised system for allocation of cases to judges, which does impartial allocation of all administrative cases (with no exceptions). Choice of a judge for a case depends on specialization of judges and random numbers generated by the computer. This ensures complete transparency of distribution of cases among judges. In response to requests from people, a new website of the court has been created and launched. All information about activities of the court is regularly uploaded to this website (Piličiauskas, 2011a).

All these techniques increase the openness of the courts, but do not perform the tasks of legal education of citizens. The analysis of Lithuanian administrative courts site was found to be adequate depths and convenient legal information not only for professional lawyers, but also ordinary citizens who intend to defend or protect their interests in court, the Vilnius Regional Administrative Court's website (http://www.vaateismas.com). This site contains not only the necessary information about the court structure, jurisdiction, functions, history, statistics and business area, where judges and court personnel all phone numbers, but also useful advice on how, during the time needed to go to court on the form provided by complaint, which is accessing the file, order, and so on. Want to ask about court procedures, the proposed section "Questions – Answers". Web site contains links to other Lithuanian courts, state agencies, pre-trial institutions and the judiciary legislation. Website can be accessible for disabled people - they are adapted to a specific version. Cover page and the information available to foreigners - it is published also in English (Bilevičienė, Bilevičiūtė, 2012).

E-Fine

Implementation of the project "E-fine" aimed at creation of e-services information system for administration of fines levied on natural and legal persons without formal disputing is currently in progress. The aim of this 8.5 million LTL (of these 7.3 million are resources from the EU funds) project is to encourage voluntary payment of fines, improve the process of administration of fines levied without formal disputing, and provide instruments to pay them conveniently. Presently only the State Tax Inspectorate, the State Social Insurance Fund Board, and the Customs of the Republic of Lithuania extract taxes in arrears. More than 60 other state institutions make decisions on recovery and pass them for bailiffs. Upon consolidation of recovery in the single institution (the State Tax Inspectorate), the project "E-fine" will enable unification of different procedures of administration and recovery, improve efficiency of recovery of fines, and encourage voluntary payment of fines. The project being implemented is designed to allow for distance payment of fines, that is, it will no longer be necessary to deliver receipts or other payment confirmation documents to relevant institutions, as all information about the imposed fines will be consolidated at the website of the State Tax Inspectorate. This procedure will enable the users of the E-fine service to timely receive information about the recovery procedures applied and save money by paying the fines remotely and within the period specified. Moreover, this will reduce the number of cases passed for bailiffs by mistake, because information about the levied and paid fines will be recorded in information systems (GLIMST-EDT, 2012).

In order to find out the opinion of public, etc. every person of Lithuania's position on public participation in the examination of administrative cases of necessity, the Lithuanian Supreme Administrative Court (SACL) has fulfilled a public online public opinion poll on public representatives of the Lithuanian Institute of the implementation of the administrative courts. The survey was SACL's website, 2011 August 19 - 16 October. Questionnaires, which consisted of 10 questions, 689 people completed the online (Visuomenės atstovų...). The survey results showed that 65% of respondents consider that an examination of public representatives in administrative cases, 67% of respondents said that it would increase public confidence in the Lithuanian administrative courts. 41% of respondents believe that the administrative cases involved public hearing should be called a representative of the assessor, by 24% - by public judge. 34% of the respondents have the opinion that public representatives should be appointed (several candidates), certain specialists in the field according to which category the file will be analysed, 27% - are selected at random. The results of this analysis show that both the public participation in administrative proceedings provided the necessary public legal education (Bilevičienė, Bilevičiūtė, 2012).

Solutions and Recommendations

Technologies that affect social-legal practice must satisfy the following criteria: simplicity (a technology should not be overly complex), flexibility, adaptability (possibility to adapt to changes in social-legal environment), reliability (reliance on stability of performance of technology), cost-effectiveness (be useful but not too expensive), ease of use (though being well-made a technology will fail if it is inconvenient for people who will have to use it). Manifestation of social technologies in law is related to condition of social and legal scientific knowledge (factors of science) and to efficiency of social legal activity, which

has been determined by sought methods to make decisions towards achievement of social and legal aims in society. Implementation of public relations policy and online availability of information from Lithuanian administrative justice institutions have been analysed in the article.

For expenditure on management to be reasonable, justice institutions must cooperate and improve information exchange, protect citizens and adhere to security measures:

- Complicated processes result in overload and data delays: electronic document system should be the first important step;
- Incompatibility between systems necessitates data repetition leading to mistakes, therefore unification shall provide for better and faster decision-making;
- Privacy and security issues often obstruct cooperation among parties concerned.

By consolidating the related processes and improving public online access to the legal system, justice institutions would improve their productivity:

- Staff of justice institutions could safely access data at other institutions;
- Citizens could obtain information without calling help and support;
- It would be easier for different departments to work together.

Information technologies make functioning of the justice system more efficient and useful, accelerate service provision, and simplify work processes. The administrative procedure is the complicate process that needs not only legal knowledge. Accordingly the collection and perception of information has the supplementary importance. Bringing the wide system of administrative e-justice, we could save the time, because the interaction between citizen and state servant. Also, the documents could be presented by e-mail and out-of-hours. Disabled persons have better opportunity to familiarize with trial procedure. The input of material resources decreases, the environment is protecting. Finally, such reforms should generally release and accelerate the trial procedure.

FUTURE RESEARCH DIRECTIONS

Subjects of social technologies can include social relations, social processes, and the system of methods and tools to understand and regulate these relations and processes. However, application of social technologies in Lithuanian administrative justice has not been analysed in depth yet. Lithuania saw only one conference where these issues were discussed from the theoretical point of view. Analysing statistical information on case-law regarding administrative cases one can see that the numbers of such cases are increasing. As administrative justice is complex and hearing of administrative offences and application of penalties can be subject to both the Code on Administrative Transgressions of Law and the Law on Administrative Proceedings, citizens of Lithuania find it problematic to understand the norms of these legal acts. However, most citizens encounter administrative offences from time to time. Therefore, provision of information to and legal education of the public contribute to development of civil society. The aspects of administrative justice dealt with in the article have not been analysed previously.

CONCLUSION

Issues of administrative proceedings are complicated due to problems with classification of administrative offences, variations in scope of application of individual principles of administrative proceedings in different administrative cases,

and insufficient level of the legislative framework. Citizens of Lithuania have a right to complete and correct information about administrative law and administrative process. Manifestation of social technologies in law is not possible without application of ICT. The first steps towards use of public relations and information and communication technologies in court activities have already been taken.

E-Justice expands attitude at definition of justice in Europe. Today, citizens, enterprises, trials and other institutions are not only recipients of legal information. E-Justice should provide for them the opportunity to interact directly among them. Although, e-Justice could has influence on most fields of civil, criminal and administrative law. That is the most important in context of international cooperation in Europe.

Lack of integration capabilities across jurisdictions, agencies, and organizations hinders justice — it also means that very often justice agencies fail to provide the right services to the right people. By streamlining the justice enterprise and its connected data transmission, people are safer and have equal access to services. Organizations find that outcomes and performance indicators improve because new tools exist for cases to be solved, and criminals are caught and prosecuted more efficiently and quickly. Effective integrated justice solutions collect, analyze, and circulate information across multiple agencies and organizations in the justice community. Using the latest applications that are designed to work together, electronic data collection is more reliable and cost efficient, freeing up officials to detect and investigate crime, instead of managing paper work.

Administrative courts of Lithuania provide the public with information about court activities on websites of courts. The information, however, focuses on procedures (such as allocation of cases), presentation of court schedules, cases, etc. with almost no coverage of peculiarities of administrative proceedings.

REFERENCES

Adler, M., & Henman, P. (2001). E-justice: A comparative study of computerization and procedural justice in social security. *International Review of Law Computers & Technology*, *15*(2), 195–212. doi:10.1080/13600860120070510

Aleknonis, G. (2010). Komunikaciniai teisės žinoti ir laisvės informuoti aspektai. *Social Sciences Studies*, *2*(6), 7–21.

Augustinaitis, A., & Petrauskas, R. (2010). Pilietinių technologijų vaidmuo šiuolaikinėje visuomenėje. In Socialinės technologijos'10: Iššūkiai, galimybės sprendimai: Konferencijos medžiaga, 2010 m. lapkričio 25-26 d. (pp. 205-212). Vilnius-Net.

Bilevičienė, T., & Bilevičiūtė, E. (2012). Information systems of administrative justice - As social tool for implementation of publicity principle. In *Artificial intelligence driven solutions to business and engineering problems* (pp. 108–119). ITHEA.

Chang, A., & Kannan, P. K. (2008). *Leveraging web 2.0 in government*. Retrieved March 18, 2013 from http://faculty.cbpp.uaa.alaska.edu/afgjp/PADM601%20Fall%202009/Leverging%20Web%202.0.pdf

Commission of the European Communities. (2008). *Communication from the commission to the council, the European parliament and the European economic and social committee: Towards a European e-Justice strategy COM(2008)329 final*. Retrieved March 18, 2013 from http://ec.europa.eu/civiljustice/docs/com_2008_329_en.pdf

Council of the European Union. (2008). *European e-justice action plan*. Retrieved May 5, 2013 from http://register.consilium.europa.eu/pdf/en/08/st15/st15315.en08.pdf

Council of the European Union. (2012). *Report from the working party on e-law (e-justice) to Coreper/council, 6575/12*. Retrieved December 29, 2012 from http://register.consilium.europa.eu/pdf/en/12/st16/st16575.en12.pdf

Deviatnikovaitė, I., & Kalašnykas, R. (2007). Kategorijų kontrolė, valdžia ir socialinės technologijos turiningųjų požymių ypatumai teisėtumo užtikrinimo aplinkoje. *Jurisprudencija: Mokslo Darbai*, *6*(96), 85–89.

European Commission Communication from the Commission. (2010). *Europe 2020: A strategy for smart, sustainable and inclusive growth COM(2010) 2020 final*. Retrieved February 28, 2013 http://eur-lex.europa.eu/LexUriServ/LexUriServ.do?uri=COM:2010:2020:FIN:EN:PDF European Commission. (2011). *Communication from the commission to the European parliament, the council, the European economic and social committee and the committee of the regions: Building trust in EU-wide justice: A new dimension to European judicial training: COM(2011) 551 final*. Retrieved October 28, 2013 from http://ec.europa.eu/justice/criminal/files/2011-551-judicial-training_en.pdf

European Commission Communication from the Commission to the European Parliament. the Council, the European Economic and Social Committee and the Committee of the Regions. (2010). *A digital agenda for Europe COM(2010) 245 final/2*. Retrieved February 28, 2013 from http://eur-lex.europa.eu/LexUriServ/LexUriServ.do?uri=COM:2010:0245:FIN:EN:PDF

GLIMSTEDT. (2012). *Teisės žinios 2012 Nr. 5(5)*. Retrieved February 28, 2013 from http://www.glimstedt.lt/e-laikrastis/e-laikrastis-glimstedt-teises-zinios-5-e-paslaugos/2952

Institutas, T. (2004). Administracinių teismų vieta teismų sistemoje: užsienio šalių patirtis ir jos pritaikymo Lietuvoje galimybės. *Mokslinis tyrimas.* Retrieved February 28, 2013 from http://www.teise.org/docs/upload/adm%20teismai.pdf

Justice, I. (2010). *A Microsoft white paper.* Retrieved February 28, 2013 http://www.microsoft.com/government/ww/safety-defense/solutions/Pages/integrated-justice.aspx

Kargaudienė, A. (2007). Socialinės įtakos mechanizmai: Naujos galimybės paveikti administracinės teisės normų įgyvendinimo procesą. *Jurisprudencija. Mokslo Darbai, 6*(96), 27–31.

Kurpuvesas, V. (2007). Socialinės technologijos administracinėje justicijoje. *Jurisprudencija: Mokslo darbai, 6*(96), 72–77.

Lietuvos Respublikos Administracinių bylų Teisenos Įstatymas. (1999). *Nr. VIII-1029.* Nauja įstatymo redakcija nuo 2001 m. sausio 1 d Nr. VIII-1927 2000.09.19.

Lietuvos Respublikos Administracinių Teisės Pažeidimų Kodeksas. (2012). Redakcija 2012-11-06.

Lietuvos Respublikos Teismų ir Teismų Savivaldos Institucijų 2010 Metų Veiklos Apžvalga. (2011). *Vilnius.* Retrieved February 28, 2013 from http://www.teismai.lt/dokumentai/bendroji_informacija/teismu%20veiklos%20apzvalga%202010.pdf

Lietuvos Respublikos Visuomenės Informavimo Įstatymas. (1996). Nr. I-1418.

Lietuvos Respublikos Vyriausybės Nutarimas. (2003). Dėl bendrųjų reikalavimų valstybės ir savivaldybių institucijų ir įstaigų interneto svetainėms aprašo patvirtinimo, 2003 m. balandžio 18 d. Nr. 480.

Lietuvos Respublikos Vyriausybės Nutarimas. (2011). Dėl elektroninės informacijos saugos (kibernetinio saugumo) plėtros 2011–2019 metais programos patvirtinimo, 2011 m. birželio 29 d. Nr. 796.

Lietuvos Statistikos Departamentas. (2012). Informacinės technologijos Lietuvoje: Information technologies in Lithuania 2012. Vilnius.

Lietuvos Vyriausiasis Administracinis Teismas. (2012). *Statistika.* Retrieved March 13, 2013 from http://www.lvat.lt/veikla/statistika.aspx

Maurer, M. (2007). Court automation in Austria. *Masaryk University Journal of Law and Technology, 2,* 313–318.

Piličiauskas, R. (2011a). *Atvirai visuomenei - Atviri teismai.* Retrieved from http://www.lvat.lt/atvirai-visuomenei-atviri-teismai.aspx

Piličiauskas, R. (2011b). Viešojo intereso gynimas administraciniuose teismuose. In *Konferencijos Viešasis interesas ir jo gynimas medžiaga.* Retrieved February 28, 2013 http://www3.lrs.lt/pls/inter/w5_show?p_r=7992&p_d=111939&p_k=1

Pranevičienė, B. (2007). Teisėtų lūkesčių principo samprata ir teisėtų lūkesčių apsaugos modeliai Europos Sąjungos administracinėje erdvėje. *Jurisprudencija. Mokslo Darbai, 6*(96), 43–48.

Respublika, L. (2013). *Nacionalinė teismų administracija.* Retrieved February 28, 2013 from http://www.teismai.lt

Salovaara, I., & Augusiak, A. (2011). *A guide to careers in administrative law.* Cambridge, MA: Bernard Koteen Office of Public Interest Advising, Harvard Law School.

Teisėjų Taryba. (2007). Nutarimas dėl informacijos apie teismų veiklą teikimo visuomenei ir visuomenės informavimo priemonėms taisyklių patvirtinimo 2007 m. balandžio 27 d. Nr. 13P-60.

Teisėjų Taryba. (2008). Nutarimas dėl bylų paskirstymo naudojant informacines technologijas laikinųjų taisyklių patvirtinimo 2008 m. spalio 10 d. Nr. 13P-178-(7.1.2).

Teismų Taryba. (2005). Nutarimas dėl teismų sprendimų, nuosprendžių, nutarimų ir nutarčių skelbimo internete tvarkos patvirtinimo 2005 m. rugsėjo 9 d. Nr. 13 P – 378.

Torres, L., Pina, V., & Royo, S. (2005) E-government and the transformation of public administrations in EU countries: Beyond NPM or just a second wave of reforms? *Documento de Trabajo, 2005-01*. Retrieved February 28, 2013 from http://www.dteconz.unizar.es/DT2005-01.pdf

Trumputis, U. (2010). Žmogaus individualūs interesai kaip viešojo intereso pagrindas. *Social Sciences Studies*, 2(6), 123–137.

Urmonas, A. (2007). Socialinių technologijų konceptualių modelių pritaikymo administracinėje teisėje paieška. *Jurisprudencija. Mokslo Darbai*, 6(96), 9–15.

Valančius, V. (2007). *Žmonės vis dažniau gina savo teises administraciniuose teismuose*. INFOLEX. Retrieved February 28, 2013 http://infolex.lt/portal/start.asp?act=news&Tema=50&str=18935

Valančius, V., & Norkus, R. (2006). Lietuvos administracinės ir baudžiamosios justicijos sąlyčio aspektai. *Jurisprudencija. Mokslo Darbai*, 4(82), 91–98.

Vilniaus Apygardos Administracinio Teismo Pirmininko Įsakymas. (2010). Dėl bylų paskirstymo teisėjams naudojant informacines technologijas taisyklių patvirtinimo, 2010 m. kovo 5 d. Nr. T- 29.

Visuomenės Atstovų Dalyvavimas Nagrinėjant Administracines Bylas. (2011). *LVAT įvykdytos apklausos rezultatai*. Retrieved February 28, 2013 http://www.lvat.lt/media/77038/statistika.pdf

Vyriausybei Atskaitingų Institucijų Funkcijų Analizės ir Biudžeto Programų Vertinimo Paslaugos. (2011). Horizontali elektroninės valdžios politikos funkcijų peržiūra, Bandomosios funkcijų peržiūros ataskaita. 2011 m. sausio 3 d. Parengė viešoji įstaiga „Europos socialiniai, teisiniai ir ekonominiai projektai pagal 2009 m. gruodžio 29 d. paslaugų sutartį Nr. MPT-09-077 su Lietuvos Respublikos Ministro Pirmininko tarnyba.

Wyld, D. C. (2008). *Government in 3D: How public leaders can draw on virtual worlds*. Retrieved February 28, 2013 from http://faculty.cbpp.uaa.alaska.edu/afgjp/PADM601%20Fall%202009/Wyld3dReport.pdf

Xanthoulis, N. (2009). *Introducing the concept of 'e-justice' in Europe: How adding an 'E' becomes a modern challenge for Greece and the EU*. Retrieved February 28, 2013 from http://effectius.com/yahoo_site_admin/assets/docs/Introducing_the_concept_of_e-justice_in_Europe_by_Napoleon_Xanthoulis.20775004.pdf

ADDITIONAL READING

Agenda, D. new Regulation to enable cross-border electronic signatures and to get more value out of electronic identification in Digital Single Market Reference: IP/12/558 Event Date: 04/06/2012. Retrieved December 16, 2012 from http://europa.eu/rapid/press-release_IP-12-558_en.htm.

Bilevičienė, T., & Kažemikaitienė, E. (2005). Teisinės informacijos pateikimo būdai Lietuvos valstybinių institucijų interneto svetainėse Vyriausybės nustatytų reikalavimų kontekste. In Informacinės technologijos 2005. Konferencijos pranešimų medžiaga (742-751). Kaunas: Technologija.

Bilevičienė, T., & Kažemikaitienė, E. (2006). Adaptation of Lithuanian State Institutions' Sites to Disabled Persons. In *The 4th International Conference Citizens and Governance for Sustainable Development CIGSUD'2006. Selected papers* (48-52). Vilnius: Technika.

Bilevičienė, T., & Kažemikaitienė, E. (2006). Teisinių konsultacijų suteikimo būdai Lietuvos valstybinių institucijų interneto svetainėse Vyriausybės nustatytų reikalavimų kontekste. In Informacinės technologijos 2006. Konferencijos pranešimų medžiaga (201-209). Kaunas: Technologija.

Bughin, J., Chui, M., & Manyika, J. (2012). Capturing business value with social technologies. Retrieved December 16, 2012 from http://www. mckinsey.com/insights/high_tech_telecoms_internet/capturing_business_value_with_social_technologies.

Cerrillo, I. M., Fabra, A. I., & Abat, P. (2009). *E-Justice: Using Information Communication Technologies in the Court System.* IGI Global Snippet.

Chang, A., & Kannan, P. K. (2008). Leveraging Web 2.0 in Government. Retrieved February 28, 2013 http://faculty.cbpp.uaa.alaska.edu/afgjp/PADM601%20Fall%202009/Leverging%20Web%202.0.pdf.

Dapkus, R., & Kmieliauskaitė, R. (2011). E-demokratijos plėtros perspektyvos kaimiškuosiuose regionuose. In Management theory and studies for rural business and infrastructure development. Research papers. 2011. Nr. 2 (26).

Document, B. (2009). Justice Forum Meeting on European E-Justice. 5 March 2009. Retrieved January 30, 2013 from http://www.ccbe.eu/fileadmin/user_upload/document/E-Justice_Portal/05_03_2009/English/EN_Background_document.pdf.

E-Justice Submitted in partial fulfilment of the requirements for the Degree of Bachelor of Science at the University of Hull. By Alexander Cooper, May 2009. Retrieved December 16, 2012 from http://alexcooper.co.uk/downloads/e-justice.pdf.

European Commission. (2010). Communication from the Commission to the European Parliament, the Council, the European Economic and Social Committee and the Committee of the Regions. The European eGovernment Action Plan 2011-2015. Harnessing ICT to promote smart, sustainable & innovative Government COM(2010) 743 final, Retrieved February 28, 2013 http://eur-lex.europa.eu/LexUriServ/LexUriServ.do?uri=COM:2010:0743:FIN:EN:pdf.

European Commission. (2012). MEMO. Electronic identification, signatures and trust services: Questions & Answers. Brussels, 4 June 2012. Retrieved December 16, 2012 from http://europa.eu/rapid/press-release_MEMO-12-403_en.htm.

European e-Justice internet portal offers quick answers to citizens' legal questions. (2010). IP/10/956. Brussels, 16 July 2010.

European Parliament Resolution 18 December 2008 with Recommendations to the Commission on E-Justice (2008/2125(INI)). Retrieved December 16, 2012 from http://www.europarl.europa.eu/sides/getDoc.do?type=TA&language=EN&reference=P6-TA-2008-637.

European Parliament resolution of 20 April 2012 on a competitive digital single market – eGovernment as a spearhead (2011/2178(INI)). Retrieved May 7, 2013 from http://www.europarl.europa.eu/sides/getDoc.do?type=TA&reference=P7-TA-2012-0140&language=en.

European Parliament resolution of 6 July 2011 on a comprehensive approach on personal data protection in the European Union (2011/2025(INI)). Retrieved December 16, 2012 from http://www.europarl.europa.eu/sides/getDoc.do?pubRef=-//EP//TEXT+TA+P7-TA-2011-0323+0+DOC+XML+V0//en.

ICT within the Court in the E-Justice Era. (2012). By Marco Velicogna. Retrieved May 7, 2013 from http://effectius.com/yahoo_site_admin/assets/docs/ICT_within_the_court_in_the_e-Justice_Era_by_Marco_Velicogna.207234735.pdf.

Informacinės visuomenės plėtros komiteto prie Lietuvos Respublikos Vyriausybės direktoriaus įsakymas. (2004). Dėl valstybės informacinių sistemų kūrimo metodinių dokumentų patvirtinimo, 2004 m. spalio 15 d. Nr. T-131.

Informacinės visuomenės plėtros komiteto prie Lietuvos Respublikos Vyriausybės direktoriaus įsakymas. (2008). Dėl viešojo administravimo institucijų informacinių sistemų interoperabilumo sistemos funkcionavimo taisyklių patvirtinimo, 2008 m. gruodžio 1 d. Nr. T-228.

Informacinės visuomenės plėtros komiteto prie Lietuvos Respublikos Vyriausybės direktoriaus įsakymas. (2008). Dėl viešojo administravimo institucijų informacinių sistemų interoperabilumo sistemos nuostatų patvirtinimo, 2008 m. rugpjūčio 8 d. Nr. T-139.

Informacinės visuomenės plėtros komiteto prie Lietuvos Respublikos Vyriausybės direktoriaus įsakymas. (2009) Dėl administracinių paslaugų teikimo panaudojant informacinių ir ryšių technologijų priemones rekomendacijų patvirtinimo, 2009 m. spalio 28 d. Nr. T-105.

Kiškis, M., & Kraujelytė, A. (2005). Elektroninės valdžios instrumentalizmo ir jo alternatyvų teisinė-politinė analizė. *Teisė, 2005*, 55.

Knutson, T., & Kutler, J. (2010). Social Media Problems. *Risk Professional, 28-32*. Retrieved May 7, 2013 from http://www.ipswitchft.com/Company/PressReleases/pr_0610_RiskProfessionals.pdf

Lietuvos Respublikos Vyriausybės nutarimas. (2003). Dėl viešo naudojimo kompiuterių tinkluose neskelbtinos informacijos kontrolės ir ribojamos viešosios informacijos platinimo tvarkos patvirtinimo, 2003 m. kovo 5 d. Nr. 290.

Lietuvos Respublikos Vyriausybės nutarimas. (2005). Dėl Lietuvos informacinės visuomenės plėtros strategijos patvirtinimo, 2005 m. birželio 8 d. Nr. 625.

Lietuvos Respublikos Vyriausybės nutarimas. (2006). Dėl Lietuvos respublikos elektroninių ryšių tinklų ir informacijos saugumo įstatymo koncepcijos patvirtinimo, 2006 m. gruodžio 6 d. Nr. 1211.

Lietuvos Respublikos Vyriausybės nutarimas. (2009). Dėl viešojo administravimo institucijų informacinių sistemų sąveikumo sistemos naudojimo teikiant viešąsias ir administracines paslaugas elektroninėje erdvėje, 2009 m. gruodžio 16 d. Nr. 1659.

Lietuvos Respublikos Vyriausybės nutarimas. (2011). Dėl elektroninės informacijos saugos (kibernetinio saugumo) plėtros 2011–2019 metais programos patvirtinimo, 2011 m. birželio 29 d. Nr. 796.

Malinauskaitė, A. (2012). Elektroninė forma ir elektroninis parašas: Lietuvos teisinė bazė globaliame kontekste. Teisės problemos, 1 (75), 66-97.

Pandurangan, K. (2009). *E-Justice: Practical Guide for the Bench and the Bar*. Universal Law Publishing.

Petrauskas, R., Bilevičienė, T., & Kiškienė, A. (2008). E-Inclusion as the Part of E-Government Development in Lithuania, *Viešoji politika ir administravimas, 23*, 48-58.

Rights, H., & Sales, T. How Corporations Can Avoid Assisting Repressive Regimes. (2012). By Cindy Cohn, Trevor Timm, & Jillian C. York, April 2012. Electronic Frontier Foundation. Retrieved May 7, 2013 from https://www.eff.org/sites/default/files/filenode/human-rights-technology-sales.pdf.

Van Opijnen, M. (2011). European Case Law Identifier: Indispensable Asset for Legal Information Retrieval. In M. A. Biasiotti & S. Faro (Ed.), from *From Information to Knowledge. Online access to legal information: methodologies, trends and perspectives. IOS Press, December 2011.* Retrieved May 7, 2013 from http://www.legalaccess.eu/IMG/pdf/marc_van_opijnen_ecli_indispensableasset.pdf.

Velicogna, M., Errera, A., & Derlange, S. (2011). E-Justice in France: the e-Barreau experience. *Utrecht Law Review, 7 (1), 163-187*, Retrieved May 7, 2013 from www.utrechtlawreview.orq.

KEY TERMS AND DEFINITIONS

Administrative Justice: Is the body of law that governs the activities of administrative agencies of government. Government agency action can include rulemaking, adjudication, or the enforcement of a specific regulatory agenda.

E-Government: Refers to the use by government agencies of information technologies (such as Wide Area Networks, the Internet, and mobile computing) that have the ability to transform relations with citizens, businesses, and other arms of government.

E-Identity: Is user identification in cyberspace by an identification code.

E-Justice: Informacinių ir komunikacinių technologijų naudojimas siekiant pagerinti piliečių teisės į teisingumą įgyvendinimą ir padidinti teisminės veiklos veiksmingumą.

E-Services: Are Internet-based customer service and online account management services and alternately as an overarching service-centric concept.

E-Signature: Any electronic means that indicates either that a person adopts the contents of an electronic message, or more broadly that the person who claims to have written a message is the one who wrote it (and that the message received is the one that was sent).

Public E-Service: Legislation that regulates the activities of public administration entities for legal and natural persons, against payment or free of charge, to assist in the implementation of their rights and fulfill duties remotely, using ICT, and through them from making their data, information and documentation.

Public Administration: Governmental system for management and policies so that government can function, the management of public programs.

Information Society: Is a society based on knowledge economy and where the information is a significant economic, political, and cultural activity.

Information Society Development Committee: Is committee which mission is to plan, organise and coordinate processes of the development of information society aimed at creating an open, educated and continuously learning society, members of which rely on knowledge and have an opportunity and capability to make effective use of modern ICT in all their fields of activity.

Chapter 18
E–Procurement System as an E–Government Platform:
Case of South Korea

Young-Jin Shin
PaiChai University, South Korea

ABSTRACT

This chapter introduces and analyzes the best practices and development methods for Information Communication Technologies (ICTs) in South Korea in the realm of e-Government. To the present, national informatization in South Korea has focused on e-Government. This is because e-Government can lead to transformation in national information infrastructure and the public services sector, leading to increased efficiencies. Thus, firstly, this chapter focuses on defining the key concepts of e-Government. Secondly, it analyzes public document systems for the best practices of e-Government in South Korea in the following categories: Government for Citizens (G4C), Government e-Procurement Systems (GePS), the governance system, the On-Nara Business Process System, and the Home Tax Service (HTS). E-Government has reduced the number of documents and therefore reduced costs. In particular, the e-Procurement system has proven effective. This chapter explains the theoretical concepts of e-Government in South Korea via a literature review. Finally, this chapter analyzes instances of success and suggests avenues for future e-Government growth.

DOI: 10.4018/978-1-4666-4900-2.ch018

INTRODUCTION

Most governments the world over have used ICT to improve the efficiency of public affairs and the quality of citizens' service. With e-Government, it is possible to provide essential universal services to people in many countries. Because of its potential to revitalize public service delivery, e-Government is considered a major national strategy in advanced countries.

Recently, the UN declared South Korea the leading country for in as far as e-Government development is concerned. This was because South Korea had already extensively invested in erecting a robust national information infrastructure during the past decades with programs such as Basic Computerized Administrative Plan (1978~1987), National Basic Information plan (1987~1996) and so on. These programs are requisite for affluent development of e-Government. In addition, South Korea has implemented various national informatization plans such as Cyber Korea21 (1999~2002), e-Korea Vision 2006(2002~2006) and u-Korea (2007~2013). There have also been efforts regarding the e-Government 11 tasks (2001~2002), e-Government 31 roadmap tasks (2003~2007), and e-Government 12 tasks and e-Government support projects (2008~2012). In this process, South Korea has brought transparency to government affairs and efficiency to public services. E-Procurement systems in particular have achieved good e-Government service for governments, businesses and citizens. It has also caused a reduction of administrative documents and sped up delivery of documents.

The first part of this chapter provides an overview of domestic and overseas e-Government systems. The second part covers the implementation and best practices in South Korea in the following categories: Government for Citizen (G4C), Government e-Procurement System (GePS), Governance System, On-Nara Business Process System (On-Nara), Procurement System, and Home Tax Service(HTS), and so on. The third part tries to predict the direction of e-Government in the future. Finally, this chapter examines the way South Korea has tried to use e-Government through mobile e-Government or TV e-Government to create ubiquitous e-Government or smart e-Government during the last 12 years.

OVERVIEW OF E-GOVERNMENT

The Concept of E-Government

There have been many approaches to explaining e-Government within international organizations over the years. Some say e-Government is a type of government to maximize citizens' convenience based on the government's innovative use of information communication technologies (ICTs). Therefore, e-Government is part of an e-Democracy endeavor that fosters self reflective government and improves national responsiveness to issues of public interest. The genesis of e-Government can be traced to 'electronic banking' in the report 'Reengineering' at the National Performance Review of the USA in 1991. After this inception, different countries have taken different approaches in tackling the e-Government question (see Table 1).

In general, the concept of e-Government aims to supply high-quality public services for stakeholders and government, business and citizens utilizing ICTs. The basic framework of e-Government is to embody a small and efficient government with ICTs developed toward providing better public services. The major focus of e-Government would thus be to maximize citizen's convenience and to lead e-Democracy. In addition, e-Government aims to generally improve national competitiveness and economic activation with global usage of ICTs in the different socio-economic value chains (Shin, 2006).

Table 1. Concept of e-Government {© MOPAS (2005); Shin (2010}

Organization	Details
UN	E-government as a permanent commitment by government to improve the relationship between the private citizen and the public sector through enhanced, cost effective and efficient delivery of services, information and knowledge. It is the practical realization of the best that government has to offer
World Bank	E-government as the use by government agencies of information technologies such as Wide Area Networks, the Internet, and mobile computing that have the ability of transform relation with citizens, business, and other arms of government
OECD	E-government as the use of ICT and particularly the internet, as a tool to achieve a better level is simply better government. It is more about government than about "e" It enables better policy outcomes, higher quality services and greater engagement with citizens

The Goal of E-Government

The ideal goal of e-Government is to realize strong democracy through e-Democracy and this is done through technology platforms such as e-Voting systems. E-Government intends to improve online citizens' services by fostering the increase of efficiency levels and effectiveness in the public service delivery frameworks. This can only be achieved if there is requisite information policy framework ensuring that whatever the government does should be in the know of its citizens. The pre-requisites to effective implementation of e-Government are shown in Figure 1 (the phases and levels of e-Government implementation are shown in Figure 2). The key factors influencing e-Government development are: information demand (information recognition, information literacy, etc.), information supply (transmission infrastructure, circulation infrastructure, application infrastructure, etc.), and information policy

(institutional infrastructure, propulsion system). The model can simulate movements and synergies based on the systematic interrelations of these factors.

The progress of e-Government development can be divided into 5 levels as emerging level, enhancement level, interactive level, transactional level, and connected level.

THE PROGRESS OF E-GOVERNMENT

Overseas' E-Government Trends

The world over, e-Government has been utilized for public affairs and citizens' services in many ways. So, some countries aim to improve and fast-track e-Government development by aligning e-Government to their national strategic development plans and ensure that there is adequate legal, institutional and regulatory frameworks. The USA, Canada, the UK, and Japan have all done so.

In the United States, e-Government is assessed by the Performance Evaluation Committee of the National Performance Review's (NPR) attached report 'Re-engineering Government through ICT (1993). The report has 13 projects and 49 implementation plans. It supports e-Government systems for administrative information and services and enacted a national law for ICT enforcement and public safety networks between the federal government and provincial government (Kim, 2003). The Clinton administration enacted the national information highway business NII (National Information Infrastructure) with a variety of information and business promotions starting from 1993. This was done in order to increase national competitiveness and to improve the quality of life for the people.

NPR has been providing information related to the electronic portal civil service (Firstgov. gov) shared by all federal government websites

Figure 1. Pre-requisites of e-Government {© Kim, Seang Tae (2007)}

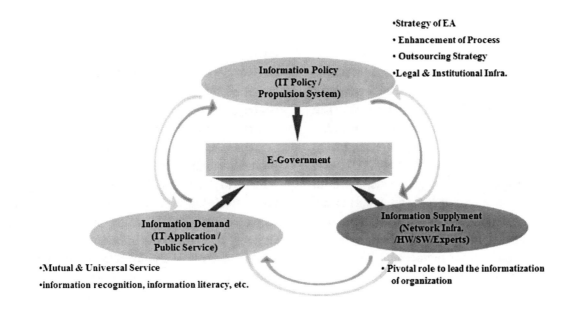

Figure 2. Phases and levels of e-Government {© UN (2005); S.T.Kim (2007)}

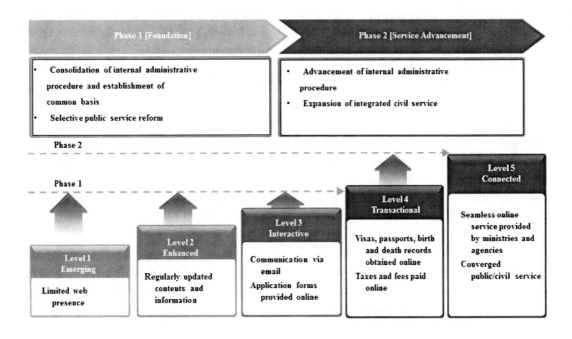

since 1999 (Govinfo.library.unt.edu/npr/library/reports/it.html).

Further, the Bush administration proposed 'active small government' in a blueprint for new beginnings' new national management vision over 10 years. The administration announced 5 e-Government reform plans to realize e-Government in August 2001 and the plan began in 2002. The president's agenda with OMB was also included in government innovation strategies (Kim, 2003). In addition, the e-Government Act (2002) was enacted to supply administrative rules for both off-line and on-line contents. This law is based on institutional foundations such as the improving customer service, integrating duplicate systems, reduction of paperwork, increasing productivity and realizing cost savings through active utilization of ICTs. The government tried to improve the efficiency and transparency through the 'Open Government Plan [1] in 2009' as a means of achieving their e-Government goals (NIA, 2012; Shin, 2013).

Canada started Government Online Services (GOL) in 1999 and began implementing the program for promoting e-Government in 2000. 'Connecting Canadian' had been implemented as a strategy to construct ICT infrastructure and to connect Canadian websites. It was also done in order to close the digital divide by means of distance education, distance schools, distance libraries, and private organizations until 2005. In addition, Canada increased the efficiency of government affairs in conjunction with 450 federal services and has implemented the Service Canada program to broaden online service (NIA, 2012).

In United Kingdom former Prime Minister, Tony Blair (1999), had implemented e-Government plans to perform most government, business and citizen transactions electronically. The UK plans, based on the 26 core information goals, seek to become the world leader in the global knowledge-based economy. For this, the United Kingdom reset British government ICT strategy announced 'Digital Britain' for advanced ICT

based public service in January 2010. Therefore, The UK government has implemented the project for constructing smarter, cheaper and greener public ICT infrastructures and has improved the quality of public service in 2011. In addition, the British government tried to expand the public sector network, to build cloud services and data centers, and to share the public services of the Digital Britain project (Shin, 2013).

Japan launched an administrative information promotion plan as a part of the administrative reforms in December 1994 and has ultimately implemented e-Government for paperless electronic administration. Japan established the 'e-Japan strategy' to develop the information technology sector while announcing a new development policy for the rebirth of Japan in October 2000. In addition, it announced the e-Japan strategy and established the e-Japan 2002 program as an annual program. The main elements of the program were to seek to create an environment to actively utilize ICT, while expanding e-Commerce and protecting information. Japan also announced 'i-Japan 2015'[2] to establish a digital society focused on the citizen as a response to the new ICTs in 2009. In addition, the government of Japan extended the application of ICTs by planning a new ICT strategy in 2010. The government tried to promote value creation and innovation to reform the whole economy and society with digital technology (MOPAS, 2010).

E-GOVERNMENT INITIATIVES IN SOUTH KOREA

South Korea's e-Government project started with the promotion of automation of statistical analysis work in the economy planning board (EPB). This project was supported by Committee on Coordination for Development of Computerized Organization under the Ministry of Science and Technology (MOST) in 1967. South Korea constructed its ICT infrastructure through its basic computerized administration plan (1978~1987), national basic information plan (1987-1996), and national master Plan (1996-1998). In the beginning, e-Government focused on the administrative framework but it changed its direction of national informatization plans by going to Cyber Korea21 (1999-2002), e-Korea Vision 2006 (2002-2006), Broadband ICT Korea Vision 2007 (2003-2007), and u-Korea (2007-2013) (see Table 2).

South Korea realized the importance of e-Government during the Kim Dae-Jung administration (1998-2002). This lead e-Government to improve public services without restructuring and downsizing the public sector via 11 e-Government initiatives (4 front offices, 4 back offices, 3 core infrastructures). The purpose of e-Government was to enhance public productivity, to change business surroundings and to improve public services between government and government (G2G), government and business (G2B), and government to citizens (G2C). G2G consisted of national financial management and personnel management systems. G2B was a government e-Procurement system to provide public services online for procurement transactions such as e-Bidding, e-Contract, e-Applications, and so on. Government to citizens (G2C) provided public services for citizens to modify the roles and scope

of e-Government. In particular, the G4C system is a well-developed e-Government website that provides e-Registration and e-Application. This was an initiative to not only construct information systems but also to supply online public services for the stakeholders (see Table 3).

The Roh Moo-Hyun administration (2003-2007) wanted Korea to be the top country in the world in as far as e-Government development is concerned as detailed in the targets for 3 of the goals in the 31 Road map priority tasks, U-Korea (IT839 Strategy, u-Government, etc.), and so on. The Roh administration had tried to improve working patterns, public services, information resource management, and the legal system. Until now, the priority tasks have been designated as the 3 projects in matters of business process re-engineering/information Strategy Planning (BPR/ISP), the 7 projects in pre-development and the 31 projects in systems development. More than 90% of these projects are on schedule for e-Government. The Lee Myung-Bak administration (2008-2012) planned and initiated 12 tasks for e-Government and e-Government supported tasks (NIA, 2012). The Lee administration tried to support e-Government with the 31 roadmap

Table 2. E-Government Plan in South Korea {© MOPAS (2012)}

Phase	Level	Division	Details
Phase 1: Constructing Infrastructure	Emerging Level (1987-1992)	Construction of public informatization infrastructure	- Constructing of Public DB and Connecting partial system - Computerizing main work in each department
	Enhanced Level (1993-2000)	Connection of partial system	- Law for promoting informatization(1995) - After public computerizing, achievement selected connection for main work
Phase 2: Embodying e-government	Interactive Level (2001-2002)	Construction of e-Gov infrastructure	- Law for promoting computerization of public works for e-Gov(2001) - Constructing e-Gov infrastructure with service for business and people and service for pubic productivity
	Transactional Level (2003-2005)	Stability and enhance of e-Gov service	- Interaction of public online service - Enhance of focused e-Gov - Propulsion of road map to progress new issue for e-Gov
	Connected Level (2006-2007)	Integration of e-Gov service	- Online service among departments /organizations - Objective of service among governments/ businesses

Table 3.The goal and key action of e-Government in South Korea {© MOPAS (2008)}

	E-Government Infra. Development (1987 ~ 2002)	Full-Fledged Implementation of E-Government (2003 ~ 2007)	Further Advancement of E-Government (2008 ~ 2012)
Goal	Digitalization of government business process, establishment of IT infra.	Expansion of e-Government services through digitalization of overall government business processes	Integration of e-Government systems for seamless delivery of public services
Key Action	- Digitalization of government business processes (patent, customs, tax, etc.) - Establishment of e-Government infra.(high-speed internet network) - 11 key initiatives (G4C, e-Procurement, etc.)	- Expansion and improvement of services for citizens and businesses - Enhanced administrative efficiency and transparency through reform of government work method - Linkage and connection among information systems	- Customer-centric citizen services and enhanced public participation - Intelligent administrative services through digital government network - Real-time public safety information network -Strengthened e-Government infra. through enhanced privacy and security

tasks to improve the efficiency in both the private and public sectors (Table 4).

In particular, South Korea regulated to promote e-Government work, to raise the productivity, transparency of administrative agency and to improve the quality of people's lives in the knowledge and information age. That is, the service system is based on the law to provide a mechanism to increase public awareness and to implement e-Government portal site (eGov.go.kr). The e-Government projects were divided as shown in the following Table 5 to embrace new and emerging technologies. Thus, the efforts of e-Government in South Korea were evaluated eventually the best in the world. That is, South Korea has achieved the transparency of government affairs and the efficiency of public services to a greater extent though e-Government (Table 5).

THE ASSESSMENT OF E-GOVERNMENT

Until now, many countries such as the USA, Canada, the UK have implemented e-Government for their national informatization efforts. So the formal assessment systems of international organizations like the UN use e-Government information to determine national e-Service as well as e-Participation rankings. The assessment leads to

a higher level of e-Government than self reported information. this chapter intends to highlight the South Korea's e-Government efforts leading to it being touted as the top country with regards to e-Government implementation is concerned.

E-Government Readiness Index by UN

For close to a decade, the UN has been assessing e-Government levels in 193 countries through the e-Government readiness index. The comparison factors consist of the Web-level Index, the Telecommunication Infrastructure Index and the Human Capital Index. The research surveyed 50,000 features of e-Government websites for how well the websites improve the access to and quality of social services. To evaluate e-Government readiness, the index has collected related materials and data as well as checked the websites of government agencies from 193 counties every May since 2002. South Korea was ranked 15th in 2002, 13th in 2003 and 1st in 2012 (MOPAS, June 27, 2012).

Global E-Government by Brown University

Brown University assessed global e-Government with 1,935 government websites in 198 countries beginning in 2001. The survey seeks to improve

Table 4. E-Government 31 roadmap tasks {© NIA (2008-2010)}

Goal	Agenda	Priority Tasks
Innovating the way Government Works	Establishing e-working Process	1. Digitalizing document processing procedures
		2. Comprehensive information of national and local public finance
		3. Realizing local e-government
		4. Building e-auditing system
		5. Realizing e-national assembly
		6. Building integrated criminal justice service system
		7. Comprehensive informatization of HR management
		8. e-diplomacy system
		9. Real-time management of national agenda
	Expanding Sharing of Administrative Information	10. Expanding of administrative information sharing
	Service-oriented BPR	11. Developing government business reference model
Innovating Civil Services	Enhancing Civil Service	12. Enhancing internet-based civil services
		13. Integrated national disaster management service
		14. Advanced architectural administration information system
		15. Integrated tax service
		16. Integrated national welfare service
		17. Comprehensive food and drug information service
		18. Comprehensive employment information service
		19. Internet-based administration appeal service
Innovating Information Resource Management	Enhancing Business Support Services	20. Single-window for business support service (G4B)
		21. Integrated national logistics information service
		22. E-commerce service
		23. Comprehensive foreigner support service
		24. Support for exporting e-government solution
	Increasing Electronic Citizen Engagement	25. Increasing online citizen participation
	Comprehensive Standardization of Information Resource	26. Building government-wide NCA
		27. Strengthening e-government communications network(e-Gov Net)
		28. Establishing government-wide ITA
	Strengthening Information Security System	29. Building Information Security System
	Strengthening Information Organization and Personnel	30. Restructuring Informatization Organizations and Personnel
Reforming the Legal system	Restructuring e-government Legislation	31. Reforming the legal system of e-government and security

Table 5. Modified e-Government supported projects (2008~2012) {© NIA (2012)}

Area	Tasks
Enhancement of national efficiency	Construction of public administration sharing system
	Construction of Integrated system for resident services
	Construction of national portal site
	Advancement of online civil service
	Linkage of multi-ministerial welfare information
Revitalization of economy	Construction of support system for cooperate competitiveness
	Integration for global logistics and trade information network
reinforcement of social safety	Construction of digital animal control system
	Reinforcement for web standardization and accessibility of e-Government
	Construction of standardization and co-utilization for meteorological data
	Construction of national security information service
	Construction of social disadvantaged support system
Delivery of new technology	Construction of smart phone-based mobile e-government
Improvement of administrative efficiency	Construction of national spatial information system
	Construction of universal statistics system for advancement of the national statistical survey system
	Construction of digital administrative collaboration system
	Construction of diplomatic information integrated management system
	Construction of online national communication system
	Construction of next generation e-HR system
reinforcement of information infrastructure	Construction of e-government standards framework and common service
	Integration of administrative service based on national EA infrastructure
	Construction of national resource openness and sharing system
	Construction of smart Work Center
reinforcement of information security system	Construction of next integrated authentication scheme
	Separation of internet and business network
	Construction of secret management system
	Construction for security control center

the quality of websites focused on administrators (president, prime minister and party governor, the royal family), the legislature (parliament, legislators, royalties), senior national judiciary (the courts), cabinets, and major institutions (health, labor, tax, education, construction, economic development, foreign affairs, foreign investment, transportation, defense, tourism, sales regulations) in each country. But it doesn't included websites from sub-agencies, committees, local governments, regional agencies, and authorities.

The survey checks the factors as like online information, electronic services, privacy and security, disability access, foreign language access, ads, user fees, premium fees, public outreach (email, search comments, broadcast, PDA, etc.). The group of countries is divided into Western Europe (20%), Africa (17%), Asia (14%), Eastern Europe (12%), the Middle East (8%), South America (7%), the Pacific, (5%), Central America (6%), North America (6%), Russia, and Central Asia (4.0%). The index is calculated as the mean of 18 scores such as online service, the extent of publications and databases (phone numbers, addresses, sites of association, publications, databases, audio material, video material), electronic services (online services, the world local government site), the degree of privacy and information protection that can be viewed, language accessibility, advertising, pricing, premium costs, and public service (e-mail, e-mail updates, search, comment, broadcasting, individual preferred site, PDA use)(West, 2004; Shin, 2013).

E-Government Assessment by Accenture Group

The Accenture Group has evaluated websites for 9 main services and 169 public services in 23 countries. The 9 main services are welfare, law and public safety, finance, defense, education, transportation, democracy, procurement and postal service. It measures the degree of service, customer service satisfaction, and customer feedback. The evaluation divides countries into four groups. The first group is Innovative Leaders. It is the top innovative countries that more than 50% e-Government maturity. The second group is called Visionary Challengers. These countries have customer relationship management (CRM) and have maturity ratings between 40% and 50%. The third group is Emerging Performers. These countries can develop customer relationship management (CRM) to maximize the potential of the online services in a wide range of services but currently have low levels of e-Government. The fourth group is called the Platform Builders. They are less than 30% mature. They suffer from low levels of online services and are not making good progress (Accenture, 2004; Shin, 2013).

Municipal E-Government by Sungkyunkwan Univ. & Rutgers Univ.

Sungkyunkwan University and Rutgers University-Newark have evaluated digital governance in the world's 100 largest cities starting from 2003. Evaluation items are divided into 5 categories consisting of; security and privacy, usability, web contents, online service, and citizen response and participation (Holzer & Manoharan, 2007; Shin, 2013). The detailed evaluation items are assessed the degree of governance as following Table 6. ICT was measured in cities having more 1,000,000 citizens. Seoul in Korea has been assessed as the best city in the world in as far as e-Government development is concerned.

THE BEST PRACTICES OF E-GOVERNEMTN IN SOUTH KOREA

The Results for Assessment of E-Government

UN ranked South Korea first in e-Government readiness rate in 2012 as well as in 2010 (MOPAS, June 27 2012). In parts of the e-Government Development Index and Online Participation Index, South Korea was ranked from 5th country in 2005 to 1st in 2012 (Table 7). Because South Korea was quick to open online service for citizens' participation, it increased the level of online services and human resources. In addition, South Korea supplied e-Government solutions for customs, procuring, patents, and so on for the stakeholders. Therefore, e-Government exports increased about 24 times between 2008 (9,820,000) and 2011. The e-Government of South Korea has been a means for national growth.

The Best Practices of E-Government

South Korea is the best country for e-Government in the world because of many investments for

Table 6. Evaluation of e-Government in world's cities {© Sungkyunkwan Univ. & Rutgers State Univ. (2003)}

Category	No. of Main Concept	Point	weight Point	Details
security & privacy	19	28	20	privacy policy, authentication, encryption, data management, use of cookies
usability	20	32	20	user-friendly design, length of homepage, targeted audience links or channels, and site search capabilities
web contents	19	47	20	access to current accurate information, public document, reports, publications, multi-media materials
online service	20	57	20	transactional services involving purchase or register, interaction between citizens, businesses and government
citizen partici-pation	14	39	20	online civic engagement, internet based policy deliberation, and citizen based performance measurement
Total	92	203	100	-

Table 7. Ranks and points of e-Government readiness index (Top 10 countries){© UN(2008-2012); MOPAS (2012. June)}

Division	2012		2010		2008	
	Rank	Points	Rank	Points	Rank	Points
South Korea	1	0.9282	1	0.8785	6	0.8317
Netherlands	2	0.9125	5	0.8097	5	0.8631
U.K.	3	0.8960	4	0.8147	10	0.7872
Denmark	4	0.8889	7	0.7872	2	0.9134
U.S.A	5	0.8687	2	0.8510	4	0.8644
France	6	0.8635	10	0.7510	9	0.8038
Sweden	7	0.8599	12	0.7474	1	0.9157
Norway	8	0.8593	6	0.8020	3	0.8921
Finland	9	0.8505	19	0.6967	15	0.7488
Singapore	10	0.8474	11	0.7476	23	0.7009

e-Government within the national plan, through enacting e-Government and constructing ICT infrastructure. South Korea is in particular leading in the area of e-Procurement systems for connecting e-Government platforms. In this chapter, five cases of e-Procurement system are presented: Government for Citizens (G4C), Government e-Procurement System (GePS), Governance Systems, On-Nara Business Management Systems

(On-Nara) and Home Tax Services (HTS) (Shin, August 2010).

Government for Citizens (G4C)

The government for citizens system (G4C, http://www.minwon.go.kr)[3] aims to ensure more convenient access to civil service and to deliver seamless government services through a single portal of e-Government. G4C has decreased the number of documents and visits to offices through online services such as civil information inquiry, petition, application, document inquiry and issuance, etc. [4] G4C allows citizens to use public services and to access administrative information in each government agency with the Internet, mobile devices (mobile phone, PDA, etc.), TV, and so on. G4C tries to achieve three goals for convenient and fast service regarding the process of civil petition while sharing administrative information and common infrastructure for e-civil service.

G4C is designed to share administrative information and to provide convenient functions concerning the number of visits and required documents regarding expenses and waiting times. Secondly, G4C is to provide various convenient functions like personalized service, integrated forms, and linkage with the electronic payment system. Thirdly, G4C is to provide other useful information by civil application, user education, etc. G4C had introduced 5 citizen services: issuance of residence certificates, issuance and perusal of building permits, issuance of mother-children family certificates, issuance of handicapped certification, and application for issuance of farmland permits in 2004. G4C has provided 24 citizens' service systems with 4,900 system service guides, 589 online applications, 22 categories of government information related with civil affairs and 3,000 online certificate issuances and miscellaneous services including about 1,200 species of civil documents, all of which can be issued to a printer. G4C will enable transparent administrative processing by ensuring accuracy, privacy, and information security.

It is also expanded to include the integration of civil services and to share public information among the government administrative agencies and other public agencies and private organizations. The reason to foster the innovation of civil affairs is to construct public information sharing system. It aims to change government affairs innovations to construct public information sharing systems in an e-Government focused on 11 tasks

and to expand the public information sharing system from e-Government's 31 roadmap tasks. The public information sharing system has operated from 2005 and so far saved about 1 trillion won in costs (May/17/2012 standards). When the service was started, it had only 17 kinds of public information, but now it is expanded to 120 kinds of information and it is utilized for approximately 290 million services by 438 institutions of administrative agency and public institution.

Therefore, e-Government has progressed to implement 'small and efficient government and to improve the efficiency of administrative affairs and the quality of public service - to share public information, to utilize information technology and to reuse information with linking, integrating and interlocking systems, to collect, store and manage the information (NIA, 2010). In addition, G4C is intended to provide a variety of civil services with smart phone apps for handling the government complaints in more than 1,800 species of civil affairs (Myung, January 1 2010).

Government E-Procurement System (GePS)

The government e-Procurement system (GePS, http://www.g2b.go.kr)[5] is the single window of public procurement integrating information infrastructure such as high speedy communication networks at home. It has functioned since 2002. GePS has become the largest e-Marketplace with total transaction volume of 43 billion dollars among 30,000 public organization and 150,000 companies. It has reduced the amount of documents, visits, and consultations between buyers and sellers. It has also made it possible for network connections to be made in organizations, procurement agencies, security companies and the e-Signature certification authority based on PPS (Public Procurement Service)'s e-Procurement system. It served over 90% of e-Contracts, 94% of e-Bidding and so on. It's connected goods and construction accounted for $25 billion of the total amount (NIA, 2010).

Governance System

Governance system has been operating since June 2007. It is designed to manage and execute the president and prime minister's instructions and to help with parliamentary focused issues. This system can reduce time needed and reduce the administrative burden of business processes and provide requisite information when needed. In addition, this system supplies information linking with the On-Nara business management system in the central government and an easy-one system in the Blue House. The governance system is closely linked to and operated by the business management system. The business management system is managed by each responsible ministry and takes the innovation of the reporting system to enact a vertical reporting system going from the President or the Prime Minister to each minister.

On-Nara Business Management System

On-Nara business management system constantly manages business and integrates government with business. The system is to manage citizen's opinions in the policy decision making process. It is to support rational decision-making and to improve the efficiency of business.

In particular, the system is implemented in conjunction 11 government-wide systems including personnel, budget, and evaluation, legislative, etc. and 4 local fiscal accounting systems like the regional administrative system (Digital Times, May 26, 2009). The government affairs management system had been constructed from 2004, and was applied in 5 ministries' pilot tests to integrate the affairs of 5 ministries in 2005.

The On-Nara government affairs management system was planned for expansion in 2006 and has been the standard government affairs management

system in 55 ministries from 2007. In addition, the government studied using the On-Nara system to upgrade other business systems. The ministry of public administration and security (MOPAS) distributed it to 71 government agencies, including 49 administrative agencies and 7 local governments (Yonhapnews, May 25, 2009).

Home Tax Service

The Home Tax Service (HTS. www.hometax. go.kr) can simply handle all national tax services submitted online tax report, issued notices, payments, handling complaints, collected taxation data through the Internet at home or office. That is, the IRS has supplied e-Services including value-added tax, withholding tax, state tax, special consumption tax, securities transaction tax, stamp duty, transportation tax and related tax from April 2002. In particular, the system is convenient for submitting year-end adjustments and income payments for retired works and labors. With HTS it is possible to receive the convenient service 24 hours a day and enjoy fast and transparent tax affairs (NIA, 2010).

E-PROCUREMENT SYSTEMS FOR E-GOVERNMENT

The Concept of E-Procurement Systems

E-Procurement aids the purchase and sale of supplies and services through the Internet (see Figure 3). It serves government to business transactions, business to business transactions and business to consumer transactions. The system manages tenders through a website (Wikipedia.org). The e-Procurement system increases efficiency and lowers costs. It is useful for buying material resources, helps the construction and planning industries, consultations and other public sector transactions. E-Procurement projects are often the

Figure 3. The six forms of e-procurement plotted in the procurement process{© UN(2012. September)}

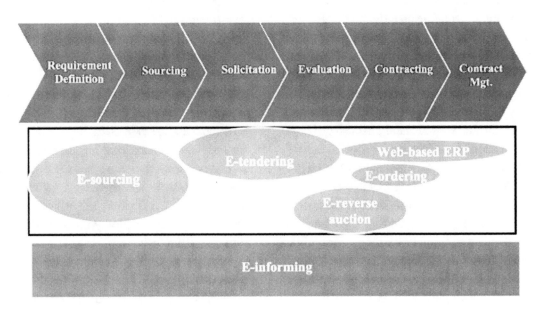

largest parts of government efforts in the digital economy (wikipedia.org).

The Case of E-Procurement Systems Overseas

The United States has increased the efficiency of its central procurement system. Many agencies use e-biding, particularly the Defense Procurement Agency under the Ministry of Defense. The Defense Procurement Agency has implemented Internet-based e-Bidding.

The US government uses the Federal Business Opportunity website to deal with MAS contracts (FedBizOpps, www.fedbizopps.gov). It also used electronic tools to screen bidders via the Central Contractor Registry (CCR), which offers the Online Representation and Certification Application (ORCA). This system electronically helps to supply proposals. It also uses an e-Buy system to publish RFQ & RFP. It tags all bids over $25,000 for review. Vendors wishing to deal with the federal government thus can search the government's requisition lists. Other government

agencies and vendors are the main users. Vendors don't need to log in separately to search for common procurement information. FedBizOpps provides government agencies and suppliers the necessary information for government contracts.

GSA Advantage is a site to search for information and prices. It specializes in the goods and services required by federal government employees. Except in the cases of Alaska, Hawaii and overseas territories, goods are delivered within 2-7 days. This site is a system where goods can be delivered quickly in the continental USA. GSA provides information such as the GSA's goods, special order information and upcoming compulsory purchases, etc. This e-Commerce system is for contractors in all government agencies in the federal government. It is possible for all people to search this system, but only dedicated members with exclusive membership can exchange purchase information among members, write lists of purchase conditions, manage a purchase history and send emails etc.

Australia and New Zealand have managed procurement through federal, state & local agencies. Australia and New Zealand are providing procurement information on individual agencies' websites or portal websites. Some of these allow electronically submitted proposals. However, dedicated procurement agencies in Australia and New Zealand do not exist. However, the Australian Ministry of Finance (Department of Finance and Deregulation) and New Zealand's Ministry of Economic Development (The Ministry of Economic Development) are performing similar duties.

The AUSTender (www.tenders.gov.au) website in Australia and the Government Electronic Tenders Service (GETS, www.gets.govt.nz) in New Zealand provide public bidding information. However, there are differences between federal agencies and state/local government procurement agencies. For example, Canberra allows contractors to submit proposals built in web a document but the system is too limited to take submissions from websites or portal procurement systems. New South Wales' state government is operating 'NSWbuy', which can accept all proposals through either the site or a portal procurement system (Seo, JW, Lee, MJ, Lim, JH, 2009.9), but other states have difficulty operating such a site.

Some countries try to operate separate e-Procurement systems in each institution. But they have also supported central government by monitoring system of e-Bidding system. In addition, each institution tried to link with the federal system to unite their e-Procurement systems. Someday we should be able to find any type of procurement information via integrated online systems.

The Case of E-Procurement Systems in South Korea

The public procurement system in South Korea, called EDI, started in 1996 and has developed into the Korea ON-line E-Procurement System (KONEPS). EDI is designed to support e-Document circulation, specifically procurement requests, change of procurement requests, accounting and contract documents. It expanded to

include the EDI/EC e-Bidding system for foreign investment in 2002.

KONEPS was also constructed as a portal for public procurement in 2002. The system is seamless and designed to eliminate all unnecessary costs and procedures by digitalizing the entire procurement process, from bid to bill (Kim & Lee, November 18 2012). KONEPS provides a convenient one-stop service, enabling users to process all necessary operations for procurement-registration, bidding, contracts, and payment-together (Chung, J. W., Nov. 18, 2012). In the G to B, the business has saved up to 6.6 trillion Won annually because with KONEPS it is possible to cut the cost for paper work as well as to reduce the number of documents (Kim & Lee, November 18 2012).

This system was evaluated deemed a best practice (2004) and received a public service award (2003) from the UN. In addition, KONEPS was recognized for its innovation in public IT service by World Information Technology Service Alliance (WITSA) in 2006. Many public officers from more than 25 countries want to visit Korea to benchmark KONEPS. KONEPS leads the global procurement market. Multiple memorandum of understanding have been signed with 19 countries on e-Procurement. This includes Vietnam, Mongolia, Costa Rica and Tunisia. KONEPS is spreading to Africa via the `KOAFEC e-Procurement Workshop` which was held from September 28 to 30 in Tunis, Tunisia (Figure 4). This showcased KOAFEC to approximately 10 African countries (MK News, 2009, 28 September). In addition, KONEP helps to introduce relevant laws and regulations and to provide consulting in developing countries regarding maintenance and to encourage collaborating with MDB like ADB, WB, AfDB, etc.

Development Plans for a Platform of E-Procurement

KONEP is a platform for e-Procurement and should be able to perform procurements efficiently

Figure 4. Exports of KONEPS worldwide {© Chung J.W. (2012. 18 November)}

* Dark gray: Importer, gray: Potential importer

for companies and users. KONEP was developed as a standard linkage model. It had no specific features for business, safety or security. However, new editions apply fingerprint recognition technology as alternative means of safeguarding business information. The e-Bidding notification system of KONEP provides the functions to search for and link to bid notice information in the G2B system (Figure 5). It is linked with e-Bidding, fee payment, joint supply, deposit payment systems.

It is possible to check the G2B system for successful bids. The final successful bidder information is linked within the e-Bidding system. In addition, the laws for the use and promotion of e-Procurement were enacted in March 2013 to systematically manage public e-Procurement. The law decides what matters must be handled electronically and then ensures safety, reliability, fairness and smooth conduct.

KONEPS needs to construct a bid center to manage all bidding affairs and to change the system to enable easy searches. The main feature of this e-Procurement system is to support the e-Procurement process, e-Announcements of competitive

bidding, e-Bidding, e-Notification of partners, creation and processing of e-Contracts, e-payment of grants, e-Document transmission/reception, etc. Therefore, KONEP is able to improve the online processes instead of using offline services for the audit and payment of public agencies. It supports business in private sector as well and helps develop the enhanced utilization and integrated management of public procurement information. Private enterprises can use mobile applications to access information like bids, contracts, inventories and other information from KONEP because mobile application with Open API will be developed by November 2013. KONEP will also open to non-profit organizations like APT management offices, social welfare organizations, etc. (PPS, 2013).

Thus KONEP will be a representative business platform in the private sector. The system will build up public procurement data until 2014 in order to produce the statistics. It will analyze all of the procurement systems in state agencies, local governments, public agencies and so on (PPS, 2013). Anticipating more demand for e-Procurement in the future, (MAS) is designed to expand to new

Figure 5. Successful bidding process {@ PPS (2013)}

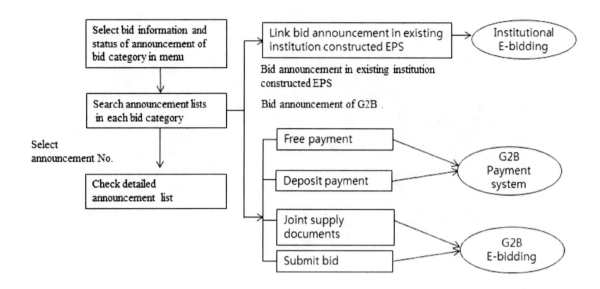

industries. It will also take on more employees to foster its plans for expanding the supply of services to industry and traders. KONEP hopes to facilitate more trade in the future - going from 15% in 2012 (3 trillion Won) to 20% in 2017 (4 trillion Won) (PPS, 2013).

In particular, KONEP helps to maintain a mutually beneficial relationship with small and medium sized enterprises, women entrepreneurs and social enterprises. It is designed to favor mid-sized business through the designation of excellent goods and preferential purchases. In addition, the trade items of KONEP's mall will be expanded from 330,000 items in 2012 to 500,000 items in 2017. This is to strengthen customized service and provide total solutions in fields like public information, facility construction and purchasing foreign goods (PPS, 2013).

THE FUTURE OF E-GOVERNMENT

Successful Factors for E-Government

So far, e-Government has progressed significantly to serve as the best information management/sharing system for citizens. Implementing e-Government has safely and effectively streamlined access to administrative information. As such, South Korea has been evaluated as the best country for e-Government in several international assessments. The most important factors for South Korea can be summarized mainly as follows; strong government leadership, ICT governance, customer-oriented e-Government service, performance-based program management, and technology support (Shin, 2007) (see Table 8).

South Korea should change the system according to the SWOT analysis as Table 9 shows. South Korea has strong factors such as a much improved ICT infrastructure, a comprehensive, strategic and systematic approach, good leadership, and so on. It is possible to leap into e-Government and use

Table 8. Critical success factors of e-Government {© MOPAS (2008)}

Category	Details
Strong Government Leadership	• The President's Leadership • Strategic and sustainable plans for 20 years • Nationwide change management program • Aligned e-Government projects with Performance Evaluation
IT Governance	• Informatization Promotion Committee chaired by the Prime Minister mediates and guides the administrative branches • Makes the national level e-Government strategies; work with NIA (National Information society Agency) • Revision of the legislative system for government process reform
Customer-oriented e-Government Services	• Service development based on the needs of citizens, company and other organizations • Civil Service closely related to everyday life
Performance-based Program Management	• Clear goals, objectives, short and long-term plans, with expected expenditure, income streams and deadlines • Qualitative, Quantitative Performance Index(KPI) for nationwide level and each project level • Designation of an officer or organizing body in charge of project performance
Technology Support	• Participation of experienced system Integration companies and specialized solution vendors • Adoption of practical technology Ex) GIS(Geographical Information System), LBS(Location-Based Service), Component Based Developing technology etc.)

Table 9. SWOT analysis for e-Government {© MOPAS (2008); Y.J.Shin (2010)}

Division	Results of SWOT
Strength	• Information communication Infrastructure • Comprehensive and systematic approach for IT development • Executive leadership, Legal Framework and National Master Plan • Strategic Partnership
Weakness	• Protection of Information security and Privacy • Weakness of trend analysis • Short period plans
Opportunity	• High contribution of It to world economic growth • Adaptation of new trends • Change of Policies
Threaten	• Recycle of Information resource • Shortage of connecting with systems • Budget and Human Resources • Increase of cyber crime

ICTs for developing the national competitiveness. The reason is that South Korea has a good chance to be a leader in the world's economy and to change the information society by way of its ICT paradigm. In addition, South Korea has invested in ICT infrastructure and has established many medium and long term plans.

Main Concerns for a Successful E-Government

South Korea should develop e-Government and expand citizens' service according to these three factors. First, South Korea should expand capability for its e-Government to quickly react to new circumstances and changes. For this, it could revise the existing law and construct a new system for e-Government anticipating the needs of future governments. Second, South Korea should be connected to various information systems for high quality public service. The government should construct a broad e-Document system to connect government and government or government and business. In addition, it needs to give universal information to regional and stratified entities. Third, South Korea should pursue global competitiveness to improve national informatization. For this, government tries to maximize efficient investment by connecting public agencies and citizens, constructing contents for individual regional conditions (MOPAS·KCC·MKE, 2012: 8).

THE FUTURE OF E-GOVERNMENT

We refer the future e-Government to m-Government, u-Government or smart government.[6] U-Korea (2005-2013) aims to provide broad practice technology for e-Government. Because the future e-Government will give us main ICT mechanisms by PC, mobile machine, wire & wireless network, RFID, ubiquitous computing and cloud computing services. In addition, South Korea published smart e-Government (Smart Gov) strategy as next generation e-Government strategy to bring about new information policies especially in the changing technology and information management landscapes. This is in accordance with the Proclamation of National Informatization Vision (2010). Therefore, the future of e-Government will pursue the ICT infrastructure based on a normalized system, and robust technology platforms with new applications and services. That is, e-Government will be changed by new ICT and new services for government, business, and citizens. It will along the four aspects in Table 10.

CONCLUSION

The information society has been affected by the new ICT paradigm connecting with various technologies for implementing e-Government. So many countries have tried to achieve efficiency of public affairs and high quality public service. E-Government has been promoted according to the best practices of government policies in advanced countries. South Korea has also implemented a step by step e-Government response to the new paradigm. Some ICT systems have resulted in the reduction of paper documents and increased the efficiency of administration related with e-Procurement system as like G4C, GePS, GS, On-Nara and HTS. South Korea could embody effective e-Government. This is thanks to the government, excellent leadership, people's participation and so on.

The UN tries to standardize e-Procurement systems globally. Therefore, e-Procurement systems must work with national bid and payment systems and exhibit online transparency. They must improve the efficiency of the procurement process. KONEPS has expanded into e-Procurement in private companies as well as all kinds of public agencies. KONEPS was already evaluated as the best system of e-Government by UN, OECD, etc. It was exported to other countries for their e-Procurement systems. In the future, KONEPS

will lead and change e-Procurement processes in the world to save costs, paper and time.

In addition, the e-Government of South Korea has been expanding into new services in conjunction with new ICT. Thus, the Korean government also provided guidelines to enable a mobile application service in the public sector (Kyonggi-maeil, April 12 2010). In order to implement e-Government using smart devices such as smart phones and tablet PCs the government introduced changes to the government business environment and to citizens' life styles. South Korea is implementing smart e-Government for the future. Smart e-Government will be pursued from 2011 to 2015. It is propelled by the four promotion strategies of disclosure, information integration, collaboration, and green IT.

For the smart e-Government as a future e-Government, first, it needs to share the public information and services in the private sector as well as in the public sector. It makes citizens participate in national policies and strategies for transparently managing public service. Second, it needs to provide customer-centric service and integrate multi-channels for linking and integrating personalized services by smart phones, tablet PCs, smart TVs and so on. Third, it needs to collaborate

Table 10. The direction of four aspects in the future e-Government {© S.T.Kim (2007); Y.J.Shin (2010)}

Aspects	Details
Infrastructure	• An integrated ICT environment on the basis of standardization infrastructure • The spread of a broadband communication network of wired & wireless infrastructure
Technology	• New services and application technology for administrative service in cyberspace (ICTS, medical and distribute fields using minimum chips)
Administrative efficiency	• Collaboration between different government ministries, central government and local government, and government and citizens • Necessary to secure transparency and raise administrative efficiency
Citizen service	• Services to reduce the digital divide and to extend access to information service & CRM • Two-way communication, e-suggestion activation, e-voting execution for e-democracy

with organizations and departments for sharing information. It aims to build a system to implement preemptive administration, customized administration, one-site administration, and convergence administration for the citizens. This is required to settle the environment for collaborating and sharing information system among organizations and departments (MOPAS, 2010.October). Therefore, South Korea will change with new paradigms to be the best leader of e-Government in the future. See Table 11.

Table 11. Performed goal of smart e-Government {© MOPAS (2010. October)}

Agenda	Performance Goals
Implementation of leading mobile e-government	Implement the world best e-government integrated wire and wireless: • Mobile service 100% 2015) • Ratio of supplying public information for private agency: 14.8%(2009) → 50%(2015) • Speed of wireless network: 1Mbps(2010) → 100Mbps(2015)
Implementation of safe and warm society	Implement ware and safe people's lives: • Conviction rate of 5 major crimes: 82.25%(2009) → 90%(2015) • Recovery rate of hazardous food s: 34%(2009) → 45%(2015)
Activation of smart work harmonized work and life	Change smart work: • Government Efficiency(IMD): 26th rank(2010) → 10th rank(2015) • Smart worker rate: 4.7%(2010) → 30%(2015)
Personalized service based on communication	Implement national tangible service National tangible implementation of custom open communication: • Online participation index(UN) maintenance of 1st rank • Satisfaction rate of e-government service: 63(2010) → 75(2015) • Use rate of e-government service: 61%(2010) → 70%(2015)
E-government infrastructure based on the strong basis	Implement e-government infrastructure based on the strong basis: • Rate of cloud service in public sector 30% attainment(2015) • Information security index: 73.9(2009) → 80(2015) • Information divide index: 30.3(2009) → 20(2015) • Information culture index: 66.2(2009) → 75(2015)

REFERENCES

Accenture. (2004). *e-Government leadership: High performance, maximum value.* Retrieved April 12, 2006 from http://www.accenture.com/Global/Research_and_Insights/By_industry/Government/HighValue.htm

Azab, N. A. (2009). Assessing electronic government readiness of public organizations. *Communications of the IBIMA, 8,* 95–106.

Cabinet Office. (2000, May). *Successful IT modernizing government in action.* Retrieved April 12, 2010 from http://www.citu.gov.uk/itprojectsreview.htm

Central, I. T. Unit. (2000). E-government - A strategic framework for public services in the information age. London: Cabinet Office.

Chung, J. W. (2012). *Korean e-procurement system booming worldwide.* The Korea Herald. Retrieved May 12, 2013 from http://khnews.kheraldm.com/view.php?ud=20121118000259&md=20121121003450_AP

Digital Times. (2009). *National e-procurement system government e-procurement system.* Retrieved April 16, 2013 from http://www.dt.co.kr/contents.htm?article_no=2009050702011857731002

DPADM. (2004). *Global e-government readiness report 2004: Towards access for opportunity.* Division for Public Administration and Development Management. Retrieved April 16, 2013 from http://www.unpan.org/egovernment4.asp

E-Government Special Committee. (2003). *e-Government white paper.* Retrieved March 28, 2013 from http://eng.nia.or.kr/english/bbs/download.asp?fullpathname=%5CData%5Cattach%5C201112221611231975%5Ce-Goverment+White+Paper+2003(english).pdf&filename=e-Goverment+White+Paper+2003(english).pdf

Hammer, M. (1995). *Reengineering the corporation: A manifesto for business revolution.* Nicholas Breadley Publishing.

Heeks, R. (1999). *Reinventing government in the information age: International practice in IT-enabled public sector reform.* London: Routledge. doi:10.4324/9780203204962

Holzer, M., & Manoharan, A. (2007). *Global trends in municipal e-government: An online assessment of worldwide municipal web portals.* Retrieved April 16, 2013 from http://www.iceg.net/2007/books/1/19_303.pdf

Jeong, M. W. (2010). *New start 0minwon 24' as government citizen service portal.* Inews24. Retrieved April 12, 2010 from http://news.inews24.com/php/news_view.php?g_serial=507556&g_menu=020200

Kim, H. S. (2005). Public innovation in ubiquitous age: Plan to implement ubiquitous public management. In *Proceeding of Entrue World 2005.* Retrieved April 15, 2013 from http://www.entrue.com/LGCNS.ENT.UI.MAIN/upload/agenda/200510/4.20051006_T1_S5_%EA%B9%80%ED%98%84%EC%84%B1.pdf

Kim, J. H., & Lee, K. H. (2012). *Procurement agency leads transparency and digitalization.* The Korea Herald. Retrieved May 12, 2013 from http://khnews.kheraldm.com/view.php?ud=20121118000258&md=20121129110627_AP

Kim, S. J. (2003). e-Government and public reform: focused on applying to construct information integrated electronic environment. In *Proceeding for Information Policy Seminar by SAPA,* (pp. 18-38). SAPA.

Kim, S. T. (2010). Prepare smart gov 3.0. *Digital Times.* Retrieved April 16, 2013 from http://www.dt.co.kr/contents.html?article_no=2010072302012369697035

Kyonggi-Maeil. (2010). *MOPAS, supply the guideline for developing mobile application service.* Retrieved June 6, 2013 from http://www.kgmaeil.net

Lee, S. K. (2003, January 1). *Global.e-government theory.* Seoul, eROK: Bobmoonsa.

Ministry of Internal Affairs and Communications (MIAC). (n.d.). *The master plan to construct e-government.* Retrieved April 12, 2010 from http://www.e-gov.go.jp/doc/040614/keikaku.html/

MOPAS. (Ministry of Public Administration and Security)eNIA (National informatization Agency). (2008). e-*Government tasks white paper 2003-2007.* Author.

MOPAS. (2012). e-*Government, 2 consecutive UN global award.* MOPAS press release. Retrieved April 16, 2013 from http://video.mospa.go.kr/view.asp?cate_id=2&vod_id=975

MOPASr.ent task(2012, August). *National informatization white paper.* Author.

News, M. K. (2009). *Korea on-line e-procurement system to advance into Africa.* Retrieved May 12, 2013 from http://news.mk.co.kr/newsRead.php?year=2009&no=506602

NIA. (2010). *National informatization white paper.* Author.

OECD. (2003). The e-Government imperative: Main findings. Policy Brief. *OECD Observer.* Retrieved April 12, 2010 from www.oecd.org/publications/Pol_brief

PPS. (2013). *Innovation plan of procurement administration for economic revival.* Retrieved May 22, 2013, from http://www.korea.kr/policy/pressReleaseView.do?newsId=155895612

Seo, J. W., Lee, M. J., & Lim, J. H. (2009). Comparative analysis of e-procurement system in main countries. *Journal of the Korean Association for Regional Information Society, 12*(3), 105–126.

Seoul, R.O.K. (2006a). *e-Government issue.* Saram & Jihye.

Seoul, R. O. K. (2006b). The evaluation and enahancement of e-government in Asia. In *Proceeding of Global e-Government Symposium.* MOPAS & NIA.

Shin, Y. J. (2010). *Construction advanced public administration system for e-government. Public Administration Focus.* NIA.

Tsekos, T. (2002). *E-government and the transitional countries.* Paper presented at the 10th NISPAcee Annual Conference. Cracow, Poland.

UN. (2008). *e-Government survey 2008.* Retrieved April 15, 2013 from http://unpan3.un.org/egovkb/global_reports/08report.htm

UN. (2010). *e-Government survey 2010.* Retrieved April 15, 2013 from http://unpan3.un.org/egovkb/global_reports/10report.htm

UN. (2012). *e-Government survey 2012.* Retrieved April 15, 2013 from http://unpan3.un.org/egovkb/global_reports/12report.htm

UN. (2012). *UN procurement practitioner's handbook.* Retrieved May 12, 2013 from https://www.ungm.org/pph/ch04s02.html

UNDEA. (2003). *e-Government readiness survey.* Fourth Caribbean Regional Consultation and High-Level Workshop on Public Sector management: Strategies for e-Government. Retrieved April 16, 2010 from http://www.unpan.org

UNDESA & ASPA. (2005). *Global e-government readiness report 2005: From e-government to e-inclusion.* UNDESA. Retrieved April 12, 2010 from http://www.unpan.org/egovernment5.asp

UNDP & UNCRD. (2007). e-Government and universal administrative information service in South Korea. *Capacity Building of Asia Pacific e-Government.* Retrieved March 17, 2013 from http://users.dcc.uchile.cl/~mnmonsal/egob/REPOS/WShopInteroperabilidad.pdf

United States Senate. (2002). *E-government act of 2002.* Retrieved April 16, 2013 from http://csrc.nist.gov/drivers/documents/HR2458-final.pdf

Sungkyunkwan Univ., & Rutgers State Univ. (2003). *Digital governance in municipalities worldwide: An assessment of municipal web sites throughout the world.* United Nations.

Waisanen, B. (2002). The future of e-government: Technology-fueled management tools. *Public Management, 84*(5), 6–9.

Weiser, M. (1984). Program slicing. *IEEE Transactions on Software Engineering, 10*(4), 352–357. doi:10.1109/TSE.1984.5010248

West, M. D. (2006). *Global e-government 2006.* Retrieved April 16, 2013, from http://www.insidepolitics.org/egovt06int.pdf

Wikipedia. (n.d.). *e-Procurement.* Retrieved May 12, 2013 from http://en.wikipedia.org/wiki/E-Procurement

Yonhapnews. (2009). *Public administration, realize good government by on-nara system.* Retrieved April 16, 2013 from http://app.yonhapnews.co.kr/YNA/Basic/article/Press/YIBW_showPress.aspx?contents_id=RPR20090525005600353&from=search

ADDITIONAL READING

Peters, R. M., Janssen, M., & Engers, T. M. V. (2004). Measuring e-Government impact: existing practices and shortcomings, Conference Proceedings, *6th International Conference on Electronic Commerce* (ICEC'2004).

Petrauskas, R., Bilevičienė, T., & Kiškienė, A. (2008). E-Inclusion as the Part of E-Government Development in Lithuania. *Viešoji Politika IR Administravimas,* Nr. 23.

Pilling, D., & Boeltzig, H. (2007). Moving toward e-Government: effective strategies for increasing access and use of the Internet among non-Internet users in the U.S., & U.K. The Proceedings of the 8th Annual International Digital Government Research Conference, 35-46.

Polit, D. F., & Hunfgler, B. P. (1995). *Nursing research: Principles and methods* (6th ed.). Philadelphia: Lippincott.

Powell, M. (2006). *Rethinking education management information systems: Lessons from and options for less-developed countries.* Infodev Working Paper No. 6. Retrieved June 20, 2010 from www.infodev.org/en/Publication.504.html.

KEY TERMS AND DEFINITIONS

E-Government: It describes the use of ICTs to facilitate the operation of government information and services.

E-Government Readiness Index: There are several international rankings of e-Government maturity. The Eurostat rankings, Economist, Brown University, and the UN e-Government Readiness Index are among the most frequently cited. The United Nations Public Administration Network conducts a bi-annual e-Government survey which includes a section titled e-Government Readiness.

E-Procurement: It is the business-to-business or business-to-consumer or business-to-government purchase and sale of supplies, work, and services through the Internet as well as other infor-mation and networking systems, such as electronic data interchange and enterprise resource planning.

KONEPS: A smart e-Procurement platform utilized in the e-Government domain in South Korea.

ENDNOTES

[1] Four strategies of 'open government plan' were selected as transparency, open government, cost saving, and securing ICT systems and expanding broadband networks.

[2] Three key strategies for I-Japan are divided into medical health (telemedicine technology utilization and the local medical association, etc.), e-Government e-local governments (such as expanding electronic mailbox), digital training and talent fostering.

[3] Government for citizen service changes the name as online civil service (Minwon 24).

[4] Civil information inquiry and application are increased up to 4,400 kinds of inquiries. Online application: 410 kinds (2005) →592 kinds (2007) Online document inquiry and issuance: 8 kinds(2005)→ 34 kinds(2007)

[5] Government e-Procurement System changed the name of Korea On-line e-Procurement system(KONEPS).

[6] Three key strategies for I-Japan are divided into medical health (telemedicine technology utilization and the local medical association, etc.), e-Government e-local governments (such as expanding electronic mailbox), digital training and talent fostering.

Chapter 19
Towards a Successful E-Government Implementation

Mehdi Sagheb-Tehrani
Columbus State University, USA

ABSTRACT

There are many different benefits that a government can obtain from encouraging the use of Information and Communication Technologies (ICTs) in its public sector delivery frameworks. Utilization of ICTs as a socio-economic stimulant has long been recognized by governments the world over. Electronic government utilizes ICTs to provide all the access to a wide range of public services. Today, different government departments and/or units at all levels of the governance hierarchy respond to millions of citizen demands electronically. The rising interest of many stakeholders in e-Government calls for a conceptual model that will guide implementation regardless of context. This chapter argues that several key success factors are appropriate and need to be considered for successful e-Government implementation. About one hundred e-Government Websites were examined upon those key success factors. Sixty-one university students took part in this investigation. Using t-test, the chapter investigates the appropriateness of the proposed model.

INTRODUCTION

In recent years, nearly all countries have integrated Information Technology (IT) and Information and Communication Technologies (ICTs) into their national economic development strategies. Gov-

ernments see IT and ICTs as ways to improve the quality of life of their citizens. The scale of activity on the part of public sectors in leveraging IT has increased in volume (Smith, 2008). E-Government is enabling government companies to provide better services to their customers. The ability to improve citizens' access to services online has made e-Government a desirable application for government organizations (Gorla, 2008; Donna,

DOI: 10.4018/978-1-4666-4900-2.ch019

Table 1. World e-Government development leaders (source: UN, 2012)

Rank		Rank		Rank		Rank	
1	Republic of Korea	2	Netherlands	3	United Kingdom	4	Denmark
5	United States	6	France	7	Sweden	8	Norway
9	Finland	10	Singapore	11	Canada	12	Australia
13	New Zealand	14	Liechtenstein	15	Switzerland	16	Israel
17	Germany	18	Japan	19	Luxembourg	20	Estonia

Yen, 2006). Governments around the world are implementing e-Government. In every part of the world - from industrialized countries to developing ones, governments are putting information online to provide better services for citizens (The Working Group, 2002; Chircu, Lee, 2005; Palmer, 2006). Transactions such as renewing drivers' licenses, applying for jobs and filing tax forms can now be conducted online, quickly and efficiently (West, 2008-2). IT and ICTs are viewed as the major platform for realizing citizens' access to the aforesaid transactions through ICTs.

Developing countries are behind in this race to provide e-Government services to their citizens. This can be due to many reasons such as lack of a good communication infrastructure, low computer literacy, and limited access to the Internet and so on (Akther, Onishi, & Kidokoro, 2007). These issues have to be addressed before developing e-Government applications. Officials should be aware of the obstacles before starting an e-Government project because such projects take a long time to accomplish and are generally very costly)The working group, 2002).

The 2012 United Nations E-Government Survey (UN, 2012) reports that many countries have put in place e-Government applications for the people to further enhance public sector efficiencies and streamline governance systems to support sustainable development. In the present recessionary time, some countries have been better able to continue to invest in IT infrastructure and service improvement for their citizens. The following table shows the world e-Government ranking in the top 20 countries worldwide.

In the following sections, the author makes an effort to disclose the concept of e-Government in a way that leads to more successful e-Government project development.

Organization of the Chapter

The next section describes the research method of this study and thereafter a section follows that attempts to clarify some of the fundamental concepts of e-Government. Next section describes data analysis and test of hypotheses and the section after this puts forward a conceptual model of e-Government and possible conclusion. The last section presents the list of references. Appendix "A" follows the list of e-Government Web sites.

RESEARCH METHOD, QUESTIONS, PROCESS AND LIMITATION

This study attempts to explain the concept of e-Government by defining various vital perceptions and their relationships involved in embracing e-Government. The research introduced here draws upon social system theory in the functionalist sociology defined by Burrell and Morgan (1979). The focus of social system theory is on the "holistic view", i.e., all parts of a system are related to each other. This chapter approaches its subject matter from an objectivist perspective. Objectivist is one of several doctrines holding that all reality is objective and external to the mind and that knowledge is reliably based on observed objects and events. Put differently, objectivism holds that reality exists independent of consciousness; that individual persons are in contact with this reality through sensory insight; that human beings can gain objective knowledge from perception through the process of concept creation and deductive and inductive logic. The conceptual model presented here is based on the "holistic view" school (Social System Theory). The methodology is based on a literature review and personal experiences as an IT consultant in numerous organizations. This study attempts to answer the following main research problems:

1. What concepts are involved in implementing e-Government in order to provide e-services for citizens?

2. What are the steps towards implementing e-Government?

Many public organizations are implementing Electronic Government (e-Government) projects. So there is a need to put forward a conceptual model focusing on steps towards successful planning e-Government projects. From the author's point of view, good research requires a sequence of well-defined steps planned in advance. Most of the research on e-Government has utilized the Internet to examine government websites. The use of the Internet has been suggested by e-Government scholars as a method to assess e-Government development (Mofleh & Wanous, 2009). As with any research, this study has limitations. The data were presented in various tables extracted from the literature review and about 100 Websites (appendix "A") were examined (see Table 3)

A questionnaire was designed based upon the E-Government model (see Figure 1). The survey

Figure 1. E-Government conceptual model

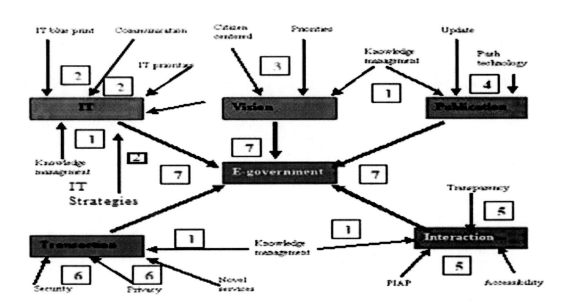

was approved by the institutional review board at the institutions. The questionnaire was comprised of thirteen questions (See Appendix B for a sample of the questionnaire). Some of the questions were designed as open-ended questions. The questionnaires were pre-tested by some students before sending them out. The questionnaire (Appendix B) was available online to 262 (see Table 2) students taking nine different courses at university A (see Table 2). For the purpose of confidentiality, the names of universities are not disclosed. The answers provided were confidential and did not affect their course performance/grade in any way. Participants were not required to identify themselves; the name of the respondent on the questionnaire was optional. In total 61 questionnaires out of 262 questionnaires (23%) were returned. After collecting the questionnaires, the author analyzed each question from each respondent and summarized the data in almost 14 tables.

So, one limitation would be the number of participants and Websites that were reviewed in this study. Furthermore, the questions in this study are based upon the author's understanding of the literature review.

CONCEPTS DEVELOPMENT

One frequently asked question regarding electronic government (e-Government) is "What is e-Government?" E-Government is more than just providing some public information and specific citizen services available to people via a Web site (Lee, Wu, Lin, & Wang, 2008; Curtin et al., 2003). E-Government serves as a portal focused mainly on access to the public sector; these portals are aimed at citizens (G2C), businesses (G2B), other governments (G2G) and anyone else who are interested in the government and its services. Over 160 countries worldwide have already begun some kind of e-Government project, creating a major market for IT vendors and service providers that are competent of helping public agencies in their technology initiatives (Greiner, 2005). E-Government is an emerging concept and recent researches focus on applying the new concept of e-Commerce and management in e-Government such as knowledge management enterprise resource planning (Raymond & Bergeron, 2006). E-Government is being considered as one of the tools that can be used to meet the many challenges faced by governments (Jupp, 2003). Governments

Table 2. Shows the basic information

No	Course Title	Term	No. of Students	Under Graduate	Returned Questionnaire
1	BUAD 2280	Spring 2010	25	Yes	2
2	BUAD 2280	Fall 2010	27	Yes	7
3	BUAD 3283	Fall 2010	9	Yes	6
4	BUAD 3284	Fall2010	29	Yes	14
5	BUAD 3281	Fall 2010	18	Yes	4
6	BUAD 2280	Spring 2011	60	Yes	12
7	BUAD 3382	Spring 2011	12	Yes	4
8	BUAD 2280	Fall 2011	59	Yes	4
9	BUAD 4387	Fall 2011	23	Yes	8
Total	9 Courses		262		61

are facing increased service expectations by their citizens. Some of the services that can be offered by e-Governments are as follows (Evolution of e-Government, 2002):

Government to Citizens (G2C)

1. Income taxes: notification of assessment
2. Job search services by labor offices
3. Social security contributions
4. Personal documents (passport and driver's license)
5. Car registration (new, used and imported cars)
6. Application for building permission
7. Declaration to the police
8. Public libraries (availability of catalogues, search tools)
9. Certificates (birth, marriage): request and delivery
10. Enrollment in higher education / university
11. Announcement of moving (change of address)
12. Health related services (e.g., interactive advice on the availability of services
    in different hospitals; appointments for hospitals)

Government to Business (G2B)

1. Social contribution for employees
2. Corporation tax: declaration, notification
3. Value Added Tax (VAT): declaration, notification
4. Registration of a new company
5. Submission of data to statistical offices
6. Customs declarations

According to a study made by (Cap Gemini, Ernst & Young, 2001) shows that in Europe the most used services are the job search, income taxes, VAT and corporate tax services; the least used are the health related services, building and environment-related permits. Further, the study emphasizes that in Europe the biggest customer of e-Government services is business (G2B, 53%) whereas services for citizen (G2C, 40%) scores significantly lower. Though US companies lead the e-Commerce initiatives among businesses, e-Government portal efforts in the US are not ahead of the world. FirstGov or USA.gov (see appendix A for URL) is the US federal government's portal, providing access to both state and federal government agency Web sites. US portal now offers Americans a complete source of information, and the options to apply for student loans and even Social Security benefits online. FirstGov has about 186 million pages across 22 different sites and receive 6 million visitors per month (Greiner, 2005). The US e-Government initiative is divided in three main groups as follows (Murra, 2003):

Government to Citizens (G2C)

1. Free online tax filing;
2. Job search;
3. Social security;
4. Personal documents (birth and marriage certificates, passport applications, driver license);
5. Immigration services;
6. Health and related services;
7. Government benefits;
8. Student loans;
9. Disaster help;
10. Other useful information (for sales, weather forecast, recreation).

Government to Business (G2B)

1. Comment on federal regulation;
2. Corporation tax;
3. Business opportunities;
4. Registration of a new company;

5. Business laws and regulations;
6. Central contractor registration;
7. Government auctions and sales;
8. Employer ID number;
9. Wage reporting;
10. Subcontracting opportunities;
11. Patents and trademarks filing;
12. Export portal.

Government to Government (G2G)

1. 2003 Federal Pay Tables;
2. Grants;
3. Background Investigation Application;
4. E-Training Initiative for Federal Workers;
5. For Sale to Government Buyers;
6. FirstGov Search for Federal Agencies;
7. Per Diem Rates;
8. Employee Directory;
9. Federal Personnel-Payroll Changes.

The US e-Government strategy is to improve the quality of the services to the citizens and businesses. According to one study by (West, 2008-1), 11% of the websites examined have no services, 12% provide one service, 10% have two services, and 67% have three or more services. Obviously, both federal and state governments are making important strides in providing services online. The United States has fallen behind many countries in Internet access and broadband usage. America delays Sweden, Denmark, Switzerland, Australia, Germany and the Netherlands in Internet subscribers per 100 inhabitants. Whereas 36 percent of Swiss residents have access to Internet subscription services, 31 percent of Americans have access to the Internet (West, 2008-1).

In this complex world in which we live, everyone must learn more about e-Government. Even our politicians may not fully understand the concept and application of e-Government. Surveys carried out by the United Nations Conference for Trade and Development (UNCTAD, 2002, UN, 2012) on the development of e-Commerce in various parts of the world identifying the need in developing countries for transparency within government operations (Mitra, 2005). Electronic commerce (EC) has revolutionized the way the business and individuals interact. In the United States and Europe, the use of the Internet in the public sector has initiated a discussion about new forms of democracy. E-Government will change the course of democracy by providing all citizens access to government operations.

Vision, Principles and Priorities

A fully implemented e-Government can break down bureaucratic barriers and move to a better service level, connection and protection that a government may want and need in every aspect of government's activity. This provides an opportunity not merely to manage business but also to get wide access to what government is doing or intending to do, and how, and why. This will allow citizens more than ever before to take part in government decisions and become more knowledgeable of the performance of their elected representatives. Citizens will have the chance to become stable players in the process of determining and making government task (McGinnis, 2003).A broad vision of e-Government should be shared by all citizens, i.e., encouraging stakeholders (citizens, officials, businesses, civil society groups and others) to participate in determining the vision. A shared vision can lead to a more successful implementation of e-Government, i.e., supporting e-Government project from beginning to end (please see Table 3).Broad categories of goals that are commonly shared by citizens are as follows (The working group, 2002):

- Improving the productivity of government
- Improving services to citizens
- Improving the quality of life for disadvantaged communities and

Table 3. Comparison of various e-Government Websitesbased upon some key concepts

Country	Continent	G2C	G2B	G2G	Vision	Publication	Interaction	Transparency	Accessibility	Transaction
Albania	Europe	A	A	NA	A	A	A	A	NA	A
Algeria	Africa	A	A	NA	A	A	A	A	NA	NA
Andorra	Europe	A	NA	NA	A	A	A	A	NA	A
Angola	Africa	A	A	NA	A	A	A	A	NA	A
Argentina	South America	A	A	A	A	A	A	A	A	NA
Australia	Australia	A	A	NA	A	A	A	A	A	A
Austria	Europe	A	A	A	A	A	A	A	A	NA
Bahamas	Noth America	A	A	NA	A	A	A	A	A	A
Barbados	North America	A	NA	NA	A	A	A	A	NA	A
Belarus	Europe	A	A	NA	A	A	A	A	A	A
Belgium	Europe	A	NA	NA	A	A	A	A	NA	NA
Canada	North America	A	A	NA	A	A	A	A	A	A
China	Asia	A	NA	NA	A	A	A	A	NA	NA
Columbia	South America	A	NA	NA	A	A	A	A	NA	NA
Congo	Africa	A	NA	NA	A	A	A	A	NA	NA
Cuba	Noth America	A	NA	NA	NA	NA	A	NA	NA	NA
Czech Republic	Europe	A	NA	NA	NA	A	A	A	NA	NA
Denmark	Europe	A	A	NA	A	A	A	A	NA	NA
Dominican Republic	North America	A	NA	NA	A	A	A	NA	NA	NA
Egypt	Africa	A	A	NA	A	A	A	A	A	A
El Salvador	South America	A	NA	NA	A	A	A	NA	NA	NA
Estonia	Europe	A	NA	NA	A	A	A	A	A	A
Fiji	Australia	A	A	NA	A	A	A	A	A	A
Finland	Europe	A	NA	NA	A	A	A	NA	NA	NA
Gambia	Africa	A	A	NA	A	A	A	A	NA	A
Georgia	Europe	A	A	NA	A	A	A	A	A	A
Germany	Europe	A	A	NA	A	A	A	A	NA	NA
Greece	Europe	A	A	NA	A	A	A	A	A	A
Guatemala	South America	A	A	NA	A	A	A	A	NA	NA
Guinea	Africa	A	NA	NA	NA	A	A	A	NA	NA
Haiti	North America	A	A	NA	A	A	A	A	A	A

continued on following page

Table 3. Continued

Country	Continent	G2C	G2B	G2G	Vision	Publicat-ion	Interac-tion	Transpar-ency	Accessibil-ity	Transact-ion
Honduras	North America	NA	A	NA	A	A	A	A	NA	A
Hungary	Europe	A	A	NA	A	A	A	A	A	A
Iceland	Europe	A	A	NA	A	A	A	A	A	A
India	Asia	A	A	NA	A	A	A	A	A	NA
Indonesia	Asia	A	A	A	A	A	A	A	A	A
Ireland	Europe	A	A	NA	A	A	A	A	A	A
Israel	Asia	A	A	NA	A	A	A	A	NA	A
Italy	Europe	A	A	A	A	A	A	A	A	A
Jamaica	North America	A	NA	NA	A	A	A	A	A	NA
Jordan	Asia	A	A	NA	A	A	A	A	NA	NA
Kazakhstan	Asia	A	A	NA	A	A	A	A	A	A
Kenya	Africa	A	A	NA	A	A	A	A	A	NA
Kuwait	Asia	A	A	NA	A	A	A	A	A	A
Latvia	Europe	A	A	NA	A	A	A	A	NA	NA
Lebanon	Asia	A	A	NA	A	A	A	A	A	A
Liberia	Africa	A	A	NA	A	A	A	A	A	A
Lithuania	Europe	A	A	NA	A	A	A	A	A	A
Luxembourg	Europe	A	A	NA	A	A	A	A	NA	A
Madagascar	Africa	A	A	NA	NA	A	A	A	A	NA
Malawi	Africa	A	NA	A	A	A	A	A	A	A
Mali	Africa	A	A	NA	A	A	A	A	NA	NA
Marshall Islands	Australia	A	NA	NA	A	A	NA	A	NA	A
Mauritania	Africa	A	A	NA	NA	A	A	A	NA	A
Mauritius	Africa	A	A	A	NA	A	A	A	A	A
Mexico	N.America	A	A	NA	NA	A	A	A	A	A
Micronesia	Australia	A	A	A	A	A	NA	A	A	NA
Nepal	Asia	A	NA	A	A	A	A	A	NA	NA
New Zealand	Australia	A	A	A	NA	A	A	A	A	A
Nicaragua	N.America	A	A	A	A	A	A	A	A	NA
Niger	Africa	A	A	NA	A	A	A	A	A	A
Norway	Europe	A	A	A	NA	A	A	A	A	A
Oman	Asia	A	A	A	NA	A	NA	A	A	NA
Pakistan	Asia	A	NA	A	NA	A	A	A	NA	NA
Palau	Australia	A	A	NA	NA	A	A	A	A	NA
Panama	N.America	A	NA	NA	NA	A	A	A	NA	NA
Poland	Europe	A	A	NA	NA	A	A	A	NA	A
Qatar	Asia	A	NA	NA	NA	A	NA	A	A	NA

continued on following page

Table 3. Continued

Country	Continent	G2C	G2B	G2G	Vision	Publication	Interaction	Transparency	Accessibility	Transaction
Republic of Korea	Asia	A	A	NA	A	A	A	A	NA	A
Republic of Moldolva	Europe	A	NA	NA	A	A	A	A	NA	A
Romania	Europe	A	NA	NA	NA	A	A	A	NA	NA
Russian Federation	Asia	A	A	NA	NA	A	NA	A	A	NA
Rwanda	Africa	A	NA	NA	NA	A	NA	NA	NA	NA
Samoa	Asia	A	A	NA	A	A	A	A	A	NA
Saudi Arabia	Asia	A	A	A	A	A	A	A	A	A
Senegal	Africa	A	A	NA	A	A	A	A	A	NA
Serbia	Europe	A	A	A	A	A	A	A	A	NA
Singapore	Asia	A	A	A	A	A	A	A	A	A
Slovakia	Europe	NA	NA	A	A	NA	A	A	A	NA
Slovenia	Europe	NA	NA	A	A	A	NA	A	A	NA
Somalia	Africa	NA	NA	NA	NA	NA	NA	NA	NA	NA
South Africa	Africa	A	A	A	A	A	A	A	A	NA
Spain	Europe	A	A	A	A	A	A	A	A	NA
Sudan	Africa	A	A	A	NA	A	A	A	A	NA
Swaziland	Africa	A	A	A	A	A	A	A	A	NA
Sweden	Europe	A	A	A	A	A	A	A	A	A
Switzerland	Europe	A	A	A	A	A	A	A	A	A
Tong	Asia	A	A	A	NA	A	A	A	NA	NA
Togo	Africa	A	A	A	A	A	A	A	A	NA
Trinidad and Tobago	South America	A	A	A	A	A	NA	A	A	NA
Tunisia	Africa	A	A	A	A	A	A	A	A	NA
Turkmenistan	Europe	NA	NA	NA	NA	NA	NA	NA	NA	NA
Uganda	Africa	A	A	A	A	A	A	A	A	NA
Ukraine	Europe	A	A	A	A	A	A	A	A	A
United Republic of Tanzania	Africa	NA	NA	NA	A	A	A	A	A	NA
Uzbekistan	Europe	NA	A	NA	A	A	NA	A	A	NA
Zambia	Africa	NA	NA	NA	A	NA	A	NA	A	NA
Zimbabwe	Africa	A	A	A	NA	A	A	NA	A	A

A = Available

NA = Not available

- Improving the legal system and law enforcement.

Putting it differently, e-Government would make government become closer to this vision: an institution of the citizens, run by citizens, owned by citizens and for the citizens. Fighting corruption should be included in the vision. This may be announced to the public as "anti-corruption" goal of e-Government. More, a challenge for public sectors is to recognize today's trends and apply effective tools for creating and implementing policies that optimize the role of IT in their societies. These strategies are often novel, a result of the spread of relatively new technologies, such as the Internet, mobile devices, opens sources (e.g., Linux, games, information) viewing movies via Internet, and e-mailing. This means that government agencies will need to choose wisely the most appropriate strategies. Naturally, each government's vision should also be accompanied by a short list of priority areas for the e-Government project. Improvements in the following areas are recommended:

- Employee productivity
- Service delivery
- Information security
- IT infrastructure
- Data management
- IT management
- Human resource management
- Disaster recovery/management and
- Others.

Up to 2007, research not only confirms the historic role governments played in affecting the employment of IT, but more significantly that IT is considered to be a main component of a national economic development policy. Today, no advanced nation can ignore the role of IT strategies in its economy (Ghapanchi, Albadvi & Zarei, 2008; Haigh & Griffiths, 2008; Cortada, Gupta, Le Noir, 2007).

One strategy is the effective use of IT by government agencies themselves to improve their internal productivity and increase their ability to serve citizens (as in providing 24 x 7 services). By providing citizens convenient access to information around the clock over the Internet, a government encourages citizens to access public services, data, and application forms using PCs and the Internet. This action encourages citizens to utilize that technology in other ways in their private and professional lives. Another popular tactic is requiring suppliers to provided their services using online procurement systems. In addition to helping lower the costs of acquiring these by a government, it makes suppliers start using the Internet and related technologies in an "e-business" environment (Abramson and Harris, 2003). In recent years connectivity has been all about making it possible for individuals, firms, and other institutions to access mobile (wireless) networks and the Internet. Wireless Internet service should be available all over cities in any country. This should be one of the main strategies for any government. Costs of these services to individuals and organizations should be affordable for all citizens. The expansion of the Internet plays a vital role in the economic development activities of the public sector. This is a development that is attracting renewed attention to the topic of IT by economists and public policy experts (Breznitz, 2007; Baumol, Litan, & Schramm, 2007). This reality is made more passionate by the fact that more people and firms dependent on IT to go about their job and private lives has enlarged over the past quarter century.

Publications

The ability to search for a specific website is a basic tool needed by citizens. In this regard, one significant new development has been the formation of online service portals. This service is an important advantage for ordinary citizens because it reduces the need to log on to various websites to order services or find information (please see Table 3). Citizens can connect in "one-stop" shopping, and locate what they require through a single site that integrates a range of government Web sites. One of the main dissatisfaction for citizens is going through enormous amounts of information to locate useful material (Haigh & Griffiths, 2008). Admission to updated publications, contact information and databases are vital to citizen access to information and improve democratic responsibility. Another way that e-Government Websites can provide the available information to citizens is by personalizing the Web site or letting citizens register to receive update publications. This is known as "push technology" (Murru, 2003). All these services utilize IT to expand access to government information, so that citizens do not need to go to the government offices in person and wait in long lines. This is the leading frame of e-Government. Naturally, knowledge is required on how to manage publications, how to present information clearly online and how users likely to use the information.

Interaction, Transparency and accessibility

A state should aim to have broadband connections for all public administrations. Broadband services can be offered on various technological platforms. Public Internet Access Points (PIAP), preferably with broadband connections, should be provided for all citizens in their communities. Internet is a perfect tool for obtaining public access to government information. Accessible and clear information can improve citizens' understand-

ing and knowledge and may lead them to take part in the decision-making process, developing democracy. With the increase of the Internet, the value of well designed e-Government Web site will become even more obvious(please see Table 3). Making it easier for citizens to access public information will improve participation and democracy. Knowledge is required on how citizens or government officials look for information and like to receive it.

E-Government sites should also consider disability access. World Wide Web Consortium (W3C) has introduced some standards regarding disability access. There has been some progress in this area on US government websites (see Table 4). Further, e-Government sites should provide foreign language accessibility as well. Public outreach is one of the most important characteristics of any e-Government project. Put another way, one of the most promising benefits of e-Government is its ability to draw citizens closer to their governments. In my examination of US Citizenship and Immigration (USCIS) websites, a visitor to the USCIS Web site cannot email or phone a person in any particular department.

Transaction

The goal of transaction is to provide government services online (please see Table 5). Government agencies can computerize particular processes and procedures, such as fine collection, tax collection and credit card purchases. By providing these services online, government can attempt to restrict corruption and improve citizens' trust in government. Further, this can lead to increased

Table 4. Percentage of state and federal sites meeting W3C disability accessibility

	2003	2004	2005	2006	2007	2008
Federal	47%	42%	44%	54%	54%	25%
State	33	37	40	43	46	19

Source: West 2008-2: 5.

Table 5. Assessment of e-Government privacy and security statements

	2001	2002	2003	2004	2005	2006	2007	2008
Prohibit commercial marketing	12%	39%	32%	40%	64%	58%	64%	53%
Prohibit cookies	10	6	10	16	21	16	32	40
Prohibit sharing personal information	13	36	31	36	65	54	37	51
Share information with law enforcement	--	35	35	39	62	49	50	49
Use computer software to monitor traffic	8	37	24	28	46	60	65	57

Source: West, 2008-2:4.

productivity in both private and public sectors. Knowledge of efficiency and security is required for designing such a computerized system. In the study by West (2005-1), it is mentioned that there are several novel services available on US state portals, such as live online help desk and state tourism sites featuring online planning for travelers. At the same time, the study mentioned some aspects of e-Government privacy and security issues.

RESEARCH FINDINGS

Data Analysis

The questionnaire was pre-tested and refined after the pre-test. The questionnaire (Appendix B) was available online to 262 (see Table 6) students taking nine different courses. All the courses were conducted as face-to-face (FTF). The online platform (D2L) was utilized as a supplement to the courses. In total 61 questionnaires out of 262 questionnaires (23%) were returned. After collecting the questionnaires, the author analyzed each question from each respondent and summarized the data in the following tables.

The first item in the questionnaire was related to gender of respondents. As Table 7 shows, about 44% of respondents were male and (56%) were female.

Table 6. Shows the basic information

Factors	#	%
Total questionnaires returned	61	23
Total questionnaires not returned	201	77
Total Undergraduate participants	**262**	**100**

Table 7. Shows gender

Factors	#	%
Male	27	44
Female	34	56
Total	**61**	**100**

The next question was focusing on Internet usage. As Table 8 shows 57% responded that they used Internet daily, while 43% reported they used Internet weekly.

The next question asked, why you think there should be e-services by the USA government to the citizens (*one may choose more than one option*). Table 9 shows 23% reported convenient, 18% responded faster services and 17% reported less cost for all. 16% reported available anytime and anywhere, and 15% responded more productive and efficient.

The next question was focusing on why you think there should not be any e-services by the USA government to the citizens (*one may choose more than one option*). Table 10 shows 44% reported privacy issue, 24% reported computer il-

Table 8. Shows Internet usage

Factors	#	%
Daily	35	57
Weekly	26	43
Monthly	0	0
Yearly	0	0
Total	**61**	**100**

Table 9. Shows e-services by USA government

Factors	#	%
Convenient	45	23
Less cost for all	34	17
Faster service	36	18
More Transparent	12	6
Available any time, any where	31	16
More productive and efficient	30	15
No way to ignore application of IT regarding our daily tasks	9	4.5
Other	1	0.5
Total	**198**	**100**

Table 10. Shows factors for not having e-services by USA government

Factors	#	%
Privacy issue	44	44
Lack of access to Internet	12	12
Lack of access to a computer	16	16
Computer illiterate	24	24
Other	4	4
Total	**100**	**100**

literate, 16% reported lack of access to a computer and 12% responded lack of access to Internet.

Question five was about if USA e-Government system (www.usa.gov) provide services (such as: Free online taxing, Job search, Immigration services, Student loans, Disaster help, and ...) for citizens? Table 11 shows 90% responded yes while 10% reported no.

Table 11. Data about USA e-Government system

Factors	#	%
Yes	55	90
No	6	10
Total	**61**	**100**

Question six asked, Does USA e-Government system provide services (such as: Corporation online taxing, Business opportunities, Business law and regulation, Government auctions, Export portal, patents and trademarks filing, and ...) for businesses? Table 12 shows 90% responded yes while 10% reported no.

The next question was focusing on if USA e-Government system provides services for other governments? Table 13 shows 77% responded yes while 23% reported no.

Question eight asked, Does USA e-Government system (www.usa.gov) allow citizens more than ever before to take part in government decisions and become more knowledgeable of the performance of their elected representatives. Table 14 shows 82% responded yes while 18% reported no.

Table 12. Data about USA e-Government system services

Factors	#	%
Yes	55	90
No	6	10
Total	**61**	**100**

Table 13. Shows USA e-Government system services for other government

Factors	#	%
Yes	47	77
No	14	23
Total	**61**	**100**

Table 14. Shows USA e-Government system services for citizens participation

Factors	#	%
Yes	50	82
No	11	18
Total	**61**	**100**

Question nine asked, Does USA e-Government system (www.usa.gov) allow citizens to search for a specific Web site? Table 15 shows 87% responded yes while 13% reported no.

Question ten asked, Does USA e-Government system (www.usa.gov) allow citizens to register to receive updated publications? Table 16 shows 93% responded yes while 7% reported no.

Next question asked, Have citizens access to broadband connection, i.e., Public Internet Access Points (PIAP)? Table 17 shows 87% responded yes while 15% reported no.

Question twelve was focusing on, if USA e-Government system considers disability access? As Table 18 shows, about 87% of respondents yes and 13% responded no.

Last question asked, if USA e-Government system provide foreign language accessibility?

Table 15. Shows USA e-Government system services regarding citizens searching the Web

Factors	#	%
Yes	53	87
No	8	13
Total	**61**	**100**

Table 16. Shows USA e-Government system services regarding citizens receiving information

Factors	#	%
Yes	57	93
No	4	7
Total	**61**	**100**

Table 17. Shows USA e-Government system services regarding citizens access to Internet

Factors	#	%
Yes	53	87
No	8	13
Total	**61**	**100**

Table 18. Shows USA e-Government system regarding disability access

Factors	#	%
Yes	53	87
No	8	13
Total	**61**	**100**

As Table 19 shows, about 84% of respondents yes and 16% responded no.

Questions 2-3 contribute to the most of the concepts in the proposed conceptual model. In other words, this supports all the seven propositions in the study. Question four contributes to the propositions 5-7. So, this means that the findings support those propositions. Questions 5-13 contribute to the propositions 3-7. One can see. The findings support those propositions in the study.

Hypothesis Testing

RQ (Research Question): What concepts are involved in implementing e-Government in order to provide e-services for citizens?

Table 19. Shows USA e-Government system regarding foreign language accessibility

Factors	#	%
Yes	51	84
No	10	16
Total	**61**	**100**

Q.Why you think there should be e-services by the USA government to the citizens? (Table 20)

Based upon the facts, one has to do the Chi square test using the following formula:

$$x^2 = \sum \left| \frac{(f0 - fe)^2}{fe} \right|$$

With k-1 degree of freedom, where (k=7)

Table 20. Shows e-services by USA government

Factors	#	%
Convenient	45	23
Less cost for all	34	17
Faster service	36	18
More Transparent	12	6
Available any time, any where	31	16
More productive and efficient	30	15
No way to ignore application of IT regarding our daily tasks	9	4.5
Other	1	0.5
Total	198	100

k is the number of categories, (k= 8)

f_0 is an observed frequency in a particular category

f_e is expected frequency in a particular category (197/8= 25.6)

$\alpha = 0.05$

df (k-1)= 14.067 (using table critical value of Chi square)

H_0: neutral response, i.e.,there should be no e-services by the USA government to the citizens.

Ha: non-neutral, i.e., the main factor of e-services by the USA government to the citizens is convenient.

After inserting all values in the formula then (see Table 21)

$x^2=67$

As the value of 67 lies in the region to right 14.067, then H0 is rejected at the 0.05 significant level in favor of Ha, i.e., the data support H5-7. So, one can conclude that the main factor of e-services by the USA government to the citizens is convenient.

Table 21.

Factors	f0	fe	(f0-fe)	(f0-fe)2	(f0-fe)2 / fe
Convenient	45	24.75	20.25	410.0625	16.568
Less cost for all	34	24.75	9.25	85.5625	3.457
Faster service	36	24.75	11.25	126.5625	5.114
More Transparent	12	24.75	-12.75	162.5625	6.568
Available any time, any where	31	24.75	6.25	39.0625	1.578
More productive and efficient	30	24.75	5.25	27.5625	1.114
No way to ignore application of IT regarding our daily tasks	9	24.75	-15.75	248.0625	10.023
Other	1	24.75	-23.75	564.0625	22.79
Total	**198**		**0**		**67.212**

Q. Why you think there should not be any e-services by the USA government to the citizens. (Table 22)?

Based upon the facts, one has to do the Chi square test using the following formula:

$$x^2 = \sum \left| \frac{(f0 - fe)^2}{fe} \right|$$

With k-1 degree of freedom, where (k=4)

k is the number of categories, (k= 5)
f_0 is an observed frequency in a particular category
f_e is expected frequency in a particular category (100/5= 20)
$\alpha = 0.05$
df (k-1)= 9.488 (using table critical value of Chi square)
H_0: neutral response, i.e., there should be any e-services by the USA government to the citizens.
Ha: non-neutral, i.e., so the main factor of there should not be any e-service by the USA government to the citizens is privacy issue.

After inserting all values in the formula then

x^2=46

Table 22. Shows factors for not having e-services by USA government

Factors	#	%
Privacy issue	44	44
Lack of access to Internet	12	12
Lack of access to a computer	16	16
Computer illiterate	24	24
Other	4	4
Total	100	100

As the value of 46 lies in the region to right 9.488, then H0 is rejected at the 0.05 significant level in favor of Ha, i.e., the data support all the hypothesis. So the main factor of there should not be any e-service by the USA government to the citizens is privacy issue.

Q. Does USA e-Government system provide services (such as: Free online taxing, Job search, Immigration services, Student loans, Disaster help, and …) for citizens (Table 23)?

Based upon the facts, one has to do the Chi square test using the following formula:

$$x^2 = \sum \left| \frac{(f0 - fe)^2}{fe} \right|$$

With k-1 degree of freedom, where (k=1)

k is the number of categories, (k= 2)
f_0 is an observed frequency in a particular category
f_e is expected frequency in a particular category (61/2= 30.50)
$\alpha = 0.05$
df (k-1)= 3.841 (using table critical value of Chi square)
H_0: neutral response, i.e., Shouldn't be any USA e-Government system provide services (such as: Free online taxing, Job search, Immigration services, Student loans, Disaster help, and …) for citizens?
Ha: non-neutral, i.e., so the main factor of should any USA e-Government system provide

Table 23. Data about USA e-Government system

Factors	#	%
Yes	55	90
No	6	10
Total	61	100

services (such as: Free online taxing, Job search, Immigration services, Student loans, Disaster help, and …) for citizens is yes.

After inserting all values in the formula then

$x^2 = 39$

As the value of 39 lies in the region to right 3.84, then H0 is rejected at the 0.05 significant level in favor of Ha, i.e., the data support all the hypothesis. So the main factor of should any USA e-Government system provide services (such as: Free online taxing, Job search, Immigration services, Student loans, Disaster help, and …) for citizens is yes.

Applying the same hypothesis test for the rest of questions will support the conceptual model.

CONCEPTUAL MODEL

Designing an efficient and successful e-Government project is a very challenging and demanding process (Sagheb-Tehrani, 2007). Researchers who proceed without theory rarely conduct top-quality research. Concepts are the main building blocks of theory. A concept can be an idea expressed as a symbol or in words (Neuman, 2003). Thus, the conceptual model presented here may contribute to the theory of correlated fields. Figure 1 shows an e-Government conceptual model with its relationships.

The conceptual model may suggest a number of propositions regarding the impacts of some concepts related to e-Government. In this section, seven particular research proposals are stated in general terms. The aim is to suggest important issues that need to be investigated further. Deeper discussion of the research propositions may also reveal that potential efforts are often complex with both positive and negative connotations.

Hypothesis 1: Knowledge management is required to shape the concepts of IT, vision, publication, interaction and transaction.

Hypothesis 2: The concept of IT is based upon other concepts such as: IT blue print, communication, IT priorities and IT strategies.

Hypothesis 3: The concept of vision is derived by concepts of citizen centered and vision priorities.

Hypothesis 4: The concept of publication is formed by the concepts of update, personalizing and push technology.

Hypothesis 5: The concept of interaction is created by the concepts of PIAP, transparency and accessibility.

Hypothesis 6: The concept of transaction is based upon the concepts of security, privacy and novel services.

Hypothesis 7: The concept of e-Government is generated by the concepts of IT, vision, publication, interaction and transaction.

CONCLUSION

All government or business operations require an effective management, as is the case with regards to e-Government implementation. One may say that there is no "one size fits all" IT strategy that works for all societies. To be able to deliver a project within a budget and on time and to coordinate effectively between all partners requires skillful management (The working group, 2002).

This study has introduced a conceptual model of e-Government. The chapter has argued that several key success factors are appropriate for e-Government implementation. About one hundred e-Government websites were examined upon those key success factors (please see Table 3). Also, the study supported the hypotheses by utilizing Chi square. The conceptual model allows one to broadly comprehend the concept of e-Government. This helps to design more successful e-Government projects. Further, this work may supply a basis for future research in the associated disciplines. One direction would be to use the conceptual model presented here in a case study. Moreover, the propositions launched here are meant to provide a starting point for supplementary research on this subject. Research in this theme should make a contribution to the knowledge of e-Government development so that these projects can be implemented more effectively.

REFERENCES

Abramson, M. A., & Harris, R. S. (2003). *The procurement revolution*. London: Rowland and Littlefield.

Akther, M. S., Onishi, T., & Kidokoro, T. (2007). E-government in a developing country: Citizen-ceteric approach for success. *International Journal of Electronic Goverance, 1*(1), 38–51. doi:10.1504/IJEG.2007.014342

Baumol, W. J., Litan, R. E., & Schramm, C. J. (2007). *Good capitalism, bad capitalism and the economics of growth and prosperity*. New Haven, CT: Yale. doi:10.2139/ssrn.985843

Breznitz, D. (2007). *Innovation and the state: Political choice and strategies for growth in Israel, Taiwan, and Ireland*. New Haven, CT: Yale.

Burrell, G., & Morgan, G. (1979). *Social paradigms and organization analysis*. Boston: Heineman.

Cap Gemini & Ernest & Young. (2001). *Web-based survey on electronic public services*. Retrieved March 13, 2013 from http://europa.eu.int/information_society/eeurope/news_library/documents/bench_online_services.doc.

Chircu, A.M., & Lee, D., & Hae-Dong. (2005). E-government: Key success factors for value discovery and realization. *Electronic Government, 2*(1), 11–24. doi:10.1504/EG.2005.006645

Cortada, J. W., Gupta, A. M., & Le Noir, M. (2007). *How the most advanced nations can remain competitive in the information age*. IBM.

Curtin, G. G., Sommer, M. H., & Vis-Sommer, V. (2003). *The world of e-government*. New York: The Haworth Press.

Donna, E., & Yen, D. C. (2006). E-government: Evolving relationship of citizens and government domestic, and international development. *Government Information Quarterly, 23*(2), 207–235. doi:10.1016/j.giq.2005.11.004

Evolution of e-Government in the European Union. (2002). *Report commissioned by the Spanish Presidency of the Council of the European Union*. Retrieved March 6, 2013 from http://www.map.es/csi/pdf/egovEngl_definitivo.pdf

Ghapanci, A., Albadavi, A., & Zarei, B. (2008). A framework for e-government planning and implementation. *Electronic Government: An International Journal, 5*(1), 71–90. doi:10.1504/EG.2008.016129

Gorla, N. (2008). Hurdles in rural e-government projects in India: Lessons for developing countries. *Electronic Government: An International Journal, 5*(1), 91–102. doi:10.1504/EG.2008.016130

Greiner, L. (2005). *State of the marketplace: e-Government gateways*. Faulkner Information Service. Retrieved February 6, 2012 from http://www.faulkner.com/products/faulknerlibrary/00018297.htm

Haigh, N., & Griffiths, A. (2008). E-government and environmental sustainability: Results from three Australian cases. *Electronic Government: An International Journal, 5*(1), 45–62. doi:10.1504/EG.2008.016127

Jupp, V. (2003). Realizing the vision of egovernment. In *The world of e-government*. Academic Press.

Lee, T.-R., Wu, H.-C., Lin, C.-J., & Wang, H.-T. (2008). Agricultural e-government in China, Korea, Taiwan and the USA. *Electronic Government: An International Journal, 5*(1), 63–70. doi:10.1504/EG.2008.016128

Magro, M. J. (2012). A review of social media use in e-government. *American Scientist, 2*(2), 148–161.

McGinnis, P. (2003). Creating a blueprint for e-government. In *The world of e-government*. Academic Press.

Mitra, A. (2005). Direction of electronic governance initiative within two worlds: Case for a shift in emphasis. Electronic Government, 2(1).

Mofleh, S. I., & Wanous, M. (2009). Reviewing existing methods for evaluating e-government websites. *Electronic Government: An International Journal, 6*(2), 129–142. doi:10.1504/EG.2009.024438

Murra, M. E. (2003). *E-government: From real to virtual democracy*. Boston University. Retrieved February 8, 2013 from http://unpan1.un.org/intradoc/groups/public/documents/other/unpan011094.pdf#search='egovernment%3Afrom%20Real%20to%20virtual%20democracy

Neuman, W. L. (2003). *Social research methods: Qualitative and quantitative approaches* (5th ed.). Boston: Allyn & Bacon.

Palmer, I. (2003). *State of the world: e-Government implementation*. Retrieved February 8, 2013 from http://www.faulkner.com/products/faulknerlibrary/00018297.htm

Raymond, L., Uwizeyemungu, S., & Bergeron, F. (2006). Motivations to implement ERP in e-government: An analysis from success stories. *Electronic Government: An International Journal, 3*(3), 225–240. doi:10.1504/EG.2006.009597

Sagheb-Tehrani, M. (2007). Some steps towards implementing e-government. *Journal of ACM. Computers & Society, 37*(1), 22–29. doi:10.1145/1273353.1273356

Smith, A. D. (2008). Business and e-government intelligence for strategically leveraging information retrieval. *Electronic Government: An International Journal, 5*(1), 31–44. doi:10.1504/EG.2008.016126

Stern, S., & Ibarra, P. (2011). Digital government creating the social media game plan. *Government Finance Review, 27*(5), 8–14.

UN. (2012). *United Nations e-government survey 2012: E-government for people department of economic and social affairs*. Retrieved May 8, 2013 from http://www2.unpan.org/egovkb/datacenter/CountryView.aspx

UNCTAD. (2002). *Reports on e-commerce and development of the United Nations conference on trade and development*. New York: United Nations.

Vietor, R. H. K. (2007). *How countries compete: Strategy, structure, and government in the global economy*. Cambridge, MA: Harvard Business School.

West, D. (2008a). *Improving technology utilization in electronic government around the world*. Retrieved February 8, 2013 from http://www.brookings.edu/reports/2008/0817_egovernment_west.aspx

West, D. (2008b). *State and federal e-government in the United States*. Retrieved October 13, 2010 from http://www.brookings.edu/reports/2008/0826_egovernment_west.aspx

Working Group. (2002). *Roadmap for e-government in the developing world*. Los Angeles, CA: Pacific Council on International Policy.

World Bank. (2007). *Country brief: Russian federation, economy*. Retrieved May 6, 2007 from http://web.worldbank.org

ADDITIONAL READING

Potnis, D., & Pardo, T. (2008). The United Nations e-Government Readiness Index: a work in progress, *Proceedings of the 2008 international conference on Digital government research.*

Prybutok, V., Zhang, X., & Ryana, S. (2008). Evaluating leadership, IT quality, and net benefits in an e-Government environment. *Information & Management, 45,* 143–152. doi:10.1016/j.im.2007.12.004

Pudaruth, S., Moloo, R. K., Mantaye, A., & Bibi, J. N. (2010). A Survey of E-Learning Platforms in Mauritius. *Proceedings of the World Congress on Engineering 2010 Vol. I WCE 2010,* June 30 - July 2, 2010, London, U.K. Retrieved January 16, 2011 from www.iaeng.org/publication/WCE2010/WCE2010_ pp415-420.pdf.

Pudjianto, B., & Hangjung, Z. (2009). Factors Affecting e-Government Assimilation in Developing Countries. Retrieved April 11, 2011 from Available from www.cprsouth.org/wp-content/uploads/drupal/Boni%20Pudjianto.pdf.

KEY TERMS AND DEFINITIONS

E-Government: The use of Information and Communication Technologies (ICTs) in the diverse government business processes.

Government to Business (G2B): This is a form of e-Government that details technology platforms for information interchange between government agencies and business entities. G2B platforms may be utilized to outline platforms for government-business interaction such as e-Procurement systems.

Government to Citizens (G2C): This is a form of e-Government that makes it possible for government agencies and citizens to exchange information. An example of such a platform may be a technologgy platform allowing citizens to comment on various decisions that the government is about to take.

Government to Government (G2G): This is a form of e-Government that makes it possible for government agencies to exchange information to aid them in decision-making.

Information Technology (IT): Platforms in the technology realm used for managing and accessing different information resources.

APPENDIX A

List of some related links to electronic governments

http://www.keshilliministrave.al/?fq=brenda&r=&kid=43
http://www.cg.gov.dz/index.php
http://www.govern.ad/
http://www.angola.org/
http://www.argentina.gob.ar/
http://www.australia.gov.au
http://www.austria.gv.at
http://www.bahamas.gov.bs
http://www.gov.bb/
http://www.belarus.by/en/
http://www.belgium.be/en/
http://www.canada.gc.ca
http://english.gov.cn/
http://wsp.presidencia.gov.co/En/Paginas/Presidency.aspx
http://www.congo-site.com/
http://www.cubagob.cu/
http://www.vlada.cz/en/default.htm
http://www.denmark.dk/en
http://dominicanrepublic.com
http://www.egypt.gov.eg/english/
http://www.presidencia.gob.sv/
http://valitsus.ee/en/government
http://www.fiji.gov.fj/
http://government.fi/etusivu/en.jsp
http://www.un.int/wcm/content/site/gambia/
http://embassy.mfa.gov.ge/index.php?lang_id=GEO&sec_id=5&lang_id=EN
http://www.new-york-un.diplo.de/Vertretung/newyorkvn/en/Startseite.html
http://www.greeceun.org/greeceun/content/Folder.aspx?d=3&rd=12106234&f=1272&rf=629020616
&m=-1&rm=0&l=1
http://www.guatemalaun.org/index.cfm
http://www.un.int/guinea/Guinea_pgs/mst_fm6.htm
http://www.un.int/wcm/content/site/haiti/
http://www.un.int/wcm/content/site/haiti/
http://www.mfa.gov.hu/kulkepviselet/New_York_ENSZ/en/
http://www.iceland.is/iceland-abroad/un/nyc/
http://www.un.int/india/
http://www.indonesiamission-ny.org/index.html
http://www.irelandunnewyork.org/home/index.aspx?id=81115
http://israel-un.mfa.gov.il/media-center

http://www.italyun.esteri.it/Rappresentanza_ONU/
http://www.un.int/jamaica/
http://www.un.int/wcm/content/site/jordan
http://www.kazakhstanun.org/
http://kenyaun.org/index.html
http://www.kuwaitmission.com/
http://www.un.int/wcm/content/site/latvia
http://unifil.unmissions.org/Default.aspx?tabid=1499
http://www.liberia-un.org/index.html
http://mission-un-ny.mfa.lt/
http://newyork-un.mae.lu/en
http://www.nationsonline.org/oneworld/madagascar.htm#News
http://www.malawi.gov.mw/
http://www.maliembassy.us

APPENDIX B:

Student Questionnaire

The following questionnaire is designed to conduct a research regarding the expectations that influence the satisfaction level of citizens' on USA e-Government system (www.usa.gov). The following questionnaire will be used to gain a better understanding of e-Government. The answers you provide are confidential and will not affect your grade in any way Please answer the following questions based on your experience, opinions and knowledge. There is no right or wrong answers. All responses are confidential and will be analyzed at the aggregate level. Your cooperation will be really appreciated. I am the only person who will have access to data. I will destroy the data after 5 years when the research gets published in a journal. Your participation is totally voluntary and you may quit anytime during the questionnaire. This research has been approved by Human Subject Committee of BSU. If you have any questions about your rights as a human research subject, please contact HSC (218-755-2027). If you have any questions about the research, please contact me (Tel: 218-755 2751 or email:mtehrani@bemidjistate.edu).

Thank you in advance for taking the time to complete this questionnaire ☺

Name:... Date: Course:

1. Sex:
   - Female
   - Male
2. Internet usage:
   - Daily
   - Weekly
   - Monthly
   - Yearly

3. Why do you think there should be e-services by the USA government to the citizens (*you may choose more than one option*)?
    ◦   Convenient
    ◦   Less cost for all
    ◦   Faster service
    ◦   More transparent
    ◦   Available any time, any where
    ◦   More productive and efficient
    ◦   No way to ignore application of information technology regarding our daily tasks
    ◦   Other.......

4. Why do you think there should not be any e-services provided by the USA government to the citizens (*you may choose more than one option*)?
    ◦   Privacy issue
    ◦   Lack of access to Internet
    ◦   Lack of access to a computer
    ◦   Computer illiterate
    ◦   Other..........

5. Does USA e-Government system (www.usa.gov) provide services (such as: Free online taxing, Job search, Immigration services, Student loans, Disaster help, and ...) for citizens?
    ◦   Yes
    ◦   No

6. Does USA e-Government system (www.usa.gov) provide services (such as: Corporation online taxing, Business opportunities, Business law and regulation, Government auctions, Export portal, patents and trademarks filing, and ...) for businesses?
    ◦   Yes
    ◦   No

7. Does USA e-Government system (www.usa.gov) provide services for other governments? (such as: Background Investigation application, For sale to other government buyers, and....).
    ◦   Yes
    ◦   No

8. Does USA e-Government system (www.usa.gov) allow citizens more than ever before to take part in government decisions and become more knowledgeable of the performance of their elected representatives.
    ◦   Yes
    ◦   No

9. Does USA e-Government system (www.usa.gov) allow citizens to search for a specific Web site?
    ◦   Yes
    ◦   No

10. Does USA e-Government system (www.usa.gov) allow citizens to register to receive updated publications?
    ◦   Yes
    ◦   No

11. Have citizens access to broadband connection, i.e., Public Internet Access Points (PIAP)?

○   Yes

○   No

12. Does USA e-Government system (www.usa.gov) consider disability access?

○   Yes

○   No

13. Does USA e-Government system (www.usa.gov) provide foreign language accessibility?

○   Yes

○   No

Thank you

Chapter 20
Critical Perspectives of E–Government in Developing World:
Insights from Emerging Issues and Barriers

Gbenga Emmanuel Afolayan
University of York, UK

ABSTRACT

This chapter utilizes extensive literature reviews to assess the different perspectives of e-Government development in developing world contexts. In order to do that, the chapter presents a case study from Jordan assessing the design and reality gaps of e-Government interventions using the ITPOSMO model. The chapter posits that e-Government for development is likely to grow only if there is deliberate cognisance of culture, real work practices, and of the broader technical and socio-political environment with which the e-Government projects are introduced and applied in the developing world.

INTRODUCTION

The debate on the new ICTs raises numerous conceptual and contextual questions. For example, how can we explain the new ICTs as part of government and development discourse? What are the issues and barriers that ICT-led development has in the delivery of public services within the wider debates of e-Government and ICT4D in developing countries? This chapter addresses these questions by investigating and critiquing the e-Government and ICT4D literatures. Using design-reality and ITPOSMO model, this chapter analyses the design and reality gaps that are responsible to the total failure of 'Drivers and Vehicles Licensing (DVL), a specific fast track ICT project in Jordan. It then seeks to understand emerging issues and barriers that shape this e-Government project.

DOI: 10.4018/978-1-4666-4900-2.ch020

The chapter argues that e-Government-for development is a potential tool to sustain public administration agendas but there remain some implementation barriers which hamper the full exploitation of its promising opportunities. This chapter begins by setting out the overview of the information age and e-Government, before investigating and critiquing ICT4D literature. Using the design-reality framework and ITPOSMO model, the chapter analyses how 'Drivers and Vehicles Licencing Department' has been affected in Jordan, and together with its underlying barriers/burdens that result in failure. It concludes that e-Government for development is likely to grow only if there is deliberate cognisance of culture, real work practices, and of the broader technical and socio-political environment with which the e-Government projects are introduced and applied in developing world.

CRITICAL OVERVIEW OF THE INFORMATION AGE AND E-GOVERNMENT

Information age marks a period in human history and it is defined by exponential growth in the collection, analysis, shaping, storing, duplication and transmission of information through electronic means (Webster, 2006; Castell, 2000). It is a period that some scholars perhaps see as an age of information revolution and access to information, not an information age (Loader and Dutton, 2003). It provides clues about how digital and networked technologies already in use might have influenced the future shape, socio-economic relationships, and conduct of human institutions, human activities, citizen-government relationships and international exchange (Lips, 2010; Hood and Margetts, 2007; Heeks, 1999).

Advancement in ICTs has altered the politics, economics, sociology and culture of knowledge creation and distribution, which perhaps make it as part of a continuing process that dates back at least a century and a half (Castells, 1989). Thus, the characterisation of information age is based on the access to information, network logic, widespread proliferation of emerging ICTs and the capabilities that those technologies provide and will provide humankind (Castell, 1999). As Webster notes, however, there are enormous problems in measuring what is meant by an information age. Even with the proliferation of new and emerging ICTs, Webster asks, has society changed profoundly enough to warrant calling the present—or the near term future—an information age? (Webster, 2006). Defining information age revolves around a mix of positive and negative point of view. Therefore, the contending issues about the meaning and quality of information, together with the relationship between the citizen and the government, are portentous ones for the information age.

On the other hand, e-Government has become a general phenomenon in this information age. Numerous claims have been made about the contribution of e-Government to poverty alleviation and development of public services (Lips, 2010; Chadwick, 2006; Evans and Yen, 2006; Heeks, 2001; 1999; Castell, 1999). In line with global trends, developed and developing countries have been initiating e-Government strategies and projects in improving the standards of service delivery and increasing the efficiencies of government, the latter typically with support from donor organisations such as the World Bank or bilateral donor organisations. Under the label "ICT4D" (Information and Communication Technologies for Development), these donor organisations are stressing the relevance of ICTs in general, and e-Government in particular, as a way to promote development and reduce poverty (Schuppan, 2009). In so doing, expectations are high because e-Government is perceived as strengthening the performance of government and public administration, and an efficient and effective administration of government is a necessary precondition for socio-economic development.

The foregoing claims are particularly relevant to developing world, where public administration is characterised with inefficiency, limited capacity, and poorly trained workforces (see Ndou, 2004; Cocchiglia & Vernaschi, 2006). This implies that e-Government, in general, has the potency to solve administrative problems, however because e-Government and its related institutional concepts were developed in industrialized countries, the current assumptions do not warrant such general claims. This is because there is a need for a critical debate about the strengths and limitations of e-Government, one that poses questions that hitherto have been unasked or neglected for developing countries. Therefore, when introducing e-Government in developing world, it is expected that different and more far-reaching efforts will be necessary than in developed countries.

Further, in spite of its surging popularity, for surprisingly large numbers of people – including the poor, the elderly, the undereducated, and many minorities – cyberspace is still an inaccessible, often weakly perceived domain. Lacking the necessary technical savvy, the income to get a personal computer at home, jobs that provide reliable internet access, and facing government policies that assume their needs will be addressed by the private sector, people excluded fail to benefit from the benefits that ICTs could provide them. A profound irony thus exists within developing world and many other societies: those who enjoy reliable access to the internet face an information overload, while many others are deprived of knowledge that could assist them in obtaining jobs, lower consumer prices, entertainment, and many other necessities and conveniences (for more analysis on these inequalities, see Stiglitz, 2012). Hence, as the number of different internet users has risen, the opportunity costs of those lacking access have grown proportionately.

It then becomes obvious that e-Government is a concept that must first be taken in the context of the individual citizen and their relationship to their government (Schuppan, 2009). There are different interpretations of the concept, although it undoubtedly crosses borders with noteworthy ease, making it one of the fastest spreading ideas for public sector change in history (Evans and Yen, 2006). Historically, for example, as ICT increases and is available to the individual citizen, the power of the citizen increases (Ibid.). E-Government is the modern step in this evolution that empowers the individual citizen to protect his rights and have his voice heard by his government. While each culture has its own history, it appears that as ICT improves, the relative power position of both 'citizens and consumers' improves relative to that of the government (Hofstede, 1997; Chadwick, 2006).

Simply put, e-Government is the use of technology to enhance the access to and delivery of government services to benefit citizens, business partners and employees (Silcock, 2001). From a technical standpoint, Jaeger and Thompson note that e-Government initiatives revolve around several types of electronic and information systems, for example, database, networking, discussion support, multimedia, automation…and personal technologies (2003). Like e-commerce, that facilitates businesses more efficiently (B2B) and brings customers closer to businesses (B2C), e-Government fosters the interaction between government and citizens (G2C), government and business enterprises (G2B), government and employees (G2E) and inter-agency relationships (G2G) more friendly, useful, bi-directional, transparent, and economical (World Bank, 2012; see also ITU, 2008). This means e-Government affects every aspect of how an organisation delivers service to the public. As a result, there is a real possibility for change in government's interaction with the outside world, both in terms of disseminating information to citizens and businesses and collecting information from them (Marggets, 2006; Silcock, 2001), with regards to differences in each country's specific historical, political, economic and institutional setting.

Therefore, e-Government offers itself a degree of comparative investigation and it is not only seen as a means of improving quality and responsiveness of the services provided to citizens, but also expanding the reach, transparency and accessibility of these services (UN, 2004; Marggets, 2006; ITU, 2008). For this and other reasons, a number of e-Government projects are being implemented in developing economies. Behind the hi-tech glamour of these projects, however, lies a dirty truth – the majority of projects are failures; some of which can result in total or partial failure or success (Heeks, 2006). The study of the way in which e-Government becomes a technology of ordering then unveils at the same time hurdles, risks and inner contradictions. These ideas will be developed in the next section where the idea of 'Information, Communication and Technology for Development' (ICT4D) will be discussed.

ICT4D (INFORMATION, COMMUNICATION AND TECHNOLOGY FOR DEVELOPMENT)

Before examining these issues further, we will examine a framework for the use of ICTs particularly in developing contexts that has some prominence in the discourse of development practice. ICT4D is a framework for the application of tools and techniques to the practice of development. It is a multidisciplinary field within the practice of development and can be summarised as the use of ICTs to reach development objectives (Hoods & Margetts, 2007; Unwin, 2009a). Their potential for accumulation of searchable knowledge and information are responsible for what many are now calling the advent of the 'Information Age' (Castells, 2000). Besides, ICT4D aims at empowering people and communities by answering the difficult questions of not only "what should be done" in the practice of development but also "how we should do it" (Unwin, 2009b: 33).

Consequently, the diffusion of ICTs has had a profound impact on the lives of the people and on some poorer people world-wide (Cocchiglia & Vernaschi, 2006). There are economic interests, political prestige, international structures and ongoing techno-optimistic discourses in place to buttress the mainstream ICT4D field (Kleine & Unwin, 2009). Nevertheless, high-profile ICT4D rhetoric has championed initiatives that see development in ways that are in line with the understanding of key international donors, governments and IT companies (Ciborra, 2005). Typically, these perspectives focus on economic growth or, by extension, on achieving the Millennium Development Goals by promoting economic growth and thereby seeking to reduce poverty (Avgerou, 2003).

Apparently, ICT is seen as a critical empowering infrastructure for future advancement within four of Sen's (1999) five developmental indicators: economic opportunities, political freedoms, social facilities, and transparency guarantees – and in the development of 'knowledge societies' as a key accelerator for development (UNESCO, 2005). This universal role of ICT as both medium and channel for cultural and economic exchange brings a growing necessity for an informed critique, at policy level, of its conception and practice in those areas of the world whose real cost for such argument is presently most inadequate, and where citizens are often least positioned to condemn when the accompanying benefits do not occur. This kind of a policy-level critique is all the more important since, as with all methods of empowering social infrastructure, ICT has the potency to form new inequalities, as well as intensify prevailing ones, and as Thompson (2004) has previously argued, even to structure and reproduce marginalization itself. This can happen both at the macro-level, by structurally integrating communities into broader, uneven networks of capital, production, trade and communication (Castells 1997, 1998; Wilson and Wong, 2007), as well as at the micro-level, where the unmoving debate of software can 'smuggle' entire, perhaps unfitting value structures into new environments (Danowitz, et al., 1995).

Additionally, Thompson (2005) has critiqued the ICT4D discourse for the hidden political and economic agendas of Western domination it represents. The vested interest in highlighting the digital divide issue, which might lead to a relationship of dependency between economic interests in the developed world and the developing world, has also been criticised (Wade, 2004). Escobar (1995, 2001) has long been a critic of development which takes majority of market-inspired forces capitalism asserts as the dominant hegemony for development, often at the expense of other models and local economies. As a field already acquainted with such uncertainties, there is thus an essential condition for the developmental community to engage with and critique the ICT within the developmental context: to continue to ask often challenging questions about whether ICT-led initiatives are truly ballooning equitable access to the freedoms and life-chances that establish the basis of contemporary developmental initiatives – or just creating or intensifying more inequality. For example, the flow of foreign direct investment into some countries in developing world has not been sufficient, despite the large multinational presence (see Ndou, 2004; Roy, 2005). This observation calls for a more structural investigation that looks beyond the tracking of 'deliverables' and short-term functional benefits so ideal by ICT projects, to include a wider political economy of developmental ICT in developing world.

Therefore, understanding and examining the underlying situations through which multimillion dollar ICT projects aimed at helping billions of poor people around the world becomes no less than a legitimate exercise. The next section will briefly map-out the e-Government strategy in Jordan before it analyses the opportunities and barriers/burdens associated with her public administration agenda of e-Government for development through Heeks' ITPOSMO model.

JORDAN'S E-GOVERNMENT STRATEGY

Jordan's e-Government development plans include the following five major foundations (a) introduction of e-services; (b) infrastructural development (c) education and training; and (d) legal change (e) establishment of management and organisational framework (Ciborra, 2003; MoICT, 2001, 2003a; Elsheikh, Cullen & Hobbs, 2008). Jordania eGovernment strategy is centred on the following broad objectives: increasing the transparency of government by increasing availability of information; increasing the responsiveness and the participation of government agencies by providing more information and services to the public; creating a new mode of contact between governments and the public; bridging the digital divide through the promotion of ICTs skills development in firms and individuals; and boosting e-commerce activities in the region (Ciborra, 2003; MoICT, 2003b).

Jordan's e-Government project is being implemented by a task force, an eight-member public/private committee headed by the 'Ministry of ICT' (Ciborra, 2003, 2005). Apart from attracting investment in the ICT sectors, and setting the ICT strategy plan for the telecom and postal sector, the Ministry of ICT is responsible for setting the telecom policy and coordinating the e-Government for development initiative (Al-Jaghoub & Westrup, 2003; Al Nagi & Hamdan, 2009). Specifically, the Ministry issues the technical standards and articulates the policy for the various government agencies to bring their data, services and transactions on-line (Ministry of ICT, 2001). Consequently, the creation of new jobs in the ICT sector and the launch of a software industry were given a priority (Reach, 2001) and there was diffusion of ICT in rural areas and the promotion of eLearning (Ministry of ICT, 2001).

Several fast track projects such as motoring services, taxation services, and land registry were launched in 2001 (Ciborra, 2005). For example, four government departments are involved: The

Department of Land & Survey (DLS); and three under the umbrella of the Ministry of Finance – the Income Tax Department (ITD); the Drivers & Vehicles Licensing Department (DVLD); and the General Sales Tax Department (GSTD). The legal change gave room to the creation of partnerships between foreign ICT multinationals and local educational institutes for the provision of necessary ICT skills, such as the training course that Microsoft Corporation agreed to provide to IT students of the Yarmouk University (Cited in Al-Jaghoub and Westrup, 2003). Finally, loans and aid from international agencies are being used to create ICT enabled public services and reduce a possible digital divide between rich and poor (UNDP, 2000a, b).

Just like any other developing country, Jordanian public administration is not a "green-field site" as far as IT is concerned (Ciborra, 2005). Over the years, each ministry, department and agency has been implementing several ICT-led programmes. There are ministries or areas more advanced than others and a variety of infrastructures, often incompatible or plainly not integrated or networked. Thus, when considering the fast track projects, the one at ITD is relatively more advanced, or ranks higher on the "technical readiness" scale. In other services (e.g. sales tax) new systems have been introduced, but due to lack of involvement and user participation, there is resistance to acceptance (Ibid.). In line with the foregoing, the ICT readiness within the government administration is uneven: it is a matter of technologies; the de facto autonomy of the Ministries; the different practices in systems implementation; sometimes untimely user involvement and training; the need for a profound culture change towards the new techniques of working, and so on (Ciborra, 2005; Elsheikh et al., 2008).

An important question that one could then ask now is: what does this mean for the idea of the ICT4D framework presented in the earlier section? It is evident that there are problems of policy and implementation in the Jordanian e-Government

strategy. It then means that the idea is flawed because it fails to understand the issues of context. A valuable example of a critical critique of this kind is Wilson's (2004) questioning of mindless assumptions about the general benefits associated with ICT diffusion. As an alternative, Wilson underlines the need to see 'developmental' ICT as profoundly embedded within social structures, and proposes an idea of internet diffusion comprising, first, social, economic and political structures, second, institutions, third, politics, and fourth, government policy (comprising the oppositions public/private, competition/monopoly, foreign/domestic, and centralized/decentralized – all fundamental struggles that are of particular importance to developmental ICT).

As shown in this example, ICT could still benefit directly from such a 'policy' critique from within development studies, by including an analysis of these factors within the business cases and investment assessments of developmental ICT-led initiatives as a set of conditions to be met before the release of funding – private or public. All these point to the fact that ICT4D is still a helpful framework, if it is vernacularized in the context of developing world. Next, we can then conceptualize 'design-reality gap' before we turn to the ITPOSMO model advanced by Heeks (2006) in later section.

METHODOLOGY

After reviewing the extant literature on e-Government and ICT for development, the chapter will make use of a combination of design-reality gap and ITPOSMO model. This approach will be used to explore empirically within a developing country context. The approach is applied to a case study of DVLD failure in one of the Jordan's public agencies, analysing the situation before and during e-Government implementation of the affected public services through a mix of previously published works (Heeks, 2002, 2003;

Hawari & Heeks, 2010 and unpublished doctoral theses (Alomari, 2010; Kanaan, 2009), observation and document analysis.

Unfortunately, this implies that there are some limitations to this chapter. Exclusively using unweighted data means that the scope of the results is limited only to information that is available in the case study. Thus, the level of detail to which the methodology can be tested is minimal and the results cannot be taken as more than a robust suggestion. Yet, the chapter shows the relevance and applicability of the e-Government development outcomes and design-reality approach to understanding DVLD failure. Further study can be undertaken applying the approach to other DVLD cases, as well as case studies of success.

DESIGN-REALITY GAP

How could this concept be framed? To do this, we need to simultaneously assess the current system and the future system. Meanwhile, defining the existence of the current and the future system simultaneously is not feasible. It is rather easy to evaluate the current 'reality' in a particular situation. But in order to evaluate the future, we must evaluate instead the representation of an intended future—an envisioned future that is represented in a design for the system. Overall, the foregoing is based on an assessment of the match or mismatch between local reality ("where we are now") and system design ("where the design wants to get us"). We refer to this as the design–reality gap (Heeks, 2002).

Practically, because the expectations about the future and perceptions of reality are subjective, it could be argued that every individual information system stakeholder has their own design and their own form. Included in this conceptual framework are the two key stakeholders—the designers (creators of the dominant information system design) and the users (those that populate the local reality). These major stakeholders are

specifically important to an understanding of 'failure' (Sauer, 1999) given their dislocation, in both psychological and physical terms, as part of the implementation process of the information system. The simplification, however, enforces limits—for example, "limiting subjective partial failures to a consideration of the objectives of these two stakeholder groups alone" (Heeks, 2002: 104).

What could then be the significant perspectives of this design–reality gap between the designers' dominant design and the local context (reality) of the users? The perspectives could be based on: e-Government literature, direct delineation of components of an information system (IS) and case studies. All these three bases are explored here. Overall, as pointed out earlier, the design is a representation of an intended future. As noted by Heeks (2002), design contains elements with either explicit or implicit inscriptions. These elements are:

1. Components from the designers' own context: Information system design is a situated action "taken in the context of particular, concrete circumstances" (Suchman, 1987, p. viii). This action draws elements of that context into the design. For example, "Our technologies mirror our societies. They reproduce and embody the complex interplay of professional, technical, economic and political factors" (Akrich, 1992, p. 3). In particular, designers are component of and characterised by that context. Thus, their own cultural values, objectives and goals will be inscribed in the design (Shields & Servaes, 1989; Braa & Hedberg, 2002).

2. Imagined assumptions about the situation of the user: This revolves around assumptions about the users' activities, skills, culture, and objectives, and assumptions about the user organization's structure, infrastructure, among others. (Suchman, 1987; Wynn & deLyra, 2000).

All these two elements determine the potency and feasibility of the design of information systems. Let us now turn to the ITPOSMO model advanced by Heeks (2006), in an attempt to ascertain its nexus with design-reality gap within the purview ICT for development in developing world.

ITPOSMO MODEL

Having discussed the fundamental ideas revolving around the 'mixed' discourse of ICT for development and design-reality gap in the previous sections, this section will briefly explore the nexus between Heeks' ITPOSMO model and design-reality gap to analyse the case of Jordan's e-Government strategy in the section that follows.

ITPOSMO model explains the gap between the rhetoric and reality of change (design-reality gap). The use of this model is twofold. First, it identifies various sets of critical factors that account for the success and failure of prevailing ICT-based reforms (evaluation ex post). Second, it helps to identify potential factors that should be considered, if government organizations want to commence ICT-based reform (evaluation ex ante) (Heeks, 2002; 2006). It is clearly understandable that the more gaps found, the more likely failure addressed to the e-Government project and vice-versa.

The seven dimensions summarised by the ITPOSMO acronym – are necessary and sufficient to provide an understanding of design-reality gaps:

- **I**nformation (data stores, data flows and the informal information used by the people with the system)
- **T**echnology (both hardware and software)
- **P**rocesses (the activities undertaken by the users and others)
- **O**bjectives and values (*Objectives* component manifest issues of self-interest and politics; the *values* component manifest culture: i.e. what the users and others feel are the right and wrong ways to do things)

- **S**taffing and skills (covers the 'number 'of staff [quantitative aspect] with e-Government system, and the 'competencies' of those staff [qualitative aspect] and other users)
- **M**anagement systems and structures (operation and use of the e-Government system, as well as the way in which the stakeholder agencies/groups are structured)
- **O**ther resources (time and money are particularly required to implement and operate e-Government system—see Heeks, 2006: 5-6).

Analysis of e-Government failure and success case studies across the world reveals that ITPOSMO model can be applied in practice to a wide range of case studies, particularly in developing countries (Heeks, 2001; Elsheikh, Cullen & Hobbs, 2008; Hawari & Heeks, 2010; Weerakkody & El-Haddadeh, 2011). An example of such case study analysis is given later in the chapter. For each of the seven dimensions, the gap between design and reality can be assessed and ranked (e.g. low, medium, high). All in all, ratings will give a sense of incompatibility between design and reality and, hence, a view of the likelihood of failure.

ANALYTICAL SUMMARY

Taking a simple, unweighted approach to each of the seven dimensions, we can aggregate the gaps to get an overall design-reality gap score of 55 prior to e-goverment project implementation. Comparing this to Table 1 (adapted from Heeks, 2006), we can see that the prediction for the project—that it 'may well fail', leaning close to 'will almost certainly fail', matches well with the actual outcome. Table 2 (as shown below) outlines a summary of the individual dimensional gap scores and compares them to the ratings provided by Heeks (2003). It then considers four dimensions (technology, processes, objectives and values, and staffing and

Table 1. Predicted e-Government project outcomes from overall design-reality gap scores

Overall Design-Reality Gap Score	Likely eGovernment Project Outcome
57-70	E-Government project will almost certainly fail unless action is taken to close design-reality gaps
43-56	E-Government project may well fail unless action is taken to close design-reality gaps
29-42	E-Government project might fail totally, or might well be a partial failure unless action is taken to close design-reality gaps
15-28	E-Government project might be a partial failure unless action is taken to close design-reality gaps
0-14	E-Government project may well succeed

Source: Adapted from Heeks (2006)

Table 2. Design-reality gap dimensions as likely causes of failure in the pre-implementation

Dimension	Gap Score	Likelihood as Cause of Failure
Information	8	Likely
Technology	8.5	Very likely
Process	8	Very likely
Objectives and Values	9	Very likely
Staffing and skills	8.5	Very likely
Management systems and structures	8	Likely
Other resources	5	Possible

NB: Adapted from Heeks (2003)

skills) as the most likely causes of DVLD project failure, the scores on all but the 'other resources' dimension are so close as to point to a wide base of risk factors for the project.

In analysing design-reality gaps during DVLD implementation, it should be pointed out that neither information system design nor contextual reality are static. They change repeatedly and thus so too do design-reality gaps. Successful e-Government project implementation is possible even when initial gaps are large, if measures can be taken to change system design and/or change situational realities in order to ensure gap closure (Heeks, 2006). Our next analytical step for the Jordanian case is to analyse what happened to the initial gaps during DVLD implementation. But it is very important for us to firstly provide the information about the application description of information systems, application drivers and stakeholders for DVLD implementation before the analysis.

Application Description

The application was the planned introduction of computers into the Drivers and Vehicles Licencing Service to replace the previously-manual processes of gathering, processing and storing of data relating to drivers and vehicles and bringing the data, services and transactions on-line (Ministry of ICT, 2001). The main software was a series of packages for registration and analysis of vehicles' and drivers' details. These facilitated an intra-agency communication and cooperation with local, regional and national databases that relied on common data items, with a view to having the development of a holistic view of a security strategy (Ciborra, 2005).

Application Drivers

Within the DVLD, there was a general awareness that the existing information systems did not allow the Service to monitor and analyse current licencing trends properly, or to make traffic decisions in an effective and timely manner. Thus, the King of Jordan, top officials of the state, public-private committee and the newly created Ministry of ICT (MoICT) were a key driving force behind the application as they sought improvements in the Service's performance. There was also a general external support (from the World Bank to the UN, and the donors of various leading Western and Far East countries) for the programme, with the combined commitment expressed by the top of the state (King himself, government officials and MoICT). They all wedded to modernisation of the public sector, and with citizens—becoming used to rapid social and economic progress and general efficient services to the citizens (MoICT, 2000, 2003a; Ciborra, 2005)

Stakeholders

The project was initiated by an eight-member public/private committee headed by the newly formed MoICT and Ministry of Finance (Ministry of ICT, 2000). Other key stakeholders include King Abdullah II of Jordan, who has been instrument to the ICT-led development (Elsheikh et al., 2008). Ordinary citizens (Jordanians) are the ultimate source of much of the data and also the ultimate intended beneficiaries of the project (Ciborra, 2005). Further, Jordan's e-Government program is administered by the MoICT. e-Government program management office was established by the MoICT to give support for the program and manage its functions which include e-services, shared services, operation management, technology services, and change management. These functions are interlinked, and do not operate independently (World Bank, 2002). National Information Technology Centre is another party,

which acts effectively in the implementation of MoICT policies and strategies related to government's adoption of ICTs on one hand, and will be accountable for the development of all ICT resources in Jordan on the other hand.

ITPOSMO ANALYSIS OF THE JORDANIAN CASE STUDY

With the conceptual background and analytical summary set in the previous sections, we can now return to the question with which this chapter is based on, namely, what opportunities and barriers/burdens do the eGovernment for development offer developing country like Jordan?

This case study illustrates use of the design-reality gap approach (Heeks, 2006) in relation to computerisation of the Drivers and Vehicles Licensing in Jordan. It is a typical application where the idea of electronic service comes to the fore to provide better service to the Jordanians, decreased transactions costs and opportunity for restructuring old-fashioned operation about drivers and vehicles licencing (Ciborra, 2005). The ITPOSMO analysis compared the assumptions/requirements within the application design of Drivers and Vehicles Licensing Department (DVLD), with the reality pertaining just before that design was implemented along the seven 'ITPOSMO' dimensions as follow:

1. **Information**: Gap rating: 6.5. The design was built on the pre-existing data and a new set of data capture forms and systems within the DVLD service because it is a fast track project. Indeed, DVLD's real-time design approach mismatches the traditional style of working. Overall, then, there was some, but limited, progress in closing informational design-reality gap.
2. **Technology**: Gap rating: 6. The design assumed the use of a broad range of software and hardware, with personal computers

(PCs) in the DVLD and other departments concerned. The initial reality was manual operations. Internet diffusion is somewhat low due to the fact that local phone calls are expensive and the fact that PC's prices are expensive. And this includes 0.7 percent of Jordanian population in terms of internet account subscribers and 1.9 percent in terms of internet users (Al-omari, 2006). All these led some gap between design and reality to remain.

3. **Processes**: Gap rating: 6. The design assumed pre-existing 'Drivers and Vehicles Licencing service processes with some changes made to the way in which data was gathered, processed, stored and output, with many previous human processes being changed to computerised processes (Ciborra, 2005). Unfortunately some of the changes effected were relatively mismatched (for example, mapping of Drivers and Vehicles Licencing and processes onto software functionalities). Consequent upon this, many initial suggested process redesigns were infeasible or inappropriate to Jordanian ways of working. Where attempts were made to redesign the DVLD system to compensate for inability to change working processes, these were drawn into heavy customisation of the software that went well beyond basic configuration as well as integration. This created its own problems. All these, enable some measure of design-reality gap in this particular Jordanian public agency operations.

4. **Objectives and values**: Gap rating: 8.5. The design assumed that the objectives of the fast track project were shared by all the stakeholders in Jordan. In theory, most departments supported the system because they believed that these initiatives may attract the creation of new jobs in the ICT sector and the launch of a software industry (Ciborra, 2005). But in practice, there was lack of institutional

framework and operational leadership across government agencies, along with limited financial support, to coordinate and implement the ICT-led initiatives (UNDP, 2006). For example, where management input was required, it was passed down to some junior staff member like a hot potato. As a result, these enable huge measure of the mismatch between system design and actual objectives on this dimension.

5. **Staffing and skills**: Gap rating: 7.5. The design assumed the ongoing presence during and after implementation of a suitable workforce for an emerging ICT sector (Ministry of ICT, 2000). However, a problem of loss of skilled ICT emerged later (Nusseir, 2001), which fell well short of good practice. It was evident that this was different from the initial reality before computerisation. There was lack of training for the staff (UNDP, 200b). As a result, many workers did not have a clear idea about the nature and use of the systems. Even where there was training, it therefore failed to change staff attitudes. It also failed to impart necessary skills. Some that were trained were employed without consideration of their IT skills, education or experience. Combined with the poor quality of the training, this left them unable to work on the system. Consequently, while there was diffusion of skills, it was shallow and, for some elements, short-lived when skills pick up on training emaciated through disuse. Gap closure was therefore rather limited.

6. **Management systems and structures**: Gap rating: 7.5. The design proposed some improving changes to pre-existing structures, with the Ministry of Post and Telecommunications being renamed 'Ministry of ICT'. This was done in order to issue the technical standards and articulate the policy for the various agencies to bring their data, services and transactions online (Ministry of ICT, 2001). However,

managerial responsibilities and the system of centralised control and decision-making remained. Unfortunately, there was intended change to organisational reality which fell short in practice (UNDP, 2000b). As a result, decisions were left unmade, and problems were left unsolved because more junior staff were not authorised to make decisions. Where senior staff did become involved—and partly because of the integrative and data-sharing nature of DVLD applications—they were sometimes drawn into conflict with each other. Overall, this intended new structural reality did not function as necessary and there was only limited progress in closing the management systems and structures gap.

7. **Other resources**: Gap rating 5. The key success to the fairly generous allowances for the project was the close involvement of public and private sector organisations. However, in terms of time, the explicit design requirement proved much too short and implementation. Even this required an enormous workload from the concerned personnel (Ciborra, 2002; 2005), still it was not enough to match the implicit design requirement for implementation of good quality DVL system. Consequently, corners were sometimes cut during implementation, with so many activities done with a hurry rather being done well. One cannot say that

there was any gap closure here. In terms of money, both design requirement and reality changed leaving small gap between the two—the required money for DVL implementation was available, even though the estimated final cost of DVL perhaps could have over-run the original cost.

Based on the findings of eGovernment project as revealed in Jordanian case, we shall now turn to the discussion on design-reality gap score of 47 points (see Table 3) following the DVLD implementation as revealed by the basic and un-weighted approach. This will enable us to unpack the underlying issues and barriers that result in the failure of the computerisation of 'Drivers and Vehicles Licensing' service in Jordan.

DISCUSSING THE DESIGN-REALITY GAP SCORE OF DRIVERS AND VEHICLES LICENSING (DVL) IMPLEMENTATION IN JORDAN

From the above analysis, one could say that the overall computerisation of DVLD service (with the design-reality gap of 47 points) can be classified as a failure. The justification for this has been offered through a more overarching understanding: the design-reality gap model. Undoubtedly, it is an essential application where the idea of eService for development is indispensable: better service

Table 3. Post-Implementation Design-reality gap dimensions as likely causes of failure

Dimension	Gap change	Gap score	Likelihood as cause of failure
Information	-1.5	6.5	Likely
Technology	-2.5	6	Possible
Process	-2	6	Possible
Objectives and Values	-.5	8.5	Very likely
Staffing and skills	-1	7.5	Likely
Management systems and structures	-.5	7.5	Likely
Other resources	0	5	Possible

to the Jordanians, decreased transaction costs and prospect for streamlining the obsolete office operations. Yet, as noted by Ciborra (2005), a number of unintended potential risks emerged, which appear to indicate that this application will be much more complex to implement as opposed to initial plan. Generally, DVLD case is, in itself, an application that causes several difficulties of transferring Western e-Government models and methodologies to organisations operating in developing countries. Consequently, there is a low technical readiness and employees are not very technically savvy for this application (Elsheikh et al, 2008). Overall, our analysis has shown that a set of assumptions and requirements were designed into DLV and its broader project. These suggestively mismatched the realities to be found in an ideal public institution. For example, required information was not present; the technology infrastructure was much more basic, work processes were far from best practice, among others (Cibora, 2005; Kanaan, 2009).

Another key issue is what happens during implementation. Can the project team work to change institutional reality (public) through the introduction of the new system and/or alter the system design to moderate the more extreme mismatches to reality? There was indeed an attempt do this in the case of 'Drivers and Vehicles Licencing (DVL) but the impact was far too limited, leaving the base of skills, data, technology etc within the DVLD too far-removed from what a successful DVL system would require (Ciborra, 2002, 2005). The explanation for this can be offered through the number of 'dependencies' which cast a shadow on the easiness of implementation. For example, having any type of transport or vehicle license encompasses internal transaction with different agencies/ministries, including local municipalities and so on. Another worry is on the change management and training efforts. These are to be expected: to resolve resistance issue, to educate the computer illiterate or to change the manage-

ment model. The latter will involve a radical cultural transformation (Caldow, 2001). In Jordanian context, it implies the transition from a military culture to a business/market culture (Ciborra, 2005). Thus, their failure to close design-reality gaps enables us to know why this project failed: the model therefore acts as post hoc investigation tool focusing basically on identification of risk. However, the design-reality gap model could also be useful for risk mitigation; pointing to the ways to move forwards from the present situation by closing actual dimensional gaps and so increasing the likelihood of project success.

Hence, successful implementation and delivery of public services demand the change of some parts of the Jordan from a security apparatus into a transparent service agency, where a driving licence is not a public security but a quasi-commercial product (Ibid.). Taken together, even in the analysis phase, an unexciting application, chosen because of its low risk and high return in terms of engaging the citizens into the notion and experience of e-Government, turns out to be one of the obstacles of e-Government in a developing country. Again, DVLD case shows the two impacts of ICTs: ordering and revealing. ICT-led development allows an unprecedented ordering of transactions within the government and between the government and outside agencies, firms and individuals (i.e. citizens as customers). By implication, e-Government projects can expose the institutions in which they are being implemented. Likewise, however, its arrangement can continue only by revealing the nature of the government, and more in general of the Jordan state, and the differing necessities for its change.

One way to resolve this puzzle is to change the current reality to make it more closely stick firmly to the assumptions and requirements of DVL system design, in line with the contextual reality of developing country like Jordan. Examples could include:

- **Information**: Widening the base of data gathered within the DVLD, to reduce the number of blank fields in the DVLD database.
- **Technology**: Better investment in IT infrastructure to make the technology reality more closely match the infrastructural requirements inscribed into the DLV design.
- **Process**: More skilful planning of improvements to DVLD's work processes to bring them at least somewhat closer to drivers and vehicles licencing norms
- **Objectives and values**: Implementation of a simultaneous programme of institutional change, aiming to engage internal stakeholders in the DVLD project, and to nudge institutional culture more towards DVLD-like values.
- **Staffing and skills**: An appropriately-undertaken training programme that would teach purpose and skills; and would offer a well-resourced post-training support system. Through this, match real skills more closely to required skills.
- **Management systems and structures**: Leadership from the top that would drive synergy between actual system/structures and those assumed within system design
- **Other resources**: Adequate time and more money should be allowed for the service.
- Design-reality gap closure recommendations like these along each dimension, as above-listed, do set an agenda for risk mitigation. Nevertheless, we must take cognisance attention of these two things:

First of all, the design-reality gap model is blind to the quality of design and of reality—it tells us nothing whether stakeholders would see them as 'good' or 'bad' but rather emphasize on the fact that the mismatches between design and reality increase the risk of failure. Thus, we may wish to question DVLD system; asking whether this is the most tangible method for a Jordanian public agency. If DVLD matched its reality to the demands of licencing service design, would this place it in the most effective business position or not? Does some of the resistance to DVL derive not from personal interest, but from a legitimate and valid concern; of which the issue of customer payments might be one example? (see, Ciborra, 2002). Generally speaking, resistance appears to be a bad thing in the information systems literature but perhaps it is not at all times. Probably, resistance is sometimes, at least in part, a pointer that the offered system is taking the institution in the unconformable direction (Hawari & Heeks, 2010).

Too, how possible are the kind of gap closure suggestions made above in a developing world context? Due to a fundamental lack of expertise that several businesses in the developing nations might find themselves (see, Rajapakse & Seddon, 2005), there are serious barriers to both redesign and altering current realities (see, Elsheikh, et al., 2008). To cap it all, culture is also relevant to this case. Cultural problems are related to DVL failures. Other studies, too, identify a significant role for culture in implementation of services in Jordan (Elsheikh et al., 2008; El-Sawah et al., 2008; Kanaan, 2009). As Heeks (2003) notes, the main reason behind e-Government projects failure in most, if not all, developing countries is the gap experienced between the design and reality of information systems implementation. However, Jordan mainly relies on experts globally to set up e-Government initiatives. This mostly results in little consideration of the specific national context of Jordan in terms of the social issues such as traditions, customs, values, orientations, and attitudes, as well as the cultural issues including organisational culture, geography, literacy, gender segregation, and religion (Elsheikh et al., 2008).

Though general views on cultural issues are challenging thoughts (Shoib & Nandhakumar, 2003; Hofstede, 2003), they can create distortions that homogenise culture at a national level. Hitherto, culture has institutional, group and individual mechanisms. All these offer a single cultural profile though; individuals will often be subject to multiple, potentially conflicting and cultural streams; because culture is dynamic. We should not reject these ideas entirely. What this suggests is potentially deep institutional forces in Jordan—and perhaps in some other developing country contexts—that run counter to the values inscribed into DVL systems design. This offers us a valuable supplement to the case research reported above, by implying reasons why it may be difficult to close the gap on the 'objectives and values' dimension. Given the centrality of this dimension to motivation for any e-Government project, the dilemma of such gap closure may in turn make it hard to find the drive force for closing gaps in other ITPOSMO dimensions. The list of gap closure thoughts outlined earlier may thus be practical in theory, but tougher to attain in practice.

CONCLUSION

This chapter supports the view that ICTs have the potential to trigger the development of public services, in spite of the implementation challenges associated with them. Using design-reality and ITPOSMO model, it analyses the Jordanian case as the one that seeks to use the new ICTs as a tool for development of its public services (Ciborra, 2005). Developing drivers and vehicles licencing systems can deliver benefits to citizens in developing countries (Ciborra, 2005). However, high failure rates continue to block the delivery of such benefits (Elsheikh et al., 2008; Kanaan, 2009). Research to date, though, often appears partial, focusing on only some parts of system outcome and/or focusing on particular implementation factors.

This chapter thus sought to identify conceptual models that provide a more holistic perspective to the focus of the study. We demonstrate that these frameworks for data gathering, analysis and presentation are related to the outcome of DVLD initiatives. And we integrate it with Heek's three-

way outcome categorisation of total failure, partial failure and success in order to provide a final classification (2002). Our second focus revolves around how we can understand why e-Government project outcomes (DVLD initiatives outcomes) occurred. For this, we describe development of the design-reality gap model and show how it can be used to analyse why DVLD initiatives largely failed. Its explanation is that DVLD initiatives failed due to too large gap between DVL design and institutional/country reality—a gap that remains unclosed during implementation, and which exists on several dimensions.

One could see that the DVLD initiative was a participatory project (private-public partnership) that ensure that the design and implementation process involve a broad range of stakeholders (Ministry of ICT, 2001). Taking a clue from the standard practices of the international agencies, other specific gaps recognised early in the Jordan's ICT-led initiative were somewhat reduced in order to increase the chances of DVLD success, though existing work practices, cultural, technical and socio-political influences still remain a 'quandary' (Ciborra, 2005). Combined together, the Jordan case demonstrates a total failure, as assumed by design-reality gap approach. Some of those certain dimensions resonate individual factors that earlier studies have considered. However, the design-reality approach symbolises an expansion beyond those studies because it is more methodical and inclusive; drawing together all the dispersed aspects of which earlier work has characteristically concentrated on only one or two items. It is also helpful to track the changing risks and likelihood of success or failure over ICT-inspired development project's lifecycle. It is more critical, illuminating the root cause of problems in a reliable way for all factors, and through reference to a strong theoretical underpinning that draws on sociological thoughts of technology. And it is also more contextual, avoiding the implicit "one-size-fits-all" belief that reinforces some earlier ICT-led development analyses and, instead, allowing a sensitivity not just to different national settings but to different institutional settings; a sensitivity that is mostly pertinent to the work on developing nations.

We therefore believe that this approach, if more widely used in the context of developing world by other researchers and by practitioners as a means to understand, and act on, the processes of DVL implementation, it offers the opportunity to address the persistently-high failure rate of e-Government-for-development projects. Therefore, when questioning how e-Government initiatives can be positioned in the developing context, it is important to consider consensual agreement, history, real work practices, technical, socio-political cultural factors, for the common good of any e-Government projects.

REFERENCES

Akrich, M. (1992). The description of technical objects. In *Shaping technology/building society*. Cambridge, MA: MIT Press.

Al-Jaghoub, S., & Westrup, C. (2003). Jordan and ICT-led development: Towards a competition state? *Information Technology & People*, *16*(1), 93–110. doi:10.1108/09593840310463032

Al-Omari, H. (2006). E-government architecture in Jordan: A comparative analysis. *Journal of Computer Science*, *2*(11), 846–852. doi:10.3844/jcssp.2006.846.852

Alomari, M. K. (2010). *Predictors for successful e-government adoption on the Hashemite Kingdom of Jordan: The deployment of an empirical evaluation based on citizen-centric perspectives*. (Unpublished Phd Thesis). Griffith University, Canberra, Australia.

Al Nagi, E., & Hamdan, M. (2009). Computerization and e-government implementation in Jordan: Challenges, obstacles and successes. *Government Information Quarterly*, *26*, 577–583. doi:10.1016/j.giq.2009.04.003

Avgerou, C. (2003). The link between ICT and economic growth in the discourse of development. In *Organizational information systems in the context of globalization*. Boston: Kluwer Academic Publishers. doi:10.1007/978-0-387-35695-2_23

Braa, J., & Hedberg, C. (2002). Developing district-based health care information systems. *The Information Society*, *18*(2), 113–127. doi:10.1080/01972240290075048

Caldow, J. (2001). *Seven e-government leadership milestones*. Washington, DC: IBM Institute for Electronic Government.

Castells, M. (1989). *The informational city: Information technology, economic restructuring and the urban regional process*. Oxford, UK: Blackwell.

Castells, M. (1997). *The information age: Economy, society and culture: The power of identity*. Oxford, UK: Blackwell.

Castells, M. (1998). *The end of millennium*. Oxford, UK: Blackwell.

Castell, M. (1999). *Information, technology, globalization and social development*. UNRISD Discussion Paper No. 114. UNRISD.

Castells, M. (2000). *The rise of the network society* (2nd ed.). Malden, MA: Blackwell.

Chadwick, A. (2006). Executives and bureaucracies: E-government. In *Internet politics: States, citizens and new communications technologies* (pp. 177–203). New York: Oxford University Press Inc.

Ciborra, C. (2003). *Unveiling e-government and development governing at a distance in the new war*. Information System Working Paper 126. London school of Economic and Political Science. Retrieved May 5, 2013 from www.is.lse.ac.uk/wp/pdf/wp126.pdf

Ciborra, C. (2002). *The labyrinths of information: Challenging the wisdom of systems*. Oxford, UK: Oxford University Press.

Ciborra, C. (2005). Interpreting e-government and development: Efficiency, transparency or governance at a distance? *Information Technology & People*, *18*(3), 260–279. doi:10.1108/09593840510615879

Cocchiglia, M., & Vernaschi, S. (2006). E-government for development. *Journal of E-Government*, *2*(2), 3–18. doi:10.1300/J399v02n02_02

Danowitz, A. K., Nassef, Y., & Goodman, S. E. (1995). Cyberspace across the Sahara: Computing in North Africa. *Communications of the ACM*, *38*(12), 23–28. doi:10.1145/219663.219674

El-Sawah, S., El Fattah Tharwat, A. A., & Rasmy, M. H. (2008). A quantitative model to predict the Egyptian ERP implementation success index. *Business Process Management Journal*, *14*(3), 288–306. doi:10.1108/14637150810876643

Elsheikh, Y., Cullenm, A., & Hobbs, D. (2008). E-government in Jordan: Challenges and opportunities. *Transforming Government: People. Process and Policy*, *2*(2), 83–103.

Escobar, A. (1995). *Encountering development: The making and unmaking of the third world*. Princeton, NJ: Princeton University Press.

Escobar, A. (2001). Culture sits in places: Reflections on globalism and subaltern strategies of localization. *Political Geography*, *20*(2), 139–174. doi:10.1016/S0962-6298(00)00064-0

Evans, D., & Yen, D. (2006). E-government: Evolving relationship of citizens and government, domestic, and international development. *Government Information Quarterly*, *23*, 207–235. doi:10.1016/j.giq.2005.11.004

Hawari, A., & Heeks, R. (2010). Explaining ERP failure in a developing country: A Jordanian case study. *Journal of Enterprise Information Management*, *23*(2), 135–160. doi:10.1108/17410391011019741

Heeks, R. (1999). Reinventing government in the information age. In *Reinventing government in the information age: International practice in IT-enabled public sector reform* (pp. 9–21). London: Routledge. doi:10.4324/9780203204962

Heeks, R. (2001). *Understanding e-governance for development*. Manchester, UK: University of Manchester.

Heeks, R. (2002). Information systems and developing countries: Failure, success, and local improvisations. *The Information Society: An International Journal*, *18*(2), 101–112. doi:10.1080/01972240290075039

Heeks, R. (2003). *Design-reality gap analysis*. Retrieved May 28, 2013 from www.egov4dev.org/success/techniques/idfailure_drg.shtml

Heeks, R. (2006). *Implementing and managing egovernment: An international text*. London: Sage.

Hofstede, G. (1997). *Cultures and organizations: Software of the mind*. New York: McGraw-Hill.

Hofstede, G. (2003). *Culture's consequences* (2nd ed.). London: Academic Press.

Hood, C., & Margetts, H. (2007). Exploring government's toolsheds. In *The tools of government in the digital age* (pp. 4–25). Basingstoke, UK: Palgrave.

ITU. (2008). *Electronic government for developing countires*. ICT Applications and Cybersecurity Division Policies and Strategies Department, ITU Telecommunication Development Sector.

Jaeger, P. T., & Thompson, K. M. (2003). E-government around the world: Lessons, challenges, and future directions. *Government Information Quarterly*, *20*, 389–394. doi:10.1016/j.giq.2003.08.001

Kanaan, R. K. (2009). *Making sense of e-government implementation in Jordan: A qualitative investigation*. Leicester, UK: De Montfort University.

Kleine, D., & Unwin, T. (2009). Technological revolution, evolution and new dependencies: What's new about ict4d? *Third World Quarterly*, *30*(5), 1045–1067. doi:10.1080/01436590902959339

Lips, M. (2010). Rethinking citizen-government relationships in the age of digital identity: Insights from research. *Information Polity*, *15*, 273–289.

Margetts, H. (2006). E-government in Britain—A decade on. *Parliamentary Affairs*, *59*(2), 250–265. doi:10.1093/pa/gsl003

Ministry of ICT. (2000). *Launching e-government in Jordan: Readiness and approach*. Retrieved May 4, 2013 from www.mopc.gov.jo/egovment_n_egoreport.htm

Ministry of ICT. (2001). *Implementing Jordan's information and communications technology strategies – 2002 work plan*. Amman, Jordan: Ministry of ICT.

MoICT. (2003a). *Ministry of information and communications technology web-site*. Retrieved May 3, 2013 from www.moict.gov.jo

MoICT. (2003b). *E-government program in Jordan*. Retrieved May 3, 2013 from www.moict.gov.jo/moict/program_overview.aspx

Ndou, V. D. (2004). E-government for developing countries: Opportunities and challenges. *The Electronic Journal on Information Systems in Developing Countries*, *18*(1), 1–24.

Nusseir, Y. (2001). *Science and technology and competitiveness: The seventh Jordanian science week: Science and technology as means for investment incentive and sustainability*. Amman, Jordan: The Higher Council for Science and Technology.

Rajapakse, J., & Seddon, P. (2005a). *Why ERP may not be suitable for organizations in developing countries in Asia* (Working Paper No. 121). Retrieved May 28, 2013 from www.pacis-net.org/file/2005/121.pdf

Reach. (2001). *Launching Jordan's software & IT industry*. Amman, Jordan: Reach.

Roy, S. (2005). *Globalisation, ICT and developing nations*. New Delhi: Sage.

Sauer, C. (1999). Deciding the future for IS failures: Not the choice you might think. In *Rethinking management information systems*. Oxford, UK: Oxford University Press.

Sen, A. (1999). *Development as freedom*. Oxford, UK: Oxford University Press.

Schuppan, T. (2009). E-government in developing countries: Experiences from sub-Saharan Africa. *Government Information Quarterly*, (26): 118–127. doi:10.1016/j.giq.2008.01.006

Shields, P., & Servaes, J. (1989). The impact of the transfer of information technology on development. *The Information Society*, *6*(1–2), 47–57. doi:10.1080/01972243.1989.9960068

Shoib, G., & Nandhakumar, J. (2003). Cross-cultural IS adoption in multinational corporation. *Information Technology for Development*, *10*, 249–260. doi:10.1002/itdj.1590100404

Silcock, R. (2001). What is e-government? *Parliamentary Affairs, 54*, 88–101. doi:10.1093/pa/54.1.88

Stiglitz, J. (2012). *The price of inequality: How today's divided society endangers our future.* New York: W. W. Norton & Company.

Suchman, L. (1987). *Plans and situated actions.* Cambridge, UK: Cambridge University Press.

Thompson, M. (2004). Discourse, 'development' and the 'digital divide': ICT and the World Bank. *Review of African Political Economy, 31*(99), 103–123. doi:10.1080/0305624042000258441

Thompson, M. P. A. (2005). ICT, power, and developmental discourse: A critical analysis. *The Electronic Journal of Information Systems in Developing Countries, 20*(4), 1–26.

UN. (2004). *Global e-government readiness report 2004–Towards access for opportunity.* New York: UN.

UNDP. (2000a). *Jordan human development report 2000.* New York: UNDP.

UNDP. (2000b). *Project of the government of Jordan. Information Technology in Higher Education, SPPD document, project number: JOR/2000/001/A/08/13.* New York: UNDP.

Unwin, T. (2009a). Introduction. In *ICT4D: Information and communication technology for development.* Cambridge, UK: Cambridge University Press.

UNESCO. (2005). *Towards knowledge societies.* Paris: UNESCO Publishing.

Unwin, T. (2009b). Development agendas and the place of ICTs. In *ICT4D: Information and communication technology for development.* Cambridge, UK: Cambridge University Press.

Wade, R. H. (2002). Bridging the digital divide—New route to development or new form of dependency? *Global Governance, 8,* 443–466.

Wade, R. H. (2004). Bridging the digital divide: New route to development or new form of dependency. In C. Avgerou, C. Ciborra, & F. Land (Eds.), *The social study of information and communication technology: Innovation, actors, and contexts* (pp. 185–206). Oxford, UK: Oxford University Press.

Webster, F. (2006). *Theories of the information society* (3rd ed.). London: Routledge.

Weerakkody, V., & El-Haddadeh, R. (2011). Exploring the complexities of e-government implementation and diffusion in a developing country: Some lessons from the State of Qatar. *Journal of Enterprise Information Management, 24*(2), 172–196. doi:10.1108/17410391111106293

Wilson, E. J., & Wong, K. R. (2007). *Negotiating the net in Africa: The politics of internet diffusion.* London: Rienner.

World Bank. (2012). *E-government.* Retrieved from http//go.worldbank.org/6WT3UPVG80

Wynn, E., & deLyra, J. (2000). A strange attractor in the chaos of global IS development. In *Proceedings of the IFIP WG9.4 Conference 2000.* Cape Town, South Africa: IFIP.

ADDITIONAL READING

Lee, J.H., Kim, H.J., & Ahn, M.J. (2011). The willingness of e-Government service adoption by business users: The role of offline service quality and trust in technology, doi:10.1016/j.giq.2010.07.007. *Government Information Quarterly,* xxx–xxx, Article in press

Maumbe, B., & Ntombovuyo, N. (2009). Crafting an E-Government Development Model for South Africa: A Strategic New Direction for the Western Cape Province, Proceedings of the International Conference on Information Resources Management (CONF-IRM), paper 7, Retrieved April 30, 2011, from http://aisel.aisnet.org/confirm2009/7

Mutula, S. M. (2011). A model for building e-Government trust. In Adomi, E.E (Ed.) (2011). Frameworks for ICT policy: government, social and legal issues. Hershey: Information Science Reference.

Papadopoulou, P., Nikolaidou, M., & Martakos, D. (2010). What Is Trust in E-Government? A Proposed Typology. Proceedings of the 43rd Hawaii International Conference on System Sciences (HICSS-43- 2010), Koloa, Kauai, Hawai.

Pardo, T., & Styrin, E. (2010). Digital Government Implementation: A Comparative Study in USA and Russia, Americas Conference on Information Systems, *AMCIS 2010 Proceedings,* Paper 330, Retrieved April 19, 2011, from http://aisel.aisnet.org/amcis2010/330.

KEY TERMS AND DEFINITIONS

Developing World: This is an economy that has limited developed (low) standards of living, undeveloped (or partialy developed) industrial base and very low Human Development Index (HDI).

E-Government: This is the use of Information and Communications Technologies in the different public service business value chains.

ICT4D: This is an acronym standing for ICT for Development – Initiatives done through the utilization of ICTs in a bid to achieve socio-economic development.

ICTs: This is an acronym that stands for Information and Communications Technology – detailing technology platforms utilized in the management of information through its 'Information Lifecycle'.

Information Age: These are times where everything in the socio-economic values chains is being driven by information and ICTs virtually lie at the center of everything.

Chapter 21
What is Needed to Advance Transformational E–Government and Why:
A Different Approach to Project Management

Shauneen Furlong
University of Liverpool, UK

ABSTRACT

Throughout the millennia, project management methodologies were developed, and as projects were completed, both theoreticians and practitioners contributed to the development of project management science and codification. Throughout this time, project management science grappled with the problem of delineating project activities from on-going operational activities. Projects require project management while operations require business process management or operations management (PMI, 2008). In the project methodology world, a project is defined as unique, temporary, a definite start and finish (PMI, 2008). Without this definition, the science of project management cannot be applied. It is this definition that provides the credence for the creation and application of project management processes, tools, and techniques. However, the science of project management exists irrespective of a project. In fact, it is the application of project management to any endeavor that creates a project. Effective project management that will drive the design and implementation of transformational e-Government must be enhanced. This chapter proposes project management enhancements to the design, direction, management, and implementation of e-Government projects that focus on project problems rather than methodological

DOI: 10.4018/978-1-4666-4900-2.ch021

processes. The enhanced project management solution provides the tools and educates the user to take into account the impact of the holistic, synergistic challenges and barriers that surround and influence e-Government projects – heretofore, in an unmanageable way that has inhibited change instead of promoting it. The enhanced project management solution is "exogenous" of the e-Government solution; it is its external driver.

INTRODUCTION

Transformational e-Government is the continuous innovation in the delivery of services, citizen participation and governance through the transformation of external and internal relationships by the use of technology; especially the Internet. When introduced, it offered the hope and promise to revitalize and modernize public services; reinvigorate and improve services to citizens, business and governments; and, create an exciting environment for employees to work and contribute. Countries, world-wide are inexorably engaged and urged forward by both push and pull motivational pressures to use technology to improve democratic participation, social harmony and economic sustainability. However, it has not achieved the international worldwide success anticipated. E-Government has high rates of failure; by some measures, more than 60-80% are partial or total failures (United Nations, 2003).

E-Government and especially transformational e-Government progress remains slow and halting and shackled to time honoured approaches to project management, especially in the information communication technology (ICT) domain. (e-Government being the traditional transactional and service focused improvements through the application of ICTs whereas transformational e-Government encompasses the reform and modernization of the business process reengineering opportunities and enterprise wide reform as well as what and how the government achieves its mandate). Ineffective project management is one of most significant reasons for transformational e-Government failure (Aikens, 2012b; Misuraca, 2009). There are a number of reasons and ex-

amples for transformational e-Government project failures including: the lack of capacity to manage unanticipated transparent and concealed organizational opposition; the inability to effectively and precisely identify current, changing, disparate, and conflicting key information requirements; and lack of insight into the obstacles in obtaining parochially coveted information. These are in addition to a recent (2012) review of literature (developed and developing countries) that outlines the most common issues and problems that cause e-Government failure to be: cultural barriers; infrastructure; resources; socio-economic barriers; security and privacy; and e-integration (Zhao, 2012).

The objective of this chapter is to introduce the need for and provide enhancements to the well-established international project management bodies of knowledge; these enhancements will enable transformational e-Government project managers to be more effective, results oriented and successful. This chapter reports upon the e-Government failure rate, and project management's contribution, and proposes changes based upon an international compendium of ten transformational e-Government challenges that revamp traditional project management methodologies by redirecting their focus from project management processes to project management products, results, and accountability.

This chapter also introduces the concept that project management does not begin with the creation of a project. This redirection is based not on the definition of a project but rather on the recognition that project management (particularly ICT work) means working in a milieu of complexity and uncertainty wherein the application of the science of project management to any endeavour thereby creates a project. Futuristic projects will be created; they will not be defined; they will be created by evolution, unintended consequences, and iteration that solve problems and produces project results. This fundamentally different concept challenges the current assumption and practice that insists that a project is defined before the science of project management is applied. Accordingly it deemphasizes; streamlines; and prioritizes processes that flow out of project definition. Instead it targets project management toward problem solving, results, and accountability. It places individuals and interaction over processes; project iteration over project life-cycles; and simplistic 'perpetual beta' results over full operational sign-off.

Since the science of project management is based on the premise of the existence of projects, project management processes are built that start, plan, execute, control, and end projects. And thus the emphasis of the processes is on the techniques and science of project methodology as opposed to the emphasis on successful delivery of project products, services, or results and on the solving of problems and barriers to project success. This chapter offers enhancements to project management methodologies to contribute to transformational e-Government success and postulates that the science of project management is required to bring a project to life.

The next section presents the background which outlines the context and literature review supporting the need for more effective project management. This section is followed by a discussion of the current project management methodologies, problems and solutions, and introduces a compendium of 10 synergistic and holistic e-Government challenges that are not currently effectively served by project management. This chapter concludes with a section on future research and a conclusion that confirms the need for a modern up-to-date relevant methodology that highlights the challenges of our current age.

BACKGROUND

Transformational e-Government has not been the success hoped for around the world and a number of the barriers preventing success have been identified and analyzed (Weerakkody, Janssen & Dwivedi, 2011; Sharif & Irani, 2010; Ziemann & Loos, 2009; Dawes, 2009; United Nations, 2010; United Nations, 2008; World Bank, 2002; Nordfors, Ericson, Lindell & Lapidus, 2009; Oxford Institute, 2007). It has been harder, slower and more complicated to deliver than what was originally expected, specifically from a business transformational agenda (BCS Thought Leadership, 2005; Roy, 2006). Transformational e-Government promised hope for government transformation, public sector renewal and revitalization of the role of bureaucracies in the 21st century. e-Government delivered primarily on the transactional success of using the Internet to allow citizens closer and more direct access to government programs (Weerakkody, Janssen & Dwivedi, 2011); important and valuable, but not of the significance and benefit that was predicted. Transformational e-Government remains slow and halting (Aikins, 2012b) and shackled to the time honoured approaches of managing existing organizational assets rather than reaching out to create new management capacities that business transformation demands and technology affords.

Even in Canada, where e-Government was rated by Accenture number one in the world for five years in a row (Accenture, 2005, 2006, 2007; Government of Canada Foreign Affairs & International Trade, 2006), it is seen as being primarily a transactional success as opposed to a transformational one (Roy, 2006). Internationally, there has been a high and critical failure rate related to IT solutions (Aikins, 2012b; Fraser, 2006). More recently the failure in IT solutions that was the bane of transactional processing is now appearing in e-Government initiatives (Heeks, 2008; Arif, 2008; Janowski, Estevez & Ojo, 2007; Aikins, 2012b). E-Government failures are often hushed up (Heeks, 2003) and as Misuraca (2009) points out, the majority of e-Government projects are failures as high as 70-80% and are not meeting the 'messianic' expectations. Failures are costly; as per Irani, Al-Sebie & Elliman (2006), the United Kingdom Parliamentary Office of Science and Technology reported that cancelled or over-budgeted e-Government projects were greater than 1.5 billion British pounds.

There are a number of reasons for the lack of transformational e-Government success, including unanticipated organizational opposition, difficulties in communicating requirements and obstacles to obtaining information from different government departments and agencies (Kamal, Weerakkody & Irani, 2011). However, there is some support for the belief that one of the most significant reasons for transformational e-Government failure is ineffective project management (Aikins, 2012b; Misuraca, 2009). The literature and this chapter refer to the dearth of peer-reviewed information on the effective role of project management and its impact on transformational e-Government project success even though there are non-peer reviewed business publications and country audits (British Computer Society, 2004; Fraser, 2006) that identify ineffective project management as an important cause of ICT failure.

The literature review finding is that ineffective project management is a leading cause of e-Government failure. And the reason for this ineffectiveness is a result of the use of the traditional project management methodologies that do not meet the demands of transformational e-Government for results, accountability, and problem solving.

The following introduces the current project management approach as it applies to project management as a discipline and science, and why it has been less than effective. It does not undertake to examine in detail the limitations of the project management approach (with the application and recycling of the following processes and knowledge areas) to the comprehensive management involved in managing and successfully delivering an e-Government project. Governments continue to rely heavily (in the absence of an alternative) on the codified concepts of project management in its quest to develop and implement transactional and transformational e-Government projects in spite of the project high failure rate.

This section discusses project management as a holistic discipline as opposed to an examination of the specific criteria and iterative approaches used in developing project management methodologies. Project management science is described in the North American focused PMBOK and the European focused PRINCE2 (2009). The fundamental scientific codification sets out project management concepts in terms of project processes and project knowledge areas. By cycling through the processes and knowledge areas project management spans the full array of information that must be merged to develop an e-Government project. PMBOK 2008, the 4th edition describes the process groups to be initiating, planning, executing, monitoring and controlling, and closing. The knowledge areas are integration, scope, time, cost, quality, human resource, communications, risk and procurement.

Project management as derived from generic project management methodologies is a systems approach to planning scheduling and controlling project activities; it began its modern accelerated in growth in the 1960s (Kerzner, 2001). The systems approach creates a project management framework that is constructed from process groupings and knowledge areas. The implementation of this approach ensures that the work of project management activities is performed efficiently and effectively and is measured by such features as planning, cost, schedule management, scope control, and communications.

In transformational e-Government, the project management systems approach is not enough. Instead, in transformational e-Government, project management must discover the interrelated sets of challenges and barriers that impede transformational e-Government project success and respond to and cope with them from a 'results achieved' perspective. The project management systems approach must become a basic entry level to the transformational e-Government project management regime and project results must be the project drivers that are measured by the effective management of objectives, stakeholders, clients, technical and subject matter experts, resources, and functional support services (Kerzner, 2001).

There are many reasons cited for project management failure and many of them are attributed to one or more breakdowns in the traditional project management systems approach (Aikins, 2012). But when a project meets key stakeholder (user) requirements, many other project short-comings are overlooked such as cost overruns, late schedules, and scope creep. However, in the author's opinion, transformational e-Government project management must result in success by ensuring that project management evolves from a system activity approach to a system results approach that starts with identifying an interrelated set of transformational e-Government project barriers and challenges. This research is focused on informationally enhancing the project management process in order to upgrade the traditional systems activities approach and support the project results orientation.

To address the difficulties currently experienced specifically in e-Government projects, it can be argued that modern project management growth that began in the 1960s (Kerzner, 2001) now needs to be radically accelerated; become less process bound and more results driven. Transformational e-Government project management could take on the functions and features of other management professions similar to the example of accounting and finance. By comparison, accounting equates to enhanced supporting project processes and finance equates to project results. Processes supporting results should far outweigh processes supporting activities.

Transformational e-Government project management should ensure that information management and information technology (IT) that has long been relied upon to assist governments in carrying out their mandates (Movahedi, Tan, & Lavassani, 2010) delivers on the demand for 'faster, better, cheaper' IT solutions. These demands are not abating as governments evolve from transactional management to e-Government transformation. Creating transformational e-Government citizen centric solutions and organizations requires (Schwester, 2009; Elliman & Irani, 2007):

- focusing on and targeting citizen centric requirements, cultures, and mores;
- responding to a broad and deep plethora of specific citizen demands;
- using technology as an agent to integrate technical architectures and information structures, and information from subject matter experts;
- managing technology to blend new and legacy systems, redesigned processes, and differently motivated human resources, while supposedly achieving cost and time savings;
- recognizing the lack of tools and skilled resources; and,
- evolving governments from paternalistic and hierarchical structures to collaborative and networked organizations.

Transformational e-Government project resources are consumed in enormous quantities and qualified, certified personnel are employed in planning and delivering transformational e-Government projects; still projects fail. Consequently and by default, attention must be focused on the effectiveness of project management tools -- generic project management guides and methodologies. As well the wide-spread development and use of bespoke methodologies instead of the use of existing generic project management methodologies is evidence of the need to find effective methodologies. It has been estimated that there are 1000 'brand name' methodologies used by organizations globally (Wells, 2012).

Further, even when project management is declared to be successful (the completed iron triangle), often less than a third of projects deliver any benefits. Perhaps only 10% of projects deliver what was wanted (Young, 2012).

The overview of trends in the development and use of project management methodologies starts with the management of projects in early history. Throughout the millennia project management techniques were developed and deployed (Gauthier, 2012). For example, they were used in 2570 BCE to build the Great Pyramid of Giza and in 208 CE they were used to build the great Wall in China. Then, as now, elements of project management science were codified: for instance, in 1917 the Gantt chart was developed; in 1958 the program evaluation review technique (PERT) was adopted; in 2008 the fourth edition of PMBOK was released; and PRINCE2 was released in 2009 (OGC, 2009).

Throughout this era as projects were completed and the science of project management evolved, the problem of delineating project activities from ongoing operations activities proved to be essential to the identification, development, and codification of project management bodies of knowledge. In the past, as now project activities are deemed to be different than operations activities. PMBOK 2008 states that this delineation is required because projects require project management while operations require business process management or operations management (PMI 2008).

Hence, in the project methodology world, it is concluded that a project must be defined before project management activity can begin. A long established definition of a project is ascertained to be that a project is unique in nature, temporary, with a definite beginning and end, and its purpose is said to create a unique product, service, or result (PMI, 2008; Kerzner, 2001). And it is this definition that provides the credence for current project management methodologies. Since, if no project exists, project management cannot exist, and there is, therefore, no basis for a meaningful theory of project management. The definition of a project, then, is the platform on which the project management bodies of knowledge are created.

Based upon the definition of a project and the differentiation of project work from operational work, project management - as defined in generic project management methodologies, is a systems approach to planning scheduling and controlling project activities; it began its modern accelerated in growth in the 1960s (Kerzner, 2001). This systems approach created project management frameworks and methodologies that are reflected in process groupings and knowledge areas.

Trends in the system approach processes lead to the creation, control, and analysis of an array of data points that often overwhelm and even misinform the project manager, the project team, and key project stakeholders. The systemic processes are primarily compliance and administratively driven and the array of data points that they generate are difficult to maintain, analyse, and distribute. For example such data points are;

- **PVB:** planned value
- **PMB:** performance measurement baseline
- **BAC:** budget at completion
- **EV:** earned value
- **AC:** actual cost
- **SV:** schedule variance
- **CV:** cost variance
- **SPI:** schedule performance index
- **CPI:** cost performance index
- **EAC:** cost at completion
- **ETC:** estimate to complete the remaining work
- **TCPI:** to complete performance index

Other project processes create data points for cost benefit analysis; control charts, bench marking, statistical sampling, and flowcharting. A full outline of project management processes can be found in two world-wide methodologies; 'A guide to the Project Management of Knowledge' (PMI, 2008) or PRINCE2 (OCG, 2009).

In all, the trend in the systems approach to project management now ensures that project management methodologies are replete with, knowledge areas processes, activities, inputs, outputs, tools and techniques. The objective of the methodologies is to ensure that the compliance and administrative work of project management is performed efficiently and effectively and this includes such features as planning, cost, schedule management, scope control, and communications.

Transformational e-Government project management has adopted the broad project management components such as standardized frameworks, governance, certifications, and qualifications that were developed in the past and in different industries. And academics, researchers, and practitioners continue to compile knowledge, skills, tools, and techniques that form the basis of the science of project management. This science has been encoded into project methodologies or guides that are generally accepted by theoreticians and practitioners and they are heavily promoted by government decision-makers and contracting authorities. But most practitioners perceive that the prime purpose of project management methodologies is to manage administration and compliance rather than support and guidance (Wells, 2012).

Hence, transformational e-Government project management must turn the trend in project management. The systems based approach incorporated in the generic project management methodologies is not enough for transformational e-Government. Instead, in transformational e-Government; project management must become more results focused and less prescription focused. It must discover any interrelated and holistic sets of challenges and barriers that impede transformational e-Government project success; it must respond to and cope with them from a 'results achieved' perspective. The project management systems approach must de-

volve to a basic entry level to the transformational e-Government project management regime and project success and results must be the project drivers that are measured by the effective management of objectives, stakeholders, clients, technical and subject matter experts, resources, and functional support services (Kerzner, 2001).

Transformational e-Government projects success and results rather than the adherence to project processes must provide the assurance that information management and information technology (IT), that has long been relied upon to assist governments in carrying out their mandates (Movahedi, Tan, & Lavassani, 2011), delivers on the demand for 'faster, better, cheaper' government solutions. These demands are not abating as governments evolve from transactional management to e-Government transformation.

Of the reasons cited for project management failure many of them are attributed to one or more breakdowns in the traditional project management systems approach (Aikins, 2012b). However, in the author's opinion, transformational e-Government project management must result in success by ensuring that project management evolves from a system activity approach to a system results approach that starts with identifying an interrelated set of transformational e-Government project barriers and challenges. This research is focused on informationally enhancing the project management process in order to upgrade the traditional systems activities approach and support the project results orientation.

To address the difficulties currently experienced specifically in e-Government projects, it can be argued that modern project management growth that began in the 1960s (Kerzner, 2001) now needs to be radically accelerated; become less process bound and more results driven. Transformational e-Government project management could take on the functions and features of other management professions similar to the example of accounting and finance. By comparison, accounting equates to enhanced project processes and finance equates to project results. Processes supporting results should far outweigh processes supporting activities.

E-GOVERNMENT PROJECT MANAGEMENT METHODOLOGIES: PROBLEMS AND SOLUTIONS

The current more popular international project management methodologies, PRINCE2 and PMBOK, along with a litany of others, do not meet the needs of e-Government. E-Government failure is disappointing, and much research has been dedicated to examine why and if project management could be the culprit. Clearly, project management plays a significant role. This paper introduces the proposition that current parlance and management culture accepts that the science of project management is only enacted once a project has been identified; common practice does not acknowledge that it is the application of the science of project management to any operational endeavour that creates a specific project. The project is born through the application of the project management principles by bringing rigour and discipline and specificity to a challenging and complex, though often vague, operational endeavour and objective. In addition, the science of project management expressed through popular methodologies does not address nor assist with the synergistic compendium of ten international barriers to e-Government success recently studied (Furlong, 2011; Furlong, 2012).

This chapter describes these barriers and introduces how project management methodologies fail to address them and how an e-Government tailored project management solution could mitigate them. In fact, this paper concludes that these elements must be tackled in order to advance upon the transformational e-Government agenda that so many countries strive to attain.

This section outlines the current situation and the inadequacy of the current project management methodologies and their failings; introduces the compendium of ten barriers each requiring attention; and, offers preliminary solutions to governments and commercial organizations to digest.

By way of explanation, this paper focused on two internationally used project management methodologies. The PMBOK Guide (PMI, 2008) and PRINCE2 (OCG, 2009) provide roadmaps for project managers to deliver projects with neither methodology being the complete solution for the project management world. PMBOK gives a wider perspective to project management, while PRINCE2 gives a more delivery-based approach.

In these world-wide methodologies and other more parochial ones, methodologies, time-honoured project management processes associated with project integration, scope, schedule, cost, quality, resource, communications, risk, and procurement are often used as safeguards that split management and control of the projects and thereby water-down accountability for project development and implementation success. In no case is there a domain within the methodologies that directly and specifically provides the transformational e-Government project manager with the tools to cope with the intrinsic problems that impede transformational e-Government (Furlong, 2011; Furlong, 2012).

The objective of this paper is revamp project management methodologies by transforming them from process-bound mechanisms to a problem and results oriented instrument. Akin to the early medical profession's emphasis on procedure (e.g. in order to preclude the adage that the operation was a success but the patient died) the project management profession has too long suffered from the use of project management methodologies that focus on procedures and processes instead of those that focus on results and accountability. Futuristic transformational e-Government project management methodologies must contribute to the successful management of transformational e-Government projects. They must move well beyond the generic body of knowledge that is generally recognized as good practice. Instead, the enhanced methodologies must address the very caveat that existing methodologies hedge against; that is, the embracement of the responsibility for management to obtain successful results for transformational e-Government projects. The enhanced methodologies must reach above and beyond the goals to provide professional project management certification; standardization of processes, skills, tools, and techniques; and ethical codes of conduct. They must address a higher objective. The required methodology must enhance the science of transformational e-Government project management so that the project team can be held accountable for results achieved. The project manager and team are not stewards of the administrative procedures; they are responsible for project success and outcomes.

Various key transformational e-Government organizations (United Nations, 2010; West, 2007) have completed studies that identify the causes of transformational e-Government project failure and, just as importantly, they have identified, described, and analyzed the reasons for project development and implementation success. Current project management methodologies unwittingly allow the project manager to escape his accountability by retreating behind the mantra - 'we're on budget; we're on time; you changed the requirements'. These processes protect him at the expense of project results oriented success as opposed to process oriented success.

Definition of the Compendium of 10 International Challenges to Transformational E-Government Success

The following summarizes the author's compendium of ten international challenges and barriers (resulting from PhD research and a survey with 67 countries) that prohibit e-Government transformation (Furlong, 2011), and offers enhancements to the project management process to address these

limitations in an e-Government environment. The author postulates that the complete compendium of challenges must be addressed (over and above the traditional project management activities) for any chance of e-Government progress and success.

Requirement to Manage Diverse and Conflicting Stakeholder Interests within a Governance Framework

Stakeholder interests are usually conflicting because e-Government applications are usually developed with one or more departments and central agencies. Each of these departments and agencies has a unique legislative mandate, accountability regime, culture, history and background, and more recently security requirements. .

Challenge to Continuously Adapt to and Blend Technology, People and Processes

Today's system environment is more organic that it was in the past; previously, system solutions were applied to a corporate service environment. Today's systems are at the core of company performance, not on the periphery. They are significantly affected by evolving priorities and circumstances, and are more integrated with the operational environment including technological developments, the capacity of the resource experts, and constantly changing and evolving business processes.

Outdated Business Models that Reward Traditional Applications

Most business models do not recognize that collaborative and unprecedented solutions do not meet the criteria for performance measurement targets, accurate costing and resource utilization, and work plan deliverables whose solutions are not known until they are negotiated and well into the implementation stage. Promises of cost and resource reductions along with improved efficiency and effectiveness gains the funder's attention more than promises of transformation and innovation.

System Development Models Affected by Political Realities and a New Relationship with the Private Sector

Most system development models do not recognize the 'stop and start' reality of projects affected by political cycles and funding priorities, and the need for system development fragments to be reused instead of continuously 'starting over'. Though cancelling projects is generally due to changing systems objectives, it is critical to recognize the waste of precious resources and time, and the inability to recover and reuse these efforts. However, public service has been impacted significantly through private sector contracting and outsourcing arrangements. The integration of private and public sector resources is now mandatory.

Lack of Access to Lessons Learned and a Body of Knowledge for Government Wide Projects

Project managers are designing and implementing system solutions that are often unprecedented and government wide, and yet they have no facility to neither access the knowledge nor benefit from the experience gained from other project managers in similar circumstances. The problem is that there is no way to harness previous experience and no demand to conduct and access lessons learned.

Promises of Interoperability, Integration, and Cost and Resource Savings

The e-Government environment is predicated upon a collaborative and partnership based environment that requires sharing both work and accountability responsibilities, and it is usually argued (and ultimately funded) under a banner of promised cost savings and resource reductions.

Proliferation of Information and the Challenge to Judiciously Access and Manage Information

The information age exacerbates project management because of the massive and exponentially produced data that must be sorted out to effectively implement system solutions. The interconnectedness of information and system requirements is so overwhelming that projects suffer from the weight of information. Mining through this data to retrieve the relevant information produces a 'spin and churn' that can be non-productive; and this along with the lack of authoritative control to wind through the layers of information can derail the project.

Lack of a Comprehensive Holistic Approach to Project Management as the Driving Force

Project management often plays the role of arbitrator, as it is often the agent that brings the disparate parties together to deliver a solution that was not driven by either party. This is usually the case with citizen centric applications as they cross the program interests of each of the contributing organizations. Project management needs to drive the solution to change the business processes of the affected departments and turn the solution into a government wide enterprise.

Limited Access to Vital Subject Matter Expertise

Within governments, knowledge is either so vastly spread or not available that it is difficult for the project manager to understand the implications of systems design. The knowledgeable personnel are difficult to locate and approach given hierarchical and organizational limitations, and are frequently reassigned and no longer accessible.

Organizational Environment not Presupposed to Enterprise Wide Transformation

Departments do not necessarily act as units of a government enterprise; they are vertically based with individual objectives and resource reward mechanisms. Accountability of each department is to its Minister and senior officials, and to the government acts for which it was created.

Description of the Potential Project Management Improvements to Address the Compendium of 10 International Challenges to Transformational E-Government Success

The following section discusses the key enhancements required to project management methodologies to transform them from administrative and compliance processes to results and accountability driven mechanisms.

Requirement to Manage Diverse and Conflicting Stakeholder Interests within a Governance Framework

Project management within transformational e-Government is currently a staff function that incorporates the established project management methodologies that are in use throughout the government project centers of excellence or other such government management control units. However, this staff function must integrate with the work standards and processes applicable to particular governmental operating units. The interaction of the project staff function and the operating unit line function is a key stakeholder requirement, particularly when the situation is complicated by conflicting stakeholder interests.

The existing methodologies handle this requirement by leaving the project manager and team to sort out the procedures for working amid the danger of duplicate activities; unclear or vague responsibilities; and confused reporting lines. They do little to ensure that senior and other appropriate levels of management effectively participate in the development, delivery, and operations of transformational e-Government portfolios of programs and projects. Rating and weighting the impact of stakeholders throughout the life of the project is key to project management success.

The project initiating and planning processes described in the project management methodologies do not effectively lay out how the project team can gain a complete understanding of the existing transformational e-Government processes and how the stakeholders interact externally and internally. The process of collecting requirements and creating a project scope document and a work breakdown structure does not sufficiently take into account the impact that stakeholders have throughout the life of the project.

An information enhanced project management aid could categorize and 'weigh' the stakeholders influence. It could relate their interests to reporting requirements. It could monitor and incorporate changes to their interests and changing degree of influence. It could provide 'intelligence' to the project manager on the implications of accommodating changing interests; i.e. impact on other interests and additional time, cost, and reporting requirements. It could highlight to the governance committees the complexities and interdependence of stakeholder interests and the impact on project success and accountability without impeding development. It could highlight, for example, the gap between the interest in considering a government as a single enterprise versus the reality of managing different and competing departmental or ministerial interests and accountabilities. It could also relate interests of the delivery agent (responsible department) with the product – for example, to highlight the inappropriate assignment of accountability to a third party not directly involved in the product line.

Challenge to Continuously Adapt to and Blend Technology, People and Processes

Transformational e-Government projects are dependent upon robust and flexible ICTs; therefore, transformational e-Government project management methodologies should include specific procedures to reflect this reality. The procedures should ensure that project managers consult with industry to test the viability of the proposed ICT enabled change; outline the need for a comprehensive and well-evidenced examination of the use of applications for meeting requirements of proposed transformational changes; and include an open and constructive relationship with ICT suppliers and providers. ICTs need to remain aligned with e-Government technology, people and processes.

An informationally enhanced project management methodology could highlight the impact of systems and projects on organizational business processes and the issues associated with personnel revising their workplace practices. It could assist in mapping and managing the business process changes resulting from the implementation and evolution of the project. It could also relate the organizational objectives to those particular practices, and identify potential technology enabled support; for example, offer an automated checklist to the project manager to recognize the organizational and personnel impact. It could revisit the changes and implications along the project implementation process as they are not static and are adjusted as the project evolves. Ultimately, technology could be designed to contribute to the core performance as these systems form the new basis of the organization's capacity to meet its mandate.

Outdated Business Models that Reward Traditional Applications

Transformational e-Government business models must incorporate the decision-making structure that ensures strong and effective leadership of the ICT effort in support of the business change. Current practices too often reward applications that are easier to measure or understand or cost; not necessarily criteria that leads to complicated innovative changes for a transformational objective.

If the feasibility analysis and project approval process could become part of the overall project management methodology, technological improvements could be developed to help support a shift in the business model criteria to fund the more controversial e-Government projects. This could involve changing the criteria from performance specificity and delivery measures to rewarding more innovative and transformational based applications.

System Development Models Affected by Political Realities and a New Relationship with the Private Sector

Key project stakeholders are interested in a project's results and products rather than the procedures that were used to carry out the project. Project delivery is a product that enables sponsors to assess the rate and quality of progress; and it permits the users to ascertain that their original request represents their actual needs, and reflective improvements.

The project management methodology could be expanded to subsume system development approaches that meet partnership and transformational solutions. Technology could be provided to assist the management of information based projects, which would address the system elements and project management environment, and contribute to the negotiated effort of finding and delivering a project based solution.

System development and the identification of requirements has become a more 'moving target'. The relationship between government officials who express their requirements and the private sector capacity to lock them down is strained. The scope and requirements shift is due to changing political interests, funding levels, relationships, accountability regimes, resource availability, and individual influences just to name a few, and this is becoming increasingly difficult for the private sector to carry the cost of chasing requirements.

Lack of Access to Lessons Learned and a Body of Knowledge for Government Wide Projects

There are many reasons why lessons learned are not a factor: lack of time; incentives; resources; management support; the capacity and knowledge to collect store and access the information. Useful lessons learned often focus around risks, issues, change requests, and ICT provider concerns. But just as importantly, methods of ensuring that project managers see the value in applying lessons learned to the uniqueness of their specific project. They must include their evaluation in the scope of 'getting things done'. Analyzing lessons learned, in the form of a formal literature review, for example often results in getting things right the first time.

Recent popular language discusses a 'wicked problem' to describe a problem that is difficult or impossible to solve because of incomplete, contradictory, and changing requirements that are often difficult to recognize. The term 'wicked' is used, not in the sense of evil but rather its resistance to resolution. Moreover, because of complex interdependencies, the effort to solve one aspect of a wicked problem may reveal or create other problems.

Project managers are rewarded for getting things done, and in this current regime action is better than thought or discussion – the perceived error of focusing on doing as being more important than reflecting. But lessons learned can lead to correct action and contribute to getting these things done and they can avoid the cost and effort of project rework through planning, training, and communicating.

Lessons learned are not just theories; they can achieve results and cannot be ignored as they have in the past. The new methodology would ensure that the reflection on lessons learned would become inherent.

A key feature where additional information could benefit the project manager is in having access to the experience and knowledge attained from actual 'on-the-ground' applications. The project management methodology could be expanded to support the overall project management and implementation of new solutions, and contributing to building a repository of experience could be of immense value towards the successful implementation of future projects. This approach could encompass the need to access and document experiences from individual projects for a historical database but more importantly, targeted as the agent to influence the design and implementation of future projects.

Promises of Interoperability, Integration, and Cost And Resource Savings

Interoperability, integration, and cost and resource savings in transformational e-Government requires a multi-layered multi-faceted backroom technology that is required to participate in a technology-driven public sector economy, and yet delivering upon pre-established savings or systemic approaches before deliverables are available often leads to inaccurate estimating that damages the transformational agenda.

The project management methodology could be strengthened to provide project managers and governments the tools to achieve interoperability and integration. (Focusing on achieving cost savings is another matter, and perhaps not reasonable in the short term due to the high costs required to design and implement new systems.) Using technology to have access to the information required to deliver on interoperability and integration would be extremely helpful to the project manager. Having automated access to an understanding of the systems and processes required to accomplish interoperability and their interrelationships, as well as the business processes and systems to achieve integration would contribute greatly to e-Government progress and ultimate success.

Proliferation of Information and the Challenge to Judiciously Access and Manage Information

The transformational e-Government project manager faces, from the project outset, the onerous task of compiling indigenous information associated with managing a project. The project manager has to develop and manage all the detail associated with the processes, dates, tasks, costs, and people. He spends his time addressing these requirements and serving another master rather than 'getting the job done' and driving the project to success. However, these labours apply to both internal and external activities constantly focusing on administration and chasing estimates and managing relationships with the governance committees instead of being the prime user of this information. He collects and reports and becomes subservient to information management. This has been a traditional onerous effort by the project manager and he becomes mired in the numbers and irrelevant measures by running to placate the bookkeepers and governance players who usually are not wedded to the product output. (Hence, the interest in the tiresome, nagging detail, and not necessarily relevant administration).

The transformational e-Government project manager, in order to focus on project results, must optimize the use of available Internet tools to manage the collection, access, and storage of project information. But the transformational e-Government project manager can no longer be the focus of the management of information; no longer be the omnipotent information manager.

He must become the sage in receipt of this data, assembled by others so that he can effectively analyze project process and results. The project manager must 'stop rowing and start steering' or risk being swamped by the ubiquitous proliferation of project management information. He suffers from the ease to follow the bureaucratic requirements instead of challenging them in the name of product success and outcome. He unwittingly becomes the bottleneck of information – in and out; a key stakeholder who needs it most. Other people must assemble and manage the changing and interdependent data, so that the project manager as prime user may read and analyze the information, and no longer 'feed the beast'.

The management of transformational e-Government information must use Internet based and technological tools to harness the power collective intelligence requires. Rather than being a handler of information the transformational e-Government project manager must become a key intelligent user that understands the social, cultural, economic information environment in which transformational e-Government operates. The transformational e-Government project manager must prioritize results over processes, and be resolved to use the project information to detect and solidify unstated assumptions and 'blind alleys' and interfering governance committee members not committed to the final product.

A broader project management methodology could benefit from the aid of better information and support in managing the interrelationships, location and access of information as it pertains to all facets of project management; this includes the horizontal and user related content information as well as the process related information required to manage the project itself. Content information would also assist in assessing the implications of changing and evolving requirements, users and stakeholder and governance committee reporting requirements.

Lack of a Comprehensive Holistic Approach to Project Management as the Driving Force

In the management of transformational e-Government projects there are very few material individual or group incentives for performance albeit there is a long established commitment to public service. The individual driving criteria may erroneously be to the mechanistic project management reporting scheme and not to the project success; reporting successfully on measures such as timing or cost controls rather than on results.

Concomitantly, few government organizations have created a 'risk culture' that rewards well-managed risk taking within the domain of transformational e-Government project management. As a result the project manager tends to operate in a cocoon of project methodology processes that demonstrate performance and afford protection against possible criticism; the propensity to hide behind governance committees and their announced performance measures.

Transformational e-Government project managers and those organizations with related responsibilities for project contracting and associated decision-making often become entangled in project management methodology processes such as 'earned value management' (EVM) –esoteric to all except some specialists. Yet, there is no process dedicated to the realization of project results by the transformational e-Government project manager.

Furthermore, in enterprise wide government applications, when the project spans numerous departments and agencies each having varying degrees of interest and accountability, the project manager is often left to be the 'driver' and 'prime user'; an unnatural occurrence yet imperative for project success. This situation is exacerbated when central agencies or special programmes fund the government wide initiative instead of the participating funders.

The project management scope and tools for overall responsibility for project success could be expanded to recognize the project manager as the holistic driver, negotiator and consensus builder. In this capacity, he needs authority and information on the delicate interests both overt and unarticulated on the issues and complications that could derail or promote project success. Technology support and an expansion to and recognition of the scope and responsibilities of project management could contribute to project success.

Limited Access to Vital Subject Matter Expertise

There is likely no factor that contributes more to the success of any transformational e-Government project than having an in-depth and complete definition of the project's scope of work and, as importantly, having the ability to identify and measure the inevitable scope changes that occur during the life of the project.

Project management methodologies rely heavily on scope processes and this includes the use of subject matter expertise. But the methodologies do not recognize the need to build capacity and capability within the project to develop scope and deliver project results based upon pragmatic subject matter expertise.

Instead transformational e-Government project management methodologies often look to 'historical organizations assets' that contain subject matter expertise, rather than having direct interaction with subject matter experts.

To be effective in the development and delivery of transformational e-Government project management, methodologies must incorporate procedures that broaden and deepen project management skills in managing ICT programs, as demanded by the information and digital age. This includes an adoption of subject matter expertise.

During the management of transformational e-Government projects, subject matter expertise is often developed by and inculcated into third-party consultants; because of this, they often become *de facto* project managers that hoard critical corporate knowledge. This becomes an issue that must be addressed by transformational e-Government methodologies.

The project management scope could be expanded to recognize the importance and difficulties in having access to the subject matter expertise within the client area for the project team when and as required. Though these personnel do not form part of the project team, they do influence the success of the project, and in an informationally enhanced environment, a project management methodology could include the facility to identify, manage, and have access to this expertise as required.

Organizational Environment not Presupposed to Enterprise Wide Transformation

In transformational e-Government there are usually a number of groups with a divergence in attitudes that are involved. And so there is the potential for problems caused by disparate vested interests. Power struggles can arise from: conservative verses risk-adverse approaches to project management; personal and organizational fear of the loss of power, authority, and influence; and ineffective communications around the boundaries and interfaces of impacted organizations. In some cases organizations are dedicated to maintaining existing parochial organizational arrangements and they are diametrically opposed to operational change.

The project management scope could be expanded to recognize the interdependencies and breadth of a government enterprise, and could use technology to help tag and identify the relationships and associated transformational e-Government activities.

FUTURE RESEARCH

Transformational e-Government success through enhanced project management could be further developed by future research in the following areas:

Corroborate the impact of project management on transformational e-Government success: Further work is required to determine the culpability and impact of project management in transformational e-Government success and failure. Though a few private sector studies and academic literature attributes approximately up to an 85% failure rate in e-Government due to project management, an additional academic and private/public sector focused literature review is required as corroborating evidence to support this statement, and understand in more detail the precise aspect of project management that falls short of contributing to project success.

In addition, further work is required to determine the relevance and suitability of current project management methodologies to meet the needs of transformational e-Government systems, especially in the developing world contexts. This examination would include the identification of the governance environments that requires and benefits from the step-by-step planning process for project management and product development. In addition, it would address the project manager and stakeholder/user needs to adopt a more results driven systems thinking approach to project management and outcome and system success. These are only two elements that could be examined through the lens of project management in the 21st century; this work would further develop this concept and examine the relevancy and currency of the most commonly used project management methodologies.

Test 'insitu' the impact of the proposed enhancement to project management methodologies on e-Government applications: Further work is required to test the effectiveness of proposed enhancements to project management methodologies on actual e-Government applications. This could be achieved by setting up a base rating of the effectiveness of existing e-Government applications by e-Government experts. These experts would participate in the design of the criteria, and develop a standardized measurement of success and failure.

These e-Government experts would conduct two reviews; the initial review would be to assign a rating based upon the standardized measurement developed above to each e-Government application selected. They would then conduct a secondary review and produce a rating based upon the incorporation of the enhancements had they been in effect. In this way the e-Government application would be retrospectively examined with the proposed enhancements applied to an actual e-Government project (post implementation).

A comparison between the two ratings would be a proxy for the potential impact had the enhancement been applied during project implementation i.e. 'insitu'. This approach is recommended as the incorporation of non-tested project management enhancement to a 'live' system is not feasible, nor recommended.

Corroborate the relevance and impact of the individual and composite e-Government challenges and barriers, and the feasibility of project management enhancements to address them: Further work is also required to update and test the current validity of the synergistic compendium of the ten transformational e-Government challenges outlined in this chapter. This compendium would benefit by an assessment by current e-Government project managers and interested international parties to corroborate and update these findings and their applicability to evolving e-Government environments. This examination could take place by conducting a focused literature review and survey and/or structured interviews probing in detail the challenges that hinder success in today's complex organizational, systemic and political

environment. It would also re-examine the appropriateness and flexibility of project management methodologies as a mitigating agent and whether other solutions may be entertained; for example policy and procedural improvements or changes to the system development methodologies.

Conduct a case study analysis of country-wide transformational e-Government project failures: This field of research would also benefit by the development of a lessons learned repository of the key factors and results of a number of country-wide transformational e-Government project failures. This could be achieved by developing a case study summary for critical and representative projects, interviewing key players, and the examination of documentation. At a global level, the following are desired:

- Additional research and additional follow-up is required with the Project Management Institute (PMI), USA to share the findings of e-Government challenges and limitations within PMBOK to serve e-Government and its project management needs. (The author is approaching the Project Management Institute and Project Manager Working Groupl);

- Follow up with IBM would also be of value based upon the IBM Fellowship granted the author to revisit their interest in designing a technologically enabled and informationally enhanced project management methodological support;

- Opportunities to share these findings and consult on the feasibility of these project management enhancements with public and private sector officials, academics, international think tanks, and interested organizations; and

- Additional effort is also required within the international e-Government/project management domain to promote research, international knowledge sharing, and peer reviewed publications.

CONCLUSION

E-Government has not been the success originally envisioned around the world when it was originally initiated. Even in Canada, where e-Government was rated number one in the world for five years (Accenture, 2005), the revolutionary changes to Government administration and democracy have not materialized. Many champions of technology in government and industry alike are convinced that we have only begun to scratch the surface of digital innovation (Roy, 2006). E-Government's first decade has arguably been much more transitional than transformational. And around the world, progress has been less. Why has e-Government not attained the promised success?

This chapter analyzes the challenges to advancing transformational e-Government around the world and explores the feasibility of improved project management. It uncovers impediments not previously documented, summarizes a list of ten challenges that impede e-Government success, and assesses the feasibility of using project management to address some of these impediments and advance e-Government progress.

This research has shown that transformational e-Government is not living up to promises made; progress is stalling and project failure rates are high. The conclusion is that project management methodologies, originally designed to address the industrial and manufacturing age, do not adequately respond to the needs of today's e-Government initiatives. They have to be revamped from an administrative compliance methodology to a results based accountability methodology. Project management has not yet evolved to a state where it can become a force in the solution. It does not bring value from technology, and does not facilitate radical changes to organizational arrangements, reengineered business processes, or more client-focused human resource behaviour. This failing introduces the possibility of considering the use of an informationally enhanced project management methodology to potentially address some of these issues and highlights the need for technological support within the project management discipline.

REFERENCES

Accenture. (2005). *Leadership in customer service: New expectations, new experiences.* Retrieved March 23, 2013 from http://www.accenture.com/Countries/Canada/Services/By_Subject/Customer_Relationship_Management/R_and_I/LeadershipNewExperiences.htm

Accenture. (2006). *Leadership in customer service: Building the trust.* Retrieved March 15, 2013 from http://www.accenture.com/Global/Services/By_Industry/Government_and_Public_Service/PS_Global/R_and_I/BuildingtheTrustES.htm

Accenture. (2007). *Leadership in customer service: Delivering on the promise.* Retrieved March 15, 2013 from http://nstore.accenture.com/acn_com/PDF/2007LCSDelivPromiseFinal.pdf

Aikins, S. K. (2012a). Foreword. In *Managing e-government projects: Concepts, issues and practices.* Hershey, PA: IGI Global.

Aikins, S. K. (2012b). Preface. In *Managing e-government projects: Concepts, issues and practices.* Hershey, PA: IGI Global.

Aikins, S. K. (2012c). *Improving e-government project management: Best practices and critical success factors, managing e-government projects: Concepts, issues, and best practices.* Hershey, PA: IGI Global.

Aikins, S. K. (Ed.). (2012d). *Managing e-government projects: Concepts, issues, and best practices.* Hershey, PA: IGI Global.

Arif, M. (2008). Customer orientation in e-government project management: A case study. *The Electronic. Journal of E-Government, 6*(1), 1–10.

BCS Thought Leadership. (2005). *Why are complex IT projects different?* Retrieved March 16, 2009 from www.bcs.org/server.php?show=conWebDoc.2619.

British Computer Society (BCS). (2004). *Parliamentary report on IT project waste management of IT projects: Making IT deliver for department of work and pension customers.* Retrieved August 26, 2004 from http://www.bcs.org/content/conWebDoc/1762

Dawes, S. S. (2009). Governance in the digital age: A research and action framework for an uncertain future. *Government Information Quarterly, 26,* 257–264. doi:10.1016/j.giq.2008.12.003

Elliman, T., & Irani, Z. (2007). Establishing a framework for e-government research: Project VIEGO. *Transforming Government: People. Process and Policy, 1*(4), 364.

Fraser, S. (2006). *Report of the auditor general of Canada to the house of commons.* Retrieved November 8, 2013 from http://www.oag-bvg.gc.ca/internet/English/parl_oag_200611_03_e_14971.html

Furlong, S. (2011). *Transformational e-government success through enhanced project management.* (Ph.D. Thesis). Liverpool, UK.

Furlong, S. (2012). Project management: An e-government driver? In *Handbook of research on e-government in emerging economies: Adoption, e-participation, and legal frameworks.* Hershey, PA: IGI Global. doi:10.4018/978-1-4666-0324-0.ch027

Gauthier, J., & Lavagnon, A. (n.d.). Foundations of project management research: An explicit and six-facet ontological framework. *Project Management Journal, 43* (5), 5-23.

Government of Canada Foreign Affairs and International Trade Canada. (2006). *Government on-line final report.* Retrieved March 8, 2013, from http://www.dfait-maeci.gc.ca/department/gol-annual-report-en.asp

Heeks, R. (2008). *e-Government for development – Success and failure in e-government projects, e-government for development information exchange, coordinated by the University of Manchester's Institute for Development Policy and Management.* Retrieved May 4, 2013 from http://www.egov4dev.org/success/sfrates.shtml

Irani, Z., Al-Sebie, A., & Elliman, T. (2006). Transaction stage of e-government systems: Identification of its location & importance. In *Proceedings of the 39th Hawaii International Conference on System Sciences.* IEEE.

Janowski, T., Estevez, E., & Ojo, A. (2007). *A project framework for e-government.* New York: United Nations International Institute for Software Technology, UNU-IIST.

Kamal, M., Weerakkody, V., & Irani, Z. (2011). Analyzing the role of stakeholders in the adoption of technology integration solutions in UK local government: An exploratory study. *Government Information Quarterly, 28,* 200–210. doi:10.1016/j.giq.2010.08.003

Kerzner, H. (2001). *Project management: A systems approach to planning, scheduling and controlling* (7th ed.). Hoboken, NJ: John Wiley and Sons Inc.

Misuraca, G. (2009). e-Government 2015: Exploring m-government scenarios, between ICT-driven experiments and citizen-centric implications. *Technology Analysis and Strategic Management, 21*(3), 407–424. doi:10.1080/09537320902750871

Movahedi, B., Tan, R.-X., & Lavassani, K. M. (2010). Organizational development in electronic government adoption: A process development perspective. *International Journal of Electronic Government Research, 7*(1), 51–63. doi:10.4018/jegr.2011010104

Nordfors, L., Ericson, B., Lindell, H., & Lapidus, J. (2009). *e-Government of tomorrow – Future scenarios for 2020*. Gullers Group.

Office of Government Commerce (OGC). (2009). *Managing successful projects with PRINCE2 projects in controlled environments*. London: TSO London, Office of Government Commerce.

Oxford Institute. (2007). *Breaking barriers to e-government: Overcoming obstacles to improving European public services*. Retrieved March 16, 2013 from http://www.egovbarriers.org/downloads/deliverables/solutions_report/Solutions_for_e-Government.pdf

PRINCE2 Pocketbook. (2009). *TSO information and publishing solution*. Norwich, UK: Author.

Project Management Institute (PMI). Inc. (2008). *a guide to the project management body of knowledge*. Paper presented at PMBOK. Newtown Square, PA.

Roy, J. (2006). *E-government in Canada: Transformation for the digital age*. Ottawa, Canada: University of Ottawa Press.

Schwester, R. (2009). Examining the barriers to e-government adoption. *Electronic. Journal of E-Government, 7*(1), 113–122.

Sharif, A., & Irani, Z. (2010). The logistics of information management within an e-government context. *Journal of Enterprise Information Management, 23*(6), 694–723. doi:10.1108/17410391011088600

United Nations. (2008). *UN e-government survey 2008 from e-government to connected governance*. New York: Department of Economic and Social Affairs, Division for Public Administration and Development Management, United Nations.

United Nations. (2010). *E-government survey 2010 – Leveraging e-government at a time of financial and economic crisis*. Retrieved June 30, 2013 from http://www2.unpan.org/egovkb/global_reports/10report.htm

Weerakkody, V., Janssen, M., & Dwivedi, Y. K. (2011). Transformational change and business process reengineering (BPR): Lessons from the British and Dutch public sector. *Government Information Quarterly, 28*, 320–328. doi:10.1016/j.giq.2010.07.010

Wells, H. (2012). How effective are project management methodologies? An explorative evaluation of their benefits in practice. *Project Management Journal, 43*(6), 43–58. doi:10.1002/pmj.21302

West, D. (2007). *Global e-government*. Providence, RI: Brown University.

World Bank. (2002). *The e-government handbook for developing countries*. Washington, DC: Centre for Democracy and Technology.

Young, R., Young, M., Jordan, E., & O'Connor, P. (2012). Is strategy being implemented through projects? Contrary evidence from a leader in new public management. *International Journal of Project Management, 30*, 887–900. doi:10.1016/j.ijproman.2012.03.003

Zhao, F., Scavarda, A., & Waxin, M. (2012). Key issues and challenges in e-government development: An integrative case study of the number one eCity in the Arab world. *Information Technology & People, 25*(4), 395–422. doi:10.1108/09593841211278794

Ziemann, J., & Loos, P. (2009). Transforming cross-organisational processes between european administrations: Towards a comprehensive business interoperability interface. In *Handbook of research on ICT-enabled transformational government: A global perspective*. Hershey, PA: IGI Global. doi:10.4018/978-1-60566-390-6.ch006

ADDITIONAL READING

Furlong, S., & Al-Karaghouli, W. (2011, January). *Delivering Professional Projects: The Effectiveness of Project Management in Transformational Initiatives*, Emerald Publishing.

Organisation for Economic Cooperation and Development (OECD). (2001). The Hidden Threat to E-Government: Avoiding large government IT failures, Public Management website, Paris, France.

Weerakkody, V. (2009). *Handbook of Research on ICT Enabled Transformational Government: A Global Perspective, Information Science Reference*. New York: Brunel University. doi:10.4018/978-1-60566-390-6

KEY TERMS AND DEFINITIONS

E-Government: Focuses on the use of new information and communication technologies by governments as applied to the full range of government function through the networking potential offered by the Internet and related technologies has the potential to transform the structures and operation of government.

E-Government Projects: Refers to the initiatives of government using information technologies enterprise-wide that have the ability to transform relations with citizens, businesses, and other arms of government. These projects serve a variety of different ends: better delivery of government services to citizens, improved interactions with business and industry, citizen empowerment through access to information, and more efficient government management.

ICTs: This is an acronym that stands for Information and Communication Technology(ies) meaning different technology platforms that are used to managing different information resources in the e-Government realm.

Project Management: The discipline of planning, organizing, and managing resources to bring about the successful completion of specific project goals and objectives.

Project Management Methodology: The various prescriptive ways in which projects are initiated, planned and executed unto completion.

Public Sector Reform: Consists of deliberate changes to the structures and processes of public sector organizations with the objective of getting them to run better. Structural change may include merging or splitting public sector organizations while process change may include redesigning systems, setting quality standards and focusing on capacity-building.

Transformational Government: The term used to describe computer-based information and communications technologies to enable radical improvement to the delivery of public services and describes a government reform strategy which aims to avoid the limitations which have come to be seen as associated with a traditional e-Government strategy.

Compilation of References

(2003). Towards a definition of electronic government: A comparative review. InGil-Garcia, J., & Luna-Reyes, L. (Eds.), *Techno-legal aspects of the information society and the new economy: An overview*. Badajoz, Spain: Formatex.

Abbes, S. B., Scheuermann, A., Meilender, T., & d'Aquin, M. (2012). *Characterizing modular ontologies*. Paper presented at the International Conference on Formal Ontologies in Information Systems (FOIS). Graz, Autriche.

ABC4Trust Project. (2009). *ABC4Trust*. Retrieved March 23rd, 2011, from http://abc4trust.de/

Aboelmaged, M. G. (2010). Predicting e-procurement adoption in a developing country: An empirical integration of technology acceptance model and theory of planned behaviour. *Industrial Management & Data Systems, 110*(3-4), 392–414.

About MWater. (2012). MWater. Retreived July 9, 2013 from http://mwater.info/Site/About_mWater.html.

Abramson, A. M., & Means, E. G. (2001). *E-government, price water house coopers endowment for the business of government*. London: Rowman & Littlefield Publishers Inc.

Abramson, M. A., & Harris, R. S. (2003). *The procurement revolution*. London: Rowland and Littlefield.

Accenture. (2004). *e-Government leadership: High performance, maximum value*. Retrieved April 12, 2006 from http://www.accenture.com/Global/Research_and_Insights/By_industry/Government/HighValue.htm

Accenture. (2005). *Leadership in customer service: New expectations, new experiences*. Retrieved March 23, 2013 from http://www.accenture.com/Countries/Canada/Services/By_Subject/Customer_Relationship_Management/R_and_I/LeadershipNewExperiences.htm

Accenture. (2006). *Leadership in customer service: Building the trust*. Retrieved March 15, 2013 from http://www.accenture.com/Global/Services/By_Industry/Government_and_Public_Service/PS_Global/R_and_I/BuildingtheTrustES.htm

Accenture. (2007). *Leadership in customer service: Delivering on the promise*. Retrieved March 15, 2013 from http://nstore.accenture.com/acn_com/PDF/2007LCSDelivPromiseFinal.pdf

ADB. (2009). *Improving public services through information and communication technology (Technical Assistance Report)*. Asian Development Bank.

ADDITIONAL READING

Adejuwon, K. D. (2012). From e-government to e-governance: Whither African public administration? *Advances in Arts. Social Sciences and Education Research, 2*(1), 63–75.

Adelakun, O. M. (2002). Stakeholder process approach to information systems evaluation. In *Proceedings of the Eighth Americas Conference on Information Systems*. IEEE.

Adler, M., & Henman, P. (2001). E-justice: A comparative study of computerization and procedural justice in social security. *International Review of Law Computers & Technology, 15*(2), 195–212. doi:10.1080/13600860120070510

Agarwal, N., Lim, M., & Wigand, R. (2011). *Finding her master's voice: The power of collective action among female Muslim bloggers*. Paper presented at the 19th European Conference on Information Systems. Helsinki, Finland.

Ahmed, A. S. (2005). *Automating government with e-governance*. Retrieved April 15, 2013, from http://www.linuxjournal.com/article/7591

Aikins, S. K. (2010). Participatory e-planning: Bridging theory and practice through improvements in technology. In Ch.G. Reddick (Ed.), Politics, democracy and e-government, participation and service delivery (pp. 131-150). Hershey, PA: IGI Global.

Aikins, S. K. (2012a). Foreword. In *Managing e-government projects: Concepts, issues and practices*. Hershey, PA: IGI Global.

Aikins, S. K. (2012b). Preface. In *Managing e-government projects: Concepts, issues and practices*. Hershey, PA: IGI Global.

Aikins, S. K. (2012c). *Improving e-government project management: Best practices and critical success factors, managing e-government projects: Concepts, issues, and best practices*. Hershey, PA: IGI Global.

Aikins, S. K. (Ed.). (2012d). *Managing e-government projects: Concepts, issues, and best practices*. Hershey, PA: IGI Global.

Ajayi, L. (2007). *ICT business in Nigeria: Challenges and opportunities*. Retrieved March 12, 2013 from www.nitpa.org/articles/globalit/NCS_Paper.pdf

Ajzen, I. (1991). The theory of planned behavior. *Organizational Behavior and Human Decision Processes*, *50*, 179–211. doi:10.1016/0749-5978(91)90020-T

Akman, I., Yazici, A., Mishra, A., & Arifoglu, A. (2005). E-government: A global view and an empirical evaluation of some attributes of citizens. *Government Information Quarterly*, *22*(2), 239–257. doi:10.1016/j.giq.2004.12.001

Akrich, M. (1992). The description of technical objects. In *Shaping technology/building society*. Cambridge, MA: MIT Press.

Akşam. (2012). *Fotoğraft çek büyükşehire yolla yönetime ortak ol*. Retrieved February 13, 2013 from http://www.aksam.com.tr/guncel/fotografi-cek-buyuksehire-yolla-yonetime-ortak-ol/haber-109272

Akther, M. S., Onishi, T., & Kidokoro, T. (2007). E-government in a developing country: Citizen-ceteric approach for success. *International Journal of Electronic Goverance*, *1*(1), 38–51. doi:10.1504/IJEG.2007.014342

Al Nagi, E., & Hamdan, M. (2009). Computerization and e-government implementation in Jordan: Challenges, obstacles and successes. *Government Information Quarterly*, *26*, 577–583. doi:10.1016/j.giq.2009.04.003

Albrecht, W. S., Albrecht, C. C., & Albrecht, C. O. (2004). Fraud and corporate executives: Agency stewardship and broken trust. *Journal of Forensic Accounting*, *5*(1), 109–130.

Aleknonis, G. (2010). Komunikaciniai teisės žinoti ir laisvės informuoti aspektai. *Social Sciences Studies*, *2*(6), 7–21.

Alford, J., & O'Flynn, J. (2008). Public value: A stocktake of a concept. In *Proceedings of Twelfth Annual Conference of the International Research Society for Public Management*. Barcelona: IRSPM.

Al-Jaghoub, S., & Westrup, C. (2003). Jordan and ICT-led development: Towards a competition state? *Information Technology & People*, *16*(1), 93–110. doi:10.1108/09593840310463032

Al-Khouri, A. M. (2013). e-Government in Arab countries: A 6-staged roadmap to develop the public sector. *Journal of Management and Strategy*, *4*(1), 80–107. doi:10.5430/jms.v4n1p80

Al-Kibisi, G., de Boer, K., Mourshed, M., & Rea, N. (2001). Putting citizens on-line, not inline. *The McKinsey Quarterly*, (2): 64.

Allen, A. B., Juillet, L., Paquet, G., & Roy, J. (2001). E-governance and government online in Canada: Partnerships, people and prospects. *Government Information Quarterly*, *18*, 93–104. doi:10.1016/S0740-624X(01)00063-6

Almarabeh, T., & AbuAli, A. (2010). A general framework for e-government: Definition maturity challenges, opportunities, and success. *European Journal of Scientific Research*, *39*(1), 29–42.

Alomari, M. K. (2010). *Predictors for successful e-government adoption on the Hashemite Kingdom of Jordan: The deployment of an empirical evaluation based on citizen-centric perspectives*. (Unpublished Phd Thesis). Griffith University, Canberra, Australia.

Al-Omari, H. (2006). E-government architecture in Jordan: A comparative analysis. *Journal of Computer Science*, *2*(11), 846–852. doi:10.3844/jcssp.2006.846.852

Amagoh, F. (2009). Information asymmetry and the contracting out process. *The Innovation Journal: The Public Sector Innovation Journal*, *14*(2), 1–14.

Aman, A. C. (2005). Privatization, prisons, democracy, and human rights: The need to extend the province of administrative law. *Indiana Journal of Global Legal Studies*, *12*(2), 511–550. doi:10.1353/gls.2005.0000

Amit, R., & Zott, C. (2001). Value creation in e-business. *Strategic Management Journal*, *22*, 493–520. doi:10.1002/smj.187

Amor, D. (2000). *The e-business (r) evolution: Living and working in an interconnected world*. Upper Saddle River, NJ: Prentice Hall PTR.

Anatolia News Agency. (2010). *Turkcell sees future in mobile wallet*. Hürriyet Daily News Economy Er-Sectors - HDN ISTANBUL. Retrieved February 13, 2013 from http://www.hurriyetdailynews.com/turkcell-sees-future-in-mobile-wallet.aspx?pageID=438&n=turkcell-sees-future-in-mobile-wallet-2010-05-12

Anatolia News Agency. (2012). *Turks surpass EU citizens in using mobile internet*. Hürriyet Daily News, ANKARA. Retrieved February 13, 2013 from http://www.hurriyetdailynews.com/turks-surpass-eu-citizens-in-using-mobile-internet.aspx?pageID=238&nID=357 15&NewsCatID=344

Anatolia News Agency. Istanbul. (2012). *Turkey fails to tax mobile internet applications*. Hürriyet Daily News. Retrieved February 13, 2013 from http://www.hurriyetdailynews.com/turkey-fails-to-tax-mobile-internet-applications.aspx?pageID=238&nID=25913&NewsCatID=344

Andersen, E. S., Grude, K. V., & Hague, T. (2004). *Goal directed project management*. Kogan Page.

Angelov, S., & Grefen, P. (2008). An e-contracting reference architecture. *Journal of Systems and Software*, *81*(11), 1816–1844. doi:10.1016/j.jss.2008.02.023

Annor-Frempong, F., Kwarteng, J., Agunga, R., & Zinnah, M. M. (2006). Challenges and prospects of infusing information communication technologies (ICTS) in extension for agricultural and rural development in Ghana. In *Proceedings of the Annual Conference of the International Association of Agricultural and Extension Education*. Academic Press.

Anthony, R. N. (1965). *Planning and control systems: A framework for analysis*. Boston: Harvard University Graduate School of Business Administration.

Apostolou, D., Stojanovic, L., Lobo, T. P., Miro, J. C., & Papadakis, A. (2005a). Configuring e-government services using ontologies. *IFIP International Federation for Information Processing*, *189*, 1571–5736. doi:10.1007/0-387-29773-1_10

Apostolou, D., Stojanovic, L., Lobo, T. P., & Thoensen, B. (2005b). Towards a semantically driven software engineering environment for e-Government. *IFIP International Federation for Information Processing*, *3416*, 157–168.

Arif, M. (2008). Customer orientation in e-government project management: A case study. *The Electronic. Journal of E-Government*, *6*(1), 1–10.

Armitage, C. (2012). *Council uses phone apps to give power to the people*. Herald, Newcastle. Retrieved February 13, 2013 from http://www.theherald.com.au/story/409807/council-uses-phone-apps-to-give-power-to-the-people/

Arokoyo, T. (2008). *ICTs in the transformation of agricultural extension: The case of Nigeria*. Retrieved May 16, 2013 from http://www.cta.int/observatory2003/case_studies/Case_study_Nigeria.pdf

Aspray, W., Bromley, A., Campbell-Kelly, M., & Williams, M. R. (1990). *Computing before computers* (W. Aspray, Ed.). Ames, IA: Iowa State University Press.

Atkinson, R. D., & Castro, D. (2008). *Digital quality of life: Understanding the personal & social benefits of the information technology revolution.* The Information Technology and Innovation Foundation. Retrieved March 28, 2013 from http://www.innovationfiles.org/

Auer, S., & Herre, H. (2006). Rapid OWL - An agile knowledge engineering methodology. In *Proceedings of at Sixth International Andrei Ershov Memorial Conference - Perspectives of System Informatics PSI'06.* Novosibirsk, Russia: PSI.

Augustinaitis, A., & Petrauskas, R. (2010). Pilietinių technologijų vaidmuo šiuolaikinėje visuomenėje. In Socialinės technologijos' 10: Iššūkiai, galimybės sprendimai: Konferencijos medžiaga, 2010 m. lapkričio 25-26 d. (pp. 205-212). Vilnius-Net.

Avgerou, C. (2003). The link between ICT and economic growth in the discourse of development. In *Organizational information systems in the context of globalization.* Boston: Kluwer Academic Publishers. doi:10.1007/978-0-387-35695-2_23

Awad, M. A. (2005). *A comparison between agile and traditional software development methodologies.* Retrieved May 20, 2013 from http://pds10.egloos.com/pds/200808/13/85/A_comparision_between_Agile_and_Traditional_SW_development_methodologies.pdf

Axetue Team. (2011, October 12). *Google Earth gets a billion downloads.* Retrieved August 16, 2012 from http://www.axetue.com/2011/10/12/google-earth-billion-downloads

Aykut, A. (2008). Assessment of the Turkish local e-governments: An empirical study. *International Journal of Human Sciences.* Retrieved from http://ssrn.com/abstract=1259378

Azab, N. A. (2009). Assessing electronic government readiness of public organizations. *Communications of the IBIMA, 8,* 95–106.

Aziz, M. (2011). Implementing ICT for governance in a post-conflict nation: A case study of Afghanistan. In D. Piaggesi, K. J. Sund, & W. Castelnovo (Eds.), *Global strategy and practice of e-governance: Examples from around the world* (pp. 185–208). Hershey, PA: IGI Global. doi:10.4018/978-1-60960-489-9.ch011

Bacharach, S. B. (1989). Organizational theories: Some criteria for evaluation. *Academy of Management Review, 14*(4), 496–515.

Bachmann, R., & Inkpen, A. C. (2011). Understanding institutional-based trust building processes in inter-organizational relationships. *Organization Studies, 32*(2), 281–301. doi:10.1177/0170840610397477

Bachu, V. R., Polepalli, K.R., & Reddy, G.S. (2006). eSagu: An IT based personalized agricultural extension system prototype - Analysis of 51 farmers' case studies. *International Journal of Education and Development using ICT, 2*(1).

Backus, M. (2001). E-governance in developing countries`. *IICD Research Brief, 1*(1).

Baguma, R. (2005). *Affordable e-governance using free and open source software.* Retrieved March 12, 2013 from http://cit.mak.ac.ug/iccir/downloads/SREC_05/Rehema%20Baguma_05.pdf

Baker. (2011). *The app. model and the web.* Retrieved February 13, 2013 from https://blog.lizardwrangler.com/2011/08/09/

Baldoni, B., Fuligni, S., Mecella, M., & Tortorelli, F. (2009). The Italian e-government service oriented architecture: Strategic vision and technical solutions. *Electronic. Journal of E-Government, 7*(4), 318–390.

Barber, B. (1984). *Strong democracy.* Berkeley, CA: University of California Press.

Barker, D. R., & Barker, L. L. (2012). Criteria for evaluating models of intrapersonal communication processes. In *Communication Yearbook 15.* London: Routledge.

Basu, S. (2004). E-government and developing countries: An overview. *International Review of Law Computers & Technology, 18*(1), 109–132. doi:10.1080/13600860410001674779

Baumol, W. J., Litan, R. E., & Schramm, C. J. (2007). *Good capitalism, bad capitalism and the economics of growth and prosperity.* New Haven, CT: Yale. doi:10.2139/ssrn.985843

BCS Thought Leadership. (2005). *Why are complex IT projects different?* Retrieved March 16, 2009 from www.bcs.org/server.php?show=conWebDoc.2619.

Beck, H., & Pinto, H. S. (2003). *Overview of approach, methodologies, standards, and tools for ontologies. Agricultural Ontology Service.* UN FAO.

Beck, K. (2000). *Extreme programming explained: Embrace change.* Reading, MA: Addison Wesley Longman, Inc.

Bedi, K., Singh, P. J., & Srivastava, S. (2001). *Government net: New governance opportunities for India.* New Delhi: Sage.

Beers, P. J., Boshuizen, H. P. A. E., Kirschner, P. A., & Van den Bossche, P. (2002). *Decision-support and complexity in decision making.* Paper presented at the 5th Junior Researchers of EARLI Conference. Amsterdam, The Netherlands.

Bellamy, C., & Taylor, J. A. (1998). *Governing in the information age.* Buckingham, UK: Open University Press.

Benčina, J. (2007). Web-based decision support system for the public sector comprising linguistic variables. *Informatica, 31*, 311–323.

Betts, M., Black, P., Christensen, S. A., Dawson, E., Du, R., & Duncan, W. et al. (2010). Towards secure and legal e-tendering. *Journal of Information Technology in Construction, 11*, 89–102.

Beynon-Davies, P. (2005). Constructing electronic government: The case of the UK inland revenue. *International Journal of Information Management, 25*(1), 3–20. doi:10.1016/j.ijinfomgt.2004.08.002

Bhatnagar, S. (2002). Egovernment: Lessons from implementation in developing countries. *Regional Development Dialogue, 24*, 164–174.

Bhattacherjee, A. (2012). *Social science research: Principles, methods, and practices* (2nd Ed.). Reterived February 5, 2013 form http://scholarcommons.usf.edu/oa_textbooks/3/

Bhuiyan, S. (2009). E-government in Kazakhstan: Challenges and its role to development. *Public Organization Review, 10*, 31–47. doi:10.1007/s11115-009-0087-6

Bidgoli, H. (2002). *Electronic commerce: Principles and practice.* San Diego, CA: Academic Press.

Bikshapathi, K. RamaRaju, P., Bhatnagar, S., & Ahmedabad, I. (2006). E-procurement in government of Andhra Pradesh India. Washington, DC: World Bank.

Bilevičienė, T., & Bilevičiūtė, E. (2012). Information systems of administrative justice - As social tool for implementation of publicity principle. In *Artificial intelligence driven solutions to business and engineering problems* (pp. 108–119). ITHEA.

Block, C., & Neumann, D. (2008). A decision support system for choosing market mechanisms in e-procurement. In *Negotiation, auctions, and market engineering* (pp. 44–57). Berlin: Springer. doi:10.1007/978-3-540-77554-6_3

Boer, L., Harink, J., & Heijboer, G. (2001). *A model for assessing the impact of electronic procurement forms.* Paper presented at the 10th International Annual IPSERA Conference. Jönköping, Sweden.

Bontas, E. P., Mochol, M., & Tolksdorf, R. (2005). Case studies on ontology reuse. In *Proceedings of the 5th International Conference on Knowledge Management IKNOW05.* IKNOW.

Borras, J. (2004). International technical standards for e-government. *Electronic. Journal of E-Government, 2*(2), 75–80.

Borst, W. N. (1997). *Construction of engineering ontologies for knowledge sharing and reuse.* (PhD thesis). Centre for Telematica and Information Technology, University of Twente, Twente, The Netherlands.

Bose, S., & Rashel, M. R. (2007). *Implementing e-governance using OECD model (modified) and gartner model (modified) upon agriculture of Bangladesh.* Paper presented at the 10th International Conference on Computer and Information Technology. Dhaka, Bangladesh.

Bothma, C. (2000). *E-commerce for South African managers.* Irene: Interactive Reality.

Boyce, S., & Pahl, C. (2007). Developing domain ontologies for course content. *Journal of Educational Technology & Society*, *10*(3), 275–288.

Braa, J., & Hedberg, C. (2002). Developing district-based health care information systems. *The Information Society*, *18*(2), 113–127. doi:10.1080/01972240290075048

Brabham, D. C. (2008). Crowdsourcing as a model for problem solving: An introduction and cases. *Convergence: The International Journal of Research into New Media Technologies*, *14*(1), 75–90. doi:10.1177/1354856507084420

Breznitz, D. (2007). *Innovation and the state: Political choice and strategies for growth in Israel, Taiwan, and Ireland*. New Haven, CT: Yale.

Bri, F. D. (2009). An e-government stages of growth model based on research within the Irish revenue offices. *Electronic Journal of E-Government*, *7*(4), 1339–1348.

British Computer Society (BCS). (2004). *Parliamentary report on IT project waste management of IT projects: Making IT deliver for department of work and pension customers*. Retrieved August 26, 2004 from http://www.bcs.org/content/conWebDoc/1762

Brooker, P. (2008). *Non-democratic regimes*. Hampshire, UK: Palgrave Macmillan.

Bruggink, M. (2003). Open source in Africa: Towards informed decision-making. *IICD Research Brief, 7*.

Brun, A., Ronchi, S., Fan, X., & Golini, R. (2010). What is the value of an IT e-procurement system? *Journal of Purchasing and Supply Management*, *16*(2), 131–140. doi:10.1016/j.pursup.2010.03.013

Bruno, G., Esposito, E., Mastroianni, M., & Vellutino, D. (2005). Analysis of public e-procurement web site accessibility. *Journal of Public Procurement*, *5*(3), 344.

Brusa, G., Caliusco, M. L., & Chiotti, O. (2006). A process for building a domain ontology: An experience in developing a government budgetary ontology. In *Proceedings of the Second Australasian Workshop on Advances in Ontologies*, (Vol. 72). IEEE.

Burrell, G., & Morgan, G. (1979). *Social paradigms and organization analysis*. Boston: Heineman.

Butler, T., Feller, J., Pope, A., Emerson, B., & Murphy, C. (2008). Designing a core IT artefact for knowledge management systems using participatory action research in a government and a non-government organisation. *The Journal of Strategic Information Systems*, *17*, 249–267. doi:10.1016/j.jsis.2007.10.002

Butler, T., Feller, J., Pope, P., Barry, P., & Murphy, C. (2004). Promoting knowledge sharing in government and non-government organizations using open source software: The pKADS story. *Electronic. Journal of E-Government*, *2*(2), 81–94.

Bwalya, K. (2010). E-government adoption landscape Zambia: Contexts, issues and challenges. In C. G. Reddick (Ed.), *Comparative e-government* (pp. 241–258). New York: Springer.

Bwalya, K. J., & Healy, M. (2010). Harnessing e-government adoption in the SADC region: A conceptual underpinning. *Electronic Journal of E-Government*, *8*(1), 23–32.

Bwalya, K. J., Zulu, S. F., Grand, B., & Sebina, P. M. (2012). E-government and technological utopianism: Exploring Zambia's challenges and opportunities. *Electronic Journal of E-Government*, *10*(1), 16–30.

Cabinet Office. (2000, May). *Successful IT modernizing government in action*. Retrieved April 12, 2010 from http://www.citu.gov.uk/itprojectsreview.htm

Cai, T., Wang, S., & Xu, Q. (2013). Scheduling of multiple chemical plant start-ups to minimize regional air quality impacts. *Computers & Chemical Engineering*, *54*, 68–78. doi:10.1016/j.compchemeng.2013.03.027

Cai, T., Zhao, C., & Xu, Q. (2012). Energy network dispatch optimization under emergency of local energy shortage. *Energy*, *42*, 132–145. doi:10.1016/j.energy.2012.04.001

Caldow, J. (2001). *Seven e-government leadership milestones*. Washington, DC: IBM Institute for Electronic Government.

Camara, G., & Onsrud, H. (n.d.). *Open-source geographic information systems software: Myths and realities*. Academic Press.

Câmara, G., Souza, B. R., Pedrosa, B., Vinhas, L., Monteiro, A., Paiva, J., et al. (2000). *TerraLib: Technology in support of GIS innovation.* II Workshop Brasileiro de Geoinformática, GeoInfo2000, InstitutoNacional de PesquisasEspaciais, São Paulo.

CapGemini & Ernest & Young. (2001). *Web-based survey on electronic public services.* Retrieved March 13, 2013 from http://europa.eu.int/information_society/eeurope/news_library/documents/bench_online_services.doc.

Carbo, T., & Williams, J. G. (2004). Models and metrics for evaluating local electronic government systems and services. *Electronic. Journal of E-Government*, 2(2), 95–104.

Carlsson, S. A. (2010). Design science research in information systems: A critical realist approach. In A. Hevner, & S. Chatterjee (Eds.), *Design research in information systems* (pp. 209–233). New York: Springer. doi:10.1007/978-1-4419-5653-8_15

Carter, C. R., Kaufmann, L., Beall, S., Carter, P. L., Hendrick, T. E., & Petersen, K. J. (2004). Reverse auctions--Grounded theory from the buyer and supplier perspective. *Transportation Research Part E, Logistics and Transportation Review*, 40(3), 229–254. doi:10.1016/j.tre.2003.08.004

Castell, M. (1999). *Information, technology, globalization and social development.* UNRISD Discussion Paper No. 114. UNRISD.

Castells, M. (1989). *The informational city: Information technology, economic restructuring and the urban regional process.* Oxford, UK: Blackwell.

Castells, M. (1996). *The rise of the network society.* Malden, MA: Blackwell.

Castells, M. (1997). *The information age: Economy, society and culture: The power of identity.* Oxford, UK: Blackwell.

Castells, M. (1998). *The end of millennium.* Oxford, UK: Blackwell.

Centeno, C., van Bavel, R., & Burgelman, J. C. (2004). eGovernment in the EU in the next decade: The vision and key challenges, based on the workshop held in Seville. In Proceedings of eGovernment in the EU in 2010: Key policy and research challenges. Brussels: European Commission, Directorate General Joint Research Centre, EUR 21376.

Center for Democracy and Technology. (2002). *E-government handbook.* Washington, DC: World Bank.

Center for Technology in Government. (2012). *Definition of e-government.* Retrieved March 12, 2012 from http://www.ctg.albany.edu/publications/reports/future_of_egov?chapter=2

Central, I. T. Unit. (2000). E-government - A strategic framework for public services in the information age. London: Cabinet Office.

Chadwick, A. (2009b). Web 2.0: New challenges for the study of e-democracy in an era of informational exuberance. *I/S: A Journal of Law and Policy for the Information Society, 5*(1), 9-41.

Chadwick, A. (2006). Executives and bureaucracies: E-government. In *Internet politics: States, citizens and new communications technologies* (pp. 177–203). New York: Oxford University Press Inc.

Chadwick, A. (2009a). The internet and politics in flux. *Journal of Information Technology & Politics*, 6(3-4), 195–196. doi:10.1080/19331680903028743

Chan, C. M. L., Shan-Ling, P., & Tan, C. W. (2003). Managing stakeholder relationships in an e-government project. In *Proceedings of Ninth Americas Conference on Information Systems.* Academic Press.

Chandler, S., & Emanuels, S. (2002). Transformation not automation. In *Proceedings of 2nd European Conference on EGovernment.* Academic Press.

Chandler, A. (1977). *The visible hand – Managerial revolution in American business.* Boston: Harvard University Press.

Chandrasekaran, B., Josephson, J. R., & Benjamins, V. R. (1999). Ontology of tasks and methods, (acrobat), Banff knowledge acquisition workshop. *IEEE Intelligent Systems, 14*(1), 20–26. doi:10.1109/5254.747902

Chang, A., & Kannan, P. K. (2008). *Leveraging web 2.0 in government*. Retrieved March 18, 2013 from http://faculty.cbpp.uaa.alaska.edu/afgjp/PADM601%20Fall%202009/Leverging%20Web%202.0.pdf

Chang, K.-S. (2011). *Enhancing transparency through e-procurement*. Retrived February 12, 2013 from http://www.oecd.org/dataoecd/47/30/49311011.pdf

Chang, H. H., Tsai, Y.-C., & Hsu, C.-H. (2013). E-procurement and supply chain performance. *Supply Chain Management: An International Journal, 18*(1), 34–51. doi:10.1108/13598541311293168

Charalabidis, Y., & Askounis, D. (2008). Interoperability registries in e-government: Developing a semantically rich repository for electronic services and documents of the new public administration. In *Proceedings of the 41st Hawaii International Conference on System Sciences*. IEEE.

Charalabidis, Y., Gionis, G., & Loukis, E. (2010). *Policy processes support through interoperability with social media*. Paper presented at the 5th Mediterranean Conference on Information Systems 2010. Haifa, Israel.

Charalabidis, Y., Loukis, E., & Androutsopoulou, A. (2011). *Enhancing participative policy making through simulation modelling – A state of the art review*. Paper presented at the European Mediterranean Conference on Information Systems 2011. Athens, Greece.

Checkland, P. (1981). *Systems thinking, systems practice*. Chichester, UK: John Wiley & Sons.

Checkland, P., & Scholes, J. (1990). *Soft systems methodology in action*. Chichester, UK: John Wiley & Sons.

Chen, Y. N., Chen, H. M., Huang, W., & Ching, R. K. H. (2006). E-government strategies in developed and developing countries: An implementation framework and case study. *Journal of Global Information Management, 14*(1), 23–46. doi:10.4018/jgim.2006010102

Chen, Y., & Dorsey, A. (2009). E-government for current and future senior citizens. In C. G. Reddick (Ed.), *Strategies for local e-government adoption and implementation, comparative studies* (pp. 306–322). Hershey, PA: IGI Global. doi:10.4018/978-1-60566-282-4.ch016

Chilimo, W. L., Ngulube, P., & Stilwell, C. (2011). Information seeking patterns and telecentre operations: A case of selected rural communities in Tanzania. *Libri, 61*(1), 37–49. doi:10.1515/libr.2011.004

Chircu, A.M., & Lee, D., & Hae-Dong. (2005). E-government: Key success factors for value discovery and realization. *Electronic Government, 2*(1), 11–24. doi:10.1504/EG.2005.006645

Choudrie, J., Ghinea, G., & Weerakkody, V. (2004). Evaluating global e-government sites: A view using web diagnostic tools. *Electronic. Journal of E-Government, 2*(2), 105–114.

Choudrie, J., & Weerrakody, V. (2007). Horizontal process integration in e-Government: The perspective of UK local authority. *International Journal of Electronic Government Research, 3*(3), 22–39. doi:10.4018/jegr.2007070102

Christenses, S., & Duncan, W. (2006). Maintaining the integrity of electronic tendering by government-reflections on the capacity of the Australian legal framework to meet this challenge. *eLaw Journal, 13*(8).

Chui, M., Manyika, J., Bughin, J., Dobbs, R., Roxburgh, C., Sarrazin, H., et al. (2012). *The social economy: Unlocking value and productivity through social technologies*. Retrieved June 27, 2013 from http://www.markleweeklydigest.org/2012/07/the-social-economy-unlocking-value-and.html

Chung, J. W. (2012). *Korean e-procurement system booming worldwide*. The Korea Herald. Retrieved May 12, 2013 from http://khnews.kheraldm.com/view.php?ud=20121118000259&md=20121121003450_AP

Chun, S. A., Shulman, S., & Sandoval, A. R. (2010). Government 2.0: Marking connections between citizens, data and government. *Information Polity, 15*(1–2), 1–9.

Chu, P. Y., Hsiao, N., Lee, F. W., & Chen, C. W. (2004). Exploring success factors for Taiwan's government electronic tendering system: Behavioral perspectives from end users. *Government Information Quarterly, 2*(2), 219–234. doi:10.1016/j.giq.2004.01.005

Ciborra, C. (2003). *Unveiling e-government and development governing at a distance in the new war*. Information System Working Paper 126. London school of Economic and Political Science. Retrieved May 5, 2013 from www.is.lse.ac.uk/wp/pdf/wp126.pdf

Ciborra, C. (2002). *The labyrinths of information: Challenging the wisdom of systems*. Oxford, UK: Oxford University Press.

Ciborra, C. (2005). Interpreting e-government and development: Efficiency, transparency or governance at a distance? *Information Technology & People*, *18*(3), 260–279. doi:10.1108/09593840510615879

Clarke, K. C. (1986). Advances in geographic information systems. *Computers, Environment and Urban Systems*, *10*, 175–184. doi:10.1016/0198-9715(86)90006-2

Clutterbuck, P., Rowlands, T., & Seamons, O. (2009). A case study of SME web application development effectiveness via agile methods. *The Electronic Journal of Information Systems Evaluation*, *12*(1), 13–26.

Cocchiglia, M., & Vernaschi, S. (2006). E-government for development. *Journal of E-Government*, *2*(2), 3–18. doi:10.1300/J399v02n02_02

Coffey International Development (CID). (2007). *The role of communication in governance: Detailed analysis*. Retrieved March, 15, 2009 from http://www.icdev.info/portal/documents/GovernanceSummaryPaper_003.pdf

Colle, R. (2005). Building ICT4D capacity in and by African universities. *International Journal of Education and Development using ICT*, *1*(1).

Commission for Communications Regulation. (2008). *Postal strategy statement (2008-2010)*. Dublin: Commission for Communications Regulation.

Commission of the European Communities. (2006). *i2010 eGovernment action plan: Accelerating eGovernment in Europe for the benefit of all*. SEC(2006) 511.

Commission of the European Communities. (2008). *Communication from the commission to the council, the European parliament and the European economic and social committee: Towards a European e-Justice strategy COM(2008)329 final*. Retrieved March 18, 2013 from http://ec.europa.eu/civiljustice/docs/com_2008_329_en.pdf

Commission of the European Communities. (2009). *European eParticipation summary report*. Retrieved from http://ec.europa.eu/information_society/newsroom/cf//document.cfm?action=display&doc_id=1499

Commission of the European Communities. (2010). *A digital Agenda for Europe*. SEC(2010) 245.

Communication Commission of Kenya (CCK). (2012). *Quarterly sector statistics report fourth quarter of the financial year 2011/12, April- June 2012*. Retrieved December 12, 2012 from http://cck.go.ke/resc/downloads/sector_statistics_report_q3_11-12.pdf

Compeau, D. R., & Higgins, C. A. (1995). Computer self-efficacy: Development of a measure and initial test. *Management Information Systems Quarterly*, *19*(2), 189–211. doi:10.2307/249688

Compeau, D. R., Higgins, C. A., & Huffs, S. (1999). Social cognitive theory and individual reactions to computing technology: A longitudinal study. *Management Information Systems Quarterly*, *23*(2), 145–158. doi:10.2307/249749

Comscore. (2011). *Google/IPSOS (ourmobileplanet.com), informa and netsize 2011 guide*. Retrieved February 13, 2013 from http://txt4ever.wordpress.com/2011/12/30/1715/

Conklin, J. (2003). Dialog mapping: Reflections on an industrial strength case study. In P. Kirschner, S. Buckingham Shum, & C. Carr (Eds.), *Visualizing argumentation: Software tools for collaborative and educational sensemaking*. London: Springer Verlag. doi:10.1007/978-1-4471-0037-9_6

Conklin, J., & Begeman, M. (1989). gIBIS: A tool for all reasons. *Journal of the American Society for Information Science American Society for Information Science*, *40*(3), 200–213. doi:10.1002/(SICI)1097-4571(198905)40:3<200::AID-ASI11>3.0.CO;2-U

Connolly, C., Chambers, C., Eagleson, E., Matthews, D., & Rogers, T. (2010). *Augmented reality effectiveness in advertising*. Retrieved July 6, 2013 from http://edgd. asee.org/conferences/proceedings/65th%20Midyear/ Connolly_Chambers_Augmented_Reality_%20Effectiveness%20in%20Advert.pdf

Constantinides, E. (2009). *Social media/web 2.0 as marketing parameter: An introduction*. Paper presented at the 8th International Congress Marketing Trends. Paris, France.

Constantinides, E. (2010). Connecting small and medium enterprises to the new consumer: The web 2.0 as marketing tool. In *Global perspectives on small and medium enterprises and strategic information systems: International approaches*. Hershey, PA: IGI Global. doi:10.4018/978-1-61520-627-8.ch001

Cordella, A. (2005). *The role of information and communication technology in building trust in governance: Towards effectiveness and results*. Washington, DC: Inter-American Development Bank.

Cordella, A. (2007). e-Government: Towards the e-Bureaucratic. *Journal of Information Technology, 22*, 265–274. doi:10.1057/palgrave.jit.2000105

Cordella, A., & Willcocks, L. (2010). Outsourcing, bureaucracy and public value: Reappraising the notion of the 'contract state'. *Government Information Quarterly, 27*(1), 82–88. doi:10.1016/j.giq.2009.08.004

Cortada, J. W., Gupta, A. M., & Le Noir, M. (2007). *How the most advanced nations can remain competitive in the information age*. IBM.

Cortes, E. C., Espinosa, S. J., & Tari, J. J. (2006). E-government maturity at Spanish local levels. In *Proceedings of the European and Mediterranean Conference on Information Systems* (EMCIS). Costa Blanca, Spain: EMCIS.

Cotterill, S. (2009). Local e-government partnerships. In C. G. Reddick (Ed.), *Strategies for local e-government adoption and implementation, comparative studies* (pp. 105–122). Hershey, PA: Information Science Reference. doi:10.4018/978-1-60566-282-4.ch006

Council of the European Union. (2008). *European e-justice action plan*. Retrieved May 5, 2013 from http://register. consilium.europa.eu/pdf/en/08/st15/st15315.en08.pdf

Council of the European Union. (2012). *Report from the working party on e-law (e-justice) to Coreper/council, 6575/12*. Retrieved December 29, 2012 from http://register.consilium.europa.eu/pdf/en/12/st16/st16575.en12.pdf

Courtney, J. F. (2001). Decision making and knowledge management in inquiring organizations: Toward a new decision-making paradigm for DSS. *Decision Support Systems, 31*(1), 17–38. doi:10.1016/S0167-9236(00)00117-2

Cova, B., & Dalli, D. (2009). Working consumers: The next step in marketing theory? *Marketing Theory, 9*(3), 315–339. doi:10.1177/1470593109338144

Cova, B., Dalli, D., & Zwick, D. (2011). Critical perspectives on consumers' role as 'producers': Broadening the debate on value co-creation in marketing processes. *Marketing Theory, 11*(3), 231–241. doi:10.1177/1470593111408171

Cressey, D. R. (1953). *A study in the social psychology of embezzlement: Other people's money*. Glencoe, IL: Free Press.

Croom, S. R. (2000). The impact of web-based procurement on the management of operating resources supply. *Journal of Supply Chain Management, 36*(1), 4–13. doi:10.1111/j.1745-493X.2000.tb00065.x

Croom, S., & Brandon-Jones, A. (2007). Impact of e-procurement: Experiences from implementation in the UK public sector. *Journal of Purchasing and Supply Management, 13*(4), 294–303. doi:10.1016/j.pursup.2007.09.015

Cross, N. (2001). *Keynote speech: Design/science/research: Developing a discipline*. Paper presented at the 5th Asian Design Conference. Seoul, Korea.

Csetenyi, A. (2000). Electronic government: Perspectives from e-commerce. In *Proceedings of the 11th International Workshop on Database and Expert Systems Applications* (DEXA'00). IEEE Press.

Cuenca-Grau, B., Parsia, B., Sirin, E., & Kalyanpur, A. (2005). Automatic partitioning of OWL ontologies using e-connections. In *Proceedings of the 2005 International Workshop on Description Logics* (DL-2005). DL.

Curtin, G. G., Sommer, M. H., & Vis-Sommer, V. (2003). *The world of e-government*. New York: The Haworth Press.

Dada, D. (2006). The failure of e-government in developing countries: A literature review. *Electronic Journal of Information Systems in Developing Countries, 26*(7), 1–10.

Danowitz, A. K., Nassef, Y., & Goodman, S. E. (1995). Cyberspace across the Sahara: Computing in North Africa. *Communications of the ACM, 38*(12), 23–28. doi:10.1145/219663.219674

d'Aquin, M., Sabou, M., & Motta, E. (2006). Modularization: A key for the dynamic selection of relevant knowledge components. In *Proceedings of First International Workshop on Modular Ontologies*, ISWC2006. Athens, GA: ISWC.

David, S., & Asamoah, C. (2011). Video as a tool for agricultural extension in Africa: A case study from Ghana. *International Journal of Education and Development using ICT, 7*(1).

David, M., & Michael, B. (2004). Usability and open source software. *First Monday.*

Davila, A., Gupta, M., & Palmer, R. (2003). Moving procurement systems to the internet: The adoption and use of e-procurement technology models. *European Management Journal, 21*(1), 11–23. doi:10.1016/S0263-2373(02)00155-X

Davis, F. (1989). Perceived usefulness, perceived ease of use, and user acceptance of information technology. *Management Information Systems Quarterly, 13*(1), 319–340. doi:10.2307/249008

Davis, F. D. (1993). User acceptance of information technology: System characteristics, user perceptions and behavioural impacts. *International Journal of Man-Machine Studies, 38*(3), 475–487. doi:10.1006/imms.1993.1022

Davis, F. D., Bagozzi, R. P., & Warshaw, P. R. (1992). Extrinsic and intrinsic motivation to use computers in the workplace. *Journal of Applied Social Psychology, 22*(14), 1111–1132. doi:10.1111/j.1559-1816.1992.tb00945.x

Dawes, S. S. (2008, December). Th e evolution and continuing challenges of e-governance. *Public Administration Review*, 86–102. doi:10.1111/j.1540-6210.2008.00981.x

Dawes, S. S. (2009). Governance in the digital age: A research and action framework for an uncertain future. *Government Information Quarterly, 26*, 257–264. doi:10.1016/j.giq.2008.12.003

De Boer, L., Harink, J., & Heijboer, G. (2002). A conceptual model for assessing the impact of electronic procurement. *European Journal of Purchasing & Supply Management, 8*(1), 25–33. doi:10.1016/S0969-7012(01)00015-6

De Kervenoael, R., & Koçoğlu, I. (2011). E-government strategy in Turkey: A case for m-government? In *Handbook for e-government in emerging economies – Adoption, continuance, usage, e-participation and legal frameworks.* Hershey, PA: IGI Global Publishing.

De Kervenoael, R., Palmer, M., & Cakici, N. M. (2010). Exploring civil servant resistance to m-government: A story of transition and opportunities Turkey. In *Mobile information communication technologies adoption in developing countries: Effects and implications.* Hershey, PA: IGI Global Publishing. doi:10.4018/978-1-61692-818-6.ch010

De Reuck, J., & Joseph, R. (1999). Universal service in a participatory democracy: A perspective from Australia. *Government Information Quarterly, 16*(4), 345–352. doi:10.1016/S0740-624X(00)86839-2

Del Gallo, U. (2009). *The lynchpin of integrated communications: A new paradigm for postal operators.* Retrieved May 20th, 2011, from http://www.accenture.com/SiteCollectionDocuments/PDF/Accenture_Postal_Lynchpin_of_Integrated_Communications.pdf

Del Monte, A., & Papagni, E. (2007). The determinants of corruption in Italy: Regional panel data analysis. *European Journal of Political Economy, 23*(2), 379–396. doi:10.1016/j.ejpoleco.2006.03.004

Deladoss, P. R., Pan, S. L., & Huang, J. C. (2003). Structurational analysis of e-government initiatives: A case study of SCO. *Decision Support Systems, 34*(3), 253–269. doi:10.1016/S0167-9236(02)00120-3

Deloitte & Touche. (2001). The citizen as customer. *CMA Management, 74* (10).

DePriest, D. (2012). The fifth dimension: How augmented reality is launching worlds within our world. In *Proceedings of TCC.* TCC.

Dept. for Communities and Local Government. (2008). *Delivering digital inclusion: An action plan for consultation*. London: Communities and Local Government Publications.

Deridder, D. (2002). A concept-oriented approach to support software maintenance and reuse activities. In *Proceedings of 5th Joint Conference on Knowledge-Based Software Engineering*. IEEE.

Desa. (2010). *E-government survey 2010*. Retrieved February 13, 2013 from http://books.google.com.tr/books?id=IPsnu3nBeksC&pg=PA28&lpg=PA28&dq=%22desa+2010+e.government+survey+2010%22&source=bl&ots=RbnJTiBwT_&sig=22jJP9oCD61-dEVIxbgvDAVIJ6I&hl=tr&sa=X&ei=4dwwUaWFCs3Zsgb-6YDwDA&ved=0CDcQ6AEwAg#v=onepage&q=%22desa%202010%20e.government%20survey%202010%22&f=false

Deviatnikovaitė, I., & Kalašnykas, R. (2007). Kategorijų kontrolė, valdžia ir socialinės technologijos turiningųjų požymių ypatumai teisėtumo užtikrinimo aplinkoje. *Jurisprudencija: Mokslo Darbai, 6*(96), 85–89.

Dewan, S., & Riggins, F. J. (2005). The digital divide: Current and future research directions. *Journal of the Association for Information Systems*. Retrieved March 12, 2013 from http://misrc.umn.edu/workingpapers/fullpapers/2005/0524_120605.pdf

Dewan, S., & Kraemer, K. L. (2000). Information technology and productivity: Evidence from country-level data. *Management Science, 46*(4), 548–562. doi:10.1287/mnsc.46.4.548.12057

Dezayas, H. (2008). *So, how much paper does our local government use?* Penn-Trafford Star.

Dias, M. G. B., Anquetil, N., & Marcal de Oliveira, K. (2003). Organizing the knowledge used in software maintenance. *Journal of Universal Computer Science, 9*(7), 641–658.

Digital Times. (2009). *National e-procurement system government e-procurement system*. Retrieved April 16, 2013 from http://www.dt.co.kr/contents.htm?article_no=2009050702011857731002

Dillon, T., Chang, E., Hadzic, M., & Wongthongtham, P. (2008). Differentiating conceptual modelling from data modelling, knowledge modelling and ontology modelling and a notation for ontology modeling. In *Proceedings of the Fifth Asia-Pacific Conference on Conceptual Modeling*. Australian Computer Society Inc.

Dillon, A., & Morris, M. (1996). User acceptance of information technology: Theories and models. In *Annual review of information science and technology* (pp. 3–32). Medford, NJ: Information Today, Inc.

DiMaggio, P., & Hargittai, E. (2001). *From the 'digital divide' to `digital inequality':Studying internet use as penetration increases*. Princeton, NJ: Princeton University.

Dinev, T., Hart, P., & Mullen, M. R. (2008). Internet privacy concerns and beliefs about government surveillance – An empirical investigation. *The Journal of Strategic Information Systems, 17*, 214–233. doi:10.1016/j.jsis.2007.09.002

Dinsdale, G., Chhabra, S., & Rath-Wilson, J. (2002). *A toolkit for e-government: Issues, impacts and insights*. Canadian Centre for Management Development.

Dobbins, T. (2007, November 14th). *Industrial relations in the postal sector - Ireland*. Retrieved October 20th, 2010, from http://www.eurofound.europa.eu/eiro/studies/tn0704018s/ie0704019q.htm

Dombeu, J. V. F., Huisman, M., & Szpak, Z. (2011). A framework for semantic model ontologies generation for e-government applications. In *Proceedings of the Fifth International Conference on Digital Society*, (pp. 152-158). ICDS.

Donna, E., & Yen, D. C. (2006). E-government: Evolving relationship of citizens and government domestic, and international development. *Government Information Quarterly, 23*(2), 207–235. doi:10.1016/j.giq.2005.11.004

Doran, P. (2009). *Ontology modularization: Principles and practice*. (PhD Thesis). University of Liverpool, Liverpool, UK.

Doyle, T. (2010). *Information and communications technology procurement for border management*. Washington, DC: Border Management Modernization.

DPADM. (2004). *Global e-government readiness report 2004: Towards access for opportunity.* Division for Public Administration and Development Management. Retrieved April 16, 2013 from http://www.unpan.org/egovernment4.asp

Dravis, R. (2002). *Open source software: Perspective for development.* InfoDev, TheDravis Group. Retrieved April 15, 2013, from http://www.infodev.org/en/Document.21.pdf

Drigas, A., & Koukianakis, L. (2009). Government online: An e-Government platform to improve public administration operations and services delivery of the citizens. In *Proceedings of WSKS*, (pp. 523-532). WSKS.

Drucker, P. (1954). *The practice of management.* New York: Harper.

Drucker, P. (1969). *The age of discontinuity: Guidelines to our changing society.* London: Pan Book Ltd.

Drucker, P. F. (1999). *Management challenges for the 21st century.* Oxford, UK: Butterworth-Heinemann.

Dubelaar, C., Sohal, A., & Savic, V. (2005). Benefits, impediments and critical success factors in B2C E-business adoption. *Technovation*, *25*(11), 1251–1262. doi:10.1016/j.technovation.2004.08.004

Dwivedi, Y., Williams, M., Ramdani, B., Niranjan, S., & Weerakkody, V. (2011). *Understanding factors for successful adoption of web 2.0 applications.* Paper presented at the 19th European Conference on Information Systems. Helsinki, Finland.

Eakin, D. (2003). Measuring e-procurement benefits. *Summit: Canada's Magazine on Public Sector Purchasing.*

Eddowes, L. A. (2004). The application of methodologies in e-government. *Electronic. Journal of E-Government*, *2*(2), 115–126.

Eele, G., Somboja, J., Likwelile, S., & Ackroyd, S. (2000). Meeting international targets in Tanzania. *Development Review Policy*, *18*(1), 1467–7679.

E-Governance Practices, Strategies and Policies of European Cities. (2004). Retrieved October 2012 from http://www.intelcitiesproject.com

E-Government Special Committee. (2003). *e-Government white paper.* Retrieved March 28, 2013 from http://eng.nia.or.kr/english/bbs/download.asp?fullpathname=%5CData%5Cattach%5C201112221611231975%5Ce-Goverment+White+Paper+2003(english).pdf&filename=e-Goverment+White+Paper+2003(english).pdf

Eicher, C. K. (2007). *Agricultural extension in Africa and Asia.* East Lansing, MI: Michigan State University, Department of Agricultural Economics.

Eisenhardt, K. (1989). Agency theory: An assessment and review. *Academy of Management Review*, *14*(1), 57–74.

Elliman, T., & Irani, Z. (2007). Establishing a framework for e-government research: Project VIEGO. *Transforming Government: People. Process and Policy*, *1*(4), 364.

Ellis, A. (2004). Using the new institutional economics in e-government to deliver transformational change. *Electronic. Journal of E-Government*, *2*(2), 126–138.

El-Qawasmeh, E. (2011). Assessment of the Jordanian e-government: An empirical study. *Journal of Emerging Trends in Engineering and Applied Sciences*, *2*(4), 594–600.

El-Sawah, S., El Fattah Tharwat, A. A., & Rasmy, M. H. (2008). A quantitative model to predict the Egyptian ERP implementation success index. *Business Process Management Journal*, *14*(3), 288–306. doi:10.1108/14637150810876643

Elsheikh, Y., Cullenm, A., & Hobbs, D. (2008). E-government in Jordan: Challenges and opportunities. *Transforming Government: People. Process and Policy*, *2*(2), 83–103.

Ensan, F. (2010). *Semantic interface-based modular ontology framework.* New Brunswick, Canada: The University of New Brunswick.

EPA. (n.d.). *Our mission and what we do.* US EPA. Retrieved August 16, 2012 from http://www.epa.gov/aboutepa/whatwedo.html

Epstein, J. M. (1999). Agent-based computational models and generative social science. *Complexity*, *4*(5), 41–60. doi:10.1002/(SICI)1099-0526(199905/06)4:5<41::AID-CPLX9>3.0.CO;2-F

Escobar, A. (1995). *Encountering development: The making and unmaking of the third world.* Princeton, NJ: Princeton University Press.

Escobar, A. (2001). Culture sits in places: Reflections on globalism and subaltern strategies of localization. *Political Geography, 20*(2), 139–174. doi:10.1016/S0962-6298(00)00064-0

ESRI. (2011). *Geographic information systems as an integrating technology: Context, concepts, and definitions.* Retrieved March 24, 2013 from http://www.colorado.edu/geography/gcraft/notes/intro/intro.html

Essig, M., & Arnold, U. (2001). Electronic procurement in supply chain management: An information economics based analysis of electronic markets. *Journal of Supply Chain Management, 37*(4), 43–49. doi:10.1111/j.1745-493X.2001.tb00112.x

Esteves, J., & Joseph, R. C. (2008). A comprehensive framework for the assessment of eGovernment projects. *Government Information Quarterly, 25,* 118–132. doi:10.1016/j.giq.2007.04.009

Estevez, E., Janowski, T., & Ojo, A. (2007).*Planning for e-government -A service-oriented agency survey* (Research Report No. 361). Centre for Electronic Government, United Nations University-International Institute for Software Technology (UNU-IIST).

ESTI. (2009). *Directive 2009/140/EC of the European parliament and of the council.* Retrieved September 2, 2011, from http://www.etsi.org/website/document/aboutetsi/ec_directives/2009_140.pdf

Etzioni, A. (1999). *The limits of privacy.* New York: Basic Books.

European Commission Communication from the Commission to the European Parliament. the Council, the European Economic and Social Committee and the Committee of the Regions. (2010).*A digital agenda for Europe COM(2010) 245 final/2.* Retrieved February 28, 2013 from http://eur-lex.europa.eu/LexUriServ/LexUriServ.do?uri=COM:2010:0245:FIN:EN:PDF

European Commission Communication from the Commission. (2010). *Europe 2020: A strategy for smart, sustainable and inclusive growth COM(2010) 2020 final.* Retrieved February 28, 2013 http://eur-lex.europa.eu/LexUriServ/LexUriServ.do?uri=COM:2010:2020:FIN:EN:PDF

European Commission. (2011). *Communication from the commission to the European parliament, the council, the European economic and social committee and the committee of the regions: Building trust in EU-wide justice: A new dimension to European judicial training: COM(2011) 551 final.* Retrieved October 28, 2013 from http://ec.europa.eu/justice/criminal/files/2011-551-judicial-training_en.pdf

European Commission. (2005). *Inclusive e-government - No citizen left behind.* Retrieved December 20, 2010 from http://ec.europa.eu/information_society/activities/einclusion/policy/egov/index_en.htm

European Commission. (2010 a). A digital agenda for europe (COM(2010) 245 final/2). Brussels: European Commission.

European Commission. (2010). *e-Inclusion.* (E. I. Society, Producer). Retrieved September 19th, 2011 from http://ec.europa.eu/information_society/activities/einclusion/index_en.htm

European Communities. (2008). *Draft document as basis for EIF 2.0.* Official Publications of the European Communities. Retrieved February 13, 2013 from http://ec.europa.eu/idabc/servlets/Docb0db.pdf

Evans, L. L. (2010). *Social media marketing – Strategies for engaging in Facebook, Twitter and other social media.* Que Publishing.

Evolution of e-Government in the European Union. (2002). *Report commissioned by the Spanish Presidency of the Council of the European Union.* Retrieved March 6, 2013 from http://www.map.es/csi/pdf/egovEngl_definitivo.pdf

Factsheets: GPS Advanced Control Segment (OCX). (n.d.). Retrieved November 6, 2011 from http://www.losangeles.af.mil/library/factsheets/factsheet.asp?id=18676

Fang, Z. (2002). E-government in digital era: Concept, practice, and development. *International Journal of the Computer, the Internet and Management, 10*(2), 1-22.

Federal Trade Commission. (2010). *Protecting consumer privay in an era of rapid change: A proposed framework for businesses and policymakers.* Washington, DC: Federal Trade Commission.

Fedorowicz, J., & Dias, M. (2010). A decade of design in digital government research. *Government Information Quarterly, 27,* 1–8. doi:10.1016/j.giq.2009.09.002

Feller, J., Finnegan, P., & Nilsson, O. (2008). Openning public administration: Exploring open innovation archetypes and business model impacts. In L. Gonzalo, A. M. Bernardos, J. R. Casar, K. Kautz, & J. I. DeGross (Eds.), *Open IT-based innovation: Moving towards cooperative IT transfer and knowledge diffusion* (pp. 483–500). New York: Springer. doi:10.1007/978-0-387-87503-3_27

Fensel, D. (2004). *Ontologies: A silver bullet for knowledge management and electronic commerce.* Berlin: Springer.

Fernandez-Lopez, M., Gomez-Perez, A., Pazos-Sierra, A., & Pazos-Sierra, J. (1999). Building a chemical ontology using methodology and the ontology design environment. *IEEE Intelligent Systems & Their Applications, 4*(1), 37–46. doi:10.1109/5254.747904

Ferro, E., & Molinari, F. (2010a). Making sense of gov 2.0 strategies: No citizens, no party. *Journal of eDemocracy and Open Government, 2*(1), 56-68.

Ferro, E., & Molinari, F. (2010b). Framing web 2.0 in the process of public sector innovation: Going down the participation ladder. *European Journal of ePractice, 9,* 20-34.

Ferro, E., Caroleo, B., Cantamessa, M., & Leo, M. (2010). *ICT diffusion in an aging society: A scenario analysis.* Paper presented at the 9th International Federation for Information Processing, WG 8.5 International Conference on Electronic Government. Lausanne, Switzerland.

Filho, J. R., & Mota, F. P. B. (2012). Public e-procurement implementation: Insights from the structuration theory. In K. Vaidya (Ed.), *Inter-organizational infromation systems and business management: Theories for researcher.* Hershey, PA: IGI Global.

Finat, J., Delgado, F.J., Martìnez, R., Hurtado, A., Fernández, J.J., San José J.I., & Martìnez, J. (2010). Constructors of geometric primitives in domain ontologies for urban environments. *Journal of Information Technology in Construction.*

Finger, M., & Pécoud, G. (2003). From e-government to e-governance? Towards a model of e-governance. *Electronic. Journal of E-Government, 1*(1), 1–10.

Fink, D. (2006). Value decomposition of e-commerce performance. *Benchmarking: An International Journal, 13*(1/2), 81–92. doi:10.1108/14635770610644592

Finkle, A. (2005). Relying on information acquired by a principal. *International Journal of Industrial Organization, 23*(3-4), 263–278. doi:10.1016/j.ijindorg.2004.12.001

Foley, P., & Ghani, S. (2005). *The business case for e-government.* Paris: OECD.

Fonou Dombeu, V. F., Huisman, M., & Szpak, Z. (2011). A framework for semantic model ontologies generation for e-government applications. In *Proceedings of ICDS 2011: The Fifth International Conference on Digital Society.* ICDS.

Fonou-Dombeu, J. V., & Huisman, M. (2010a). Integrating e-government services: A stepwise ontology-based methodology framework. In *Proceedings of the 6th International Conference on eGovernment* (ECEG 2010). ECEG.

Fonou-Dombeu, J. V., Huisman, M., & Szpak, Z. (2011a). A framework for semantic model ontologies generation for e-government application. In *Proceedings of the 5th International Conference on Digital Society.* Gosier, France: Academic Press.

Fonou-Dombeu, J.V., & Huisman, M. (2011b). Combining ontology development methodologies and semantic web platforms for e-government domain ontology development. *International Journal of Web & Semantic technology, 2*(2), 12-25.

Fonou-Dombeu, J. V., & Huisman, M. (2010b). Investigating e-government knowledge base ontology supporting development projects monitoring in sub Saharan Africa. *International Journal of Computing and ICT Research, 4*(1), 20–29.

Fonou-Dombeu, J. V., & Huisman, M. (2011c). Semantic-driven e-government: Application of uschold and king ontology building methodology for semantic ontology models development. *International Journal of Web & Semantic Technology*, 2(4), 1–20. doi:10.5121/ijwest.2011.2401

Ford, T. C., Colombi, J. M., Graham, S. R., & Jacques, D. R. (2007). A survey on interoperability measurement. In *Proceedings of the 12th International Command and Control Research and Technology Symposium*. Retrieved February 13, 2013 from http://www.dtic.mil/cgibin/GetTRDoc?Location=U2&doc=GetTRDoc.pdf&AD=ADA481314

Forrester, J. (1961). *Industrial dynamics*. Cambridge, MA: Productivity Press.

Fraser, S. (2006). *Report of the auditor general of Canada to the house of commons*. Retrieved November 8, 2013 from http://www.oag-bvg.gc.ca/internet/English/parl_oag_200611_03_e_14971.html

Fuks, K., Kawa, A., & Wieczerzycki, W. (2009). *Improved e-sourcing strategy with multi-agent swarms*. Paper presented to Computational Intelligence for Modelling Control & Automation, International Conference. Vienna, Austria.

Furlong, S. (2011). *Transformational e-government success through enhanced project management*. (Ph.D. Thesis). Liverpool, UK.

Furlong, S. (2012). Project management: An e-government driver? In *Handbook of research on e-government in emerging economies: Adoption, e-participation, and legal frameworks*. Hershey, PA: IGI Global. doi:10.4018/978-1-4666-0324-0.ch027

Gangemi, A., Pisanelli, D. M., & Steve, G. (1999). An overview of the ONIONS project: Applying ontologies to the integration of medical terminologies. *Data & Knowledge Engineering*, 31(2), 183–220. doi:10.1016/S0169-023X(99)00023-3

Gartner Group. (2000, May 23). Key issues in e-government strategy and management. *Research Notes, Key Issues*.

Gauld, R. (2007). Principal-agent theory and organizational change. *Policy Studies*, 28(1), 17–34. doi:10.1080/01442870601121395

Gauthier, J., & Lavagnon, A. (n.d.). Foundations of project management research: An explicit and six-facet ontological framework. *Project Management Journal*, 43(5), 5-23.

Gaynor, G. H. (2002). *Innovation by design*. New York: American Management Association.

Gelb, E., & Bonati, G. (2007). Evaluating internet for extension in agriculture (1997). In *ICT in agriculture: Perspectives of technological innovation*. Jerusalem, Israel: Hebrew University of Jerusalem. Retrieved June 2, 2013 from http://departments.agri.huji.ac.il/economics/gelb-sum-12.pdf

Gelb, E., & Parker, C. (2007). Is ICT adoption for agriculture still an important issue? In *ICT in agriculture: Perspectives of technological innovation*. Jerusalem, Israel: Hebrew University of Jerusalem. Retrieved March 23, 2013 from http://departments.agri.huji.ac.il/economics/gelb-gelb-parker.pdf.

Gervautz, M., & Schmalstieg, D. (2012). Anywhere interfaces using handheld augmented reality. IEEE Computer Society, 26-31.

Ghapanci, A., Albadavi, A., & Zarei, B. (2008). A framework for e-government planning and implementation. *Electronic Government: An International Journal*, 5(1), 71–90. doi:10.1504/EG.2008.016129

Ghosh, R. A., Krieger, B., Glott, R., & Robles, G. (2002). *Open source software in the public sector: Policy within the European Union*. Maastricht, The Netherlands: International Institute of Infonomics, University of Maastricht.

Gintis, H., Bowles, S., Boyd, R., & Fehr, E. (2005). *Moral sentiments and material interest*. Cambridge, MA: MIT Press.

GLIMSTEDT. (2012). *Teisės žinios 2012 Nr. 5(5)*. Retrieved February 28, 2013 from http://www.glimstedt.lt/e-laikrastis/e-laikrastis-glimstedt-teises-zinios-5-e-paslaugos/2952

Godse, V., & Garg, A. (2009). *From e-government to e-governance*. New Delhi: Computer Society of India.

Gómez-Pérez, A. (1995). Some ideas and examples to evaluate ontologies. In *Proceedings of 11th Conference on Artificial Intelligence for Applications*, (pp. 299-305). AI.

Gomez-Perez, A., & Benjamins, V. R. (1999). Overview of knowledge sharing and reuse components: Ontology and problem-solving methods. In *Proceedings of the IJCAI-99 Workshop on Ontologies and Problem-Solving Methods* (KRR5). Stockholm, Sweden: IJCAI.

Goodchild, M. F. (2010). Twenty years of progress: GIScience in 2010. *Journal of Spatial Information Science, 1*, 3–20.

Google Discontinues Google Earth Plus. (n.d.). Retrieved August 16, 2012 from http://www.techpluto.com/google-earth-live/

Google Earth Plus Discontinued. (n.d.). Retrieved August 16, 2012 from http://www.gearthblog.com/blog/archives/2008/12/google_earth_plus_discontinued.html

Google Earth Product Family. (n.d.). Retrieved August 16, 2012 from http://earth.google.com/products.html

Google Earth. (n.d.). *Meet the browser*. Retrieved from http://google-latlong.blogspot.com/2008/05/google-earth-meet-browser.html

Goold, B. J. (2009). Building it In the role of privacy enhancing technologies (PETs) in the regulation of surveillance and data collection. In B. J. Goold, & D. Neyland (Eds.), *New directions in surveillance and privacy* (pp. 18–38). Cullompton, UK: Wilan Publishing.

Gorla, N. (2008). Hurdles in rural e-government projects in India: Lessons for developing countries. *Electronic Government: An International Journal, 5*(1), 91–102. doi:10.1504/EG.2008.016130

Gorry, G. A., & Morton, M. S. (1971). A framework for management information systems. *Sloan Management Review, 13*(1), 55–70.

Gottschalk, P. (2007). Sharing knowledge in law firms. *International Journal of Innovation and Learning, 4*(3), 255–273. doi:10.1504/IJIL.2007.012381

Government of Canada Foreign Affairs and International Trade Canada. (2006). *Government on-line final report*. Retrieved March 8, 2013, from http://www.dfait-maeci.gc.ca/department/gol-annual-report-en.asp

Graham, S., & Aurigi, A. (1997). Virtual cities, social polarisation, and the crisis in urban public space. *Journal of Urban Technology, 4*(1), 19–52. doi:10.1080/10630739708724546

Grant, G., & Chau, D. (2005). Developing a generic framework for e-government. *Journal of Global Information Management, 13*(1). doi:10.4018/jgim.2005010101

Grant, T. S., Wix, T. S., Whitehead, C. J., & Blair, J. D. (1991). Strategies for assessing and managing organisational stakeholders. *The Academy of Management Executive*, 61–75.

Gregor, S. (2006). The nature of theory in information systems. *Management Information Systems Quarterly, 30*(3), 611–642.

Gregor, S., & Jones, D. (2007). The anatomy of a design theory. *Journal of the Association for Information Systems, 8*(5), 312–335.

Greiner, L. (2005). *State of the marketplace: e-Government gateways*. Faulkner Information Service. Retrieved February 6, 2012 from http://www.faulkner.com/products/faulknerlibrary/00018297.htm

Grey, J., Huisman, M., & Goede, R. (2006). *An investigation of the suitability of agile system development methodologies for the development of data warehouses*. (Msc. Dissertation). North-West University, Potchefstroom, South Africa.

Grönroos, C. (2008). Service logic revisited: Who creates value? And who co-creates? *European Business Review, 20*(4), 298–314. doi:10.1108/09555340810886585

Gruber, T. R. (1993). A translation approach to portable ontology specifications. *Journal of Knowledge Acquisition, 5*(2), 199–220. doi:10.1006/knac.1993.1008

Gruber, T. R. (1995). Toward principles for the design of ontologies used for knowledge sharing. *International Journal of Human-Computer Studies, 43*(5/6), 907–928. doi:10.1006/ijhc.1995.1081

Gruninger, M., & Fox, M. S. (1995). Methodology for the design and evaluation of ontologies. In *Proceedings of Workshop on Basic Ontological Issues in Knowledge Sharing*. Montreal, Canada: IEEE.

GTN. (2003). *Centre for international development at Harvard University: Government procurement.* Retrived February 14, 2013, form http://www.cid.harvard.edu/cidtrade/issues/govpro.html

Guijarro, L. (2007). Interoperability frameworks and enterprise architectures in e-government initiatives in Europe and the United States. *Government Information Quarterly, 24*(1), 89–101. doi:10.1016/j.giq.2006.05.003

Guler, E. (2012). *Obama versus Turkish politicians: Who fares better on social media?* Hürriyet Daily News, Ankara. Retrieved February 13, 2013 from http://www.hurriyetdailynews.com/obama-versus-turkish-politicians-who-fares-better-on-social-media-.aspx?pageID=238&nid=33906

Gunasekaran, A., McGaughey, R. E., Ngai, E. W. T., & Rai, B. K. (2009). E-procurement adoption in the southcoast SMEs. *International Journal of Production Economics, 122*(1), 161–175. doi:10.1016/j.ijpe.2009.05.013

Haigh, N., & Griffiths, A. (2008). E-government and environmental sustainability: Results from three Australian cases. *Electronic Government: An International Journal, 5*(1), 45–62. doi:10.1504/EG.2008.016127

Halfawy, M. R., Vanier, D. J., & Hubble, D. (2004). Integration of municipal information systems for sustainable management of infrastructure assets. *Environmental Informatics Archives, 2*, 375–386.

Hammer, M. (1995). *Reengineering the corporation: A manifesto for business revolution.* Nicholas Breadley Publishing.

Hansen, H. S., & Reinau, K. H. (2006). The citizens in e-participation. In M. A. Wimmer, H. J. Scholl, A. Gronlund, & K. V. Andersen (Eds.), *Electronic government* (pp. 70–82). Berlin: Springer. doi:10.1007/11823100_7

Hao, X., & Qi, P. (2011). Analysis on corruption and collusive behaviors in government procurement in a game theory perspective. *Journal of Management and Strategy, 2*(2), 38. doi:10.5430/jms.v2n2p38

Harding, R. (2006). Ecologically sustainable development: Origins, implementation and challenges. *Desalination, 187*(1-3), 229–239. doi:10.1016/j.desal.2005.04.082

Harink, J. H. A. (2003). *Internet technology to purchase.* (PhD thesis). University of Twente, Twente, The Netherlands.

Harris, S., Gibbons, J., Davies, J., & Crichton, C. (2008). *Semantic technologies in electronic government: Tutorial and workshop.* Retrieved May 2, 2013, from http://www.cs.ox.ac.uk/people/jeremy.gibbons/publications/semantech-egov.pdf

Harrison, T. M., Santiago, G. G., Burke, B., Cook, M., Cresswell, A., & Helbig, N. … Pardo, T. (2011). Open government and e-government: Democratic challenges from a public value perspective. In *Proceedings of the 12th Annual International Conference on Digital Government Research.* College Park, MD: DGR.

Hawari, A., & Heeks, R. (2010). Explaining ERP failure in a developing country: A Jordanian case study. *Journal of Enterprise Information Management, 23*(2), 135–160. doi:10.1108/17410391011019741

Hayes, R., & Abernathy, W. (1980, July-August). Managing our way to economic decline. *Harvard Business Review*, 67–77.

Heeks, R. (2001). *Understanding e-governance for development.* Retrieved March 12, 2012 from http://www.sed.manchester.ac.uk/idpm/research/publications/wp/igovernment/igov_wp11.htm

Heeks, R. (2003). *Design-reality gap analysis.* Retrieved May 28, 2013 from www.egov4dev.org/success/techniques/idfailure_drg.shtml

Heeks, R. (2005). *Foundations of ICTs in development: The onion-ring model.* Retrieved March 12, 2013 from http://www.sed.manchester.ac.uk/idpm/research/publications/wp/di/short/DIGBriefing4Onion.pdf

Heeks, R. (2008). *e-Government for development – Success and failure in e-government projects, e-government for development information exchange, coordinated by the University of Manchester's Institute for Development Policy and Management.* Retrieved May 4, 2013 from http://www.egov4dev.org/success/sfrates.shtml

Heeks, R. (1999). *Re-inventing government in the information age: International practice in IT enabled public sector reform.* London: Routledge. doi:10.4324/9780203204962

Heeks, R. (2001). *Understanding e-governance for development*. Manchester, UK: University of Manchester.

Heeks, R. (2002). Information systems and developing countries: Failure, success, and local improvisations. *The Information Society: An International Journal*, *18*(2), 101–112. doi:10.1080/01972240290075039

Heeks, R. (2006). *Implementing and managing egovernment: An international text*. London: Sage.

Heeks, R. (2010). Do information and communication technologies (ICTs) contribute to development? *Journal of International Development*, *22*(5), 625–640. doi:10.1002/jid.1716

Heeks, R. B. (2001). *Building e-governance for development (iGovernment paper no.12)*. Manchester, UK: University of Manchester.

Hefetz, A., & Warner, M. (2004). Privatization and its reverse: Explaining the dynamics of the government contracting process. *Journal of Public Administration: Research and Theory*, *14*(2), 171–190. doi:10.1093/jopart/muh012

Hevner, A. R., March, S. T., & Park, J. (2004). Design science in information systems research. *Management Information Systems Quarterly*, *28*(1), 75–105.

Hiller, J., & Belanger, F. (2001). *Privacy strategies for electronic government*. Arlington, VA: The Pricewaterhouse Coopers Endowment for the Business of Government.

Hinkelmann, K., Thonssen, B., & Wolff, D. (2010). Ontologies for e-government. In *Theory and applications of ontology: Computer applications* (pp. 429–461). IEEE. doi:10.1007/978-90-481-8847-5_19

Hirst, P. (2002). Democracy and governance. In J. Pierre (Ed.), *Debating governance, authority, steering and democracy* (pp. 13-33). Oxford, UK: Oxford University Press. Retrieved December 2012 from http://fds.oup.com/www.oup.co.uk/pdf/0-19-829514-6.pdf

Ho, A. (2002). Reinventing local governments and the e-government initiative. *Public Administration Review*, *62*(4), 434–444. doi:10.1111/0033-3352.00197

Hobbs, J. E. (1996). A transaction cost approach to supply chain management. *Supply Chain Management: An International Journal*, *1*(2), 15–27. doi:10.1108/13598549610155260

Hofstede, G. (1997). *Cultures and organizations: Software of the mind*. New York: McGraw-Hill.

Hofstede, G. (2003). *Culture's consequences* (2nd ed.). London: Academic Press.

Holmes, D. (2001). eGov: eBusiness strategies for government. London: Nicholas Brealey.

Holzer, M., & Manoharan, A. (2007). *Global trends in municipal e-government: An online assessment of worldwide municipal web portals*. Retrieved April 16, 2013 from http://www.iceg.net/2007/books/1/19_303.pdf

Homburg, V. (2008). *Understanding e-Government: Information systems in public administration*. Oxon, UK: Routledge.

Honeycutt, C., & Herring, S. C. (2009). *Beyond microblogging: Conversation and collaboration via Twitter*. Paper presented at the 42nd Hawaii International Conference on System Sciences. Waikoloa, HI.

Hood, C. (1991). A public management for all seasons? *Public Administration*, *69*, 3–19. doi:10.1111/j.1467-9299.1991.tb00779.x

Hood, C., & Margetts, H. (2007). Exploring government's toolsheds. In *The tools of government in the digital age* (pp. 4–25). Basingstoke, UK: Palgrave.

Howard, M. (2001). E-government across the globe: How will 'e' change government?. *Government Finance Review*, 6-9.

Hristozova, M. H. (2003). *EXPLODE: Extreme programming for lightweight ontology development*. (MSc Thesis). University of Melbourne, Melbourne, Australia.

Hsieh, J. J.-A., Rai, A., & Keil, M. (2008). Understanding digital inequality: Comparing continued use behaviour models of the socio-economically advantaged and disadvantaged. *Management Information Systems Quarterly*, *32*(1), 97–126.

Huduma. (2013). *About Huduma*. Retrieved January 25, 2013, from HTTP://huduma.OR.KE

Hult, G. T. (2003). An integration of thoughts on knowledge management. *Decision Sciences*, *34*, 189–195. doi:10.1111/1540-5915.02264

Hürriyet Daily News. (2010). *Vodafone Turkey presents cell phones for 1 TL*. Retrieved February 13, 2013 from http://www.hurriyetdailynews.com/vodafone-turkey-presents-cell-phones-for-1-tl.aspx?pageID=438&n=vodofone-presents-cell-phones-for-one-lira-2010-07-23

Hürriyet Daily News. (2011a). *Turkish marketing world discusses e-trade draft law*. Retrieved February 13, 2013 from http://www.hurriyetdailynews.com/turkish-marketing-world-discusses-e-trade-draft-law.aspx?pageID=438&n=turkish-marketing-world-discuss-e-trade-draft-2011-01-28

Hürriyet Daily News. (2011b). *Digital sales not making up for losses over piracy*. Retrieved February 13, 2013 from http://www.hurriyetdailynews.com/digital-sales-not-making-up-for-losses-over-piracy.aspx?pageID=238&nID=7924&NewsCatID=345

Hürriyet Daily News. (2012a). *Revenues for Turkey's telecom firms up 6 pct*. Retrieved February 13, 2013 from http://www.hurriyetdailynews.com/revenues-for-turkeys-telecom-firms-up-6-pct.aspx?pageID=238&nID=21623&NewsCatID=345

Hürriyet Daily News. (2012b). *Turkey's 3G faster than US 4G: Reports*. Retrieved February 13, 2013 from http://www.hurriyetdailynews.com/turkeys-3g-faster-than-us-4g-reports.aspx?pageID=238&nID=34452&NewsCatID=374

IBM Business Consulting Services. (2003). *How e-government are you? e-Government in France: State of play and perspectives*. Retrieved March 30, 2012 from http://www-07.ibm.com/services/pdf/bcs_egovernment.pdf

Iivari, J., & Hirschheim, R. (1996). Analyzing information systems development: A comparison and analysis of eight is development approaches. *Information Systems*, *21*(7), 551–575. doi:10.1016/S0306-4379(96)00028-2

Ikeda, M., Seta, K., Kakusho, O., & Mizoguchi, R. (1998). Task ontology: Ontology for building conceptual problem solving models. In *Proceedings of ECAI98 Workshop on Applications of Ontologies and Problem-Solving Model*, (pp. 126-133). ECA.

Information Policy. (2006). *Comparing e-governance and e-government*. Retrieved on January 12, 2013 from http://www.i-policy.org/2006/06/comparing_e-Gove.html

Infoxchange Australia. (2011). *Technology for social justice*. Retrieved from www.infoxchange.net.au

Institutas, T. (2004). Administracinių teismų vieta teismų sistemoje: užsienio šalių patirtis ir jos pritaikymo Lietuvoje galimybės. *Mokslinis tyrimas*. Retrieved February 28, 2013 from http://www.teise.org/docs/upload/adm%20teismai.pdf

Irani, Z., Al-Sebie, A., & Elliman, T. (2006). Transaction stage of e-government systems: Identification of its location & importance. In *Proceedings of the 39th Hawaii International Conference on System Sciences*. IEEE.

Irani, Z., Elliman, T., & Jackson, P. (2007). Electronic transformation of government in the UK: A research agenda. *European Journal of Information Systems*, *16*(4), 327–335. doi:10.1057/palgrave.ejis.3000698

ISO. (1998). Ergonomic requirements for office work with visual display terminals. *ISO 9241-11*.

ISO. (1999). Human centred design processes for interactive systems. *ISO 13407*.

ISO. (2003). ISO/TS 16071 ergonomics of human-system interaction. *Ergonomics of Human-System Interaction*.

ISO/IEC. (1989). ISO/IEC 7498-2:198. *Information processing systems-Open systems interconnection*.

ISO/IEC. (1996). ISO/IEC 10181:1996. *Information technology - Open systems interconnection*.

ISO/IEC. (1998). ISO/IEC 2788:1998. *Information technology-Security techniques*.

Ittner, C., & Larcker, D. (2003, November). Coming up short on non-financial performance measurement. *Harvard Business Review*, 88–95. PMID:14619154

ITU. (2008). *Electronic government for developing countires*. ICT Applications and Cybersecurity Division Policies and Strategies Department, ITU Telecommunication Development Sector.

Iversen, J., Mathiassen, L., & Nielsen, P. (2004). Managing process risk in software process improvement: An action research approach. *Management Information Systems Quarterly*, 28(3), 395–434.

Jackson, M. (2003). *Systems thinking: Creative holism for managers*. West Sussex, UK: John Wiley & Son Ltd.

Jaeger, P. T., & Thompson, K. M. (2003). E-government around the world: Lessons, challenges, and future directions. *Government Information Quarterly*, 20(4), 389–394. doi:10.1016/j.giq.2003.08.001

Jaeger, P., & Bertot, J. (2010). Transparency and technological change: Ensuring equal and sustained public access to government information. *Government Information Quarterly*, 27, 371–376. doi:10.1016/j.giq.2010.05.003

Janowski, T., Estevez, E., & Ojo, A. (2007). *A project framework for e-government* (Research Report No. 359). Centre for Electronic Governmen, United Nations University-International Institute for Software Technology (UNU-IIST).

Jarrar, M., Deik, A., & Farraj, B. (2011). *Ontology-based data and process governance framework-The case of e-government interoperability in Palestine*. Retrieved March 18, 2013 from http://www.jarrar.info/publications/JDF11.pdf

Jensen, M. C., & Meckling, W. H. (1976). Theory of the firm: Managerial behavior, agency costs and ownership structure. *Journal of Financial Economics*, 3(4), 305–360. doi:10.1016/0304-405X(76)90026-X

Jeong, M. W. (2010). *New start 0minwon 24' as government citizen service portal*. Inews24. Retrieved April 12, 2010 from http://news.inews24.com/php/news_view.php?g_serial=507556&g_menu=020200

Johannessen, J.-A., Olaisen, J., & Olsen, B. (2002). Aspects of a systemic philosophy of knowledge: From social facts to data, information and knowledge. *Kybernetes*, 31(7/8), 1099–1120. doi:10.1108/03684920210436363

Johnson, H., & Kaplan, R. (1987). *Relevance lost – The rise and fall of management accounting*. Boston: Harvard Business School Press.

Jorgensen, D. J., & Cable, S. (2002). Facing the challenges of e-government: A case study of the city of Corpus Christi, Texas. *S.A.M. Advanced Management Journal*, 67(3), 15.

Jupp, V. (2003). Realizing the vision of egovernment. In *The world of e-government*. Academic Press.

Jurisdisca, I., Mylopoulos, J., & Yu, E. (2004). Using ontologies for knowledge management: An information systems perspective. *Knowledge and Information Systems Archive*, 6(4), 380–401. doi:10.1007/s10115-003-0135-4

Justesen, S. (2004). Innoversity in communities of practice. In *Knowledge networks, innovation through communities of practice* (pp. 79–95). Hershey, PA: Information Science Publishing.

Justice, I. (2010). *A Microsoft white paper*. Retrieved February 28, 2013 http://www.microsoft.com/government/ww/safety-defense/solutions/Pages/integrated-justice.aspx

Kaaya, J. (1999). Role of information technology in agriculture. In *Proceedings of FoA Conference*, (vol. 4, pp. 315-328). FoA.

Kachwamba, M. A. (2011). Impact of e-government on transaction cost and FDI Inflows: A proposed conceptual framework. *International Journal of Business and Management*, 6(11), 285. doi:10.5539/ijbm.v6n11p285

Kaisara, G., & Pather, S. P. (2009). *E-government in South Africa: e-Service quality access and adoption factors. Informatics & Design Papers and Reports*. Cape Peninsula University of Technology.

Kamal, M., Weerakkody, V., & Irani, Z. (2011). Analyzing the role of stakeholders in the adoption of technology integration solutions in UK local government: An exploratory study. *Government Information Quarterly*, 28, 200–210. doi:10.1016/j.giq.2010.08.003

Kamar, N., & Ongo'ndo, M. (2007). *Impact of e-government on management and use of government information in Kenya*. Paper presented at the World Library and Information Congress: 73rd IFLA General Conference and Council. Durban, South Africa.

Kamel, S. (1998). *Decision support systems and strategic public sector decision making in Egypt*. Retrieved June 13, 2013 from http://www.sed.manchester.ac.uk/idpm/research/publications/wp/igovernment/documents/igov_wp03.pdf

Kameswari, V. L. V., Kishore, D., & Gupta, V. (2011). ICTs for agricultural extension: A study in the Indian Himalayan region ICTs for agricultural extension. *Electronic Journal of Information Systems in Developing Countries*, 48(3), 1–12.

Kanaan, R. K. (2009). *Making sense of e-government implementation in Jordan: A qualitative investigation*. Leicester, UK: De Montfort University.

Kaplan, R., & Norton, D. (1996, January-February). Using the balanced scorecard as a strategic management system. *Harvard Business Review*, 3–13.

Kaplinsky, R., & Morris, M. (2000). *A handbook for value chain research*. Ottawa, Canada: International Development Research Centre.

Kargaudienė, A. (2007). Socialinės įtakos mechanizmai: Naujos galimybės paveikti administracinės teisės normų įgyvendinimo procesą. *Jurisprudencija. Mokslo Darbai*, 6(96), 27–31.

Karokola, G., & Yngström, L. (2009). Discussing e-government maturity models for developing world – Security view. In *Proceedings of the 8th ISSA 2009 Conference on Information Security*. Johannesburg, South Africa: ISSA.

Kassahun, A. E., Molla, A., & Sarkar, P. (2012). Government process reengineering, what we know and what we need to know. In S. Chhabra, & M. Kumar (Eds.), *Strategic enterprise resource planning models for e-government, applications and methodologies* (pp. 1–25). Hershey, PA: IGI Global. doi:10.4018/978-1-4666-1740-7.ch086

Kassen, M. (2013). *Globalization of e-government: Open government as a global agenda, benefits, limitations and ways forward*. Retrieved 17 April 2013 from http://idv.sagepub.com/content/early/2013/01/18/0266666912473620

Kauffman, R. J., & Mohtadi, H. (2004). Proprietary and open systems adoption in e-procurement: A risk-augmented transaction cost perspective. *Journal of Management Information Systems*, 21(1), 137–166.

Kayed, A., & Colomb, R. (2000). Extracting ontological concepts for tendering conceptual structures. *Eng.*, 40(1), 71–398.

Kayed, A., & Colomb, R. (2005). Using BWW model to evaluate building ontologies in CGs formalism. *Information Systems*, 30(5), 379–398. doi:10.1016/j.is.2004.03.002

Keen, P. G. W. (1999). *Electronic commerce relationships: Trust by design*. Englewood Cliffs, NJ: Prentice-Hall.

Kehagias, D., Kontotasio, D., Mouratidis, G., Nikolaou, T., Papadimitriou, I., & Kalogirou, K. … Normann, I. (2008). *Ontologies, typologies, models and management tools*. OASIS Deliverable. Retrieved March 16, 2013 from www.oasis-project.eu%2Fdocs%2FOFFICIAL_DELIVERABLES%2FSP1%2FD1.1.1%2FOASISDeliverableD1_1_1_version_4%25205.doc&ei=LOvfUb6wHayr0gXmw4HADg&usg=AFQjCNE4ZcnK1XU_G02SdgCFKLwgEDZlnA&bvm=bv.48705608,d.d2k

Kelly, G., Mulgan, G., & Muers, S. (2002). *Creating public value: An analytical framework for public service reform*. Retrieved Nov 2, 2009 from http://www.cabinetoffice.gov.uk/strategy/seminars/public_value.aspx

Kenny, S., & Shannon, P. (2010). Using soft systems methodology to support extension program development in the dairy industry. *Extension Farming Systems Journal*, 6(1), 124–129.

Keohane, R. O., & Nye, J. S. Jr. (2000). Introduction. In *Governance in a globalization world*. Washington, DC: Brookings Institution Press.

Kerzner, H. (2001). *Project management: A systems approach to planning, scheduling and controlling* (7th ed.). Hoboken, NJ: John Wiley and Sons Inc.

Khan, G. F., Young, H. Y., & Park, H. W. (2012). Social media use in public sector: a comparative study of the Korean & US government agencies. In *Proceedings of the 8th International Conference on Webometrics, Informatics and Scientometrics & 13th COLLNET Meeting*. Retrieved 17 April, 2013 from http://collnet2012.ndsl.kr/wsp/submission/submitted.jsp

Kharbat, F., & El-Ghalayini, H. (2008). *Building ontology from knowledge base systems, data mining in medical and biological research*. InTech.

Kim, H. (1999). *Representing and reasoning about quality using enterprise models*. (PhD thesis). Dept. of Mechanical and Industrial Engineering, University of Toronto, Toronto, Canada.

Kim, H. S. (2005). Public innovation in ubiquitous age: Plan to implement ubiquitous public management. In *Proceeding of Entrue World 2005*. Retrieved April 15, 2013 from http://www.entrue.com/LGCNS.ENT.UI.MAIN/upload/agenda/200510/4.20051006_T1_S5_%EA%B9%80%ED%98%84%EC%84%B1.pdf

Kim, J. H., & Lee, K. H. (2012). *Procurement agency leads transparency and digitalization*. The Korea Herald. Retrieved May 12, 2013 from http://khnews.kheraldm.com/view.php?ud=20121118000258&md=20121129110627_AP

Kim, K., & Prabhakar, B. (2000). Initial trust, perceived risk, and the adoption of internet banking. In *Proceedings of International Conference on Information Systems* (pp. 537-543). Brisbane, Australia: Association for Information Systems.

Kim, S. J. (2003). e-Government and public reform: focused on applying to construct information integrated electronic environment. In *Proceeding for Information Policy Seminar by SAPA*, (pp. 18-38). SAPA.

Kim, S. T. (2010). Prepare smart gov 3.0. *Digital Times*. Retrieved April 16, 2013 from http://www.dt.co.kr/contents.html?article_no=2010072302012369697035

Kim, V. A., & Henriksen, H. Z. (2006). E-government maturity models: Extension of the Layne and Lee model. *Government Information Quarterly*, 23(2), 232–245.

King, R., & Kendall, G. (2003). *The state, democracy & globalization*. Hampshire, UK: Palgrave Macmillan.

Kitchenham, B. A., Travassos, G. H., Mayrhauser, A., Niessink, F., Schneidewind, N. F., & Singer, J. et al. (1999). Towards an ontology of software maintenance. *Journal of Software Maintenance: Research and Practice*, 11(6), 365–389. doi:10.1002/(SICI)1096-908X(199911/12)11:6<365::AID-SMR200>3.0.CO;2-W

Kleine, D., & Unwin, T. (2009). Technological revolution, evolution and new dependencies: What's new about ict4d? *Third World Quarterly*, 30(5), 1045–1067. doi:10.1080/01436590902959339

Kline, S. J. (1995). *Conceptual foundations for multidisciplinary thinking*. Palo Alto, CA: Stanford University Press.

Klitgaard, R. (1988). *Controlling corruption*. Berkeley, CA: University of California Press.

Knublauch, H. (2002). *An agile development methodology for knowledge-based systems including a Java framework for knowledge modeling and appropriate tool support*. (PhD Thesis). University of Ulm, Ulm, Germany.

Knudsen, D. (2003). Aligning corporate strategy, procurement strategy and e-procurement tools. *International Journal of Physical Distribution & Logistics Management*, 33(8), 720–734. doi:10.1108/09600030310502894

Kolsaker, A., & Lee-Kelley, L. (2006). Mind the gap: E-government and e-democracy. In M. A. Wimmer, H. J. Scholl, A. Gronlund, & K. V. Andersen (Eds.), *Electronic government* (pp. 96–106). Berlin: Springer. doi:10.1007/11823100_9

Kolstad, I., & Wiig, A. (2009). Is transparency the key to reducing corruption in resource-rich countries? *World Development*, 37(3), 521–532. doi:10.1016/j.worlddev.2008.07.002

Kowalski, S., & Yngström, L. (2011). Secure e-government services: Towards a framework for integrating it security services into e-government maturity models. Information Security South Africa, 1-9.

Kreps, D., & Richardson, H. (2007). IS success and failure - The problem of scale. *The Political Quarterly*, 78(3). doi:10.1111/j.1467-923X.2007.00871.x

Krippendorff, K. (1980). *Content analysis: An introduction to its methodology*. Thousand Oaks, CA: Sage Publications.

Krishna, S., & Wlashan, G. (2005). Implementing public information systems in developing countries: Learning from a success story. *Information Technology for Development*, 11(2), 123–140. doi:10.1002/itdj.20007

Kroukamp, H. (2005). E-governance in South Africa: Are we coping. *Acta Academia*, 37(2), 52–69.

Kunakornpaiboonsiri, T. (2013). *GEBIZ: Enhancing Singapore procurement system.* Alphabet Media Pte Ltd. Retrieved February 1, 2013, from http://www.futuregov. asia/articles/2013/feb/28/gebiz-enhancing-singapore-procurement-system/# Leipold, K. (2007). *Electronic government procurement (e-GP) opportunities and challenges.* Retrived February 18, 2013, from http://www.uncitral.org/pdf/english/congress/Leipold.pdf

Kunz, W., & Rittel, H. (1979). *Issues as elements of information systems. Berkeley, CA.* Berkley: Institute of Urban & Regional Development, University of California.

Kurpuvesas, V. (2007). Socialinės technologijos administracinėje justicijoje. *Jurisprudencija: Mokslo darbai, 6*(96), 72–77.

Kushchu, I. (2007). *Mobile government: An emerging direction in e-government.* Hershey, PA: Idea Group Publishers. doi:10.4018/978-1-59140-884-0

Kyonggi-Maeil. (2010). *MOPAS, supply the guideline for developing mobile application service.* Retrieved June 6, 2013 from http://www.kgmaeil.net

Lallana, E. (2008). *e-Government interoperability.* Retrieved February 13, 2013., from http://unpan1.un.org/intradoc/groups/public/documents/UN-OTHER/UN-PAN032094.pdf

Lallana, E. C. (2007). e-Government interoperability: A review of government interoperability. New York: United Nations Development.

Landes, D. S. (1999). *The wealth and poverty of nations.* New York: W. W. Norton & Co.

Larsson, A., & Moe, H. (2011). *Who tweets? Tracking microblogging use in the 2010 Swedish election campaign.* Paper presented at the 19th European Conference on Information Systems. Helsinki, Finland.

Laskowski, S. J., Autry, M., Cugini, J., & Yen, W. K. (2004). *Improving the usability and accessibility of votingsystems and products.* Washington, DC: National Institute of Standards and Technology.

Lathrop, D., & Ruma, L. (2010). *Open government, collaboration, transparency and participation in practice.* Sebastopol, CA: O'Reilly Media.

Laudon, K. (1997, June). Extensions to the theory of markets and privacy: Mechanics of pricing information. In *Privacy and self-regulation in the information age.* Retrieved February 10th, 2011 from http://www.ntia.doc. gov/reports/privacy/privacy_rpt.htm

Layne, K., & Lee, J. (2001). Developing fully functional e-government: A four stage model. *Government Information Quarterly, 18*(2), 122–136. doi:10.1016/S0740-624X(01)00066-1

Lee, S. K. (2003, January 1). *Global.e-government theory.* Seoul,eROK: Bobmoonsa.

Lee, T. Y., Yee, P. K., & Cheung, D. W. (2009). E-government data interoperability framework in Hong Kong. In *Proceedings - 2009 International Conference On Interoperability For Enterprise Software and Applications* (IESA 2009). IESA. http://dx.doi.org/10.1109/I-ESA.2009.12

Lee, T., Hon, C. T., & Cheung, D. (2009). XML schema design and management for e-government data interoperability. *Electronic. Journal of E-Government, 7*(4), 381–390.

Lee, T.-R., Wu, H.-C., Lin, C.-J., & Wang, H.-T. (2008). Agricultural e-government in China, Korea, Taiwan and the USA. *Electronic Government: An International Journal, 5*(1), 63–70. doi:10.1504/EG.2008.016128

Leipold, K., Klemow, J., Holloway, F., & Vaidya, K. (2004). The World Bank e-procurement for the selection of consultants: Challenges and lessons learned. *Journal of Public Procurement, 4*(3), 319–339.

Lesur, M. (2007). *Digital opportunities for the postal industry.* Microsoft Corporation.

Liao, L., Qu, Y., & Leung, H. K. N. (2005). *A software process ontology and its application.* Paper presented at the ISWC2005 Workshop on Semantic Web Enabled Software Engineering. New York, NY.

Lietuvos Respublikos Administracinių bylų Teisenos Įstatymas. (1999). *Nr. VIII-1029.* Nauja įstatymo redakcija nuo 2001 m. sausio 1 d Nr. VIII-1927 2000.09.19.

Lietuvos Respublikos Administracinių Teisės Pažeidimų Kodeksas. (2012). Redakcija 2012-11-06.

Lietuvos Respublikos Teismų ir Teismų Savivaldos Institucijų 2010 Metų Veiklos Apžvalga. (2011). *Vilnius.* Retrieved February 28, 2013 from http://www.teismai.lt/dokumentai/bendroji_informacija/teismu%20veiklos%20apzvalga%202010.pdf

Lietuvos Respublikos Visuomenės Informavimo Įstatymas. (1996). Nr. I-1418.

Lietuvos Respublikos Vyriausybės Nutarimas. (2003). Dėl bendrųjų reikalavimų valstybės ir savivaldybių institucijų ir įstaigų interneto svetainėms aprašo patvirtinimo, 2003 m. balandžio 18 d. Nr. 480.

Lietuvos Respublikos Vyriausybės Nutarimas. (2011). Dėl elektroninės informacijos saugos (kibernetinio saugumo) plėtros 2011–2019 metais programos patvirtinimo, 2011 m. birželio 29 d. Nr. 796.

Lietuvos Statistikos Departamentas. (2012). Informacinės technologijos Lietuvoje: Information technologies in Lithuania 2012. Vilnius.

Lietuvos Vyriausiasis Administracinis Teismas. (2012). *Statistika.* Retrieved March 13, 2013 from http://www.lvat.lt/veikla/statistika.aspx

Lindgren, I., & Jansson, G. (2013). Electronic services in the public sector: A conceptual framework. *Government Information Quarterly, 30,* 163–172. doi:10.1016/j.giq.2012.10.005

Lin, H. K., Harding, J. A., & Shahbaz, M. (2004). Manufacturing system engineering ontology for semantic interoperability across extended project teams. *International Journal of Production Research, 42*(24), 5099–5118. doi:10.1080/00207540412331281999

Lips, M. (2010). Rethinking citizen-government relationships in the age of digital identity: Insights from research. *Information Polity, 15,* 273–289.

Li, Y. H., & Huang, J. W. (2009). Applying theory of perceived risk and technology acceptance model in the online shopping channel. *World Academy of Science. Engineering and Technology, 53*(29), 919–925.

Lofstedt, U. (2005). E-government – Assessment of current research and some proposals for future directions. *International Journal of Public Information Systems, 1*(1), 39–52.

London Economics. (2010). *Study on the economic benefits of privacy-enhancing technologies (PETs).* London: European Commission.

Louise, P., Nordstokka, U., Friesen, C., Sigaloff, C., Moerbeek, K., & van Loon, L. (Eds.). (2011). *Co-creation guide: Realising social innovation together.* Retrieved February 13, 2013 from http://www.euclidnetwork.eu/resources/doc_view/158-co-creation-guide-realising-social-innovation-together.html

Loukis, E., Macintosh, A., & Charalabidis, Y. (2011). Editorial of the special issue on e-participation in southern Europe and the Balkans: Issues of democracy and participation via electronic media. *Journal of Balkan and Near East Studies, 13*(1), 1–12. doi:10.1080/19448953.2011.550814

Low Income Networking AndCommunications Project. (2003). *Building an open source office: GRO case study part II, 2003.* Welfare Law Center.

Luna-Reyes, L. F., Pardo, T. A., Gil-Garcia, J. R., Navarrete, C., Zhang, J., & Mellouli, S. (2010). Digital government in North America: A comparative analysis of policy and program priorities in Canada, Mexico, and the United States. In C. G. Reddick (Ed.), *Comparative e-government* (pp. 139–160). New York: Springer. doi:10.1007/978-1-4419-6536-3_7

Lwoga, E. T. (2010). Bridging the agricultural knowledge and information divide: The case of selected telecenters and rural radio in Tanzania. *Electronic Journal of Information Systems in Developing Countries, 43*(6), 1–14.

Macintosh, A., & Whyte, A. (2008). Towards an evaluation framework for eparticipation. *Transforming Government: People. Process and Policy, 2*(1), 16–30.

Mägli, M., Jaag, C., Koller, M., & Trinkner, U. (2010). *Postal markets and electronic substitution: Implications for regulatory practices and institutions in Europe.* Zürich: Swiss Economics SE AG.

Magro, M. J. (2012). A review of social media use in e-government. *American Scientist, 2*(2), 148–161.

Maheshwari, B., Kumar, V., Kumar, U., & Sharan, V. (2007). E-government portal effectiveness: Managerial considerations for design and development. In *Proceedings of International Congress of E-Government*. E-Government.

MAJIDATA. Retreived July 9, 2013 from http://www.majidata.go.ke/index.php?MID=MQ==.

Maragoudakis, M., Loukis, E., & Charalabidis, Y. (2011). *A review of opinion mining methods for analyzing citizens' contributions in public policy debate*. Paper presented at the 3rd International Federation for Information Processing, Conference on e-Participation. Delft, The Netherlands.

Marche, S., & McNiven, J. D. (2003). E-government and e-governance: The future isn't what it used to be. *Canadian Journal of Administrative Sciences*, *20*(1), 74–86. doi:10.1111/j.1936-4490.2003.tb00306.x

Margetts, H. (2006). E-government in Britain—A decade on. *Parliamentary Affairs*, *59*(2), 250–265. doi:10.1093/pa/gsl003

Markaki, O., Charilas, D., & Askoumis, D. (2010). Evaluation of the impact and adoption of e-government services in the Ballrans. In *Comparative e-government*. New York: Springer. doi:10.1007/978-1-4419-6536-3_5

Markus, M. L., Majchrzak, A., & Gasser, L. (2002). A design theory for systems that support emergent knowledge processes. *Management Information Systems Quarterly*, *26*(3), 179–212.

Marx, G. (2003). A tack in the shoe: Neutralizing and resisting the new surveillance. *The Journal of Social Issues*, *59*(2), 369–390. doi:10.1111/1540-4560.00069

Matavire, R., Chigona, W., Roode, D., Sewchurran, E., Davids, Z., Mukudu, A., & Boamah-Abu, C. (2010). Challenges of e-government project implementation in a South African context. *The Electronic Journal Information Systems Evaluation*, *13*(2), 153–164.

Matavire, R., Chigona, W., Roode, D., Sewchurran, E., Davids, Z., Mukudu, A., & Boamah-Abu, C. (2010). Challenges of e-government project implementation in South African context. *The Electronic Journal of Information Systems Evaluation*, *13*(2), 153–164.

Matthew, K., Patrick, K., & Denise, K. (2013). The effects of fraudulent procurement practices on public procurement performance. *International Journal of Business and Behavioral Sciences*, *3*(1), 17–27.

Maurer, M. (2007). Court automation in Austria. *Masaryk University Journal of Law and Technology*, *2*, 313–318.

McCue, C., & Roman, A. V. (2012). E-procurement: Myth or reality? *Journal of Public Procurement*, *12*(2), 212–238.

McGinnis, P. (2003). Creating a blueprint for e-government. In *The world of e-government*. Academic Press.

McKay, J., & Marshall, P. (2004). *Strategic management of business*. Milton, UK: John Wiley & Sons.

McKee, L. (2000). *Implications of the OpenGIS® specification for regional science: An open GIS consortium (OGC)*. Retrieved November 2012 from http://www.opengeospatial.org/pressroom/papers

McKnight, D. H., Choudhury, V., & Kacmar, C. (2002). Developing and validating trust measures for e-commerce: An integrative typology. *Information Systems Research*, *13*(3), 334–359. doi:10.1287/isre.13.3.334.81

Media Coverage of Geospatial Platforms. (2007). Retrieved September 17, 2013 from http://www.geospatialweb.com/figure-4

Meneklis, B., Kaliontzoglou, A., Douligeris, C., & Polemi, D. (2005). Engineering and technology aspects of an e-government architecture based on web services. In *Proceedings of the ECOWS '05 Proceedings of the Third European Conference on Web Services*. ECOWS.

Meneklis, V., & Douligeris, C. (2010). Bridging theory and practice in e-government: A set of guidelines for architectural design. *Government Information Quarterly*, *27*, 70–81. doi:10.1016/j.giq.2009.08.005

Mergel, I. A., Schweik, C. M., & Fountain, J. E. (2009). *The transformational effect of web 2.0 technologies on government*. Retrieved March 12, 2013 from http://ssrn.com/abstract=1412796

Mergel, I. (2010). Government 2.0 revisited: Social media strategies in the public sector. *American Society for Public Administration*, *33*(3), 7–10.

Mingers, J., & White, L. (2010). A review of the recent contribution of systems thinking to operational research and management science. *European Journal of Operational Research, 207*(3), 1147–1161. doi:10.1016/j.ejor.2009.12.019

Ministry of Agriculture. Food Security and Cooperatives (MAFSC). (2009). *Ten pillars of Kilimo Kwanza (implementation framework)*. Retrieved May 9, 2013 from http://www.tzonline.org/pdf/tenpillarsofkilimokwanza.pdf

Ministry of ICT. (2000). *Launching e-government in Jordan: Readiness and approach*. Retrieved May 4, 2013 from www.mopc.gov.jo/egovment_n_egoreport.htm

Ministry of ICT. (2001). *Implementing Jordan's information and communications technology strategies – 2002 work plan*. Amman, Jordan: Ministry of ICT.

Ministry of Internal Affairs and Communications (MIAC). (n.d.). *The master plan to construct e-government*. Retrieved April 12, 2010 from http://www.e-gov.go.jp/doc/040614/keikaku.html/

Ministry of Water and Irrigation. December (MWID). (2008). Ministerial strategic plan. Author.

Misuraca, G. (2009). e-Government 2015: Exploring m-government scenarios, between ICT-driven experiments and citizen-centric implications. *Technology Analysis and Strategic Management, 21*(3), 407–424. doi:10.1080/09537320902750871

Mitra, A. (2005). Direction of electronic governance initiative within two worlds: Case for a shift in emphasis. Electronic Government, 2(1).

MMAJI. (2013). *MMAJI water application: About MMAJI*. Retrieved February 2, 2013, from HTTP://MMAJI.WORDPRESS.COM

Mnkandla, E. (2009). *About software engineering frameworks and methodologies*. Paper presented at the IEEE Africon Conference. Nairobi, Kenya.

Mofleh, S. I., & Wanous, M. (2009). Reviewing existing methods for evaluating e-government websites. *Electronic Government: An International Journal, 6*(2), 129–142. doi:10.1504/EG.2009.024438

MoICT. (2003a). *Ministry of information and communications technology web-site*. Retrieved May 3, 2013 from www.moict.gov.jo

MoICT. (2003b). *E-government program in Jordan*. Retrieved May 3, 2013 from www.moict.gov.jo/moict/program_overview.aspx

Momanyi, L. (2005). An analysis of water governance in Kibera, Kenya (2004/2005). Academic Press.

Monga, A. (2008). E-government in India: Opportunities and challenges. *JOAAG, 3*(2), 52–61.

Moon, M. J. (2002). The evolution of e-government among municipalities: Rhetoric or reality? *Public Administration Review, 62*(4), 424–433. doi:10.1111/0033-3352.00196

Moore, M. H. (2003, May). *The public value scorecard: A rejoinder and an alternative to strategic performance measurement and management in non-profit organizations by Robert Kaplan*. Retrieved August 2011, from http://oueli.voinovichcenter.ohio.edu/alumni/public_value_scorecard.pdf

Moore, M. H. (1995). *Creating public value: Strategic management in government*. Cambridge, MA: Harvard University Press.

MOPAS. (2012). *e-Government, 2 consecutive UN global award*. MOPAS press release. Retrieved April 16, 2013 from http://video.mospa.go.kr/view.asp?cate_id=2&vod_id=975

MOPAS. (Ministry of Public Administration and Security)eNIA (National informatization Agency). (2008). *e-Government tasks white paper 2003-2007*. Author.

MOPASr.ent task(2012, August). *National informatization white paper*. Author.

Moraa, H., Otieno, A., & Salim, A. (2012). *Technology in solving society's water problems*. Academic Press.

Moreira, A., Gerhardt, G., & Ladner, A. (2010). *Impact of web 2.0 on political participation*. Paper presented at the Electronic Government and Electronic Participation, Ongoing Research and Projects of International Federation for Information Processing eGOV and ePart 2010. New York, NY.

Movahedi, B., Tan, R.-X., & Lavassani, K. M. (2010). Organizational development in electronic government adoption: A process development perspective. *International Journal of Electronic Government Research*, 7(1), 51–63. doi:10.4018/jegr.2011010104

Mtega, W., & Malekani, A. (2009). Analyzing the usage patterns and challenges of telecenters among rural communities: Experience from four selected telecenters in Tanzania. *International Journal of Education and Development using ICT, 5*(2).

Mtega, W. P. (2012). Access to and usage of information among rural communities: A case study of Kilosa District Morogoro Region in Tanzania. *Partnership. The Canadian Journal of Library and Information Practice and Research, 7*(1).

Mtega, W. P., & Msungu, A. C. (2013). Using information and communication technologies for enhancing the accessibility of agricultural information for improved agricultural production in Tanzania. *Electronic Journal of Information Systems in Developing Countries, 56*(1), 1–14.

Murra, M. E. (2003). *E-government: From real to virtual democracy*. Boston University. Retrieved February 8, 2013 from http://unpan1.un.org/intradoc/groups/public/documents/other/unpan011094.pdf#search='egovernment%3Afrom%20Real%20to%20virtual%20democracy

Murray, A. (2010). *Information technology law, the law and society*. Oxford, UK: Oxford University Press.

Muthaiyah, S., & Kerschberg, L. (2008). Achieving interoperability in e-government services with two modes of semantic bridging: SRS and SWRL. *Journal of Theoretical and Applied Electronic Commerce Research, 3*(3), 52–63. doi:10.4067/S0718-18762008000200005

National Research Council (U.S.), Committee on the Future of the Global Positioning System, National Academy of Public Administration. (1995). *The global positioning system: A shared national asset: Recommendations for technical improvements and enhancements*. Washington, DC: National Academies Press. Retrieved November 6, 2011 from http://books.google.com/books?id=FAHk65slfY4C

Nawaz, M., Issa, M., & Hyder, S. I. (2007). e-Government services maturity models. In *Proceeding of the 2007 Computer Science and IT Education Conference*, (pp. 511- 519). IEEE.

Ndou, V. D. (2004). E-government for developing countries: Opportunities and challenges. *The Electronic Journal on Information Systems in Developing Countries, 18*(1), 1–24.

Neely, A. (1998). *Measuring business performance*. London: Profile Books Limited.

Neely, A., Adams, C., & Kennerley, M. (2002). *The performance prism: The scorecard for measuring and managing business success*. London: Prentice Hall.

Neuman, W. L. (2003). *Social research methods: Qualitative and quantitative approaches* (5th ed.). Boston: Allyn & Bacon.

Neupane, A., Soar, J., Vaidya, K., & Yong, J. (2012). *Role of public e-procurement technology to reduce corruption in government procurement*. Paper presented to 5th International Public Procurement Conference (IPPC5). Seattle, WA.

Neupane, A., Soar, J., & Vaidya, K. (2012). Evaluating the anti-corruption capabilities of public e-procurement in a developing country. *The Electronic Journal on Information System in Developing Countries, 55*(2), 1–17.

Neupane, A., Soar, J., & Vaidya, K. (2012b). The potential of e-procurement technology for reducing corruption. *International Journal of Information Technology and Management, 11*(4), 273–287.

News, M. K. (2009). *Korea on-line e-procurement system to advance into Africa*. Retrieved May 12, 2013 from http://news.mk.co.kr/newsRead.php?year=2009&no=506602

Nexleaf Analytics. (2012). *Mobile phone applications for the water, sanitation and hygiene sector*. Author.

Ngai, E., Lai, K. H., & Cheng, T. (2008). Logistics information systems: The Hong Kong experience. *International Journal of Production Economics, 113*(1), 223–234. doi:10.1016/j.ijpe.2007.05.018

NIA. (2010). *National informatization white paper*. Author.

Nicola, G. (1998). Formal ontology in information systems. In *Proceedings of FOIS'98*. Amsterdam: IOS Press.

Noam, E. M. (1997). *Privacy and self-regulation: Markets for electronic privacy*. Retrieved February 10th, 2011, from http://www.citi.columbia.edu/elinoam/articles/priv_self.htm

NOMAD. (2012). *Policy formulation & validation through non-moderated crowd-sourcing*. Retrieved February 20, 2013 from http://www.nomad-project.eu/

Nordfors, L., Ericson, B., Lindell, H., & Lapidus, J. (2009). *e-Government of tomorrow – Future scenarios for 2020*. Gullers Group.

Nour, P., Holz, H., & Maurer, F. (2000). *Ontology-based retrieval of software process experiences*. Paper presented at the ICSE Workshop on Software Engineering over the Internet. New York, NY.

Novakouski, M., & Lewis, G. A. (2012). *Interoperability in the e-government context*. Software Engineering Institute. Retrieved February 13, 2013 from http://www.sei.cmu.edu/reports/11tn014.pdf

Noy, N. F., & McGuinness, D. (2001). Ontology development 101: A guide to creating your first ontology. *Stanford Knowledge Systems Laboratory Technical Report KSL-01-05 and Stanford Medical Informatics Technical Report SMI-2001-0880*.

Nusseir, Y. (2001). *Science and technology and competitiveness: The seventh Jordanian science week: Science and technology as means for investment incentive and sustainability*. Amman, Jordan: The Higher Council for Science and Technology.

Nygren, K. G. (2009). The rhetoric of e-government management and the reality of e-government work- the Swedish action plan for e-government considered. *International Journal of Public Information Systems, 2*, 135–146.

O'Reilly, T. (2005). *What is web 2.0? Design patterns and business models for the next generation of software*. Retrieved December 13, 2012, from http://www.oreilly.com/lpt/a/6228

O'Connell, R., & Read, V. (2009). *Safer social networking principles for the EU*. London: The Home Office Internet Task Force.

OECD. (2001). *Engaging citizens in policy-making: Information, consultation and policy participation (Puma Policy Brief No. 10)*. Paris: OECD.

OECD. (2002). *ICT and business performance – Empirical findings and policy implications*. Paper presented at the Workshop on ICT and Business Performance. New York, NY.

OECD. (2003). *The e-government imperative*. Paris: OECD.

OECD. (2003). The e-Government imperative: Main findings. Policy Brief. *OECD Observer*. Retrieved April 12, 2010 from www.oecd.org/publications/Pol_brief

OECD. (2003a). *Implementing e-government in OECD countries: Experiences and challenges*. Paris: OECD.

OECD. (2007). *Giving knowledge for free: The emergence of open education resources, centre for educational research and innovation*. OECD. Retrieved May 2011 from http://www.oecd.org/document/41/0,3343,en_2649_35845581_38659497_1_1_1_1,00.html

OECD. (2007). *Good governance for development (GfD) in Arab countries*. Paris: OECD.

OECD. (2010). *Policy rounddables: Collusion and corruption in public procuremnet*. Retrived February 12, 2013, from http://www.oecd.org/daf/competition/cartelsandanti-competitiveagreements/46235884.pdf

Office of Government Commerce (OGC). (2009). *Managing successful projects with PRINCE2 projects in controlled environments*. London: TSO London, Office of Government Commerce.

Office of Government Commerce. (2005). *Managing successful projects with PRINCE2: The PRINCE2 manual*. Stationery Office Books.

Official Google Blog. (2011). *Google Earth downloaded more than one billion times*. Retrieved from http://google-blog.blogspot.com/2011/10/google-earth-downloaded-more-than-one.html

O'Flynn, J. (2007). From new public management to public value: Paradigmatic change and managerial implications. *The Australian Journal of Public Administration, 66*(3), 353–366. doi:10.1111/j.1467-8500.2007.00545.x

Ojha, A., Palvia, S., & Gupta, M. (2008). A model for impact of e-government on corruption: Exploring theoretical foundations. In J. Bhattacharya (Ed.), *Critical thinking in e-governance*. New Delhi: Gift Publishing.

Okot-Uma, R. W. O. (2000). *Electronic governance: Re-inventing good governance. Londo*. Commonwealth Secretariat.

Olbrich, S. (2012). Reflecting ten years of e-government: A plea for a multimethodological research agenda. In *Transformational government through egov practice: Socioeconomic, cultural, and technological issues*. London: Emerald.

Organization for Economic Co-Operation & Development. (2003). *Engaging citizens online for better policy-making*. Paris: OECD Publication.

Organization for Economic Co-Operation & Development. (2004a). *Evaluating public participation in policy making*. Paris: OECD Publication.

Organization for Economic Co-Operation & Development. (2004b). *Promise and problems of e-democracy: Challenges of online citizen engagement*. Paris: OECD Publication.

Organization for Economic Co-Operation and Development (OECD). (2001). *Understanding the digital divide*. Retrieved February 25, 2013 from www.oecd.org/bookshop/

Orihuela, L., & Obi, T. (2007). E-government and e-governance: Towards a clarification in the usage of both concepts. In T. Obi (Ed.), *E-governance: A global perspective on a new paradigm* (pp. 26–33). Amsterdam: IOS Press.

Osimo, D. (2008). *Web 2.0 in government: Why and how?* Luxembourg: Office for Official Publications of the European Communities.

Oxford Institute. (2007). *Breaking barriers to e-government: Overcoming obstacles to improving European public services*. Retrieved March 16, 2013 from http://www.egovbarriers.org/downloads/deliverables/solutions_report/Solutions_for_e-Government.pdf

Ozacar, T., Ozturk, O., & Unalir, M. O. (2011). ANEMONE: An environment for modular ontology development. *Data & Knowledge Engineering, 70*(6), 504–526. doi:10.1016/j.datak.2011.02.005

Pablo, Z. D., & Pan, S. L. (2002). A multi-disciplinary analysis of e-overnance: Why do we start? In *Proceedings of the 6th Pacific Conference on Information Systems (PACIS 2002)*. Tokyo, Japan: PACIS.

PADGETS. (2010). *Policy gadgets mashing underlying group knowledge in web 2.0 media*. Retrieved February 20, 2013 from http://www.padgets.eu/

Palmer, I. (2003). *State of the world: e-Government implementation*. Retrieved February 8, 2013 from http://www.faulkner.com/products/faulknerlibrary/00018297.htm

Palvia, S. C. J., & Sharma, S. S. (2006). *E-government and e-governance: Definitions/domain framework and status around the world, foundations of e-government*. New Delhi: Computer Society of India.

Panayiotou, N. A., Gayialis, S. P., & Tatsiopoulos, I. P. (2004). An e-procurement system for governmental purchasing. *International Journal of Production Economics, 90*(1), 79–102. doi:10.1016/S0925-5273(03)00103-8

Papadomichelaki, X., Magoutas, B., Halaris, C., Apostolou, D., & Mentzas, G. (2006). A review of quality dimensions in e-government services. In M. A. Wimmer, H. J. Scholl, A. Gronlund, & K. V. Andersen (Eds.), *Electronic government* (pp. 128–138). Berlin: Springer. doi:10.1007/11823100_12

Pardo, T. A., & Scholl, H. J. (2002). Walking atop the cliffs: Avoiding failure and avoiding risk in large scale e-government projects. In *Proceedings of Hawai'i International Conference on System Sciences*. IEEE.

Parikh, T. S., Patel, N., & Schwartzman, Y. (2007). A survey of information systems reaching small producers in global agricultural value chains. In *Proceedings of IEEE Conference on Information and Communication Technologies for Development* (ICTD 2007). IEEE.

Parker, D., & Hartley, K. (2003). Transaction costs, relational contracting and public private partnerships: A case study of UK defence. *Journal of Purchasing and Supply Management, 9*(3), 97–108. doi:10.1016/S0969-7012(02)00035-7

Parlak, B., & Sobaci, Z. (2010). A comparative analysis of local agenda 21 websites in Turkey in terms of e-participation. In C. G. Reddick (Ed.), *Politics, democracy and e-government, participation and service delivery* (pp. 75–94). Hershey, PA: IGI Global. doi:10.4018/978-1-61520-933-0.ch005

Payne, A., Storbacka, K., & Frow, P. (2008). Managing co-creation of value. *Journal of the Academy of Marketing Science, 36*, 83–96. doi:10.1007/s11747-007-0070-0

PCI Security Standards Council. (2010, October). *Payment card industry (PCI) payment application data security standard: Requirements and security assessment procedures.* Retrieved September 08, 2011, from https://www.pcisecuritystandards.org/documents/pa-dss_v2.pdf

Pedersen, S. M., & Pedersen, J. L. (2006). Innovation and diffusion of site-specific crop management. In *Contemporary management of innovation* (pp. 110–123). Houndmills, UK: Palgrave Macmillan.

Pellegrini, L., & Gerlagh, R. (2008). Causes of corruption: A survey of cross-country analyses and extended results. *Economics of Governance, 9*(3), 245–263. doi:10.1007/s10101-007-0033-4

Perrott, B. E. (1996). Managing strategic issues in the public service. *Long Range Planning, 29*(3), 337–345. doi:10.1016/0024-6301(96)00030-1

Pierre, J., & Peters, B. (2000). *Governance, politics and the state.* London: Macmillan.

Piličiauskas, R. (2011a). *Atvirai visuomenei - Atviri teismai.* Retrieved from http://www.lvat.lt/atvirai-visuomenei-atviri-teismai.aspx

Piličiauskas, R. (2011b). Viešojo intereso gynimas administraciniuose teismuose. In *Konferencijos Viešasis interesas ir jo gynimas medžiaga.* Retrieved February 28, 2013 http://www3.lrs.lt/pls/inter/w5_show?p_r=7992&p_d=111939&p_k=1

Pi, S. M., Liao, H. L., & Chen, H. M. (2012). Factors that affect consumers' trust and continuous adoption of online financial services. *International Journal of Business and Management, 7*(9), 108–119. doi:10.5539/ijbm.v7n9p108

Plummer, J., & Slaymaker, T. (2009). *Rethinking governance in water services.* Academic Press.

Porter, M. (1980). *Competitive strategy.* Cambridge, MA: Harvard Business School.

Porter, M. E. (1985). *Competitive advantage.* New York: Free Press.

PPS. (2013). *Innovation plan of procurement administration for economic revival.* Retrieved May 22, 2013, from http://www.korea.kr/policy/pressReleaseView.do?newsId=155895612

Prahalad, C. K., & Ramaswamy, V. (2000). Co-opting customer competence. *Harvard Business Review, 78*(1), 79–87.

Pranevičienė, B. (2007). Teisėtų lūkesčių principo samprata ir teisėtų lūkesčių apsaugos modeliai Europos Sąjungos administracinėje erdvėje. *Jurisprudencija. Mokslo Darbai, 6*(96), 43–48.

Pries-Heje, J., & Baskerville, R. (2008). The design theory nexus. *Management Information Systems Quarterly, 32*(4), 731–755.

PRINCE2 Pocketbook. (2009). *TSO information and publishing solution.* Norwich, UK: Author.

Project Management Institute (PMI). Inc. (2008). *a guide to the project management body of knowledge.* Paper presented at PMBOK. Newtown Square, PA.

Punie, Y., Misuraca, G., & Osimo, D. (2009). *Public services 2.0: The impact of social computing on public services. JRC Scientific and Technical Reports.* European Commission, Joint Research Centre, Institute for Prospective Technological Studies.

Purnomo, S., & Lee, Y. (2010). An assessment of readiness and barriers towards ICT program implementation: Perceptions of agricultural extension officers in Indonesia. *International Journal of Education and Development using ICT, 6*(3).

Quirk, B. (2000). *From managing change to leading transformation.* Paper presented at the E-Government Summit. London, UK.

Rahim, M. M. (2008). Identifying factors affecting acceptance of e-procurement systems: An initial qualitative study at an Australian city council. *Communications of the IBIMA, 3*(2), 7–17.

Rahman, H. (2011). *e-Governance framework at the local government level: Empowerment of community people and improvement of e-governance at the grass roots.* (PhD Thesis). Empresarial University of Costa Rica, Costa Rica.

Rahman, H. (2010). *Developing successful ICT strategies: Competitive advantages in a global knowledge-driven society. Hershey, PA.* USA: Idea Group Inc.

Rahman, H. (2012). Preface. In *Cases on progressions and challenges in ICT utilization for citizen-centric governance.* Hershey, PA: IGI Global.

Rahman, H. (2013). Data mining technologies to improve early warning systems in the Bay of Bengal: A Bangladesh perspective. In *Ethical data mining applications for socio-economic development.* Hershey, PA: IGI Global. doi:10.4018/978-1-4666-4078-8.ch004

Rajapakse, J., & Seddon, P. (2005a). *Why ERP may not be suitable for organizations in developing countries in Asia* (Working Paper No. 121). Retrieved May 28, 2013 from www.pacis-net.org/file/2005/121.pdf

Ramal, M. F., Meneses, R., & Anquetil, N. A. (2002). Disturbing result on the knowledge used during software maintenance. In *Proceedings of Working Conference on Reverse Engineering,* (pp. 277-287). Richmond, VA: IEEE.

Raymond, L., Uwizeyemungu, S., & Bergeron, F. (2006). Motivations to implement ERP in e-government: An analysis from success stories. *Electronic Government: An International Journal, 3*(3), 225–240. doi:10.1504/EG.2006.009597

Reach. (2001). *Launching Jordan's software & IT industry.* Amman, Jordan: Reach.

Respublika, L. (2013). *Nacionalinė teismų administracija.* Retrieved February 28, 2013 from http://www.teismai.lt

Reunis, M. R. B., Santema, S. C., & Harink, J. H. A. (2006). Increasing e-ordering adoption: A case study. *Journal of Purchasing and Supply Management, 12*(6), 322–331. doi:10.1016/j.pursup.2007.01.006

Richardson, D. (2004). *How can agricultural extension best harness ICTs to improve rural livelihoods in developing countries?* Retrieved May 9, 2013 from http://departments.agri.huji.ac.il/economics/gelb-how-11.pdf

Ridgway, V. (1956). Dysfunctional consequences of performance measurements. *Administrative Science Quarterly, 1*(2), 240–247. doi:10.2307/2390989

Riley, C. G. (2003). *The changing role of the citizen in the e-governance & e-democracy equation.* Commonwealth Center for E-Governance.

Rittel, H. W. J., & Weber, M. M. (1973). Dilemmas in a general theory of planning. *Policy Sciences, 4*(2), 155–169. doi:10.1007/BF01405730

Rogers, E. M. (1995). *Diffusion of innovations.* New York: Free Press.

Rowe, G., & Frewer, L. J. (2000). Public participation methods: A framework for evaluation. *Science, Technology & Human Values, 25*(1), 3–29. doi:10.1177/016224390002500101

Rowe, G., & Frewer, L. J. (2004). Evaluating public-participation exercises: A research agenda. *Science, Technology & Human Values, 29*(4), 512–557. doi:10.1177/0162243903259197

Rowe, J. (2005). Process metaphor and knowledge management. *Kybernetes, 34*(6), 770–783. doi:10.1108/03684920510595481

Roy, J. (2006). *E-government in Canada: Transformation for the digital age.* Ottawa, Canada: University of Ottawa Press.

Roy, S. (2005). *Globalisation, ICT and developing nations.* New Delhi: Sage.

Ruiz, F., Vizcaíno, A., Piattini, M., & García, F. (2004). An ontology for the management of software maintenance projects. *International Journal of Software Engineering and Knowledge Engineering, 14*(3), 323–349. doi:10.1142/S0218194004001646

Rumbaugh, J., Balha, M., & Premelani, W. (1991). *Object oriented modeling and design.* Upper Saddle River, NJ: Prentice Hall.

Sabucedo, P., Rifon, L. E. A., Corradini, F., Polzonetti, A., & Re, B. (2010). Knowledge-based platform for e-government agents: A web-based solution using semantic technologies. *Journal of Expert Systems with Applications, 37*(5), 3647–3656. doi:10.1016/j.eswa.2009.10.026

Saebo, O., Rose, J., & Flak, L. S. (2008). The shape of eParticipation: Characterizing an emerging research area. *Government Information Quarterly*, *25*(3), 400–428. doi:10.1016/j.giq.2007.04.007

Saekow, A., & Boonmee, C. (2009). A practical approach to interoperability practical implementation support (IPIS) for e-government interoperability. *Electronic Journal of E-Government*, *7*(4), 403–414.

Saekow, A., & Boonmee, C. (2009). A pragmatic approach to interoperability practical implementation support (IPIS) for e-government interoperability. *Electronic. Journal of E-Government*, *7*(4), 403–414.

Sagheb-Tehrani, M. (2007). Some steps towards implementing e-government. *Journal of ACM. Computers & Society*, *37*(1), 22–29. doi:10.1145/1273353.1273356

Sahi, G., & Madan, S. (2012). Information security threats in ERP enabled e-governance: Challenges and solutions. In S. Chhabra, & M. Kumar (Eds.), *Strategic enterprise resource planning models for e-government, applications and methodologies* (pp. 158–170). Hershey, PA: IGI Global.

Salhofer, P., & Ferbas, D. (2007). A pragmatic approach to the introduction of e-government. In *Proceedings of the 8th Annual International Digital Government Research Conference*, (pp. 183-189). Philadelphia, PA: Academic Press.

Salhofer, P., Stadlhofer, B., & Tretter, G. (2009). Ontology driven e-government. *Electronic. Journal of E-Government*, *7*(4), 415–424.

Salin, A. S. A. P., & Abidin, Z. Z. (2011). *Information and communication technologies and local governance trend–A case study of a smart city in Malaysia*. Kuala Lumpur, Malaysia: IACSIT Press.

Salovaara, I., & Augusiak, A. (2011). *A guide to careers in administrative law*. Cambridge, MA: Bernard Koteen Office of Public Interest Advising, Harvard Law School.

Sanati, F., & Lu, J. (2009). Multilevel life-event abstraction for e-government service integration. In *Proceedings of the 9th European Conference on E-Government 2009* (ECEG 2009), (pp. 550-558). London, UK: ECEG.

Sanford, C., & Rose, J. (2007). Characterizing eParticipation. *International Journal of Information Management*, *27*(6), 406–421. doi:10.1016/j.ijinfomgt.2007.08.002

Sanga, C., Churi, A. J., & Tumbo, S. (2007). *Status, opportunities, potential and challenges of technology-mediated open and distance education (Tech-MODE) for agricultural education and improved livelihoods: A case study of Tanzania, July 2007*. Retrieved March 28, 2013 from http://www.col.org/SiteCollectionDocuments/TechMODE_report_online.pdf

Sanga, C.A., Kalungwizi, V.J., & Msuya, C.P. (2013). Building agricultural extension services system supported by ICTs in Tanzania: Progress made, challenges remain. *International Journal of Education and Development using ICT*, *9*(1), 80-99.

Sang, M. L., Tan, X., & Trimi, S. (2005). Current practices of leading e-government countries. *Communications of the ACM*, *48*(10), 99–104. doi:10.1145/1089107.1089112

Sarantis, D., & Askounis, D. (2009). Electronic criminal record in Greece: Project management approach and lessons learned in public administration. *Transylvanian Review of Administrative Sciences*, *25* (E), 132-146.

Sarantis, D., & Askounis, D. (2010). Electronic government interoperability framework in Greece: Project management approach and lessons learned in public administration. *Journal of US-China Public Administration*, *7*(3).

Sarantis, D., Charalabidis, Y., & Askounis, D. (2011). A goal-driven management framework for electronic government transformation projects implementation. *Government Information Quarterly*, *28*, 117–128. doi:10.1016/j.giq.2009.10.006

Sauer, C. (1999). Deciding the future for IS failures: Not the choice you might think. In *Rethinking management information systems*. Oxford, UK: Oxford University Press.

Schiavo-Ocampo, S., & Sundaram, P. (2001). *To serve and preserve: Improving public administration in a competitive world*. Manila, Philippines: Asian Development Bank.

Schilling, M. A. (2010). *Strategic management of technological innovation*. Columbus, OH: McGraw-Hill.

Schlicht, A., & Stuckenschmidt, H. (2008). A flexible partitioning tool for large ontologies. In *Proceedings of the 2008 IEEE/WIC/ACM International Conference, on Web Intelligence and Intelligent Agent Technology*. IEEE.

Scholl, H. J. (2003). E-government: A special case of ICT-enabled business process change. In *Proceedings of the 36ᵗʰ Hawaii International Conference on System Sciences* (HICSS'03). Waikoloa, HI: IEEE.

Scholl, H. J. (2001). Applying stakeholder theory to e-government. In *Towards the e-society: e-commerce, e-business and e-government*. Boston: Kluwer Academic Publishers.

Schuppan, T. (2009). E-government in developing countries: Experiences from sub-Saharan Africa. *Government Information Quarterly*, *26*, 118–127. doi:10.1016/j.giq.2008.01.006

Schwaninger, M., Ulli-Beer, S., & Kaufmann-Hayoz, R. (2008). Policy analysis and design in local public management a system dynamics approach. In *Handbook of transdisciplinary research* (pp. 205–221). Springer. doi:10.1007/978-1-4020-6699-3_13

Schwester, R. (2009). Examining the barriers to e-government adoption. *Electronic. Journal of E-Government*, *7*(1), 113–122.

Scialabba, N. (2000). *Factors influencing organic agriculture policies with a focus on developing countries*. Paper presented at the IFOAM 2000 Scientific Conference. Basel, Switzerland.

Scott, M., Golden, W., & Hughes, M. (2004). Implementation strategies for e-government: A stakeholder analysis approach. In *Proceedings of the 12th European Conference on Information Systems*. Turku, Finland: IEEE.

Segole, J. (2010). South *African government interoperability framework using enterprise architecture to achieve interoperability*. Retrieved March 18, 2013 from http://www.gif4dev.net/wp-content/uploads/2010/05/South-Africa-Julius-Segole.pdf

Selwyn, N. (2002). E-stablishing and inclusive society? Technology, social exclusion and UK government policy making. *Journal of Social Policy*, *31*(1), 1–20. doi:10.1017/S0047279402006487

Sen, A. (1999). *Development as freedom*. Oxford, UK: Oxford University Press.

Seo, J. W., Lee, M. J., & Lim, J. H. (2009). Comparative analysis of e-procurement system in main countries. *Journal of the Korean Association for Regional Information Society*, *12*(3), 105–126.

Seoul, R. O. K. (2006b). The evaluation and enahancement of e-government in Asia. In *Proceeding of Global e-Government Symposium*. MOPAS & NIA.

Seoul, R.O.K. (2006a). *e-Government issue*. Saram & Jihye.

Shackleton, P., Fisher, J., & Dawson, L. (2005). *From dog licences to democracy: Local government approaches to e-service delivery in Australia*. Paper presented at the Thirteenth European Conference on Information Systems. Regensberg, Germany.

Shah, A. (2006). *Corruption and decentralized public governance*. Washington, DC: World Bank. doi:10.1596/1813-9450-3824

Shailendra, C., Jain, P., & Sushil, S. S. (2007). *E-government and e-governance: Definitions/domain framework and status around the world*. ICEG. Retrieved March 28, 2013 from http://www.iceg.net/2007/books/1/1_369.pdf

Shang, S. S. C., & Lin, S. F. (2009). Understanding the effectiveness of capability maturity model integration by examining the knowledge management of software development processes. *Total Quality Management & Business Excellence*, *20*(5), 509–521. doi:10.1080/14783360902863671

Sharif, A., & Irani, Z. (2010). The logistics of information management within an e-government context. *Journal of Enterprise Information Management*, *23*(6), 694–723. doi:10.1108/17410391011088600

Sharon, D. (2008). *Introduction to digital government research in public policy and management, digital. government*. Academic Press.

Shields, P., & Servaes, J. (1989). The impact of the transfer of information technology on development. *The Information Society*, *6*(1–2), 47–57. doi:10.1080/01972243.1989.9960068

Shim, J. P., Warkentin, M., Courtney, J. F., Power, D. J., Sharda, R., & Carlsson, C. (2002). Past, present, and future of decision support technology. *Decision Support Systems*, *33*(2), 111–126. doi:10.1016/S0167-9236(01)00139-7

Shin, D.-H. (2006). Effective design in the development of public information infrastructure: A social constructionist approach. *Information Polity*, *11*, 85–100.

Shin, Y. J. (2010). *Construction advanced public administration system for e-government. Public Administration Focus*. NIA.

Shoib, G., & Nandhakumar, J. (2003). Cross-cultural IS adoption in multinational corporation. *Information Technology for Development*, *10*, 249–260. doi:10.1002/itdj.1590100404

Siau, K., & Long, Y. (2004). A stage model for e-government implementation. In M. Khosrow-Pour (Ed.), *Innovations through information technology*. Hershey, PA: Idea Group Inc.

Siau, K., & Long, Y. (2005). Synthesizing e-government stages models – A meta-synthesis based on meta-ethnography approach. *Industrial Management & Data Systems*, *105*(4), 443–458. doi:10.1108/02635570510592352

Sicilima, N. (2003). Strengthening the linkage among researchers, farmers and extension as a means towards enhancing adoption of agricultural technologies. In *Proceedings of the Second Collaborative Research Workshop on Food Security*. TARP II-SUA.

Sife, S. A., Kiondo, E., & Lyimo-Macha, J. G. (2010). Contribution of mobile phones to rural livelihoods and poverty reduction in Morogoro region: Tanzania. *The Electronic Journal of Information Systems in Developing Countries*, *42*(3), 1–15.

Silcock, R. (2001). What is e-government? *Parliamentary Affairs*, *54*, 88–101. doi:10.1093/pa/54.1.88

Simon, H. A. (1960). *The new science of management decision*. New York: Harper Brothers. doi:10.1037/13978-000

Sims, J. (2011, April). *Tolbert traces cause of digital inequality to lack of skills and money*. Cambridge, MA: Harvard Kennedy School.

Singh, J., & Sirdeshmukh, D. (2000). Agency and trust mechanisms in consumer satisfaction and loyalty judgments. *Journal of the Academy of Marketing Science*, *28*(1), 150–167. doi:10.1177/0092070300281014

Skidmore, D. (2005). *Governance of open source software projects*. Melbourne, Australia: Center for Public Policy, University of Melbourne.

Smith, A. D. (2008). Business and e-government intelligence for strategically leveraging information retrieval. *Electronic Government: An International Journal*, *5*(1), 31–44. doi:10.1504/EG.2008.016126

Sommerville, I. (2007). *What is software?* (8th ed.). Reading, MA: Addison-Wesley.

Song, H. J. (2006). E-government in developing countries: Lesson learnt from the republic of Korea. Bangkok: United Nation Educationa, Scientific and Cultural organization, UNESCO.

Sourouni, A.-M., Lampathaki, F., Mouzakitis, S., Charalabidis, F., & Askounis, D. (2008). *Paving the way to eGovernment transformation: Interoperability registry infrastructure development*. Paper presented at the DEXA eGOV 2008 Conference. Torino, Italy.

Spano, A. (2009). Public value creation and systems management control systems. *International Journal of Public Administration*, *32*(3-4), 328–348. doi:10.1080/01900690902732848

Stamer, R. T. (2006). *Reducing costs of exchange by combating corruption in procurement*. Paper presented to 10th ISNIE Conference. Boulder, CO.

Sterman, J. D. (1994). Learning in and about complex systems. *System Dynamics Review*, *10*(2-3), 291–330. doi:10.1002/sdr.4260100214

Stern, S., & Ibarra, P. (2011). Digital government creating the social media game plan. *Government Finance Review*, *27*(5), 8–14.

Stiglitz, J., Orszag, P., & Orszag, J. (2000). *The role of government in a digital age*. Retrieved March 12, 2012 from http://www.ccianet.org/digital_age/report.pdf

Stiglitz, J. (2003). Democratising the international monetary fund and the world bank: Governance and accountability. *Governance: An International Journal of Policy, Administration and Institutions, 16*(1), L11–L139. doi:10.1111/1468-0491.00207

Stiglitz, J. (2012). *The price of inequality: How today's divided society endangers our future*. New York: W. W. Norton & Company.

Stuckenschmidt, H., & Klein, M. C. A. (2004). Structure-based partitioning of large concept hierarchies. In *International semantic web conference (LNCS)* (Vol. 3298, pp. 289–303). Berlin: Springer.

Suarez-Figuearoa, M. C., & Dellschaft, K. E. Montiel-Ponsoda, Villazon-Terrazas, B., Yufei, Z., Aguado de Cea, G., … Sabou, M. (2008). *NeOn deliverable, NeOn Methodology for building conceptualised ontology networks*. NeOn Project. Retrieved May 20, 2013 from http://www.neon-project.org

Subedi, M. S. (2006). Corruption in Nepal: An anthropological inquiry. *Dhaulagiri Journal of Sociology and Anthropology, 1*(0), 110–128. doi:10.3126/dsaj.v1i0.283

Suchman, L. (1987). *Plans and situated actions*. Cambridge, UK: Cambridge University Press.

Sungkyunkwan Univ., & Rutgers State Univ. (2003). *Digital governance in municipalities worldwide: An assessment of municipal web sites throughout the world*. United Nations.

Sureephong, P., Chakpitak, N., Ouzrout, Y., & Bouras, A. (2008). An ontology-based knowledge management system for industry clusters. In *Proceedings of International Conference on Advanced Design and Manufacture* (ICADAM 2008). Sanya, China: ICADAM.

Swanson, B. E., & Rajalahti, R. (2010). *Strengthening agricultural extension and advisory systems: Procedures for assessing, transforming, and evaluating extension systems*. Washington, DC: World Bank-Agriculture and Rural Development.

Szeremeta, J. (2002). *Benchmarking e-government: A global perspective*. Paper presented at the International Congress on Government Online 2002. Ottawa, Canada.

Szymanski, S. (2007). *How to implement economic reforms: How to fight corruption effectively in public procurement in SEE countries*. Paris: OECD.

Tai, Y.-M., Ho, C.-F., & Wu, W.-H. (2010). The performance impact of implementing web-based e-procurement systems. *International Journal of Production Research, 48*(18), 5397–5414. doi:10.1080/00207540903117915

Tapscott, D. (1995). *The digital economy: Promise and peril in the age of networked intelligence*. New York: McGraw Hill.

Tapscott, D. (1996). *The digital economy*. New York: McGraw Hill.

Tauber, A. (2010). Requirements and properties of qualified electronic delivery systems in egovernment: An Austrian experience. *International Journal of E-Adoption*, 45–58. doi:10.4018/jea.2010010104

Taylor-Gooby, P. (2008). Choice and values: Individualised rational action and social goals. *Journal of Social Policy, 37*(2), 167–185. doi:10.1017/S0047279407001699

Taylor, P. (2005). Do public sector contract catering tender procedures result in an auction for lemons? *International Journal of Public Sector Management, 18*(6), 484–497. doi:10.1108/09513550510616724

Taylor, S., & Todd, P. A. (1995). Assessing IT usage: The role of prior experience. *Management Information Systems Quarterly, 19*(2), 561–570. doi:10.2307/249633

Teicher, J., & Dow, N. (2002). E-government in Australia: Promise and progress. *Information Polity, 7*(4), 231–246.

Teich, J., Wallenius, H., & Wallenius, J. (1999). Multiple-issue auction and market algorithms for the world wide web. *Decision Support Systems, 26*(1), 49–66. doi:10.1016/S0167-9236(99)00016-0

Teinowitz, I. (2011). *Trust of government agencies drops, but folks still love the USPS*. AOL Inc.

Teisėjų Taryba. (2007). Nutarimas dėl informacijos apie teismų veiklą teikimo visuomenei ir visuomenės informavimo priemonėms taisyklių patvirtinimo 2007 m. balandžio 27 d. Nr. 13P-60.

Teisėjų Taryba. (2008). Nutarimas dėl bylų paskirstymo naudojant informacines technologijas laikinųjų taisyklių patvirtinimo 2008 m. spalio 10 d. Nr. 13P-178-(7.1.2).

Teismų Taryba. (2005). Nutarimas dėl teismų sprendimų, nuosprendžių, nutarimų ir nutarčių skelbimo internete tvarkos patvirtinimo 2005 m. rugsėjo 9 d. Nr. 13 P – 378.

Temple Consulting Group. (2012). *MAIS: Municipal accounting and information system*. Retrieved November 2012 from http://findaccountingsoftware.com/directory/temple-consulting/mais-municipal-accounting-and-information-system/

Tennert, J. R., & Schroeder, A. D. (1991). *Stakeholder analysis. American Society for Public Administration. Center of Democracy and Technology. (2002). The e-government handbook for developing countries*. Author.

Teo, T. S. H., Lin, S. J., & Lai, K. H. (2009). Adopters and non-adopters of e-procurement in Singapore: An empirical study. *Omega-International Journal of Management Science, 37*(5), 972–987. doi:10.1016/j.omega.2008.11.001

The Protégé Ontology Editor and Knowledge Acquisition System. (2013). Retrieved May 20 2013 from http://protege.stanford.edu/

Thieme, J. (Ed.). (2001). *A best practices review: Local e-government services*. Madison, WI: Legislative Audit Bureau.

Thompson, D., & Malaviya, P. (2012). *When co-creation backfires: The effects of disclosing consumers source on advertising persuasiveness*. Academic Press.

Thompson, M. (2004). Discourse, 'development' and the 'digital divide': ICT and the World Bank. *Review of African Political Economy, 31*(99), 103–123. doi:10.1080/0305624042000258441

Thompson, M. P. A. (2005). ICT, power, and developmental discourse: A critical analysis. *The Electronic Journal of Information Systems in Developing Countries, 20*(4), 1–26.

Thompson, R. L., Higgins, C. A., & Howell, J. M. (1991). Personal computing: Toward a conceptual model of utilization. *Management Information Systems Quarterly, 15*(1), 124–143. doi:10.2307/249443

Thomson, J. D. (2012). E-government management practice, enterprise resource planning. In S. Chhabra, & M. Kumar (Eds.), *Strategic enterprise resource planning models for e-government, applications and methodologies* (pp. 40–55). Hershey, PA: IGI Global.

Tibenderana, P., & Ogao, P. (2008). Information and communication technologies acceptance and use among university community in Uganda: A model for hybrid library services end-users. *International Journal of Computing and ICT Research, 1*(1), 391–410.

Timmers, P. (2007). *Agenda for eDemocracy – An EU perspective*. Brussels: European Commission.

Tlagadi, P. (2007). *E-governance for improved service delivery*. Paper presented at the Free State SMS Conference. Retrieved on January 12, 2013 from http://www.fs.gov.za/INFORMATION/Events/2007/Premier/SMS%20Conference/Presentations/Tlagadi.pdf

Tolbert, C., & Mossberger, K. (2003). The effects of e-government on trust and confidence in government. In *Proceedings of the 2003 Annual National Conference on Digital Government Research*. Digital Government Society of North America.

Torres, L., Pina, V., & Royo, S. (2005) E-government and the transformation of public administrations in EU countries: Beyond NPM or just a second wave of reforms? *Documento de Trabajo, 2005-01*. Retrieved February 28, 2013 from http://www.dteconz.unizar.es/DT2005-01.pdf

Tran, A. (2009). *Can procurement auctions reduce corruption? Evidence from the internal records of a bribe-paying firm*. Cambridge, MA: Harvard University.

Trumputis, U. (2010). Žmogaus individualūs interesai kaip viešojo intereso pagrindas. *Social Sciences Studies, 2*(6), 123–137.

Tschumperlin, J. (2009). Model-driven semantic interoperability using open standards: A case study, New Zealand education sector architecture framework (ESAF). In *Proceedings of the 10th Annual International Conference on Digital Government Research: Social Networks: Making Connections between Citizens, Data and Government*, (pp. 63-72). Academic Press.

Tsekos, T. (2002). *E-government and the transitional countries*. Paper presented at the 10th NISPAcee Annual Conference. Cracow, Poland.

UN Global E-Government Readiness Report. (2004). *Towards access for opportunity*. New York: United Nations Department of Economic and Social Affairs/Division for Public Administration and Development Management, UNPAN/2004/11.

UN Global E-Government Readiness Report. (2005). *From e-government to e-inclusion*. New York: United Nations Department of Economic and Social Affairs/Division for Public Administration and Development Management, UNPAN/2005/14.

UN. (2002). *Benchmarking e-government: A global perspective - Assessing the UN member states*. New York: United Nations Division for Public Economics and Public Administration.

UN. (2004). *Global e-government readiness report 2004–Towards access for opportunity*. New York: UN.

UN. (2006). *E-procurement: Economic and social commission for Asia and the Pacific Asian development bank institute public procurement service of the Republic of Korea*. New York: United Nations Publication.

UN. (2008). *e-Government survey 2008*. Retrieved April 15, 2013 from http://unpan3.un.org/egovkb/global_reports/08report.htm

UN. (2010). *e-Government survey 2010*. Retrieved April 15, 2013 from http://unpan3.un.org/egovkb/global_reports/10report.htm

UN. (2012). *e-Government survey 2012*. Retrieved April 15, 2013 from http://unpan3.un.org/egovkb/global_reports/12report.htm

UN. (2012). *UN procurement practitioner's handbook*. Retrieved May 12, 2013 from https://www.ungm.org/pph/ch04s02.html

UN. (2012). *United Nations e-government survey 2012: E-government for people department of economic and social affairs*. Retrieved May 8, 2013 from http://www2.unpan.org/egovkb/datacenter/CountryView.aspx

UN/ASPA. (2001). *Benchmarking e-government: A global perspective*. Retrieved March 16, 2009 from http://www.unpan.org/e-government/ Benchmarking%20E-gov%20 2001.pdf

UNCTAD. (2002). *Reports on e-commerce and development of the United Nations conference on trade and development*. New York: United Nations.

UNDEA. (2003). *e-Government readiness survey*. Fourth Caribbean Regional Consultation and High-Level Workshop on Public Sector management: Strategies for e-Government. Retrieved April 16, 2010 from http://www.unpan.org

UNDESA & ASPA. (2005). *Global e-government readiness report 2005: From e-government to e-inclusion*. UNDESA. Retrieved April 12, 2010 from http://www.unpan.org/egovernment5.asp

UNDESA. (2005). *UN global e-government readiness report 2005: From e-government to e-inclusion*. New York: United Nations Publication.

UNDP & UNCRD. (2007). e-Government and universal administrative information service in South Korea. *Capacity Building of Asia Pacific e-Government*. Retrieved March 17, 2013 from http://users.dcc.uchile.cl/~mnmonsal/egob/REPOS/WShopInteroperabilidad.pdf

UNDP. (2000a). *Jordan human development report 2000*. New York: UNDP.

UNDP. (2000b). *Project of the government of Jordan. Information Technology in Higher Education, SPPD document, project number: JOR/2000/001/A/08/13*. New York: UNDP.

UNDP. (2007). *WGF: A mapping and baseline report, improving water governance in Kenya through the human rights based approach*. Retrieved June 26, 2013 from http://ebookbrowse.com/baseline-report-hrba-kenya-pdf-d107548951

UNESCO. (2005). *Towards knowledge societies*. Paris: UNESCO Publishing.

United Nations Department of Economic and Social Affairs. (2012). *United Nations e-government survey 2012*. New York: UN.

United Nations. (2003). *UN global e-government survey 2003*. Retrieved March 28, 2011, from http://unpan1.un.org/intradoc/groups/public/documents/un/unpan016066.pdf

United Nations. (2008). *UN e-government survey 2008 from e-government to connected governance*. New York: Department of Economic and Social Affairs, Division for Public Administration and Development Management, United Nations.

United Nations. (2010). *E-government survey 2010 – Leveraging e-government at a time of financial and economic crisis*. Retrieved June 30, 2013 from http://www2.unpan.org/egovkb/global_reports/10report.htm

United Nations. (2010). *UN global e-government survey 2010: Leveraging e-government at a time of financial and economic crisis*. Retrieved February 25, 2013 from http://www.unpan.org/DPADM/E-Government/UNE-GovernmentSurveys/tabid/600/language/en-US/Default.aspx

United Nations. UN Global E-Government Survey. (2008). From e-government to connected governance. New York: United Nations Publication.

United Nations. UN Global E-Government Survey. (2010). Leveraging e-government at a time of financial and economic crisis. United Nations.

United States Senate. (2002). *E-government act of 2002*. Retrieved April 16, 2013 from http://csrc.nist.gov/drivers/documents/HR2458-final.pdf

Unwin, T. (2009a). Introduction. In *ICT4D: Information and communication technology for development*. Cambridge, UK: Cambridge University Press.

Unwin, T. (2009b). Development agendas and the place of ICTs. In *ICT4D: Information and communication technology for development*. Cambridge, UK: Cambridge University Press.

Urmonas, A. (2007). Socialinių technologijų konceptualių modelių pritaikymo administracinėje teisėje paieška. *Jurisprudencija. Mokslo Darbai, 6*(96), 9–15.

Uschold, M. (1996). Building ontologies: Towards a unified methodology. In *Proceedings of Expert Systems 96, the 16th Annual Conference of British Computer Society Specialist Group Expert Systems*. Cambridge, UK: BCS.

Uschold, M., & King, M. (1995). Towards a methodology for building ontologies. In *Proceedings of IJCAI95 Workshop on Basic Ontological Issues in Knowledge Sharing*. Montreal, Canada: IJCAI.

Uschold, M., & Grunninger, M. (1996). Ontologies: Principles, methods and application. *The Knowledge Engineering Review, 11*(2). doi:10.1017/S0269888900007797

Vaidya, K., Sajeev, A., Johnston, J., & Cox, M. A. (2008). *Assimilation of public procurement innovation: An empirical analysis in light of transaction cost theory*. Paper presented to Annual Conference of International Purchasing and Supply Education and Research Association. Perth, Australia.

Vaidya, K. (2007). *Electronic procurement in the Australian public sector: The organizational assimilation process and its impact on public procurement performance*. University of New England.

Vaidya, K., & Hyde, M. (2011). Inter-organisational information systems assimilation: An empirical evaluation in light of the diffusion of innovation theory. *International Journal of Business Information Systems, 7*(3), 247–268. doi:10.1504/IJBIS.2011.039330

Valančius, V. (2007). *Žmonės vis dažniau gina savo teises administraciniuose teismuose*. INFOLEX. Retrieved February 28, 2013 http://infolex.lt/portal/start.asp?act=news&Tema=50&str=18935

Valančius, V., & Norkus, R. (2006). Lietuvos administracinės ir baudžiamosios justicijos sąlyčio aspektai. *Jurisprudencija. Mokslo Darbai, 4*(82), 91–98.

Van Der Wal, Z., De Graaf, G., & Lasthuizen, K. (2008). What's valued most? Similarities and differences between the organisational values of the public and private sector. *Public Administration, 86*(2), 465–482. doi:10.1111/j.1467-9299.2008.00719.x

Van Themat, C. (2004). The digital divide: Implications for South Africa. *South African Journal of Information Management, 6*(3), 12–19.

VanderMeer, A., & VanWinden, W. (2003). E-governance in cities: A comparison of urban information and communication technology policies. *The Journal of the Regional Studies Association, 37*(4), 407–419. doi:10.1080/0034340032000074433

Varian, H. R. (1996, December 6th). *Economic aspects of personal privacy in US dept of commerce privacy and self-regulation in the information age.* Retrieved February 10th, 2011 from http://people.ischool.berkeley.edu/~hal/Papers/privacy/

Vassilakis, C., Laskaridis, G., Lepouras, G., Rouvas, S., & Georgiadis, P. (2002). Transactional e-government services: An integrated approach. *Lecture Notes in Computer Science, 2456,* 276–279. doi:10.1007/978-3-540-46138-8_44

Veenstra, A. F. V., Bram, K., & Marijin, J. (2009). Barriers for transformation: Impediments for transforming the public sector through e-government. In *Proceedings of ECIS 2009.* ECIS.

Venkatesh, V., Morris, M., Davis, G., & Davis, F. (2003). User acceptance of information technology: Toward a unified view. *Management Information Systems Quarterly, 27*(3), 425–478.

Vietor, R. H. K. (2007). *How countries compete: Strategy, structure, and government in the global economy.* Cambridge, MA: Harvard Business School.

Vijayasarathy, L. R., & Turk, D. (2008). Agile software development = a survey of early adopters. *Journal of Information Technology,* 1-8. Retrieved May 17, 2013 from http://www.aom-iaom.org/jitm_pdfs/jitm_08/article3.pdf

Vilniaus Apygardos Administracinio Teismo Pirmininko Įsakymas. (2010). Dėl bylų paskirstymo teisėjams naudojant informacines technologijas taisyklių patvirtinimo, 2010 m. kovo 5 d. Nr. T- 29.

Visuomenės Atstovų Dalyvavimas Nagrinėjant Administracines Bylas. (2011). *LVAT įvykdytos apklausos rezultatai.* Retrieved February 28, 2013 http://www.lvat.lt/media/77038/statistika.pdf

Vyriausybei Atskaitingų Institucijų Funkcijų Analizės ir Biudžeto Programų Vertinimo Paslaugos. (2011). Horizontali elektroninės valdžios politikos funkcijų peržiūra, Bandomosios funkcijų peržiūros ataskaita. 2011 m. sausio 3 d. Parengė viešoji įstaiga „Europos socialiniai, teisiniai ir ekonominiai projektai pagal 2009 m. gruodžio 29 d. paslaugų sutartį Nr. MPT-09-077 su Lietuvos Respublikos Ministro Pirmininko tarnyba.

Wade, R. H. (2002). Bridging the digital divide—New route to development or new form of dependency? *Global Governance, 8,* 443–466.

Wade, R. H. (2004). Bridging the digital divide: New route to development or new form of dependency. In C. Avgerou, C. Ciborra, & F. Land (Eds.), *The social study of information and communication technology: Innovation, actors, and contexts* (pp. 185–206). Oxford, UK: Oxford University Press.

Waisanen, B. (2002). The future of e-government: Technology-fueled management tools. *Public Management, 84*(5), 6–9.

Walker, H., & Brammer, S. (2012). The relationship between sustainable procurement and e-procurement in the public sector. *International Journal of Production Economics, 140*(1), 256–268. doi:10.1016/j.ijpe.2012.01.008

Walls, J. G., Widmeyer, G. R., & Sawy, O. A. (1992). Building an information systems design theory for vigilant EIS. *Information Systems Research, 3*(1), 25–59. doi:10.1287/isre.3.1.36

Wang, S., & Ariguzo, G. (2004). Knowledge management through the development of information schema. *Information & Management, 41,* 445–456. doi:10.1016/S0378-7206(03)00083-1

Ware, G. T., Moss, S., Campos, J. E., & Noone, G. P. (2012). Corruption in procurement. In A. Graycar, & R. Smith (Eds.), *Handbook of global research and practice in corruption.* Chichester, UK: Edward Elgar Publishing.

Waring, A. (1996). *Practical systems thinking.* Hampshire, UK: Canage Learning.

Warkentin, M., Gefen, D., Pavlou, P., & Rose, M. (2002). Encouraging citizen adoption of e-government by building trust. *Electronic Markets, 12,* 157–162. doi:10.1080/101967802320245929

Watex System. (2012). Kenya Turns to Satellite Technology to Quench Thirst for Water. *HumanIPO.* Retrieved June 9, 2013 from http://www.humanipo.com/news/493/Kenya-turns-to-satellite-technology-to-quench-thirst-for-water.

Web Services Interoperability Organisation. (2007, December 25). *Basic profile version 2.0.* Retrieved September 14, 2011 from http://www.ws-i.org/Profiles/BasicProfile-2_0(WGD).html

Weber, S. (2000). *The political economy of open source software.* Berkeley, CA: University of California.

Webster, F. (2006). *Theories of the information society* (3rd ed.). London: Routledge.

Weerakkody, V., & Dhillon, G. (2008). Moving from e-government to t-government: A study of process re-engineering challenges in a UK local authority context. *International Journal of Electronic Government Research,* *4,* 1–16. doi:10.4018/jegr.2008100101

Weerakkody, V., & El-Haddadeh, R. (2011). Exploring the complexities of e-government implementation and diffusion in a developing country: Some lessons from the State of Qatar. *Journal of Enterprise Information Management,* *24*(2), 172–196. doi:10.1108/17410391111106293

Weerakkody, V., Janssen, M., & Dwivedi, Y. K. (2011). Transformational change and business process reengineering (BPR): Lessons from the British and Dutch public sector. *Government Information Quarterly,* *28,* 320–328. doi:10.1016/j.giq.2010.07.010

Weinberg, G. (1975). *An introduction to general systems thinking.* New York: John Wiley & Sons.

Weiser, M. (1984). Program slicing. *IEEE Transactions on Software Engineering,* *10*(4), 352–357. doi:10.1109/TSE.1984.5010248

Wells, H. (2012). How effective are project management methodologies? An explorative evaluation of their benefits in practice. *Project Management Journal,* *43*(6), 43–58. doi:10.1002/pmj.21302

Wen, W., & Wei, L. (2007). *Decision-making analysis of e-procurement with the rough set theory.* Paper presented to International Conference on Wireless Communications, Networking and Mobile Computing. Shanghai, China.

Wescott, C. G. (2001). E government in the Asia pacific region. *Asian Journal of Political Science,* *9*(2), 1–24. doi:10.1080/02185370108434189

Wescott, C. G. (2001a). e-Government in the Asia-Pacific region: Progress and challenges. *Systemics. Cybernetics and Informatics,* *3*(6), 37–42.

Wescott, C. G. (2001b). *E-government in the Asia-Pacific region.* Asian Development Bank.

West, D. (2008a). *Improving technology utilization in electronic government around the world.* Retrieved February 8, 2013 from http://www.brookings.edu/reports/2008/0817_egovernment_west.aspx

West, D. (2008b). *State and federal e-government in the United States.* Retrieved October 13, 2010 from http://www.brookings.edu/reports/2008/0826_egovernment_west.aspx

West, M. D. (2006). *Global e-government 2006.* Retrieved April 16, 2013, from http://www.insidepolitics.org/egovt06int.pdf

West, D. (2007). *Global e-government.* Providence, RI: Brown University.

West, D. M. (2004). E-government and the transformation of service delivery and citizen attitudes. *Public Administration Review,* *64*(1), 15–27. doi:10.1111/j.1540-6210.2004.00343.x

West, D. M. (2008). *Improving technology utilization in electronic government around the world, 2008.* Washington, DC: Government Studies at Brookings, The Brookings Institution.

Whipple, J. M., & Roh, J. (2010). Agency theory and quality fade in buyer-supplier relationships. *International Journal of Logistics Management,* *21*(3), 338–352. doi:10.1108/09574091011089781

White House. (2010). *DRAFT national strategy for trusted identities in cyberspace: Creating options for enhanced online security and privacy.* Washington, DC: The White House.

Whitley, E. A. (2009). *Informational privacy, consent and the control of personal data.* London: Elsevier. doi:10.1016/j.istr.2009.10.001

Whitley, E. A. (2009). Perceptions of government technology, surveillance and privacy: The UK identity cards scheme. In N. Daniel, & B. Goold (Eds.), *New directions in privacy and surveillance* (pp. 133–156). Cullompton, UK: Willan.

Widodo, A. P., Istiyanto, J. E., Wardoyo, R., & Santoso, P. (2013). E-government interoperability framework based on a real time architecture. *International Journal of Computer Science Issues, 10*(1), 469–477.

Wikipedia. (n.d.). *e-Procurement.* Retrieved May 12, 2013 from http://en.wikipedia.org/wiki/E-Procurement

Williamson, O. E. (1981). The economics of organization: The transaction cost approach. *American Journal of Sociology, 87*(3), 548–577. doi:10.1086/227496

Wilson, B. (1984). *Systems: Concepts, methodologies and applications.* Chichester, UK: John Wiley & Son.

Wilson, E. J., & Wong, K. R. (2007). *Negotiating the net in Africa: The politics of internet diffusion.* London: Rienner.

Wimmer, M. A. (2002). Integrated service modelling for online one-stop government. *Electronic Markets, 12*(3), 149–156. doi:10.1080/101967802320245910

Working Group. (2002). *Roadmap for e-government in the developing world.* Los Angeles, CA: Pacific Council on International Policy.

World Bank Web Site. (2012). *Full definition of e-government.* Retrieved March 12, 2012 from http://web.worldbank.org/WBSITE/EXTERNAL/TOPICS/EXTINFORMATIONANDCOMMUNICATIONANDTECHNOLOGIES/EXTEGOVERNMENT/0,contentMDK:20507153~menuPK:6226295~pagePK:210058~piPK:210062~theSitePK:702586~isCURL:Y,00.html

World Bank. (2001). *Issue note: E-government and the World Bank.* Washington, DC: World Bank.

World Bank. (2002). *The e-government handbook for developing countries.* Washington, DC: Centre for Democracy and Technology.

World Bank. (2003). *World development indicators.* Washington, DC: World Bank.

World Bank. (2007). *Country brief: Russian federation, economy.* Retrieved May 6, 2007 from http://web.worldbank.org

World Bank. (2012). *E-government.* Retrieved from http//go.worldbank.org/6WT3UPVG80

World Bank. (2012). *Kenya: About MajiVoice.* Retrieved July 1, 2013 from WWW.MAJIVOICE.COM

World Bank. (n.d.). *Definition of e-government.* Retrieved 12 July, 2011 from http://go.worldbank.org/M1JHE0Z280

Wyld, D. C. (2008). *Government in 3D: How public leaders can draw on virtual worlds.* Retrieved February 28, 2013 from http://faculty.cbpp.uaa.alaska.edu/afgjp/PADM601%20Fall%202009/Wyld3dReport.pdf

Wynn, E., & deLyra, J. (2000). A strange attractor in the chaos of global IS development. In *Proceedings of the IFIP WG9.4 Conference 2000.* Cape Town, South Africa: IFIP.

Xanthoulis, N. (2009). *Introducing the concept of 'e-justice' in Europe: How adding an 'E' becomes a modern challenge for Greece and the EU.* Retrieved February 28, 2013 from http://effectius.com/yahoo_site_admin/assets/docs/Introducing_the_concept_of_e-justice_in_Europe_by_Napoleon_Xanthoulis.20775004.pdf

Xiao, Y., Xioa, M., & Zhao, H. (2007). An ontology for e-government knowledge modelling and interoperability. In *Proceedings of IEEE International Conference on Wireless Communications, Networking and Mobile Computing (WiCOM 2007).* Shanghai, China: IEEE.

Xinzhang, C., & Yonggang, W. (2011). *E-government, government procurement and the development of e-commerce: Korean experience and its implications.* Paper presented to E -Business and E-Government (ICEE). Shanghai, China.

Yaghoubi, N. M., Haghi, A., & Khazaee, S. (2011). E-government and citizen satisfaction in Iran: Empirical study on ICT offices. *World Applied Sciences Journal, 12*(7), 1084–1092.

Yang, J., & Zhang, R. (2009). The research and analysis of e-procurement for iron and steel enterprises. In *Proceedings of Information Management, Innovation Management and Industrial Engineering.* IEEE. doi:10.1109/ICIII.2009.158

Yannis, K., & Marco, S. (2003). Ontology mapping: The state of the art. *The Knowledge Engineering Review, 18*(1), 1–31. doi:10.1017/S0269888903000651

Yim, N.-H., Kim, S.-H., Kim, H.-W., & Kwahk, K.-Y. (2004). Knowledge based decision making on higher level strategic concerns: System dynamics approach. *Expert Systems with Applications, 27*, 143–158. doi:10.1016/j.eswa.2003.12.019

Yonck, R. (2008). The future of advertising and you. *Mensa Bulletin,* 32-33.

Yonhapnews. (2009). *Public administration, realize good government by on-nara system.* Retrieved April 16, 2013 from http://app.yonhapnews.co.kr/YNA/Basic/article/Press/YIBW_showPress.aspx?contents_id=RPR20090525005600353&from=search

Young, R., Young, M., Jordan, E., & O'Connor, P. (2012). Is strategy being implemented through projects? Contrary evidence from a leader in new public management. *International Journal of Project Management, 30*, 887–900. doi:10.1016/j.ijproman.2012.03.003

Yuan, M. (2011). A design of e-government SMS platform-based on web. *International Conference on Management and Artificial Intelligence.* Retrieved March 1, 2011, from http://www.ipedr.com/vol16/24-A10019.pdf

Zarei, B., Ghapanchi, A., & Sattary, B. (2008). Toward national e-government development models for developing countries: A nine stage model. *The International Information & Library Review, 40*(3), 199–207. doi:10.1016/j.iilr.2008.04.001

Zeithaml, V. A., Parasuraman, A., & Berry, L. L. (1990). *Delivering quality service: Balancing customer perceptions and expectations.* New York, NY: The Free Press.

Zhao, G., Gao, Y., & Meersman, R. (2004). An ontology-based approach to business modeling. In *Proceedings of the International Conference of Knowledge Engineering and Decision Support.* IEEE.

Zhao, F., Scavarda, A., & Waxin, M. (2012). Key issues and challenges in e-government development: An integrative case study of the number one eCity in the Arab world. *Information Technology & People, 25*(4), 395–422. doi:10.1108/09593841211278794

Zhou, Z., & Hu, C. (2008). Study on the e-government security risk management. *International Journal of Computer Science and Network Security, 8*(5), 208–213.

Ziemann, J., & Loos, P. (2009). Transforming cross-organisational processes between european administrations: Towards a comprehensive business interoperability interface. In *Handbook of research on ICT-enabled transformational government: A global perspective.* Hershey, PA: IGI Global. doi:10.4018/978-1-60566-390-6.ch006

Zwick, D., Bonsu, S. K., & Darmody, A. (2008). Putting consumers to work: "Co-creation" and new marketing govern-mentality. *Journal of Consumer Culture, 8*(2), 163–196. doi:10.1177/1469540508090089

About the Contributors

Kelvin Joseph Bwalya is a Senior Lecturer in Computer Information Systems at the Department of Library and Information Studies, University of Botswana. He is also a Senior Research Fellow at the University of Johannesburg, and a Senior IT reviewer for the Tertiary Education Council, Botswana. He has a PhD in Information Systems (Information Management) from the University of Johannesburg, Masters in Computer Science from the Korea Advanced Institute of Technology, and Bachelors in Electronics from Moscow Power Engineering Technical University. His research interests include all aspects of computer information systems (e-Government, database design, process modeling, virtual reality, knowledge management systems, community informatics, etc.) and competitive intelligence.

* * *

Gbenga Emmanuel Afolayan, with degrees in counselling and Economics, human rights, social justice and development, and public policy and management, has an interdisciplinary educational background. While she is interested in various areas, such as capitalism, colonialism, women's human rights, social justice and development, ICTs for development, gender and social movement, governance and public management issues, particularly within developing societies—stretching from Africa to other continents where African descendants can be found—the unifying theme of her research hinges on the relationship between culture, ICT for development, political-economic relations, and their particular articulations that gave rise to the phenomenon of women's rights movement on a mass scale. Through this relationship, she is now involved in different trends that revolve around gender, natural resources, electronic governance and development, social movements and women's rights, and social-political transformation in Africa.

H. B. Akanbi-Ademolake (CLN) holds Certificate and Diploma in Cooperative studies from Federal Cooperative College, Eleyele Ibadan, B.Sc. (ED) Library Studies from University of Ado-Ekiti, and MLIS from University of Ibadan. Mrs. H. B. Akanbi-Ademolake is an Assistant Lecturer in the Department of Library and Information Science, Faculty of Communication and Information Sciences at the University of Ilorin, Nigeria. She is a member of the Nigeria Library Association and presently the Treasurer of the Kwara State chapter. Her research interest is in the area of knowledge management. She has both national and international publications to her credit.

Eglė Bilevičiūtė, Mykolas Romeris University, Faculty of Law, PhD, Professor, is teaching students of Mykolas Romeris University in such subjects: law of research and studies, administrative procedure, social changes and administrative law, crime investigation. She defended her doctoral thesis "Lithuania Criminalistic Information System: Modern State and New Model" and received her PhD in Social Science (Law) in 2003. She was granted as associated professor in 2007. She has enough experience in implementation and preparation of national and international projects. She is experienced in processing of data and she knows statistical methods for social scientific researches. Her current research interest includes law of research and studies, management of research, administrative law, forensic science, legal informatics, implementation of IT in law. Major Fields of Scientific Research: research management and law, environmental law, administrative law and procedure, law informatics and IT law, criminalistics, criminal procedure.

Tatjana Bilevičienė, Mykolas Romeris University, Faculty of Economics and Finance Management, PhD, Assistant Professor, graduated in 1974 of Faculty of Electronic Technique of Leningrad Electro Technique Institute and acquired the profession of engineer of electronic technique (summa cum laude of high education equal for Master degree). In 2009, she defended Doctoral Thesis at Mykolas Romeris University and was graduated as PhD (management and administration). She is teaching students of Mykolas Romeris University. Teaching subjects: information technologies, methods of statistical analysis, statistical management technologies, market research. From 2002, Tatjana Bilevičienė published more than 50 scientific articles in Lithuanian and foreign journals and two textbooks. Scientific research fields: mathematics (statistics), informatics, IT, management and administration, education. Major Fields of Scientific Research: Mathematics (statistics), IT, management and administration, knowledge management.

Tianxing Cai (TX) is currently a research associate in the Department of Chemical Engineering, Lamar University. He received his BS in Chemistry from Shanghai University in 2006 after which he entered Amkor Technology, the world's leading supplier of outsourced semiconductor interconnect services, working as senior quality and laboratory engineer for five years. TX entered Lamar University to start the graduate study in 2011. After getting the master degree in 2012, he became a research associate in the Department of Chemical Engineering of Lamar University until now. He was once and has been the member of Chinese Semiconductor Association, Chinese Electro Plating Association, Chinese Indoor Environment Control Association, Chinese Chemical Analysis Association, Chinese ESD Control Association, American Institute of Chemical Engineers, the Society of Petroleum Engineers, Society for Industrial and Applied Mathematics, American Society of Civil Engineers, Institute of Electrical and Electronics Engineers, Mathematical Association of America and American Mathematical Society. His current research involves the simulation, modeling, optimization and algorithm development to achieve industrial optimal operation and sustainable development.

Yannis Charalabidis is Assistant Professor in the University of the Aegean, in the area of e-Governance Information Systems, coordinating policy making, research, and pilot application projects for governments and enterprises worldwide. A computer engineer with a PhD in complex information systems, he has been employed for several years as an executive director in Singular IT Group, leading software development and company expansion in Europe, India, and the US. He also serves as the scientific manager at the Greek Interoperability Centre, hosted at Decision Support Systems Laboratory, of the National Technical University of Athens, delivering high quality research in the area of interoperability. He has also been the coordinator or technical leader in numerous FP6, FP7, and National research projects in the areas of e-Business and e-Governance. He is a contributing member in several standardization and technology policy committees. He writes and teaches on Government Service Systems, Enterprise Interoperability, Government Transformation, and Citizen Participation.

Liam Church is the CEO of Escher Group and is responsible for successfully positioning the company as the global leader in digital point of service for postal organizations. Under Liam's direction, Escher Group has revolutionized how technology is utilized to promote business growth and increase profitability. As an innovator, Liam strategically elevated and expanded the company's core competencies into interactive services, including cutting-edge near field communications solutions. His unique vision for the company is driving record sales and expanding Escher Group's presence into multiple new markets across the globe. Prior to his leadership at Escher, Mr Church was Chief Executive Officer at a successful wealth management company and held numerous senior positions during his 22-year tenure with the postal service in Ireland. A trusted thought leader, Liam provides council and mentorship to senior executives and government officials throughout the world.

Ronan de Kervenoael is a Marketing Lecturer at Sabanci University in Turkey and network Lecturer at Aston University. His wider research interests lie under the umbrella of consumer behaviour and retailing, including the study of social, cultural, and technological transformations in how consumers (re)organize their lives and become producers of their experiences. His work has been published in *Environment & Planning A, World Development, Service Industries Journal, Telecommunication Policy.*

Jean Vincent Fonou Dombeu Completed his PhD in Computer Science at the School of Computer, Statistical and Mathematical Sciences of the North-West University, South Africa and his is currently a Senior Lecturer in the Department of Software Studies at the Vaal University of Technology, South Africa. He received an MSc. in Computer Science at the University of KwaZulu-Natal, South Africa, in 2008, BSc. Honour's and BSc. in Computer Science at the University of Yaoundé I, Cameroon, in 2002 and 2000 respectively. His research interests include: Biometric for Personal Identification, Ontology, Agent Modelling, and Semantic Knowledge representation in e-Government. Dr. Fonou-Dombeu has published articles on Semantic Web development in e-Government and presented papers at international conferences in South Africa, France, Slovenia and Italy.

Shauneen Furlong is an independent consultant and part-time professor who lectures on e-Government and project management with the University of Toronto and University of Ottawa. Over the last couple of years, she has presented and worked in the United Kingdom, Middle East, Europe, East Africa, Egypt, China, Canada, Washington and Turkey. Shauneen has executive level management experience in a number of Government of Canada central agencies and departments over a period of 20 years, lastly as Executive Director, Government On-Line, Government of Canada. She has published articles and peer reviewed papers for international journals and conferences. She was awarded an IBM Fellowship; has a Ph.D. in Computer Science; a MA in Business Administration Economics; a MBA in Project Management; a BA in Philosophy; and is a Project Manager Professional (PMP). Dr. Furlong was nominated by IT World Canada as being one of Canada's key e-Government drivers, and was profiled by Computer World Canada.

Baby Ashwin Gobin was born in Mauritius in 1979. She received a B.Eng. (Hons) in Computer Science and Engineering in 2002 and a MSc in E-Business in 2006 from the University of Mauritius. She worked as Business Analyst, Software Engineer and Marketing Executive before joining the University of Mauritius as Lecturer in 2009. She is currently working on her PhD thesis, entitled "AOM – An Agile Methodology for the Development of Ontology Modules." Her other research areas are: Information Systems Development, Impact of IT on Society, Technology Acceptance Models.

Magda Huisman is a Professor of Computer Science and Information Systems at the North-West University (Potchefstroom Campus) where she teaches software engineering, IT project management, management information systems, and decision support systems. She received her Ph.D degree in Computer Science and Information Systems at the Potchefstroom University for CHE in 2001. Prof. Huisman is actively involved in research projects regarding systems development methodologies. She has published her research in journals such as *MISQ, Information & Management, IADIS International Journal on Csomputer Science and Information Systems, IJWEST,* and *Lecture Notes in Computer Science.* She presented 22 peer reviewed full-length papers at various international conferences. She was the supervisor for 16 Masters degree students and 4 Ph.D students who completed their studies successfully under her guidance. Her current research interests are in the use and effectiveness of systems development methodologies and the diffusion of information technologies.

Malongo R. S. Mlozi is a Professor in the Department of Agricultural Extension and Education. He has B.Sc.(General Agriculture) from West Virginia University, Morgantown, WV, USA; M.Phil.(Agricultural Extension) from West Virginia University, Morgantown, WV, USA; and PhD (Agricultural Extension and Education) from University of British Columbia, Canada. He teaches Research Planning and Management, Methods of Social Research, Formal and Non-Formal Education, Agricultural Extension, Issues in Urban Agriculture, Extension Methods and Methods of Adult Education. His research interests are in urban Agriculture-Livestocks and Crops, Agricultural Extension, Agricultural Education, Rural Development and Peri-urban Farming Systems. He has several publications in peer reviewed Internatinal journals. Furthermore, he has supervised many Masters and PhD students at SUA.

Maria Moloney is an IT consultant with Escher Group Ltd and a lecturer at Trinity College Dublin. After earning a BSc degree and an MSc degree in Information Systems, she is currently reading towards a PhD at Trinity College Dublin. Her research interests include informational privacy, e-Government, and information systems design theory.

Hilda Moraa spearheads iHub Research innovation and entrepreneurship studies, and is currently working on leading an in-house study on African ICT Hubs. Hilda received her bachelor's degree in "Business in Information Technology" at Strathmore University and is currently enrolled as a master's student at Jomo Kenyatta University studying entrepreneurship. Hilda's experience in quantitative research, market research, management consulting, and operations research in a fast-paced high-exposure environment has been invaluable in designing and managing research projects. She is the co-founder of My_Order, which won the Mobile Boot Camp Competition 2010.

Arjun Neupane is a Ph.D. candidate of School of Information Systems, Faculty of Business and Law, University of Southern Queensland (USQ), Toowoomba, Australia. He received his Master of Information Technology from the USQ, Australia. Mr. Neupane research interests are electronic procurement, E-government, business information system, ICT4D, and software engineering. He has published international journals and conference proceedings.

Bongani Ngwenya is currently Dean, Faculty of Business, MBA Thesis Defense Panel Chair, Lecturer, and Master's thesis supervisor at Solusi University, Zimbabwe. Has 27 years of work experience, both in the public and private sector. PhD in Business Management and Administration finalist, with specialization in Strategic Management (A Grounded Theory Research), with North West University, Mafeking Campus in South Africa. My research interests are mainly in the areas of Organisational Decision-Making Research and in Business in general.

Albert Otieno Orwa, as a statistician, Albert's main role at iHub Research entails entry, visualization of graphics and analysis of various projects. He explains complex ideas and findings in a way that can easily be understood. Albert holds a BSc. In Applied Statistics with Computing and is currently working on his masters in social statistics. He is passionate about research.

Rafiat Ajibade Oyekunle is a Lecturer at the Department of Information and Communication Science, University of Ilorin. She holds a B.Sc. degree in Public Administration from ABU Zaria and M.Inf.Sc. Information Science from the University of Ibadan. Her research interests include: information communications, e-business, and social informatics. She is a registered member of Nigeria Computer Society (NCS) and has a number of national and international publications to her credit.

Malgorzata Pankowska is an Assistant Professor of the Department of Informatics at University of Economics in Katowice, Poland. She received the qualification in econometrics and statistics from the Karol Adamiecki University of Economics in Katowice in 1981, the Ph.D. degree in 1988, and the Doctor Habilitatus degree in 2009, both from the Karol Adamiecki University of Economics in Katowice. She participated in EU Leonardo da Vinci Programme projects as well as gave lectures within the Socrates Program Teaching Staff Exchange in Braganca, Portugal, Trier, Germany, Brussels, Belgium, in Vilnius, Lithuania, and in Ostrava, Czech Republic. She is a member of ISACA and the Secretary in the Board of the Polish Society for Business Informatics. Her research interests include virtual organization development, ICT project management, IT outsourcing, information governance, corporate architecture, and business information systems design and implementation.

Hakikur Rahman is an academic over 27 years has served leading education institutes and established various ICT4D projects funded by ADB, UNDP, and World Bank in Bangladesh. He is currently serving as a Post Doctoral Researcher at the University of Minho, Portugal, under the Centro Algoritmi. He has written and edited over 25 books, more than 50 book chapters, and contributed over 100 articles on computer education, ICTs, knowledge management, open innovation, data mining, and e-government research in newspapers, journals, and conference proceedings. Graduating from the Bangladesh University of Engineering and Technology in 1981, he has done his Master's of Engineering from the American University of Beirut in 1986 and completed his PhD in Computer Engineering from the Ansted University, BVI, UK, in 2001.

Isabel Ramos is an Assistant Professor at Information Systems Department of University of Minho, Portugal. She coordinates a research group in Knowledge Management. She also has research work in the field of Requirements Engineering. Isabel Ramos is associate editor of the *International Journal of Technology and Human Interaction* and Secretary of the IFIP TC8 (Information Systems). Her research and teaching interests include: requirements engineering, knowledge management, organizational theory, sociology of knowledge, history of science, research methodology. She is responsible for the user studies in two funded R&D projects. Isabel Ramos is author of more than three dozen scientific papers presented at international conferences and published in scientific and technical journals. She advises the work of several PhD and Master Students.

Mehdi Sagheb-Tehrani is an Associate Professor in Business Information Technology at the College of Business, Bemidji State University (BSU), USA, and is currently on the leave from BSU to Columbus State University. He taught at the graduate level and Computer Business Application, Advanced Structured Application Development, Corporate Information Management, e-Commerce and Web Page development, MIS and Systems Analysis at the undergraduate level. Before joining BSU, he taught MIS, Expert Systems, Business Network Systems Management, Virtual Business and Advanced Topics in Information Technology at the graduate level and Project Management, Internet Applications, Introduction to Computers, C++, Visual Basic and COBOL programming at the Undergraduate level. He received his PhD in Informatics (Old name – Information and Computer Science) from Lund University-Sweden, in 1993. He has published over 47 papers in various international journals, conference proceedings, book chapters and a book (Management of IT). Before joining academia, he was IT Manager as well as Consultant in a number of organizations, including IRISL, Cutting Tools Manufacturing, NI Register Organization, IDP Company (formerly IBM), etc.

Anne Salim is currently a researcher at iHub, where she leads the program on M-Governance. The study has focused on the role of mobile devices for enhancing transparency in governance of the water sector. Prior to working with iHub, Anne was involved in business development at SemaSoft. She also has experience working with the Embassy of Mexico in Kenya, and Pablo Tours. Anne studied Business Information Technology from Strathmore University and her interests include applying Design Thinking processes to Kenya, as well as facilitating Hackathon events.

Camilius Aloyce Sanga is a Senior Lecturer at the Department of Informatics and Computer Centre, Sokoine University of Agriculture, Tanzania. He holds BSc in Computer Science from University of Dar es Salaam and MSc. Computer Science from Osmania University. In addition, he has PhD in Computer Science from the University of the Western Cape, South Africa. His research interest is in the area of Information and Communication Technology for Development (ICT4D). He has published papers in proceedings of International conferences in ICT. He has also published journal papers in many peer reviewed International Journals (http://scholar.google.com/citations?user=vuJQthUAAAAJ&hl=en). Furthermore, he has co-authored two books as well as co-authored book chapters in the following books: *Information and Communication Technology: Changing Education* published by ICFAI University Press (India) and *Technology-Mediated Open and Distance Education for Agricultural Education and Improved Livelihood in Sub-Saharan Africa* published by Commonwealth of Learning (Canada). In addition, he has co-authored book chapter in the forthcoming book titled *Technology Development and Platform Enhancements for Successful Global E-Government Design* by IGI-Global (USA).

Egemen Şekeralp is the Chief Marketing Officer of Pordiva İnformation Technologies in Turkey a company that gave life to many projects on mobile technologies such as mobile integrations, applications, and augmented reality. He has a Masters Degree in Marketing and E-commerce from the University of Notre Dame in Australia. His research interests are consumer behaviour, evolution of life styles, social media, technology and mobile technology.

Kosheek Sewchurran is Associate Professor – Innovation Management and Information Systems at UCTs Graduate School of Business (GSB). Co-Convenor of the MPhil in Inclusive Innovation studies at GSB. Leader of a research program aimed at reinventing the style of organizing for ICT work in collaboration with the Department of Trade and Industry (DTI) and Johannesburg Centre for Software Engineering (JCSE) and National team of PhD and MPhil students. Board Member of CAPACIT1000, a non-profit organization involved in sector development of the ICT industry and alleviating unemployment among graduates in South Africa. Member of the international editorial review board at *International Journal of Managing Projects in Business*. Member of the international editorial review board at International Journal of Information Technologies and Systems Approach (IJITSA).Member of the international editorial review board "TAPROOT Series," a cutting edge publication series of the DST/NRF SARCHI Chair in Development Education. NRF rated researcher ("Y") in Organizing Practices for High Innovation and Complex Contexts. Prior responsibilities include over a decade in large scale industrial expansion projects in the Aluminium Smelting, Casting and Rolling Business Sector spanning various professional roles from Program Management, Planning Specialist, Software Engineer, Enterprise Architect. And HOD – Department of Information Systems in Faculty of Commerce at UCT.

Young-Jin Shin is an assistant professor of Pai Chai University, South Korea. Dr. Shin is a well-known policy advisor to e-government as well as information policy. She worked as a reach professor at Korea University, expert advisor on Ministry of Public Administration and Security. She was one of members, work group of project of indicator development of information security in Ministry of Information Communication. She received a doctoral degree in public administration from Sungkyunkwan University.

Jeffrey Soar is the Chair in Human Centred Technology, School of Management and Enterprise at the University of Southern Queensland. He holds Honorary Professor positions at Jiangxi Institute of Economic Administrators, The University of Queensland, and Curtin University. In 12 years in academia, Prof Soar has been awarded more than 20 grants and research commissions including national competitive grants. Prof Soar's research has guided national policy in Australia, New Zealand, and other nations. Through international agencies, he has developed information strategy for the Pacific Islands and other developing nations. Jeffrey came to academia from a career at the highest senior executive levels in the public sector. In New Zealand he had nation-wide responsible for IT and telecommunications services to national emergency response agencies; he also successfully managed New Zealand's largest public sector technology project involving infrastructure, data services, telephony, radio telecommunications, applications development, and implementation.

Lefkothea Spiliotopoulou is a PhD Candidate and a Research Associate in the Information Systems Laboratory at the Department of Information and Communication Systems Engineering, University of the Aegean. She is also a Teaching Assistant in the undergraduate course "Software Engineering." She holds a Bachelor Degree from University of the Aegean, Department of Information and Communication Systems Engineering and a Master of Science in "Technologies and Management of Information and Communication Systems" from the University of the Aegean, Department of Information and Communication Systems Engineering. She is actively taking part in European and National Projects. Her research interests lie in the area of e-Government, e-Participation, Policy Modeling, and Opinion Mining.

Adetayo Oluseyi Tella graduated from the Department of Library, Archival and Information Studies, University of Ibadan, Nigeria, 2011. He has enrolled in the same Department as a graduate student. His research areas include Library and Media, Open Source and Library, etc. He is married with children.

Adeyinka Tella is a Senior Lecturer in the Department of Library and Information Science, Faculty of Communication and Information Sciences, University of Ilorin, Nigeria. Tella was a Commonwealth Scholar who finished his PhD in September 2009 from the Department of Library and Information Studies, University of Botswana, where he was awarded small grant for thesis writing for the PhD student's category in 2007 by the Council for Development in Social Science Research in Africa (CODESRIA). He has written and published articles mostly in International reputable refereed journals together with chapters in books. He is one of the contributors to an information science reference *Cases on Successful E-learning Practices in the Developed and Developing World: Methods for the Global Information Economy* and Editor of another information science reference text *Library and Information Science in Developing Countries: Contemporary Issues*. Currently, he is the Associate Editor *International Journal of Library and Information Science*, and Editor-in-Chief of *International Journal of Information Processing and Communication*. He is also editorial board member, for *Library Philosophy and Practice* and *Malaysian Journal of Educational Technology*. Tella is an external examiner for Library and Information Science PhD candidates at the Annamalai University, Alagapa University, and Bharathidasan University, Trichy, in India. Tella has just been awarded a Post-Doctoral Research Scholarship by the University of Kwazulu-Nata in South Africa in April 2012. His re-search areas include e-learning, information literacy, information communication technology and management, information system evaluation and psychology of information.

Siza D. Tumbo is an Associate Professor in Agricultural Engineering at Sokoine University of Agriculture (SUA), Tanzania. He holds a BSc. in Agricultural Engineering from Sokoine University of Agriculture (1991), MSc in Light Current Engineering from University of Dar-es-Salaam (1996) and PhD in Biological and Agricultural Engineering from Pennsylvania State University (2000). His broad area of knowledge is in Agricultural Engineering and his specialty is in Bio-systems Information, Computing and Automation. His research interests are in Modeling and Simulation of Agricultural and Engineering Systems; Development and Use of Decision Support and Intelligent Systems; Electronic Instrumentation, Automation, Measurement, and Control; Social and Economic Research for Improved Uptake and Up-Scaling of Engineering Technologies; General Agricultural and Natural Resources Engineering Related Researches. Dr. Tumbo is a member of ASABE, TSAE, and IET.

Samuel C. Avemaria Utulu is a PhD student at the Department of Information Systems, University of Cape Town, South Africa. He has worked as a systems librarian in two universities in Nigeria and currently works as the Senior Librarian in charge of the serials and government document librarian at the Redeemer's University, Nigeria where he was granted study leave until 2014. His research interests include open access publishing, Webology, e-readiness assessment, library and information service modeling, and process analysis and improvement.

Kishor Vaidya is an Associate Professor (Adjunct) at the University of Canberra, Australia. Dr Vaidya is also an Adjunct Senior Lecturer at the University of Southern Queensland, Australia. His research interests include Inter-Organizational Information Systems (IOIS), especially e-Procurement, public procurement, application of organizational theories in IOIS and business management, and program evaluation. He has currently developed his research interests in issues pertaining to the use of technologies in reducing corruption in public procurement. Most recently, Dr Vaidya is working on an action-oriented/Web analytical research project to assess the impact of various Internet marketing strategies (including search engine optimization) on the conversion rate of e-commerce Websites (StudentBusinessOnline.com).

Index

CPSIA information can be obtained at www.ICGtesting.com
Printed in the USA
BVOW04*2254151213

338884BV00008BA/57/P